THE INSIDERS' GUIDE ®
TO
Maine's
Mid-Coast

THE INSIDERS' GUIDE TO

Maine's
Mid-Coast

by
Carol des Lauriers Cieri
and
Donna Gold

Co-published and marketed by:
Bangor Daily News Enterprises
491 Main St.
Bangor, Maine 04401
(207) 990-8132

Insiders' Publishing
105 Budleigh St.
P.O. Box 2057
Manteo, NC 27954
(919) 473-6100
www.insiders.com

Sales and Marketing:
Falcon Publishing, Inc.
P.O. Box 1718
Helena, MT 59624
(800) 582-2665
www.falconguide.com

•

SECOND EDITION
1st printing

•

Copyright ©1998
by Bangor Daily News Enterprises

•

Printed in the United States
of America

•

Publications from The Insiders' Publishing
series are available at special discounts for
bulk purchases for sales promotions,
premiums or fundraisings. Special editions,
including personalized covers, can be
created in large quantities for special
needs. For more information, please write
to Karen Bachman, Insiders' Publishing,
P.O. Box 2057, Manteo, NC 27954, or call
(800) 765-2665 Ext. 241.

ISBN 1-57380-067-8

Bangor Daily News Enterprises

President
John P. Bishop

Director of Special Publications
Joe Brooks

Treasurer
Arlene Boyle

Project Coordinator
Jayne Jamo

Sales Manager
James Walker

Account Representative
Carol Brooks

Insiders' Publishing

Publisher/Editor-in-Chief
Beth P. Storie

Advertising Director/
General Manager
Michael McOwen

Creative Services Director
Giles MacMillan

Art Director
David Haynes

Managing Editor
Dave McCarter

Project Editor
Dan DeGregory

Project Artist
Bart Smith

Insiders' Publishing
An imprint of Falcon Publishing Inc.
A Landmark Communications company.

Preface

Congratulations! You've made a great choice in deciding to spend some time in Maine.

You'll find a coast of rocks and islands, engaging activities, challenges for body and soul and people who brave snow and ice, short summers and long winters to make a life in this rugged, beautiful, mysterious land.

Not long ago we made the same choice, leaving more urban settings for coastal Maine. It wasn't long before we found ourselves falling in love and settling into old homes close to the fog-bound coast, sending our roots into small coastal towns. We came for the same reason you probably have come: not only because Maine's Mid-Coast is so beautiful in both summer and winter, but also because it is so removed. Here we find peace, privacy and time to attend to what is important to us. We can walk a rocky shoreline, wander a woodland, maybe even see a deer or a fox — the business of the human race hasn't totally upset the balance of nature here. We also find tradition — gravestones with generations of family names; people who remember roads before they were paved, the forest when it was field and the neighbor's house when it was woods. As we come to the close of the 20th century, we find a need to ground ourselves in tradition, to feel the soil and smell brine.

No, we ourselves are not Mainers. We were not born here, our parents are not Mainers, and it's doubtful our children will be considered Mainers. We are, however, Maine lovers and have made every attempt to portray the state we love: the Maine of woods and coast, of hard-working people, of artists and musicians, of small-business people and many service workers — a people so remarkable for their resilience, independence and attention to each other, that when the 1998 ice storm crashed power lines for as many as 16 days during the coldest weeks of the year, not a soul on the coast died from exposure, even though shelters were surprisingly under-used. Neighbors checked in on each other, loaned out generators and wood, hauled water to the elderly and made sure that all were safe, fed and relatively warm.

In particular it is coastal Maine that we love, and we've given it an odd label by calling it Maine's Mid-Coast. No other travel guide will call it that. Most guides consider mid-coast Maine to begin in Wiscasset, or even farther south in Bath and Brunswick, and extend north only as far as Searsport, or perhaps Bucksport, at the mouth of the Penobscot River. We've pushed it into the Down East region. So Maine's Mid-Coast, extending from Waldoboro to Gouldsboro and inland just beyond Bangor to Orono, is something of a marriage of convenience between part of the mid-coast and part of Down East. (And we've thrown in part of Central Maine — Bangor and Orono — just to add a spicy, urban triangle to the relationship!)

We hope you'll use this guide to help you understand who Mainers are and why Maine is so special. As you wander throughout the Mid-Coast region, we hope you'll find this guide offers some depth to what you see — some background on the churches and farmhouses, the forts and foundations, the birds and moose, the trees and flowers, even the rocks and sand you might happen upon. We also hope this guide leads you to some of our special places — the inns with views we covet, the restaurants we particularly look forward to visiting, the cafes where we meet our friends, and the museums, shops and galleries we haunt. To make this guide even more useful, we have considered the totality of your life here as a newcomer, offering you options for child care and healthcare, choices for radio listening and TV viewing, even telling you about school districts and the real estate market.

With this book you have embarked on a voyage of discovery. As our mothers always say, enjoy it in good health.

About the Authors

Carol des Lauriers Cieri

After five years in national and international news at *The Christian Science Monitor*, Carol des Lauriers Cieri left Boston for Camden, Maine, in 1989.

Since then she's written and edited for a weekly newspaper, a fly-fishing magazine and a computer-imaging magazine.

Now a freelance writer, her work has appeared in a variety of publications including Continental's in-flight magazine, *Maine Boats and Harbors*, *Arriving*, *California Fly Fisher*, *Service News* and *Imaging World*.

She was born in Tokyo — her father was in the U.S. Air Force, her mother in the U.S. State Department — and she's been a bit of a nomad ever since. The family lived in Washington, D.C., Ohio, Virginia and Wisconsin. She attended four colleges in six years, spending two terms in a tutorial with a professional writer. In a bout of career anxiety, she finished law school and then, naturally, went to work as a journalist.

She's settled down now in a big old house in Lincolnville, with her husband, Paul; daughter, Emma; and a black cat named Agnes. Paul's a registered Maine guide, and they like nothing better than noodling down back roads . . . when they should be scraping, painting and shoring up the barn.

Donna Gold

As a born New Yorker, Donna Gold soaked up Manhattan living for about a decade, exploring the city and searching out stories for *Smithsonian*, *Natural History*, *American Photographer* and other publications. She took it all in, as if she knew someday it would end.

In 1984, it did. Gold found herself standing on a ramshackle balcony in Central Maine, visiting friends who lived beside the Kennebec River. She realized then and there that not only was there life outside the city, but that the life could be quite fine.

By October, Gold's desk no longer faced a row of steel safety bars, but rather a field of cows. Never mind that by January she found herself wearing gloves indoors to keep frostbite away — she had already gone cross-country skiing under the full moon.

In the 13 years since then, Gold has ventured through Maine the way she once did New York (though opting for four-wheel drive instead of a two-wheeled bike). She has driven from Kittery to Madawaska, Newfield to Lubec, reviewing art and theater, writing profiles and feature stories about artists, education and travel for the *Boston Globe*, *Maine Times*, *Portland Press Herald* and *Maine Sunday Telegram*, and researching her two books for Country Roads Press, *Country Roads of Maine* and *Country Towns of Maine*.

Since 1989, her desk has looked over the edge of Penobscot Bay from the old shingled inn she shares with her family — poet and novelist William Carpenter; their son, Daniel Carpenter-Gold; and their cat, Kitty.

Photo: Bangor Daily News

The city of Belfast, at the mouth of the Penobscot River, is a popular spot for Maine visitors.

Acknowledgments

Carol . . .

Some of Maine — the best part, I think — has no artificial veneer developed for tourists, no slick PR sensibility. The result is a quirky informality that can be a stumbling block when putting together a book like this, where all the i's are dotted, all the t's crossed.

When tracking down information, particularly during the off-season, you learn to be imaginative, to try the local general store, the town office or the nearest hotel for suggestions. And they bend over backward for you! You hear those native Maine accents, those pregnant pauses, that dry sense of humor, and you share in the richness of a civic life that's driven by a desire to help, not to impress or to profit. That's part of the joy and charm of the state, and I was glad to be reminded of it. The fact is, I've found more of what I love and respect in Maine than I have anywhere else, and that's what drove my work on this book. I wanted to help you find what I did.

So first I must thank the hundreds of Mainers I met in my travels by car or by phone. Thanks, too, to readers who spurred me on. And thanks to the staff at Insiders' Publishing Inc., whose tried-and-true format is sure to help travelers on their way.

More particularly, thanks to publisher Beth Storie, a joy from the start, for being straight, funny and wonderfully professional. Thanks to editor Dan DeGregory, who consistently saw through the eyes of someone from away, which I know will be a blessing for readers.

How can I thank Joe Brooks of the *Bangor Daily News*, who kept his head — and his heart — when everyone around him was losing theirs? Charlie Campo and his crew at the *BDN* library were a great help, and parts of this book could not have been written but for Lew Dietz's Maine classic *Night Train from Wiscasset Station* and *Maine Forms of American Architecture*, edited by Deborah Thompson. I found the *Maine Times* and *Down East*

magazine to be great resources, and real estate broker David Brown, former president of the Bangor Board of Realtors, did a yeoman's job explaining the area's housing market.

Thanks too to dear Donna, for commiserating, encouraging and inspiring; for her good sense and her great skill.

And to Doug Hayward of Black Crow Photography in Rockland, Maine, who took my photo for the back cover. Here's the credit they couldn't fit next to it, Doug, and thanks.

To former colleague Tim Seymour of Tim Seymour Designs in Camden, Maine, who graciously bailed me out when power outages during an ice storm made my computer eat whole chapters the day they were due.

To Milton Mayer, Dr. Stephen Rogers, Dr. Cronin and David Anable, for the hard lessons.

To Robert Massa, for all he was. To Nan Tellier, C.S., and my parents, for their insight and support.

And finally, and always to Paul and to Emma, who made a wilderness blossom like a rose.

Donna . . .

My thanks go out to the many, many people who have had the patience to answer my multitude of questions with kindness and grace. There are the kind people at the chambers of commerce in the Mid-Coast region, especially those in Camden, Bar Harbor and on Deer Isle, who helped me dig up numbers and names in the deepest of winter. There are the libraries — Buck Memorial Library in Bucksport, Belfast Free Library, Thorndike Library at the College of the Atlantic in Bar Harbor, and the Maine State Library in Augusta — and the many librarians who helped me first by offering reference material and second by withholding frowns when said material came back late.

There are the staff members of the Department of Labor, the Department of Marine Resources, the Maine State Museum, the Department of Conservation, the Maine Geologic Survey and many another location who provided me with information and ideas. Thanks. And thanks to the winter rangers at Acadia National Park for cheerful and good information, and to the folks at Maine Audubon, the Natural Resources Conservancy and the Abbe Museum for their continual help. Thanks to William David Barry, Wanda Morin and Darwin Davidson for your special help.

Thanks, too, to those around me who kept things in perspective: to Joe Brooks, for being so very grounded, and for representing us so well in Augusta; to Carol, for reaching out to the reader with her concise lyricism; to Dan, for his steady focus on the book; to Carol B., for your cheery support and genuine concern for the region; and to those who have added levity and distraction, especially Jane Lor and her boys — Jerrod, Ivan, Michael and Justin. Thanks also to my parents and my brother Ron for still asking me, "Now which book is this?"

And finally thanks to my Maine family: to Daniel, who helps me explore Maine with a child's eye, then delights me with Lego creations upon our return home; and to Bill, my guide to sea, sky and e-mail.

MAINE'S PREMIERE OCEANFRONT RETIREMENT COMMUNITY

PENOBSCOT SHORES is a spectacular independent retirement community on twenty magnificent acres overlooking Penobscot Bay. Penobscot Shores offers you a full range of services -- Maintenance, health, fitness, dining, housekeeping and transportation; leaving you free to enjoy the many recreational and cultural offerings of Mid-Coast Maine! Penobscot Shores has an apartment or cottage that is sure to meet your needs! Refer to the Real Estate section of this book for more information on Penobscot Shores.

Penobscot Shores combines the location you want and the lifestyle you desire!

Mail in the coupon below for more information

Table of Contents

Directory of Maps

Maine's Mid-Coast

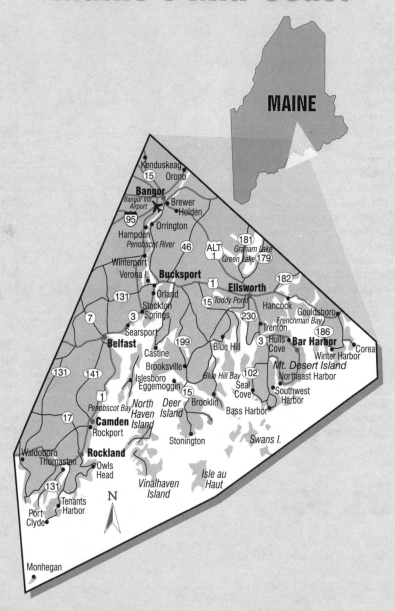

Waldoboro to
Stockton Springs

Inland to Bangor

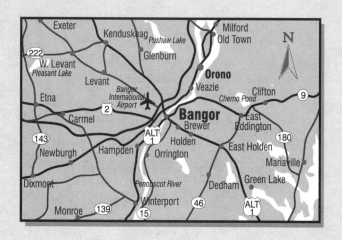

Bucksport to Gouldsboro

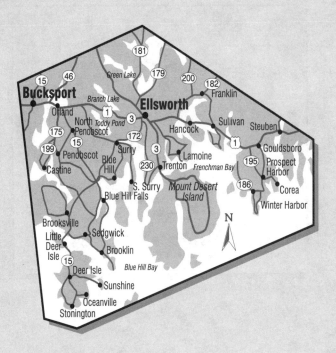

Mount Desert Island

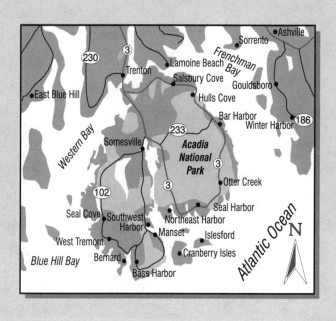

Photo: Bangor Daily News

Fall is a great time of year to visit and relax in Maine.

How to Use This Book

It's a fact of life that most visitors to Maine's Mid-Coast travel on U.S. Highway 1. For this reason, we've organized the listings in most chapters (exceptions are noted in each respective chapter's introduction) geographically, following that highway's path northward and eastward. The first section runs from Waldoboro to Stockton Springs. The second section allows for a jog inland to Bangor along U.S. Highway 1A. The third section picks up U.S. 1 back where we left it, on the coast at Bucksport, and extends to Gouldsboro. The fourth section covers Mount Desert Island, a destination in itself for many visitors. These towns and their locations may mean nothing to you now, so check our maps to get your bearings.

Because the area this book covers is so wide, we retained these four geographic sections throughout all applicable chapters and arranged entries as you would encounter them on U.S. 1. We thought this arrangement would help you find the restaurants, accommodations, attractions, etc. nearest you. The only exception is the Shopping chapter: We still orient you by geographic region, but within each we list antique shops, specialty-food sources and book shops alphabetically. We figured if you were on the hunt for those items, distance would be less of a factor.

A number of special places appear repeatedly throughout the book. For instance, a park might be described in the Attractions chapter as well as in the Parks and Recreation chapter, while a separate entry geared toward children might appear in the Kidstuff chapter. We trimmed some repetition for space reasons, but we left some in to save you the trouble of flipping back and forth between chapters. Check the Index if you want to read every reference to a particular place, or simply rely on the numerous cross-references that dot this guide.

The State of Maine has one area code: 207; use that for all instate toll calls. Where we take you to New Brunswick or Nova Scotia on daytrips, we list the proper area code.

Now, addresses. This was a source of continued frustration. All Insiders' Guides endeavor to provide street addresses — obviously they are the most practical references for visitors — but Maine is just not like other states. As we explain in the Getting Here, Getting Around chapter, many businesses don't have street numbers, just a street name. Folks figure the towns they're in are so small that, once you get there, you can't miss your destination. This is the way people here think, and it might take some getting used to. All you can do is get yourself to town and look around. Don't hesitate to stop and ask, or call, for directions if you get lost. Finally, to complicate matters, street addresses are most often insufficient to use as a mailing address because the Postal Service organizes some rural delivery by routes, not roads. If you do need to write to a company or organization listed in this book, call first for a mailing address.

Other chapters you might enjoy reading ahead of time are History, The Maine Experience, Architecture and Our Natural World. They'll help you see and appreciate the story behind the scene, and we've written them to be easy reads. No footnotes, we promise. The rest of the book is arranged so you can dip into selected chapters, depending on your itinerary.

We hope you'll keep this book in your backpack or your car, not on the shelf at home. Read it, mark it up and dog-ear those pages. Wear it out, and when your trip is over, don't forget to write. Tell us about your favorite discoveries. We'd also like to know when a place doesn't live up to our description. Write us c/o Insiders' Guide, P.O. Box 2057, Manteo, NC 27954, or visit us on the Internet (www.insiders.com).

Maine's past is a wild
one — a history of men,
women and wilderness.

History

In Maine, history seeps through the landscape. Perhaps you've already noticed stone walls snaking through Maine's forests and old cribs or pilings rising from the mud flats of tidal rivers. Perhaps you've taken a walk by the shore and been surprised to find banks built from heaps of broken shells.

What is forest today probably was field a hundred years ago; the stone wall confirms the fact. Quiet rivers were crowded with ships navigating the treacherous, rocky stretches; their silent banks once rang with the pounding of shipbuilders' hammers. Solitary island shores were the dining rooms of Maine's Native Americans; the banks of shells were their garbage heaps, now such a rich source of information that only trained archaeologists should sift through them.

Maine's past is a wild one — a history of men, women and wilderness. As hunters and gathers, fishermen, pioneer farmers, lumberjacks and sailors, they faced land, sea and sky with little more than two hands, a brave heart and a clever mind.

Circles of Stone

Before sailing ships graced the coast of Maine, there were dugout canoes. Before there were roads, there were trails. Before there were fields and forests as we know them today stood towering pines 6 feet in diameter.

And long before all that, there was ice. Mammoths and mastodons roamed as far as Georges Bank, now deep in the Atlantic Ocean. When the ice broke, as it did several times during the last ice age, the melt flooded Maine's coastline, and bearded seals and walruses swam as far inland as the present-day Bangor suburb of Orrington.

During the ice age, possibly more than 15,000 years ago, North America became populated by brave trekkers who crossed the Bering Strait via a land bridge formed between Siberia and Alaska. These first Americans began walking in China and kept going for generations, branching southward and eastward, eventually reaching the southernmost tip of South America, eastern Brazil and maritime Canada. We know that these men and women were living in Maine by about 9000 B.C., for archaeologists have discovered campfire-like circles of stones and projectile points in the northwestern part of the state, beyond Rangeley.

By 6500 B.C. a more complex picture of life in Maine emerged. The knives, spear points and adzes (axlike tools for dressing wood) found by archaeologists are similar to tools found along the eastern seaboard as far south as the Carolinas, suggesting that those living here were part of a larger, coastal culture.

After 3,000 years, the cultures regionalized, and Maine life looked different than elsewhere. Archaeologists know this, in part, from the results of a major dig on the island of North Haven at what is known as the Turner Farm Site. Layer by layer, this dig uncovered more than 5,000 years of habitation topped by copper beads fashioned by post-contact Natives from worn-out European copper kettles. The archeological site is closed now, but a replica of it stands in the excellent exhibit, *12,000 Years in Maine,* at the Maine State Museum (see subsequent discussion).

Red Paint and Burnt Offerings

Early Mainers fished for swordfish, probably out of dugout canoes made from the thick white pines of the ancient forest. The vessels must have been strong, and their paddlers intrepid, for evidence suggests they traveled between Nova Scotia and the New England coast — a formidable journey — trading arrowheads and stones such as those discovered in Labrador, the Lake Champlain region and Ontario as well as on the Mid-Coast's North Haven Island.

These early coastal dwellers fed themselves from land and sea and made a spiritual connection with the universe, creating images of sea creatures barely longer than a finger; arrowheads carved in rock crystal; and delicate, tiny decorations on spear points so fragile, they probably were not functional. These people also sprinkled red ocher dust over their dead before burial and so are known as the Red Paint people.

The Red Paint culture apparently vanished around 1800 B.C., but the Susquehanna culture, which reached southwestward to Pennsylvania, emerged. The Susquehannas didn't bury their dead, but rather burned them and placed tools in the funeral pyre. Archaeologists have found charred remains of bone and antler tools as well as copper beads from this era.

The Susquehannas farmed as early as 1000 B.C. They also made pots — and a bit of magic. The conical ceramic containers found on the coast seem to be self-stirring: When heated, the liquid inside swirls.

Gradually, a culture similar to those encountered by the first European explorers emerged. However, because so much changed in the early years of contact with whites, and native tribes were so devastated by disease, scholars can only speculate about pre-contact culture.

For instance, researchers long assumed that Maine's tribes flocked to the coast in summer — much like Maine's visitors today — and retreated inland in winter (but to the woods, not New York or Philadelphia). More recent evidence suggests, however, that tribes most likely remained on the coast throughout the winter. And why not? Winters on the coast are actually milder than inland; there's a warming offshore breeze that keeps snow to a minimum; and while forest animals hibernate, seagoing animals get more active. The best fishing season in the Gulf of Maine, then as now, is from January through March.

Native Sailors and Traders

The Wabanaki (the collective name for the natives who met the first Europeans) were cosmopolitan people, capable of traveling between Mount Desert Island and Quebec City or Nova Scotia by canoe and portage, using heavy dugouts for ocean travel and lighter birch-bark canoes for river and lake voyages. Trade was practiced early here. Though little is known about the Norse gold coin (c. 1065) found in Brooklin, on the Blue Hill Peninsula, archaeologists speculate that it represents the beginning of trade with Europeans who were venturing westward across the Atlantic. (The Norse lived for a year at L'Anse aux Meadows, on the northern tip of Newfoundland.)

European explorers ventured into the region in earnest in the 16th century, with European fishermen in their wake. The explorers wrote glowing accounts, most likely offered to generate interest in the region so as to raise money for further explorations.

The fishermen left few accounts (Who raves about great fishing grounds?). We do know, however, that scores of vessels came to the islands off Maine to fish in spring, leaving their catch on the islands to dry on racks, then returning in the fall to gather the dried fish.

The first recorded European visitor to Maine was Giovanni Verazzano, who sailed from Spain in 1524 and landed near Cape Fear, North Carolina, while searching for a route to India. He sailed north as far as southern Maine, around Cape Small, where he reported the natives hostile and rude and grumbled that they would only accept knives, fish hooks and tools in trade. Apparently, they lowered baskets from cliffs to conduct the trade and derided the whites in loud, vulgar and abusive ways.

But Verazzano returned to Spain with tales of Norumbega, a "city of gold," and fueled interest in the search for a strait to India. The next year, in 1525, Estevan Gomez sailed from Spain and explored Passamaquoddy Bay, Mount Desert Island, Somes Sound, Blue Hill,

FYI

Unless otherwise noted, the area code for all phone numbers listed in this guide is 207.

Jericho Bay, Eggemoggin Reach and the Penobscot River as far inland as Bangor. He found no passage and no gold, but he did find friendly natives. When Andre Thevet, a seagoing monk and a friend of explorer Jacques Cartier (who was busy on the St. Lawrence River to the north) came to Maine in 1555, he found the natives very friendly: He spent five days partying with the Abenaki on the shores of Penobscot Bay, "drinking" tobacco through lobster claws. We don't know whether he left with the pipes, but he is credited with introducing tobacco to France. Thevet's account of his journey is published in John S.C. Abbott's *History of Maine* (B.B. Russell: Boston: 1875). We also found Thevet's account in Roger F. Duncan's excellent, if romantic, *Coastal Maine: A Maritime History* (W.W. Norton & Co.: New York: 1992), from which much of the information for this chapter has come:

As you enter this river there appears an island [Vinalhaven] *surrounded by eight small islets. These are near the country of the Green Mountains. About three leagues into the river, there is an island four leagues in circumference which the natives called Aiayascon* [Islesboro]. *It would be easy to plant on this island, and to build a fortress, which would hold in check the whole surrounding country. Upon landing we saw a great multitude of people coming down upon us in such number that you might have supposed them to be a flight of starlings. The men came first, then the women, then the boys, then the girls. They were all clothed in the skins of wild animals.*

The trading had begun. In 1580 John Walker, an Englishman, landed at Penobscot Bay and left with some 300 dry hides — one reportedly as large as 18 feet square (probably a moose hide, although the size seems too large to be plausible). Maine natives were likely the middlemen, exchanging furs for metal goods and spreading unrest up and down the Gulf of Maine because of their efforts to control the fur trade.

We frequently forget 16th-century contact, but Europeans who arrived in Maine between 1602 and 1610 were amazed to be greeted by native men traveling in 40-foot-long, multi-masted sailboats (known as shallops) and donning modified Basque garb. When Capt. George Waymouth, an early explorer, sailed by Cape Neddick, in the Yorks in southern Maine, in 1602, he and his crew were astonished to meet "eight Indians in a Basque-shallop with mast and sail, an iron grapple, a waistcoat and breeches of black serge . . . hose and shoes on his feet" (from John Brereton, *A Briefe And True Relation of the Discouerie of the North Part of Virginia: Being a most pleasant, fruitfull and commodious soile: made this present yeere, 1602* (Da Capo Press: New York: 1973)).

Not all Natives knew of the Europeans.

According to the oral tradition of the Micmacs, one of the four surviving Maine native tribes, seeing the ships was a baffling sight: "The Indians saw the ship. The children thought the thunder had torn a big tree up. They went home, and said to those there, 'See what the storm did last night! . . . The thunder has pitched a big tree up, roots and all.'" (from Micmac legend, recorded in Bunny McBride's *Our Lives in Our Hands: Micmac Indian Basketmakers* (Tilbury House: Gardiner, Maine: 1990)).

Waymouth's second expedition in 1605 made it to St. George, where the crew had another encounter with the native people. Crew member James Rosier raved about the fishing, the whales, the "raine deare staggeres, fallow deare, and the tabacco, wild vines, strawberries, raspberries, gooseberries, currant trees, rose bushes, peare, ground nuts . . ." His account, *A True Relation of Captain George Waymouth, His Voyage, Made This Present Yeere 1605; In The Discouerie Of The North Part Of Virginia*, appears in George Parker *Winship's Sailors Narratives of Voyages Along the New England Coast, 1524-1624* (Houghton Mifflin & Co.: Boston: 1905). We found it in *A History of Maine: A Collection of Readings on the History of Maine, 1600-1976*, edited by Ronald F. Banks (Kendall/Hunt Publishing Co.: Dubuque, Iowa: 1976, fourth edition).

Rosier's account continues:

This day, about five a clocke in the afternoon, we in the shippe espied three Canoeas coming towards us, which went to the island adjoining where they went ashore, and very quickly had made a fire, about which they stood beholding our ship: to whom we made signes with our hands and hats, . . . because we had not seene any of the people yet. They sent one Canoe with three men, one of which, when they came neere unto us, spake in his language very lowd and very boldly, seeming as though he would know why we were there, and by pointing with his oare towards the sea, we conjectured he meant we should be gone. But when we shewed them knives and their use, by cutting of stickes and other trifles as combs and glasses, they came close aboard our ship, desirous to entertaine our friendship. . . .

The British took advantage of the friendship, kidnapping five men as specimens to bring back to Europe. Among them was the man we know as Squanto, who returned to live with the Pilgrims at Plymouth.

First Colonies

St. Croix, an island in the St. Croix River near the Canadian border, was the first permanent European settlement. It was chosen by Pierre du Guast, Sieur de Monts, in 1604. From there, explorer Samuel de Champlain visited the coast, naming Mount Desert Island and Isle au Haut, recording his encounters, returning with excellent maps. But the winter was shockingly harsher than winters at that same latitude in France, and the colony, isolated in a salty river that could never quite freeze enough to safely pass over, was a poor choice. Nearly half the settlers died; the rest retreated to Nova Scotia.

In 1607, Capt. George Popham established a colony at Popham, near the Indian settlement of Pemaquid, just south of the Mid-Coast area. It too failed after a year, but from lack of leadership more than hardship.

Later, Capt. John Smith tried to start a colony on Monhegan; it also failed.

It was left to the fishermen to establish the first permanent European settlements in Maine. By the 1620s fishermen began to spend winter in Maine — first on Damariscove Island, off the Boothbay Peninsula, and then on Monhegan and other islands — braving the cold to take advantage of the season's excellent fishing. These were not colonies as much as independent habitations. As Roger F. Duncan writes, "These were rough and ready people. They faced the cold, the fog, the gales, and the rough seas to get cargoes of fish ashore. They cured fish, and they ate, drank, roughhoused, and fought. . . . In these practically anarchic fishing settlements, maritime Maine was born."

But when Europeans began to settle in

earnest in New England, tensions rose. Epidemics had already coursed through the tribes. The epidemic of 1617 to 1618 was catastrophic, especially on the heels of one from 1611 to 1613. The intertribal warfare that ensued as a result of the drastic change in each tribe's fortunes merely amplified the decimation.

Overlapping Charters

There also were tensions between the British and the French. France gave Sieur de Monts rights to the area from Newfoundland to New York City and established a trading post in Castine (originally called Pentagoet) by 1613. The British were dividing the same territory. The Puritans of the Massachusetts Bay Company settled much of southern Maine and claimed the land ranging to the St. Croix River. Samuel Waldo, who later settled the Medomak River near Waldoboro, received a patent for the area. The Pilgrims were granted trading rights up the Kennebec River to Cushnoc, where Augusta is today. In 1626, Gov. William Bradford of Massachusetts received a charter for his own trading post in Castine, which the French continually raided and ultimately seized. The French set up a fort there to control their interests in Maine, which they then claimed reached southwest to the Kennebec River.

In the midst of the confusion, one thing became certain: The land north of Massachusetts, between the Piscataqua and St. John rivers, or thereabouts, was called Maine, whether because it was the mainland destination for merchant ships and fishing folk on the islands, or because the French thought it looked like a hand ("main" in French).

In 1642, the British gave Sir Ferdinando Gorges a charter to much of the territory. The capital, Gorgeana (now York), was the first English city chartered in the New World. After Gorges died, Massachusetts bought out Gorges' heirs — in effect, laying claim to all of Maine.

Until 1820, when Maine entered the Union as a "free state" to balance out slave-holding Missouri, the fate of Maine rested with Massachusetts, though its far reaches were continually a point of contention — and battles. Between 1667 and 1676, for instance, Castine (by then given its permanent name from the colorful Baron de Castin) changed hands from British to French to Dutch to British again. As the maritime gateway Downeast and up the Penobscot River, it was a strategic site. The population was a mix of French and British — families, fur traders and fishermen. Rumor has it that many of the early settlements were populated by fugitives or debtors who shared their wives as they did their boats.

A Century of Massacres

And what about the original inhabitants? The British settlers arrived to find the tribes of Maine already decimated by epidemics and fighting for their lives. These tribes — now known as the Penobscot, Passamaquoddy, Maliseet and Micmac — joined together as the Wabanaki Confederacy and formed an alliance with the French in Canada against the encroaching British. Beginning with King Philip's War in 1675, Maine saw nearly a century of bloody massacres that collectively came to be known as the French and Indian War.

These battles were waged over more than the land. As religious refugees, the Puritan British were in the region to stay. The Catholic French, on the other hand, were traders (read transient); they befriended the natives and sought to convert their allies to Catholicism. Thus the war was waged over religion as well as land and lumber.

The first battle, in 1676, just about cleared the region around Damariscotta and Pemaquid of its European settlers, who either were killed or escaped to Monhegan. Then a truce was negotiated between the British and the Penobscot Chief Medicant. The British soon betrayed the truce, launching more skirmishes. By 1678, Castine was in French hands again, remaining so through another spate of battles. In 1692, York Village was attacked. Forty or more settlers were killed; those who survived were forced to march to Canada. The rhythm continued for half a century: Warfare prompted an exodus, which was followed by uneasy peace, British resettlements, then warfare again, with the French frequently egging on the Wabanaki. Then, in 1724, a survivor of the York massacre avenged himself by destroying Norridgewock, the Wabanaki's inland retreat on the Kennebec River north of Skowhegan. With their settlement destroyed and their protector, the Jesuit Fr. Rasle, murdered, the tribes were more or less defeated.

Again, settlers filtered back, though skirmishes continued. In 1731 they built a paper mill in Westbrook, near what is now Portland. In 1735 a group of farmers from Bremen, Germany, sailed across the Atlantic lured by Samuel Waldo's promise to settle in a fine city on the St. George River. Finding wilderness instead, they nevertheless settled and eventually built Waldoboro. (See our Architecture chapter for information about the German Meeting House.)

In 1745, men from Kittery joined Samuel Waldo and a New England regiment to defeat the French at Louisbourg, on Cape Breton Island, Nova Scotia. The defeat signalled the end of the French claim to Maine. But when Britain chose to restore the fort to France in exchange for Madras, India, the colonists were enraged. They had already been irritated by tariffs on goods such as molasses — essential to life in New England — and by the Broad Arrow Policy, which mandated that all white pines with trunks 24 feet or larger in circumference — the tallest and best mast trees in New England — be reserved for the King of England. A rebellion was brewing.

Revolution

By the early 1760s, eight families lived in Castine, and a sawmill was built in Carver's Harbor on Vinalhaven. Soon, much of the land east of the Penobscot River was claimed, and the townships of Bucksport, Orland, Penobscot, Sedgwick, Blue Hill, Surry, Trenton, Sullivan, Mount Desert and Steuben were established. By 1772, Camden, Belfast, Lincolnville and Bangor were settled. These towns were large geographically but small in the number of settlers: seven families on Deer Isle; 10 on Mount Desert Island; five at

Naskeag, in Brooklin; and one family with five sons on Islesboro. Twelve families lived in Bangor at that time.

These settlers were not fishing folk, but rather farmers and lumbermen — many of whom headed to the coast in the wake of forest fires inland. But they also were versatile, independent folk; they picked up the work their coastal predecessors had done for most of the past two centuries, plying the deep ocean waters off the Grand Banks for cod and herring and the inland lakes and rivers and shad and salmon. Settlers built ships and erected sawmills; they sent lumber from the Maine woods to the budding cities down the coast. Machias, just east of the Mid-Coast region, was already well-populated by June 1775 when a British ship arrived in port accompanied by a British warship, the cutter *Margaretta*. The ships were to return with lumber for the British Gen. Gage. It was one thing to send lumber to Boston but quite another to send it into the hands of the British army. The folks of Machias met at a town meeting, declared they would never contribute lumber to the British and erected a liberty pole and planned to capture the *Margaretta*. Midshipman Moor, who captained the boat, was hit by two musket balls and was forced to surrender. He was carried to the Burnham Tavern (it still stands in the center of town) where he died. The *Margaretta* was appropriated by the patriots and renamed the *Machias Liberty*. (Machias forever carries the honor of launching the first naval battle of the American Revolution.) Later that year, Falmouth (now Portland) was burned. The war on Maine's coast mostly consisted of British and Tory blockades and raids against American patriots and neutrals who attempted to ship lumber and supplies down the coast.

Then came the disastrous Penobscot Expedition of 1779, arguably the worst naval disaster in United States military history (with the possible exception of Pearl Harbor). To stage a presence along the Penobscot River,

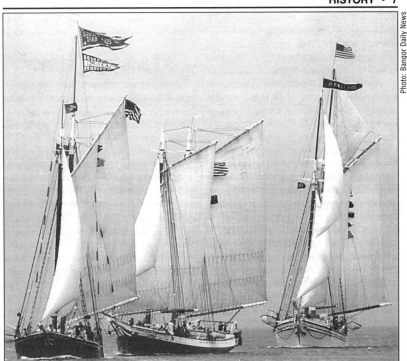

Schooner races along the coast of Maine during summer paint pictures
of the past for spectators who visit the coastline.

the British began building Fort George in June 1779. Fearful that the British could control shipping from Maine to Massachusetts with a base in Castine, the Americans quickly arranged an expedition. Paul Revere was commander of the land artillery under Solomon Lovell. Dudley Saltonstall was commodore of the fleet. Twenty-one armed vessels and two-dozen unarmed transport vessels headed from Boston to Castine. About 900 men were aboard the ships when they anchored off Castine on July 25, 1779.

The British were desperate. They had few men, and the walls of fort they were constructing were barely tall enough to protect the soldiers' knees. Saltonstall didn't believe it, swearing, "I'm not going to risk my fleet in that damned hole."

A few days later a party of about 500 converged on Castine near the British fort. The British prepared to surrender, but the Americans never attacked. As Duncan writes, "Saltonstall remained in terror of three guns."

Weeks passed before the Americans were ready to attack. By that time British reinforcements had arrived. The Americans still had the advantage, though they still did not fight. When they saw the ships approaching, they fled instead, sailing up the Penobscot River, where they were promptly trapped. Rather than give the boats to the British, the Americans burnt their ships — 17 of them — and ran home through the woods. Back in Boston they faced a serious investigation. Saltonstall took most of the blame. Revere was acquitted, but his honor definitely was tarnished. Peleg Wadsworth, assistant commander of the land forces, made his way to Camden where he called in the militia and eventually was able to halt westward movements of British troops in Castine.

Castine, meanwhile, remained a British

stronghold, welcoming Tories from down the coast. From there they raided many Mid-Coast towns, burning buildings, capturing American patriots along the way and forcing them to complete construction of Fort George.

A Tory detachment burned the sawmill and shipyard Jonathan Buck had erected in Bucksport. The patriots in Belfast were forced to evacuate. But when a British detachment led by Camden Tory John Long attempted to take the harbor, two clever men pretended to be an entire regiment to buy time for the town. Duncan's account offers a flavor of this war of neighbors:

The party burned one house, found Mrs. Ogier pretending convincingly to be sick in her bed so saved her house, burned the town's sawmill. Then they set fire to the gristmill, which held goods belonging to the inhabitants of Belfast, who had had to abandon their homes. A Belfast cripple named Daw put out the fire. The British set it afire again threatening Daw ferociously; again Daw put it out. The soldiers beat him and set the fire again, and once again Daw put it out. The soldiers gave up, saying, "Well, we'll let it alone as the damned rebels will starve if we burn their mill." About this time the militia mobilized and fired on the British as they retreated.

After the war, John Long was in Ott's tavern in Camden one cold day. Robert Jameson, a local patriot/citizen, came in and bade Ott build up the fire, as he wanted to burn someone. Ott thought he was joking but built up the fire. Jameson seized Long like a stick of wood and threw him into the fire. He got out, scorched, blistered, and burned. "There," said Jameson, "burn the harbor village again, will you."

When peace was declared, the Tories of Castine realized they would have a hard time reintegrating into the young democracy. Instead they dismantled their homes and built barges, moving their homes onto the flat-bottomed boats and sailing farther east, across

the Passamaquoddy Bay to St. Andrews, New Brunswick, where the structures remain today.

A Land In Its Infancy

After the war, many soldiers were given land in the Maine wilderness as a reward for three years' service. And Maine was still most definitely wilderness. In 1790, its population was less than 100,000, and seven-eighths of that population lived in York, Cumberland and Lincoln counties. Though Maine was part of Massachusetts, its per-capita income was but half of Massachusetts's.

The settling of Maine might have been good for the new Americans, but it was hard for the first Americans. Accustomed to having territory in which to hunt and fish, Maine's native tribes found themselves losing most rights and retreating to small reservations in northern and eastern Maine, including the Penobscot Reservation, on Indian Island in the Penobscot River, a few miles north of Orono.

Lumbering and the shipping of lumber products — pine planks, boards and shingles, spruce masts and spars, ash oars and oak staves — were the most important trades, followed by fishing and farming. Shipbuilding was just beginning.

Farmers cleared the forests, cutting as much as 150 cord a year; grew grains; and raised cattle, sheep, oxen and horses. They also hunted game and wild fowl.

Life was rough, as expressed by French nobleman Francois Alexandre Frederic, Duc de la Rochefoucauld-Liancourt, who came to the United States in 1795 and 1796, touring the East Coast from south to north. In Maine, his party stayed as guests of Maj. Gen. Henry Knox, who had built his sumptuous mansion, Montpelier, on the banks of the St. George River in Thomaston about 10 years earlier. (The original mansion fell into disrepair and was destroyed; later, a reproduction was built. See our Attractions chapter.) Frederic was none

---

INSIDERS' TIP

To find out more about Maine's Native Americans, or to purchase their wood-splint or sweet-grass baskets, visit the Abbe Museum, in Acadia National Park, or the Hudson Museum, at the University of Maine in Orono.

too pleased with his visit however. As reported in Banks's *A History of Maine*, he wrote:

In short, of all America, the province of Maine is the place that afforded me the worst accommodation. And, considering how little reason I found to praise the accommodations of many other places, what I have now said of Maine must be regarded as an affirmation that the condition of human life in that place is exceedingly wretched . . . this country is still in its infancy and in a languid and cheerless infancy.

There might be another side to the story: The folks who run Montpelier say Frederic arrived penniless, with nothing more than the clothes on his back, and Knox helped him get back on his feet. (There's gratitude for you!)

Maine did not have much to offer a pioneer. Summers were not warm, winters were very cold; the growing season was short, the soil rocky and thin. Population centers were far apart, and communication difficult.

But the rudiments of the social fabric already were in place. When Gen. George Washington died on December 14, 1799, the word got out. The population of Maine, even in the wilderness, joined the rest of the nation in wearing black crepe on their right arm for 30 days.

War . . . Again

Gradually, but slowly, the shipping and shipbuilding recovered, with Maine ships and crews sailing to China, India, the East Indies and around Cape Horn to the Northwest Coast. Meanwhile, the French and British were at war. Americans, being neutral, attempted to trade with both parties but got caught in the cross fire, and American men were impressed into the British navy.

To oppose this action, President Thomas Jefferson initiated the 1807 Embargo Act, forbidding any trade with foreign ports — a problem for Maine, because it's economy relied upon the shipping industry. Portland had been the nation's sixth-largest port since 1790; Wiscasset, too, had grown into a thriving port until the passage of the Embargo Act, but was ruined by the war. Castine was deeply hurt, despite the ships that managed to "blow off course" to the West Indies, where they traded their loads and blew back on course.

By 1809 the embargo was modified, but war was declared in 1812 — an act immensely unpopular in New England. The Maine coast was blockaded, and coasters and fishermen were captured as were the towns of Castine and Bangor, where 17 vessels were burned and a host of men and animals captured. Briefly, Castine became a port of entry for Nova Scotia. Fort George was rebuilt, and a canal was dug across the isthmus leading to Castine. (A sign now posted at the narrow entrance to the town serves as a reminder that ships once sailed around this mud flat.)

From Castine, the British raided surrounding towns, but without inflicting great damage. For the most part, the British were not cruel conquerors, but rather friendly neighbors. A good amount of food and fuel were smuggled from the United States to Britain via Castine.

Shipping News

The war ended in 1815; but until 1830, American ships were not allowed to trade between the West Indies and Britain. Again Maine was affected. By the time restrictions were lifted, the wealth had become concentrated in fewer hands. Shipping became focused on the large ports — Boston and New York. Maine's shipping declined, but not its shipbuilding. Waldoboro, once a strong port with its own customs house (now a library), became one of several shipbuilding towns. Portland remained a busy port, however, with seven distilleries turning molasses into rum and farmers from as far away as New Hampshire bringing in goods for export.

Boats from Bath, Wiscasset, Waldoboro, Rockland and Camden would load up with timber and food supplies — salt fish, apples, potatoes, butter, cider, even livestock — bound for the Caribbean and return with rum, molasses, sugar and coffee. Boats sailed to China for tea, silk and porcelain; the Northwest for sea otter fur; and the Caribbean and India to exchange ice for hides used in Maine's shoe factories.

Gradually, Maine entered a golden age, when new ports, new cargo and hence new needs were continually springing up around the globe. With cargo moving mostly by ship, each new need challenged shipbuilders to make vessels roomier, tighter, faster, larger, or even smaller. Maine's marine architects met each demand. The tea trade with India and China in the 1830s and '40s prompted a need for large but swift boats to bring tea to New York and Boston before it lost flavor in the ships' damp holds. When gold was discovered in California, the need for speed only increased.

In 1836, Maine shipbuilders constructed 157 vessels, more than a quarter of the ships built in the country that year. By 1855 Maine's new ships increased to 388, more than a third of the total U.S. production.

When the need came for larger boats — weighing more than 500 tons — Maine kept pace. Of the large boats, 56 percent were built in Maine.

From 1835 until the depression of 1857, when the United States led the world in ocean commerce, Maine led the nation. Good navigation skills, astute reading of the weather and brave use of sails — tempting the cloth to fill but not tear in heavy winds — were all essential to seamanship. But a fast boat mattered immensely to sailing profits, especially after 1848, when gold was discovered in California, and then in 1851, in Australia. It was the age of clipper ships — three-masted, square-rigged ships of streamlined design that sacrificed space for speed.

The fastest of the clippers was *Red Jacket*, a 251-foot-long, 2,035-ton clipper built in Rockland in 1853. Schools were let out to mark her launch. Though her crew was called "indifferent," they found she could average 17 knots per day. On her maiden voyage, she flew into Liverpool, England, outrunning all tugs. Capt. Asa Eldridge backed the huge clipper along the pier while still under sail, a difficult feat even with a smaller ship. *Red Jacket's* record of 13 days, one hour and 25 minutes never has been beaten by a single-hulled vessel.

The *Red Jacket* was perhaps the pinnacle of Maine shipbuilding, though the industry remained strong for many years thereafter. When the gold rush slowed, grain was transported. Rather than speed, room was essential. For this, the roomy but slower Down Easters were

built to ply waters around the globe. Later, after rails overtook transcontinental traffic, came the schooner — swift and compact — built with two, then three, then four, then five and six masts to keep up the speed. They could be maintained by a small crew and thus were economical. Though schooners came off the ways all along the coast, Waldoboro was the center of the multi-masted fleet.

For the passenger trade, however, steamers were used throughout the 19th century. They ran between Boston, Portland and Rockland (you could switch for Belfast and Bangor from there) and eventually brought the high society of Boston, New York and Philadelphia to Mount Desert Island.

FYI

Unless otherwise noted, the area code for all phone numbers listed in this guide is 207.

A Sailor's Life

Seafaring was not an easy life. Food consisted of hard tack, a kind of biscuit soaked in rum; the berths were cramped; and the work was hard and constant. Danger was rampant: hurricanes; gales; diseases such as yellow fever and malaria; accidents on the boat; and ruthless pirates who adhered to the motto "dead cats don't meow." Still, shipping out was the dream of many children.

Consider the autobiographical account of one such Rockland child. Pearl S. Spear's *The Old Sailor's Story, Written by Himself* was put on paper when he was past 80 years old and published in 1888 by Southworth Press of Portland. We found it in *Growing Up in Maine: Recollections of Childhood from the 1780s to the 1920s*, edited by Charles and Samuella Shain (Down East Books: Camden, Maine: 1991).

The son of a captain, Pearl grew up hearing stories from both his parents (both of whom sailed). So perhaps it's no surprise that he first stowed away on a friend's schooner in 1821, when he was just 9 years old; he was put ashore that time. Later on, he headed down to Spear's Wharf at the shore in Thomaston (now called South End in the City of Rockland). There at the wharf, settled in the mud and waiting for the tide to come, lay the high-decked, full-rigged brig *Iddo*, with half her cargo of lime aboard. Pearl stowed away.

A citizen-initiated fund-raising effort led to the construction of a memorial to Korean War veterans in Bangor. The memorial opened in 1996.

That time he made it aboard but suffered a seasickness that a mate attempted to cure not with medicine or copper bracelets, but with a dozen lashes from "the oil of tarred hemp." Then Pearl was sent to cook for the crew.

The brig was pitching into it quite lively, and the boy cook was as sick as could be. We had boiled salt mackerel and potatoes for breakfast, hardbread and coffee sweetened with 'Longlick' (molasses). So the boy, what with getting a 'good licking,' and the smell of bilgewater, fragrant food, etc., became entirely prostrate, and didn't care if they threw him overboard, or what they did. He got into the long boat, which was stowed and lashed on the main hatch, amid-ships, and hid under an old tarpaulin and went to sleep.

Mercifully, Pearl's duties were taken on by a friend, but a day later he was found and again given of the oil of tarred hemp.

A year later, Pearl was bound for Alexandria, with a promotion to a sailor and getting six dollars a month. Upon returning home, he wrote:

Now I tell you this child feels himself quite a somebody, as he stands there at the helm, as we'll haul up around Owl's Head, with white trowsers, blue jacket and new tarpaulin hat on, one fine May morning.

A few voyages later, the crew came down with yellow fever. It was January, the vessel was coming up the Chesapeake, sailing through the ice in a track cut for vessels. With the crew shorthanded, and all sick with the fever, it fell to Pearl to run onto the ice and help pull the boat through, even though his feet were so swollen from the fever that he couldn't get his shoes on. He nearly lost his feet to frostbite on that journey, and yet he kept sailing, traveling to China before he settled down to work on coasters that served the eastern coast.

Lumbering

In 1844, when Henry David Thoreau traveled from Boston to Bangor, the town he described as "a star on the edge of night," he arrived not on a big sailing ship — a 10-day journey — but on a coastal steamer, taking just one day. There, he took a room and set about getting a guide to take him north to Katahdin, or west and north to Greenville and up Moosehead Lake, where he explored Maine's great north woods.

The woods, however, were being cut, its trees sent downriver to sawmills and then to shipyards, or farther south to build homes in cities like Boston, which had depleted its own woods. Much of the lumber was shipped via Bangor, then known as the Queen City, which led the world in lumber exports in the mid-19th century. At one time, kids could make a game of crossing the Penobscot River by walking over docked ships from Bangor to Brewer. Since wood floats, ships could be loaded to the decks with lumber — and they were.

Shipping on the "Bangor" River — the Penobscot — was quite a feat given the turns of the river, a few well-placed ledges, escaped boards of lumber floating every which way, rafts of ice, booms of logs and ships towed three abreast and nine deep, not to mention other schooners, steamers and sidewheelers. Sawdust from the mills and logs made the river's bottom rise so high that the channel had to be dredged several times.

Bangor was the queen of the frontier — both tawdry and elegant. It was the source of supplies and send-off for the lumbermen who worked in the woods in winter, sliding the huge trunks out on the snow and on the river in spring, walking on logs and guiding them downstream to the docks. In town, unwatered rum cost 3¢ per dipper and was relished by those who had survived another bout in the woods. Champagne was poured into wash tubs while land prices skyrocketed during the 1830s. Pine and rum fueled the town. As historian Stewart H. Holbrook wrote in *Holy Old Mackinaw*, "One sniffed the air and found the perfume of pine in it. In the shops one smelled rum and molasses. Lumbermen sweetened the loggers' beans and tea with molasses; they made it into rum for the loggers' entertainment."

Those who rode the speculation wave of the north woods built mansions along State Street in Bangor (many are still standing). Those who merely worked the woods flocked to Skyblue House, Fan Jones's famous Bangor bordello. With its blue chimney visible for miles,

it was the centerpiece of Haymarket Square. Today the famous house and its surrounding taverns are gone, replaced by bank offices.

Far north of Bangor, the woods remained so uncharted that no clear boundary had been established between Maine and British Canada. By the 1830s, territorial arguments were brewing. To preserve the lumbering center amid fears of yet another war, work began for Fort Knox (see Attractions), built on a promontory where the river bends at Bucksport and leads north to Bangor. The earthwork-style fort, made of the granite from nearby Mount Waldo and covered with sod to help drain rainwater, took years to build. But the ensuing so-called "Aroostook War" never amounted to anything, and the fort remained unused except for some training exercises.

The Civil War and Its Aftermath

Maine had something of a personal stake in the Civil War, for Abraham Lincoln's first vice president was Hannibal Hamlin, a Hampden lawyer who also had been a senator from Maine. At the time, vice-presidential candidates were nominated by the party separate from presidential candidates, and Lincoln and Hamlin hadn't even met when they were slated as a pair. It was said at the time, however, that Hamlin was Lincoln's best insurance against assassination, for Hamlin was the greater abolitionist of the two. That thought must have resounded through the nation's collective conscience after 1864, when political maneuvering brought Andrew Johnson to the position of vice president. It wasn't long after Lincoln lost his "insurance" that he also lost his life.

During the Civil War, Maine saw little action on her territory, though an offshore block-

---

INSIDERS' TIP

As you look out at the islands along Maine's Mid-Coast, think of the centuries of paddlers that crossed the waters: early Native Americans in dugout canoes, early European fishermen in shallops using hand lines, and centuries of settlers who farmed and fished from the islands and rowed to the mainland only for necessary supplies.

ade reduced fishing. Maine soldiers, however, saw plenty of trouble. Nearly 80,000 men enlisted, about 1,000 under the leadership of Brewer's Joshua Lawrence Chamberlain, a 33-year old professor at Bowdoin College in Brunswick. Chamberlain commanded the 20th Maine in the battle of Gettysburg and later was awarded the Congressional Medal of Honor for a pair of brilliant maneuvers during that battle, though 130 Maine men were killed and wounded that day. In all, some 8,000 Maine men died during the Civil War. Many more men and their families chose not to return to the northland, instead moving westward, where opportunities seemed greater than in Maine's harsh climate and poor soil.

The lumber industry also moved west. Even though Bangor's lumber production grew after the war, hitting its peak in 1873, it couldn't compare with Midwestern towns. Paul Bunyan, whom Bangor had claimed as its own for a time, had moved on, joined by so many Maine families that the state actually lost population. According to Holbrook: "Saginaw and Muskegon in Michigan would cut more boards in a month than Bangor did in a year, a single sawdust plant would rise on the Columbia River in the Pacific Northwest that could cut twice as much lumber as all of Bangor's four hundred and ten saws." The Queen was dethroned.

Along with its people, Maine continued to export its natural resources, sending granite, sawdust-packed ice and lime to build the cities of the eastern seaboard. Granite from quarries in Rockland, Vinalhaven, Frankfort and Stonington was used to build the bridges, museums, offices and streets of Boston, New York, Philadelphia and Washington, D.C. Lime, quarried from a vein behind Thomaston, was used for making mortar, plaster and cement. It was shipped down the East Coast in very tight schooners, for even a little water intrusion would cause the lime to burn, endangering not only the cargo, but also the entire wooden ship.

One resource Maine did not export was its lumber. Instead, the state began piling up its softwood supply and turning it into paper. From Madawaska to Westbrook and in Bucksport on the Penobscot River, paper mills were being built. (You still can tour the Champion Paper Mill in Bucksport; see our Attractions chapter.)

Population loss and industrial development left Maine open for an influx of immigrants. Swedes settled in Aroostook County and west in Monson; Scots-Irish and other Europeans settled along the coast to work in the paper mills, woolen mills and shoe factories that were being built along Maine's cascading rivers, both coastal and inland; French Canadians streamed in from the north, also to work in the mills; Italian, Finnish and Portuguese stone cutters came to work the quarries; and Eastern European Jews flocked to Bangor and branched out — among them, Ruby Cohen, father of U.S. Secretary of Defense William S. Cohen.

Rusticators

Lumber, granite and lime might seem ungainly exports, but Maine had another less physical, even less tangible, resource. It was the call of the wild, the call of her natural beauty, though a tame call since a steamer could take you there. Maine's call was heralded in the 1840s by writer Henry David Thoreau, who traveled inland and into the great north woods, and even earlier, in the mid-1830s, by artist Thomas Doughty, who painted images of Mount Desert Island. Doughty's paintings, exhibited in an 1836 Boston exposition, brought more painters to Maine. Their images of a wild and mountainous coast lured visitors to Maine in search of an essence, purity and sense of grandeur. These visitors, who frequently stayed for a summer, became known as rusticators, or seekers of a rustic experience. They were hoping to find something uniquely American in the wilderness, searching for an identity separate from Europe. These first rusticators stayed with farmers and fishermen. They continued to come after the Civil War and after the Industrial Revolution, seeking simply a respite from the cities, longing for what urbanites saw as a simple, land-based life. (We provide a sketch of the rusticators in our Acadia National Park chapter.)

The southern Maine town of Portland already had exerted a national influence. Writers like Henry Wadsworth Longfellow, John Neal and Seba Smith had broadcast Maine to the nation. Their stories brought artists and adventurers to the coast of Maine. The very wealthy followed close on their heels. The well-heeled folk built huge mansions and called them cottages as if they were minuscule, unheated bungalows, then developed summer societies in Camden, Castine, Hancock Point, Gouldsboro and on the islands — Islesboro, North Haven, Isle au Haut and, most dramatically, Mount Desert Island.

These were influential people, able to maneuver a portion of the island first into a national monument and eventually into Acadia National Park. They not only begged favors off the government, but also were able to assist. During World War I, amateur radio enthusiast Alessandro Fabri, a wealthy summer resident, built a powerful transmitter in his Bar Harbor home. From there, he was able to communicate via Morse code with other enthusiasts and with ships at sea, reporting on explosions and submarine attacks and, on October 6, 1918, transmitting the news of Germany's first offer of peace.

While summer society continued to visit the Mid-Coast throughout the 1920s, the postwar establishment of the income tax took its toll. A worse impact was the stock-market crash of October 1929 that destroyed many a summer person's equity — and kicked off the Great Depression. Until then, life in these towns had been quite luxurious: elegant mansions, numerous summer parties and hours of shopping in branch stores of Boston's finest merchants and at stands selling exotica from China, Japan, Turkey, Spain — and Maine. Each summer, members of Maine's Wabanaki tribes settled in a row of tents on the shores of Bar Harbor, offering canoe trips and making and selling a variety of wood-splint baskets as well as birch boxes and canoes.

By the onset of World War II, folks didn't have to own a mansion to visit Maine in summer. A car was useful, however, as were a few bucks to pay for a week or so in one of the many tourist cabins, such as those at Moody's Diner in Waldoboro, that had sprung up along U.S. Highway 1.

During the war, sailing yachts were used to patrol the coast; on land, Mainers kept watch for German submarines and spies. What they found could be the substance of a novel or two. Consider the incident late at night on No-vember 29, 1944, when Harvard Hodgkins, a high school student, was driving down Hancock Point, coming home from a dance. He noticed two men dressed in city clothes, carrying suitcases. The boy and his father, a sheriff, later followed the men's tracks to other shore and found a rubber boat: The pair were German spies.

After World War II, there was yet another exodus, similar to the one that followed the Civil War. Servicemen and women who had seen the world as youths chose to leave the state in search of greater opportunity elsewhere. Then came the summer of 1947, when it hardly rained a drop during July, August and September. Water supplies dwindled, and the forest floors dried. Never before on record had the Mid-Coast experienced so dry a summer and fall. Fire was imminent.

On the afternoon of October 17, 1947, a fire started in a cranberry bog near Hulls Cove on Mount Desert Island. At first it was relatively contained — only 169 acres burned in three days. Then the wind came up, fanning the fire and spreading it across 2,000 acres. Help came from Bangor and the University of Maine, and even more helpers flew in from other national parks in the East — to no avail. Two days later the wind increased to gale force and shifted, directing the fire toward Bar Harbor, directly at the line of cottages known as Millionaire's Row. It took fewer than three hours for the fire to travel 6 miles and destroy 67 summer cottages, 170 permanent homes and five large hotels. The blaze raged for 10 days in all and smoldered for weeks more, burning 17,188 acres — more than 10,000 of them in Acadia National Park.

The park eventually recovered, with deciduous trees taking the place of the old spruce and fir forests. But summer society never recovered. The scourge of fire, combined with the increased equality of postwar society, had changed things dramatically.

Today you'll find society and national figures like Martha Stewart and Casper and Jane Weinberger joining the Rockefellers as residents of Mount Desert Island mansions. But you'll also find numerous hotels — many old cottages that survived the fire have been turned into accommodations — and motels for urban summer visitors.

Cannons were installed along the coast many years ago to protect against attack during the Revolutionary War. Today, many of these no-longer-operative pieces of weaponry still adorn their original sites.

Other things also changed in following years. Most obvious, perhaps: Maine's traditional resource-based industries were shrinking.

Once there were so many poultry-processing plants in town and poultry raisers out of town that Belfast literally had chicken feathers flying through the air. Now? Nary a chicken to be found. Rockland used to be differentiated from Camden with the disparaging adage: Camden by the sea, Rockland by the smell (of its fish-processing plants). There's no smell left in Rockland, just some empty warehouses. Cafes and galleries line its streets. Perhaps most telling, Camden's Knox Woolen Mill now is the site of a large plant owned by the credit card firm MBNA. Like the rest of the nation, Maine is becoming a service-based economy.

The poultry industry left in the late '70s, overlapping with the back-to-the-landers who arrived early in that decade, seeking farms and land-based lives. These former urbanites, like the rusticators before them, sought respite and adventure. Some may have been following Helen and Scott Nearing's image of "the good life" as delineated in their several books on the topic, among them *Living the Good Life*. Some were following Zen practitioners settled in Blue Hill. Many came on their own and did live off the land, at least for a while.

Today's Maine is still long on the romance of land and sea but actually quite short on farmers and commercial fishermen. Of the state's 630,000 workers, only about 2,000 people fish — that includes hauling lobster traps. There are slightly more farmers — about 5,500 people work or own farms. As for lumbermen, now that machinery does most of the job, only about 1,800 people log each year. And yet, like stone walls that so frequently trail through the woods, the independent spirit is still visible in Maine — among the farmers, fishermen, mechanics, home builders, boat builders, cabinet makers, artists, crafters and small and home-based business owners.

Historical Societies

Intimate, but public, Maine's historical societies thrive on the state's fascination with its past. We know of no town without a historical society, though not all towns have managed to find a building in which to house their collections. Should you be visiting Maine in summer when they're more likely to be open, stop in: The artifacts and photos reveal the life behind these events.

You'll find some historical collections in old one-room schoolhouses, others in period homes or barns. Franklin's is in an old church; Ellsworth's, in an old jail. Days and hours of operation vary. Some have no phones; if they do, expect it to ring in someone's house. Frequently, the contact number is the society's president or secretary.

The following is a rundown of historical societies in the Mid-Coast region.

Waldoboro to Stockton Springs

Waldoborough Historical Society Museum, Maine Highway 220, south of U.S. Highway 1, Waldoboro, no phone

Friendship Museum, Maine Highway 220 and Martin's Point Road, Friendship, 832-4818

Cushing Historical Society Museum, Hathorn Point Road, Cushing, 354-6431 (for information)

Thomaston Historical Society, at the Maj. Gen. Henry Knox Museum, Knox Street, Thomaston, 354-2295

INSIDERS' TIP

Stand at the banks of the Penobscot, St. George or Medomak rivers and picture the scene a century ago: The waters were filled with coastal steamers and schooners, even some clipper ships — carrying rum, maybe lumber, ice or granite, and sailing for parts unknown.

Marshall Point Light and Lighthouse Museum, Marshall Point Road (Maine Highway 131), St. George, 372-6450 (see our Lighthouses chapter)

Monhegan Museum, Monhegan Island Lighthouse, Monhegan, 596-7003 (see our Offshore/Islands chapter)

The Old Homestead, Ash Point Drive, off Maine Highway 73, Owls Head, 594-7646

Vinalhaven Historical Society Museum, High Street, Vinalhaven, 863-4410 or 863-4318

The **Schoolhouse Museum of the Lincolnville Historical Society**, Maine Highway 73, just off U.S. Highway 1, Lincolnville Beach, 789-5445

Islesboro Historical Society, Main Road, Islesboro, 734-6733

Sailors' Memorial Museum and Lighthouse, Grindle Point, Islesboro, 734-2253 (see Lighthouses)

Belfast Museum, 6 Market Street, Belfast, 338-2078 or 338-1875

Searsport Historical Society, U.S. Highway 1, Searsport, 548-6663

Inland to Bangor

Bangor Historical Society, 159 Union Street, Bangor, 942-5766

Kinsley House Museum Hampden Historical Society, 83 Main Road (U.S. Highway 1A), Hampden, 862-2027

Hannibal Hamlin House, Fifth and Hammond streets, no phone

Brewer Historical Society, at Clewley Museum, 199 Wilson Street, Brewer, 989-7468

Bucksport to Gouldsboro

Bucksport Historical Society Museum, Main Street, Bucksport, 469-3623

Orland Historical Society, Main Street (Maine Highway 175), Orland, 469-2476

Castine Historical Society, at the Abbott School, Town Common, Castine, 326-8786

Holt House, Water Street, Blue Hill, no phone

Brooksville Historical Society Museum, Maine Highway 176, Brooksville Corner, 326-4137

Shakespeare School, Maine Highway 15, Deer Isle, no phone

Salome Sellers House, Maine Highway 15A, Sunset, Deer Isle, no phone

Ellsworth Historical Society, State Street, Ellsworth, no phone

Franklin Historical Society, Sullivan Road (Maine Highway 200), Franklin, 565-3635 or 565-3323

Old Town House (Gouldsboro Historical Society), U.S. Highway 1, Gouldsboro, 963-5530

Mount Desert Island

Bar Harbor Historical Society, 33 Ledgelawn Avenue, Bar Harbor, 288-3807

Mt. Desert Island Historical Society, Maine Highway 102, Somesville, 244-9012

Frenchboro Historical Society, Frenchboro, Long Island, 334-2929

The appeal of the Mid-Coast area is its sweep and grandeur — mountains that meet the sea, lakes that shimmer in the sunset and rocky peninsulas that reach like fingers into Penobscot Bay.

Area Overview

Maine: The Way Life Should Be

That's one of the state's tourism slogans, and it says volumes. Maine is a summer day from childhood where the yellow sun, blue water and green pines go on forever. It's small towns, high school basketball tournaments and the best lobster in the world. It's three-masted schooners, Acadia National Park and blueberries.

We've sliced Maine's Mid-Coast into four regions and diced it into even smaller bits, so you can find just the right bed and breakfast, diner and farmer's market. Still, the appeal of the area is its sweep and grandeur — mountains that meet the sea, lakes that shimmer in the sunset and rocky peninsulas that reach like fingers into Penobscot Bay.

To help you get acclimated, let's consider the state in broad strokes. Maine has a population of 1.2 million in an area of 33,215 square miles. That's about the size of the other five New England states combined. Almost 90 percent of Maine's land is forested. In fact, wood product processing has been the principal industry for more than 300 years, with paper-making leading the way. The state is known for its potatoes, apples, blueberries and, of course, lobsters. While the commercial fishing industry is on the decline, there's an upsurge of interest in cranberry growing. Maine's been slow to climb out of the 1990-91 recession, but manufacturing is making a comeback. General Electric has completed two expansions to its facilities in Bangor; Brewer Automotive Components finished a major expansion to its plant; and Nautica, the clothing manufacturer, added 265,000 square feet to its Rockland facility. Meanwhile, MBNA, the country's second-largest credit card company, has six sites in Maine, three of which are in the Mid-Coast region. It employs nearly 3,000 Mainers and expects that number to grow by another 2,000 by 2001.

The state's summer climate is one of the most comfortable in the continental United States. The humidity is relatively low, the sun shines more than 60 percent of the time, and summer temperatures average 70 degrees. Average rainfall is 43 inches. Winter temperatures average 20 degrees. Snow usually doesn't fall until mid-December, and the annual average is 60 to 90 inches, with more falling in the northern inland sections of the state. The coastal regions are tempered by onshore breezes, which make it warmer in the winter and cooler in the summer.

If you're deciding when to travel, remember that black flies and mosquitoes can make some country pursuits almost unbearable in June. July and August are the most popular months. If you want to avoid the crowds, try September and October; some attractions might be closed, but the fall foliage is spectacular. In winter, off-season accommodations rates can be a real boon to the hardy traveler, especially when it means cross-country skiing in Acadia National Park or tobogganing at Camden's Snow Bowl.

Much of Maine's natural beauty is unspoiled by development, and many areas look just as they did decades ago. Pictures of the Aldermere Farm in Rockport 20 years ago show the area almost entirely unchanged. This timeless quality has attracted more than tourists. Actor Mel Gibson made quite a splash when he filmed part of his feature *The Man Without a Face* in Camden/Rockport. Parts of *Forrest Gump*, Stephen King's *Thinner* and the sequel to the TV special *Sarah, Plain and Tall* were filmed here as well.

If Maine's scenery is grand, so is the character of its people. The legendary Margaret Chase Smith was the first woman to serve in the United States Senate, and she was the first senator to oppose Sen. Joseph McCarthy and his Committee on Un-American Activities. Her political career began in 1935 when she took her late husband's seat in the U.S. House of Representatives. Smith ran successfully for the Senate in 1949 and was re-elected every six years until retiring in 1972. The independence she manifested has been a hallmark of politics in this state. That, and sheer intellectual capacity, distinguished the careers of the late Sen. Edmund Muskie, a towering figure in Maine and national politics, as well as former Senate Majority Leader George Mitchell and current Defense Secretary William S. Cohen. All came from modest roots, and while they were respected for their moderation, they weren't afraid to take strong positions. Cohen, a Republican, sat on the Senate Judiciary committee that investigated the Watergate scandal in the late 1970s, and he voted to impeach then-President Richard Nixon.

Political celebrities aren't the state's only asset, although former Defense Secretary Casper Weinberger and his wife, Jane, live on Mount Desert Island. A number of Roosevelts have homes here, as do domestic diva Martha Stewart, movie star John Travolta and singer/songwriter Don McClean. Other sightings include visitors Walter Cronkite, Danny DeVito, Billy Joel, Christie Brinkley and John F. Kennedy Jr. If this list is incomplete, it's because most folks here don't much care about famous people, and that's probably why they come. We give them space.

Getting There . . .

The area we cover in this book is a constellation of tiny towns, all with fewer than 10,000 people and most with a fraction of that. Only **Bangor** weighs in at 33,000, making it the third-largest city in the state and the commercial and cultural center of the region. Its quality of life is beginning to draw attention. MacMillan's *Places Rated Almanac*, a national city-rating guide, ranks Bangor 110th out of 351 municipalities surveyed. The city has the 16th-lowest crime rate in the country, and when compared to other metro areas with 100,000 people or fewer, it places first in a field of 17.

This comes just three years after the city was named one of the top 10 municipalities in the country by *World Trade* magazine.

Rockland also has distinguished itself, having been written up in *The 100 Best Small Towns in America* by Norman Crampton. When the book first came out in 1995, however, a local newspaper writer with a long history in the area wondered in print whether Crampton had ever actually been to Rockland:

"In the wild and woolly days of the 1970s and '80s, such an idea would have been unthinkable," wrote the inimitable Emmet Meara in the *Bangor Daily News*. "Let's chart the city's progress from the night one of the members of the NSKK Motorcycle Club drove his gleaming Harley up the ramp into the Golden Spike, the club's home bar. The Spike was so bad that even the police hated to go in. Every Labor Day, the rumor was that the Hell's Angels were coming. They never did, but it said a lot that Rockland was where they were expected."

Meara reported there were times Rockland's crime rate vied with Portland, a city eight times its size. That was then. This is now. Rockland's crime rate has dropped several years in a row, and it is an altogether different city. Now there are espresso bars, chic clothing stores and funky, fabulous restaurants. The city bills itself as the schooner capital of the world, the lobster capital of the world and, more recently, an art mecca. The Farnsworth Museum (see our Attractions and Arts chapters) is expanding to house the works of the Wyeth family (N.C., Andrew and Jamie); the new facility is expected to draw thousands of visitors a year.

Camden never had a past to overcome, except perhaps that it was the setting for the movie version of *Peyton Place*. It has always had a civil, sophisticated mix of locals, summer people and retirees. A number of business executives and CIA and State Department personnel have retired here, and they're the force behind the town's phenomenally successful Camden Conference, a decade-old international forum held in February (see our Annual Events chapter). The U.S. National To-

---

www.insiders.com

See this and many other **Insiders' Guide®** destinations online — in their entirety.

Visit us today!

Although relatively quiet in winter, downtown Bar Harbor bustles with visitors in summer.

boggan Championships are held at the Snow Bowl the same month, which gives you a sense of the scope of this high-powered little community. The summer sight of schooners nestled in Camden's picturesque harbor is enough to make anyone want to move here. The shopping's great, as is the 5,500-acre Camden Hills State Park.

Bar Harbor is similar in size to Camden, but its location next to Acadia National Park, one of the most visited national parks in the country, makes it far more crowded in the summer. Many Bar Harbor businesses shut down in winter (we discovered this the hard way while researching this book), but Acadia is just as appealing in the off-season. Those four towns may be the highlights of the Mid-Coast area as we've defined it, but let's look more carefully at the terrain between them. We've divided the area into four sections: Waldoboro to Stockton Springs; Inland to Bangor; Bucksport to Gouldsboro; and Mount Desert Island.

Waldoboro to Stockton Springs

Waldoboro is home to cultural landmark Moody's Restaurant (see our Restaurants chapter), Morse's Sauerkraut, Borealis (for-merly Bodacious) Breads and the first ocean-going five-masted schooner, built in 1888. First settled in 1740, the little community attracted German immigrants who were distressed to find that Samuel Waldo had not been entirely truthful with them about the level of civilization to be found there in the early days. You, however, will not be distressed. The town itself is small, with a population of about 4,000, but there are some fine bed and breakfasts, good restaurants and beautiful countryside to explore.

Inland are a sprinkling of small towns worth exploring as well — **Union** and **Warren** among them. Down the peninsulas, life slows down. The roads can be excellent for biking, and along the way you'll catch glimpses of rivers and bays through forests and across the fields of saltwater farms. Towns such as **Friendship** and **Cushing** are sleepy and pleasant, but don't expect shops all decked out for tourists. Those cluster on U.S. Highway 1, the Mid-Coast's main tourist strip. A trip down the St. George Peninsula is rewarded by the Marshall Point Lighthouse near **Port Clyde**, the point of departure for the mail boat to the island of **Monhegan** (see our Offshore/Islands chapter). There was a time when the population clustered at the tips of these peninsulas because boats, not cars, were the primary means of transportation. Consequently, many of the houses you'll pass are old and exquisite.

Thomaston is our next stop on U.S. 1. Once you put the state prison behind you, massive white-clapboard sea captains' houses line the center of town in an impressive display of architectural pyrotechnics. The blocks of buildings that form the downtown area hold restaurants and bookstores, so don't speed past. At the head of the St. George River stands Montpelier, a splendid 1930 reproduction of a 30-room mansion built by Maj. Gen. Henry Knox in the 1790s.

We've told you something about Rockland already but should add that it's the departure point for the state-run ferry to **Vinalhaven** (see Offshore/Islands), upscale **North Haven** and tiny **Matinicus**. In Rockport, don't miss Aldermere Farm, home of the Belted Galloways (a.k.a. Oreo-cookie cows). To get there, turn right on Chestnut Street in front of the Camden Post Office and continue for a mile or so, passing a cemetery on the left. Inland, the towns of **Hope**, **Appleton** and **Searsmont** are windows on the way Maine used to be. If you like touring rural America, get out your map and go!

Continuing north on U.S. 1, **Lincolnville Beach** (not to be confused with Lincolnville Center a few miles inland) has restaurants, shops and one of the few sand beaches around. The **Islesboro** ferry leaves from here as well (see Offshore/Islands). **Belfast** is next on our tour. The town thought it would never get over the closing of its poultry and shoe enterprises, but MBNA opened a processing center in town and lifted spirits considerably. The town has long had great art galleries, an impressive theater group and wonderful restaurants, but the pace of development is picking up, particularly along the waterfront. The housing stock is impressive as well. Historic properties abound, including the imposing James P. White House (1840). **Searsport's** heritage as a shipbuilding town can be seen in its deep-water port, in the rows of exquisite sea captains' houses and in the Penobscot Marine Museum. The town's claim that it's the antique capital of Maine may be a long shot, but summer traffic stalls here as cars and vans pull in and out of the string of shops and flea markets that line the highway. **Stock-**

ton Springs escaped the path of U.S. 1, so it feels like a real place where real people live and work and play. There are restaurants, accommodations and Cape Jellison, with its Fort Point State Park, to explore. And all at your own pace!

Inland to Bangor

The highway inland to Bangor will take you along the south branch of the Marsh River and then along the beautiful Penobscot. The towns of **Prospect** and **Frankfort** are barely bends in the road, but **Winterport** and **Hampden** have little commercial centers. Bangor is the major hub here, with the towns of **Brewer**, **Veazie** and **Orono** clustering around it like satellites. The result is a broad commercial district that includes a downtown area on the upswing, the Maine Mall (see our Shopping chapter) and the University of Maine in Orono (see our Education and Spectator Sports chapters).

Bucksport to Gouldsboro

The Bucksport-to-Gouldsboro stretch of the Mid-Coast area takes you through Ellsworth, **Hancock** and **East Sullivan**. **Bucksport** has a small downtown stretch from which you can see Fort Knox, and farther upriver, the massive Champion International paper mill (see our Attractions chapter). Beyond it is the Blue Hill Peninsula, with Penobscot Bay on one side and Blue Hill Bay on the other. Here you'll find elegant **Castine** village, with its over-arching elms and white-clapboard homes. Helen and Scott Nearing built their good life on nearby **Cape Rosier**, while E.B. White wrote his fine New Yorker essays and children's books from **North Brooklin**. The area is alive with writers, artists, craftsmen and musicians, so go slowly and keep an eye out for galleries and studios.

Little Deer Isle and **Deer Isle** are connected to the mainland by a bridge and a causeway (Maine Highway 15). Drive all the way to the end and you'll find **Stonington**, a fishing community that retains some of the grit and grace of old-time Maine. Here you'll take the mail boat to **Isle au Haut** (see our

Photo: Mary (Dysart) Hartt

Moose are part of the wildlife that you'll discover in Maine's Mid-Coast region.

Offshore/Islands chapter) and its tiny sliver of Acadia National Park.

Back on U.S. 1, the next town we consider is **Ellsworth**, with its odd, split character. First you pass through a handsome, old downtown area that includes a block of three-story buildings built in 1845 and the offices of the formidable *Ellsworth American* weekly newspaper. But then the road takes a sharp turn to the right toward Mount Desert Island, taking you through a strip of commercial development that rivals any you'd find in major metropolitan areas across the country. From there U.S. 1 swings north again, and once you get to open road, you might as well be in a different state.

The area beyond Ellsworth is often referred to as Downeast Maine, and it really does have a distinct character: little or no commercial development along the highway, magnificent vistas and even glimpses of Frenchman Bay off to the right. This stretch culminates on the Schoodic Peninsula, which ends at Schoodic Point, another part of Acadia National Park. Mount Desert Island dominates the views from the west side of the peninsula, while the east side looks out on open ocean. None but the most dedicated tourists get this far north, so you'll find a Maine that's unalloyed — cheaper, less crowded and more real somehow.

Mount Desert Island

The last area we explore is **Mount Desert Island** (a.k.a. MDI). Follow Maine Highway 3 from U.S. 1 in Ellsworth to MDI, the land of Bar Harbor and Acadia National Park, to which we've devoted an entire chapter of this book. The whole area is rich with activity. Acadia is one of the most visited destinations in Maine, so while it turns Bar Harbor into a tourist town in the summer, the west side of the island, often called the quiet side, retains a calm demeanor. And there's plenty to explore. Check out our Attractions chapter for details.

Getting Along

If you've lived in a small town, Maine will seem mighty familiar. "They'll know what toothpaste you're using before the week is up," said one of our mothers when we moved here. She'd grown up in a small town in Wisconsin, and she wasn't far wrong. No one much cared about our toothpaste, but a man who moved to town when we did had this story: A few days after he'd bought his house, he and his wife decided to wallpaper the dining room. As they stood in line at the hardware store, they discussed whether to buy and apply sizing — that critical first element — to the walls. "Oh no," interjected the clerk, "That wall's been sized." Somehow she knew who they were, what house they'd bought, and she remembered selling sizing to the previous owners for that particular room.

Similarly, there are butchers at small grocery stores who will advise you on what to serve your guests because they know what your guests were served last night at Mrs. So-n-So's house. A friend of ours was shooed home because, said the butcher, "you have plenty of meat in your freezer. Now use it up before it goes bad." This can be charming — and it can be unnerving.

"I have to live in this town," is what people say when they temper their response to some civic scandal, but that tempering brings an air of much-needed civility. Which is not to say tempers never flare. There's nothing like a good zoning or school controversy to divide and alienate towns and families; hard feelings can last for years. Still, when you see a town pull together to raise money for two women with breast cancer, to fight off the Postal Service's attempt to shut down their post office, or to build up some town facility, you know that this is indeed the way life should be. Tiny Camden, for instance, raised $3.1 million for a 9,000-square-foot underground addition to its handsome library at the head of its harbor. No less than former First Lady Barbara Bush gave the keynote address. Camden is unusual in its resources, but not in its community spirit.

Another aspect of this small-town atmosphere is that families who have lived here for generations have a solid sense of identity. They don't bother buying expensive clothing or houses or cars to telegraph how important they are. They tend to look more at who you are than what you have. This translates into an easy egalitarianism, which can, at times, turn into reverse snobbery. If you're not from here, you're "from away."

How long do you have to live here to be from here? An old saw says there are daytrippers, summer people and year-rounders . . . and then there are natives — *they* are from here. What if you too were born here? That doesn't mean you're *from* here. "Just because a cat's had kittens in the oven, doesn't mean they're biscuits," as the saying goes.

That attitude's softened considerably, but it flares up in various forms when people here feel that newcomers are changing the character of their state, a character as complex as it is precious. The late Lew Dietz, in his classic book on Maine, *Night Train at Wiscasset Station*, wrote "The [state's] bedrock characteristic, it seems to me, is a stubborn independence of thought and action. Call it the frontier syndrome, or, if you will, a persistent strain of primitive, old-fashioned Americanism."

Photo: Bangor Daily News

Two fishermen row to shore after a day of pulling lobster traps aboard the *Miss Judy*.

Dietz also calls it "prickly pride," adding, "It may well be that a fair share of Maine's people today are engaged in trades, services and industry, but it is from its cadres of fishermen, woodsmen, trappers and farmers that Maine attitudes continue to be nurtured. It was the predisposition to resent all privileges based on wealth and class which colored Maine frontier attitudes. And this prejudice persists to this day."

Dietz wrote that 20 years ago, but his words are still right on target, and it's one of the hardest lessons newcomers and relocating businesses have to learn. One recent arrival, a big company from outside New England, hired a local contractor to do some work but was distressed to find the owner working along with his crew. That's common practice here, but the company though it inappropriate — he was supposed to be the manager! — and asked him to stop. Needless to say, it caused some hard feelings.

Tread Lightly

While this book tracks U.S. Highway 1 in its path up the coast, we urge you to explore beyond it. There's great charm on the back roads of Maine, but you'll see hardship as well. Just don't judge too harshly as you pass. Amy Willard Cross could be describing Maine in this excerpt from *The Summer House*:

The houses that are old and worn down are owned by the real people who collect rotting and rusting machinery, be it tractors, cars or old plows in a pile on the front lawn. For country people, used to making do, those piles are a savings account whose balance is shown to all — and it's a wealth the summer folk can not understand.

As you travel, remember that tourism is a two-edged sword — it brings jobs, but it also brings traffic jams. Of course, there's a natural tension between the tourists eating ice-cream cones in the sun and the people who hustle two or three jobs in that same summer sun just to cover winter's fuel bills. Keeping body and soul together here without a trust fund requires an incredible work ethic and persistent frugality. It is wise for visitors to know and respect this — and tread lightly. The rewards are extraordinary. Read on and see. . . .

As you drive, you will see painted crosswalks in the small towns. These are sacrosanct, and it is a point of honor to slow and stop if a pedestrian shows the slightest inclination to cross the street.

Getting Here, Getting Around

We were going to start this chapter with cheery, encouraging words on how easy it is to get around the Mid-Coast area, until we really thought about our first days in the region.

First, flying here can be cumbersome because Bangor and Portland, the sites of our two major airports, are not major destinations. You'll probably have to fly to a larger airport and transfer from there. Even then, you might end up flying into Boston and taking a commuter plane.

Plans for rail service into Maine are in the works but incomplete, and while one of the two bus lines will get you here, there isn't much in the way of public transportation once you arrive. Car rental information is listed subsequently, if that will help. Bike rental information is in our Parks and Recreation chapter.

We did have a car when we moved here, but then we had a dickens of a time finding an accurate map of our little town. The first time we traveled off the main roads, we found ourselves hopelessly lost and hopelessly late. Riding over those unmarked dirt roads in the dark was an experience we swore we'd never repeat. Other times, when we stopped to ask directions, we got the definite impression that if we didn't know where we were, maybe we shouldn't be there.

We'd like to spare you similar discomfort. This chapter sketches out the various ways you might get here as well as what to expect once you arrive. You might have to work a little harder than you would in, say, a Midwestern suburb; but then, that's not where you wanted to spend your vacation, was it?

By Car

If license plates are any indication, most visitors drive here. If you plan to come by car, find yourself a good map. We both swear by DeLorme's *Maine Atlas and Gazetteer*, 865-4171, an 11-by-15-inch book of 70 maps that depict the state in excruciating detail.

That said, most of the places you'll be trying to find want you to find them, so they'll put small signs at major intersections with pointers and mileage. While the state has chosen to minimize the size of these roadside signs (billboards are outlawed), once you get used to looking for them, you'll be amazed at how convenient they are. Researching our Campgrounds chapter took us into the uncharted wilds, but not once did we get lost.

One more thing. Many businesses don't have street addresses — just a street name and a town or city name; and yes, we're sorry to say that there is frequently more than one name for some roads. Don't be put off by this. Just get yourself to the town and keep an eye out for signs. If you get baffled, call or ask. The state is in the process of assigning street names and addresses to prepare for an Emergency 911 system, but most towns are nowhere near finished. Beware of towns where they've just finished assigning addresses. Confusion reigns: Printed references may be wrong, and residents themselves can't always remember their new address.

Highways and Byways

Interstate 95 (a.k.a. Maine Turnpike) is the major entry point to Maine and the fastest route to the Mid-Coast area. The Kittery-to-Portland stretch of the Maine Turnpike can be congested during summer, so try to avoid traveling during the Friday afternoon/Sunday afternoon crunch.

U.S. Highway 1 runs from the New Hampshire border (it actually originates in South Florida) to the Canadian border and parallels I-95 for about a third of the way, but we don't advise exiting I-95 until Brunswick — the section from Kittery to Brunswick is just too congested during summer. Beyond Brunswick, U.S. 1 traffic picks up considerably, barely slowing down until it hits Rockland, and you'll pass some beautiful forested coastline along the way.

If you're bound for destinations between Waldoboro and Camden, take I-95 to Exit 9, marked "Coastal Route 1." (If you get on the Maine Turnpike at the New Hampshire/Maine border and stay on it straight up the coast, you'll pay $2.05 at the toll booth, which is about 3 miles beyond the exit.) That gets you off the toll road, but you should stay on I-95 and then take Exit 15A. Stay on I-295 for about 7 miles, then get off at Exit 22 in Brunswick, which will take you to U.S. 1, the major two-lane thoroughfare along the coast.

Maine Highway 90 is a favorite shortcut if you're heading to Camden; it branches off the loop of U.S. 1 that swings through the center of Rockland.

Travelers bound for Bangor might best stay on I-95 and take it all the way to the Queen City. If you're headed for Bar Harbor and beyond, you also can take I-95 to Augusta, then Maine Highway 3 west to Belfast and north along U.S. 1 to Ellsworth, where Maine 3 cuts south toward Mount Desert Island. **Maine Highway 3** is the causeway to Mount Desert Island, and it can clog terribly in the summer season. Try to time your travel to avoid peak hours.

The other major road in the area is **U.S. Highway 1A**, another two-lane route that turns inland from U.S. 1 at Stockton Springs. It runs in a kind of triangle, taking you north to Bangor, then south, back to U.S. 1 in Ellsworth.

Mind Your Manners

The remaining roads are not nearly as busy as the aforementioned, but they have their own challenges. We've barreled down Maine Highway 52 toward Belfast, only to join a line of stopped cars as the cows from a dairy crossed the road. On back roads we've stopped to gawk at moose and swerved to avoid foxes. On U.S. 1, we've slowed to avoid an enormous beaver and slammed into deer.

Animals aren't the only creatures to watch out for. As you drive, you will see painted crosswalks in the small towns. These are sacrosanct, and it is a point of honor to slow and stop if a pedestrian shows the slightest inclination to cross the street. If you notice people looking at your license plates, it's because they are gauging whether you know the rules — and whether you'll respect them.

The fact is, visitors from big cities often have a hard time here. Metro driving is based on taking chances and taking advantage. You'll never get home if you don't. Small-town driving is based on giving way, and people think less of you if you don't. We talked with a police chief who was new to a small coastal town. He said he was sure the main intersection needed a traffic light, but after watching for most of an afternoon, he wasn't so sure. The key was that people slowed to let others turn in front of them. They'd both wave and smile and drive off, glad that they live in a place like this. It's a matter of good manners, really.

> ## FYI
>
> Unless otherwise noted, the area code for all phone numbers listed in this guide is 207.

INSIDERS' TIP

When you start traveling back roads, keep an eye on your odometer and on your map. Look at the mileage key and estimate the distance to the next intersection you're trying to find. If there's no road sign, your odometer can help determine whether it's the one you're looking for.

Another thing: People here don't use their car horns. Ever. Well, maybe a tiny tap as you wave to a friend, but not in anger or impatience. A recent visitor from New Jersey couldn't get over this. "It's so quiet without all those horns," she said.

While courtesy seems to be the rule of the road, we've often thought much of it comes from the habits of winter driving. You'll never see the black ice that can send you careening, so drivers tend to be considerate and don't crowd each other. Those in a hurry tend not to tailgate. Slow drivers pull over so others can pass. If you do get into trouble in the ice and snow, you'll be amazed at how helpful people are. The first car by almost always stops.

One last point: People here have strong feelings about private property, so don't go wandering down fire roads or unmarked dirt roads. They are probably not public ways; they are probably somebody's driveway.

By Air

If you plan to fly here, you have a choice of Portland International Airport or Bangor International Airport (see subsequent entries). The Portland airport is most convenient for destinations in the southern part of the Waldoboro-to-Stockton Springs stretch, while Bangor works best from about Belfast north. Of course, your choice might depend on what airline you are flying and what flights are available.

Speaking of flights, if you can manage it, fly through Cincinnati, Atlanta, Pittsburgh or Newark. We've had trouble flying in through Boston; Logan Airport gets jammed up in foul weather and can be somewhat unreliable during the holidays.

Two other airports that might figure into your plans include Knox County Regional Airport in Owls Head and Hancock County-Bar Harbor Airport in Trenton (see subsequent entries).

Bangor International Airport
287 Godfrey Blvd., Bangor • 942-0384

The BIA is a five-minute drive (about 3 miles) from downtown and about a mile from a Concord Trailways bus station. As the northernmost international airport, it frequently handles private and commercial planes that wish to clear U.S. Customs, Immigration & Naturalization and Department of Agriculture inspections in a relatively small airport. The following airlines offer passenger service: Delta Airlines, (800) 221-1212; USAir/ USAir Express, (800) 428-4322; Continental Airlines, (800) 525-0280; Business Express, (800) 345-3400.

The airport itself is relatively small and easy to get around. Creature comforts include a coffee shop and lounge, a news/gift shop and an ATM as well as an outpost of The Grasshopper Shop (see Shopping). Children can play in an area set aside for them on the second level.

While you're on the second level, look for a display window near the lounge and bathrooms. The BIA processed 60,000 troops during the Gulf War in 1991, and the city gave them an incredible welcome. The military had contracted with civilian airlines to handle much of the transport. The planes landed comfortably on BIA's 11,000-foot-long runway and then were refueled quickly so the troops could clear customs. High school bands, veterans groups and ordinary citizens — sometimes outnumbering the soldiers 3- or 4-to-1 — met 222 flights at all hours of the day and night. Memorabilia and plaques collected from the troops are on display.

Long- and short-range parking is available within easy walking distance of the terminal, and long-term rates (for two or three weeks) are available.

Taxis line up in a queue outside the terminal for local destinations, but you can call ahead and negotiate long-distance trips (see the subsequent "Taxis and Limousines" section).

INSIDERS' TIP

A new state law requires that you turn on your car lights any time you use your windshield wipers.

---

www.insiders.com

See this and many other **Insiders' Guide®** destinations online — in their entirety.

Visit us today!

The Airport Shuttle, 942-1111, will pick you up at the airport and take you just about anywhere (including New York City, says the owner). It charges about what a taxi will charge. Fares to Mount Desert Island, for instance, are $65 for one person, $75 for two people, $85 for three and $95 for four.

Some of the area hotel and motel chains have shuttles. There's a list in the baggage claim area, but it's best to ask when you make your reservations.

The city bus (see the subsequent "Public Transportation" section) stops here, as does the West Coastal Connection bus (see the "By Bus" section).

Rental car companies with facilities at the airport are: Avis Rent A Car, 947-8383 or (800) 831-2847; Budget Car & Truck Rental, 945-9429 or (800) 527-0700; Hertz Rent A Car, 942-5519 or (800) 654-3131; National Car Rental Interrent, 947-0158 or (800) 227-7368.

Hancock County-Bar Harbor Airport
Maine Hwy. 3, 12 miles outside Bar Harbor, Trenton • 667-7329

This airport is served only by Colgan Air, (800) 523-3273, a year-round carrier that's recently become a Continental Connection. Fly to Boston, then pick up a Colgan connection. There's no landing fee for private planes. On-site services include fuel, maintenance and repairs, storage and tie-down. The Unicom frequency is 123.0. This facility offers flight training and rental planes.

Budget Car & Truck Rental, 667-1200 or (800) 527-0700, and Hertz Rent A Car, 667-5017 or (800) 654-3131, operate out of the terminal, and Airport Taxi, 667-5995, serves the airport full time. Some of the larger hotels and motels in Bar Harbor offer courtesy service as well; inquire when you make a reservation.

Knox County Regional Airport
Ash Point Dr., 2 miles south of Rockland, Owls Head • 594-4131

This tiny airport is served only by Colgan Air, (800) 523-3273, which operates year round and is now a Continental Connection. Again the trick is to fly into Boston, then pick up a Colgan connection. Private planes can land without charge, but there is a fee for overnight parking. Per-night fees are: $3, single-engine aircraft; $5, twin-engines up to 7,500 pounds; $8, twin-engines more than 7,500 pounds.

Two different vendors offer fuel, and full maintenance service is available. While the airport doesn't offer storage, a private hangar nearby does; call Omni Leasing, 594-5191.

You can rent a plane from Down East Air, 594-2171, and you can take lessons through the Knox County Flying Club, 594-0680.

At the Knox County airport (often called simply "Owls Head" by many locals, but referred to as Rockland by the airlines), Budget Car & Truck Rental, 594-0822 or (800) 527-0700, and Enterprise Rent A Car, 594-9093 or (800) 325-8007, have offices on the field. Schooner Bay Taxi, 594-5000, has offices in the terminal. The Samoset Resort will send a courtesy car, and other lodgings might as well. Just ask.

Portland International Jetport
1001 Westbrook St., Portland • 772-0690

You have a greater choice of airlines coming into Portland than into Bangor. Carriers include Business Express, (800) 638-7333; Continental/Continental Express Airlines, (800) 525-0280; Delta Airlines, (800) 638-7333; USAir/USAir Express, (800) 428-4322; United Airlines, (800) 241-6522; Northwest Airlines, (800) 225-2525; Pine State Airlines, (800) 353-6334; and Northeast Airways, (800) 983-3247.

Like many small hubs, Portland has a news/gift shop, another gift shop, a restaurant and lounge and ATMs. Long- and short-term parking is available, and it's close to the terminal.

A number of rental cars have offices here: Avis Rent A Car, 874-7500 or (800) 831-2847; Budget Car & Truck Rental, 774-8642 or (800) 527-0700; Hertz Rent A Car, 774-4544 or (800) 654-3131; and National Car Rental Interrent, 773-0036 or (800) 227-7368.

There's a shuttle as well. Mid-Coast Limo, 236-2424 or (800) 937-2424, offers daily van service to and from the airport, serving the stretch along U.S. 1 from Brunswick to Lincolnville. Reservations must be made 24 hours in advance, and fares vary depending on your location. The fare to Camden, for instance, is $45.

By Bus

Our first instinct was to advise against taking the bus to this area. We so love the freedom of a car to noodle around on back roads and down the peninsulas. Then we realized what fun it is to get off at a bus stop, walk to our lodgings and explore the area on foot. That is perfectly possible in many towns where the following two bus lines stop. In Camden, for instance, the Whitehall Inn will pick you up at the bus stop. In Lincolnville, The Spouter Inn is across the street from the bus stop, and it can arrange bike rentals (see our Accommodations chapter).

Generally, however, this kind of trip will take some coordinating. Pick the area you want to visit and call around to lodgings. Find out how far they are from the bus stop. Explain your plan and ask whether it's feasible to enjoy the area on foot.

Some of our suburban friends commute for hours. This would be a great way to shed the car for a few blissful days. (Of course, in a few towns, you could rent a car. See the subsequent "Rental Cars" section.)

Concord Trailways
South Station, 700 Atlantic Ave., Boston • 945-4000, (800) 639-5150
Logan International Airport, 600 Tower Rd., Boston • 945-4000, (800) 639-5150

Concord Trailways runs two routes a day from Boston. One is a four-hour express from either South Station or the airport in Boston to Bangor, with one stop in Portland. The six-hour coastal route also runs from Boston to Bangor, but it stops in Portland, Brunswick, Bath, Wiscasset, Damariscotta, Waldoboro, Rockland, Camden/Rockport, Lincolnville Beach (a flag stop), Belfast and Searsport. Between Boston and Bangor, Concord shows two movies on small video screens. This company also offers connections to New York City.

Concord doesn't take reservations, the schedules change two or three times a year, and the rates change independently of the schedules, so call for the latest information.

INSIDERS' TIP

If you're stuck in a traffic jam, don't just sit there, frustrated. You're on vacation! Look at your map, look through this book, look around you. There might be a park nearby, a string of shops or some country-road detour you could take that would interest and occupy you until traffic starts moving more freely.

Photo: Bangor Daily News

The *Queen Elizabeth II* visits Bar Harbor nearly every summer.

Greyhound/Vermont Transit Bus Line

South Station, 700 Atlantic Ave., Boston • 945-3000, (800) 894-3355
Logan International Airport, 600 Tower Rd., Boston • 945-3000, (800) 894-3355

Greyhound/Vermont Transit also originates in Boston (at the airport or South Station) and runs to Bangor, but it does not stop at the towns already served by Concord Trailways (see previous entry). Its route is inland, with stops in Lewiston, Augusta and Waterville. This company also handles questions about the West Coastal Connection bus, which leaves Bangor once a day at 3:30 PM for Calais, with stops in Ellsworth, Hancock, Sullivan and Gouldsboro. There is service to Bar Harbor during the summer months.

Schedules change seasonally, and rates change as well. No reservations are required, but do call ahead.

Taxis and Limousines

There are few taxi and limo companies in most of the small towns that make up Maine's Mid-Coast. The widest array is in Bangor, but no matter where you are, your best bet is to call ahead to be sure you can get where you need to go. And while you're on the phone, ask what the trip will cost you. In Bangor, the rates are set at $1.20 a mile. In other areas, it's catch as catch can. Most companies map out their areas in zones and charge flat rates based on where you are and where you want to go.

Waldoboro to Stockton Springs

In the Rockland/Camden area, try Schooner Bay Taxi, 594-5000, in Owls Head; Don's Taxi Service, 236-4762, in Camden; and Belfast Taxi Service, 338-2943, in Belfast.

Inland to Bangor

In Bangor, call Town Taxi, 945-5671; Dick's Taxi, 942-6403; or Airport/River City Taxi, 947-8294.

Bucksport to Gouldsboro

Superior Limo & Port Taxi, 469-1155 or (800) 340-1155, operates out of Bucksport, running limousines and station wagons. In Ellsworth, try Towne Taxi, 667-1000, or Ellsworth Taxi, 667-2722. In Trenton, Airport

Taxi, 667-5995, runs to and from the Bangor and Bar Harbor airports, Mount Desert Island towns, Blue Hill, Castine and Deer Isle, and the Rockland/Camden area.

Mount Desert Island

In Bar Harbor, there's the Bar Harbor Cab Co., 288-4020; and O'Pooch Taxi Crab, 288-3898.

Public Transportation

There's precious little public transportation outside Bangor, Rockland, Camden and Bar Harbor. Here's a rundown of what's available.

Waldoboro to Stockton Springs

Coastal Trans Inc.
46 Summer St., Rockland • 596-6605

Coastal Trans, a nonprofit, offers door-to-door service in Knox, Lincoln and Sagadahoc counties. Call a day in advance to make arrangements. Most trips cost $1.50 each way.

In Camden, Coastal Trans runs The Camden Shuttle from June to October along U.S. 1, between parking lots south and north of town. The schedule indicates buses leave the lots on the hour and half-hour, with two or three stops in between. The lots are at the Camden Hills State Park to the north and near The Country Inn to the south. The service is free.

Inland to Bangor

The Bus
481 Maine Ave., Bangor • 947-0536

The Bus serves Bangor, Brewer, Hampden, Veazie, Old Town and the University of Maine.

While you'd best call for the booklet outlining its schedule, the service is described as a hub system, with buses leaving downtown Bangor every half-hour from 6:15 AM to 5:45 PM. Buses will stop at any safe intersection; just flag them down. A ride will cost you 75¢ in Bangor and as much as $1.25 in outlying areas.

Bucksport to Gouldsboro and Mount Desert Island

Downeast Transportation
194 Main St., Ellsworth • 667-5796

Downeast Transportation serves Hancock County, including Ellsworth and Mount Desert Island. It operates buses and commuter vans year round, with expanded hours and service during the summer. Round-trip fares range from $2 for travel within towns to $2.50 for service between neighboring towns to $5 for longer rides. An all-day family pass costs $10, and books of tickets are available at a discount. Call ahead for a schedule if you expect to use this service while you're here. The bus also makes weekly runs to Bangor from Ellsworth ($7) and Bar Harbor ($9), with stops at major bus terminals, the shopping mall, the hospital and the airport.

On Mount Desert Island, free shuttle buses pick up campers at the campgrounds along U.S. 1 and take them into Bar Harbor.

Rental Cars

If you pass through one of the aforementioned airports (see "By Air") on your way to the area, check this chapter's airport entries for available rental cars and shuttles. This section addresses rental cars that aren't attached to airports. Let's say you're visiting Aunt Tilley in Rockport. She picks you up at the bus drop-off, and as the two of you drive to her house,

---

INSIDERS' TIP

The central block of Camden's downtown area is called Main Street. The section north of that intersection is called High Street; the section south of that intersection is called Elm Street. It's all called U.S. Highway 1.

she talks a little about what she's been doing. You realize she has a busy life: bridge, the garden club, chamber concerts, a foreign-affairs luncheon. You can't walk everywhere you want to go, and she can't drive you. Solution? Rent a car.

U-Save Auto Rental, (800) 272-8728, has franchises in Rockland, 594-2268; Rockport, 236-2320; Belfast, 338-2515; and Bucksport, 469-2258. National Car Rental has an office at Shepard Motors in Rockland, 594-8424. Enterprise Rent A Car, (800) 325-8007, has offices in Bangor, 990-0745, and Ellsworth, 667-1217. Avis Rent A Car, (800) 831-2847, has an office in Bangor, 947-8383. In Trenton, Acadia Auto Rental, 667-6130, is one of the U-Save franchises, and it rents pickups and vans as well as cars. Apex Custom Lease Corp., 667-7360, in Ellsworth, advertises low weekly and monthly rates.

To enhance your visit to
Maine's Mid-Coast,
look, listen, view, smell,
touch, taste —
and read.

The Maine Experience

Maine offers more than a place to explore: It is history, legend, tall tale, precise research and many ways of life — of birds and bears, 18th-century midwives, 19th-century sailors and 20th-century storytellers.

To enhance your visit, look, listen, view, smell, touch, taste — and read. Take along a book of Maine paintings and see how many of the vistas pictured within are ones you have seen. Are you traveling with kids? Bring *Charlotte's Web* and *Blueberries for Sal*, and be sure to attend one of Maine's many summer fairs — and its even more numerous blueberry fields. Pop an audio tape of Sarah Orne Jewett's stories into your car cassette player and imagine yourselves living in the self-sufficient world of 19th-century Maine. Bring home a carton of lobsters for those who couldn't come with — and add a video reminding you how to open 'em up and extract the meat.

Atlases

The Maine Atlas and Gazetteer (a.k.a. *DeLorme Atlas*), DeLorme Mapping Co.

Maine has few major but many minor roads. It's on the interlacing of the tiniest ones — roads most maps entirely dismiss — that you'll find the fun of driving in Maine. DeLorme has perfected a road atlas, charting everything from dirt roads in the north woods to boat landings along the coast at 2 miles to the inch. Need to get from Waldoboro to Belfast in midsummer? Look on pages 13 and 14 to find how to avoid the inevitable jams along U.S. Highway 1. The drive might not be any shorter, but you'll get an inside look at Maine in the process. We don't dare leave home without it!

Guides

Appalachian Mountain Club guides

These no-nonsense, fit-in-your-pocket guides were the ones your parents used before you came around. They're small, venerable, but updated fairly frequently. Use them to plan hikes (though most mountains outside Acadia National Park are also outside the Mid-Coast region) and some good canoe or kayak trips.

A Birder's Guide to Maine by Elizabeth Cary Pierson, Jan Erik Pierson and Peter D. Vickery

This excellent guide tells you where to go and, as important, when to go to see a wide array of birds in Maine, many of which are migratory. Have you been longing to find the rare Barrow's goldeneye duck? This guide's authors know that a whole flock winters in Belfast Harbor.

A Cruising Guide to the Maine Coast by Hank and Jean Taft and Curtis Rindlaub

This is the definitive guide to Maine harbors and islands. It's a treat even for the nonsailor, for what it has to say about the history and lore of the land. But it's really for the folks traveling by boat — filled with information on passages, anchorages and showers. Don't sail Maine waters without it!

Maine, A Guide Downeast edited by Dorris A. Isaacson

In 1937, the Works Project Administration (WPA) sought to create a series of national portraits by commissioning specific area guides, employing writers in the process. As you can imagine, the guide became outdated rather quickly. But in 1970, Dorris Isaacson, president of the Maine League of Historical Societies and Museums, updated the Maine guide by adding to rather than altering it. By now, it's again a period piece — and also out of print — but it's still so clear and comprehensive a portrait of the people, the places and the culture of Maine that we use it as a backdrop to all our travels. Though both editions are hard to find, it's worth combing secondhand bookstores for either or both. Or check your local library before you leave — you might find a copy to take along.

Maine Forever: A Guide to Nature Conservancy Preserves in Maine by Ruth Ann Hill

The Nature Conservancy is an international, private, nonprofit conservation organization that preserves and maintains natural areas for our benefit. Years ago, the Maine chapter issued a guide to its more than 75 sanctuaries, along with specific directions of how to get to them. You won't necessarily find these highlighted on maps, so appreciate the solitude. Tread lightly and be amazed.

Literature

Novelists

A debate has raged in Maine for years now: Just who is a Maine writer? Are you a Maine writer if you live here and write about other places? Live elsewhere and write about Maine? Must you have been born here? Must your parents have been born here?

More interesting than the debate itself is the fact that there is a debate — that there are so many writers who live (or once lived) in Maine, there's room for this kind of jealousy. We discuss many authors and their works subsequently — and leave out too many more: Kenneth Roberts' historical dramas *Arundel* and *Trending into Maine*; Lura Beam's *A Maine Hamlet*; Louise Dickinson Rich's *We Took to the Woods*; and works by Elizabeth Ogilvie,

Gladys Hasty Carroll and others. There are so many writers that a whole trip to Maine could be organized around the state's literary landmarks.

So, who's a Mainer? Compared to Maine's first residents, the Wabanaki, every writer is very much "from away." It isn't easy to find collections of Wabanaki stories, which is why we want to mention *Giants of The Dawnland: Eight Ancient Wabanaki Legends*, collected by Alice Mead and Arnold Neptune. Read all about Gluskap, the trickster hero of the region, and his Grandmother Woodchuck. The publisher is the minuscule Loose Canon Press of Cumberland Center, Maine.

Read! There's no equaling the insight.

FYI

Unless otherwise noted, the area code for all phone numbers listed in this guide is 207.

Mary Ellen Chase (1887-1973)

Born in Blue Hill, Chase was 12 years old when she met Sarah Orne Jewett (see subsequent entry) and determined to follow in her footsteps. Chase wrote numerous books about the lives of her ancestors and the ways of her early years. Among the most famous are *Silas Crockett* and *A Goodly Heritage*, centered on Jonathan Fisher, Blue Hill's first pastor and astonishing Renaissance man.

Carolyn Chute (1948-)

The Beans of Egypt, Maine reveals the shadowed side of Maine's beauty and has already become a classic of Maine literature. Chute, raised outside Portland, has written two more novels, *Letourneau's Used Auto Parts* and *Merry Men*. In 1996, she launched a movement of the poor and under-represented, which she calls the Second Maine Militia. *Merry Men*, Chute's most recent effort, offers a fascinating if fierce insight into tensions between Mainers and those "from away."

Robert Tristram Coffin (1892-1955)

If you want to have a Christmas like the one we had on Paradise Farm when I was a boy, you will have to hunt up a salt-water farm on the Maine coast, with bays on both sides of it, and a road that goes around all sorts of bays, up over Misery Hill and down, and through the

fir trees so close together that they brush you and your horse on both cheeks. . . . You must have a clear December night, with blue Maine stars snapping like sapphires with the cold, and the big moon flooding full over Misery and lighting up the snowy spruce boughs like crushed diamonds.

Coffin may be the best literary purveyor of the Maine winter — both its glory and its meanness. Born in Brunswick and raised nearby on a saltwater farm, Coffin wrote poetry as well as prose, was both a student and teacher at Bowdoin College and garnered a Pulitzer Prize for his efforts.

Nathaniel Hawthorne (1804-1864)

Yes, Hawthorne was a Maine transplant, at least for a time. He came to Maine with his widowed mother at age 12 and spent some of his happiest days fishing in the local streams, tramping through the forests and listening to the talk of travelers at his uncle's store in Raymond, on the shores of Sebago Lake. The tales he heard as a boy can be found throughout his work. Later, some years after leaving Bowdoin College in Brunswick (Hawthorne was a classmate of Henry Wadsworth Longfellow there), he took a tour of Maine. He traveled to Montpelier, in Thomaston (see our Attractions chapter), with his classmates Horatio Bridge and Jonathan Cilley, who had just been elected to the U.S. Congress. Hawthorne was feeling quite the underachiever, despite the fact that his *Twice-Told Tales* already had been something of a success. He was still far from writing *The Scarlet Letter* or even *The House of the Seven Gables*, the book inspired by Montpelier. You can read about this journey through Maine in *Passages from the American Notebooks of Nathaniel Hawthorne*.

Sarah Orne Jewett (1849-1909)

In her time, Sarah Orne Jewett was thought to be one of the best writers in the nation. Her star is again rising. She's most famous for *The White Heron*, but *The Country of the Pointed Firs* and *Deephaven* take their setting from a time when Jewett summered in the Mid-Coast region (in Martinsville, just down the St. George Peninsula from Tenant's Harbor). Her delicate character sketches speak volumes about Maine and bring to life the myriad personalities who built the homes you still see as you travel her back roads.

Stephen King (1947-)

We're not so sure what kind of overall image King actually presents of Maine outside the state, but we do know that instate he has improved Maine's image immensely. His success as a writer has been translated into generous donations to the Bangor Public Library, Bangor athletics and the work of the National Poetry Foundation, located at his alma mater, the University of Maine. In early 1997, King and wife Tabitha pledged $4 million to the university — half for scholarships. Notable works include *Thinner*, *The Running Man*, *The Shining*, *Carrie*, *The Stand* and *Skeleton Crew*.

Ruth Moore (1903-1989)

Born on remote Gott's Island, Moore spent her childhood poking about in archeological digs and wandering the small island off Mount Desert Island. Before her death she enjoyed a renaissance, following the Blackberry Press reissue of *Spoonhandle*, a volume of her letters and other work. She once wrote:

Gott's Island was a perfect microcosm of the world. Three miles around and a mile wide, but on it were rich and poor, young and old, and everything in between. Good guys and bad guys, hard-working and lazy people, cowards and heroes, they were all there. And I said to myself, "Why, they're just like people everywhere, only more so." I knew then that I never wanted to write about anything else.

Sanford Phippen (1942-)

In a biographical statement for the anthology *Maine Speaks* (see the subsequent "Anthologies" section), Phippen writes about Hancock, his home town: "Hancock has a summer colony, Hancock Point, where I used to work as a boy mowing lawns, delivering milk and eggs, and helping my parents and relatives caretake a number of summer places."

Hancock was and is a great storytellers town filled with legends and myths of sea captains, fishermen, farmers, Nazi spies, summer people, steamboat and train workers, famous names and town characters.

Phippen's latest book, *The Kitchen Boy,* continues his lifelong tale of the relationship of summer people to Mainers.

E.B. White (1899-1985)

Essayist, short-story writer and children's book writer, Elwyn Brooks White is one of the most famous writers to live in Maine. There is of course, Wilbur, that "Some Pig" from the timeless *Charlotte's Web*, who took the prize at the Blue Hill Fair, up the road from White's North Brooklin home. But White also wrote wonderfully engaging essays about life on his Maine farm. His collection *One Man's Meat* has just been reprinted. Another book that the "lover of all things Wilbur" might be interested in is *The Annotated Charlotte's Web*, with copious notes by Peter Neumeyer.

Photo: Bangor Daily News

Although horror author Stephen King has an office in Bangor, he creates most of his books at a desk in his home.

Poets

The poets of Maine's Mid-Coast range from the Penobscots, Passamaquodies, Micmacs and Malaceets, who spoke in legend and verse long before a sail appeared over the horizon, to current U.S. Secretary of Defense William Cohen (1941-), author of mystery novels as well as several books of poetry, including *Sons and Seasons*. These wordsmiths are hard to restrict.

Kate Barnes (1932-)

With parents Henry Beston (see the subsequent "Naturalists" section) and Elizabeth Coatsworth (see this section's subsequent entry), Kate Barnes probably had no choice but to write. "I never wake up in the morning without being happy to be exactly where I am," she once wrote. Perhaps that's why she was recently chosen poet laureate of Maine.

Philip Booth (1925-)

Booth, the child of a Dartmouth College professor, spent summers in an ancestral Castine home. He later taught English at Syracuse University and has since retired to the quiet streets of Castine, where he sails summers. Booth is now familiar with every rock and nook of the region, and not at all unfamiliar with its people, as is clear from the following excerpt from the poem "Eaton's Boatyard," named for the boatyard that is still a major presence in Castine:

> To make do, making a living:
> to throw away nothing,
> practically nothing, nothing that may
> come in handy;
> within an inertia of caked paintcans,
> frozen C-clamps, blown strips of tar, and
> pulling-boat molds,
> to be able to find,
> for whatever it's worth,
> what has to be there:
> the requisite tool

Amy Clampitt (1920-1994)

Naturalist and poet Clampitt summered in Corea, just east of Schoodic, and wrote richly of the minutiae of the natural world. Look for her musings on Maine in her books *The Kingfisher*, *What the Light Was Like* and others. Listen to her careful evocation of the fog in her poem "Fog":

> vagueness comes over everything,
> as though proving color and contour

alike dispensable: the lighthouse
extinct, the islands' spruce-tips
drunk up like milk in the
universal emulsion; houses
reverting into the lost
and forgotten; granite
subsumed, a rumor
in a mumble of ocean.

Elizabeth Coatsworth (1893-1986)

In Maine the dead
melt into the forest
like Indians, or, rather,
in Maine the forests, shadow round the
dead
until the dead are indistinguishably mingled
with trees; while underground,
roots and bones intertwine.

So begins "Lost Graveyards," a tale of how the pioneers of Maine cleared the forest only to find the forest encroaching back on their very graves.

Children's book writer, essayist, short-story writer, novelist and poet, Coatsworth came to Maine with husband Henry Beston (see the subsequent "Naturalists" section). She is probably best known for her children's books, like *The Cat Who Went to Heaven*, *Chimney Farm Bedtime Stories*, *Lighthouse Island* and *Under the Green Willow*, but she was also a fine poet.

Leo Conellan (1928-)

A hearty, sensitive Irish boy raised in Rockland's "clear, blue lobster-water country," Conellan is the author of several books of poetry, including one with that title. He has the native view: unromantic of place yet somehow still romantic of people. Of Rockland, which he calls "Lime City" — it once exported lime down the eastern seaboard — he writes:

Lime City has become hamburger stands
now
and unskilled crime committed
from despair's overwhelming fatigue.
— from "Clear Blue Lobster-Water Country"

Marsden Hartley (1877-1943)

Best known as a painter (see subsequent entry), Hartley was also a poet. Born and raised in Lewiston, he spent many summers painting in various coastal Maine spots and added to the literature of the coast as well. His poems are published as *The Collected Poems of Marsden Hartley*.

Henry Wadsworth Longfellow (1807-1882)

Longfellow was born in Portland into some degree of comfort. His father was an attorney, a member of the U.S. Congress and president of the Maine Historical Society. When Henry entered Bowdoin College, where his father was a trustee, he already had a published poem under his belt. Longfellow later taught at Bowdoin College and then at Harvard, gaining fame for poems such as "Evangeline," written about the dispersal of the Acadians from Nova Scotia to northern Maine, "Hiawatha" and "Paul Revere's Ride."

Robert Lowell (1917-1977)

Troubled and brilliant, Lowell had an extensive relationship with Maine's Mid-Coast. He lived with his first wife, writer Jean Stafford, in Damariscotta Mills (see the novel *The Mills of the Kavanaughs*); later, he summered in Castine with his second wife, writer Elizabeth Hardwick, who still summers there. His "Skunk Hour," set in Castine and touching on Holbrook Island Sanctuary (see Parks and Recreation), is a poem filled with loneliness and hope.

Edna St. Vincent Millay (1892-1950)

Her mother gave her daughters piano lessons, encouraged their talents, taught them about nature and divorced her school-superintendent husband because of his compulsive gambling. At age 19, Millay, a poor Rockland girl (a tablet at 200 Broadway in Rockland indicates her birthplace), was "discovered" by wealthy summer people at a gathering at Camden's Whitehall Inn after reading her poem "Renascence," set on the Camden Hills:

All I could see from where I stood
Was three long mountains and a wood;
I turned and looked another way,
And saw three islands in a bay.
So with my eyes I traced the line
Of the horizon, thin and fine,
Straight around till I was come
Back to where I'd started from;
And all I saw from where I stood
Was three long mountains and a wood.

Millay was sent to Vassar on that poem,

excerpted above. She became worldly in Greenwich Village and Europe, and was the first woman to win a Pulitzer Prize for poetry. The room in which she read the poem is now a memorial to the poet (see our Accommodations chapter).

Edwin Arlington Robinson (1869-1935)

Robinson's "Tilbury Town" was the central Maine town of Gardiner, south of Augusta. It's not Mid-Coast, but poems such as "Richard Cory" offer a sardonic glimpse at the tight world of the small town. Robinson, like Edna St. Vincent Millay (see previous entry), won a Pulitzer Prize in poetry.

Anthologies

The Maine Reader: The Down East Experience, 1614 to the Present edited by Charles and Samuella Shain

This is a portrait in a book. A veritable taste-of-the-town sampler, it includes all manner of excerpts: historical accounts; contemporary poetry; the journals of Hawthorne, Thoreau and James Russell Lowell; and the stories of humorist John Gould and Carolyn Chute.

Maine Speaks: An Anthology of Maine Literature, The Maine Literature Project

Virtually a history lesson through literature, this anthology includes works from early Native American legends to contemporary poets like William Carpenter and Sylvester Pollet and naturalists such as Susan Hand Shetterly. Created as both text and trade book, the anthology serves students as well as travelers.

White Pine and Blue Water: A State of Maine Reader edited by Henry Beston

From seafaring to farming, Beston's 1950 anthology is a graceful way to know Maine through historical and recent journal excerpts and novelistic accounts that Beston calls "Mirrors held up to Maine."

Children's Writers

Perhaps it's that Maine retains enough of the 19th-century rural ideal so often pictured in children's books; perhaps it's simply that you don't need a six-figure income to live here.

INSIDERS' TIP

Blue Hill is home to writers Jan William van der Wetering and Helen Yglesias.

Whatever the reason, many children's book writers make their homes in Maine. Some, like Eloise Ensor, have written delightful books as almost an afterthought in their lives (check out her *Good Golly Miss Molly and the 4th of July Parade* and *Nellie, the Lighthouse Dog*, after a visit to the Port Clyde peninsula).

Other children's book writers living in the region, like the great-spirited Ashley Bryan, really do not reflect Maine in their writings. We've listed a few of the classic Maine children's book writers, who very much crystallize life here.

Margaret Wise Brown (1910-1952)

The author of *Goodnight Moon* summered on Vinalhaven (no wonder she has such a delicate hand on magic). Brown's delightful picture book *Little Island* is most evocative of Maine, and it won her the Caldecott Medal in 1947. She wrote that book under the pen name Golden MacDonald.

Barbara Cooney (1917-)

Barbara Cooney was recently named a Maine State Treasure. Visit Maine in June and July, and you will see the Lupine Lady's work featured in Cooney's *Miss Rumphius*, whose title character vowed to see the world, live by the shore and do something universally meaningful. Miss Rumphius became the Lupine Lady, carpeting the region, according to Cooney, with a glorious array of these lavender, purple and violet flowers.

Rachel Field (1894-1942)

Field summered on Sutton's Island, one of the Cranberries off Mount Desert Island. Perhaps *Hitty: Her First 100 Years* was influenced by her time on this immensely serene island. That book has been reissued this decade. As she once wrote, "There's something about islands, I don't know what it is, but I simply cannot keep them out of the things I write, I always find them there along with pointed trees, toadstools, children, and patchwork quilts."

Robert McCloskey (1914-)

People make pilgrimages to South Brooksville, off Blue Hill, to the place little Sal visited the day her tooth fell out in *One Morning in Maine*.

McCloskey, a children's book writer and illustrator, lived on an island in Penobscot Bay for many years and based his stories on his quiet family life: picking blueberries (*Blueberries for Sal*), digging for clams and sailing on Penobscot Bay. He has since retired inland.

By the way, Condon's garage, depicted in *One Morning in Maine*, is still around, and South Brooksville has changed little from McCloskey's drawings.

Kate Douglas Wiggin (1856-1923)

Rebecca's Sunnybrook Farm is not in the Mid-Coast area, but parts of it are in Bar Mills and Hollis and on the banks of the Salmon River in southern Maine. Never mind; Rebecca of Sunnybrook Farm is one unforgettable image of rural Maine.

History

Interested in Isle au Haut? Read *Here on the Island* by Charles Pratt. Is it coastal schooners that fascinate you? Find *Sailing Days on the Penobscot* by George S. Wasson for tales of harrowing voyages up the boat- and wreck-strewn Penobscot River to Bangor.

Or does sailing around the world fascinate you? Check out *Log of the Skipper's Wife*, edited by James W. Balano, of Bucksport, from his mother's diaries as the skipper's wife; or *A Bride's Passage: Susan Hathorn's Year Under Sail*, written by Catherine Petroski based on Hathorn's journal recounting her first year of marriage and her first pregnancy, both spent on the water.

Do you want to understand the life of a lighthouse keeper? Philmore Wass is a great storyteller. Find his account of his family's life on an offshore lighthouse — *Lighthouse in My Life: Story of a Maine Light Keepers Family* —

Photo: Bangor Daily News

Archaeological digs are frequent sights along Maine's rocky coast.

and enjoy the details. There's even a lighthouse counterpart for children: *Keep the Lights Burning Abbie*, by Peter and Connie Roop, tells the story of a 15-year-old girl who kept the lights going during a long storm that came up while her lighthouse-keeper father was off-island getting supplies.

Or is it simply islands that delight you? Then *Islands of the Mid-Maine Coast*, a four-volume series of histories of islands by Charles B. and Carol Evarts McLane, is indispensable. Sometimes the histories are simply lists of who lived where and what they had, but even that is interesting.

There are also thick histories of Maine. For our History chapter, we have relied on *Coastal Maine, A Maritime History* by Roger F. Duncan and *A Maritime History of Maine* by William Hutchinson Rowe.

Mount Desert Island has many of its own specific histories, including *Rockefeller's Roads*, the photographic essay *Lost Bar Harbor* and the fictional *My Dear Sarah Anne: Letters from a Century Ago*, written and illustrated by Teisha Smedstad; the latter gives a taste of the elegant rusticating life.

Growing Up in Maine: Recollections of Childhood from the 1780s to the 1920s edited by Charles and Samuella Shain

Using autobiographical accounts of Maine childhoods — walking miles without shoes to school, watching river drives, going to church and shipping out on schooners — we find out how life really was. The result is one of the best insights into the state.

A Midwife's Tale: The Life of Martha Ballard, Based on Her Diary, 1785-1812 by Laurel Thatcher Ulrich

This book is set in central Maine, just south of Augusta — not exactly the Mid-Coast region, yet we can only imagine that the life of this 18th-century midwife must have been echoed elsewhere, hopefully by as wise and discreet a woman. In 1997, the history was made into a movie.

Molly Spotted Elk by Bunny McBride

This 1995 biography of a Penobscot dancer offers insight into the life of the Native American tribe living closest to the Mid-Coast region, just north of Orono on Indian Island. Molly broke through the barrier of the rushing Penobscot River that keeps the island separate from white culture and found her way to France as a dancer, only to be forced on a trek across the Pyrenees to escape the Nazis.

Our Lives in Our Hands: Micmac Indian Basketmakers by Bunny McBride

These stories feature the creators of the baskets you see in Bar Harbor and at the Hudson Museum in Orono.

Naturalists

Maine has lured many a philosopher and naturalist. As in other sections in this chapter, we've listed the notable ones subsequently, but we also want to mention a couple of children's books just recently issued. Both happen to be about puffins. *Project Puffin: How We Brought Puffins Back to Egg Rock,* by Stephen W. Kress as told to Pete Salmansohn, tells how Kress had a dream of bringing the puffins back to Eastern Egg Rock, off Maine's Mid-Coast. It took a number of years, but he succeeded. While we're on the subject of puffins, take a look at Bruce McMillan's *Nights of the Pufflings*, which tells of the Icelandic children who help baby puffins, known as pufflings, find their way to sea.

Henry Beston (1888-1968)

Writer and amateur naturalist Beston came to Nobleboro with his wife, Elizabeth Coatsworth (see this chapter's previous "Poets" section), establishing a farm and generating a small writing dynasty. He wrote *Northern Farm* about Maine. The farm was passed on to daughter Kate Barnes (see "Poets") and is now owned by poet, publisher and bookstore owner Gary Lawless. Beston's writings about natural events and the human response are cogent and precise.

Rachel Carson (1907-1964)

Carson was summer resident of Southport Island, in the Sheepscot River, just south of our Mid-Coast area. Her *The Edge of the Sea* is incomparable as a direct portrait of Maine, gracefully incorporating marine biology and geology into poetic descriptions such as this discussion of walking through a coastal forest:

In the quiet of that place even the voice of the surf is reduced to a whispered echo and the sounds of the forest are but the ghosts of sound — the faint sighing of evergreen needles in the moving air; the creaks and heavier groans of half-fallen trees resting against their neighbors and rubbing bark against bark; the light rattling fall of a dead branch broken under the feet of a squirrel and sent bouncing and ricocheting earthward.

Helen (1904-1995) and Scott Nearing (1893-1993)

The Nearings are hard to categorize; they came to Cape Rosier, homesteaded on a bit of its stony land and created a movement that has outlasted both of these long-lived people. *The Good Life: Helen and Scott Nearing's Sixty Years of Self-Sufficient Living* is their most famous book on Maine. (See our Attractions chapter for more details on the Nearings.)

Linda Tatelbaum (1947-)

Linda Tatelbaum wrote *Carrying Water as a Way of Life* and became the literary heir to the Nearings. Her book about 20 years of homesteading — juggling hauling water from the well with teaching at Colby College in Waterville — is a meditation upon choices. It resonated strongly when she published it in 1997 and again when the rest of Maine lived it during the January 1998 ice storm, when hauling water did become a way of life.

Henry David Thoreau (1817-1862)

No, Thoreau did not write about Maine's Mid-Coast, but he wrote about Maine, and his reflections on nature — among them *The Maine Woods* — surely mean something to all Mainers. A beautifully illustrated child's edition, *Into the Deep Forest with Henry David Thoreau*, has just been published.

Audio Tapes

Drive the St. George Peninsula and listen to Jewett's *Country of the Pointed Firs*; drive through Brooklin and Blue Hill with *Charlotte's Web* on the tape player; or cruise around the Penobscot while listening to trickster tales of Maine's Native Americans. It's a connecting experience you'll never forget.

You'll find a number of Maine books on audio cassette, especially children's books. Check your local library for White's *Charlotte's Web* and McCloskey's *One Morning in Maine*, *Blueberries for Sal* or *Keep the Light Burning Abby*, the harrowing, true tale of the lighthouse keeper's daughter in a storm off Matinicus Rock.

Audio Bookshelf, Heather Fredericks

In launching Audio Bookshelf, Heather Fredericks has galvanized Maine literature simply by recording it. The productions, created in Northport, a hamlet just south of Belfast on U.S. Highway 1, are beautifully done. Fredericks' choices of stories and poetry are a delight, and her pairing of local actors — men and women with excellent voices — to recite regional stories, such as those of Sarah Orne Jewett, are well matched. The result has been a stunning success, with Maine travelers reaping the benefits. Fredericks' tapes and her broadcasts on Maine Public Radio have helped renew interest in Maine and New England literature.

Six Micmac Stories, Nimbus Audio

The Micmacs are a Maine tribe that also lives in Canada. This story tape includes some rather wild tales, some of them trickster tales and some of the hero Gluskap.

Artists

Maine has served several roles for artists. In the mid-19th century, Americans took their inspiration from the wilderness. Artists joined explorers, moving north and west, including into Maine's wilderness.

More artists than writers have flocked to Maine for its penetratingly clear northern light and the fog that obscures it. Go to your local art museum; chances are you'll find at least one image of Maine. Many of these will be by famous artists — Winslow Homer, Edward Hopper, John Marin, Andrew Wyeth and Maine's own Marsden Hartley have all painted Maine extensively.

But there are many more. Wyeth's dad, N.C., and his son, Jamie, are both Maine artists. Early visitors to the Mid-Coast region were Thomas Cole, Fitz Hugh Lane, Frederic Edwin Church, Alvan Fisher and William Stanley Hazeltine — all associated with Mount Desert Island. Monhegan Island lured still more artists, especially George Bellows, Robert Henri, Rockwell Kent, Alfred Bricher, Leon Kroll, Leo Meissner, Reuben Tam, even Zero Mostel. Karl Shrag as well as Emily and William Muir came to Stonington. Fairfield Porter worked in Penobscot Bay. John Marin lived east of our area; William and Margaret Zorach, west; and William Kienbusch resided on the Cranberries.

Contemporary Mid-Coast artists include Alan Magee, Celeste Roberge, James Fitzgerald, Dozier Bell, Alan Bray, Neil Welliver, Eric Hopkins, Alex Katz, Lois Dodd, Yvonne Jaquette, Robert Indiana and Richard Estes.

There really are too many notable artists to speak about comprehensively without writing an entire book, so we'll highlight a healthy handful. For more on Maine art, you can read the books already written. For essays and critiques, try *Maine Art Now*, a compendium of contemporary Maine artists written by *Maine Times* art reviewer Edgar Allen Beam.

For luscious images and more information about the historical figures in the art world, see the companion volumes *Paintings of Maine* and *Paintings of New England*, both written by Carl Little and edited by Arnold Stolnick. Or, look for Little and Stolnick's latest collaborative volume, the elegant *Art of the Maine Islands*, showing images of various islands, some small enough to hold just a seal or two.

In 1946, the Skowhegan School of Painting and Sculpture opened in central Maine. It offered young painters, mostly graduate students, a lakeside summer of work — intense work punctuated by critiques from more experienced artists. Many an artist thrived at the school, and so did Maine in response, for many artists came to Skowhegan and stayed. Ben Shahn took a summer place near the school;

his wife, Bernadina, also paints. Their daughter Abby Shahn is one of the state's foremost abstract painters.

Others migrated to the coast. Among the artists associated with the school, Neil Welliver, Alex Katz and Lois Dodd live in Lincolnville, and children's book author and illustrator Ashley Bryan lives on the Cranberry Islands.

Cross-fertilization of the Maine and American art worlds continues. Visit the Farnsworth Museum of Art (see our Arts chapter) in Rockland, the University of Maine Museum of Art in Orono, or the Portland Museum of Art in Portland; also stop by galleries to see the next Marins and Hartleys emerge.

George Bellows (1882-1925)

Bellows was so moved by his summer on Monhegan with Robert Henri (see subsequent entry) that he returned home with a dozen canvases and 30 drawings. Bellows painted not only the dramatic rocks and woods, but also the people on the docks, hanging with their animals and conducting their daily work — building ships and launching them; bringing in fish and cleaning them.

Frederick Edwin Church (1826-1900)

Church was greatly influenced by his teacher, Thomas Cole. After Cole died, Church wasted little time in following Cole's wake to Mount Desert Island. There, Church painted the coastal waters and jagged rocks of the island as well as the radiant hues the setting sun casts over the east. When he returned to New York — his paintings were shown in an 1851 exhibit there — Church was compared to J.M.W. Turner. Church kept venturing to Maine, and in the antebellum years, he was transforming landscapes into political allegories, using the gathering of storm clouds as a call for the Union's ascendancy.

Thomas Cole (1801-1848)

Cole was the leader of what was known as the Hudson River School. Born in England, Cole's family migrated to New York when he was young. There, he associated with New York-based writers William Cullen Bryant, Washington Irving and James Fenimore Cooper. Like Henry David Thoreau and Ralph Waldo Emerson, Cole talked about the wilderness and its powerful ability to instruct and inspire. Though he painted the bulk of his work in the Hudson River Valley, in 1844 Cole took a steamer to Mount Desert Island, which he found to be a glorious wilderness in miniature. Many of his paintings and sketches of this wilderness are at The Art Museum of Princeton University, but a few are housed in Maine.

Marsden Hartley (1877-1943)

Marsden Hartley is Maine's modernist. He was born Edmund Hartley, in Lewiston, an industrial city on the Androscoggin River. His mother died when he had just turned 8 years old. Four years later, his father married Martha Marsden, and Hartley changed his name to carry his stepmother's. By his admission, he grew up solitary and confused — an intellectual and a homosexual in a city of mills. He took art classes, though, and managed to get enough recognition to propel him to New York, to the studio of photographer Alfred Stieglitz. (Stieglitz had the 291 Gallery and had already been working with painter John Marin; see subsequent entry.) Their relationship continued throughout Hartley's life. Hartley spent many years in Europe as well as in New York, but toward the end of his life, he spent summers in Maine on Georgetown Island (south of our Mid-Coast region) and in Brooksville before settling in Corea, just beyond Schoodic Point. Look for his strong use of color and dramatic form to convey the power of his connection to Maine and its people.

Robert Henri (1865-1929)

Henri went to Monhegan Island to paint. He was the inspiration for what came to be known derisively as The Ashcan School, because he and his followers (known to one another as The Eight) focused on the realities of life. Henri and some of his artist friends first came to Boothbay Harbor for the summer, taking a day's excursion to Monhegan, which already was beginning to be known to artists at that time. After that day Henri wrote, "So much in so small a place one could hardly believe it." Later, Henri spent summers on Monhegan, accompanied by George Bellows (see previous entry), Rockwell Kent and other artists.

Photo: Bangor Daily News

A schooner glides past the lighthouse at the end of a breakwater
that protects the inner harbor at Rockland.

Winslow Homer (1836-1910)

One of the most famous and influential of all Maine artists, Winslow Homer settled south of the Mid-Coast area, south of Portland in Prout's Neck, where there are no outer islands to shield the fury of the water lapping at Maine's rocky coast. He came to stay after the Civil War, painting throughout the year, creating powerful, metaphysical images of the direct confrontation of the forces of nature — rock against sea. The Portland Museum of Art has a large collection of Homer's works; the Farnsworth also has some (see The Arts).

Edward Hopper (1882-1967)

Hopper, a student of Robert Henri, came to Monhegan for three summers starting in 1916, painting the lighthouse and the rocks. He continued to paint in the region, finding in Rockland something of the lonely desolation of the city that is part of Hopper's trademark. But more of his work was of southern Maine, around Portland.

Rockwell Kent (1882-1971)

Having already spent a year on Monhegan, Kent, a contemporary of George Bellows (see previous entry), returned there in 1940 and bought a house. While on Monhegan he cre-

ated his stylized prints and paintings of the area. The Portland Museum of Art and the Farnsworth (see The Arts) recently divided a major bequest of paintings from Intel heiress Elizabeth Noyes, so both museums have strong collections of Monhegan paintings.

Fitz Hugh Lane (1804-1865)

Though he was lame, probably from childhood polio, Lane's impairment didn't keep him from being an adventurer-artist. He was happy and comfortable on boats and painted while aboard, whether at anchor or cruising offshore. Lane came to Castine in 1848 at the invitation of the local doctor, painting the great clipper ships in the harbor as well as Maine's entrancing combination of fog and light. Lane returned to Maine several consecutive summers, traveling also to Mount Desert Island and Camden. His "Shipping in Downeast Waters," a luminist vision of sunset off Maine's coast, can be found at the Farnsworth Museum in Rockland (see The Arts). His paintings revel in atmosphere, beautifully capturing the absolute hush that happens in harbors at the quiet of the tide.

John Marin (1870-1953)

More than any other painter, John Marin was a painter of energies — a jazz artist who used line and color as rhythm. He painted the thriving jazz culture of New York in the 1920s and used that same approach to paint the oncoming storms, the waves and the energy of sky and sea during the many summers he spent on the coast of Maine. Marin left New York in the summer, pushing north and east, until he came to southern Maine in 1914 and to Stonington in 1919, at that time reached by steamer from Rockland. The steamer passed many islands along the way, and many more of Maine's most glorious isles were but a brief boat trip across the harbor from Stonington. Marin remained there summers until 1933, when he moved farther Downeast to Cape Split, a quiet fishing village to this day.

Louise Nevelson (1900-1988)

We can't forget Maine's own sculptress, whose family emigrated from Russia to Rockland before she was 5 years old. Like Marsden Hartley (see previous entry), Louise Nevelson had a hard time being different in Maine. She once told an interviewer, "Think of 1905 when you have a name like BER-li-AWSKY, and you come to Maine. Many of the people in Maine were very rich, believe it or not. And many of them had very beautiful homes. And they needed foreigners like I needed ten holes in my head." She left for New York early in her life, but her brother remained in Rockland, so Nevelson returned frequently. Thanks to gifts from her brother, his wife, Lillian Berliawsky, and Nevelson herself, the Farnsworth has a good collection of her work (see The Arts), including a wonderful early landscape she painted of Rockland.

N.C. Wyeth (1882-1945)
Andrew Wyeth (1917-)
Jamie Wyeth (1946-)

Across Muscongus Bay from Monhegan, N.C. Wyeth spent summers in Port Clyde and later in Cushing farther south. Maine was a respite for the popular illustrator. There he created the paintings of his heart, such as "Island Funeral" — paintings about a way of life he knew and loved rather than the knights-in-armor illustrations he was paid to paint for children's novels.

N.C. launched a dynasty of painters. Son Andrew met his wife in Cushing and settled there for summers. There he continues to paint his dry, pointed, poignant images of rural Maine. Andrew's son Jamie has become a popular painter in his own right, creating portraits of island people and landscapes from his home on Monhegan. The three Wyeths will be featured at the Farnsworth Museum's new Wyeth Center, slated to open in 1998 in a former church in downtown Rockland (see our Arts chapter).

William Zorach (1887-1966)
Margueritte Zorach (1887-1968)

The Zorachs eventually settled south of the Mid-Coast region, but like John Marin they first came to the fishing village of Stonington in 1919. William was primarily a sculptor, and Margueritte, a painter. But neither stayed confined to their chosen media. Though both created lovely landscapes, they were known for their figures. Rather than using the landscape as a symbol, their paintings of people symbolize emotions of love, industry and devotion. The Farnsworth Museum (see The Arts) has a large mural by Margueritte Zorach hanging in the entrance.

Photographers

Eliot Porter's book *Summer Island*, published in a Sierra Club series of portraits of the wilderness, might contain more than anyone need know of coastal Maine's beauty. His island, Great Spruce Head, is part of a small archipelago in Penobscot Bay. Of course there are more photographers, among them Kosti Ruohomaa, whose "Night Train at Wiscasset Station" is an immensely evocative portrait of Maine. Photography innovator Berenice Abbott lived out her life in Maine and created some powerful images of U.S. Highway 1.

Abbott (1898-1991) stood at the center of several photographic movements. In Paris, in the 1920s, she created lasting photographs of 20th-century artists such as James Joyce and Edna St. Vincent Millay (see the previous "Poets" section). Later she pioneered stop-motion photography. When she came to Maine, it was the worker and the life of the road that fascinated her.

Films

The Maine Film Commission's job is to get more films shot in Maine — instead of those that pretend to be shot in Maine, such as *The Beans of Egypt, Maine* and many Stephen King movies. But King has shot his share of films in Maine: *Pet Sematary* was filmed in Hancock; *The Langoliers* was filmed at the Bangor International Airport; and *Thinner* was filmed in Thomaston, Camden, Lincolnville and Belfast. Coming in 1999 is the ABC television production of King's *Storm of the Century*, filmed in Southwest Harbor during winter and spring 1998.

Carousel was filmed a bit south of the Mid-Coast area in Boothbay Harbor, and the classic *Peyton Place* was filmed primarily in Camden and a bit in Rockland. Peyton Place is replayed yearly in Camden.

Other films that feature Maine include *The Man Without a Face*, shot in Rockport and Deer Isle, and *Forrest Gump*, whose title character runs across the nation and ends up at Port Clyde. And then there's *The Hunt for Red October*, which culminates with a submarine skulking the waters of the Penobscot River, moving upriver toward Bucksport.

Videos

Documentaries of Mid-Coast life — shipbuilding and lumbering, early automobiles and unchanged towns — can be found by contacting Northeast Historic Films (see our Arts chapter).

Some of our favorites include the following: *From Stump to Ship* shows footage of the old logging camps and how woodsmen used horses to bring logs from the woods to the rivers, where they were floated downriver to sawmills. *Our Lives in Our Hands* is about Micmac basketmakers. And *Berenice Abbott: A View of the 20th Century* is about Abbott's pioneering life from France to New York to Maine.

Available commercially and in libraries, but also sold or loaned from Northeast Historic Films, is *The Robert McCloskey Library*, a video including some images of his Maine books.

For delightful images of Wabanaki legends, ask the folks at Northeast if they can help you find copies of *Frog Monster* and other videos produced by students at the Indian Island Elementary School, on Indian Island.

And don't miss *How to Eat a Lobster*, a delightfully funny video that demonstrates not only how to eat a lobster, but also tells about its life cycle, including how it is trapped from the sea. It was created by humorist Alan Smith, who knows the business well, and put out by Blue Ribbon Enterprises of Ellsworth.

THURSTON'S LOBSTER POUND

Look for our yellow awning on Steamboat Wharf Road in Bernard and enjoy lunch or dinner at our working wharf overlooking scenic Bass Harbor.

* BOILED LOBSTER * MUSSELS *
*CLAMS * CHOWDERS * SANDWICHES *
* BEER & WINE *

11 am to closing during the season
244-7600

Steamboat Wharf Road
Bernard, ME 04612

Restaurants

Are you in for a treat! The chefs we talked with are incredibly enthusiastic about their menus and their clientele. They are searching out the finest, freshest local ingredient and experimenting with healthy new combinations. Even the most expensive restaurants are finding ways to accommodate light eaters and limited budgets.

We've flushed out the best and brightest eateries and fine-dining establishments, from fabulous hot dog stands to jackets-suggested restaurants, and we present these choices with the same enthusiasm and pride as the chefs we spoke with.

We've tried to indicate the clientele various restaurants cater to but found this almost impossible to determine. As we talked with restaurant managers, it became clear that Mainers don't have the luxury of niche restaurants. If there's a good place to eat nearby, locals use it as they wish, dressing up for an anniversary or dressing down for a bite to eat on the way to a movie. We've tried to flag the really dressy places — Marcel's at the Samoset Resort, for instance, suggests that male diners wear jackets — but most restaurants welcome the range of customers they get and try to create atmospheres that work for any occasion. Maine's Mid-Coast isn't a place where we dress to the nines and go somewhere to make the scene. Actually, the whole idea kind of grates on Yankee sensibilities. Mainers don't flaunt.

A word about the menu items mentioned: We do think it's helpful to know the kind of dishes a restaurant serves, but don't walk in expecting a particular entree mentioned here. Some restaurants do have long-standing specialties, but others change their menus daily, weekly or seasonally. Some chefs won't let their customers get attached to one dish or another — they say it gets boring to make the same thing over and over!

When business slows in the winter, many restaurants close up for days, weeks or months at a time. We tried to indicate the times restaurants expect to close, but they tend to be pretty relaxed about changing their game plans. It's always best to call ahead, especially from January through March.

Also, some restaurants have summer and winter hours, but they don't have definite dates when they switch from one to the other. The decision is based on their reading of the traffic, and it's generally made on the fly ... another reason to call ahead. If it's any consolation, off-season prices might be lower, especially along the coast.

Price-code Key

The following key represents the price range for the average cost of dinner for two, excluding cocktails, beer, wine, appetizers or desserts. Many restaurants take credit cards and reservations, but many don't. Unless otherwise noted, all restaurants in this chapter accept at least Visa and MasterCard as methods of payment.

$	Less than $20
$$	$20 to $40
$$$	$40 to $60
$$$$	$60 and more

Reservations are noted only if recommended or required. Also, we haven't covered most national chain restaurants; They're predictable and easily found in the Yellow Pages.

Since so few restaurants have carved out a reputation based on the kind of food they serve, we've arranged these listings geographically rather than by category. Given the distances covered here, the real question always is, how far do we have to drive?

Waldoboro to Stockton Springs

Nobleboro Dinner House
$$, no credit cards • U.S. Hwy. 1, No. 40, Nobleboro • 563-8506

Owner/chef Shepard Brown relishes his customers, from the guy who wears his cap through dinner to the dressed-up retirees — and they relish his food. The menu changes monthly, but always includes steak, seafood, duck, lamb and vegetarian dishes. Brown likes to play with entree names, with specials like Mixed Precipitation, broiled scallops with sesame seeds and honey-soy-garlic sauce, and Greta's Rubber Duck, boneless duck baked in horseradish, peppercorns and bread crumbs. (Greta is Brown's daughter, and she makes an honorary appearance on most of his menus.) Brown makes his own desserts and brags about the Indian pudding, the lemon sponge, the pies and the cheesecake. Locals rave about the place, which is how we found it

The Nobleboro Dinner House serves beer and wine. It's open for dinner daily year round except Tuesdays and during the month of March. Reservations are suggested as the dining room seats just 24.

Moody's Diner
$, no credit cards • U.S. Hwy. 1, Waldoboro • 832-7785

A third-generation Moody runs this Maine landmark. Opened in 1927, recent renovations were done carefully to improve the kitchen space but make little mark on the dining area. Moody's sells classic diner fare, such as hot turkey sandwiches, meat loaf and crab cakes, and the sort of desserts found in nostalgic cookbooks, such as tapioca pudding, Grape-Nuts custard and pies of every variety (try the walnut).

Prices are ridiculously low, which is a good thing since Moody's doesn't accept credit cards. The place is open 24 hours a day, 365 days a year.

> ## FYI
> Unless otherwise noted, the area code for all phone numbers listed in this guide is 207.

Pine Cone Cafe
$$ • 13 Friendship Rd., Waldoboro • 832-6337

Laura Cabot's Pine Cone Cafe serves regional American cuisine with ethnic influences. The place is charming, with its light wood, signature flower arrangements and Eric Hopkins watercolors. From the outdoor dining area diners can look down the Medomak River as they enjoy Muscongus Bay Crabcakes or Chevre Chicken Roll with spinach, sun-dried tomatoes and pine nuts. Cabot's black truffle/mustard vinaigrette is a favorite — try it on a mixed green salad, then buy some to take home.

The Pine Cone Cafe is open year round daily except Mondays. It serves a light breakfast, lunch and dinner.

Thomaston Cafe & Bakery
$ • 88 Main St., Thomaston • 354-8589

The Thomaston Cafe is a marvel. The owners bend over backward to use fresh, locally grown organic produce, chemical- and hormone-free chicken and eggs from free-range hens. No canned, processed or frozen foods here. The result is *not* heavy-handed natural-foods fare sold to granola-heads. Eleanor Masin-Peters and Herb Peters serve simple, elegant comfort food in what's become a local gathering place. Crab cakes with home fries are a favorite, as are an increasing number of vegetarian entrees. Try the quesadillas with shrimp and local goat cheese in the summer. Breakfasts are a treat as well, with fresh-squeezed orange juice, espresso, pastries, quiche and excellent corned beef hash cakes and eggs.

The Thomaston Cafe is open Monday through Saturday year round for breakfast and lunch.

Hannibal's Cafe on the Common
$-$$ • 289 Common Rd., Union • 785-3663

Hannibal's opened in 1993 in the tiny town of Union some 15 miles inland from U.S. Highway 1, the primary tourist route. Chef/owner Mark Hannibal has managed to thrive by excelling at what his small-town regulars expect

Dana's Grill
Since 1938

Everyone's Favorite Summer Time Place

290 State St.	72 Summer St.	Marina Road
Bangor	Bangor	Hampden
945-6428	**945-3899**	**990-3307**
(Year Round)	Seasonal	Seasonal
	(April 15 - Sept. 20)	(Mother's Day - Labor Day)

Visit our web site at:
www.mainguide.com/bangor/danasgrill
for a Full Menu & History

from a diner while spicing up the mix with off-beat, even elegant additions. We had stuffed squab there once on Valentine's Day, but we've also had great Reubens. Hannibal, a Culinary Institute of America graduate, is equally adept at both, and the simple country decor seems to accommodate a jacket and tie as easily as jeans. It also serves local brews on tap as well as a wide range of wines from $4 a glass to $30 a bottle. The result is a restaurant popular with locals, but it draws customers from all over the area.

This cafe happily accommodates special diets. Vegetarian entrees abound, and one recent visitor left perfectly delighted that she'd been able to have a dairy-free breakfast without a lot of fuss.

Housed in an 1839 farmhouse, Hannibal's is family-friendly, with a full complement of high chairs, booster seats and an imaginative children's menu. Where else could a 5-year-old order "ants on a log?" (That's raisins on peanut butter-filled celery sticks, for non-parents.)

The cafe is open Tuesday through Friday year round for lunch and dinner; Saturday for breakfast, lunch and dinner; and Sunday for breakfast and lunch.

Brown Bag
$ • 606 Main St., Rockland • 596-6372

Open since 1987, the Brown Bag is one of the most popular breakfast and lunch spots in the Rockland area. (A Brown Bag franchise also can be found in Brewer at 272 State Street, 989-9980.) Everything's made from scratch (this place even roasts its own meats for sandwiches), and while Brown Bag isn't a health-food restaurant, its emphasis is on good, wholesome, homemade food. Try the veggie Reuben or any sandwich with roast turkey. While there are heart-smart choices on the menu, extravagant baked goods abound as well.

Be aware this is a very casual place. Diners choose their drinks, stand in line to place their orders, then pick it up when they hear their name called. The decor is country. A large picnic table in the center welcomes all comers, but the best seats in the house are the booths in the side dining area. Don't forget to clear your table when you leave.

The Brown Bag is open seven days a week year round.

Cafe Miranda
$ • 15 Oak St., Rockland • 594-2034

Incredibly cheap and incredibly good, Cafe Miranda is also incredibly popular, with a range of customers from skate punks to local millionaires. Sit at the tables, or better yet, sit at the counter and watch the chef/owner and his assistant assemble the ingredients for a handwritten, 50-item menu. The food might best be called international — everything from a drop-dead spaghetti-and-sausage dish to duck with Thai seasonings. Many dishes push the gastronomic envelope; less adventuresome eaters might best ask the wait staff for suggestions.

The tables sport those kitschy salt-and-pepper sets great Aunt Adeline used to collect, and one of the bathrooms is decorated in early Elvis. Beyond those touches of humor, everything else is perfectly respectable, with changing art exhibits on the wall. Oh yes, there are cruets of extra-virgin olive oil and balsamic vinegar on the tables — perfect to drizzle over the focaccia served as an appetizer. Fabulous. Beer and wine are available as are various ports and sherries.

Cafe Miranda is open year round for dinner. Reservations are suggested. Carmen's Patio, a lunch spot next to the restaurant, serves salads and Tex-Mex style entrees in the summer from 11:30 AM to 2:30 PM.

Jessica's European Bistro
$$ • 2 S. Main St. (Maine Hwy. 73), Rockland • 596-0770

Jessica's fills a gracious Victorian home on the Rockland/Owl's Head line. Swiss owner/chef Hans Bucher calls the food "neighborhood bistro," but it's pretty fancy for Maine: lobster ravioli, for instance, in a sherry, garlic, coriander and tarragon sauce. Another popular dish is veal Zurich — medallions of veal in a white wine mushroom sauce. Still, the prices are reasonable, given the high quality, and there's enough variety that penny-pinchers can manage to have a lovely dinner without spending an arm and a leg.

Jessica's has a full bar and is open year round for dinner. It accepts reservations. Many customers dress for dinner, but Bucher says please come as you are. All those ties drive him crazy.

Second Read Books and Coffee
$ • 328 Main St., Rockland • 594-4123

A hip little Rockland breakfast and lunch spot, Second Read is a gem: light woods; lots of used books to pore over; and excellent food including hearty soups, chili and stews in the winter, lighter sandwiches in the summer and vegetarian choices year round. Breakfasts tend to be a choice of one of 16 kinds of coffee; espresso, cappuccino or latte; 30 flavors of tea; and something spectacular from the bakery. The scones have a killer reputation.

Open year round, Second Read draws customers from Rockland's growing art community, and it's a natural spot to grab a bite after exploring the Farnsworth Museum (see our Attractions and Arts chapters) up the street.

Wasses Hot Dogs
$, no credit cards • 2 N. Main St., Rockland • 594-7472

This spic-and-span hot dog stand has been on the same corner of N. Main Street for more than 30 years. Keith Wass bought it 26 years ago, and that was the start of what's become a local hot dog empire. He now has year-round stands on Park Street in Rockland, 594-4347; Union Street in Camden, 236-6551; near Wal-Mart on Camden Street in Rockland, 593-9345; a drive-through in the Reny's parking lot (U.S. Highway 1 and Maine Highway 3) in Belfast, 338-6431; and a seasonal stand on Main Street in Thomaston, 354-8741. Everywhere the drill is the same: a sparkling white trailer accented with red, a menu of hot dogs and toppings, drinks and a few sweets for dessert.

www.insiders.com
See this and many other Insiders' Guide® destinations online — in their entirety.
Visit us today!

Photo: Bangor Daily News

A makeshift yoke helps this blueberry raker remove the crop from the field.

Now, before you dismiss this as pretty pedestrian fare, you should know these aren't just any hot dogs. They have natural casings, they're precooked and then fried to order in peanut oil on the same grill as the onions. Which brings us to those toppings. A plain dog is $1.20 including tax, but cheese sauce, chili, bacon and sauerkraut are extra. Look for brownies and Rice Krispies squares for dessert.

Wasses is open for lunch Monday through Saturday, except the Main Street location in Rockland, which is open seven days a week. The wagons don't accept reservations. Are you kidding? Wasses prides itself on serving a customer a minute.

Marcel's
$$-$$$ • Samoset Resort, 220 Warrenton St., Rockport • 594-0774

Marcel's, part of the Samoset Resort, is as fancy as it gets on the coast of Maine. It overlooks Penobscot Bay, and its linen tablecloths, candles and flowers only enhance the French-American cuisine. Specialties include salmon roasted on a cedar plank, steak Diane and rack of lamb. The Caesar salad is top-notch, and desserts such as bananas Foster are prepared tableside.

Marcel's is open year round for breakfast

and dinner. Reservations are requested, and jackets are suggested.

Rockport Corner Shop
$, no credit cards • 5 Central St., Rockport • 236-8361

There were months when we came here once a week to meet a dear pal for breakfast. We saw the same friendly faces huddled over coffee and newspapers, the waitress knew what we wanted without asking, and we felt happy as clams. Finally, we were regulars somewhere!

Come for breakfast: for waffles, an omelette or great coffee cake. Come for lunch: for lentil burgers, grilled chicken sandwiches or a grinder. Booths and a sit-down counter make the place seem cozy, and pictures of old Rockport hang on the walls. The wait staff is friendly and good-natured, and they know enough to keep it mellow in the morning. Coffee and tea is a help-yourself affair; refills are now free.

The Corner Shop is open for breakfast and lunch seven days a week except for a few weeks in February or March. Although it doesn't accept credit cards, personal checks, even from out of state, are just fine. The place just changed hands; we hope the new owners don't change a thing.

The Sail Loft
$$$ • 1 Main St., Rockport • 236-2330

There's no place like The Sail Loft. Open since 1962, it's understated, even elegant, without being pretentious. The varnished tables and chairs shine like the brightwork on a fine yacht, but the paneling is rough weathered board. The restaurant is right on Rockport's harbor, so it overlooks one of the prettiest coves in Maine, but a massive boat crane and working lobster boats are part of the view.

The food also walks that delicate balance between highbrow and down-home. The lobster is fresh off the dock, and the clam chowder recipe has been unchanged for decades. Wonderful duckling and sophisticated pasta dishes round out the menu. Little blueberry muffins are a staple in the bread basket, and Sunday brunch here is an event. Try fresh-squeezed orange juice and eggs Benedict with crabmeat.

The Sail Loft is open seven days a week for lunch and dinner; closed Tuesdays and Wednesdays in the winter. Sunday brunch starts at noon. Reservations are accepted. In the summer, ask for a window seat; in the winter, ask for a table near the fireplace.

The Helm
$$ • U.S. Hwy. 1, Rockport • 236-4337

Inside you'll find a pleasant French-American restaurant and full bar. Ask to sit in the Greenhouse for views of a pool in the Goose River out back — and try the French stew, bouillabaisse or Cajun chicken sandwich. Outside is a take-out counter with some of the best burgers, deep-fried potato wedges, onion rings and shakes in town.

The Helm is open for lunch and dinner seven days a week from April to November. It accepts reservations for the restaurant.

Fitzpatrick's Cafe
$ • 20 Bay View Landing, Camden • 236-2041

Fitzie's is a favorite local hangout, with a friendly atmosphere and a cast of regulars. Come in the morning for pancakes with real maple syrup while you pore over the newspapers. Or grab a burger, fries and a beer for lunch. The menu's listed on boards behind the counter, and it's extensive, including all manner of soups, chowders and sandwiches.

Figure out what you want, give your order, and wait for your name to be called. If the weather's warm, it's nice to take your tray out to the deck off the second floor.

Fitzpatrick's is open year round for breakfast, lunch and dinner. Reservations would be, well, silly.

Atlantica Gallery & Grille
$$ 41 Bay View Landing, Camden • 236-6011

Atlantica's expanded with the recent renovation on what was Sharp's Wharf. It now seats 68 on two levels. The owners are the same — three young, enthusiastic entrepreneurs. Yes, they serve fresh Atlantic seafood, but always with a twist, most often an Asian twist. Try the seafood puff pastry: scallops, shrimp, fish, mushrooms in a pastry shell with a sherry cream sauce. For lunch, the fish tacos are excellent, with lots of cilantro and lime. Dessert might be blackberry crêpes or crème brûlée du jour.

Oil lamps, fresh flowers and views of Camden harbor make this place pleasant in the evening, but if the weather's nice, ask to be seated on the upper or lower deck.

Atlantica's open for lunch and dinner daily in summer and Tuesday through Saturday in winter. Reservations are suggested.

Camden Bagel Cafe
$, no credit cards • Brewster Building, Mechanic and Washington Sts., Camden • 236-2661

A local gathering place, the Bagel Cafe is relaxed, low-key and sells great bagels: a dozen different kinds each day, served plain, toasted and with cream cheeses. Try a sesame bagel with vegetable cream cheese or jalapeño cream cheese. Cheddar-dill bagels aren't on the menu all the time, but they're a favorite.

The Bagel Cafe is open for breakfast and lunch (until 5 PM) daily year round, and on slow winter afternoons, customers are welcome to curl up with a cup of tea and a book. Sundays, it closes at 2 PM.

Camden Deli
$ • 37 Main St., Camden • 236-8343

There are two salient facts about this New York-style deli, and both are hidden from the

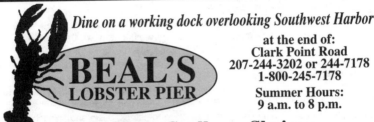
casual passerby. First, the food is excellent — soups, sandwiches and great desserts. Second, the back of the deli holds a small eating area with a wall of windows overlooking Camden Harbor. It's one of the prettiest views around.

Try "The Selectman" sandwich, with turkey, havarti, pesto, tomatoes and onions, grilled. And don't miss the Perky Bars: peanut butter with chocolate. The selection of sodas is wide, and beer and wine are sold here. This is a good place to put together the fixin's for a picnic.

Camden Deli is open year round for breakfast, lunch and dinner.

Cappy's Chowder House
$ • 1 Main St., Camden • 236-2254

Seafood is the attraction here, as is the chowder. Cappy's sits in the middle of town and is heavily decorated with nautical paraphernalia outside and in, making it a natural draw for tourists. It's a favorite with families too — there's so much for the kids to look at. Lobster and broiled salmon are favorites, and we've had great French toast for breakfast.

Cappy's is open for breakfast, lunch and dinner daily in the summer. It's closed Wednesdays in the winter and serves just lunch and dinner except Sundays, when it serves all three meals.

Frogwater Cafe
$$ • 31 Elm St., Camden • 236-8998

Frogwater falls somewhere between fine dining and burgers: It's casual American food with Mediterranean influences. That is, the menu might include salmon in a potato crust as well as a lush warm orzo salad. For an appetizer, try the Brie and vegetables in a puff pastry. Desserts and bread are baked in-house.

In a storefront on Camden's main street, Frogwater is open for dinner Monday through Saturday year round. Reservations are accepted until 5 PM daily in summer.

Marriner's Restaurant
$ • 35 Main St., Camden • 236-2647

"Down Home, Down East, No Ferns, No Quiche." That's the sign outside Marriner's, and it pretty much describes the niche this little place fills in the town of Camden. It disarms the yacht club crowd, says the manager … this is a place where millionaires sit elbow to elbow with guys from the mill.

Open since 1942, Marriner's serves great breakfasts and great diner food for lunch and dinner. Try muffins or pancakes, any of the soups and chowders or the lobster and crabmeat rolls. Baked stuffed haddock and grilled fish are favorites at dinner.

Marriner's serves breakfast and lunch in

the winter; breakfast, lunch and dinner in the summer. It's open seven days a week year round, except Sundays from January through March. Reservations are necessary only for the two big tables in the front windows.

Peter Ott's
$-$$ • 16 Bayview St., Camden • 236-4032

Named after an old colonial tavern, Peter Ott's has been a popular gathering place for visitors and locals, couples and families since 1974. The pleasant, wood-panelled dining room can seat as many as 100 people. Favorite foods include teriyaki sirloin, lobster and other local seafood specials like Annie's Fresh Basil Fettucini served with sea scallops, fresh broccoli and mushrooms in a light Alfredo sauce. Peter Ott's has made a name for itself with elaborate desserts such as ice cream pies and frozen mousse pie. It was at Peter Ott's that Eleanor Klivans, now a nationally known dessert maker, developed her confections with the help of Ott's co-owner, Carolyn Mays. Many of her recipes are still on the dessert menu.

Ott's is open nightly year round. There is a full bar, but no smoking is allowed. Ott's does not take reservations.

The Waterfront
$$ • Bayview St., Camden • 236-3747

Set off the street and hugging the harborline, The Waterfront is the place to come when the weather's nice. The partially covered deck is heavenly on sunny summer days. In the winter, two working fireplaces and oil lamps add atmosphere. The prices tend to drop a bit then too. Not surprisingly, the focus here is seafood, but with a Mediterranean slant. Try the mussels with white wine, shallots and butter, the crab cakes with remoulade sauce or any of the salads, which are large and meal-size.

The Waterfront is open year round for lunch and dinner.

Zaddik's Pizza
$ • 20 Washington St., Camden • 236-6540

Pizza lovers unite! Zaddik's has an array of choices, all made fresh daily. Look for traditional, Mediterranean, Greek, even Thai toppings, including artichokes, feta cheese, sun-dried tomatoes, pesto and spinach. Brightly painted, fresh and well-lighted, Zaddik's has a slight Southwestern motif, and its casual atmosphere attracts all manner of customers, especially families.

Open for dinner daily year round except Mondays, Zaddik's serves beer and wine and delivers within a 3-mile radius of downtown Camden.

FYI

Unless otherwise noted, the area code for all phone numbers listed in this guide is 207.

The Dining Room at Whitehall Inn
$$ • 52 High St., Camden • 236-3391, (800) 789-6565

If you want a taste of the elegant Whitehall Inn (see Accommodations) without staying there, try having dinner in its dining room. The atmosphere is classic country inn, with candles, flowers, linen and waiters in black and white, and the food is excellent. Try the veal St. Millay, sautéed veal with a wine, mushroom and cream sauce, or any of the many seafood dishes. While there are some regular specialties, the menu changes every three days to make the best use of local foods.

The Whitehall has a full bar and one of the top wine lists in the state. It's open from Memorial Day to mid-October. Reservations are accepted.

Chez Michel
$$ • U.S. Hwy. 1, Lincolnville • 789-5600

Owner/chef Michel Hetuin has a hit on his hands. The atmosphere is pleasantly ca-

---

INSIDERS' TIP

While most dining in Maine is both informal and inexpensive, it's also quite popular. Don't forget to call ahead to reserve a table, especially for dinner in summer.

An old-fashioned Maine lobster bake includes buttered baked potato, steamed corn, succulent Maine lobster and a plateful of steamed clams.

sual: light, airy and nice enough that diners can dress up if they like, but don't feel they have to. However, the real reason people from all over come here again and again is the food. Try garlic steak, rare with lots of garlic; bouillabaisse; or pork chops St. Vincent, with a mustard and onion cream sauce we've been struggling to imitate at home for years. The wine list is extensive, there's a full bar, and the desserts are excellent — usually a choice of pies and a few special French creations.

Chez Michel is open for lunch and dinner Tuesday through Sunday from April through October. It accepts reservations. If the weather's nice, ask for a seat on the second-floor deck.

Lobster Pound
$$ • U.S. Hwy. 1, Lincolnville • 789-5550

Here's a favorite with tourists and dyed-in-the-wool locals for standard American restaurant fare: roast beef, ham, steaks, but especially lobster. The restaurant is on the ocean's edge, the decor is casual/nautical, and customers have a choice of inside or outside dining. An all-day luncheon menu allows those who eat a little less to have a good meal for $7.95. The Lobster Pound is open for lunch

and dinner seven days a week from May through October.

Whale's Tooth Pub and Restaurant
$$ • U.S. Hwy. 1, Lincolnville Beach • 789-5200

Check out our Nightlife chapter for information about after-dark activity at this pub. Just be sure to come early and stay late: The food is as good as the fun. The menu includes fresh lobster, steaks, prime rib, fish and vegetarian fare, but a real specialty is the British-style fish and chips served in newspapers with malt vinegar.

Whale's Tooth Pub is open year round for dinner Wednesday through Monday and for lunch Saturday and brunch Sunday. Reservations are requested for parties of six or more.

Youngtown Inn
$$-$$$ • Maine Hwy. 52, Lincolnville • 763-4290

Under the attentive hands of Manuel and Mary Ann Mercier since 1992, the Youngtown Inn has become one of the finest restaurants in the Mid-Coast area. The decor is light and elegant, but not so formal as to feel restrictive. The menu is classical French with a dash of American innovation, and the food is consis-

How to Eat a Maine
Lobster

1.

Twist off the claws.

2.

Crack each claw with a nutcracker, pliers, knife, hammer or rock.

3.

Separate the tail from the body by arching the back until it cracks. Break off the tail flippers.

4.

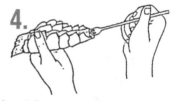

Insert fork and push the tail meat out in one piece. Remove and discard the black vein which runs the entire length of the tail.

5.

Unhinge the back shell from the body.

6.

Open the body by cracking it apart sideways. Maine lobster meat lies in the four pockets (or joints) where the small walking legs are attached. The small walking legs also contain excellent meat which can be removed by sucking on the ends of the legs.

tently excellent. We have friends in the neighborhood who will eat nowhere else. Try the Maine scallops in puff pastry and the filet mignon with Portobello ragout. For dessert, crème brûlée is a favorite, and the fresh fruit sorbets are inspired.

A lovely setting for private parties and weddings, the Youngtown Inn is open for dinner year round. From Memorial Day to Labor Day, it's closed Sundays and Mondays. Reservations are recommended.

The Hideaway Diner
$, no credit cards • 1285 Atlantic Hwy. (U.S. Hwy. 1), Northport • 338-1374

This modest little diner in a log building with flowered curtains is a slice of small-town Maine. Best of all, the food's homey, inexpensive and made from scratch, even the breads, biscuits (they're spectacular) and soups. We like Saturday breakfast best. Try the corned beef hash or the pancakes. This place is lively but not irritating, and families are welcome. For dinner, the always fresh fisherman's plat-

ter of haddock, scallops, clams and shrimp is a favorite. The Hideaway is open Tuesday through Sunday year round for breakfast, lunch and dinner.

Darby's
$$ • 155 High St., Belfast • 338-2339

The menu at this friendly local gathering spot is varied, with steaks and burgers as well as great pad Thai and Moroccan lamb. The extensive wine list — some 25 choices — is a reflection of the owner's interest in the subject. Like many restaurants in small towns, Darby's candles and low lighting can be the basis for a dress-up evening or a bite to eat on the way to the movies. Open since 1985, Darby's has a full bar and is open daily year round for lunch and dinner. It accepts reservations, especially in summer.

Ninety Main
$ • 90 Main St., Belfast • 338-1106

The atmosphere here is casual but refined, and that also describes the food. Specialties include Thai mussels, blueberry chicken (served in summer) and lamb of the day. For dessert, try the chocolate torte with raspberry sauce. There's a full bar and outdoor seating in summer. (See our Nightlife chapter for details about Ninety Main after dark.)

Ninety Main is open for lunch and dinner daily and Sunday brunch year round. Its bakery offers a continental breakfast in the morning. Reservations are accepted.

Nickerson Tavern
$$ • U.S. Hwy. 1, Searsport • 548-2220

Nickerson Tavern, in a handsome 1835 sea captain's home, has been a tavern since 1927, but the atmosphere these days is more relaxed with white tablecloths than rowdy with red-checked vinyl. Male diners would be perfectly comfortable in a jacket and tie in the winter, but summers tend to be more casual. The food is eclectic but not too nouveau. Raspberry hazelnut chicken and all manner of fresh fish are favorites. There's a full bar and a very nice wine list. Nickerson Tavern is open for dinner daily from April through December. Reservations are recommended.

Periwinkles Bakery
$, no credit cards • 225 Main St. (U.S. Hwy. 1), Searsport • 548-9910

We remember the day one of our sisters-in-law first discovered this place. She'd gone antiquing in Searsport and came home with a selection of baked goods. Everything was fabulous. We scouted the place for ourselves and found it based in the back of a large, handsome old sea captain's house. A sign on the road makes it easy to spot. Look for the "open" flag.

Inside, Periwinkles looks like a little British tea room. For breakfast, try the scones and great European pastries. Lunch has a definite British cast — delicious Cornish pasties and English sausage rolls as well as quiches, homemade soups and sandwiches, most on a croissant. The pizza is spectacular, made with seasoned Italian bread dough and one or two choices of toppings.

Periwinkles is open for breakfast and lunch. During July and August, it's open seven days a week — the schedule varies the rest of the year. It's closed altogether in January.

Inland to Bangor

Colonial Winterport Inn
$$ • 114 Main St. (U.S. Hwy. 1A), Winterport • 223-5307

Owner/chef Duncan McNab has three degrees from the Cordon Bleu Paris cooking school, and it shows in the French-American food he prepares. Chicken Winterport, a house specialty, is a boneless breast of chicken in a lobster bisque sauce. Duck a l'orange and poached salmon are other favorites. The Colonial Winterport Inn is open year round for dinner by reservation only on Wednesday, Thursday and Saturday. It also offers buffets Friday evenings and at Sunday brunch. The dinners are a fixed price for five courses, while the buffets offer a variety of choices. Sunday buffets are especially lavish, offering Belgian waffles, sausages with apples and onions and baked beans with pecans and apples plus fresh fruit, juice and muffins. All that for $5.49! The inn is open for lunch Monday through Friday in summer.

Dysart's Restaurant
$ • Coldbrook Rd., Hermon • 942-4878

This Bangor-area institution — a truckstop open all day every day — is actually in Hermon, just off I-95 Exit 44. The menu includes steak, burgers, fries and a great chicken/cheddar/bacon sub. For dessert, try the Oreo ice cream or peanut butter pie. Dysart's has been here since 1967, and it's going strong.

Harborside Restaurant
$$ • 9 S. Main St., Brewer • 989-2040

In business for 16 years, this 450-seat riverside restaurant is an institution in Brewer. While it boasts of being the only outdoor lobster pound in the Bangor area, it also has banquet facilities, private meeting rooms and a full bar. A covered deck seating 120 is delightful in the summer, with its views of the river.

Good food is what grows restaurants this size, so you can count on great seafood and steaks. The seafood chowder's a treat, and an in-house bakery makes the desserts from scratch.

The Harborside is open for breakfast, lunch

and dinner. The atmosphere is casual, and a children's menu ($2.95 for kids entrees) makes it nice for families. Reservations are suggested for parties of six or more.

Three Sisters Cafe
$, no credit cards • 415 Wilson St., Brewer • 989-3133

Owner Emily Weatherall is positively joyous about Three Sisters. That must be the reason it's grown so popular since opening in 1995. The cafe is casual and friendly, with '60s folk and blues playing in the background, but the real draw is Weatherall's food — tasty and innovative, made with the freshest, healthiest ingredients she can find. She does serve meat in some sandwiches, but the vegetarian choices really shine: The roasted eggplant with pesto is killer. Try the smoked tofu and avocado sandwich as well. Her bakery churns out desserts, muffins and pastries, which are real favorites for breakfast.

Three Sisters is open Monday through Saturday year round for continental breakfast and lunch, and Friday evenings for live acoustic music. The clientele is a mix that includes groups of high school students, and Weatherall wants to keep it that way, so for now, she's not selling beer or wine. Customers are welcome to bring their own. Reservations might be wise — there are just 35 seats.

The Bagel Shop
$, no credit cards • 1 Main St., Bangor • 947-1654

This downtown kosher deli is at the heart of Bangor. Behind its gleaming windows sit lawyers in suits and homeless people in sweats enjoying bagels, spectacular sandwiches and a pea soup to die for. The atmosphere's friendly and welcoming — there's even a smoking and nonsmoking dining room. Everything's made from scratch, and the variety's stunning. When was the last time you saw lime ricky, that old soda fountain favorite, on a menu? Or a tongue sandwich? The manager told us this is a popular stop for Jewish tourists from New York. No wonder.

The Bagel Shop is open year round for breakfast, lunch and early dinners (most evenings it closes at 6 PM) from Sunday through Friday. Reservations aren't necessary.

City Limits
$$ • 735 Main St., Bangor • 941-9888

This restaurant recently opened in the old house that once held the much-loved Sequino's, an Italian restaurant that closed down suddenly a few years ago. City Limits moved in and has had a fast start for a relative newcomer. It's upscale but casual, and specializes in seafood and Italian dishes. Try the Greek scallops, with fresh vegetables and feta over angel hair pasta, or the Savory Spinach Salad. There's a full bar and an extensive wine list. If you like lots windows, ask to be seated in the garden room, a solarium with masses of beautiful plants. It's heavenly in a snowstorm.

City Limits is open year round for lunch and dinner. Reservations are accepted but aren't necessary.

Dana's Grill
$, no credit cards • 72 Summer St., Bangor • 945-3899
$, no credit cards • Turtle Head Marina, Marina Rd., Bangor • 990-3307
$ • 290 State St., Bangor • 945-6428

The first Dana's Grill opened in 1938 on Summer Street. Now it has three locations, each seating some 100 people. Only the State Street location is actually a restaurant; the others serve take-out. Summer Street has large decks with tables and chairs just a quarter-mile from the river, while the location at Turtle Head Marina has picnic tables.

The food at all locations is classic fast-food fare — fried seafood, hamburgers and hot dogs — only Dana's uses all fresh products. Dana's Grill makes its own onion rings, and its lobster roll is one of the best in the area. To drink, you'll find soda, lemonade and shakes (no alcohol). For dessert, try Gifford's ice cream in a range of flavors, sundaes, splits and cookies.

Needless to say, these are casual spots, but you'll see all kinds — from suits to hard hats. All three locations are open for lunch and dinner. Summer Street and Turtle Head are open seasonally, from April to September; State Street is open year round.

The Greenhouse Restaurant
$$ • 193 Broad St., Bangor • 945-4040

With 200 plants decorating three dining rooms and views of the Penobscot River, the Greenhouse is popular with the professional set for both lunch and dinner. It specializes in regional American cuisine with a continental influence, so look for Châteaubriand, souffles, rack of lamb in a Dijon crust and charbroiled prime rib with fresh horseradish sauce. Owner Arthur Howard was trained in the old school of culinary arts, and that experience comes out in wonderful ways. Take his version of the traditional Paris-Brest dessert, originated by a pastry chef on the Pullman train between those two railroad stops. To a pâté choux circle filled with pastry cream, Howard adds Amaretto flavoring and decorates it more richly than the usual powdered-sugar dusting. The result is an impressive special-occasion treat.

The Greenhouse has a full bar and is open Tuesday through Saturday year round for lunch and dinner. Reservations are accepted.

The Ground Round
$ • 248 Odlin Rd., Bangor • 942-5621

Open until after midnight, the Ground Round has fed many a weary traveler when the rest of Bangor was buttoned up tight. The menu is a little bit of everything, from Black Angus steaks to taco salads and baby-back ribs. Buffalo wings are favorite appetizers.

Open since 1977, The Ground Round has a full bar and a casual, friendly atmosphere. It's open for lunch and dinner seven days a week year round.

Intown Internet Cafe
$ • 56 Main St., Bangor • 942-0999

Owner Steve Stimpson spent four years in Little Italy in New York City learning his trade. A Maine native, he's come back to Bangor with more than a thousand recipes and a zest for the cafe life. This is a warm, friendly place that serves subs, soups, chowders and a mean Pecan Turtle Latte. It has the feel of a social club or a good bar, only there's no alcohol served.

Like any good Internet cafe, Stimpson has seven computers set up (all IBM; three Macs are due this summer) for customers

INSIDERS' TIP

When you order a lobster in Maine, it's usually served whole. So you'll most likely be extracting the meat yourself. Never cracked open a lobster? Check out the directions in this chapter, or ask your server.

Photo: Bangor Daily News

In nice weather, patrons can enjoy lunch or dinner alfresco at many Bar Harbor restaurants.

to use. The cost is $5 an hour, $3 a half-hour and $2 for 15 minutes or less. Student rates are $3.50 an hour. Sundays, the rate drops to $3 an hour for anyone with reservations. Steve and his staff are happy to tutor users for free. Stuck on that resume? Bring it here for help.

The Intown Internet Cafe is open year round for breakfast, lunch and dinner.

The Lemon Tree
$$ • 167 Center St., Bangor • 945-3666

Innovative and excellent, The Lemon Tree has made a name for itself in three short years and just doubled its space. The menu is international, the style is bistro, the scale is small, but amenities include tablecloths, flowers and candles. While the neighborhood isn't much to brag about, we saw patrons from as far away as Camden. The food is fabulous! Look for entrees such as New Orleans crunchy pecan chicken and Gorgonzola and jalapeño cream sauce atop spinach pasta. Try the lemon torte pie or the chocolate tuxedo brownie pie for dessert.

The Lemon Tree is open daily year round for dinner, and Monday through Friday for lunch. Listen for live jazz and blues Friday and Saturday nights; no cover charge.

Miller's Other Room
$-$$ • 427 Main St., Bangor • 942-6361

The parking lot's packed, but that's no surprise. Miller's has an all-you-can-eat buffet of more than 200 items, including a low-fat section and a dessert bar. It's a bargain at $6.99 for lunch, $10.99 for dinner. Other menu choices include steaks, seafood and chops. The lobster pie and prime rib are specialties. Miller's has a full bar and is open daily year round for lunch and dinner. Reservations are accepted but not required.

New Moon Cafe
$ • 21 State St., Bangor • 990-2233

Next to the Bagel Shop and across from the Grasshopper Shop (see Shopping), the New Moon Cafe is sure to benefit from West Market Square traffic. Part-owner Paul Noonan grew up in the area, but he's been across the country a few times, and been to Europe. No, he says, there's no place like the New Moon in Bangor. We'd say it's more like Portland or Boston, with it's sleek oak, copper and stone.

The food has a big-city sophistication as well. Look for sandwiches of smoked turkey, havarti and honey mustard, or boursin and roast beef. The bread is European-style baked in Portland. Desserts include cheesecake, tiramisu or biscotti. And, of course, all kinds of coffee, cappuccino and latte.

Adjacent to the cafe is a room with computers (five to start, three more to come) for patrons to use. The fee is $6 an hour, $5 for students. Discounts are available for frequent users. The computers may be reserved, as can the room itself — for business meetings or network gaming.

The New Moon is open year round for breakfast, lunch and dinner.

Oriental Jade
$ • Bangor Mall Blvd., Bangor
• 947-6969

If you have a yen for Asian foods, this is the place for you. From dim sum to curry, Oriental Jade serves all manner of Chinese, Japanese and Thai dishes. The Pu Pu Platter is popular, as are a wide variety of lobster specialties. And try a mai tai to start. Here, those luscious frozen tropical drinks are made from scratch — no bar mixes.

Open nearly 20 years, Oriental Jade seats 300 and offers a full menu, a full bar, take-out and delivery. On Friday and Saturday nights, the 50-item buffet is $9.99. That must be one of the best deals in town.

The restaurant is open for lunch and dinner year round. Reservations are recommended.

Pilot's Grill
$$ • 1528 Outer Hammond St., Bangor
• 942-6325

Open since 1940, Pilot's offers casual fine dining. It attracts a cast of regulars but also is favored by local motel guests. House specialties include baked stuffed lobster, baked stuffed shrimp, prime rib and steaks. For dessert, try the lemon meringue pie or the cheesecake. Pilot's Grill is open daily year round for lunch and dinner, closed Sundays in the winter. It accepts reservations.

Sea Dog Brewing Co.
$$ • 26 Front St., Bangor • 947-8004

Expecting pub fare? Think again. Bangor's Sea Dog offers the best of native Maine food with an international flair. The menu is extensive — this is the place to go when you can't agree on what kind of food you want. While choices change seasonally, you might find baked stuffed mushrooms Gruyère offered as an appetizer and grilled Atlantic salmon, barbecued pork and Oriental vegetable stir-fry as entrees. Try the espresso cheesecake for dessert. You'll have great views of the Penobscot River from here as well. Sea Dog is open daily year round for lunch and dinner and offers brunch Sundays.

Taste of India
$ • 68 Main St., Bangor • 945-6865

One of our favorite restaurants in Bangor, Taste of India offers just that. The menu is extravagant in scope, with lamb, chicken, rice, seafood and vegetarian specialties. The best choice here is a sampler plate such as the Mix Grill, a selection of seekh kabab, boti kabab, chicken Tikka and Tandoori chicken served on a bed of greens and tomatoes with rice, dal and chutney. Smaller, less spicy portions are prepared for children. And for those on restricted diets, low-cholesterol and low-sodium preparations are available as well. Beer and wine are served, and take-out is available. Taste of India is open daily year round for lunch and dinner, except Sundays for dinner only.

Thistle's
$$ • 175 Exchange St., Bangor
• 945-5480

Relaxed and casual, Thistle's still manages an air of refinement. Chalk it up to hanging plants, the paintings and wine posters on the wall and the menu. House favorites include quesadillas (at lunch) and salmon in any form (at dinner). The bread and desserts are made in-house by a pastry chef. Try the banana custard, a pastry cream with bananas and Graham cracker crumbs.

Thistle's is open seven days a week for lunch and dinner. It recommends reservations.

Pat's Pizza
$ • 11 Mill St., Orono • 866-2111
$ • 662 Main Rd. N., Hampden
• 947-6488
$ • Bar Harbor Rd., Ellsworth • 667-6011

Pat Farnsworth opened Pat's in 1931, but it wasn't until 1955 that he started serving pizza. Since then the restaurant's become an institution, making an average of 1,000 pies a day. (Pepperoni's the runaway favor-

ite.) There are 15 franchises: In our Mid-Coast area look for a Pat's in Hampden and Ellsworth. Popular with families and students from the nearby U-Maine campus, Pat's also serves hamburgers, lasagna, chicken and veal parmigiana as well as beer and wine. It's open daily year round for breakfast, lunch and dinner.

The Lucerne Inn
$$ • Bar Harbor Rd. (U.S. Hwy. 1A), Lucerne • 843-5123, (800) 325-5123

Most tables in the dining room offer views of Phillips Lake, and while the pleasant ambiance attracts prom dates and retirees, most guests are middle-age business people. They come for the salmon, the rack of lamb and, of course, the lobster. For dessert, the chocolate French silk pie with raspberry coulis is a favorite.

The Lucerne Inn (see also our Accommodations chapter) has a full bar and is open daily year round for dinner and Sunday brunch (try the Belgian waffles). Reservations are accepted.

Bucksport to Gouldsboro

Crosby's
$, no credit cards • Maine Hwy. 46 (off U.S. Hwy. 1), Bucksport • 469-3640

Your picnic is prearranged at Crosby's: Order up your fried clams, lobster rolls, burgers and ice cream, then settle into one of the tables beside this long, shingled take-out stand just off U.S. 1 and wait for your meal to be called. Crosby's is a favorite local hangout for moderately priced lunches, treats and early dinners. Situated just off U.S. Highway 1 outside Bucksport, it's also becoming known to visitors as a great place to stop, have a snack and get your bearings. It's open from May to September.

Dockside Restaurant
$ • Main St., Bucksport • 469-7600

We have a friend who just can't wait to meet us at the Dockside: He says it's the only place he knows that will still serve hamburgers medium rare, the way he likes them. What we most like here is the view: overlooking the Penobscot River just as it turns a corner around Fort Knox. But we also like the down-home cooking, like steak and eggs at 5:30 AM, to send us off on a holiday excursion. Once, while dining on liver and onions, BLTs, fried clams and fried onion rings, we saw whales swimming up the river. Breakfast, lunch and dinner are served daily, except in winter when there's no supper Mondays and Tuesdays. There's a cocktail lounge on the premises.

L'Ermitage
$$ • 219 Main St., Bucksport • 469-3361

Tucked into a home on Main Street in Bucksport, the surprising L'Ermitage seats 39 people. You might not expect to finds sophisticated continental cuisine in such a hidden location, but L'Ermitage has been serving it for a dozen years and has developed a fine reputation. The chef-owners say they are most proud of their steak Chasseur, a filet mignon with hunter's sauce and specialty mushrooms.

L'Ermitage is open Wednesday through Sunday for dinner year round. Smoking is allowed. There's a full bar.

MacLeod's
$-$$ • Main St., Bucksport • 469-3963

When folks in Bucksport and the surrounding areas want a night out, they frequently go to MacLeod's, where owner George MacLeod offers basic good food with friendly service at reasonable rates. Try a one-plate meal, salmon, salad and new potatoes, and you'll squeeze in at the lowest end of the price code. Or splurge just a bit for Cajun-grilled swordfish, a heaping pile of barbecued spare ribs, or filet mignon topped with a green peppercorn sauce.

New for 1998 is MacLeod's Cafe, where you can settle in for a cappuccino and over-size blueberry muffin or other baked goods, down a smoothie or buy a pint of soup and focaccia bread to go. Tables are spaced at a good distance, so you can have a private conversation without feeling as if your neighbor is listening in (it's a small town after all!). But frequently, it's the neighbors who feel as if we're listening in, as we wander the restaurant time and again to gaze at the museum's

worth of historic shipping and shipbuilding photographs hanging on the walls. Especially note the chains of schooners being towed up the Penobscot River as if they were but toy boats in a bathtub and the ferry barge loaded with old Model Ts as it crossed the river in the days before the Waldo-Hancock Bridge was built.

George MacLeod is a local hero for his work in restoring Fort Knox; if you see him, ask how it's going. There's a full bar as well as a separate bar room here.

MacLeod's is open daily for lunch and dinner, though it may scale back from weekend lunches in winter. Expect the cafe to be open mornings for beverages and baked goods, and for lighter fare during the day.

Bah's Bake House
$ • Water St., Castine • 326-9510

Even in winter, Bah's is bustling. Is it the spicy Thai noodles? The gingerbread? The fresh coffee? It's all that and more. Whether your palate is partial to pâtés and wraps or meatball subs and liverwurst, you'll find excellent fare at Bah's.

In summer, the space triples when guests settle outside on Bah's broad deck overlooking part of Castine and its harbor. Pick up a paper or simply gossip while waiting for the staff to prepare your soup and pâté or your sub. Or come in the morning and nibble on some great pastries while Bah and Co. prepare you a picnic lunch to go. We're talking casual here: Order from the counter; someone will bring you the food.

While Bah's sells wine and beer by the bottle, it does not have a liquor license — you cannot drink on the premises. There's a small smoking section, or you can smoke outside on the porch.

Bah's is open daily year round for breakfast, lunch and light dinners.

The Breeze
$, no credit cards • Castine Dock, at the end of Main St., Castine • 326-9034

Order a hamburger or lobster roll at this outdoor stand and settle on the nearby dockside picnic table to watch the boat traffic in Castine Harbor. Many folk from around the region come here to grab a lunch or light dinner in summer, turning the docks into a community picnic — of several surrounding communities, mind you, with a handful of "from away" visitors thrown in. You'll find standards such as hamburgers, hot dogs, fried clams and ice cream plus non-standards such as veggie burgers at this busy stand, which is open in summer from around June into September.

Castine Inn
$$$ • Main St., Castine • 326-4365

The well-known Castine Inn (see our Accommodations chapter) is renowned for Tom Gutow's gourmet food. Tom came to Castine in 1997 with years of restaurant experience in France and at some of New York City's favorite dining spots. While he has kept such local, homey specialties — crab cakes and oysters on the half-shell — that former owners Mark Hodesh and Margaret Parker had on the menu, he has added some complex gourmet dishes — still using regional food — such as lobster salad with basil cucumbers and tomato glaze as an appetizer, or seared sea scallops with celery root puree and a cilantro vinaigrette sauce as an entree.

Meals are served in the inn's pleasant dining rooms surrounded with murals of Castine painted by former owner Parker. On balmy summer evenings, the porch overlooking the garden (and with views of Castine Harbor in the distance) is a lovely place to settle with a drink or for dinner. The full menu also is available in the wood-panelled tavern room.

Breakfast and dinner are served daily from May through December, assuming there are guests in the inn. After October, the restaurant scales back to weekends. Smoking is not allowed anywhere on the premises.

Dennett's Wharf
$-$$ • Sea St., Castine • 326-9045

The memory of eating mussels in a good garlic broth on a porch beside Castine Harbor helps us through winter. Dennett's Wharf is Castine's standard for basic seafood — lobsters, mussels, fried clams and fish. It's also a good place for thick, juicy Dennettburgers or large spinach salads.

The wide porch overlooking the harbor accommodates many a table filled with folks who flock here by land and sea in summer because there just aren't enough places to enjoy a meal outdoors in Maine. Other patrons prefer eating indoors beneath the restaurant's tall, barn-like ceiling littered with dollar bills. Want to know how all those bills stay up on the ceiling? Give Gary Dennett one and he'll show you. The restaurant's long bar commonly is filled with sailors as well as locals. By the way, don't miss the cabinet of cakes and pies.

Lunch and dinner are served daily from May through sometime in September; call for the exact closing date.

The Blue Hill Inn
$$-$$$ • Union St., Blue Hill • 374-2844

When public television planned a series of great inn cooking, it made sure to include The Blue Hill Inn. The food is *that* classic. Come at 6 PM to sample an assortment of cheeses and to mingle with the guests at this venerable lodging (see our Accommodations chapter). At 7 PM guests retire to the dining room to enjoy an extravagant multi-course meal. The night's dinner might include a field mushroom souffle followed by a lemon-herb ice to clear the palette. Then, choose from two entrees, which change nightly. You might dine on wolf fish baked with potato crust and served with fresh chervil sauce, or lobster with vanilla beurre blanc. Salads are made with local greens. After a cheese-and-fruit course, finish with chocolate profiteroles, or maybe pears soaked in port wine.

The inn's dining room is finished with antiques and candles. There is no smoking here. Older children are welcome for dinner, which is served Wednesday through Sunday from Memorial Day until the end of October (also Tuesdays in July only). Reservations are required. Ask about the inn's wine dinners and the Thanksgiving feast.

Firepond
$$-$$$ • Main St., Blue Hill • 374-9970

The Firepond is built over Mill Stream, which cascades through the heart of Blue Hill. Created in an old blacksmith shop, it is among the region's most romantic places to dine. Candles flicker on the table as water rushes beside you. The meals, some of which are prepared tableside, include interesting takes on seafood, lamb and other meats, including lobster Firepond — the meat is sauteed in a two-cheese cream sauce and served on a bed of fresh fettuccine. But the New Zealand rack of lamb marinated in burgundy herb sauce is the biggest seller. Poultry also is locally raised and organic. Look carefully — you might find ostrich on the menu.

The Firepond is open daily, serving light fare streetside on the patio during the day and dinner nightly from mid-May through October. There's music Sunday afternoons. Some years the restaurant stays open past October. There is a full bar. Reservations are advised.

Jonathan's
$$ • Main St. Blue Hill • 374-5226

We know people who are such good chefs, they seldom find it worthwhile to eat out. But when they do, Jonathan's is one of the few places they go. Asked about his cooking philosophy, owner/co-chef Jonathan Chase says he cares about keeping himself interested. For that reason, the menu changes almost daily. Jonathan also cares about keeping foods seasonal and regional, buying fish daily according to what's freshest, picking herbs and vegetables from his own kitchen garden and buying free-range chicken and rabbit locally. Preparations come from a range of ethnic cuisine, though Italian is most common. Among the standard entrees are braised lamb shank in beer and bourbon maple barbecue sauce, served with polenta or rice and vegetables; and local, farm-raised Atlantic salmon, pan-seared and topped with smoked shrimp, saffron and tomatoes.

Wines are one of Jonathan's passions; he serves 10 kinds by the glass nightly and keeps a list of about 150. There is also a full bar.

Fortunately for locals, Jonathan stays open nearly year round (it's closed in March). Jonathan's is open Wednesday through Sunday from January to May and Tuesdays as well from May through mid-June and Columbus Day through New Year's Day. Mid-June through Columbus Day, Jonathan's is open nightly for dinner. There is no smoking. Reservations are suggested.

Left Bank Bakery & Cafe
$$ • Maine Hwy. 172, Blue Hill
• 374-2201

The Left Bank transformed Blue Hill when it opened in 1987, offering fresh-baked bread daily and lunches and dinner year round and putting Blue Hill on the folk music circuit (see our Nightlife chapter). In 1996, Janet Anker and Chuck Donnelly took the reigns from the original owner, but kept the casual, welcoming atmosphere.

As a restaurant, the cafe specializes in international vegetarian food, though plenty of meat, fish and chicken also is offered. Favorite dinners include pad Thai, moussaka and vegan lasagna. A popular lunch dish is the ethnic calzone (you'll find flavors from Russia, Mexico and Greece have crept inside the Italian crust). Enjoy these dishes with beer or wine.

Since the Left Bank is also a bakery, expect homemade breads, bagels and fresh pastries. In summer, the restaurant is surrounded by gardens overflowing with vegetables, flowers and herbs, much of which eventually finds its way to the table. The Left Bank scales back its hours in winter; decisions about the schedule are made on the spot at times. In the dead of winter, the cafe closes on Tuesday, but it's open for breakfast and lunch Wednesday through Monday and for dinner Wednesday through Saturday. In the height of summer, it is open for three meals daily. Call ahead: A lovely, warm spring might mean extended hours. Children are welcome here; smoking is not. Reservations are appreciated.

Pain de Famille Bakery and Cafe
**$ • Greens Hill Place, Maine Hwy. 176
and Morgan Bay Rd., Blue Hill**
• 374-3839

Pain de Famille opened in South Brooksville a few years ago, but has since relocated to larger Blue Hill, sharing quarters with the Blue Hill Co-op. This informal cafe serves baked goods and light meals like stir-fry, tortellini, roasted vegetables, or focaccia sandwiches. There are also vegan soups and a variety of salads. Made-to-order breakfasts include omelettes and French toast, and pre-made lunches are available for take-out. All meals are surprisingly reasonably priced. Breakfast and lunch are served Monday

Photo: Bangor Daily News

Lunch by the waterside is a refreshing escape on a hot summer day.

through Saturday year round. Come summer, the cafe is open some evenings as well as Sundays; call for hours. Don't forget to take home some fresh-baked focaccia bread.

Surry Inn
$$ • Maine Hwy. 172, Surry • 667-5091, (800) 742-3414

Some meat eaters among us jump at the chance to enjoy the steak au poivre Bordelaise at the Surry Inn, a fine old establishment on the shores of Contention Cove. Come in summer and you'll be treated to a water view, perhaps colored by the sunset if you dine late. Come winter, that view will be shrouded in darkness, but the broad fireplace — large enough to dine inside! — will be blazing with warmth.

The Surry Inn's specialties, prepared with a continental flair, including duck breast stuffed with peppercorns and topped with fresh peach sauce, pork schnitzel and spicy garlic frog legs. Appetizers might include shrimp brochette with

tart apples and curry. Breads are always homemade. This friendly, homey inn is open nightly year round for dinner. There is a full bar. Smoking is not allowed. Reservations are suggested.

Bagaduce Lunch
$ • Maine Hwy. 176, North Brooksville • no phone

This take-out place is renowned for its fried clams and lobster rolls as well as for its view of the Bagaduce's reversing falls. Picnic tables are placed for an optimum view of the falls. If the tide is high, you'll also enjoy the spectacle of canoeists and kayakers whooping it up in the funnel-caused rapids (see our Parks and Recreation chapter). Bagaduce Lunch is open in summer for lunch.

The Landing
$$-$$$ • Steamboat Wharf Rd., off Maine Hwy. 176, South Brooksville • 326-8483

Owners Kurt and Verena Stoll, originally of

Switzerland, bought this portside restaurant in 1996. With the help of a new chef, they have turned dinner at The Landing into a night of delicacies, with unusual, subtle tastes and genuinely friendly, attentive service. The touches are everything here: crispy fried leeks lie across the dried cranberry salsa that's served with plank-roasted Atlantic salmon; Australian range rack of lamb comes with garlic mashed potatoes and tobacco onions; the salad is a mixture of delicate mesclun greens and fresh herbs. The menu usually includes veal, duck and occasionally lobster out of the shell. Save room for an elegant pastry — as delicate as Verena Stoll's charming accent. Come before sunset and watch the sun cast golden-rose hues across Bucks Harbor.

FYI

Unless otherwise noted, the area code for all phone numbers listed in this guide is 207.

The Stolls ask you to savor the tastes and take your time; even so, they are happy to accommodate children. They are also happy to accommodate sailors. If you're coming by boat, two guest moorings are available.

The Landing is open for dinner Tuesday through Sunday from Memorial Day through early September, possibly longer, so call ahead. There's a full bar at the restaurant. Smoking is not allowed. Reservations are recommended.

The Lookout
$$-$$$ • Flye Pt., Brooklin • 359-2188

"Upscale gourmet" characterizes The Lookout, which is named for its view: Seven picture windows look out to Blue Hill Bay from an enclosed porch on this 200-year-old house. Though the view is not to the west, time your dinner with the sunset and you'll be entranced by the shades of rose and gold cast over the bay. This family-owned establishment has been in business for 104 years as an inn and 23 years as a restaurant.

The food served here frequently is local and always is prepared with great care. Favorite meals include grilled Atlantic salmon with a curried apricot glaze and sauteed venison (imported from New Zealand) with gooseberry and port wine sauce. The meals are complemented by an extensive wine list and a full bar.

The Lookout is open for dinner seven days a week from Memorial Day to Columbus Day. Reservations are requested. There is no smoking.

Eaton's Lobster Pool Restaurant
$$, no credit cards • Blastows Cove Rd., Little Deer Isle • 348-2383

Take your lobsters down to the water for an outdoor picnic, or settle on the porch outside or beside large glass windows inside for service. Come at the right time and you'll see the sun set over the Camden Hills. When it gets chilly, a hanging fireplace warms guests at this friendly, casual restaurant. The specialty here is seafood, especially lobsters and fish, served by Eugene B. and Carolyn Eaton, who have been at the restaurant on summer nights for the past 38 years. Lobster dinner includes a tossed salad, hot roll, hot drawn butter and chips. Add steamers for a shore dinner. Don't like lobster? Try a tenderloin steak. Also on the menu are mussels (in-season), lobster salad and sandwiches such as hot dogs, hamburgers and grilled cheese. Finish off with homemade blueberry and apple pie.

There is no bar, but guests are welcome to bring their own beer, wine or spirits. There is no smoking in the restaurant, but guests may smoke on the wide strolling deck outside. This is a large place, serving 125 people inside, but it does fill up.

Eaton's is open for dinner weekends from Mother's Day weekend until Father's Day and then nightly through Labor Day. After that, it's open weekends until Columbus Day.

Goose Cove Lodge
$$$ • Goose Cove Rd., Deer Isle • 348-2508

It's hard to say which is more spectacular here, food or view. While you gaze through picture windows overlooking Penobscot Bay, the kitchen staff prepares legendary, elaborate meals.

You might begin with a bacon, onion and (local) goat cheese tartellette with mixed greens and raspberry vinaigrette. Don't want the bacon? Try the Portobello mushrooms and

roasted shallot tartellette. For an entree, you might find Provençal Duckling Duet, a leg of duck confit paired with a breast of duck, grilled medium rare, painted with an orange chive glaze and served with Israeli couscous and roasted root vegetables. About five menu items are prepared nightly, including fresh local seafood and a vegetarian dish. The produce frequently is locally grown and organic. Free-range chicken is purchased locally from a farmer who also raises shiitake mushrooms for the lodge. Goose Cove prides itself on its domestic and international wine list, with about five whites and five reds sold by the glass each night.

Breakfast is equally grand: juice; fresh fruit; homemade granola; yogurt and toppings; fresh-baked breakfast breads, muffins or scones; eggs prepared to order; and a variety of hot entries such as Black Forest ham and cheddar cheese frittata or French toast stuffed with Marscapone cheese and fresh strawberries, served with strawberry-maple syrup. And that's the regular weekday breakfast, not the even more extravagant weekend brunch.

As for lunch, you can expect lobster corn chowder; a variety of salads, including roasted salmon served over greens with smoked tomato vinaigrette; or a variety of sandwiches, from chicken salad to Maine crab cake. A children's menu is available. On most summer evenings, children can opt for the separate children's program, with a simpler meal and some activity following (expect an additional fee unless you're staying at the lodge). On Friday nights, however, children eat with their families for a soup to nuts (or rather, chowder to sundae) lobster dinner.

Goose Cove Lodge, which has been open since 1948 and under current ownership for the last seven years, is an inn (see our Accommodations chapter), but it welcomes the general public daily for breakfast, lunch, tea and dinner from mid-May until mid-October (though lunch and tea are served during July and August only). Reservations are necessary for dinner and Sunday brunch. There is no smoking.

Maggie's Clamdigger Restaurant

$-$$ • Maine Hwy. 15, Deer Isle
• 348-6423

Looking for steak, lobster and a large family restaurant? The Clamdigger is the place where Deer Isle folk gather, and all are accommodated in various nooks and crannies or in the large dining room of this rustic restaurant. Service is friendly: The wait staff has seen it all. There is a smoking section and a full-service bar.

Lunch and dinner are served April through December, with service on weekends in spring and fall and daily in summer, with the possible exception of Monday (call to be sure). This is a popular place, so reservations are advised.

Pilgrim's Inn

$$$ • The Sunset Rd., Deer Isle Village
• 348-6615

For two centuries, the Pilgrim's Inn has been a stately presence in Deer Isle Village. Standing beside a mill pond and across from Deer Isle's Northwest Harbor, it has long been recognized as one of the most handsome buildings on the island. But the Pilgrim's Inn has another identity. It's an excellent restaurant. The innkeepers grow their own produce and apply a straightforward regional philosophy to their cooking: The food is based on the season and the island's natural bounty. One seating is offered nightly in the old converted barn beside the inn (see our Accommodations chapter). The barn provides an elegant but homey backdrop to the meal, with antiques, an accent of burgundy and gray tablecloths and a mixture of local and Bennington pottery on the tables.

From appetizer to dessert, dinner courses are arranged to flow together. An extensive cocktail hour begins at 6 PM and includes about five hors d'oeuvres. Once settled at your table, depending on the night and the season, you might dine on North Atlantic salmon lightly sauteed or roasted with garden vegetables and fresh herbs, or an herb-roasted tenderloin of beef served with sauteed Maine crab cakes and festive condiments. Substitutions are available for those who don't prefer the nightly offering. There's also a full bar with a choice wine list selected by the innkeeper.

This is not a family restaurant, but if you are traveling with children, alert the owners when you make your reservation. A simpler children's meal can be provided. There is no smoking at the inn. Meals are served nightly from mid-May to mid-October. Reservations are necessary.

The Bay View Restaurant

$-$$ • Seabreeze Ave., Stonington
• 367-2274

Have your lunch or dinner overlooking Stonington Harbor at the casual Bay View Restaurant, the oldest eatery on the island. The Bay View serves regional specialties like fish chowder, lobster stew, sauteed lobster on toast points, codfish cakes, fried fish, seafood pie and old standards such as vegetarian lasagna and meat loaf. The restaurant is open daily except in winter, when it's closed two days a week; call ahead to find out which days. Desserts such as meringue shells with homemade hot fudge or hot butterscotch sauce and the old-style vinegar pie (made with vinegar, sour cream and raisins and topped with plenty of whipped cream) are also featured.

Stonington is a dry town, so you won't find liquor in any restaurant, but feel free to bring your own. There's no smoking here. Reservations can only be held for a brief time in summer.

The Lobster Deck & Seafood Market

$ • Seabreeze Ave., Stonington
• 367-6526

Settle here for an early breakfast or a relatively late dinner and enjoy this casual, family-oriented restaurant. Sit by a window to enjoy the great view of the islands of Merchant Row off Stonington, along with your good food. The restaurant is practically at the end of the road. Just keep driving, hugging the winding waterfront until you think you've gone too far — you'll find it there.

You can enjoy breakfast all day, or dine on a full lobster dinner, all while watching the lobster boats below unloading the day's catch. Also on the menu are mussels; steamers; lobster salad; rolls packed with lobster, scallops, crabmeat, clams, shrimp or tuna; crab stew; and creamy, rich lobster stew — Maine's other specialty.

The Lobster Deck is open daily in summer and possibly year round, though they won't decide that until September 1998. Picnic tables outside augment the tables inside. There is a smoking section, but as in other Stonington restaurants, no liquor is served.

Bangkok Restaurant
$-$$ • Maine Hwy. 3, Ellsworth • 667-1324

We know folks from Bar Harbor and Down East who make their way to Ellsworth for Thai food from the Bangkok Restaurant. Favorite appetizers include chicken or beef satay and fresh spring rolls. Popular entrees include spicy fried rice and hot Thai noodles, seasoned as spicy or mild as you like and served with chicken, beef, pork or vegetables. This 8-year-old restaurant has a full bar and is open for lunch and dinner daily except Sunday, when it is open for dinner only. Smoking is not permitted.

Frankie's Ellsworth
$ • 40 High St., Ellsworth • 667-7701

Snuggled next to Cadillac Mountain Sports, Frankie's has been offering specialties for light breakfasts, lunch or early dinners for 10 years. It expanded in summer 1997, leaving a little gift shop of specialty items and take-out foods in the old section. Expect an array of soups, salads and sand-wiches plus several of the following specialties: Greek spinach pie, lasagna, bean and rice burritos, spinach and tomato quiche, falafel, tofu or nut burgers. Though Frankie's menu leans toward vegetarian food, including some vegan meals, meat sandwiches are also available. No liquor is served, and no smoking is allowed in this 45-seat restaurant. Take-out orders are gladly filled, so think about stopping here for picnic fare.

Frankie's is open Monday through Saturday year round.

Helen's
$-$$ • U.S. Hwy. 1, Ellsworth • 667-2433

In Machias, farther Down East, Helen's has been an institution for years. Three years ago, it also became an institution in Ellsworth. While Helen's is known statewide for its scroll-length list of pies, it is locally beloved for the standard home cooking that few of us find at home any longer. We're talking liver and onions, fish (haddock) and chips, or the weekly New England boiled dinner special — corned beef, cabbage, turnips and potatoes. As for the pies, take a deep breath and choose from strawberry-rhubarb, raspberry, blueberry, apple, lemon meringue or chocolate pudding, to name but a few.

Lunch and dinner are served daily year round, and a children's menu is available. You'll find beer and wine at Helen's, which serves as many as 160 people at a time. There is a smoking section.

The Mex
$$ • 185 Main St., Ellsworth • 667-4494

Ellsworth's Mexican restaurant has become a meeting place for folks from Ellsworth and surrounding Mount Desert Island, Blue Hill and Down East since it opened in 1979. The service is friendly, the atmosphere bright and entertaining, with Mexican artifacts, Maine art and mosaics made by local artists and friends. The place seats 135 people. You'll find Mexican food with a local flair — The Mex has its own style. Personally, we think the mole sauce here is the best around, and we seldom venture further than this complicated spicy bean and chocolate mix, except to add a bowl of black bean soup. Friends, however, lean toward the fajitas with plump chunks of beef, fish or chicken grilled with The Mex's own marinade. Others prefer the Lazy Enchiladas smothered with tomato-based sauce, or the Red, White and Green, a beautifully prepared dish — a burrito and salad with three different (red, white and green) dressings.

The Mex serves lunch and dinner daily year round and offers relatively late hours in summer. On summer weekends, it's not a bad idea to call for reservations. This is a locals place, and when there is something happening at The Grand (see our Arts chapter), the arts center down the road, The Mex fills up.

Oak Point Lobster Pound Restaurant
$-$$ • Maine Hwy. 230, Trenton • 667-6998

Venture off the Bar Harbor Road (Maine Highway 3) just before the bridge to Bar Harbor to find this hidden but quite popular place. Lobster pounds are lobster-based restaurants, where the bluish-shelled crustaceans come from tank to table, save a brief stop at the steamer. If you want fresh lobster and an outstanding view, you'll find both here. Time your dinner right and you'll be able to watch the setting sun's colors play over the mountains and waters of Mount Desert Island. Oak Point stretches far into Western Bay, which separates the western portion of Mount Desert Island from the mainland. You'll be surrounded by windows ... and by more than 50 other diners — mostly families, many of them local. Locals keep quiet about this place so they can enjoy it for their own special outings. Still, it does get crowded in summer.

Try an Oak Point Shore Dinner with a cup of clam or fish chowder, fresh steamers and mussels and a 1.25-pound boiled lobster served with drawn butter, baked, new or french-fried potatoes, coleslaw or salad and hot biscuits. Or, ask for a simple lobster or the surf and turf, which includes a lobster tail and beef tenderloin tips. Other dishes include lobster salad and a lobster roll. Do your kids tremble at the sight of a lobster? Order them a frankfurter or hamburger. For dessert, try apple pie, blueberry pie, cheesecake or a hot fudge sundae.

Beer and wine are available. There is no smoking. There are also no reservations, but call as you leave for the restaurant — your name will be entered on the waiting list. Oak Point is open daily for dinner from mid-June through mid-October. It's also open for lunch Sundays.

Trenton Bridge Lobster Pound
$ • U.S. Hwy. 1, Trenton • 667-2977

The view across Mount Desert Narrows to Mount Desert Island from Trenton is one of the most spectacular in Maine. We're sure that a long summer twilight spent cracking lobsters beside the Narrows will only whet your appetite for more. And the prices here are so reasonable, you'll be able to afford more.

Trenton Bridge Lobster Pound serves lobster in the rough. You chose your lobster from off the ice, watch the staff weigh it, then settle down and wait for your number to be called. Trenton Bridge is among the last pounds in the state that keep lobsters on ice. That way, says Josette Pettegrow, you don't pay for water weight. Josette represents the third generation of her family to run the pound. Her son, currently in high school, makes it four generations.

To accompany your lobster, try steamed clams, clam chowder, lobster stew, coleslaw and potato salad, or dine lighter on lobster- or crabmeat-salad sandwiches. All are made on the premises. There's no liquor served, but feel free to bring your own. You may eat inside in the dining room or outside near the water at the picnic area. Smoking is permitted outside only. While the pound is open year round to purchase lobsters, it is open for lunch and dinner daily from Memorial Day weekend through Columbus Day.

The Crocker House Country Inn
$$ • Hancock Point Rd., Hancock
• 422-6806

The country flavor is strong at The Crocker House Country Inn, which focuses on fresh organic produce and local seafood served in an intimate setting — 60 seats between two dining rooms. The inn prepares good American cuisine, including some appealing appetizers. You might find oysters (farm-raised in southern Maine), pâté, wild mushroom soup, or smoked tomato cream soup. Entrees include poached salmon Florentine, veal Oscar with crabmeat and asparagus settled in Béarnaise sauce and rack of fresh lamb marinated with garlic and mustard, baked and topped with an herbed crumb dressing.

There is a small smoking section, and liquor is served. Come Friday and Saturday nights in summer for live music. You'll find dinner served here nightly from late April through October and weekends from mid-November through December. Reservations are suggested.

Armando's Restaurant
$$ • U.S. Hwy. 1, Hancock • 422-3151

The Boccias had been coming to Hancock from Long Island for many summers and had noticed the absence of native Italian food in the region. Fifteen years ago, they decided to change that, moving north and opening this family-style Italian restaurant.

Armando Boccia imports much of his food from his homeland of Naples, Italy. Expect friendly service in this rustic, fire-warmed room with bright red tablecloths and plenty of plants. One signature dish is filet mignon with brandy Dijon sauce served with fettuccine rosa (an Alfredo sauce lightened by a blend of marinara sauce). A full bar and nice wine list are available.

Armando's is open for dinner Friday and Saturday from around mid-September until mid-May, Thursday through Saturday until July

4, then Tuesday through Saturday through mid-September. Expect casual dining. A children's menu is available, and there is a smoking section. Reservations are advised on summer weekends.

Le Domaine Restaurant and Inn
$$ • U.S. Hwy. 1, Hancock • 422-3395, 422-3916, (800) 554-8498

The story of how Marianne Rose Dumas fled France during the Nazi occupation after she and her family were found hiding Jews in the basement of their Le Baux inn, is legendary in Maine. So is the restaurant Dumas opened here in 1946.

Dumas brought with her the exquisite recipes of Le Baux. Today, daughter Nicole Purslow, who learned to cook in the family kitchen and also attended Cordon Bleu in France, owns the inn (see our Accommodations chapter) and restaurant. In the style of a French country inn, guests dine on linen-covered tables amid large vessels of flowers picked from the surrounding gardens. The menu changes daily according to what is fresh. In summer, try tomato soup with basil followed by gray sole stuffed with vegetables and fennel seeds, lapin aux pruneaux (rabbit with prunes) or coquille St. Jacques. Top off your meal with wild blueberries and raspberries in thick cream or a raspberry mousse. Fish and rabbit are purchased locally, as are the vegetables (organic, if available). Herbs come from Le Domaine's gardens.

The charming, red-framed restaurant is open daily for dinner from late May until the end of October. There is no smoking in the dining room, but smoking is allowed in the full-service bar. Well-behaved children are welcome, and reservations are recommended.

Tidal Falls Lobster Pound
$, no credit cards • East Side Rd., off U.S. Hwy. 1, Hancock • 422-6818

In Europe, it's not unusual to find elegant dining in the most unusual spots, even on picnic tables beside a stream. That's what you'll find at Tidal Falls Lobster Pound, thanks to Christiane Hodgkins, whose French accent gives it all away. At the right tide, you can watch the rapids come up on this river. At any time, this is a lovely spot to enjoy mussels with garlic butter, crab rolls, crabmeat scampi, crabmeat Provençal with tomato sauce and saffron, crabmeat melts on English muffins — or simple steamed lobster. Add potato salad, coleslaw, green salad and French or garlic bread, and finish it all off with a blueberry tart. Use the basket at the end of the table to dispose of those pesky lobster shells. (Of course, you can also turn the shells into a lobster sculpture — or puppets, as we've seen some young friends do.) You bring the wine; Christiane will provide the corkscrew and glasses. And should the mosquitoes get too strong, there's no shame in retiring to the screened-in pavilion on the grounds. Tidal Falls is open evenings from June to Labor Day.

Chase's Restaurant
$-$$ • Main St., Winter Harbor • 963-7171

During a recent winter visit to Schoodic Point, we were charmed by a lunch at Chase's Restaurant, a local diner with some delicious home cooking. You'll find thick fish stew and haddock fish and chips. Crispy onion rings were only 25¢ extra. Over the plastic booths, the view through the large picture window reveals the long, splendid harbor. While one of our sons played with toys from the counterside bucket, we finished off our meal with bread pudding and pondered the bluntly worded plaque: "Be good or be gone."

Chase's is open for breakfast, lunch and dinner every day except Christmas. There is a smoking section.

Mount Desert Island

Acadia Restaurant
$, no credit cards • 62 Main St., Bar Harbor • 288-4881

"The best chowder on the island," say the ads. Locals echo the sentiment.

The Acadia Restaurant, a longtime hangout on Main Street, has a personality all its own. This venerable establishment even had a poem written about it that was set to music and performed in Carnegie Hall. The atmosphere here is all about the patrons, the wait staff, the long booths, the wall murals and the teenagers who love the hours — 6 AM to 3 AM

in summer, though only until 8 PM in the dead of winter. You can get a lobster dinner here for what you might pay for a drink elsewhere. You can also get a box lunch to go. Don't miss the ice cream pies. There is a smoking section.

Burning Tree
$$ • Maine Hwy. 3, Otter Creek • 288-9331

At the Burning Tree Restaurant in Otter Creek, 5 miles outside Bar Harbor, co-owners Alison Martin and Elmer Beal serve fish that's about as fresh as you can find it: They're on the docks when the fishing boats come in, choosing fish before it gets sent to auction in Portland. They return to The Burning Tree to fillet and prepare sole, flounder, ocean perch and monkfish in unusual, interesting ways.

A favorite is monkfish, braised and served with a white wine-based mustard sauce of fresh shiitake mushrooms and Maine shrimp. A perennial favorite is the Cajun lobster and crab au gratin, served in a delicate cheese sauce flavored with peppery Cajun spices, shallots, garlic, white wine and sherry. Again, the lobster and crabmeat are as fresh as you'll find. So are the chicken and vegetable entrees.

Beal, a native of the island, is a folk singer and teacher at nearby College of the Atlantic. The source for the restaurant's name came from a song Beal wrote years ago about the flaming maple trees of autumn. Both Beal and Martin like to keep their restaurant festive but casual and relatively intimate. Some 60 diners can be seated at tables draped with dusky rose cloths. An enclosed deck overlooking flower and herb gardens is heated by a large cookstove, and two other dining rooms are lightened by local landscapes.

Beal also makes the pastries for Burning Tree. Try a chocolate applesauce cake layered with hazelnut butter cream and iced with a dark Kahlua frosting, or go for a light lemon mousse served with reduced red wine-and-prune sauce.

The Burning Tree is open nightly except Tuesdays from early June until mid-October. Though there is no children's menu, children are welcome; smoking is not. There is a full bar with an extensive, handpicked wine list that's priced for value. Reservations are recommended.

Burwaldo's

$, Texaco cards only • 317 Main St., Bar Harbor • 288-3241

There are times when you don't want to linger — don't want to spend even an hour cooped inside eating. You just want to chow down and get out into the sunshine, or perhaps take your food with you. Burwaldo's offers basic breakfasts and lunches that you can enjoy at an old-style counter, or spread out with upstairs. Come in the morning for pancakes, waffles, omelettes, muffins or cinnamon buns; come at lunch for burgers, charbroiled chicken, steak and cheese on the grill, all kinds of sandwiches and daily specials including meat loaf and scallop chowder.

Dying for a smoke? Wander upstairs for the walk-in cigar humidor. Breakfast and lunch are served daily.

Cafe Bluefish

$$ • 122 Cottage St., Bar Harbor • 288-3696

Local chef Bobbie Lynn Hutchins keeps the cozy, den-like Cafe Bluefish open nightly year round, winning a strong place in the hearts of folks who live on the island. We well remember the smacking lips when guests returned home from an excursion to Acadia and Cafe Bluefish one November. Cafe Bluefish lives up to its name, featuring plenty of seafood prepared continental style. The Insiders'

secret, however, is that the Bluefish is also a great place for vegetarians. Favorite meals include lobster strudel, poached salmon served with a sherry-mustard sauce, curry-crusted halibut with blueberry chutney, calamari a la Greque, oven-roasted apricot chicken and vegetarian Stroganoff made with mushrooms. Beer and wine are served. You might finish off your meal with Double Cinnamon Strudel or Black & White Strudel (made with dark and white chocolate chunks).

Reservations are recommended during high-traffic times: Cafe Bluefish seats only 40. There is no smoking. Though this 8-year-old restaurant tends toward the sophisticated, ask about children's portions.

Cafe This Way

$$ • 14 Mount Desert St., Bar Harbor • 288-4483

New in 1997, Cafe This Way has already made a great splash on the Bar Harbor scene. Come here for gourmet food in a casual atmosphere — you might even find yourself lounging on a couch while you dine on grilled tuna, sirloin with a reduced black cherry sauce or Cajun grilled seafood. Cafe This Way serves breakfast and dinner daily in summer (except Sunday when there may be no dinner) and breakfast and lunch during the year. Breakfasts are eclectic, ranging from vegetarian tofu scramble to homemade corned beef hash. In summer you can dine outside on a deck; in winter, you might settle beside a fireplace. Friday nights in winter, you can settle in for the cafe's one-seating dinner for which the chef sends out from six to eight courses of whatever she pleases — true culinary indulgence.

There are high chairs and children's games here, but no children's menu. Dinner typically has a quiet atmosphere. Smoking is permitted outside at a few tables on the deck only. While there's a full bar, the wine list is so extensive that the cafe also can be considered a wine bar. Reservations are advised as this popular restaurant seats only 49. As of press time, lunch in summer (generally June through September) was still under consideration; call ahead.

Freddie's Route 66 Restaurant
$$ • 21 Cottage St., Bar Harbor
• 288-3708

Zany nostalgia is the feast for the eye at Freddie's emporium, filled with cars, trains, road signs, Elvis extravaganza and all the toys you remember having or coveting. Most come from the 1950s, but there's also a 1930s scene with an old gas pump and soapbox derby racer. The food is basic, international-style fare. You'll find lobster, seafood, steak sandwiches and onion rings, Oriental stir-fry, salads, quesadillas, spaghetti and meatballs and chicken pot pie. You'll also find milk shakes and the '57 Chevy special — a hot fudge sundae served over a brownie inside a pink 1957 Chevy convertible, which you get to keep.

Yes, atmosphere rules at Freddie's Route 66, even in the restrooms. The restaurant is open for dinner from mid-May until mid-October. A children's menu is available. Smoking is allowed at the bar. Reservations are suggested in midsummer.

George's
$$-$$$ • 7 Stephens Ln., Bar Harbor
• 288-4505

When a dear friend decided to go ahead and celebrate a major birthday, she gathered a dozen of her close friends for a really good dinner. Her choice? George's, a restaurant of ethereal simplicity in one of the alleys behind Main Street.

The menu changes daily, but a dinner might begin with a smoked salmon quesadilla,

lamb in phyllo shell with tsatsiki, or broiled Kasseri cheese with fresh garlic. This might be followed by tangerine scallops, char-grilled salmon, or Crabcake Island in Sweet Corn Sea with poblano-blueberry relish. Beef lovers might prefer beef tenderloin with Portobello, bleu cheese and Madeira-based Bordelaise. George's also offers more moderately priced selections known as "grazers:" lighter portions of such delicacies as jump-seared tuna loin, or grilled mustard shrimp. George's also has an acclaimed wine list.

There is a full bar, but no smoking is allowed. As for dress, we donned our finest for our birthday girl, but only because it was fun. George's serves dinner nightly from mid-June through October. Reservations are highly suggested.

Michelle's Fine Dining
$$-$$$ • 194 Main St., Bar Harbor
• 288-0038, (888) 670-1997

American-French gourmet with a flair for New England is how some describe the food at Michelle's in the new Ivy Manor Inn. The restaurant serves 50 in three dining rooms. In winter, cozy up by the fire; in summer, enjoy the outside deck overlooking the inn's gardens. There are many fine specialties at this new restaurant. We're intrigued by the herbed basted lobster claws appetizer, in which the lobster is lightly seared and crusted with herbs and wine, and the Baked Oyster Ivy Manor, baked with garlic and wine in a delicate Acadian seafood sauce. For entrees, consider pan-seared maple-sugared salmon, sauteed and served with glazed onions, forest mushrooms and a splash of cream; entrecote de veau (veal) grilled with calvados butter; or roasted duckling Provençal, marinated and seared in clover honey and herbs. But save room for the Chocolate Bag, a chocolate mold of a bag filled with white chocolate mousse and fruit. The restaurant offers a separate lounge, a large wine selection and dinner nightly from May through October, possibly longer, so call and ask. Reservations are advised, smoking is not.

Jordan Pond House
$$ • Park Loop Rd., in Acadia National Park • 276-3316

In the late 1800s, when Mount Desert Island was a mecca for the rich and powerful, tea houses were established throughout the woods of what became Acadia National Park. Today, Jordan Pond House (see also our Acadia National Park chapter) continues that tradition with afternoon tea and popovers served on a lawn that stretches to the glistening Jordan Pond. The location is sublime. Beyond the pond stand the pair of mountains known as The Bubbles. Closer by, lovely flower borders line the lawn.

You can also eat lunch and dinner at the Jordan Pond House. Enjoy lobster stew, seafood chowder, smoked or fresh seafood samplers and a changing entree that could be filet mignon, steamed lobster or crabmeat and havarti quiche. The same menu is served at lunch and dinner; choose a lighter or fuller portion according to your appetite.

Jordan Pond House is open daily mid-May through October for lunch, tea and dinner. (Tea time is any time between 11:30 AM and 6 PM.) At lunch, choose between lawn and indoor service; dinner is served on the screen porch or inside. Reservations are recommended for dinner but are not taken for lunch. There is a generous call-ahead policy, however. As you get underway, call the restaurant and your name will be placed on the waiting list.

The Lompoc Cafe and Brew Pub
$-$$ • 36 Rodick St., Bar Harbor • 288-9392

For years, folks in Bar Harbor have been yearning for a place like the Lompoc, a casual hangout where good food accompanies pleasant surroundings. The Lompoc is varied enough that locals return frequently; visitors do too. Meals are served inside or outside alongside the garden. Heat lamps warm the tables, extending the outdoor season. A popular boccie court occupies part of the garden.

As for the food, the Lompoc describes its fare as Mediterranean. Seasonal could be another description, for the menu changes according to the weather. In summer, you'll find a pork satay, grilled eggplant and Summer Za (as in piz-za).

Among the standards are the Persian Plate (a Middle Eastern assortment), a variety of unusual pizzas and entrees such as Indonesian peanut chicken, Cuban black bean vegetables and Sicilian pasta with fresh fennel, garlic, tomatoes and Sicilian olives. Expect unusual combinations and exotic tastes.

The Lompoc is open for lunch, dinner and late-night entertainment (see our Nightlife chapter) from May through November. It is a brewpub, so expect beers from The Atlantic Brewing Co. and other regional microbreweries on tap. An extensive wine list is available; there's also a full bar.

Maggie's Classic Scales Restaurant
$$ • 6 Summer St., Bar Harbor • 288-9007

You can be sure the fish served here will be the freshest of the lot, for Maggie once owned a fish market. Now she presides over a lovely, pink-wallpapered dining room (seating 45 only) that features refreshing quiet, fresh fish and local organic vegetables. Start with baked garlic with Fontina cheese, black bean hummus with vegetables or raw oysters. Follow that with lobster crêpes; haddock fillet with ginger sauce; scallops sauteed with bacon, fresh corn and peppers; grilled salmon with lemon herb butter; vegetarian strudel; or charbroiled Black Angus beef served with Cabernet garlic sauce. Though this is a relatively sophisticated menu, there is always a pasta dish for children. There's a full bar.

Maggie, who's been at this for 11 years, bakes her own bread and makes her own ice cream. There is no smoking. Reservations are suggested. Maggie's is open most nights from the end of May until Columbus Day weekend.

Miguel's Mexican Restaurant
$-$$ • 51 Rodick St., Bar Harbor • 288-5117

Since opening 15 years ago, Miguel's has been a popular stopping spot for locals and visitors alike. They come for northern Mexican and Tex-Mex cuisine such as the escondida, a breaded, golden-fried burrito served with guacamole and your choice of filling, and the fajitas, which include vegetarian tofitas. Back by popular demand are the blue-corn crab cakes (seasoned local crabmeat covered with blue-corn flour and sauteed to crisp the outside). Owner/chef Chris Pasha said he once tried to take the time-consuming dish off the menu but couldn't face the customer misery.

Miguel's is a bright, casual restaurant with wainscotting meeting white stucco adorned with Mexican tapestries and art. It is open mid-March through early November — Wednesday through Sunday in March, extending to Tuesday through Sunday from April until the end of May. From May through Labor Day, it's open nightly. Hours taper off again in fall. Smoking is permitted in the bar, where you can order a full meal. In midsummer you can also dine outside on the patio. Reservations are accepted for large parties only.

Parkside Restaurant
$-$$ • 185 Main St., Bar Harbor
• 288-3700

The view of flowers blooming along the border of the Parkside Restaurant is frequently enough to entice people inside this atmospheric Bar Harbor eatery. Once there, guests find sophisticated Victorian charm, with white latticework on the walls, burgundy florals on the tables, fireplaces in most rooms and fresh flowers all around. The ambiance in this 150-seat restaurant is that special Maine combination of relaxation and elegance. Many guests enjoy sitting on the porch, while others prefer to settle beside the parkside window with its view to summer antics on the green. The charm is complemented by a selection of fresh seafood dishes such as bouillabaisse, shrimp scampi or steak au poivre.

Parkside is open daily from Mother's Day weekend through mid-October. It serves lunch, light fare and dinner and offers a full bar; the management is considering offering breakfast in July and August. A children's menu is available. There is a smoking room. A limited number of reservations are taken.

The Porcupine Grill
$$ • 123 Cottage St., Bar Harbor
• 288-3884

When you settle down for an evening at the candle-lit, polished wood tables of The Porcupine Grill, expect the romantic setting to be enhanced by unusual, exciting cuisine — but leave the notion of grilled porcupines at home. The Porcupine Grill is named for the Porcupine Islands in Frenchman Bay and for the grill on which the fresh food is prepared. Owner

Tom Marinke serves seasonal items, buying local vegetables, fish and even goat cheese when he can. The menu changes frequently — at times, daily — so we can't recommend specific dishes, but there's always fresh fish on the grill as well as Black Angus beef and organic free-range poultry. Steamed lobster is always available too, and you usually can find another lobster dish.

As for specific preparations, you might find oven-roasted tomato and fennel soup, or barbecued quail with Moroccan rub on the appetizer list, and Tuscan-style mixed grill or grilled salmon fillet with mango and papaya salsa as entrees. Breads and desserts are made on the premises, and the wine list includes more than 200 bottles.

The Porcupine's wine bar is a more casual setting, created for long conversations over a glass or two or three of wine (choose from more than a dozen selections), vintage port or malt brew. The bar, Thrumcap, also offers lighter fare. It opens earlier in the day and stays open later in the night than the dining room.

Reservations are recommended. There is no smoking in the bar or restaurant. The Porcupine Grill is open for dinner nightly from July through October and Friday through Sunday most of the rest of the year.

Reading Room Restaurant
$$-$$$ • Bar Harbor Inn, Newport Dr.,
Bar Harbor • 288-3351, (800) 248-3351

When the Bar Harbor Inn was the men-only Oasis Club, the Reading Room was where the guys gathered to have a smoke while poring over the daily newspaper. Times have changed, but the atmosphere has not. The circular Reading Room, its bay windows offering vistas over Frenchman Bay and the Porcupine Islands, is still an elegant place to gather; only now, the sole restrictions are dress: Men must wear collared shirts, and neither jeans, shorts nor sneakers are allowed at dinner.

Favorite meals at the Reading Room include lobster pie, char-grilled seafood (see if the curried tomato vinaigrette is available) and filet mignon (char-grilled and served with a

---

FYI

Unless otherwise noted, the area code for all phone numbers listed in this guide is 207.

Lobster traps are stacked on a pier in a fishing village in Mid-Coast Maine.

Bordelaise sauce). Breads, rolls and desserts are baked on the premises. Come also for the Sunday champagne brunch buffet, with breakfast and luncheon offerings served along with mimosas (champagne and orange juice). The first brunch of the year is Easter Sunday, and the next is Mother's Day. Brunches continue Sundays through mid-November.

The Reading Room is open late March until early November, with breakfast and dinner served daily. There is a very small smoking area and a full bar. Reservations are suggested.

Terrace Grille
$$ • Bar Harbor Inn, Newport Dr., Bar Harbor • 288-3351, (800) 248-3351

Settle at the bright white lawn tables beneath gay yellow and white umbrellas for lunch or dinner at the Terrace Grille, on the premises of the Bar Harbor Inn. A favorite meal is the Downeast Lobster Bake, which consists of clam chowder, steamed clams and mussels, boiled lobster, red potatoes, corn on the cob and blueberry pie. Lighter meals include a variety of grilled seafood entrees and sandwiches.

The terrace is open daily for lunch and dinner, from about mid-May until late October. Lunches, only, are served inside in the Reading Room (see previous entry) during inclement weather. Smoking is allowed, as is casual dress. There is a full bar.

Two Cats
$ • 318 Main St., Bar Harbor • 288-2808

If you love lingering over long breakfasts or want to retire to a lunchtime hideaway, head to the sign of the dancing cats. Two Cats has the look and feel of a sidestreet cafe, with yellow walls trimmed in sage green and a plethora of amusing cats, and yet this place is right on Main Street.

At breakfast you might enjoy the Summer Scramble — scrambled eggs with tomatoes,

feta, scallions and herbs, served with herbed potatoes and a biscuit spread with strawberry butter. Or try pancakes or the smoked trout omelette served with creamy horseradish and red onion dill. Or simply savor the lemon-glazed blueberry muffins with a long cup of java.

Lunchtime brings homemade soup and thick sandwiches served on homemade oatmeal-molasses bread. We enjoyed The Max, which is like a Thanksgiving dinner rolled up in a sandwich — roasted turkey breast, avocado, cheddar cheese and cranberry chutney.

Smoking is not permitted. Two Cats is open daily for breakfast and lunch from Memorial Day weekend until Columbus Day.

Asticou Inn
$$-$$$ • Maine Hwy. 3, Northeast Harbor • 276-3344

For generations, the Asticou Inn has been the place to come for special Sunday dinners and celebrations. Enjoy the large (seating for 150), elegant dining room, with its Oriental carpets and sun-yellow mural-like wallpaper, overlooking Northeast Harbor. Or dine outside, practically on the edge of the harbor. While you eat, watch the fog lift from the harbor, revealing gray rocks and numerous moored sailboats. Outstanding menu items include duck in port wine, citrus chicken with orange glaze, Tournedos Excaliber and, of course, lobster.

Children are welcome and may order from the children's menu. A full bar is available. No smoking is permitted in the dining room. Come for breakfast, a simple sandwich lunch on the terrace, dinner, or the famous Sunday jazz brunch. Try the Thursday all-you-can-eat grand buffet; twice each summer, it becomes a dinner dance with live music.

Asticou Inn is a summer resort. If you're not visiting during July and August, it's likely you'll be dining across the street at Cranberry Lodge. You'll find a terrace there, too, and the same menu, but cozier surroundings. Whenever you come, reservations are a very good idea.

Main Sail Restaurant
$-$$ • Huntington Rd., Northeast Harbor • 276-5857

Take a walk around the marina at Northeast Harbor — you won't be able to miss the Main Sail Restaurant, the large, glass-enclosed building hovering over the harbor. One look at the outside will tell you all you need to know about the views from the inside: They're gorgeous. The restaurant offers seating for 250 folks on three levels, all facing the marina. There's also seating outside on a deck. Dine on seafood, poultry, Italian specialties and stir-fry in the evening, or salads and sandwiches for lunch; you also can stop by for breakfast. Come here for three "squares" daily from May through October. There's a smoking section and a full bar. Reservations are recommended in summer.

Redfield's
$$ • Main St., Northeast Harbor • 276-5283

Gourmet magazine described Redfield's food as "sophisticated and delicious with an international flair." *Bon Appetit* also has lauded this small, elegant Main Street restaurant that has developed a very select reputation in the eight years it has been open. Owners/chefs Maureen and Scott Redfield like to think of their restaurant as a French bistro, both casual and elegant. White cloths and wildflowers adorn the tables, and crisp white cafe curtains grace the windows. Even the hardwood floors are whitewashed. Jazz plays in the background, and miniature white lights dangle over the tables. The rear of the restaurant opens into Redfield's Gallery (see our Shopping chapter), owned by Scott's mother.

The clean, spare atmosphere allows guests to enjoy each other's company as well as such adventurous starters as smoked mussels and sweet potato wontons with a ginger tamari sauce, or chilled roast garlic-and-potato bisque. Come late afternoon and settle at the antique marble bar serving wine, tapas and cappuccino. Enjoy the appetizers, or keep going with an entree such as sesame-dipped rare tuna with wasabi and a ginger tamari sauce, or roast quail with wild mushroom stuffing and grain-mustard velout.

Redfield's has its own smoker and lightly flavors its seafood, poultry and other meats. Smoked lobster is frequently available. Maureen and Scott handpick their list of more than 300 wines, a few of which are offered by the glass to match to the night's dishes. Redfield's is open weekends year round and Monday through Saturday from May through October. With only 60 seats and a celebrated reputation, Redfield's fills up early; make your reservations in advance.

Deck House Restaurant and Cabaret Theater
$$-$$$ • Great Harbor Marina, Southwest Harbor • 244-5044

At the Deck House Restaurant and Cabaret Theater, you are not only a dinner guest, but also an audience member. Dining begins at 6:30 PM, where you'll sit on the second floor of a sardine factory and look out at a 180 degree view of the water. As the sun goes down, (at around 8 or 8:15 PM), the houselights dim, and wait staff magically transform from servers to singers in the Deck House's cabaret show. But the staff won't stop serving you. While you finish your meal — maybe boiled lobster, grilled swordfish, vegetable linguine or tournedos — the staff perform 13 acts, from mime to Broadway show tunes, as soloists, duets or in large groups. There's a $6-a-person charge for the theater portion (accounted for in the price code).

The Deck House moved here in 1997 from a long-standing perch in Bass Harbor. It's open for dinner seven nights a week and lunch Monday through Saturday mid-June through mid-September. For lunch, you'll enjoy standard Maine fare — lobster rolls, club sandwiches, salads — and possibly a rehearsal of the night's performance. Reservations are suggested. Smoking is not allowed.

Beal's Lobster Pier
$-$$ • Beal's Lobster Pier, Clark Point Rd., Southwest Harbor • 244-3022

When you order lobster at Beal's Lobster Pier, you'll be eating it facing the very brine it grew in. Beal's occupies its own pier, next to the Southwest Harbor Coast Guard Station, where the family has been hauling and weighing lobsters for generations. Settle at a picnic table for dinner, lunch, even breakfast (yes, some lobster diehards do find themselves enjoying the clawed crustaceans at 9 AM). With your meal, you may order clams, mussels, stone crab claws or corn on the cob. Or, choose from various fish chowders, sandwiches, lobster and crabmeat rolls, baskets of fried scallops, shrimp or fish, hamburgers or hot dogs from a snack bar at the pier. Wine and beer are available at Beal's.

As with most lobster establishments, Beal's is casual — you eat at picnic tables on the pier. Although some tables are sheltered, this is not a place to go in the rain. While the pier is open year round to sell lobsters, the eating area is open from Memorial Day to Columbus Day. Smoking is allowed.

Lindenwood Inn
$$-$$$ • Clark Point Rd., Southwest Harbor • 244-5335, (800) 307-5335

Settle beside the glass cafe tables in the sage-green dining room of the Lindenwood Inn for a refreshing, fun and sophisticated dining experience. Owner Jim King takes care of the atmosphere; Bill Morrison, a former private chef for Melanie Griffith and Don Johnson, takes care of the four menus — one for each season — featuring organic, seasonal foods.

Come warm weather, a meal might include spinach salad with roasted Portobellos and Parmesan cheese, followed by crab and cod cakes with saffron remoulade, then swordfish with cucumber salsa, perhaps capped off with a chocolate truffle torte.

Only 30 dine at a time among the soft colors and vibrant art chosen by King for the entire inn (see also our Accommodations chapter).

The Lindenwood Inn is open Tuesday through Saturday from April through New Year's Day. There is a full bar with select wines. Smoking is permitted only at the outdoor tables. Reservations are recommended.

Moorings
$$ • Shore Rd., Southwest Harbor • 244-7070

Come to the Moorings in winter, when it's most popular with locals, and the most common dish will be prime rib. Come summer, when locals give way to visitors, lobster entrees are most prevalent. Either way, you'll relish the view of Somes Sound and the Western Way from this family-style restaurant just across the road from the Hinckley Company. Other dishes here include chicken, pasta and fish served in a variety of ways.

The Moorings is open for dinner daily year round. It is also open for lunch between March and October and for breakfast in July and Au-

Photo: Mary (Dysart) Hartt

A puffin pauses for lunch on a rock off the coast of Maine.

gust. There is a smoking section and a full bar. Reservations are recommended in summer.

Seawall Dining Room
$-$$ • Seawall Rd., Manset • 244-3020

Eat close to the sea at this large beachside restaurant. Seawall Dining Room has overlooked the cobblestone beach known as Seawall (see our Acadia National Park chapter for details), just beyond Southwest Harbor, since 1959. Enjoy lobster stew, boiled lobster or a toasted lobster roll, or go for the popular clams fried in the Seawall's homemade batter. Also offered are hamburgers, hot dogs and a variety of sandwiches as well as daily specials.

Watch the sea gulls and ducks, and bring your binoculars to scan the seas for seals and dolphins (nearly every one of the 250 seats has a water view). The Seawall has a smoking section and offers a full bar. Reservations are accepted but not required. Lunch and dinner are served daily from Easter through Thanksgiving.

Thurston's Lobster Pound
$-$$ • Steamboat Wharf Rd., Bernard • 244-7600

Settle on the wharf to enjoy a lobster dinner complete with an old-fashioned lobstering experience at the largest working harbor of Mount Desert Island. As a wholesale business, Thurston's Lobster Pound has been open for more than 70 years. As a restaurant, it's nearly brand-new, but has quickly taken a strong place among the lobster pounds. After all, what could be more charming than watching the activities of Bass Harbor with the bright red shell of a lobster claw in hand?

Dine late and enjoy the setting sun color the harbor waters as you settle at a green-painted pine table inside Thurston's screened-in covered deck overlooking the harbor. Choose your lobster, and wait. It will be ready soon. Or order other seafood, or even a hamburger, perhaps with corn, cole-slaw and a blueberry cake. On cold days, vinyl windows roll down, and guests keep warm with the cozy gas fireplace. On lovely days, you can eat in the open air. Wine and beer are available.

Smoking is not permitted. Lunch and dinner are served from Memorial Day weekend until at least the end of September. (Call to see whether the restaurant will stay open into October.)

In places such as Blue Hill, pianist Paul Sullivan and Noel Paul Stookey of the famed folk trio Peter, Paul and Mary might make an appearance at local fund-raisers.

Nightlife

Nightlife? In Mid-Coast Maine? This is the land of the low-key, get-away-from-it-all vacation. Even locals have to make their own fun. We laughed at the mere thought of this chapter. Our friends laughed. Our sources laughed.

First we had to shake out the stereotypes: hanging around someone's kitchen listening to the police scanner; wandering around L.L. Bean's open-all-night store in Freeport (see Daytrips and Weekend Getaways). Most of us just rent videos, and we go to any length for good ones. (Look for some sources in this chapter.) After pressing our sources past their initial hilarity, we discovered that Mid-Coast Maine does have a social streak. It's just a matter of finding it.

In this chapter, we give a rundown of some bars, cafes, dance clubs and movie theaters, and we promise to steer you away from the really rough spots. Legend has it that years ago someone rode a Harley through a barroom in Rockland, but you won't read about that here.

That brings us to a couple of caveats. The legal drinking age in Maine is 21, and law enforcement can be tough on drunk drivers. Don't be surprised by police cars on the prowl as you drive away from a nightspot at closing time.

Finally, while the places we include are permanent fun spots, lots of activities come and go at the opera houses and grange halls in various towns, especially in summer. Contra dances and fund-raisers are just two examples.

Contra dancing is a little like square dancing, and it's very popular around here. Newcomers are welcomed like family and enthusiastically eased into the formations.

Fund-raisers can be anything from a chem-free dance at the Blue Goose hall in Northport (see subsequent entry) to benefit a community radio station, to a bean supper at a church for a family that needs help with medical bills for a sick child. In places such as Blue Hill, pianist Paul Sullivan and Noel Paul Stookey of the famed folk trio Peter, Paul and Mary might make an appearance at local fund-raisers.

The way to discover these passing fancies is to get a local newspaper as soon as you hit town, keep an eye out for posters and flyers on community bulletin boards and ask around. Then take the plunge: Dress casually (remember, you want to fit in) and don't be shy. We have friends from Florida who found a little-advertised contra dance through word-of-mouth. It was the high point of their trip here, and they left feeling they had gotten to know local people and local ways.

What more could a traveler wish for?

Waldoboro to Stockton Springs

Breakwater Cafe
Samoset Resort, 220 Warrenton St., Rockland • 594-2511

The crowd here is a mix of resort guests and locals. They come for the full bar, sandwiches, pizzas and salads and a range of music. There's country/western dancing from 7:30 to 10 PM Thursday nights, with a dance teacher on hand if you need some pointers. Sundays showcase jazz from 6 to 8:30 PM. Summer brings occasional live entertainment and lovely evenings on the patio, with its view of Penobscot Bay. We're told you can see two lighthouses from here.

Second Read Books and Coffee
328 Main St., Rockland • 594-4123

This wonderful cafe/used-book store is open on the third Friday of every month for live Celtic music and appearances by some local folk luminaries. It also offers other special live performances on an occasional basis. These are ticketed events; prices vary, and you must get them at the cafe. Call ahead to find out what's scheduled or look for notices in the local paper. Even if you aren't looking for music, this is a nice place to hang out on Friday and Saturday nights during the summer.

Strand Cinema
Main St., Rockland • 594-7266

On a block that will catapult visitors to their childhoods in the 1940s and '50s, the vintage Strand Cinema offers first-run movies, two per night, throughout the year. Admission in 1997 was $5.50 per person per show.

The Waterworks
7 Lindsey St., Rockland • 596-7950

The Waterworks is a recent arrival on the Rockland scene, and it boasts English-style pub food in an English-style pub with microbrews on tap. You'll find lots of mahogany, 10-foot-long oak trestle tables, a roaring fire in the stone fireplace and a friendly local crowd. Open seven days a week, The Waterworks offers live entertainment on Friday nights in the winter and on Thursday, Friday, Saturday in the summer. Music featured is all over the map — from blues to Scottish music to a bagpipe band. There's no cover charge.

'Gator Lounge
Navigator Inn, 520 Main St., Rockland • 594-2131

This locals' hangout is popular with the after-work crowd and packed with younger folks on the weekend. (We're told ages run from 28 to 40-ish.) Look for free hors d'oeuvres during the 4:30 to 6:30 PM "happy hour." This full bar occasionally indulges in a DJ or live entertainment — call ahead to find out what's happening. A big-screen TV makes it a popular place to watch sporting events, and a new 100-CD jukebox is a crowd-pleaser. The menu changes constantly, but expect items such as barbecued baby-back ribs, crab cakes, steak and pasta.

Bay View Street Cinema
10 Bayview St., Camden • 236-8722

This downtown theater offers two shows

FYI

Unless otherwise noted, the area code for all phone numbers listed in this guide is 207.

---

nightly of foreign and art films during summer. Come winter, it's one show nightly. Admission in 1997 was $5.50 per adult or teen per show, $3 for seniors and $3 for children 12 and younger.

Gilbert's Publick House
12 Bayview St., Camden • 236-4320

Gilbert's is under Peter Ott's restaurant, with its entrance off Sharp's Wharf on the right of the building as you face it. You can't miss it. Look for the signs, and park for free at the public landing nearby. Inside you'll find brick walls, a wooden bar, three pool tables, three dart boards and 17 beers on tap. Food is the usual bar menu: chili, sandwiches, soups, stews and pasta. This is a locals' hangout, although live entertainment and dancing on the weekends tend to draw crowds from a wider area. The J. Geils Band and Foghat were here a few years back. Cover charges vary.

Harbor Audio Video
87 Elm St., Camden • 236-6777

Open seven days a week, Harbor Audio has a notable selection of videos: some 10,000 titles with an extensive foreign and classics section. Many rent for just $1 a night. The new-release section is large with multiple copies of popular titles.

Sea Dog Brewing Co.
43 Mechanic St., Camden • 236-6863

This brewpub nestled in MBNA bank's complex on Mechanic Street is a little upscale. While it has a devoted local following, it tends to draw tourists as well, especially beer aficionados. It has a nautical theme, lots of honey-colored wood and a view of a waterfall on the Megunticook River. On the second floor, you'll find a smaller bar, pool tables, Foosball, darts and pinball. There's live entertainment — and no cover — every night during the summer and on Friday and Saturday nights in the winter. Music include blues, jazz, rock and folk.

The Waterfront
48 Bayview St., Camden • 236-3747

This restaurant/bar fronts Camden Harbor,

and there's nothing like having drinks with friends on the deck in the summer. A fireplace and a mahogany bar give the place warmth in the winter. Popular with boaters, The Waterfront draws a crowd ranging from young fishermen to well-heeled retirees. While dress is casual, leave your torn blue jeans at home. Not only is there a full bar, but you also can order anything off the restaurant menu as well as espresso and cappuccino.

Whale's Tooth Pub
U.S. Hwy. 1, Lincolnville Beach • 789-5200

Don't miss this place. It opened in 1994 and fast became a favorite local watering hole for people of all ages. A fireplace makes it cozy in the winter, while two oceanside decks make it heavenly when the weather's warm. Many of the wait staff have been here virtually from the start, so there's a real sense of community.

On Friday nights, you'll hear a piano player doing show tunes; Saturdays, there's a guitar duo playing folk and blues. It's mostly background music, but it can turn into a full-fledged sing-along depending on the crowd. There's no cover charge, and dress is always casual.

The full bar has Andrews beer on tap — which is brewed in Lincolnville Center — and the menu lists lobster stew, steaks, prime rib, fish and vegetarian fare.

The Whale's Tooth opens at noon Saturday and Sunday and 4 PM Monday through Friday; it's closed Tuesdays.

The Blue Goose
U.S. Hwy. 1, Northport • 338-3003

This funky old hall is rented by various groups for various events, from antique auctions to chem-free dances. Watch for listings in the local paper, and if there's a dance scheduled, go. They can be the talk of the town, and people of all ages come from all over to dance 'til they drop. Owner Charles Mitchell says call him at home, 223-5065, if you get no answer at the listed number.

Belfast Bay Brewing
100 Searsport Ave. (U.S. Hwy. 1), Belfast • 338-4216

Attached to The Ice Cream Barn restaurant, this brewpub was opened in August 1996.

It has a full bar with a range of microbrews and a full menu including appetizers, steaks, lobster pie and seafood Newburg. Belfast Bay Brewing definitely is not a rowdy place; the atmosphere is relaxed and casual, and it draws a range of ages.

Bruno's and Rico's
50 High St., Belfast • 338-4896

This watering hole attracts all kinds, from yuppies to granolas, the salt-of-the-earth to guys sporting ties. It's rustic and laid back, except on Friday and Saturday nights, when you'll hear live blues and rock 'n' roll for a $2 to $3 cover charge. There isn't much in the way of food, but you can enjoy a full bar and Sea Dog beer on tap.

Colonial Theatre
163 High St., Belfast • 338-1930

This downtown theater was recently resurrected by a local artist who can be credited with delightful art-deco color schemes inside and out. Look up on the roof and you'll see the famous elephant from the now-defunct Perry's Nut House. Inside, brass, mirrors, murals and uniformed ushers on the weekends add a festive touch. The Colonial has three screens and shows three Hollywood, independent or foreign films nightly, year round. Tickets cost $6 for adults and teens, $4 for seniors 60 and older and $3.50 for kids 12 and younger. Matinees cost $3.50 a person for all.

Darby's
185 High St., Belfast • 338-2339

Started in 1985, Darby's has a cozy, friendly atmosphere, a full bar, a great wine list, microbrews on tap and food worth mentioning in our Restaurants chapter. Open until 1 AM Monday through Saturday during the summer, it's a natural place to stop for a drink or dessert after a movie or a play. Come winter, the place may close earlier.

Ninety Main
90 Main St., Belfast • 338-1106

The atmosphere here is at once casual and elegant. Maybe it's the art on the walls that sets the tone. In any case, the bar draws a younger crowd (mid-20s) in the summer, but generally the clientele is a diverse group.

They come for the microbrews and a nice wine list as well as the deck for outside dining. Live entertainment includes folk, jazz and blues. Call ahead to find out what's scheduled and whether there's a cover charge.

Rollie's Cafe
37 Main St., Belfast • 338-5217

First, say it right. It's Roll-ies, not Rawlies. Now you're ready to square your shoulders and enter as local a hangout as you're likely to find in these parts. Rustic Downeast is our favorite description of the atmosphere. While the clientele represents all ages, few folks wear ties. Get the picture? You'll find a full bar as well as pizzas, fried dinners and a zillion different sandwiches. Scenes from Stephen King's *Thinner* were filmed here, so the place might look familiar.

www.insiders.com

See this and many other **Insiders' Guide®** destinations online — in their entirety.

Visit us today!

Inland to Bangor

Barnaby's Lounge
Ramada Inn, 357 Odlin Rd., Bangor • 947-6961

This full bar is open Monday to Saturday and has a popular happy hour. It's a busy yet relaxed placed with an extra-large dance floor. Wednesday draws younger folks; Thursday and Friday, an older crowd; and Saturday, a mixed group. A DJ spins music from the 1970s to '90s Wednesday through Saturday nights. Men pay a $4 cover charge on Wednesday; Thursday there's no cover; everyone pays a $2 cover on Friday and Saturday.

The Bounty Tavern
Holiday Inn Civic Center, 500 Main St., Bangor • 947-8651

The Bounty has been a hot spot for years. A DJ spins records here: rock 'n' roll Thursdays and Top-40 the rest of the time. The crowd tends to be professionals in the 21-to-45 age bracket. It's easy to meet people here, and we've been told business travelers stay at this particular Holiday Inn because of The Bounty. The time to go is later in the evening, when the scene heats up.

The Bounty is open Tuesday and Thursday through Sunday in the summer; Tuesday and Thursday through Saturday in the winter. The cover is $3 on adult nights and $5 for Sunday teen nights in the summer. When the 18-to-21 crowd is on vacation in the winter, The Bounty might do chem-free dances on nights when it's usually closed.

Dave's Movie Center
281 Hammond St., Bangor • 947-4810

While 17,000 titles might not be a record in Bangor, what is exceptional about Dave's is the range of amassed titles. This place has one of the largest selections of foreign titles around as well as many hard-to-find classics. When Dave started the business a decade ago, he collected every movie he could get his hands on. It's worth poking around to see what he found. The place might look small, but it stocks videos on three levels. Children's titles, musicals and war movies are in the basement. Foreign, religious, sports, comedy and classic films are on the first floor, while a staggering number of adult titles takes up the second floor. This homey place is family-owned and has a pleasant atmosphere. Unlike at many chain stores, the staff gets to know its customers well, and Dave's has been known to cut customers some slack if they're late returning a movie.

INSIDERS' TIP

In Maine, you can find beer and wine at most grocery and convenience stores, but hard liquor is sold only by 28 state-run stores and 190 private retail outlets licensed as agency liquor stores. To find them, check the Yellow Pages under "Liquor Stores."

Revitalization of buildings in downtown Bangor has led to the restoration of numerous classic inns, restaurants and pubs.

Dysart's Service
Coldbrook Rd., Bangor • 942-4878

This 24-hour truckstop is an old reliable in the Bangor area, open 365 days a year. You won't find alcohol or dancing, but they make a mean chicken/cheddar/bacon sub. Try the Oreo ice cream or peanut butter pie. Gas up your car, sit in the bright lights and yak with friends when the rest of Bangor has rolled up the sidewalks. You'll see lots of students during exam time and semester break.

Front Row Video
220 Union St., Bangor • 947-5066

As at Dave's (see previous entry), there are approximately 17,000 videos here, but this store focuses on new releases. There's a wide selection of titles — and lots of comedies. If the staff can't find what you're looking for, they'll call around to other Front Row stores to locate it.

Geaghan's Roundhouse
Penobscot Inn, 570 Main St., Bangor • 945-3730

Geaghan's has a local pub atmosphere. There's a full bar in the lounge with domestics, imports and microbrews on tap. You can order burgers, sandwiches and seafood platters as well. Open since 1975, this is a casual, blue-collar kind of place. A popular local jazz band, Woody Woodman and the Eastern Standard Trio, play 7 to 11 PM twice a month — on the first Friday and the third Saturday — with no cover. The dance floor is in the dining room, and it tends to be dressier than the bar. (Still, either a tie or jeans would fit in.)

G.W. Finnegan's
23 Franklin St., Bangor • 942-9194

The 21-to-35 crowd comes here for the rock, hip-hop and dance tunes spun by a DJ. The pub opened in 1989, the dance club in 1992, and they've been going strong ever since. The atmosphere is generated by a big horseshoe-shaped bar in the center, low lighting, wood beams and granite-faced walls.

Hoyts Cinemas
Bangor Cinemas 10, behind Bangor Mall, Stillwater Ave., Bangor • 942-1303

Hoyts is one of the biggest cineplexes in the area. Ten cinemas offer first-run movies. Tickets are $6.75 for adults, $5 for seniors and $4.75 for children. Two afternoon matinees are just $4.75 for everyone.

Paul's Restaurant and Speakeasy
605 Hogan Rd., Bangor • 942-6726

Paul's draws raves for its hors d'oeuvres and snacks. It's a lively, busy bar with music that's loud but not overpowering and a live interactive electronic trivia game that's hooked up to 4,000 other bars across the country. (You're up against players nationwide!) There's no cover, and just about anything goes as far as dress — from a suit and tie to torn jeans and T-shirts. A full menu of steaks, seafood and international fare is available. The Southwestern Club sandwich is a real favorite.

Pete and Larry's Lounge
Holiday Inn – Odlin Road, 404 Odlin Rd., Bangor • 947-0101

The hot night here is Sunday, when this 114-capacity lounge takes over an adjacent dining room and hosts crowds of 300. It's a young crowd, the same one that hits the Ramada on Wednesday night. Sunday aside, this lounge attracts all ages in all manner of dress, from tank tops to tuxedoes. It's small and friendly, like TV's Cheers, says the manager. A greenhouse area makes it sunny during the day and a nice spot to hit for lunch. The menu is varied too, from Caesar salad to Philly steaks and Buffalo wings.

Pete and Larry's is open seven days a week, from noon to 1 AM. On Thursday, Friday and Saturday nights, someone's usually playing a guitar — all kinds of music — from 9 PM to 1 AM. A DJ spins records from 8 PM to 1 AM Sunday and Monday, 9 PM to 1 AM Tuesday and Wednesday. There's no cover except Sunday, when it's $3.

Sea Dog Brewing Co.
26 Front St., Bangor • 947-8004

Sea Dog is a wonderful place to sit outside and gaze at the broad Penobscot River on a warm summer evening. It has a good reputation for its microbrews — the full bar offers 12 of its own concoctions plus its draft cider. The ambiance is nautical with lots of wood, and Sea Dog attracts a range of ages. Look for live entertainment — rock, jazz, blues, folk and acoustic duos — Thursday through Sunday, with a cover charge on Friday and Saturday nights. A once-a-month Sunday concert series draws bigger-name talent and carries an $10 to $12 cover charge. Popular headliners include Tom Rush, Patty Larkin, Son Seals and Paul Sullivan.

Stacey's Lounge and Brewer Motel
428 Wilson St., Bangor • 989-4940

Stacey's draws a mostly blue-collar and college crowd. When there are live bands, they tends toward country and classic rock. Cover charges are $2 Tuesday and Wednesday; $3 for men and free for women Thursday; $3 Friday; and $4 Saturday. An especially good band may mean a $4 cover charge on other nights. Monday and Tuesday are country karaoke nights from 9 PM to 1 AM.

INSIDERS' TIP

If you're visiting the area, ask your hosts for suggestions on nightlife. Hotel managers and bed and breakfast inn owners especially make it a point to know what's going on.

Talk of the Town Restaurant and Keyboard Lounge
The Roadway Inn, 482 Odlin Rd., Bangor • 947-3317

This quiet lounge draws the 30-to-60 crowd. It's open Monday to Saturday, and on Friday and Saturday you'll find someone playing oldies from the 1940s and '50s on the piano in the bar. You can sit in the lounge, listen to the music, order something from the restaurant and have the best of both worlds.

The Whig and Courier
18 Broad St., Bangor • 947-4095

No rowdy crowds here — just a friendly English pub atmosphere. The name comes from a newspaper published in Bangor in the 1800s. The exposed brick walls are adorned with pictures of the paper. Open Monday through Saturday, the full bar offers microbrews, burgers, cheese steaks and potato skins. You'll find lots of business types at happy hour and a smattering of college students as well.

Geddy's Pub
103 Park St., Orono • 866-7700

Say that "G" in Geddy's as if it's a "J" and you'll fit right in at this hoppin' college dance club. Open Wednesday to Saturday, it has a full bar and occasional live entertainment. Most of the time, a live DJ spins records from 8 PM to 1 AM. When the University of Maine is in session, Geddy's sets aside a chem-free space for the 18-to-21 crowd on Wednesday, Friday and Saturday nights.

Margarita's Mexican Watering Hole
15 Mill St., Orono • 866-4863

This full bar, restaurant and lounge is a slice of Southern California/Mexico, both in menu choices and decor. It attracts everyone from college students to senior citizens. There's a dance floor and live entertainment Wednesday through Saturday nights. The music ranges from acoustic to hard rock, and there might be a cover charge. Look for Dos Equis, Bass and Sam Adams beers on tap.

Pat's Pizza
11 Mill St., Orono • 866-2111

There's a full bar on the lower level of this local landmark, with a changing array of six beers on tap. It has low lighting, a couple of TVs, a fireplace and cozy booths. The atmosphere is homey and casual, and you'll see lots of students from the state university nearby. Of course the pizza's great, but Pat's serves subs, sandwiches and full dinners as well.

Spotlight Cinemas
University Mall, off Exit 51 of I-95, Stillwater Ave., Orono • 827-7411 (general info.), 827-0028 (office)

Six screens with Dolby™ sound feature second-run films. Call the theater to find out if it's offering art and foreign films. Tickets are $2.50 per person.

Babe's
30 Clisham Rd., Brewer • 989-1755

With a capacity of 600, Babe's is one of the biggest nightclubs in New England. Its downstairs dance floor is one of the largest in the state, and it's one of the few clubs with live rock 'n' roll bands. There are three full bars — two upstairs and one downstairs — a balcony and two pool tables. It's open Friday and Saturday nights; bands play both nights. A live or recorded DJ plays between sets, so the music is nonstop. You'll pay a $3 cover. Babe's draws all ages, all walks of life and all manner of dress. Friends say it's crowded, loud and lots of fun.

Cowboy's Tavern
554 S. Main St., Brewer • 989-6455

Cowboy's, a popular biker bar seen in Stephen King's *Pet Sematary*, is a working-class hangout frequented by Harley-Davidson riders and a number of motorcycle clubs. Open seven days a week, it has a full bar, lots of blues (and rock and country) music on the jukebox and good food. Check out anything made with its homemade barbecue and Cajun sauces. Don't expect a big place. There's room for a pool table, and that's about it.

Stevie's Restaurant and Lounge
1 Main Rd., East Holden • 989-5711

Steve's Stagecoach Lounge has moved to Felt Brook Golf Center and changed its name, but it's still a popular — if more spacious — Friday after-work hangout. Stevie's has a full bar and the usual bar fare of burgers, sandwiches, pizza and steaks. Try the Sunday brunch during football season.

Bucksport to Gouldsboro

Pete and Larry's Lounge
Holiday Inn, High St., Ellsworth • 667-9341

Weekends, folks come to dance; weeknights, they come to relax. Open seven nights a week, Pete and Larry's has a full bar, with free hors d'oeuvres during happy hour on weekdays and a DJ Thursdays, Fridays and Saturdays. You'll pay a $1 cover Friday and Saturday.

Maidee's
156 Main St., Ellsworth • 667-6554

The bar of this restaurant is inside a 1932 Worcester Deluxe Dining Car, with mahogany woodwork and a black-and-white marble-top bar. It's been around since the mid-'80s and draws a nice mix of ages. Art on the walls is by local artists and is for sale.

Renegade's
U.S. Hwy. 1, Ellsworth • 667-1573

This used to be the Oyster Bar. Now under new management, it's open seven days a week, with dancing to live rock and country bands on Friday and Saturday nights. There's a $3 cover charge on those nights. Look for karaoke Tuesdays and Thursdays. The crowd is friendly, relaxed and ranges in age from 21 to 81. Blue jeans are fine here.

Left Bank Bakery & Cafe
Maine Hwy. 172, Blue Hill • 374-2201

Folk and jazz singers seem to enjoy performing at this cafe almost as much as people enjoy listening to them. Under original owner

Arnold Greenberg's watch, the cafe developed a national reputation for presenting folk music. New owners Chuck Donnelly and Janet Anker plan to continue music seven days a week in summer and on weekends off-season, with some special concerts during the week. Tickets range from $8 to $15, depending on the performer.

Mount Desert Island

Some of the nightspots in Bar Harbor close during the off-season. The weeks or months they're closed vary from season to season, so it's best to call ahead.

Arnold's TV and Video
61 Cottage St., Bar Harbor • 288-4145

While this video store has just a few thousand titles, it's worth noting for the niche it's carved out for itself. While the chains and convenience stores try to outrace each other for the newest releases, here's a source for those films you can't find anywhere else: foreign titles, cult films and work by independent producers. Knowing you have a source for something other than the latest shoot-'em-up flick can be a real comfort when winters get long.

Geddy's Pub
19 Main St., Bar Harbor • 288-5077

Geddy's has been around since 1974, and it's a landmark in town. It has a full bar, a range of microbrews and live entertainment — acoustic guitar and a singer — most nights from 8 to 10:30 PM. Afterward, there's dancing to music played by a DJ (no cover charge). In 1996, the pub put in a wood-fired pizza oven with plans to offer a menu of burgers, pizza and grilled entrees. The clientele ranges from fishermen to the yachting crowd, and the atmosphere is rustic with barn-board walls, old signs and old pictures of Bar Harbor.

Lompoc Cafe
36 Rodick St., Bar Harbor • 288-9392

This favorite Bar Harbor hangout offers music four or five nights a week in summer, usually on weekends. Performers include local jazz musicians with some blues thrown in. Cover charges are around $2 per person.

Reel Pizza Cinerama
33 Kennebec Pl., Bar Harbor • 288-3811

Order up a pizza, settle into a couch and enjoy offbeat films — *I Shot Andy Warhol*, *Living in Oblivion* or *City of Lost Children,* for instance — otherwise known as American independent, foreign and art films. You have a choice of toppings on your white or whole wheat crust, and you can order beer or wine. The auditorium has tables and straight-backed chairs, recliners, beanbag chairs and couches. It's just like being at home — except for the big screen and stereo surround-sound. Admission in 1997 was $4.

Accommodations

Is it your dream to wake up with lobstermen working outside your window? To hear a loon's call as you cast off into sleep? To see a schooner slipping off into the sunrise? Your dream might be realized here.

When you reserve a room in the Mid-Coast region, be prepared to experience a bit of Maine: a gallery in Waldoboro; a sea captain's house in Searsport; a "cottage" of mansion proportions in Bar Harbor; or a Victorian delight just about anywhere. Step into the Roaring '20s, or lose yourself beside a colonial fireplace — it's all part of Maine.

But choose carefully. If your wish is to hike by day and return to fine food and some nightlife, you'll want a place in the thick of Bar Harbor. If you'd rather wander the seashore with little between you and the salt air, you might want to stay in Blue Hill, Deer Isle or farther Down East. Perhaps it's Maine's fishing villages that lure you; then stay in Corea, Stonington or Tenant's Harbor. Does your vacation invariably include elegance and good food? Look into Camden, Rockport, Northeast Harbor or Southwest Harbor. But if you just want to relax and retire to the past in a small Maine village, think of Waldoboro, Blue Hill, Brooksville or Gouldsboro.

Except for the Bar Harbor area, Ellsworth and Bangor, most accommodations are small bed and breakfast inns. Some chains, but not many, have made it into Maine; again, these have congregated in Bangor and the greater Bar Harbor area, including Ellsworth. One has made it down to Belfast, another to Camden.

The Insider's focus, however, is on creating a special experience. Throughout coastal Maine, old lodges and grand old hotels stand like sentinels to the coast. Built during the genteel era of long summer vacations, a few have endured. Elsewhere, in Waldoboro, Belfast and Searsport, especially, huge mansions once owned by successful sea captains have become gracious bed and breakfast inns.

On Mount Desert Island, while a few small Victorian homes have been converted into inns, so too have some of the huge mansions the summer people liked to call cottages.

We also focus on value, because we want you to have your dream without it becoming a nightmare — whether in a small family home or an exclusive cottage. Value in Maine means repeat customers. Summer on the Mid-Coast — July, to some extent, but especially August — is very popular. It's not unusual for people to book next year's room as they pay this year's check. So book ahead — early. We've heard that come midnight, Mount Desert Island is crawling with the vehicles of lost souls who didn't make reservations in time. Do they drive all night? We've never stayed awake long enough to see. (That said, of course there are last-minute cancellations. And that said — check to make sure you won't be penalized if the cancellations are yours!)

Summer is high season for most establishments on the Mid-Coast. A few keep the same rates year round, but many increase 50 percent from winter to summer. Some have very complicated rate plans, the very lowest being winter; shoulder seasons (spring and fall) are next lowest (though, increasingly, establishments are keeping rates high, or higher, during Maine's fall foliage season); and a few even raise rates from July to August.

Price-code Key

We've limited our prices to average peak-season rates, double occupancy per night. A few places have minimum stays or offer packages that include breakfast and, in some cases, dinner (a.k.a. Modified American Plan); we note their availability.

$	Less than $65
$$	$65 to $110
$$$	$110 to $155
$$$$	$155 to $200
$$$$$	$200 and more

Except where noted, all establishments accept credit cards, allow smoking outdoors only, welcome children (bed and breakfast inns say "well-behaved children") and don't allow pets. If a place is seasonal, we'll tell you when it's open; otherwise it's open year round (with from a week to a month off).

Only a few establishments are handicapped-accessible; we note those. Limited handicapped accessibility generally means a wheelchair can be moved into a room, but you might need the innkeeper's help carrying it up a two-stair entrance, and you won't be able to wheel it into a shower. Assume all rooms have private baths unless we say they don't (which in some places means just a shower stall, in other places just a bathtub). We'll tell you if you'll have a phone in your room; otherwise expect to find phones — and televisions, we might add — in public rooms only.

FYI

Unless otherwise noted, the area code for all phone numbers listed in this guide is 207.

As in other chapters, we're taking you up U.S. Highway 1 in four sections. First we lead you from Waldoboro to Stockton Springs, then into the Greater Bangor area (Winterport, Bangor, Orono and Holden). The third section moves from Bucksport to Gouldsboro (including Castine, the Blue Hill Peninsula and Deer Isle), and finally we cover Mount Desert Island.

Waldoboro to Stockton Springs

The Roaring Lion
$-$$, no credit cards • 995 Main St., Waldoboro • 832-4038

We felt instantly at home at this bed and breakfast inn. Robin and Bill Branigan have a gentle, easy way, and the atmosphere here is restful. The house itself is magnificent; it was built in 1905 and seems always to have had attentive owners. The woodwork shines; the embossed tin ceiling in the dining room is in perfect condition; and the bath has its original fixtures — a claw-foot tub and a marble sink. The four rooms are good-size; one has a working fireplace, another has a private bath. If it's a hot night, ask for the

room with a double exposure, with windows on opposite walls. Great breezes!

Full breakfasts are included, and Robin says Bill will happily accommodate special diets, including macrobiotic and vegetarian.

Le Va Tout
$-$$ • 218 Maine Hwy. 32 S., Waldoboro • 832-4969

Eliza Sweet bought this bed and breakfast inn in 1996, and her bright, pleasant manner bodes well for its future. It's a beautifully kept, beautifully landscaped 1830s cape that includes an art gallery. (The exhibit displayed when we visited was fascinating.) The gardens alone are worth the visit, particularly the arbor over two facing benches. It's a great place to spend a warm summer afternoon curled up with a book. There are five rooms, two with private baths, and rates include use of a hot tub and sauna.

Full breakfasts are served family style at a big table off the kitchen. Sweet welcomes children (she has two of her own), and she'll consider pets. She also has great maps of bike routes in the area, so bring one. She may tag along!

The Craignair Inn
$$ • Clark Island Rd., Box 533, Spruce Head • 594-7644, (800) 320-9997 (seasonal)

This inn was originally a boarding house for stone cutters who worked in nearby granite quarries, which explains why the halls are a little narrow and the rooms are small with shared baths. But don't let that be off-putting; there is so much more to enjoy here.

The owner is an antiques dealer, and the rooms are rich with her finds. The common rooms, particularly, hold beautiful examples of furniture from generations ago. (For more room and a private bath, ask to stay in the annex.)

Now, the surroundings: The Craignair is on 4 acres of shorefront, and an access road to Clark Island runs alongside it. While the 200-acre island is privately owned, guests may walk its paths and swim in one of its quarries. Cars and bikes are not allowed on the island,

so pedestrians can quietly noodle without interruption.

Full breakfasts are included in the room rate, and they're served in the inn's dining room overlooking the water. Dinner is also available.

The inn is open from mid-May to late October. Pets are welcome, and smoking is permitted in designated areas.

The East Wind Inn
$$$-$$$$ • Mechanic St., Tenants Harbor
• 372-6366

The East Wind is a classic Maine inn with a nautical air. It's right on the harbor, with wonderful water views, and its wraparound porch is a gracious indicator of what's inside. The common areas are spacious, the halls are wide, and the rooms are lovely. We were not surprised to meet guests who've been coming back here for years.

The main inn has just 13 rooms, some with private baths; a nearby annex has 10 rooms, all with private baths. Suites and apartments

are available as well. Pets are allowed, and smoking is allowed in the rooms but not in the common areas.

A full breakfast is included in the room rate, and dinner is available in the inn's splendid dining room.

The LimeRock Inn
$$$ • 96 Limerock St., Rockland
• 594-2257, (800) 546-3762

The LimeRock Inn, an 1890 Victorian mansion, has a subdued presence on a shady side street in Rockland, but the interior has the look of a luxury hotel, with lots of shining wood and gleaming brass. It's named after the street that was the main corridor for delivering lime from the kilns to the docks in the 1800s.

The inn opened in 1994, and it's run by two couples who act as hosts on alternate weeks. It's an arrangement that's worked well, giving both pairs a break from what can be a high-burnout business. Both husbands are Coast Guard captains, so either one can take guests on a cruise of Penobscot Bay in the inn's sailing yacht, the *Dory Volante*.

There are just eight rooms at the LimeRock, and they are beautifully appointed. All have private baths; some have whirlpools; some have fireplaces. The attractive reproduction furniture matches in a way antiques rarely do (and probably shouldn't). The dining area itself would put some restaurants to shame. The furnishings are lovely, the chairs are comfortable, and the table settings are elegant.

A full breakfast and afternoon tea are included in the room rate, and the breakfast menu is posted — a nice touch.

The Capt. Lindsey House Inn
$$$ • 5 Lindsey St., Rockland
• 596-7950, (800) 523-2145

Visitors may make a couple of turns to get to this inn on a one-way side street off Rockland's main drag. Once on Lindsey Street, they can't miss it. The 1835 building is mustard-colored, with green awnings and a red door. It has a self-contained air about it, like a men's club in a big city.

Inside, it even looks a little like a men's club, peppered with antiques and built for comfort. The furniture is big, the colors are rich, and the beds have down comforters. The common room has a fireplace, and tucked off the back is a snug library, a perfect place to read on a rainy day. There's a desk and a computer port as well. All nine rooms have private baths, telephones and TVs. One is fully handicapped-accessible with appropriate fittings and an entrance off a ramp from the street.

There's a minimum two-night stay during summer weekends. Children older than 10 are welcome.

Continental breakfast is included in the room rate and served in a handsome paneled dining room off the center hall. The Waterworks restaurant next door serves lunch and dinner.

The Old Granite Inn
$$-$$$ • 546 Main St., Rockland
• 594-9036, (800) 386-9036

This handsome inn — the only granite build-

ing in town — has a great location: right on U.S. Highway 1, directly across from the state ferry dock. Built between 1796 and 1840, it served as an Elks Lodge for a time. John and Stephanie Clapp restored it in 1984, sold it, bought it back in 1991, and sold it again six years later to Ragan and John Cary, who promise few changes.

Eight of its 11 rooms have private baths; some are brightly decorated, others more muted and restful. All include a full breakfast served in the dining room.

The "Captain's Quarters" at the top of the house seems wonderfully removed, but if the sound of traffic would be an annoyance, ask for rooms in the back. The inn is wheelchair-accessible. Well-behaved children are welcome.

Samoset Resort
$$$$$ • 220 Warrenton St., Rockport
• 594-2511, (800) 341-1650

This is the big resort in the area, and while it's a favorite with Mainers, it draws visitors from all over the world. The Samoset first opened in 1889 and encompasses 230 acres along Penobscot Bay. The original structure burned, and a new one was built in its place, using enormous timbers from a Portland granary.

The drive into the Samoset takes visitors past part of the golf course and approaches the main building from the back, which is not its best angle, aesthetically speaking: It looks a little industrial. But remember, most of the 150 rooms have ocean or fairway views, so the face of the resort is toward the ocean. Look up when entering the lobby; those massive exposed beams are from the granary. Look down and see cross-sections used as flooring.

The place itself is a beehive of activity, with an award-winning golf course, an indoor golf center, four outdoor tennis courts, indoor and outdoor pools, cross-country ski trails, racquetball courts and a fitness center with saunas and hot tubs. A conference center accommodates groups of up to 650 people. There's even an arrangement called "Sam-O-Camp"; for an additional fee, children can participate in supervised activities that include meals.

Breakfast, lunch and dinner are available in the hotel's various dining rooms. (See our Restaurants chapter.) Breakfast is included in some package rates.

The building is handicapped-accessible, and smoking is allowed in the rooms.

Cedar Crest Motel
**$$-$$$ • 115 Elm St., Camden
• 236-4839**

The Cedar Crest is an old reliable around here, and it deserves its excellent reputation. Family-owned and family-run, it's a great place to bring kids. There are swings and a pool, and the grounds are large enough for children to run around.

The units are spotless, the furnishings pleasant. The Cedar Crest has 37 rooms, all with private baths, TVs and telephones. Smoking is permitted in some rooms.

Breakfast is available in the motel coffee shop; it's open Tuesday through Sunday 6 AM to noon and has a faithful following among locals.

Hartstone Inn
$$-$$$ • 41 Elm St., Camden • 236-4259, (800) 788-4823

This is a lovely, peaceful place, and as ever, the personality of the owners makes all the difference. Peter and Sunny Simmons bought the 1835 mansion in 1985, renovated it and opened it as a bed and breakfast inn. They came to innkeeping later in life, and their seasoned poise serves them well. We've sat with Sunny in the front room, as a guest knocks some antique to the floor in the entry hall. Sunny doesn't flinch, she doesn't scold; she just smiles and waves off apologies. "Don't worry about it," she calls after them, "I'll take care of it." Sad to say, the Hartstone is changing hands in 1998; changes may be in the cards.

In the midst of Camden's business district, the Hartstone has eight rooms, two with fireplaces and all with private baths. Room rates include full or continental breakfasts, and dinner is offered off-season. The rooms are decorated with antiques, but there's nothing fussy about them. All have an airy, placid feel — a real comfort for travelers.

Children younger than 10 are welcome in the two housekeeping suites in the carriage house.

The Owl and Turtle Harbor View Guest Rooms
$$ • 8 Bayview St., Camden • 236-9014

These three wood-paneled rooms are snug atop a bookstore in the heart of downtown Camden. Two have harbor views; all share a balcony. They have the civilized feel of hotel rooms, with private baths, TVs and telephones, and rates include a continental breakfast.

Family-run for years, these rooms have a great location and a loyal following, so make reservations early. A two-night minimum is requested on weekends during July and August.

Lord Camden Inn
$$$-$$$$ • 24 Main St., Camden • 236-4325, (800) 336-4325

A favorite of business travelers, the Lord Camden is right in the center of Camden. Its 31 rooms have private baths, cable TV and telephones and include a continental breakfast.

Children younger than 16 stay free. Fourth-floor rooms, the priciest, have full balconies, ocean views and an elevator.

Camden Harbour Inn
$$$$-$$$$$ • 83 Bayview St., Camden • 236-4200

Built in 1874, the Camden Harbour Inn has a wonderful location with commanding views of the mountains, the harbor and Penobscot Bay. The occupant of Room B can sit up in bed and see the water. Room 29, on the third floor, also has water views plus a fireplace and a claw-foot tub. An elegant room on the ground floor in the back has a double bed, a twin bed and access to a pleasant little patio.

Antiques in the rooms and common areas contribute to the atmosphere of Old World el-

---

INSIDERS' TIP

Bar Harbor is a bustling place come summer. Stay there for a more urbane, summer-resort experience.

egance. All 22 rooms have private baths, smoking is permitted, and children older than 12 are welcome.

Breakfast is included in the room rate, and dinner is available in the inn's dining room.

Maine Stay
$$-$$$ • 22 High St., Camden • 236-9636

We arrive unexpectedly, and it's pouring rain. We ring the bell, the door swings wide, and host Capt. Peter Smith, a retired U.S. Navy officer, hurries us in. He's not a man to ask a visitor's business before making her feel welcome. His good humor and impeccable manners make everything easy, pleasant, no problem. What balm for weary travelers.

The Maine Stay has gotten lots of good press over the years, and it deserves every word. Peter, his wife, Donny, and her twin sister, Diana, run the bed and breakfast inn. They are genuine, gracious people who make it a delight to stay here, and they've cared for the 1802 house with great respect for its history. The roof is slate, interior walls are plaster, the furnishings are just right. The two front parlors have fireplaces that guests are welcome to light any time.

The Clark Suite was our favorite, with its sitting room in warm pinks and yellows and its gas fireplace. While there's nothing frou-frou about the Maine Stay, the Carriage House Room in the back of the house is described as quiet, private and romantic. Of the eight rooms available, six have private baths. (The number of private baths will increase after this year's renovation.) They all include full breakfast, afternoon refreshments and a binder full of information on the house, the area, local restaurants and activities.

Children older than 10 are welcome.

A Little Dream
$$$-$$$$ • 66 High St., Camden • 236-8742

This pretty 1888 Victorian bed and breakfast inn draws repeat visitors from all over the country and hosts a fair number of international travelers. It's no wonder. Jo Anne Ball and Billy Fontana are smart, funny and a joy to be around. They take loving care of their guests; the house is lavishly decorated and meticulously maintained. Jo and Billy do it

themselves, a rarity in Camden's upscale bed and breakfast scene. It makes a difference when the owners cook the meals and change the beds. Then you know you're truly being pampered.

For years, Jo and Billy ran Gippetto's, a specialty toy store in New York City. In the late 1980s, they turned to this, a "little" dream. What they started now has a life of its own. Guests send thank-you notes, Christmas cards and Victorian memorabilia they think Jo will like; and they coordinate future visits with couples they've met here.

The common areas and guest rooms are feasts for the eyes, rich with rare Victorian finds (this is not a place for children!). One of the suites has views of Camden's outer harbor and Curtis Island, but its bedroom has the feel of a cottage nook. All five rooms have private baths and telephones; most have televisions. A two-night minimum is requested on holiday weekends during the summer.

The Lodge at Camden Hills
$$$ • U.S. Hwy. 1, Camden • 236-8478, (800) 832-7058

Looking for water views, a working fireplace and a whirlpool bath for two? This is the place.

While our favorite is the cottage, which has all these amenities and an efficiency kitchen, a range of accommodations is available, including standard motel units. The Burgess family did major renovations on the property in the early 1990s, and the result is a cluster of modern Cape Cod-style buildings that blend nicely on their 5-acre site.

The property is a mile north of Camden and backs up to Mt. Battie and the state park. Because it's on a slope, guests in many of the 20 units can see Penobscot Bay. All rooms have TVs, telephones, private baths, small refrigerators and individually controlled heat and air-conditioning — a boon in Maine's unpredictable climate. One of the units is fully handicapped-accessible with appropriate fixtures and adequate space for wheelchairs.

John and Linda Burgess are enthusiastic, professional and committed to excellent service. Their brochure offers a guarantee that's worth noting: They will refund deposits if guests aren't satisfied with the cleanliness or comfort

The rocky coast of Maine is dotted with hundreds of inlets that have been carved over the years by the waves of the Atlantic Ocean.

of their room and the Burgesses can't make it right. They will even help arrange other accommodations in the area.

Whitehall Inn
$$-$$$ • 52 High St., Camden
• 236-3391, (800) 789-6565

The Whitehall has an elegant Yankee charm. Its character, history and sense of place are soul-satisfying at a time when many hotel rooms across the country seem to have a depressing sameness.

Built in 1834, the inn is listed on the National Register of Historic Places, and while it is fresh and clean, it feels comfortingly old. As one travel writer has said, this is a place that hasn't been renovated beyond recognition. Broad windows overlook a wide veranda complete with wooden rockers. The rambling lobby has two fireplaces, and it's carpeted with antique Orientals. The furnishings would suit the living room of a rich great-aunt. It was here, in 1912, that a young Edna St. Vincent Millay first recited her now famous work, "Renascence," and her Camden High School diploma hangs on the wall.

The guest rooms are spotless and comfortable, but like the houses of people with old money, they don't shout. There's no ostenta-tion, no pretension. There's no need for it — this is the real thing.

The Dewing family has been operating the inn since 1971, and as manager J.C. says, "We have no aspirations to standards other than the ones my mother set for us; they're pretty high." An all-weather tennis court is available for guests, and while the Whitehall is not a resort per se, this is the kind of place where the front-desk staff will help arrange any activity available in the area.

Of the 50 rooms, 45 have private baths. There are telephones in all the inn's rooms and in the lobbies of the two annex houses.

The Whitehall is open Memorial Day to late October. Breakfast is included in the room rates, and various plans and packages are available. Dinner is served in the dining room as well. Smoking is permitted.

Mt. Battie Motel
$$-$$$ • U.S. Hwy. 1, Lincolnville
• 236-3870, (800) 224-3870

The Mt. Battie is perfect for those who like the comfort of bed and breakfasts, but prefer the anonymity of motels. The landscaping is meticulous, with an abundance of flowering plants. The rooms are pristine, painted in muted colors, with gently flowered curtains and bed skirts. The housekeeping is meticulous as well.

The motel is on the uphill side of U.S. Highway 1, so some of the 22 units have bay views. All have private baths, TVs, telephones, refrigerators and in-room coffee and tea. Room rates include a continental breakfast, which may be eaten in the gazebo out back or on one of the patios. A hammock swings invitingly.

The Mt. Battie is open mid-April to November, and a two-night minimum stay is requested during weekends in July and August.

The Spouter Inn
$$$ • U.S. Hwy. 1, Lincolnville
• 789-5171

The Spouter Inn was recently expanded, and its accommodations are marvelous, carefully incorporating fireplaces, water views and whirlpool baths.

As the area around Lincolnville Beach develops into a real village, it makes good sense to stay here. Guests can walk the beach or frequent the handful of shops and restaurants nearby. The ferry to Islesboro is about a half-block away, and the inn can arrange rentals for those who might want to explore the island by bike.

The inn has seven rooms, all with private baths and cable TV hookups. (There are a couple of TVs floating around for guests to use as they like.) Room rates include a full breakfast.

Well-behaved children older than 7 are welcome. There's a two-night minimum stay from June 15 to October 15.

The Victorian by the Sea
$$$$ • Seaview Dr., off U.S. Hwy. 1,
Lincolnville • 236-3785

The bottom line in bed and breakfasts is not the beds, or the food, or the wallpaper. It's how you're made to feel when you walk in the door. While we don't normally write up new businesses, this is an established business under new ownership, and we were charmed by the new owners.

Greg and Ginny Ciraldo moved into this 1881 Queen Anne Victorian from New Jersey just two days before our unscheduled visit, and they showed us around with grace, good humor and ready warmth. That says volumes

about how comfortable you may be as one of their guests.

The inn itself has four bedrooms, two suites and more fireplaces than we could count. We especially liked The Victorian Suite. It's on the second floor, with a snug sitting room and fireplace in the turret. The Sawyer Suite would be wonderful for a family traveling with older children. (The inn welcomes children 12 and older.) It has a loft with twin beds, and an incredible bathroom with a claw-foot tub and a separate shower.

No doubt the Ciraldo's will make some changes in the year to come (we hope they paint that orange trim!). But they have enthusiasm and sincerity, which is the hallmark of real hospitality. And the house itself is lovely, with great views of Penobscot Bay.

The Youngtown Inn
$$-$$$ • Maine Hwy. 52, Lincolnville
• 763-4290

Manuel and Mary Ann Mercier have done a lovely job restoring this handsome 1810 farmhouse, the center of the Young family farm for more than seven generations. Better known for its food (see our Restaurants chapter), the inn has six rooms, two with fireplaces and all with private baths. Painted white with stencil borders, the guest accommodations are bright and airy, with floors of clear pumpkin pine.

A full breakfast is included in the room rate, and Manuel's specialties include apple-stuffed French toast, crêpes with farmer's cheese and blueberries, and scrambled eggs with smoked salmon on a potato pancake. A minimum stay of two nights is requested during summer weekends — either Friday/Saturday or Saturday/Sunday.

The Youngtown Inn is 5 miles outside Camden, but that can be a real blessing during high season. Megunticook Lake, Camden Hills State Park and Fernald's Neck Preserve are all within easy walking distance, and the swimming's great in nearby Barrett's Cove.

The Dark Harbor House
$$$$ • Main Rd., just beyond Derby St.
traveling north, Dark Harbor • 734-6669

This yellow-clapboard Colonial Revival mansion is the only hotel or motel in an exclusive summer colony on the island of Islesboro, and staying here will make guests feel they're one of the posh crowd. Owner Matt Skinner might arrange for a golf game at the private Tarratine Club or a berth for a boat. (For more about what to do and see on Islesboro, see our Offshore/Islands chapter.)

Built in 1896 for Philadelphia banker George Philler, the house has four graceful pillars at one end and a proliferation of porches. Rolling lawns and beautiful gardens make it look as if it were placed here by divine decree — or Hollywood. Despite the formal implications of all this symmetry, the Dark Harbor House has an impeccable reputation for gracious hospitality.

Open mid-May to mid-October, the hotel has 12 guest rooms, seven in the original structure and five in a recent addition. The furnishings vary from light-painted to dark mahogany. Some rooms have fireplaces, and some of the older rooms have huge claw-foot tubs and pull-chain toilets. Breakfast is included in the room rates. The hotel also serves dinner.

The Jeweled Turret Inn
$$-$$$ • 40 Pearl St., Belfast • 338-2304

This house is fascinating, and we'd stay here just for the privilege of exploring it freely. Built by a prominent local attorney in 1898, it has all kinds of rich, quirky touches. Carl and Cathy Heffentrager restored the house, and as they stripped paint, they discovered details such as bird's-eye maple paneling in the bathroom.

The name of the bed and breakfast inn comes from the jewel-like stained-glass panels in the turret over the center staircase. Our favorite room is a snug, round den in the back of the house, with rattan wainscoting and a fireplace built of rocks from every state in the Union. Of the bedrooms, we prefer the relative simplicity of the Emerald Room; it's small, cozy and has a private entrance.

The inn has seven rooms with private baths, and accommodations include a full breakfast. Children older than 12 are welcome, and there's a minimum stay of two nights during holiday weekends in the summer.

Carriage House Inn
$$ • U.S. Hwy. 1, Searsport • 548-2289

Linda and Gary Farmer came to this gra-

cious Victorian on a vacation from Los Angeles. They found the inn for sale and eventually took the plunge. The Carriage House Inn is marked on the outside by its great carriage house, now an antiques store, and by its cheery paint job. On the inside, this 19th-century sea captain's home is most marked by artist Waldo Pierce, who lived here in the 1950s.

Pierce left some paintings and lithographs (in the home) and many stories (around town) — he was quite a wild one apparently, a man who knew Hemingway from fighting with the Rough Riders. Pierce was also a sentimentalist. As thanks to the local school for educating his children through October, he donated one painting each year to the school. When the new Searsport Elementary School was built in 1990, they created a Waldo Pierce gallery on the second floor of the school library. (The gallery is open whenever there's someone in the school to show it.)

The owners of the Carriage House Inn are friendly and talkative; the three guest rooms, some with glimpses of Penobscot Bay across the street, are comfortably plush, with 19th-century decor and lots of brightly colored pillows. There are games and puzzles for children and lovely gardens for all. In winter, the inn is open by reservation only.

The Homeport Inn
$-$$ • 121 E. Main St. (U.S. Hwy. 1), Searsport • 548-2259, (800) 742-5814

Visitors want to stand outside and gawk at this house, with its large cupola, built in 1863 by a local sea captain. Some folks in Washington, D.C., thought the same and put it on the National Register of Historic Places.

Of the 10 rooms, seven have private baths, and there's a two-bedroom cottage on the water. Some rooms have decks, and many have canopied beds. This is a casual inn dressed up with formal antiques. Beyond the full breakfast, the innkeepers will not intrude. Children older than 3 are welcome, and pets are permitted in the cottage.

Recently, Searsport has become an antiques capital, with more than 30 antique stores and flea markets (bleeding over into Belfast to the south and Stockton Springs to the north) selling anything from Civil War memorabilia to last year's McDonald's toys. The Homeport is also within walking distance of the Penobscot Marine Museum, a small village's collection of maritime history (see our Attractions chapter).

Hichborn Inn
**$-$$ • Church St., Stockton Springs
• 567-4183, (800) 346-1522**

The Victorian Italianate Hichborn Inn stands on a side road of this town that was sidelined by changes in U.S. Highway 1. The re-routing nearly destroyed the town's economy but did such wonders for its tranquillity that Stockton Springs now shows signs of rebounding.

The four rooms of the Hichborn Inn welcome adult visitors to a quiet respite. Nancy Suppes, a Castine native, and husband Bruce turned the historic home into an inn a decade ago. The rooms invite romance, with lace-edged linens, hand-silkscreened wallpaper, Victorian lamps and stately furniture. Nancy glows when she tells of a young man who came to the inn with hopes of asking for his girlfriend's hand. When she agreed, Nancy sent a bottle of Moët & Chandon to the room.

Following a breakfast of fruit soup, crêpes or Dutch Babies, and special-roasted coffee, guests can wander to nearby attractions such as the Fort Point Lighthouse (down the road), the Penobscot Marine Museum in Searsport and the region's many antique stores. Or they may go farther — Mount Desert Island, Camden, Castine and Bangor are each within an hour's drive. At night, while sipping a glass of complimentary brandy by the fire, guests can enjoy musing about their own travels or the lives of the three active, artistic Hichborn daughters who lived out their lives in this home.

Inland to Bangor

Hampden Park Rest Motel
$ • 236 Main Rd., Hampden • 862-5500

This is a real, gen-u-ine Insiders' find — a pristine motel for $36 a night! The 13-room motel has been in the same family for more than 10 years; Howard and Karen Day bought it from relatives who never seemed to have raised the rates. Now they have a clientele that won't let them, and you can be the beneficiary.

The rooms aren't fancy, but they're pleasant and clean with private baths and TVs. This

is a great place for families. There's a pool, and the units are well off U.S. Highway 1A, with a huge lawn kids love — especially kids who've been cooped up in a car all day. Best of all, the room rate covers two to four people.

The Days also rent a two-bedroom cottage, including daily room service, for $400 a week or $60 to $65 a night. Remember, you read it here first.

Comfort Inn
**$$ • 750 Hogan Rd., Bangor • 942-7899,
(800) 338-9966**

Shoppers take note! The Bangor Mall is so close, it can be seen from some of the rooms. The Bangor Comfort Inn has 95 rooms with phones and TVs, and an outdoor pool. It's handicapped-accessible, allows smoking in designated rooms and permits pets. A free shuttle will take guests to and from Bangor International Airport.

Fairfield Inn by Marriott
**$$ • 300 Odlin Rd., Bangor • 990-0001,
(800) 228-2800**

For a moderately priced motel, the Fairfield has an air of luxury. The lobby has touches of mahogany, granite and marble, and there's an indoor pool, sauna, whirlpool and fitness facilities. The 153 rooms have phones and TVs; room rates include a continental breakfast. The Fairfield is handicapped-accessible and allows smoking in designated rooms.

Holiday Inn Civic Center
**$$ • 500 Main St., Bangor • 947-8651,
(800) 799-8651**

Ask for a room on the upper floors of the main building. You'll have views of downtown Bangor and the Penobscot River.

The Holiday Inn Civic Center has 122 rooms, each with phone, TV, data port and coffee maker; some also have hair dryers and ironing boards. The outdoor pool is pleasant in the summer. This particular Holiday Inn is popular with business people because of its Bounty Tavern (see our Nightlife chapter).

The inn is handicapped-accessible, allows smoking in designated rooms and permits pets. It's right across the street from the Civic Center, which is convenient if you're coming into town for an event scheduled there.

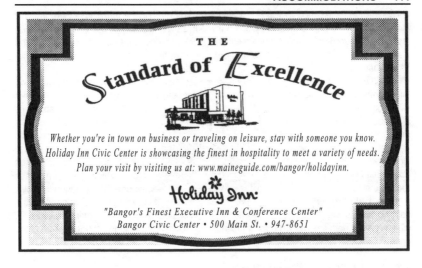

Holiday Inn – Odlin Road

$$ • 404 Odlin Rd., Bangor • 947-0101, (800) 914-0101

Ask for a room on the courtyard. This horseshoe-shaped hotel surrounds a greenscape with a pool, two kiosks and all manner of green and blooming plants. There's great poolside dining in the summer! This Holiday Inn has an indoor pool as well — a real bonus in this climate: You can swim laps or paddle around and relax no matter the weather.

The Bangor Holiday Inn has 207 rooms with phones, TVs, data ports and coffee makers, and a Jacuzzi. A fitness facility, Gold's Gym, is on the premises and is free for guests. The inn is handicapped-accessible, allows smoking in designated rooms and permits pets. A complimentary shuttle takes guests to the mall and the airport.

The Phenix Inn at West Market Square

$$ • 20 Broad St., Bangor • 947-0411

In a city peppered with chain motels and hotels, the Phenix is a delightful alternative. In the heart of the city, it feels like a small European hotel. It's great for business travelers but just as nice for weekend visitors to the city.

The rooms are different sizes and arrange-

ments; some have desks, some have four-poster beds with lovely canopies. The antique-reproduction furniture is mahogany or upholstered in leather. All 32 rooms have private baths, air-conditioning, TVs and telephones (local calls are free). The sinks (outside the bathrooms) have antique solid brass faucets.

A continental breakfast is included in the room rate. Parking is free in private lots behind the building, and there's a rear guest entrance. Pets are welcome in first-floor rooms.

Ramada Inn

$$ • 357 Odlin Rd., Bangor • 947-6961, (800) 2RAMADA

Sometimes it seems that all chains are alike, but this particular franchise was recently renovated and has won prizes for cleanliness and hospitality. The Bangor Ramada has 114 rooms with phones and TVs, an indoor pool, game room and Nautilus fitness center. It's handicapped-accessible, allows smoking in designated rooms and permits pets. A business-class room is available as well, with amenities such as a coffee maker in the room. The Ramada also offers a free shuttle to the Bangor Mall and Bangor International Airport.

Riverside Inn

$-$$ • 495 State St., Bangor • 947-3800

A mile north of downtown Bangor, The Riverside Inn is nestled next to Eastern Maine Medical Center, on the Penobscot River. Four stories high, it is crisp, pleasant and a favorite place to stay for family and friends visiting EMMC patients.

All 56 rooms have private baths, TVs and telephones, and continental breakfast is included in the room rate. There's a 24-hour cafeteria on the premises. Some rooms have great views of the river, and suites with whirlpool baths are available. An abbreviated fifth story holds two rooftop suites.

The building is handicapped-accessible. Children younger than 15 stay free, and pets are welcome for an extra charge. Smoking is permitted in some rooms.

FYI

Unless otherwise noted, the area code for all phone numbers listed in this guide is 207.

Tether's End Bed & Breakfast
$ • 50 Church Rd., Holden • 989-7886

Harry and Judy Madson have a lovely manner, and they've managed to create the kind of house in the country we all wish we could visit. Off U.S. Highway 1A, Tether's End is an unassuming 1890s home just 10 minutes from Bangor and an hour from Bar Harbor. Its gardens are extravagant, its rooms are charming, and breakfast might be gingerbread pancakes or Cheesy Apple Breakfast Pie. Guests have a choice of dishes, all served with fresh fruit, muffins and juice, and a choice of serving times, from 7 to 9 AM.

The living room has a tin ceiling and a few hand-painted chickadees flocking on the far wall. The three bedrooms and two baths upstairs are decorated with antiques. Our favorite was the smallest — the cottage room — with its blue walls, wicker furniture, quilts and cutwork pillows. There's also a small upstairs study available for guests to use. It has a long work counter, a phone, a TV, a place to plug in a laptop computer and do-it-yourself coffee and tea.

Well-behaved children are welcome; pets are not.

The Lucerne Inn
$$$ • U.S. Hwy. 1A, East Holden
• 843-5123

This inn began as a stagecoach stop halfway between Bangor and Ellsworth. Nathan Phillips had built a farmhouse here in 1812 but realized he could do better as an innkeeper. Pictures on the wall from that time attest to the fact that the inn has been thoroughly renovated since then.

While there are antiques in the common areas and guest rooms, the inn's interior is more modern than many of its counterparts'. Since it overlooks Phillips Lake and surrounding mountains, a number of the inn's 25 guest rooms share that glorious view. Other amenities include TVs, telephones, working fireplaces, whirlpool baths and heated towel bars in the private baths.

Room rates include continental breakfast. The inn is handicapped-accessible. Small pets are permitted.

High Lawn Bed & Breakfast
$-$$ • 193 Main St., Orono • 866-2272

We smile when we think of Betty Lee Comstock, who runs this bed and breakfast inn. She's full of beans, loves what she's doing and probably makes the mailman feel he should come in for coffee.

The house is elegant, the common rooms are comfortable, and best of all, Betty Lee is so relaxed. Guests never forget they're in someone's home; but then, that's the point of staying in a bed and breakfast, isn't it?

The High Lawn is a favorite of visiting professors and university guests. It has six rooms and three baths, but Betty Lee handles reservations in such a way that guests have a bath to themselves if at all possible. The furnishings include family pieces and antiques Betty Lee picked up when she was a dealer. Some rooms are limited handicapped-accessible, and children older than 13 are welcome.

A full breakfast is included, and the blueberry muffins have quite a reputation; Betty Lee had a guest call her from Germany to make sure they'd be served when he visited.

University Motor Inn
$ • 5 College Ave., Orono • 866-4921, (800) 321-4921

Here's another genuine Insiders' find. Next to the University of Maine campus, this motel is popular with parents and university visitors.

It is independently owned, and while the rooms are standard-issue motel units, they are impeccable. Some of the 48 units have views of the Stillwater River, some have limited handicapped access; all have baths, TVs and telephones. Guests may use the outdoor pool.

Owners Sharon and John Robinson are low-key and genuine. Guests are greeted at the desk like family. "We're not all new and shiny, so we go for friendliness and cleanliness," says Sharon.

Rates include a continental breakfast. Pets and smoking are permitted.

Bucksport to Gouldsboro

Best Western Jed Prouty Motor Inn
$$ • 52 Main St., Bucksport • 469-3113, (800) 528-1234

The Best Western Motor Inn clings so close to the shore of the Penobscot River, you might think you were falling in.

All but a few of the motel's 40 rooms have water views, so you can watch the river's changing moods. In summer you can watch the ospreys that occupy both towers of the Waldo-Hancock Bridge framed by your window. Huge tankers and barges get pushed up the river by bright red tugs to docks near the Champion International Paper Mill. If you come in summer, stop at the mill for a tour of the papermaking process (see Attractions) or browse through the antique shops and flea markets in town. And don't forget to visit the seemingly ancient Fort Knox (see our History and Attractions chapters), directly across the river from the mill.

Across the street from the Motor Inn is its namesake, the 1798 Jed Prouty Inn, which has just closed as an inn, but is worth a mention because it's listed on the National Register of Historic Places. Once called The Robinson House, it served as a stage stop between Castine and Bangor, hosting U.S. President Martin Van Buren and Gen. Stonewall Jackson. In 1889, writer Richard Golden set his play *Old Jed Prouty* at the tavern, giving the Yankee innkeeper the name Jed Prouty. The rather typical romantic melodrama catapulted to astounding success. It had such a long run in New York City — not to mention more than 3,000 performances on the road — that the innkeepers let fiction determine fact and changed the Robinson House to The Jed Prouty Tavern and Inn.

There are televisions and phones in every room. Call to see whether the staff can accommodate your pet.

Sign of the Amiable Pig
$-$$, no credit cards • 74 Castine Rd., Orland • 469-2561

Come to this plush, homey pre-Revolutionary War home marked by a smiling-pig weather vane for a relaxing stay in one of the few villages that remain as Maine is imagined. Orland is a quiet river town where everyone knows everyone — and they knew their parents and grandparents as well.

The Piphers retired here from the South a few years back, thought up their delightful name, opened their home to visitors and have been enjoying the company ever since. They offer three rooms in their inn; two share a bath, the third is a suite that accommodates four. They also have converted a barn into a guest house that sleeps four and is rented by the week.

The inn is less than 20 minutes by car from Castine and Blue Hill, just a few minutes from great lake swimming at Craig Brook, and within an hour's drive of Acadia National Park. Children are welcome, smoking is not. The Sign of the Amiable Pig is open year round.

The Castine Inn
$$-$$$ • Main St., Castine • 326-4365

You don't need to stay at the Castine Inn to enjoy the gardens that twine around a tiny brook, over a brick wall and through various archways. But if you enjoy these gracious gardens, you probably would want to stay at the inn. Its ample porches reflect the sociability of 1898, when it was built. The interior art, simple furniture and richly painted walls reflect contemporary Maine. There are 16 rooms plus three suites, half with harbor views. Make yourself comfortable on the ample porch, have a drink in the bar, and by all means, enjoy a gourmet dinner prepared by chef Tom Gutow, who with his wife, Amy, has owned the inn since 1997.

Those longing for the quiet of small-town

America — where stranger and native can sit together at a soda fountain and trade jokes and conversation — will find perfection in Castine.

Wander the harbor, then take a walking tour to view the wonderful architecture steeped in stories and spanning several centuries (printed guides are available everywhere in town). If you come in summer, visit the local museum and historical society. Any time of year, discover Castine's past through its historic signposts, and muse about the homes that once stood here (after the Revolutionary War, Tories in British-held Castine loaded the houses onto barges and shipped them to St. Andrews, New Brunswick; see History). And don't forget to admire Dice Head Light (see Lighthouses), the spare harborside church and the remaining earthworks of two forts.

Pentagoet Inn
$$-$$$ • Main St., Castine • 326-8616, (800) 845-1701 (out of state)

When the Pentagoet Inn was built in 1894, Castine was a bustling seaport, a major stop on the steamer route. Castine is still oriented to sea and harbor — and it's still bustling. Sailboats and motorboats are joined by a short kayaking convention in summer. When the summer sailors move out, the winter ones — students at the Maine Maritime Academy — move in.

The turreted Victorian-style Pentagoet Inn is a perfect jumping-off place from which to enjoy Castine. The 16-room inn actually consists of two buildings, a colonial annex on Perkins Street and the main building on Main.

The Perkins Street building has low ceilings, wide pine floorboards and lots of wood everywhere. Rooms are simply furnished with white coverlets, bits of lace and antiques.

The inn is similarly simple, but it draws from the Victorian era, with hooked rugs, flowered bedspreads and comfortable alcoves for sitting. Enjoy the library, the Bosendorfer piano in the sitting room, the wraparound porch and the hammocks in the back yard.

New in 1997, afternoon tea and formal high tea are served daily except Sunday from July through September. The inn also has a full bar (not to mention a full breakfast for guests).

The Pentagoet Inn is open from late May through Columbus Day. Children older than 12 are welcome. Pets are allowed in some rooms. You won't find any televisions here.

Blue Hill Farm Country Inn
$$ • Maine Hwy. 15, Blue Hill • 374-5126

Even those who work here regard the Blue Hill Farm Country Inn as home. This is a friendly, community-oriented place, as evidenced by the numerous paintings on the walls and the Maine-made items on the counters.

There are 14 simply furnished rooms — seven with private baths and seven with shared baths. The decor is real country: Quilts and braided rugs are the focus. Half the rooms are upstairs in the farmhouse (those with the shared bath) and half are on the second floor of the renovated barn. In summer, from below, in the spacious sitting and breakfast room, you might hear the strains of a chamber music concert from nearby Kneisel Hall (see our Arts chapter).

The inn is set amid 48 acres of forest veined with brooks. Guests are welcome to walk the grounds year round, or go cross-country skiing when there's snow. There is much to explore in the area. Take a shoreside drive around the Blue Hill Peninsula and across the astoundingly delicate Deer Isle Bridge, or walk through town to visit local galleries and bookstores and attend a chamber concert at Kneisel Hall or a folk concert year round at the Left Bank Cafe.

The rooms are too small for cots, but children older than 12 are welcome to stay in their own rooms.

Blue Hill Inn
$$$-$$$$ • Union St. (Maine Hwy. 177), Blue Hill • 374-2844, (800) 826-7411 (out-of-state only)

The Blue Hill Inn has been welcoming guests since 1840, just 10 years after it was built. We imagine it has honed its perfect balance of elegance and coziness since then. This is the quintessential historic inn, with Oriental rugs spread on the floor and hors d'oeuvres served daily at 6 PM in-season (mid-May through October and weekends in November).

There are 12 rooms, including two suites

Jed Prouty Motor Inn

Main Street, P.O. Box 826, Bucksport, Maine 04416

The Best Western Jed Prouty Motor Inn is located on the riverbank of the Penobscot River, overlooking historic Fort Knox State Park, and the Waldo Hancock suspension bridge. The Inn's waterfront rooms boast a picturesque "million dollar" view, which provides a relaxing and entertaining treat for our guests.

——————— *For Reservations, Call* ———————

1-207-469-3113   1-800-528-1234

and five with working fireplaces. All are large enough to incorporate writing desks. Perhaps you'll use it to chronicle your day's explorations or to copy a recipe from the inn's candle-lighted, gourmet restaurant recently featured on a public television special (see our Restaurants chapter).

New in 1997 was a luxury suite with a four-posted bed, cathedral ceiling, fireplace, kitchen with adjoining sitting area, and private deck overlooking the landscaped gardens.

Perhaps it's because the Blue Hill Inn is known as a romantic getaway that children younger than 13 — the age of Romeo and Juliet, no? — are not recommended.

John Peters Inn

$$$ • Peters Point, E. Blue Hill Rd., Blue Hill • 374-2116

Set high on a hill above Blue Hill Harbor, the white-columned, brick facade of the John Peters Inn seems almost formidable. Don't be put off — it belies an extremely relaxed, friendly, kitchen-centered atmosphere within.

There are 14 airy rooms in two buildings for adults and children older than 12. The beds are covered in lace, and fresh flowers accentuate the summer joy of this place. The four rooms in the carriage house have private extensions for outgoing calls. These rooms as well as five of the rooms in the main house

have fireplaces. Two rooms are handicapped-accessible via a portable ramp. Call ahead if you need accessibility.

You'll probably want to spend a day exploring the peninsula; then again, after the morning's famous lobster omelette (a favorite among the inn's 14 daily breakfast choices), you might just want to stay put and enjoy the elegant earthiness of this large inn. Pick out a tune on the baby grand piano or find a book in the library and cozy up — inside or out — for a delicious read. Idle away hours watching the boats on the harbor — or go there yourself aboard the inn's canoe or sailboat. There's also an unheated pool on the premises as well as a gorgeous flower garden waving with color. This is a warm-weather inn, open May 1 through October 31.

Surry Inn

$$ • Maine Hwy. 172, Surry • 667-5091, (800) 742-3414

The expansive common rooms downstairs define the Surry Inn as an inviting, cozy country inn, situated on oddly named Contention Cove. Begin your day with breakfast and perhaps a bracing swim in the cove. Explore in the inn's canoe or rowboat, indulge in a game of horseshoes, or simply watch the world go by from a wicker rocker on the expansive porch. Should you visit in winter, you might prefer to snuggle beside the fire with a good book in hand. Come evening, watch the sun set over the cove, then stay for dinner.

There are 13 simple, airy guest rooms, with white or pale paint accentuated by stencils. Five of the rooms are in a cottage on the premises. Eleven rooms have private baths; the other two share a bath. Children older than 5 are welcome. There is one room with limited handicapped accessibility.

Bucks Harbor Inn
$ • Maine Hwy. 176 and Steamboat Wharf Rd., South Brooksville • 326-8660

Set off from the road by a broad lawn, the Bucks Harbor Inn resembles an old Maine farmhouse, though it originally was built as an annex to another inn that has since closed. It stands at a tiny crossroads that barely constitutes a village but positively hums with activity in summer. Beyond the inn's own croquet lawn is The Bucks Harbor Yacht Club (check out the Thursday night square dances) and the gourmet Landings Restaurant. An equal draw is Condon's Garage, catty-corner from the inn. The garage, even the crossroads, barely have changed from when Robert McCloskey drew them in *One Morning in Maine* (see our Maine Experience chapter).

Not much changes in this town, according to innkeeper Ann Ebeling, and not much else happens, which is why it's become such a popular summer place. Watch out; you might meet your New York business partner at the general store.

Downstairs, the inn rambles in the manner of casual farmhouses. Upstairs are the inn's six light-drenched, simply decorated rooms. All share baths. There are views of the water from the third-floor sitting room. Some rooms look out to Betsy's Cove behind.

Pets — without fleas, please — are welcome off-season.

Eggemoggin Reach Bed & Breakfast
$$$ • The Herrick Rd., South Brooksville • 359-5073

From the terrace of the modern Eggemoggin Reach Bed & Breakfast, ledges cascade down to Eggemoggin Reach, a broad, river-like body of water that separates Blue Hill from Deer Isle. (The Reach is a favorite cruising spot for summer sailors.) Susie and Michael Canon chose the spot for its imposing view of the Pumpkin Island Light on a ledge off Little Deer Isle. After building a post-and-beam summer house in the style of traditional Maine summer cottages, the Canons decided to move in year round. The bed and breakfast is the result.

Walk down the steep rocks to find moorings and a dock; take hikes or a stroll along the shore; explore Blue Hill, Castine and Deer Isle; or head to Acadia National Park (within an hour's drive; see our Acadia National Park chapter for details). A canoe and rowboat are available for guests who wish to explore the surrounding waters.

The Canons have expanded the bed and breakfast since opening, and now offer 10 rooms in four buildings. Each room has a water view and private bath.

Families with teenage children, or couples who love spreading out, will enjoy the Wheelhouse Suite, which spans the inn's entire third floor and includes a king-size bed and two twin beds beneath the eaves.

For more secluded accommodations, try either the Port or Starboard Watch room — separate from the house but attached to each other. These modern rooms feature cathedral ceilings, kitchenettes, decks and wood-burning stoves.

The six rooms in the Bay Lodge are even larger, offering similar amenities, including decks or porches.

Finally, the Tuckaway Cottage offers a living room, full kitchen, bedroom and deck.

Smoking is allowed on porches. Children 12 and older are welcome. Ask about minimum stays. The B&B is open May 15 through Columbus Day.

Oakland House
$$$-$$$$, no credit cards • The Herrick Rd., Brooksville • 359-8521, (800) 359-RELAX

Those who wish to return to summer camp; to stay in a cabin in the woods between lake and sea; to boat, swim, hike or explore by day and return to share exploits with friends at night . . . this is your place. Those who wish to stay in a comfortable inn by the sea, surrounded by cottage-style, period furniture . . . this is your place too.

Oakland House was not created — it evolved. More a tradition than an inn, the Oakland House began more than 100 years ago when people came to stay in an upstairs lodge as part of a Maine farm vacation. In 1889, it became an official inn. That building, known as the Oakland House, currently houses the dining rooms and offices. Guests stay in any one of 18 cabins, which sleep from two to nine people; or they stay at the recently renovated Shore Oaks, the 10-bedroom inn open year round.

The nature of the cabins vary. Some are quite rustic, with bead-board walls, plain beds and a shower stall but no bathtub. (Remember your cabin at camp?) Others have amenities such as fireplaces or wood-burning stoves, kitchens, decks and tubs. Some are a century old; the most recent was built in the 1970s.

The Shore Oaks Inn has the airy feel of a summer cottage. Sensitive renovations have left old fixtures intact, with the delights of hot and cold running salt and fresh water (from the days when salt water was a health cure) — but don't expect to actually get salt water. Plumbing does not take kindly to brine. Rooms are simply decorated with bold quilts and coverlets, so rock, woods and sea dominate.

Wherever you stay, you'll be greeted by Jim and Sally Littlefield, members of the same family that started this domain, taking advantage of a glorious location on Eggemoggin Reach, between the Deer Isle Bridge and plump Pumpkin Island Light. They offer some boats and some moorings, in case you want to rent a larger boat.

Oakland House allows smoking in the cottages, not in the inn. Dogs may stay in some cottages (for a fee), but they must be on a leash. Some cottages have phones, many don't, and only two have televisions. Handicapped access is limited.

Plan to reserve early. Repeat customers fill the place quickly. In-season, minimum stays are one week, although there are times when a cabin is available for a shorter stay. The cottages are open from early May through late October; the inn is open year round, with some exceptions. The price-code range reflects bed and breakfast accommodations at the Shore Oaks Inn, but most people make this a vacation home, staying for at least a week and take breakfast and dinner at the Oakland House restaurant.

Inn at Ferry Landing
$$-$$$ • 108 Old Ferry Rd., Deer Isle • 348-7760

Turn left onto Old Ferry Road as you leave the rock causeway and drive from Little Deer Isle onto Deer Isle. At the end of the road, almost literally, stands the Inn at Ferry Landing, where the Deer Isle ferry used to cross before the Deer Isle Bridge was built in 1939. The bridge, of course, meant a lot to Deer Isle, which previously was rather isolated in winter (the Eggemoggin Reach would freeze in the manner that salt water frequently does). As one local elderly woman recalls, "It was loose, you know, almost spongy." She can remember her uncle driving across the frozen surface, gunning the motor to make the mile-long passage as quickly as possible.

Jean and Gerald Wheeler recently bought the six-room inn. "And we intend to be here forever," declares Jean, who adds that she's already well-known for swimming in the icy waters of the bay under most conditions. Gerald has made a name for himself locally as music director of the Episcopal Church across the reach in Blue Hill, hence the two Steinway pianos in the living room, which doubles as the inn's common room.

Guests enjoy exploring Deer Isle and Stonington (at the other end of the island) and love tracking down the many craftspeople attracted by the nearby summer craft school, Haystack Mountain School of Crafts (see our related "Deer Isle's Crafters" Close-up in Shopping). Also nearby are hiking paths, the winding roads of Blue Hill and boating opportunities of all kinds. You can even make a daytrip to Acadia National Park (see our Acadia National Park chapter for details).

Inside the main building are four rooms, all with private baths, and children older than 10 are welcome here. The annex has two rooms filled with games and toys — perfect for younger children. Usually, the annex, which sleeps seven, is rented by the week in-season.

Rooms in both the inn and annex have

Windjammers

It's one thing to gaze at the water from your room. It's another to be rocked to sleep by willowy waves night after night, or to watch the sun rise over Isle au Haut and set over the Camden Hills, casting rosy and golden rays over the still waters of Penobscot Bay.

Experience it for yourself for three to six nights at a time courtesy of Maine's windjammer cruises. The boat becomes your home and your source of adventure as it takes you and four to 38 other passengers — depending on the vessel — from island to island, through fog, wind and, sometimes, rain.

Be prepared for exposure on a windjammer cruise. Bring warm clothing and rain gear. You'll learn to rock with the waves, to call a bathroom a "head," and to take your turn sharing the two or three heads and one or two showers per vessel with other passengers. While some vessels have double beds, others offer only twin berths, so be sure to inquire about specifics. If you're traveling alone, you might find yourself with a roommate.

While accommodations can be a bit rougher than what you'd find on land, the food is not. Vessels outdo each other with their gourmet cuisine.

Also be prepared for time. Bring a sketchbook, a journal, your favorite game and plenty of reading material. A windjammer cruise is a leisurely vacation. You'll spend your time reading, thinking and looking for porpoises, seals and the occasional whale, all the while delighting in the ever-changing vistas. When not satiating your eyes, you'll be satiating your palate, chatting with other passengers and, if you wish, helping to hoist the sails and winch up the anchor.

You'll sail during the day, anchor at night and have time to stretch your legs and explore the rocky groves of Maine's offshore islands. Generally, one night of each trip is given over to an old-fashioned lobster bake — your lobster will be wrapped in salty seaweed and steamed in a sand pit. There's nothing like it.

While some windjammers are old wooden vessels with no engines (they'll be pushed, when necessary, by a yawl boat, a skiff with its own engine), others are modern replicas. Unless otherwise noted, they carry two masts. Some cruises offer themes such as hiking, painting or folk singing. Most join various schooner events on certain weeks during the summer, like races in Penobscot Bay and a folk festival on Swan's Island.

We list 15 schooners with their high-season (July and August) rates, which are per person. Remember, however, that meals and transportation (once you step on board, that is) are included. Also remember that most vessels can't take young children; call for specific policies. The cruising season for most vessels runs from Memorial Day to Columbus Day.

One more note: 10 of the following windjammers are organized into the Maine Windjammer Association; call (800) 807-WIND to receive an array of brochures.

American Eagle
North End Shipyard, Rockland • 594-8007, (800) 648-4544

Built in 1930, the *American Eagle* was originally a fishing schooner out of Gloucester, Massachusetts. Maybe that's why one trip each summer travels down to Gloucester for the schooner races there. The *American Eagle* is listed in the National Register of

— continued on next page

Historic Landmarks. The vessel carries 28 passengers 12 and older on a 92-foot-long deck for six days. There are 14 double cabins, some with double beds, as well as two heads and one shower. This captain loves to read stories to his guests. Expect to spend $715 a person in high season.

When the warm summer season arrives, so do the windjammer sailing boats along the Maine coast.

Photo: Bangor Daily News

Angelique
Head of the Harbor, Camden • 236-8873, (800) 282-9989

The *Angelique's* russet sails unfurl for vacations of three, four and six days. This lengthy modern vessel — 95 feet — with three diesel engines was built in 1980. On board you'll find two showers and three heads for 31 passengers 16 and older. You'll also find one specialty cruise with an artist and photographer on board. There's also a piano, and guitars and other instruments are most welcome. Passage is $710 a person for a weeklong cruise, more for the specialty cruise.

Grace Bailey
Town Landing, Camden • 236-2938, (800) 736-7981

Built in 1882, the schooner *Grace Bailey* originally carried hard pine from South Carolina and Georgia to Patchogue, New York, where Edwin Bailey had a lumber mill. Grace was Bailey's daughter, born in 1882. Later the *Grace Bailey* sailed to the West Indies, and still later, as the Mattie (Grace's favorite niece), she carried Maine granite to New York to be used in the construction of Grand Central Station and the New York Post Office. Now, the *Grace Bailey* is a registered National Historic Landmark. With 81 feet of deck, she carries 29 passengers and one piano, which is stored in the after cabin. She sails for six days a time for $745 a person 12 and older.

Heritage
North End Shipyard, Rockland • 594-8007, (800) 648-4544

The *Heritage* is a modern, 94-foot-long engine-less vessel, built in 1983 to carry 30 passengers. She has topsails, which are the high-flying shorter sails that fly above the larger lower sails. The *Heritage* sails on six-day cruises mostly, but occasionally takes four-day cruises. This vessel has three public heads and two cabins with private heads. There's one shower. A six-day cruise costs $715 a person 12 and older.

Isaac H. Evans
North End Shipyard, Rockland • 594-8007, (800) 648-4544

Built in 1886 as an oyster dredge boat, the *Isaac H. Evans* is a registered National Historic Landmark, carrying 20 passengers on a deck 64.5 feet long. A topsail flies over the mainsail. She sails for three-, four- and six-day cruises, all without an inboard engine. The captain plays music and does some storytelling. All cabins sleep two, and some have double beds. There is one shower. The *Isaac H. Evans* also offers

— continued on next page

three-day family cruises on which children as young as 8 can sail. A typical six-day cruise is $715 a person.

J & E Riggin
Journey's End Marina, Rockland • 594-1875, (800) 869-0604

This 70-year-old former Delaware oyster dredger is under new ownership for 1998. While plans are to focus on its food (one owner is a chef), the captain of the boat plays guitar and concertina, so expect plenty of rollicking music as well. The boat, which has two heads and one shower, is a registered National Historic Landmark. She is 90 feet long on deck and sails with 26 guests 14 and older. Plan to spend about $720 a person for a six-day cruise.

Lewis R. French
Head of Harbor, Camden • 236-9411, (800) 469-4635

Launched in 1871, the *Lewis R. French* is the oldest vessel in the windjammer fleet. It once carried lumber, firewood, bricks, granite, fish, lime and Christmas trees. Today it carries 22 passengers 16 and older on its 65-foot-long deck. This schooner sports topsails, the smaller sails that fly above the large mainsails. There are four single cabins, two heads and one shower. The *Lewis R. French* sails for three- and six-day trips. Expect to pay $725 a person for six days.

Mary Day
Head of Harbor, Camden • 236-2750, (800) 992-2218

The schooner *Mary Day* was built for passengers and launched in 1962, yet she still sails with romantic topsails. A fireplace and parlor organ might just increase the romance. She carries 30 passengers 15 and older on six-day cruises. The vessel is 90 feet long, but of shallow draft, so she can sneak into harbors other boats don't dare enter. The vessel has one shower on deck, two heads, 11 double cabins, two triples and two singles. Expect to pay about $725 a person.

Mercantile
Town Landing, Camden • 236-2938, (800) 736-7981

The two-masted schooner *Mercantile* was built in Deer Isle in 1916 to ship fish, granite and other cargo around Maine, and to bring wood to Rockport to fuel the town's lime kilns. The vessel is 80 feet long along the deck and carries 29 passengers 12 and older in 14 double cabins plus one single cabin. With russet sails and no motor, she looks quite the venerable vessel. The *Mercantile* sails for weekend and four-day trips. Expect to pay $545 a person for four days.

Mistress
Town Landing, Camden • 236-2938, (800) 736-7981

Built in 1960 on Deer Isle, the *Mistress* is used for shorter cruises of weekends and four days, as well as weeklong cruises. It's a smaller boat than other members of the fleet — 46 feet on deck — and carries only six passengers. You can go as a family (children of any age are welcome) or as a group of friends — or book a simple room and make your own friends on board. All cabins are private; each has its own lavatory and separate entrance to the deck. Passage is $560 a person for four days.

Nathaniel Bowditch
Journey's End Marina, Rockland • 273-4062, (800) 288-4098

The schooner *Nathaniel Bowditch* was built in 1922, in East Boothbay, as a private

— continued on next page

racing yacht. During World War II it was commissioned by the Navy as a coastal patrol boat. The vessel is 82 feet on deck and carries 24 guests 10 and older. The captain hails from Rangeley and is known for his storytelling acumen. The *Nathaniel Bowditch* flies topsails. There are 11 double cabins and two Pullman singles. Its one shower is on deck, and it has two heads. Six-day cruises cost $715 a person.

Stephen Taber
Windjammer Wharf, Rockland • 236-3520, (800) 999-7352

Built in 1871, the *Stephen Taber* is the oldest documented sailing vessel in continuous service. This motorless is 68 feet long on deck and carries its own fireplace and wood stove as well as 22 passengers 14 and older. There are two single cabins, eight doubles and a family cabin with four beds. As you sail, you can help on deck or in the kitchen, learning to bake using the wood-burning stove. The captain is also a bagpiper and guitarist, and you'll hear him playing the bagpipes as the vessel leaves Rockland. The six-day excursion on the *Stephen Taber* costs $745 a person.

Timberwind
Rockport Harbor, Rockport • 236-0801, (800) 759-9250

The schooner *Timberwind* was built in 1931 as a pilot schooner — a vessel that helped guide other vessels through the shoal-laden Maine waters. It was launched in Portland and has never left Maine waters. Some 20 passengers sail for three-, four- and six-day cruises ($659 a person for the latter). There are two triple cabins and seven doubles. The *Timberwind* offers family weekend cruises with children 5 and older, and these feature more time on shore. Other cruises are for passengers 16 or older. There are also sailing and hiking cruises, which also feature more land time. Bring your own musical instruments.

Victory Chimes
Journeys End Marina, Rockland • 594-0755, (800) 745-5651

You can't miss the *Victory Chimes* — it's the only three-masted schooner sailing from the region. This large vessel — 132 feet on deck — takes 40 guests for a weeklong ($715 a person) or four-day cruises. The vessel was built in Delaware of Georgia pine and launched in the Chesapeake Bay. In the 1950s it became a windjammer, but then was sold to Domino's Pizza and renamed *Domino Effect*. Now it's a windjammer again, with two showers, three cabins with private heads and four shared heads.

---

been restored and furnished with antiques. The annex features a sunroom and a suite with a wood stove, sunken tub and skylights. Expect water views beyond compare, complete with morning sunrise and evening sunset, and ask about occasional chamber concerts organized by Mr. Wheeler.

Pilgrim's Inn
$$-$$$ • The Sunset Rd. (Maine Hwy. 15A), Deer Isle Village • 348-6615

Built in Newburyport by Squire Ignatius Haskell for his bride, the purple-red clapboard house that is now the Pilgrim's Inn was the finest residence in Deer Isle in 1793, when Squire Haskell shipped it there to satisfy his more urbane wife.

It's still among the finest of Deer Isle homes. Upon entering the Pilgrim's Inn, we were immediately impressed by the low wooden beams, two 8-foot fireplaces, Dutch ovens and wide pumpkin pine floorboards — all of which give this place an unmistakably authentic feel.

Jean and Dud Hendrick bought the inn in 1982 and since have dedicated themselves to preserving its history. The inn, open from mid-

May through mid-October, offers 13 guest rooms (10 with private baths) and a separate vintage house — the same age as the inn — with two units open year round (for guests older than 10).

Some find Room No. 8 the most pleasant, with its stenciled pine furniture and antique hand-carved pine bed; others prefer No. 11, with its window seat and antique couch overlooking the mill pond. All rooms are cheery, with muted colonial colors, country antiques and braided rag rugs. Most have decorative fireplaces, and all have views of the water — either Northwest Harbor or the millpond that once served Squire Haskell's sawmill.

The Pilgrim's Inn offers B&B rates (as listed), but many take advantage of the inn's gourmet dining room (a.k.a. Pilgrim's Inn), one of Maine's noted restaurants (see our Restaurants chapter). The inn offers limited accessibility for the handicapped.

Goose Cove Lodge

$$$$ • Goose Cove Rd., Sunset
• 348-2508, (800) 728-1963 (reservations only)

Years ago, naturalist Dr. Ralph Waldron built a log cabin on Goose Cove, carved out hiking trails and stocked the library with a winter's worth of books. The library and trails remain as originally designed; the log cabin has been expanded four times, and more cabins have been built throughout the woods. The first of Waldron's guests came in 1949, and many keep coming back.

Guests come for the expansive view of the cove through the huge picture window. They come for family-friendly activities, numerous hiking trails, the tiny barred island that's accessible during low tide, the canoes and kayaks available for guests (there's a sailboat too, but you must rent that), the surprises in the woods and quiet afternoons reading by the fire. They also come for the food, which draws sighs of memory. (See our Restaurants chapter.)

Accommodations are comfortable but rustic, except for the two new luxury cottages with sun decks and fine furnishings. Other lodgings include cabins, attached cabins, two annexes and rooms at the main lodge. Most have water views and fireplaces or wood-burn-

ing stoves. Some, such as Linnea, with its stone fireplace and wraparound deck, stand close to the shore and afford unobstructed views of the many islands of Penobscot Bay.

The lodge is open from mid-May through mid-October; the luxury cottages are open year round but without services. In-season, all room rates include dinner; bed and breakfast rates apply off-season. Two-day minimum stays apply during peak summer season, though occasionally rooms come available due to last-minute cancellations.

Children are welcome here; there are even special evening programs geared for them. There is no television at the lodge. Instead, guests enjoy after-dinner entertainment — a movie, talk or slide show offered by guests — during high season.

Inn on the Harbor

$$-$$$ • Main St., Stonington
• 367-2420, (800) 942-2420

Despite a recent influx of tourists, Stonington is still a quintessential fishing town, with lobstermen rumbling their engines at 4 AM in summer. A big summer event is the lobster boat races in early August (see Annual Events).

Stonington also was once a quarrying town, known for its distinctive pink granite. (The quarry at nearby Crotch Island recently reopened; workers cut and remove glass-thin granite veneer.) Evidence of the quarrying era includes the granite blocks that support harbor buildings and the huge, green Opera House that at one time featured opera to entertain the stonecutters, many of whom were Italian immigrants.

The Inn on the Harbor, formerly known as the Captain's Quarters, overlooks the granite-walled harbor. Its four attached Victorian buildings feature new, huge decks. The views across the Deer Isle Thorofare to Merchant's Row are spectacular. (Though many a merchant has plied the waters around Stonington, the row and its island were named for the Merchant family.)

There are 13 rooms at the inn, each named after one of the windjammers that frequently pass among the islands beyond. There are sitting areas in every room and a view of the ocean from most. You'll find televisions, telephones and binoculars for in-room entertainment. There

Photo: Bangor Daily News

Castine harbor in summer is a less-crowded harbor for pleasure craft.

is one handicapped-accessible room. The decks overlooking the ocean are a bit too hazardous for young children; teens, however, are encouraged to stay here. The inn is open April 1 through New Year's. Ask about off-season specials and about the inn's espresso bar.

Pres du Port
$$, no credit cards • W. Main St. and Highland Ave., Stonington • 367-5007

Charlotte Casgrain spent 35 years as a French teacher in Connecticut but even more years coming to Stonington. In the late 1980s, she bought a home with an imposing view of Merchant's Row, right near the port — Pres du Port. She's been opening it up to guests for the summer months. Now that she's retired, her casual, offbeat lodge stays open from May to November.

Each of Charlotte's three guest rooms has a French name. Two rooms have telephones, but only one has a private bath. There's Beau Vivage (beautiful view) on a private entrance to her deck. Beau Ciel (beautiful sky) has a partial view of Stonington Harbor, with walls of pale blue and painted clouds. Other rooms in the house are painted cobalt blue, fuchsia or orange. There's also a cottage with full bath across the street where pets (with responsible owners) are allowed, and a tent site for responsible campers (who have full use of house facilities) atop a rock in the extensive garden.

Charlotte serves a buffet breakfast on a large glassed-in porch overlooking the harbor; a library full of books about Maine's geology, islands, wildflowers and birds (and many comfortable places to enjoy them); a cupboard of toys for children; and an outdoor Jacuzzi with a full view of the islands of Merchant's Row.

The Keeper's House
$$$$$, no credit cards • Lighthouse Rd., Isle au Haut • 367-2261

Much more than an inn, The Keeper's

House is an experience — possibly a hallowed one at that. It begins the moment you leave Stonington. To get to the Keeper's House, on Isle au Haut, you must take a boat. Most folks take the mail boat, an old functional vessel that chugs through one of the most glorious passages along a coast known for breathtaking beauty.

The boat docks at the inn, where you'll step back in time to a world without electricity.

This lodging has six rooms altogether, each furnished comfortably, not luxuriously, in painted antiques. The four in the Keeper's House share two baths. There are also two rooms in separate buildings. One, called the Oil House, is known as the honeymoon cottage for its seclusion, views and decks if not for its facilities, which include an outhouse.

The Garret Room, on the third floor, is the largest. It has an ocean view from two windows. On the second floor, the Keeper's Room is decorated in shades of pink and has a view of the 1907 lighthouse. (This really was a lighthouse keeper's house: The keeper needed to see the light at all hours of the night to be sure it was burning.)

Innkeepers Jeff and Judi Burke turned the house into a seasonal bed and breakfast (open mid-May through October) about 10 years ago. In addition to breakfast, they offer candlelight dinners and a box lunch, all included in the room rates, since this island of fishing folk and summer people has no other restaurants. What the island does have is utter seclusion. A portion of the island is filled with Victorian homes and more elaborate summer abodes; another portion is left to the weather-beaten wilderness cliffs of Acadia National Park (see our Acadia National Park chapter).

With borrowed bikes (available to guests), you can easily get to the park and explore Isle au Haut ("high island") from coast to coast.

Children are welcome at this establishment.

The Crocker House Country Inn
$$$ • Hancock Point Rd., Hancock
• 422-6806

Less than 10 miles from Ellsworth is the rugged, undeveloped landscape of Down East. That's not to say the area isn't also beautifully lush in summer. In fact, Hancock was the site of an old summer community; it's quiet, even private.

The Crocker House Country Inn was built as an annex to a large hotel in 1884, when this lazy community was as bustling with visitors as Bar Harbor is now. The Crocker House remains. Its 11 rooms (each with private bath) have been redecorated but in no particular theme except cozy comfort marked by country antiques. A carriage house offers a hot-tub spa, television and VCR. There's one handicapped-accessible room.

Walk around the old summer community, visit the octagonal library, marvel at the Hancock Point Post Office (open summers), which at 144 square feet might be the smallest operating post office in the United States. Or, get in your car to explore Schoodic Point, farther Down East or Mount Desert Island.

Dinner is served nightly (see our Restaurants chapter). Smoking is allowed in the bedrooms. In-room phones are available for outgoing calls only. Pets are welcome at this inn, which is open from late April through New Year's Day.

Le Domaine Restaurant and Inn
$$$ • off U.S. Hwy. 1, Hancock
• 422-3395, 422-3916, (800) 554-8498

Many come to Le Domaine for a gastronomic experience. The owners of the inn are descendants of a French family from Les Baux, site of some of the best restaurants in France (see Restaurants for details). Stay here, enjoy the region, come home for dinner, then stagger to your bed.

The seven rooms (each named for an herb) in this very French home are filled with small offerings such as books, bath soaps and fresh fruit. We like the Rosemary Room, one of four with a garden deck. Some rooms include air-conditioners; all have private baths and floral decor.

While food is the calling card, there's plenty to do aside from eating. The inn is set on 100 acres. Stroll through the gardens, wander down the back path to a small trout pond, visit the Pierre Monteux School for Conductors (see Arts) down the road and take in a summer concert, or drive up to Bartlett's Winery (see Shopping), on U.S. Highway 1 past Gouldsboro. Of course, there's also Taunton

Kimball Terrace Inn & Main Sail Restaurant

Northeast Harbor's Finest...

Overlooking Mt. Desert Island's most picturesque harbor, lies a quiet treasure, the Kimball Terrace Inn. Enjoy the wonders of Acadia National Park. Walk to our village shops. Golf and tennis are nearby. Cool off in our pool, or enjoy a cocktail on the patio or in the lounge. Enjoy dinner at the Main Sail Restaurant. Our spacious rooms have patios or balconies and beautiful views of Northeast Harbor and the Northeast Harbor Marina.

Kimball Terrace Inn, Huntington Road, Northeast Harbor, ME 04662
1-800-454-6225• 207-276-3383•Fax 207-276-4102•www.acadia/kimball

Bay to enjoy, and neither the Mount Desert Island (Bar Harbor is a 40-minute drive) nor Schoodic Point area of Acadia National Park (a 30-minute drive) is very far. (See our Acadia National Park chapter for more information.)

The inn is open from early June to mid-October. Children older than 5 are welcome. Smoking is allowed in designated areas. Pets are allowed under the discretion of the management. The listed rate is for bed and breakfast only, though most guests prefer to stay on the Modified American Plan to enjoy innkeeper Nicole Purslow's renowned dinners.

Island View Inn
$$ • U.S. Hwy. 1, Sullivan • 422-3031

Six rooms and lots of public space allow visitors to feel at home in the Island View Inn, on Sullivan Harbor in a turn-of-the-century summer cottage. Many rooms have balconies with spectacular water views, all have private baths, and there's a fireplace in the common room.

Sullivan is one of Maine's well-kept secrets.

Mount Desert Island is in sight, but you're away from the hordes. This is truly the quiet side.

Settle in and enjoy the view from the porch, or from one of three rooms with water views; walk the beach; or ask about hikes, the canoe and rowboat for loan, or the 18-foot sailboat for rent to experienced sailors.

The inn is open from Memorial Day weekend until mid-October. Well-behaved children are welcome. Smoking is limited.

Sullivan Harbor Farm
$$ • U.S. Hwy. 1, Sullivan • 422-3735

Where the road hugs Sullivan Harbor, you'll find Sullivan Harbor Farm, a small bed and breakfast built in an 1820s home. Settle on the enclosed porch for breakfast and gaze out at Mount Desert Island. Take one of the inn's canoes or kayaks out into the bay to enjoy an even closer view of the islands, mountains and bay. Then come back to the library, and read a bit about the natural history of the area.

Two of the inn's rooms have views overlooking the bay, and three have private baths. At breakfast, be sure to sample the specialty of the house, Sullivan Harbor Farm's smoked salmon — the same salmon served at Legal Seafood in Boston, the Ritz Carlton in Boston and Phoenix, and Palm Restaurant locations nationwide (see our Shopping chapter).

Larger groups and families might want to ask about the farm's two cottages, complete with kitchen facilities. The inn is open year round, though during the cold of winter, innkeepers Joel Frantzman and Leslie Harlow may take some vacation time; call ahead. Smoking is allowed outside.

Bluff House Inn & Restaurant
$-$$ • Maine Hwy. 186, South
Gouldsboro • 963-7805

People charter boats to enjoy this view: From the Bluff House you can look across Frenchman Bay to the mountains of Acadia National Park. All eight rooms here are on the second floor. The bottom floor, with its lounge and fireplace, is original.

South Gouldsboro is but a few miles from Schoodic Peninsula, where a small section of Acadia National Park is located. From here, you can kayak, canoe, hike, bike or ski. Most of the gear for most activities can be rented nearby. Or, simply bring a stash of books and relax in front of one of the most awesome views in Maine. Though no pets are allowed, kennels are nearby. There's also a BYOB restaurant open to lodge guests by reservation. A continental breakfast is offered as part of the room rate.

Sunset House Bed & Breakfast
Maine Hwy. 186, West Gouldsboro
• 963-7156, (800) 233-7156

Sometimes, in coastal Maine, you might feel like complaining: "Water, water everywhere, but nary a place to swim." Not here. Sunset House Bed & Breakfast is not only close to the ocean, but also right on a 3.5-mile-long freshwater pond, where swimming is not only delightful, but also quite warm.

Sunset House is also just a few miles from Moose Look Guide Service, which rents bicycles, canoes and kayaks.

Kathy and Carl Johnson (he's an executive chef by trade) welcome guests to this lovely inn with six guest rooms — three with private baths, three shared. It's open year round. Children 4 and older are welcome. Smoking is not.

The Black Duck Inn on Corea Harbor
$$ • Crowley Island Rd., Corea
• 963-2689

On a peninsula off the Schoodic Peninsula, Corea is one of Maine's most charming fishing villages. An absolutely secluded harbor hugs the town.

The Black Duck Inn on Corea Harbor offers four guest rooms in an old, rambling fisherman's house built in 1890 and added to ever since, most recently in 1996. Two rooms have private baths. One room has limited handicapped access. There are also two cabins nearby.

Children younger than 1 or older than 7 are welcome here. It's the grabbing, knocking-over age the innkeepers worry about because the inn is furnished with an eclectic array of antiques (including antique toys) and contemporary art.

Each room is different. Room A has a sitting room with a sleigh bed and lace curtains framing a water view. Room D has a woodsy cottage feel. The cabins, closed in winter, are on the water.

Corea is a private place; there's little to do except marvel and live. You'll have to leave town for dinner, but it's worth it for the inn's serenity and authenticity. Corea nourished painter and poet Marsden Hartley, who spent his last summers painting upstairs in the

---

INSIDERS' TIP

High season on the Mid-Coast begins anywhere from Memorial Day to the Fourth of July and usually ends on Labor Day. But because fall is so lovely here — clear, crisp days and flaming leaf colors — some establishments maintain in-season rates through Columbus Day.

steeple of a church on Maine Highway 195. It also nourished Amy Clampitt (see our Maine Experience chapter), who spent her last summers writing poetry here.

Plan to rest awhile on the large waterfront deck, or wander the 12 acres of berry-laden land that run to the harbor at one end and to an inlet off Gouldsboro Bay at the other. Discover the inspiration of land and sea.

Mount Desert Island

Acadia Hotel
$$ • 20 Mt. Desert St., Bar Harbor • 288-5721

In an 1884 Victorian building, almost on the edge of Acadia National Park and right in the heart of Bar Harbor, the Acadia Hotel offers comfortable, casual lodgings that won't drain your coffers. There are 10 sizable rooms decorated with floral-pattern wallpaper and plush modern bedcovers; each has a television and air-conditioning, but no telephone; some have Jacuzzis.

There's an optional breakfast offered through a local bakery, otherwise you're on your own to pick and choose among the numerous, inviting offerings in Bar Harbor for a morning meal. (See our Restaurants chapter for suggestions.)

Balance Rock Inn
$$$$$ • 21 Albert Meadow, Bar Harbor • 288-2610, (800) 753-0494

At this elegant, oceanside retreat, you'll feel like an invited guest at one of the finest homes from the bygone era of gilded cottages.

Balance Rock Inn was built in 1903 as a summer home for Scottish railroad tycoon Alexander Maitland. The shingle-style mansion is beyond Main Street, on a quiet lane that ends at the ocean. In the adjoining lot — wooded now — are remnants of the pink granite foundation of the home where Nelson Rockefeller was born.

The inn retains all the magnificence of the old mansion. Most of the 21 rooms have views across a stately lawn to the wide ocean dotted with the islands of Frenchman Bay. Several rooms have porches. The furnishings are classic, with canopied beds and fireplaces, yet you'll also find modern conveniences such as air conditioners and whirlpool baths (in many rooms) and saunas (in some). All rooms have televisions and phones.

Well-behaved children 4 and older are welcome at this seasonal inn, which is open from early May through late October. Enjoy afternoon tea and a swim in the outdoor heated pool. There is one handicapped-accessible apartment that's separate from the cottage. Smoking is allowed in some rooms. Pets are welcome.

Bar Harbor Hotel – Bluenose Inn
$$$$-$$$$$ • 90 Eden St., Bar Harbor • 288-3348, (800) 445-4077

The view here encompasses so much of Frenchman Bay, you'll feel almost as if you were atop Cadillac Mountain.

There's quite a story to this hotel. A fire leveled it in 1994. The owners pitched right in to rebuild it, setting up an air-filled bubble so workers could continue throughout the frigid winter to build the 52-room Mizzentop, set on the stone foundation where the old summer cottage, its namesake, once sat.

The Mizzentop is the luxury hotel, with a bar and gift shop, double sinks in each room, balconies and unrestricted water views. Stenna Nordica is the motor inn. All 45 of its rooms have water views, though some are restricted. The Rose Garden restaurant is in yet another building, along with the indoor pool.

Enjoy the amenities of a hotel, such as a spa, fitness center, room service, air-conditioning, phones, color cable television with HBO, mini refrigerators and coffee makers in each room. There are two heated pools on the premises — one indoors and one outdoors.

Smoking is permitted on the Mizzentop balconies only. The Mizzentop has one room that is completely handicapped-accessible, including a roll-in shower and bathroom handrails.

Breakfast is not necessarily included in the room rate. Ask about packages including breakfast, dinner and area activities. The hotel is open from early May through late October.

Bar Harbor Inn
$$$$ • Newport Dr., Bar Harbor • 288-3351, (800) 248-3351

More than an inn, this is a compound on nearly 8 acres right in the heart of Bar Harbor, on Frenchman Bay. So it's not without good reason that this inn calls itself an "oceanfront resort."

There are 153 rooms in three different buildings — the Main Inn, the Oceanfront Lodge and the Newport Building. Two-thirds of the rooms have water views, and many also have balconies from which you can watch the sun rise. Once the sun has risen, turn to your inn-side door and find a newspaper waiting outside.

All rooms offer air-conditioning, phones and televisions with HBO, and many have newspaper delivery. Enjoy the heated outdoor pool, spa and afternoon coffee or lemonade and cookies. Children can play on the swing set.

The Main Inn is a classic-looking building with white-trimmed porch, large lobby and fireplace. Here, in a semicircular room overlooking the bay, you'll find the Reading Room Restaurant, a favorite in Bar Harbor (see our Restaurants chapter).

The Oceanfront Lodge was built for oceanfront views. The newer Newport Building is set back a bit. There are as many as 20 different kinds of rooms, some of which are handicapped-accessible, so sound out the receptionist when you call for a reservation.

Bar Harbor Inn offers an expanded continental breakfast and special packages that include park activities or various boat trips. Smoking and nonsmoking rooms are available, but public areas are smoke-free. Three rooms are available for pets.

The inn is right behind Main Street, on a little road that ambles beside the harbor. Though most of the buildings are relatively modern, the architectural integrity of the Main Inn, along with the grandeur and spaciousness of the compound, reflect the old schooner days. This impression is echoed by the four-masted schooner that docks at the inn's private pier.

Expect the inn to stay open until the snow flies. Call for exact dates.

Bass Cottage in the Field
$-$$, no credit cards • The Field, Bar Harbor • 288-3705

On a small private road, behind the bustle of Main Street, Jean Turner has opened her cottage to guests just as her mother did before her. The Bass Cottage has been an inn for 70 years. The Oriental carpets are well-worn, and the ottoman is draped just as it might have been during the Roaring '20s heyday of socialite Bar Harbor.

This is the real thing — an old cottage where the moods are preserved as if they were ingrained in the amber of the stained-glass windows.

The gracious Ms. Turner does her best to make everyone happy and comfortable. The 10 rooms (six with baths) are bright but spare, with stamped metal ceilings and old bathroom fixtures. They are open from Memorial Day until Columbus Day. The large, glass-enclosed porch is a great spot to relax.

Morning coffee or tea is served daily, but no breakfast. There are no in-room phones or televisions, but never mind; these accommodations are unusually inexpensive for Bar Harbor. Children are welcome if they're past the midnight crying stage.

Bayview Inn
$$$$-$$$$$ • 111 Eden St., Bar Harbor • 288-5861, (800) 356-3585

Open the floor-to-ceiling windows in your room at the Bayview and you will hear the ocean lapping below. Stand for a while beside the entry gate; you'll be mesmerized by the sound.

This relatively young complex is open mid-May through late October with three options for visitors.

The hotel, which was built in the 1980s, offers 26 rooms — all with ocean views. There is one floor of handicapped-accessible rooms here. Three rooms are available for smokers.

There are also six rooms in the white brick inn, which was once the private estate of Maj. George G. McMurtry, one of Teddy Roosevelt's Rough Riders in the Spanish American War. McMurtry, who achieved the Medal of Honor for his actions in World War I, built the home in 1930. Later, he sold it to the Davis family, along with all his antiques, paintings and family memorabilia. The Davis's opened the inn to the public in 1983.

Also in the compound are six townhomes, each with either two or three bedrooms, available for a two-night minimum. The townhomes

offer kitchens, whirlpool baths, fireplaces and living and dining rooms. Children are welcome here and in the hotel.

All rooms at The Bayview have televisions and phones. Guests may enjoy the heated outdoor pool, an indoor exercise room and nearby tennis courts. Because the inn is a few miles outside Bar Harbor (close to the Blue Nose ferry terminal leading to Nova Scotia), a shuttle bus takes guests to town.

Briarfield Inn
$$$ • 60 Cottage St., Bar Harbor
• 288-5297, (800) 228-6660

Hang out for a few hours in a rocker on the porch of the Briarfield and you'll feel like a town citizen. Much passes by the porch of this funky, reasonably priced inn, which still retains something of the lazy air of the popular old watering hole it once was. Before then, however, it was the seat of elegance, owned by Evelyn Walsh McLean, who also once owned the Hope diamond. The building had gotten so run down that it was about to be demolished when school teacher (and current owner) Dana Geel rescued it. At the time, it had 12 bedrooms and 19 bathrooms.

Briarfield Inn still has 12 bedrooms, each with a private bath, many with canopied beds, most with air-conditioning and all with televi-

sions. One room has limited handicapped accessibility.

Using stained-glass windows from one old cottage and elegant wood from another, Dana assembled an unusual, eclectic home. Visit Room 12, with its own entrance, built entirely from the junk of a salvage heap. No, you wouldn't know it. . . . The old shelves, cabinets and bed boards have been pieced together and painted a purifying white. Even if there weren't a wine and cheese hour in the afternoons — or free mountain bikes — Briarfield would be one of the most reasonable places to stay in Bar Harbor. The free bikes, however, are older. You can rent a newer one for $10 a day.

On the premises, occupying the side porch, is the Elephant Museum. It's filled with everything from stuffed elephant toys and elephant teapots to miniature pachyderms carved on minuscule pieces of ivory.

Cleftstone Manor
$$$ • 92 Eden St. (Maine Hwy. 3), Bar Harbor • 288-4951

If heavy Victoriana is your style, then the Cleftstone Manor is your place. This seasonal cottage, open from late April through late October, is a bit outside town, just below the Bar Harbor Hotel and across the street from College of the Atlantic. Each of the 16 rooms is different, ranging from the heavily panelled honeymoon suite (a.k.a. the Romeo and Juliet) with a white canopied bed and love seat facing a fireplace to the relatively simple Canterbury room dressed in blue and rust tones.

Each morning, a breakfast buffet plus hot entrees are served in a breakfast room. Check out the massive wooden table that is too large for most people's living rooms but was once Joseph Pulitzer's writing desk. Afternoons, guests enjoy tea, lemonade and cookies, and each night, from 8 to 9 PM, they share the day's experiences over complimentary beverages and cheese. Children older than 8 are welcome at Cleftstone.

FYI

Unless otherwise noted, the area code for all phone numbers listed in this guide is 207.

Inn at Canoe Point
$$$$-$$$$$ • off Maine Hwy. 3, Bar Harbor • 288-9511

If you're not careful, you'll miss the subtle sign for the Inn at Canoe Point, which leads you down a winding hillside away from the bustle of the highway to a magical retreat at the shore of Frenchman Bay. Each turn in the drive frames a different view of a spot of woods beside the water; then, just where you might want to settle is an Adirondack chair, placed for your comfort.

After years of owning the Kingsleigh Inn in Southwest Harbor (see subsequent entry), Nancy and Tom Cervelli moved to Bar Harbor, purchasing this unusual inn and promising to change nothing.

The inn has only five guest rooms (each with private bath or shower), so you'll feel more like a resident of the island than a tourist here. Breakfast may be served on the porch, or in the Ocean Room, with its large fireplace and windows offering a 180-degree view of the water and woods.

A favorite room is the master suite, with a sitting area, gas fireplace and shared deck, and the Garden Room, surrounded on three sides by windows overlooking both water and forest.

This timber and stone inn is as romantic and elegant a place as you can hope for — just don't plan to bring children younger than 16.

Ivy Manor Inn
$$$-$$$$ • 194 Main St., Bar Harbor • 288-2138, (888) 670-1997

New to the scene in August 1997, the Ivy Manor Inn is a delightful, year-round inn with eight rooms, most with fireplaces and all with private baths. This 1940s-era Tudor-style home with a hint of Victoriana is right in the heart of Bar Harbor on Main Street, but set back from the bustle by a quiet garden. There's also a deck out back with more gardens where, come summer, you might enjoy your breakfast buffet of homemade granola, fresh fruit, Austrian pancakes and homemade pastries. Otherwise, you can eat inside by the fireplace. Smoking and pets are not allowed at the inn. The proprietors were considering a minimum age for child guests, but it had not been set at press time; call and ask.

Ledgelawn Inn
$$$-$$$$ • 66 Mount Desert St., Bar Harbor • 288-4596, (800) 274-5334

The Ledgelawn, with its wide porch, deep red shakes trimmed with white and gorgeous architecture, is one of the stalwart inns of Mount Desert Island. Designed by John Savage in 1904 for shoe manufacturer John Brigham, it is considered the last large summer house built on Mount Desert Street, a veritable showcase of gorgeous homes.

The stairway sweeps upward to 21 spacious rooms decorated with antiques and floral motifs. There are couches and/or chairs (perfect for settling in with a good book) as well as phones and televisions in each room. Some rooms have verandas. There's also a room with a whirlpool bath.

INSIDERS' TIP

You can get to Acadia National Park from many places along the Mid-Coast. Southwest Harbor is as close to the park's trails as Bar Harbor; and Ellsworth, Blue Hill and Gouldsboro are short drives away.

Children and pets are welcome; if you wish to smoke, it's preferred you do so in common areas or outside.

Twelve more rooms can be found in the Carriage House, which is newer but decorated in an antique style. Some rooms here have whirlpool baths, and one has a sauna.

Enjoy the wine and beer bar, the sun-bright breakfast porch and afternoon refreshments. Ledgelawn is open from early May through late October.

Manor House Inn
**$$$ • 106 West St., Bar Harbor
• 288-3759, (800) 437-0088**

Built in 1887 by a Col. James Foster, the Manor House became an inn in the 1950s and was placed on the National Register of Historic Places in 1980.

Each of the 14 large rooms has a different view of the many gardens surrounding this in-town establishment. You can leave your Victorian-decorated room, walk downtown for dinner, then return home to enjoy a good book beneath one of the bright in-room reading lights. A few rooms have fireplaces. You also will find some cottages behind the inn.

Afternoon refreshments are served, and the wraparound veranda is always busy with activity. Children 10 and older are welcome at this seasonal inn, which is open from mid-April through mid-November.

Maples Inn
**$$$ • 16 Roberts Ave., Bar Harbor
• 288-3443**

Innkeeper Susan Sinclair puts your name on the door and leaves a rolled up note on your bed to greet you upon arrival at her Maples Inn, a quiet haven on a pleasant, tree-lined side street in the heart of Bar Harbor.

The six rooms with private baths are simple and charming. What's special here are the details, such as the fluffy white bathrobes — after all, Sinclair, a former vice president at the Wells Fargo Bank in Fullerton, California, gives lessons in hospitable innkeeping. She says she named the inn for the smell, which was fragrant with maple. She has extended the arboreal motif to the names of her rooms.

A favorite room is the Red Oak, featuring nautical decor. It's known as "the treehouse" because of the myriad trees in view through the window. The view from this room, and from the compact English Holly, is of Cadillac Mountain. Another favorite is the White Birch Suite, which features a wood-burning stove. Breakfasts here are noteworthy: Susan's recipes have been featured in *Bon Appetit* and *Gourmet* magazines.

The Maples Inn welcomes children 8 and older. Ask about minimum stays.

Nannau-Seaside Bed & Breakfast
$$$ • 396 Main St., Bar Harbor
• 288-5575

In the woods and at the shore, off the beaten path but right at the edge of Acadia National Park, Nannau-Seaside Bed & Breakfast is at once peaceful, unpretentious and inviting.

The architecture of this 1904 cottage is shingle-style; it was built by the office of H.H. Richardson. The decor is eclectic, with a bent toward English floral wallpapers and wicker furnishings atop Oriental rugs.

There are five rooms in this quiet bed and breakfast inn, which is open from mid-spring through late fall and otherwise on occasional long weekends.

The second floor features an oceanfront room with a fireplace, a queen-size bed and a bay window with a distant view of the ocean. The soft colors are enhanced by the William Morris fabrics and wallpapers authentic to the original concept of the house.

Next door, alongside this rather quiet, almost forgotten part of the park, is the property once owned by George Dorr, the man who dedicated his life to the creation of Acadia.

Wander along the shore or through the gardens. Enjoy the popular kitchen garden where herbs, vegetables and fruit trees grow.

Owners Ron and Vikki Evers welcome children who are old enough to appreciate the serenity of a small bed and breakfast and ask that guests stay two nights (unless there's an unexpected vacancy).

Seacroft Inn
$$ • 18 Albert Meadow, Bar Harbor
• 288-4669, (800) 824-9694

Behind Main Street in Bar Harbor are a series of private lanes. Here elegance abuts simpler offerings. Seacroft Inn, down the road from the Balance Rock Inn (see previous entry), offers a tranquil location and basic accommodations in an old white cottage at a relatively low cost. The seven rooms each have plain, 1960s decor. Each room includes a television, refrigerator and microwave. Morning coffee is offered.

The Seacroft Inn is open year round.

Ullikana
$$$-$$$$ • 16 The Field, Bar Harbor
• 288-9552

There is a rosy glow to this quiet, charming inn, on a private lane behind Main Street. The very first summer cottage in Bar Harbor, it was built by Alpheus Hardy in 1885. He named it Ullikana, and people have guessed at its meaning ever since. Is it a Tahitian word? New Guinean? No two suggestions have been the same.

Of the inn's 10 rooms, some have views over the harbor, some have private terraces, and some have fireplaces. The rooms are furnished with brass beds, floral wall coverings and otherwise eclectic furniture. Room 3, with striped wallpaper, is among the quieter rooms. Room 6 offers a terrace looking out on Frenchman Bay.

Innkeepers Helene Harton and Roy Kasindorf are genuinely friendly. They collect antique claw-foot tubs; they also collect some fine contemporary art.

Breakfast frequently is served on the terrace. The inn is open from May to October. Children older than 8 are welcome.

Asticou Inn
$$$$$ • Maine Hwy. 3, Northeast Harbor
• 276-3344, (800) 258-3373

Come here to stay in a landmark. People remember the excitement surrounding lunch or tea at the old Asticou Inn when they were children. They remember getting dressed up in crinolines and white gloves and acting like gentlemen and ladies for great aunts and bachelor uncles.

The Asticou Inn might seem smaller when they make their return pilgrimage, but it is no less dear. They sense the mystery in the air from decades of parties and intrigue, laughter and tears.

This is one of the grand old lodges of Mount Desert Island. Overlooking the harbor at Northeast (one of the island's more posh, exclusive towns), the inn is MDI's standard of dignified luxury. There are 48 rooms, including five cottages and rooms at Cranberry Lodge across the street. All rooms have telephones, but no televisions. There is limited handicapped accessibility.

The accommodations are spacious, with

Photo: Bangor Daily News

The Blaine House mansion, named for a former Maine governor, is offered as the home for the state's chief executive. The colors are vibrant in the dining room when it is decorated for the Christmas season.

room to waltz around the white draped beds and painted floors. Those with water views are the largest; those with country views overlook the inn's driveway. A simple bed and breakfast plan is available for guests who don't prefer the Modified American Plan.

Walk across the street to visit the azalea gardens, take a stroll down the road to the Thuja Gardens, or remain at the inn for various nightly musical events ranging from Scottish bagpipers to jazz brunches (see our Restaurants chapter).

Asticou Inn is open from early May to mid-October.

Harbourside Inn
$$$, no credit cards • Harbourside Rd., Northeast Harbor • 276-3272

Some come to the Harbourside Inn with trail maps and hiking boots, others with bags of books. The west driveway of the inn leads right to Acadia National Park. According to innkeeper Geraldine Sweet, who's hiked in Acadia enough to know, you can get there from here without using a car, but you have to be a good hiker. The trail up Norumbega Mountain is a half-hour trek by foot from Harbourside Inn; Hadlock Pond is 20 minutes;

and the carriage roads are a mile away. (See our Acadia National Park chapter for more information about hiking in the park.)

Despite the name, the 14 large, bright rooms and suites of the Harbourside offer only glimpses of the water; the inn is built on a hillside overlooking a stand of old pines. The Harbourside is the real thing — built as an inn 1888 and '89. The rooms of this shingle-style cottage are old-fashioned — simple but bright and cheery with country accents — and most have fireplaces and comfortable chairs set facing the fire. Some rooms also have kitchenettes. The morning meal is a continental breakfast.

No smoking is allowed — not even on the grounds. Suites as well as public rooms have telephones, but this is an old-fashioned place — you won't find a television on the premises.

So many guests have returned over the past 20 years that many have become old friends. Children conceived at the inn have come back to play on its lawns — even though the inn does not cater to children. Among the owners, however, it's become a family affair: Geraldine's daughters-in-law have joined their elegant, gracious mother-in-law in the business; Geraldine's husband is the gardener.

This seasonal inn is open mid-June to mid-September.

Kimball Terrace Inn

$$$ • Huntington Rd., Northeast Harbor • 276-3383, (800) 454-6225

Northeast's harbor offers a spectacular vista of boats heading through the protected channel to islands beyond. The Kimball Terrace Inn, on a slope above the harbor, is well-placed to take in the view of the marina, the town and the harbor.

Open mid-April until late October, the inn has 70 rooms, most with water views and all with phones and televisions. There's also a pool and nearby public tennis courts. Smoking is allowed in some rooms. At least two rooms are handicapped-accessible.

The Maison Suisse Inn

$$$-$$$$ • Main St., Northeast Harbor • 276-5223, (800) 624-7668

The friendly, attentive owners know more about the colorful history of this inn — in the middle of Northeast Harbor's main street — than they wish to have in print. For instance, there are the tales of Gottfried Stehli (a.k.a. Mr. Fred), a trained landscape gardener who found "pruning women's hair more lucrative than pruning gardens." After accompanying Gloria Swanson on her travels for some years, he retired from Hollywood, bought this shingle-style house designed by Fred Savage, and kept the gardens going while he did the hair of the rusticators (city folk seeking a wilderness experience). His seamstress wife helped with their clothing.

Several of the 10 rooms (four suites) have claw-foot tubs, many have hand silk-screened wallpaper. Cable television is available in your room upon request. Children with "caring adult supervision" are welcome.

Breakfast is served across the street at The Colonel's Restaurant. Whether you eat a full breakfast or a portion, it's on The Maison.

The Maison Suisse Inn is open late May through late October.

The Claremont Hotel

$$$-$$$$ • Claremont Rd., Southwest Harbor • 244-5036, (800) 244-5036

Southwest Harbor has grown into a bustling town over the past decade, but the Claremont Hotel still manages to remain removed from all that.

Built in 1884, the Claremont is the island's oldest hotel and holds a deserved place on the National Register of Historic Places. Like many old hotels, it is graciously relaxed, having rambled its way into several expansions. Rooms in the main house are elegant and comfortable; those in the newer Phillips House and Clark House are posh. Everywhere, it seems, there are large bouquets of flowers.

The location — across Somes Sound from Cadillac Mountain — deserves the bouquets. You can enjoy some of New England's best scenery without leaving the grounds.

If you do wish to leave, however, you can take one of the hotel's bikes and head for town. Or you can drive to Acadia National Park (see our Acadia National Park chapter), which you can reach without having to endure the traffic or bustle of Bar Harbor.

There are 30 rooms in the inn; all have private baths. The delightful, homey rooms on the third floor incorporate the gabled architecture into the decor. One room is handicapped-accessible, others have limited accessibility. You'll find in-room phones, but no televisions.

There are also 12 separate cottages scattered along the water and in the woods, each with a fireplace or Franklin stove.

Enjoy breakfast, then relax in one of numerous sitting areas: Outdoors, try the green wicker rockers on the porch or the white wooden chairs on the lawn; indoors, hunker down in the library with a book, puzzle or card game. Have lunch at the boat house (in high season); enjoy a game of croquet on the Claremont's grounds, made famous through its annual croquet tournament (see Annual Events); take afternoon tea; and savor a formal candlelight dinner (jacket and tie required).

The Claremont Hotel is open from mid-

INSIDERS' TIP

Islands remain quintessential Maine places. For island accommodations, check out our Offshore/Islands chapter.

June through mid-October, with the cottages open slightly longer. Water view rooms are offered on a Modified American Plan only.

Kingsleigh Inn
$$$ • 373 Main St., Southwest Harbor • 244-5302

Southwest Harbor bills itself as the quiet side of MDI, but the town seems more like a burgeoning small town these days — manageable but happening. It's quite fun. The owners of the Kingsleigh Inn, Ken and Cyd Champagne Collins, reflect this energy: They're young, enthusiastic and warm.

Kingsleigh is a lovely old Maine island home with turrets, a wraparound porch with comfortable wicker furniture and flowers cascading from window boxes. Inside, the flower motif continues in the eight rooms. Check out the third-floor turret suite featuring panoramic views; you'll find an in-room telescope through which to peer over the harbor toward the horizon. There's a king-size bed, even a television in this room only, which rents for a higher rate than the other rooms. One room has limited handicapped access.

Kingsleigh welcomes children older than 12.

Lindenwood Inn
$$-$$$ • 118 Clark Point Rd., Southwest Harbor • 244-5335, (800) 307-5335

The lindens shading the lovely, waterside Clark Point Road lend their name to this harborside inn, once a sea captain's home. Those sated with antiques and Victoriana will cherish the Lindenwood Inn. It is a modern, elegant, sophisticated place, filled with simple, well-crafted furniture and bright, engaging art, both primitive and contemporary. The art contrasts well with the interesting colors (such as pale mustard and melon) of each room's painted walls.

Some rooms in the main house have water views. There are also rooms in two nearby annexes. Some rooms have phones; others have televisions, fireplaces or balconies. There are 23 rooms in all, including cottages rented by the week in July and August, and housekeeping units (where children are welcome). There is limited handicapped accessibility. Guests may enjoy the heated, in-ground pool and the hot tub.

Lindenwood Inn also features a well-regarded restaurant of the same name (see Restaurants). The inn is open from early spring through New Year's Day.

Penury Hall
$$ • 374 Main St., Southwest Harbor • 244-7102

When Gretchen and Toby Strong opened Penury Hall in 1982, launching the era of bed and breakfast accommodations on Mount Desert Island, Gretchen was town manager (she has since retired). Perhaps that's where this establishment got its odd name, referring to poverty not glory.

The hall offers three reasonably priced rooms with two shared baths. Though it sits across from the harbor, water views are available only in winter, when the trees have lost their leaves. This place feels like home; the Strongs share their living room, canoe, two playful cats and a sauna with visitors.

Credit cards are accepted for deposits and international visitors only. Mature children are welcome.

Generally there are three well-traveled avenues to satisfactory summer rentals: real estate agents, commercial cottages and classified ads.

Summer Rentals

Ah, here you must play detective. The prize is a cottage, a summer cottage. One that's safe and comfortable, clean and pleasant, airy and near or on the water. In this cottage, you can — for a week, a month or the summer — pretend you live here. Laze around in wicker chairs, read, sail, eat lobster and throw the hard, red claws off the deck. Bike back roads, pick blueberries, wave to the locals and feel you're finally having a summer like the ones you had as a kid.

Reality check: This is not as easy to find as you might hope. The really wonderful places have been in someone's family so long that they've been taken for granted and are hardly used, or loved so dearly that they're never empty, at least not when it's warm enough that pipes don't freeze. You have to do some sleuthing to find the owners of these places, and you have to somehow persuade them you wouldn't dream of nicking great Aunt Clara's china or, heaven forfend, rearrange the furniture.

Generally there are three well-traveled avenues to satisfactory summer rentals: real estate agents, commercial cottages and classified ads. We'll have listings for the first two in a minute. As for the third, see the Media chapter for newspapers and magazines. (*Down East* magazine's classified ads are particularly good for this purpose.)

We list the chambers of commerce subsequently because the men and women who answer their telephones can be saving angels, dear people who might like the sound of your voice and remember that Uncle Bert has a place he wouldn't mind letting go for a week or two in late May. If you aren't that lucky, ask how they would suggest you look for a place. Most can send you a booklet or brochure that's a good place to start. You might also get a copy of *The Maine Guide to Camp & Cottage Rentals* by contacting The Maine Publicity Bureau Inc., P.O. Box 2300, Hallowell, ME 04347, 623-0363 or (800) 533-9595.

Finally, a fourth, less-traveled avenue is what is referred to in diplomacy as the "back-channel." We can't help much on this one; we can only point you in the right direction and cheer you on. The trick is to ask everyone you know with even the slightest connection to Maine, and ask politely. You must sound earnest and reliable, someone sensitive to endangered wildflowers but able to nurse a gas refrigerator. As one Maine native told me, the key is trust. Word of mouth is your friend, so get on the telephone.

If you're dealing with real estate agents or commercial cottages, you're on equal footing and can be very specific about what you're looking for — because you'll end up paying for it. We advise a more delicate approach when dealing with private parties who might be letting a treasured family home.

Whomever you're dealing with, ask lots of questions. The range of possibilities is remarkable: in-town, wooded, lakeside, oceanside and bayside. If you're told the cottage is on water, ask what kind of water. Tidal flats can be great for toddlers, but some can smell a little, well, fishy. Deepwater frontage is pricey but wonderful if you want to dock a boat. Properties with rocky drop-offs, often called bold frontage, might boast spectacular views but might be useless for recreation — swimming is impossible, and children always want to balance on the jagged, slippery boulders.

If you plan to be in the woods, remember that in some areas in spring and early summer, blackflies and mosquitoes can be a nightmare. Ask about heating the cottage too. Chilly nights — and days! — might drive you inside, and you'll want a way to warm up. Make sure it's a technology you can handle. City visitors used to electric heat might find tending a wood stove an intimidating nuisance. We've found Mainers to be very casual about these matters. We rented a house for the winter one year, only to discover it wasn't insulated.

Finally, there are cottages, and there are *cottages*. The first is what we commonly understand — those smallish, informal and sometimes shabby places that might not be habitable when cold breezes blow. The second is a bit of Yankee understatement for huge estate-like homes that employ the architectural elements of the first, but on a much grander scale. (See the related Close-up in our Architecture chapter.)

The rates we give you in this chapter are high-season — usually June, July and August. Most cottages come furnished with linens, utensils and cookware, though some owners ask you to bring linens. Ask about a washer/dryer or the closest Laundromat. Most cottages have telephones, but ask. For some families, it's a point of honor not to have one. And while you can't assume that you'll find a TV or radio, much less cable or a VCR, some will think less of you for asking. This is one of the most beautiful places on earth, and you should be outside playing! Oh yes, children usually are welcome, but pets generally are not.

Enjoy!

FYI

Unless otherwise noted, the area code for all phone numbers listed in this guide is 207.

Waldoboro to Stockton Springs

Mahan Properties
P.O. Box 326, Waldoboro, ME 04572
• 832-5361

This company says most summer rentals in the area are booked by the same folks year after year, so real estate agents can't be of much help. Still, it has a few waterfront listings in Waldoboro, Friendship and Cushing for weekly rents ranging from $400 for a one-bedroom on a less desirable waterfront or with limited views to $800 for a three-bedroom with deepwater frontage that can accommodate boats and hardy swimmers (the bay is cold!).

Rockland/Thomaston Area Chamber of Commerce
P.O. Box 508, Rockland, ME 04841
• 596-0376

This chamber covers Cushing, Friendship,

Matinicus (Knox County area), North Haven, Owls Head, Rockland, St. George, South Thomaston, Thomaston, Vinalhaven, Warren and Washington. Staff can send you a 96-page booklet about the area as well as a great listing of private owners who are willing to rent their homes or cottages. The one for 1997 was more than 15 pages, and some of the descriptions would make you drool. Our favorite was a four-bedroom, 19th-century cape on Hawthorne Point, in Cushing, for $500 a week. It's private, in excellent condition and just 100 yards from the ocean. Amenities include two wood stoves to warm chilly evenings and a deck/porch on which to while away sunny afternoons. Generally, rates range from $300 to $2,500 a week.

Smith's Swiss Village
N. Shore Dr., Box 284, Owls Head, ME 04854 • 594-4039

Each of these three housekeeping cottages (with full kitchens) in Owls Head has a great view of Rockland Harbor and the Camden Hills. While there are weekly, monthly and seasonal rates, the cottages rent for $600 a week in July and August. Each has two bedrooms, a living room, kitchen-dining area, color cable TV and telephone.

Beloin's on the Maine Coast
HCR 60, Box 3105, Camden, ME 04843 • 236-3262

Beloin's, just off U.S. Highway 1 between Camden and Lincolnville, is an old-reliable in this area. Its 15 oceanfront cottage units are just feet from the shoreline, and they are rented on a per-night basis, with rates ranging from $98 to $185.

Camden Accommodations & Reservations
77 Elm St., Camden, ME 04843 • 236-6090, (800) 236-1920

While this company handles reservations for all kinds of inns and motels, it also books summer rentals of cottages, condos and individual homes in the Camden area. Weekly rates start at $450, average $800 and peak at around $3,500.

A local minister blesses a schooner preparing to enter one of many schooner races held in summer along Maine's coast.

Camden-Rockport-Lincolnville Chamber of Commerce
P.O. Box 919, Camden, ME 04843
• **236-4404**

This chamber covers the towns in its name and surrounding towns like Hope, Appleton, Union. It's famous for an extensive list of private homes, cottages and condos for rent. Look for rates from $400 to $2,500 a week. The 1997 list had more than 100 entries, and the word around town is that even the real estate agents use it as a source for leads. A 96-page booklet on the area includes a listing of commercial providers as well. The new editions of both come out in January.

Cedarholm Cottages
RR 3, Box 3294, Lincolnville, ME 04849
• **236-3886**

Four of Cedarholm's six cottages aren't right on the shore, but they do have water views. They range from small studios to two-bedroom units and rent on a per-night basis, with a discount for weekly rentals. Rates are $75 to $135 a night. Two new luxury cottages *are* right on the water, with two bedrooms each, big living rooms with stone fireplaces and Jacuzzis. They go for $225 to $300 a night.

Island Property
P.O. Box 300, Islesboro, ME 04848
• **734-8809**

John Oldham has been on Islesboro for more than 20 years, and while that doesn't make him a native, it does make him a very good resource on summer rentals (and real estate) on this understated tiny island. He has a list of 30 options, some with solid openings, some where the time available is at the convenience of the owner. They range from two- or three-bedroom rustic waterfront cottages for $450 to elegant summer cottages ($3,000 to $6,000), including three- or four-bedroom waterfront homes and five- or six-bedroom mansions with fireplaces and four or five smaller rooms where hired help once slept.

Belfast Area Chamber of Commerce
P.O. Box 58, Belfast, ME 04915
• **338-5900**

The Belfast chamber publishes a guide, *Gateway to Down East*, that covers Stockton Springs, Searsport, Belfast, Lincolnville and Northport. While there seem to be only a handful of commercial cottages listed, many are right on Penobscot Bay with breathtaking views of the water. While many are calculated on a nightly basis, they rent for $250 to $1,000 a week.

Wonderview Cottages
U.S. Hwy. 1, Belfast, ME 04915
• **338-1455**

Wonderview has 20 cottages on 10 acres, all with full kitchens and one to three bedrooms. A number are lined up in a row along the shore and offer beautiful views of the bay. Weekly rates range from $450 to $795.

Inland to Bangor

The Bangor Region Chamber of Commerce
519 Main St., Bangor, ME 04402
• **947-0307**

The Bangor chamber covers Bangor, Brewer, Hampden, Hermon, Holden, Old Town, Orono, Veazie, Winterport, Carmel, Eddington, Glenburn, Hudson, Kenduskeag, Levant, Milford, Newburgh, Stillwater, Bradley, Orrington and Dedham. While its 74-page booklet covers one of the state's largest cities, there is little mention of summer cottages in its pages. Real estate agents say the market just isn't mature enough, so classified ads or The Maine Publicity Bureau's list (see this chapter's introduction) are your best leads in this area.

Bucksport to Gouldsboro

Coastal Cottage Rental Co.
P.O. Box 835, Blue Hill, ME 04614
• **374-3500**

This company handles cottage rentals just as a real estate company might. It's been in the business since 1988, with listings in Blue Hill and farther east. Hate renting sight-unseen? For $5, Coastal will send you a picture catalog of more than a hundred cottages to choose from. Rates vary from $500

to $2,000, with the occasional eye-opener at $3,000.

Deer Isle-Stonington Chamber of Commerce
P.O. Box 459, Stonington, ME 04681
• **348-6124**

This chamber covers Deer Isle, Stonington and Isle au Haut. It publishes a four-page brochure that lists a handful of cottage rentals and rental agents. Weekly rates can be as low as $400, as high as $1,400.

Island Vacation Rentals
P.O. Box 446, Stonington, ME 04681
• **367-5095**

Alice Gross sold this business, but she still works a few days a week for the new owner. If you can reach her, she's a gold mine. Most customers shop for rentals over the telephone, and after years in telemarketing, Alice knows how to elicit what they're really looking for. The company handles 50 or so prime rentals — all in the Deer Isle/Stonington area — ranging from $500 to $1,400 a week.

Ellsworth Area Chamber of Commerce
P.O. Box 267, Ellsworth, ME 04605
• **667-5584**

Looking for options in Blue Hill, Castine, Ellsworth, Franklin, Hancock, Lamoine, Mount Desert Island, Orland, Sorrento, Sullivan or Surry? Ellsworth's chamber will send you a 64-page booklet on the area. It includes a listing of 25 cottages and cabins with weekly rates from $400 to $600. The next edition comes out in early January.

Mount Desert Island

Fern Farm
Huber & Jaworsky, 95 Paper Mill Rd., Manhasset, NY 11030 • (516) 627-4657

Fern Farm is just one secluded cottage on 5 acres with views of Frenchman Bay. It

INSIDERS' TIP

If you want to rent a cottage in August (the most popular vacation month), start looking at least a year in advance.

has a granite fireplace and oil heat, and its $700 per week fee includes linens and dishes. Popular with honeymooners, Fern Farm feels intimate and friendly, with its nature log, bird books, puzzles and games. Restrictions include a maximum occupancy of three, no children younger than 12 and no pets.

Bar Harbor Chamber of Commerce
93 Cottage St., Bar Harbor, ME 04609
• 288-5103

Bar Harbor's chamber covers Acadia National Park, Bar Harbor, Town Hill, Salisbury Cove and Hulls Cove. Its booklet lists individual private homes available for rent, in addition to summer cottages. Options range from $400 a week for small rustic cottages to $5,000 a week during the high season for luxurious oceanside mansions. Bar Harbor has long been a playground for the wealthy; apparently some are willing to let their houses.

Eastern Bay Cottages
RR 1, Box 1545, Bar Harbor, ME 04609
• 288-9223

There are just two cottages here, with a pebble beach and wonderful views of Eastern and Frenchman bays. One unit has a fireplace; both include a bedroom, living room, kitchen and bath. Weekly rates range from $495 to $555 for a maximum of two people each and no pets.

Emery's Cottages on the Shore
Box 172C, Bar Harbor, ME 04609
• 288-3432

Out on Sand Point, these cottages are right on the shoreline of Frenchman Bay. Some have kitchens, some don't, and there's a Laundromat on the premises. They go for $450 to $700 a week for two people.

Hinckley's Dreamwood Cottages
RR 1, Box 1180, Bar Harbor, ME 04609
• 288-3510

Hinckley's, on Maine Highway 3, offers one-, two- and four-bedroom units. The larger units are very popular with families, and they book fast. Rates range from $366 to $1,350 a week. The ocean is beyond Sand Point across the road, and there's a heated pool on the premises.

Mt. Desert Properties
P.O. Box 536, Bar Harbor, ME 04609
• 288-4523

Sharon Joyce is your contact here. She cultivates a solid selection of listings, primarily on Mount Desert Island, ranging from $700 to $4,000 a week. Her enthusiasm is contagious, as she mentions cute little rustic places on the water, 100-year-old tennis houses on the grounds of estates, and 10-bedroom waterfront mansions with private piers.

Salisbury Cove Cottages
P.O. Box 723, Bar Harbor, ME 04609
• 288-4571

These little white cottages with blue shutters are scattered across a broad green lawn. They house two to five people and include kitchenettes, heat and screened porches. Weekly rates range from $340 to $685.

Knowles Co.
One Summit Rd., Northeast Harbor, ME 04662 • 276-3322

In summer 1997, Knowles Co. reached its century mark. Knowles offers summer rentals from $500 a week to $40,000 a month. Believe it or not, the high end is not unusual; Knowles rents 15 to 20 homes for between $15,000 and $30,000 per month.

Knowles' covers high-end properties on

---

www.insiders.com

See this and many other *Insiders' Guide®* destinations online — in their entirety.

Visit us today!

INSIDERS' TIP

The notice board at Moody's Diner in Waldoboro (see our Restaurants chapter) is a great place to post a "cottage wanted" notice.

Photo: Bangor Daily News

Mount Katahdin looms in the background above a small stream in
central Maine showing the state's diverse topography.

Mount Desert Island and the Cranberries. (See our Real Estate chapter for related information.)

Mount Desert Chamber of Commerce
P.O. Box 675, Northeast Harbor, ME 04662 • 276-5040

Check with the folks here for options on Mount Desert and in Northeast Harbor, Otter Creek, Seal Harbor and Somesville. This chamber publishes a 64-page booklet with a list of real estate brokers who handle summer rentals and a handful of cottages. Expect to pay $600 to $2,000 per week.

The Davis Agency
P.O. Box 1038, Southwest Harbor, ME 04679 • 244-3891

This company has more than 100 seasonal listings of oceanfront, lakefront and wooded properties in Trenton and on Mount Desert and Swans islands. The units range in size from one bedroom to houses that sleep 13, and in price from $400 to $5,000 a week.

Harbor Ridge
39 Freeman Ridge Rd., Southwest Harbor, ME 04679 • 244-7000

These one- and two-bedroom condominiums are timeshares available for rent at $1,500 a week from mid-June through August. (They are available in the off-season as well, but that's another story.)

The 19-acre complex is situated on a ridge with views of Somes Sound and the mountains of Acadia National Park. There are four buildings containing eight units each, and each unit is a three-floor townhouse with two decks overlooking the sound and the park.

The units themselves have washers and dryers as well as fully equipped kitchens with microwaves and dishwashers. Linens are provided. The two-bedroom units sleep six; the one-bedroom units sleep four. Other amenities include an indoor swimming pool, game and exercise rooms, an outdoor hot tub and a tennis court.

It's best to make your reservations at least two months ahead, but latecomers may be accommodated.

Hinckley Real Estate
Box 920, Southwest Harbor, ME 04679 • 244-7011

Hinckley handles about 75 listings on Mount Desert Island, most of which are upper-end classic summer cottages on the waterfront. They are let for at least two weeks at a time, but leases may run as long as a season. The cottages rent from $1,100 (standard but comfortable three-bedroom homes on and off the water) to $2,500 per week (three- and four-bedroom waterfront homes with copious amenities and beautiful landscaping).

LSRobinson Co.
337 Main St., Southwest Harbor, ME 04679 • 244-5563

Martha Dodge is your contact here for summer rentals. She shares resources with the Lynam Agency in Bar Harbor — her company's sister agency — and between them they handle 300 to 400 listings on Mount Desert Island and in Lamoine and Trenton. Rates range from $500 to $4,000 for properties of every description: in-town, wooded, lakeside, oceanside and bayside. The only properties they don't handle are the more rustic — without electricity or hot and cold running water.

Southwest Harbor-Tremont Chamber of Commerce
P.O. Box 1143, Southwest Harbor, ME 04679 • 244-9264, (800) 423-9264

This chamber covers Southwest Harbor, Tremont and the west side of Mount Desert Island. A number of the cottage listings have one unit, so they aren't cottage complexes at all — just single homes available for rent. High-season weekly rates range from $375 to $1,750.

July and August are the high season along the Mid-Coast, and you'd best make reservations if you're traveling during that time.

Campgrounds

The range of campgrounds in the Mid-Coast area is impressive, from low-key backwoods and the cry of loons to high-energy RV "cities" and the ring of cellular phones. Many are right on the main roads — you can't miss them; but others are not, and we delighted in ferreting them out.

Please note our listings here are not exhaustive. We were looking for the notable and unique, which is not to say there aren't a number of fine facilities out there for you to discover.

Start by contacting the Maine Campground Owners Association, 655 Main Street, Lewiston, ME 04240, 782-5874, for a copy of its 80-plus–page directory. The *Maine Camping Guide* has descriptions of the regions of Maine and maps of those regions with the campgrounds marked. A grid on the facing page details facilities. Once you get the lay of the land, you can write or call for brochures on the ones that suit you best.

For more information about state-run facilities, contact the Maine Department of Conservation, Bureau of Parks and Lands, No. 22 State House Station, Augusta, ME 04333, 287-3821. Reservations can be made for sites in those parks, but you must call seven days in advance; Maine residents call (800) 332-1501; nonresidents call 287-3824. For camping options in Acadia, see our chapter devoted to that national park.

July and August are the high season along the Mid-Coast, and you'd best make reservations if you're traveling during that time. Some places don't take reservations, and we note those — they can be real lifesavers. You may assume you can pay with a major credit card and bring your dog unless otherwise noted. Rate schedules can be complicated, depending on whether water, electric and sewage hookups are available and for how much. We list the lowest rates in high season as a base indicator, and we also indicate the number of guests the rates include. Note that opening and closing dates will flex depending on the weather. If there's snow on the ground in April, the campground's probably closed.

Finally, the most interesting aspect of writing this chapter was discerning the atmosphere of the various campgrounds. We were amazed at the differences. If it matters to you and you're shopping by phone, ask a lot of questions and look closely at the brochures. You'll quickly learn to separate the wheat from the chaff. Stopped-up toilets, loose barking dogs and loud late-night revels four feet from your tent can spoil a vacation quicker than you can say "blueberry."

Waldoboro to Stockton Springs

Lobster Buoy Campsite
no credit cards • Maine Hwy. 73, South Thomaston • 594-7546

There's nothing fancy about this place. It's small, low-key, but the view is rich-folks Maine — the blue of Penobscot Bay and the islands. The sites are open, none is more than 150

---

yards from the Atlantic Ocean, and 400 feet of shoreline is yours to enjoy. The owners encourage campers to bring self-launched boats, canoes and sea kayaks; bikes too — there are plenty of quiet country roads to explore. Sites for tents and RVs are available. The RV sites include water and electric hookups. While there are no sewage hookups, there is a dump station.

Lobster Buoy Campsite is open May 15 to October 15; rates start at $14.50 for two adults, two children younger than 12 and a vehicle.

Megunticook Campground by the Sea
U.S. Hwy. 1, between Camden and Rockport • 594-2428, (800) 884-2428

The entrance to Megunticook Campground is right off U.S. 1, between Camden and Rockport. The brochure for this campground is elegant, and the place itself fairly shouts "good management." The grounds are neat, the 80 sites are well-laid out, and the camp store boasts fresh-ground coffee. While there are no sites actually on the ocean, a deck and picnic tables make the shoreline pleasant for all to enjoy. There's a new heated pool outdoors, and you can rent bikes and ocean kayaks.

Megunticook Campground by the Sea is open May 15 to October 15; rates start at $21 a night for two adults and two children. Water, electric, sewer and cable TV hookups are available.

Camden Hills State Park
U.S. Hwy. 1, Camden • 236-3109

You'll know you're passing Camden Hills State Park because you can smell the campfires from the road. The campground has 112 sites that are, like most state parks, very well-spaced. Some are in the woods, and some border an open field. Unlike most state parks, Camden Hills boasts flush toilets and hot showers. RVs of any size are welcome; there's a dumping station but no electric hookups. This is a busy, popular campground because the park itself is a real attraction, with 26 miles of hiking trails through more than 5,000 acres (read more about that in the Parks and Recreation chapter).

Camden Hills State Park is open May 15 to October 15; rates are $12 for Maine residents, $16 for nonresidents. You are allowed up to six people, two tents and two vehicles per site.

The Old Massachusetts Homestead Campground
U.S. Hwy. 1, Lincolnville Beach • 789-5135

This 60-acre campground is a nice surprise so close to the city of Camden. It has lots of trees, a pool, a pond with a beach and almost 2 miles of nature trails. Its 68 sites are well-spaced and nicely screened from view, and the layout here is easy to navigate. The owners have divided the area so tents and couples are in one section; pop-ups, mini motor homes, vans and more tents are in another; and trailers and motor homes in another with full hookups. According to staff, Penobscot Indians used this land when they came to the coast to fish, trap, pick fruit and canoe to the islands — so it may be one of the oldest campgrounds in the country.

The Old Massachusetts Homestead Campground is open May 1 to November 1; rates start at $19 for two adults and two children. Hookups for water, electric and sewage are available.

The Moorings
U.S. Hwy. 1, Belfast • 338-6860

The Moorings is perfect for RV campers making their way up the coast. You turn in off U.S. 1 and drive straight toward the water. The 39 sites are arranged in a rough U-shape in an open field, making it a breeze to navigate, especially for big rigs. Check in at the office, on your left as you enter — the building also houses a game room, pool table, laundry facilities and restrooms. While there's room for volleyball, tetherball and horseshoes and a playground in the middle of the U, we'd guess most campers prowl the coast during the day. The view from sites 17 to 21 is amazing — wide-open ocean!

The Moorings is open from May 15 to October 15; rates start at $25 for two adults and

FYI

Unless otherwise noted, the area code for all phone numbers listed in this guide is 207.

two children. Water and electric hookups are available at all sites, and there's a dump station for sewage.

Searsport Shores Camping Resort
216 W. Main St. (U.S. Hwy. 1), Searsport • 548-6059

Not only is this campground on the shore in Searsport, probably the flea market capital of the world, but there's also a farmers market and a great bakery (see Periwinkles in the Restaurants chapter) right across from the entrance on U.S. 1. Half the grounds is woods threaded by nature trails; the other half is a grid of more than 100 sites. The whole fronts Penobscot Bay. Tenters are accommodated along the outside ring of sites, but they are positively pampered in a tenters-only section on the beach. Searsport Shores calls itself a camping resort, so be prepared for planned activities, a pirate's boat playground and a recreation hall.

Searsport Shores is open May 15 to Columbus Day; rates start at $16 for two adults and any number of children younger than 18. Water and electric hookups are available, as are laundry facilities.

Inland to Bangor

Paul Bunyan Campground
1862 Union St., Bangor • 941-1177

Paul Bunyan is a place lots of locals use for family reunions. There's a pool, picnic shelter and ball field along with a recreation hall, pool table and video games. While the campground's literature says the place has 52 sites, we counted more like 88, including tent sites — a mix of shaded and open spots. While some Bangor natives think Paul Bunyan's not far away enough to constitute

getting away, this campground might be just the ticket for families with small children.

Paul Bunyan Campground is open April to November; rates start at $12.50 for two adults and two children. Water, electric and sewage hookups are available.

Pleasant Hill Campground
Union St., 5 mi. west of I-95, Bangor • 848-5127

Pleasant Hill is very similar to Paul Bunyan. There's lots to do, including miniature golf, swimming, volleyball, basketball, horseshoes and tetherball. You'll also find two playgrounds and a field for softball. It's no surprise, then, that Pleasant Hill attracts family gatherings and some long-term campers who stay all summer (you can tell them by the Astroturf and the hanging lanterns!). Parts of Pleasant Hill are beautifully shaded, and there are good-size pull-through sites for large RVs. Check out site No. 25; it's open, flat and grassy — great for tenters with kids.

Pleasant Hill Campground is open May 1 to Columbus Day; rates start at $14 for two adults and two children younger than 18. Water, electric and sewage hookups are available.

Bucksport to Gouldsboro

The Flying Dutchman Campground
off U.S. Hwy. 1, Verona Island • 469-3256

The advantage of this 50-site campground is location, location, location. The Flying Dutchman is on the shores of the Penobscot River, but close enough to U.S. 1 for easy access. Great views, and you won't get lost getting there. Once you're settled in, you're just 18 miles from Belfast, Bangor and Ellsworth. But if you'd rather stay put, you won't be at a loss

---

www.insiders.com

See this and many other **Insiders' Guide®** destinations online — in their entirety.

Visit us today!

INSIDERS' TIP

Just north of Rockland, there's a rest stop with picnic facilities at what used to be called Powerhouse Hill. It's a favorite stop for RVs because they can drive in, park at an angle overlooking the water and turn around at the end of the drive to exit easily.

Photo: Bangor Daily News

Where the land meets the sea — the coast of Maine — you'll discover sand beaches.

for things to do. This campground has a 38-foot heated pool, a six-person hot tub, a playground for toddlers and an all-you-can-eat pancake breakfast for $1 Sunday mornings.

New owners David and Jackie Gray say most campers are Mainers, many from a 50-mile radius. Some are seasonal, and they like the family atmosphere. Sites for tents, campers and RVs are available. Some include water/electric hookups. While there is a dump station, for another dollar a day you can get a sewer hookup and HBO. If you want to be right along the water, ask for sites 19 to 28. There isn't a beach for swimming, but the views are great.

The Flying Dutchman is open May 1 through Columbus Day. Rates start at $16 for up to three adults and any number of children 15 and younger.

Masthead Campground
no credit cards • Maine Hwy. 46, 6 mi. north of U.S. Hwy. 1, Bucksport • 469-3482

With its winding, hilly paths and smallish sites, Masthead has that wonderful, piney old-campground feel. While it's not the place to bring big RVs (up to 30 feet is OK), it's perfect for pop-ups or tents. There are 38 sites arranged around the shores of Hancock Pond;

some open, some wooded, some lakeside. This is another campground without a busy office/store/restaurant, so do your shopping and get your ice on the way in!

There's plenty to do here: volleyball, badminton, tetherball, horseshoes, even basketball. Row boats, canoes and paddle boats rent by the hour, and a toddler playground and swings will amuse the kids.

Masthead is open Memorial Day to September 15; rates start at $14 for two adults and two children. All sites have water and electric hookups.

Shady Oaks Campground
Maine Hwy. 175, just off U.S. Hwy. 1, Orland • 469-7739

This campground bursts with personality. Owner Don Nelson has a ready handshake, an equally ready smile and a knack for organized activities — potluck suppers, free Sunday pancake breakfasts, even bus trips to baseball games. He says most campers are local, and they come back for weeks at a time, year after year. He thinks of them as extended family. A board outside the office holds a sign-up sheet for a camper's Christmas party in early December. Most campers come in RVs or other motorized vehicles, and the overall layout makes it easy to get around. Tell the kids they can't bring the dog, but there is a pool.

Shady Oaks is open May 1 to October 1; rates start at $16 for two adults and two children. All sites have water and electric hookups. Sewage hookups are available at some sites, and there's an on-site dump station as well as 30-amp service for air conditioning.

Whispering Pines Campground
no credit cards • U.S. Hwy. 1, East Orland • 469-3443

If you've done a lot of camping, you will appreciate this serene little place on Toddy Pond for what it doesn't have. There's no camp store filled with things your kids just must have — and will have by the end of the week. There aren't a zillion signs and posters plastered everywhere. It does have miles of swimming, fishing and boating on Toddy Pond and a safe, family feel. Owners Dwight and Sandy Gates work to keep it that way. Dwight has insisted the jukebox company pull songs he feels are inappropriate for children. Sandy says women are perfectly comfortable camping alone or with their children here.

Whispering Pines is open May 20 to October 12; rates start at $18 for two adults and children younger than 2. Water, electric and sewage hookups are available.

Sunshine Campgrounds
off Maine Hwy. 15, 6 mi. from Deer Isle Village, Deer Isle • 348-6681

This is a tiny gem of a campground; it has 22 sites, and the office is in the owner's garage. It caters to tenters, with four walk-in–only sites, some with platforms. RV rigs are limited to 40 feet, and there are no sewage hookups. While the campground itself is not on water, it has the advantage of being the only one on Deer Isle, making it a great base camp for exploring Stonington and the sections of Acadia National Park on Isle au Haut; sea kayakers take note. Tip: Call first! You don't want to drive 40 miles off U.S. Highway 1 and down the peninsula to discover the campground is full.

Sunshine Campgrounds is open Memorial Day to October 15; rates start at $12 for a couple and their children. Only electric hookups are available. The campground uses well water.

Lamoine State Park
Maine Hwy. 184, 7 miles off Maine Hwy. 3, Lamoine • 667-4778

This 70-acre state park is just 7 miles off Maine Highway 3, the main thoroughfare onto Mount Desert Island. And it's easy to find. We're telling you that because it's a great, cheap, quiet alternative to camping on Mount Desert. Compared to commercial campgrounds, its 61 sites are wildly spacious, and a number have very nice water views. (If secluded is what you want, try No. 40. The staff calls it the honeymoon suite.) The sites are pretty spartan though: no hookups, no pay phones, but flush toilets and showers are in the works. A group site accommodating as many as 100 campers is planned as well.

There is a day-use area with wide-open spaces, swings for the kids and a boat launch. The fellow at the gate told us folks were catching striped bass from the float the day we visited. For reservations, Maine residents call (800) 332-1501; nonresidents call 287-3824.

Lamoine State Park is open May 15 to October 15; rates start at $12 for residents, $16 for nonresidents. Again, no hookups are available.

Ocean Wood Campground
no credit cards • .25 mi. off Maine Hwy. 186, Birch Harbor • 963-7194

Ocean Wood is an anomaly — and a real find. At the entrance is a gallery/restaurant, all spruced up and planted with hollyhocks. The menu sports items such as chicken/bacon/Brie sandwiches and Panacea Soup (clear chicken-garlic-ginger broth with carrots, mushrooms and chicken). A long wooded road takes you to the 72 campsites. There's no check-in at the gate, just pick any site that's not marked "Reserved," and the attendant will come 'round and collect the fee. Note: This should not indicate a laissez-faire attitude about the atmosphere. The rules are strict: no loud radios or other sounds that disturb, and no unsupervised children. At the wilderness sites, no radios, pets or guests are allowed. The brochure adds: "These principles were developed to protect this fragile coastal setting and the privacy of other campers. THEY ARE STRICTLY ENFORCED." And they are. The managers are known to kick out violators. The sites themselves are well-spaced, well-screened and quite spread out. The waterfront sites are dazzling. One Insider says he and his wife drive here from Bangor to relax; they just sit on the rocks in the sun and read Stephen King novels.

Ocean Wood is open from the first Friday in May to the last Sunday in October; rates start at $14 for two adults and four children. Water and electric hookups are available.

Mainayr Campground
no credit cards • .25 miles off U.S. Hwy. 1, Steuben • 546-2690

Mainayr is another little gem that feels like a time machine. It's one of the oldest campgrounds in the state, with 30 sites in a parklike setting along a tidal estuary called Joy Cove. (That means the water's warm enough for swimming!) You can pick blueberries and sugar pears, dig clams or buy lobsters in the camp store. Sites 29 and 30 look choice; while they don't have water or electric hookups, they're right out on a point.

Mainayr is at the far northern reach of the area we cover in this book, so it feels more "Down East" than Mid-Coast. The area around it has very little development — just a lot of small coastal fishing villages with a simplicity and charm all their own.

Mainayr is open Memorial Day to Columbus Day; rates start at $15.75 for two people and children younger than 5. Water and electric hookups are available.

Mount Desert Island

Bar Harbor Campground
no credit cards • Maine Hwy. 3, Bar Harbor • 288-5185

With 300 sites on 100 acres, this is a big (but relaxed) campground. It doesn't take reservations, and it hasn't for 30 years. That means anyone has a crack at one of its 300 sites, even during high season; just get there early enough. There are a range of sites from wooded to open-field, and you get to choose your own. The pool here is on a high bluff overlooking Frenchman Bay and the Schoodic Mountains. The sites near it are splendid, surrounded by blueberry fields, and yes, you can pick them for your pancakes.

Bar Harbor Campground is open Memorial Day to Columbus Day; rates start at $17 for four people. Water, electric and sewage hookups are available.

Mt. Desert Campground
Maine Hwy. 198, Somesville • 244-3710

The brochure is so goofy, it's hip, and the campground itself is a tenter's paradise in an astonishingly good location. Only smaller RVs are allowed here — 20 feet maximum — and no dogs during July, August and holiday weekends. This camp store is a real asset, with fresh-brewed coffee, fresh-baked pies, cookies and muffins. Groceries and camping supplies are available as well.

Established in 1958, Mt. Desert's been owned by Owen and Barbara Craighead since 1984. They scaled back the number of sites from 200 to 152 and reduced the number of cars allowed to one per site. The sites themselves are arranged along Somes Sound, the only fjord on the East Coast, and some boast startlingly good water views. (Site C23 looks choice, and it has electricity.) Nonrefundable deposits are required for reservations in July and August.

Mt. Desert Campground is open from June 20 to mid-September; rates start at $22 for two adults and two children younger than 18. Electric and water hookups are available.

As is true of the rest of Maine, there's a time-honored feel to browsing in the Mid-Coast region: The capacity for quiet, unhurried looking is still cherished.

Shopping

We know you've come to Maine to breathe the crisp air, soak in the expansiveness of sea and sky, hike the hills, paddle the waters, settle at a cove at sunset with a lobster in one hand and cracker in the other. . . . But, let's face it, the shopping is fun too. A lot of fun. Antique dealers come in droves to wade through the goods at auctions, flea markets and stores. Gallery owners and dealers interested in fine crafts, great art or unusual objects also come to Maine for the pickings. And we're sure there are bookworms who would just as soon scan the 125,000 books lining the aisles of the Big Chicken Barn outside Ellsworth as scan the waters of Frenchman Bay off Bar Harbor's Shore Path.

As is true of the rest of Maine, there's a time-honored feel to browsing in the Mid-Coast region: The capacity for quiet, unhurried looking is still cherished. Talk to shopkeepers — the woman staffing the craft store might well be the weaver of the elegant scarf you covet. The vintner has a lot to say about what foods could best accompany the wines you might be buying. That antique dealer could tell you a thing or two about the family who stocked the hutch you're considering, perhaps even about the carpenter who made it.

We've organized this chapter both by subject and by town. We start with the region's two major malls. If you're interested in antiques, books or specialty foods (is there anyone who isn't?), peruse the beginning of the chapter. First you'll find antique stores, arranged alphabetically within our four general geographic regions: Waldoboro to Stockton Springs, Inland to Bangor, Bucksport to Gouldsboro and Mount Desert Island. Bookstores follow, then specialty-food stops, each in a similar arrangement. Finally, in our "Shopping the Main Streets" section, we take a narrative tour of the stores you'll find in Waldoboro, Thomaston, Camden, Belfast, Bangor, Ellsworth, Blue Hill and on Mount Desert Island.

Major Malls

Wherever you're coming from, you probably have more substantial malls at home. Maine just is not a mall kind of place; still, these shopping centers are meccas for locals from outlying towns who might spend a weekend in Bangor just soaking up the fluorescent lights. What is commonplace for visitors can be a real treat for us.

Inland to Bangor

Bangor Mall
Hogan Rd., Bangor • 947-7333

The recently renovated Bangor Mall is hard to miss with its more than 80 shops. Anchor tenants include Sears, JCPenney and Porteous department stores, supplemented by popular clothing chains Victoria's Secret, Gap, The Limited and Casual Corner. Local favorites include My Maine Bag, which sells totes and handbags, while Treasured Maine Crafts, offers just that.

If you get hungry with all that walking, you can hit Dairy Queen for ice cream, or McDonald's for burgers and fries. Sit-down restaurants include '50s-style Bee Boppers.

The Bangor Mall has attracted a variety of businesses on its outskirts. One of the more notable nearby tenants is Borders Books, Music and Cafe, 116 Bangor Mall Boulevard, an extraordinary new chain offering more than 100,000 book titles and a dazzling array of CDs and cassettes. You'll find a cafe with live music twice a week, including Friday night jazz, and author events, discussions and workshops.

Airport Mall
Union and Griffin Sts., Bangor • 945-6222

Near (you guessed it!) the airport, this mall

has 25 stores, including Staples, the office-supply chain; Radio Shack, for home electronics; and Fashion Bug, offering ladies clothing. Twin City Coin has a large selection of sports clothing, hats, baseball cards and coins, while Bloomers sells ladies lingerie to size 4X (it carries Camille Beckman toiletries) as well as candles and a small selection of items for men.

One of the nicest ways to remember Maine is with gemstones mined here. While that includes amethysts and garnets, tourmaline is probably the runaway favorite. The Diamond Connection has some 3,000 settings of these stones in 14-carat gold. Not surprisingly, diamonds are the other specialty here. Since the store buys from one of the 10 largest suppliers in the state, you can usually find higher quality for less.

FYI

Unless otherwise noted, the area code for all phone numbers listed in this guide is 207.

Antiques

Waldoboro to Stockton Springs

Paul Fuller Antiques
Maine Hwy. 220, North Waldoboro • 832-5550

This is a truly extraordinary shop. Paul Fuller scouts Canada, the British Isles, France and Germany and brings back wonderful things he sells at reasonable prices. He also finds great local items. The last time we were there he was displaying a 5-foot-square map of Maine (c. 1862) that looked like it belonged in a museum. The only catch here is finding the shop open. Your best bet is weekends during the summer.

Beach House Antiques
U.S. Hwy. 1, Lincolnville • 789-5323

A favorite with antique buyers who wend their way up the coast, Beach House has a good selection of furniture, estate jewelry, books and tools. Owner Paul Turnbull is an active buyer, so unusual finds pop up frequently. We were especially smitten by a hand-some set of Adirondack lawn furniture, but it sold to a Midwestern antiques dealer. Beach House is open March to December.

Liberty Tool Company
Maine Hwy. 173, Liberty • 589-4771

How to tell you about Liberty Tool? The first floor is crowded with old tools, so it's a favorite with woodworkers and anyone looking for secondhand and hard-to-find implements. The second and third floors have books, furniture, kitchen items, old postcards, even a small lending library. This place is dusty and musty, but that's part of its charm. This place is about a half-hour drive from Lincolnville, and hours may be limited during the winter months, so call ahead.

Captain Tinkham's Emporium, 548-6465, on U.S. Highway 1 in Searsport, is its sister store, so you'll find similar merchandise there.

Hard Alee
51 Bayview St., Camden • 236-3373

It's about time someone gave Camden's well-to-do a place to sell their things on consignment. The owner is delightful, and the stock seems to change by the week. Look for elegant furniture, paintings, jewelry and objets d'art. Hard Alee has abbreviated hours in the winter, so call ahead.

Suffolk Gallery
47 Bayview St., Camden • 236-8868

Though it's small, we think this is one of the nicest places around. Run by a lovely British woman who buys overseas, Suffolk Gallery offers fine furniture, paintings, china and silver — all of it tasteful and understated. Suffolk Gallery is closed in the winter months.

Landmark Architectural Antiques
4 Main St., Belfast • 338-9901

The name says it all: mantelpieces, sinks, tubs and more from the 1850s to the 1950s. This is a great place to go if you own an old home and want to restore the ravages of earlier renovations. Landmark is closed during the winter months, and may be open by appointment.

Hickson's Flea Market
U.S. Hwy. 1, Searsport • no phone

With a changing array of vendors — some tacky, some wonderful — this seasonal flea market is one of the reasons Searsport fancies itself the antique capital of the state. This is the first place we saw Tupperware displayed as a collectible, but then, we found an exquisite hobnail glass vase for $25. Summer weekends are mob scenes, so get an early start.

Pumpkin Patch Antique Center
U.S. Hwy. 1, Searsport • 548-6047

Open from April to October, this group shop in a two-story barn has been in operation for more than 20 years. While its 20 to 25 dealers specialize in Americana, a number of them focus on niches such as nautical items, oak items, quilts, decoys and china.

Searsport Flea Market
U.S. Hwy. 1, Searsport • 548-2640

You can't miss this place. As you drive though town on summer weekends, the traffic starts to slow as vans negotiate the most perilous roadside parking arrangements. As with Hickson's (see previous entry), your best bet is to get an early start. This flea market is seasonal.

Searsport Antique Mall
U.S. Hwy. 1, Searsport • 548-2640

You'll find two floors with niches for 74 dealers who sell everything from Happy Meal toy collectibles to fine decoys and primitive antiques. And it's open year round!

Inland to Bangor

Alcott Antiques
30 Central St., Bangor • 942-7706

Owner Patricia Alcott has early country furniture and accessories, especially pieces in their original paint. She prefers pieces circa 1850 or earlier, although some of her rustics are later than that. She also specializes in hooked rugs. The fact that this is a group shop adds scope to Alcott's collection.

The Center Mall
39 Center St., Brewer • 989-9842

This group shop focuses on quality. You'll find 50-plus dealers in some 12,000 square feet of space. The owners chose vendors based on their specialties, so expect a well-rounded store offering everything from furniture selling for several thousand dollars to china and books selling for a fraction of that.

Lavender and Old Lace
1103 N. Main St. (U.S. Hwy. 1A), Winterport • 223-4703

Don't be put off by Beth Laverty's quarter-mile driveway. At the end of it you'll find a shop that rewards your efforts. Laverty got her start in linens and laces, and she's branched out into '30s and '40s kitchenware. In some ways, it's less of an antique shop than a store for those who want to decorate their homes with practical items from an earlier era. Either way, it's a great place to poke around. While Laverty's shop is closed in the winter months, she says she wouldn't turn you away if you showed up at her door.

Bucksport to Gouldsboro

Architectural Antiquities
Goose Falls Rd., off Maine Hwy. 176, Harborside • 326-4938

Driving through Maine, we sometimes see houses struggling for life as they settle into the mud, first along the northern side, then the western edge, sinking like stallions caught in quicksand. It's a heartbreaking sight. The folks at Architectural Antiquities can't actually rescue such homes, but they do save parts of their insides — recovering fixtures from buildings facing the wrecking ball, or from others facing the interior equivalent — renovation. John Jacobs travels around New England in search of interesting features: fireplaces, doors, windows, columns and more. He cleans them, restores them and can even guarantee some of them. Innkeepers seeking Victorian brass doorknobs, historic homeowners looking for authentic 1920s plumbing, and reno-

Photo: Mary (Dysart) Hartt

Dozens of pleasure craft are tied up at moorings or the pier at Southwest Harbor when summer season ushers thousands of tourists to Maine's picturesque coast.

vators simply wanting to add elegance in the form of an etched glass window and cut glass lighting fixtures all find their way to this Harborside shop. Original architectural features number in the thousands and are displayed in several showrooms. But call ahead — John may be off on a buying trip.

Belcher's Antiques and Gifts
Water St., Blue Hill • 374-5769
Reach Rd., Deer Isle • 348-9938

Linda Friedmann and Jean Hutchinson run two stores. The larger one operates from two rooms of an old farmhouse and two floors of a barn on the Reach Road of Deer Isle, just off Maine Highway 15. The smaller one is on Water Street in Blue Hill. Both sell antiques and quality new items. The Blue Hill shop stocks about half antiques and half local crafts, while the Deer Isle shop sells its crafts and gift items from a separate gift shop on the top floor of the barn.

Though Friedmann and Hutchinson used to make and sell rustic twig furniture with a Victorian flair, the antique business is now monopolizing their time. You might still find a few pieces of the twig furniture, but mostly you'll find an array of antiques from the 1850s to the 1940s. Look in either shop for country

antiques, nautical items, kitchen items, folk art and toys. The gift shop at the Deer Isle shop features mostly locally made crafts, sprinkled with a few mass-produced items. Both shops are open June through October and by chance or appointment at other times.

Big Chicken Barn Books and Antiques
U.S. Hwy. 1, Ellsworth • 667-7308

Not more than 25 years ago, when the chicken industry was strong, the state was dotted with huge chicken barns housing rotating stocks of chicks. But the industry folded in the 1970s, leaving massive, empty spaces begging for transformation. One of the best metamorphoses we've seen has stood on the road to Ellsworth for the past dozen years — the Big Chicken Barn.

The hulking barn fills two full floors with great old stuff. Antiques are nudged into the bottom floor, filling just about every square foot. Books line the top (see the subsequent "Book Shops" section). Currently, more than 50 antique dealers, most of whom hail from Maine, sell everything from armoires to tin zebras. It's a great source for almost anything. Whether we're looking for dining chairs, lamps or wedding gifts, the Chicken

Barn is one of our first stops. We never know for sure what we'll find, but we have found clocks, costumes, dolls, glassware, hooked rugs, jewelry, paintings, porcelain, pottery, even old sap buckets. The barn is open daily June through September, then on selected days the rest of the year. Because hours vary according to the season, it's best to call ahead.

Eagull Antiques
E. Main St., Stonington • 367-6500

Near the end of Main Street, Eagull Antiques harkens back to the days of Maine's Oriental trade. There are exotic objects, inlaid and carved furnishings from across the globe and odd fold-up chairs or tables carried by early voyagers to Maine's wild country. Most of the objects are from the 18th and 19th centuries; some are domestic, others from the Orient; and there's always one object, whether an old farm implement or a foreign tool of some sort, that puzzles even the well-versed owner.

His and Hers Antiques
U.S. Hwy. 1, Ellsworth • 667-2115

Does shopping divide you? Does he stop at every boat for sale, every 1940s convertible jeep? Does she only want to noodle through the fabrics and pottery? Here's a genuine save-your-marriage solution: an antique store packed with baby-boomer collectibles meant to unite you. Look especially for old toys, like pedal cars you once played in (or wish you could have), old dolls, perhaps model trains. Proprietor Ed Weirick is an antique-toys consultant. He also has a collection of old advertising signs, road signs, old gas pumps, soda machines, soda fountain stools and all kinds of bottles. Generally, Ed's shop is open daily Memorial Day weekend until the end of September, or by appointment — unless he's on the road consulting on toys.

Leila Day Antiques and Gallery
Main St., Castine • 326-8786

The extensive gardens through which you reach Leila Day Antiques and Gallery make coming here an awaited experience even before entering the store. Inside the restored Federal-style former home, you'll delight in the array of late 18th- and early 19th-century country and formal antiques on display. Some of the furniture here hails from around the region, but you might also find select wares from Europe and elsewhere in the United States.

That's not all. Day is the exclusive dealer for Castine folk painter Judith Payne, who creates maritime and coastal scenes of Maine. She also sells porcelain, quilts, sea chests, nautical accessories, baskets and other folk art.

Leila Day Antiques and Gallery is open daily June through October; otherwise, call for an appointment.

Liros Gallery
Main St., Blue Hill • 374-5664, 374-5370, (800) 287-5370

The draw here is the beautifully painted wooden Russian icons that have become a family passion for the owners of this gallery. You'll find pieces dating back to the 17th, 18th and 19th centuries; fine 19th- and early 20th-century paintings; and old prints and maps. Liros Gallery is small, but its vision is large.

Love Barn and Flea Market
Bucksport Rd. (U.S. Hwy. 1), Bucksport
• no phone

Come summer weekends, the attached flea market can be a hopping place, with numerous tables chock-full of toys, glassware, tools and simple junk. In the off-season we come to the two-story barn to sift through the array of well-priced goods in search of special kitchen items and collectibles. We save the best for last; the main house is lined with early 20th-century glassware and stuffed with fine oak furniture.

Mill Mall Treasures
240 State St. (U.S. Hwy. 1A), Ellsworth
• 667-8055

More than 50 antique dealers fill this mall in a mall, at the entrance to downtown Ellsworth (if you're coming from Bangor). Antique-wicker dealer E.L. Higgens (see subsequent entry) sells his glassware and other non-wicker antiques here, joining dealers selling Victorian, oak, period Americana and country furniture, along with more glassware, china, pottery, stoneware and an assortment of decorative accessories and collectibles. Mill Mall Treasures is open daily year round, except major holidays.

Moto-Car
U.S. Hwy. 1A, Ellsworth • 667-4592, 667-7376

Terry Pinkham has been collecting motor cars since he was 15 years old, and he's been selling them for almost as long. Pinkham has been at this location since 1975, buying and selling special-interest automobiles worldwide. When we last visited his lot, Pinkham had a LaSalle, a 1930s Whippet, Model A and Model T Fords, Studebakers, Corvettes and a polished 1915 Dodge ensconced in the showroom. In the last five years, Pinkham has sold his share of cars to the stars: a 1940s Ford to Kirstie Alley; a 1947 Studebaker truck to her ex-husband, Parker Stephenson; and a Mercedes Benz to Alley's friend and fellow Islesboro resident, John Travolta. But what intrigued us most were the signs he placed on his spruced and polished cars: "Don't lean unless you're nude." Moto-Car is open Monday through Saturday year round, and forever, says Pinkham, by appointment.

Old Cove Antiques
Maine Hwy. 15, Sargentville • 359-2031, 359-8585

Peg and Olney Grindall sell formal and country furniture from their store in Sargentville from Memorial Day through Labor Day and by chance or appointment the rest of the year.

You'll find tables and chairs adorned in their original paint, decorative accessories, nautical objects, paintings, quilts, hooked rugs and other folk art, decoys and other small objects, much of it bought locally from auctions and estate sales.

Old Fire House
Maine Hwy. 15, Deer Isle • 348-9978

We were just beginning to admit that our old rocker was too far gone for living room use, just beginning to wonder whether to replace it with an armchair, when lo and behold, we passed the Old Fire House just outside of Deer Isle Village. For much less than any armchair we could find, we bought a vintage wicker rocker that looks like it's always belonged in our home. Owners Arthur and Bonita Poitras are open during the summer season (say from June through September) and offer a wide range of 19th- and 20th-century antiques.

Mount Desert Island

Aquarius Arteffects and Primitive Art Gallery
Maine Hwy. 102, Town Hill • 288-4143

Is this an antique store or a world art store? Both, really. You will find rare, frequently old artifacts from across the globe, much of it sacred art, such as African masks, Indonesian spirit figures and Plains Indian pipes, as well as junk-metal folk-art sculptures, Oriental rugs and modern architectural treasures. You might also find a 14-foot carved New Guinea Asmat ancestor sculpture or a 14-inch Mexican Day of the Dead skeletal figure with its head nodding off a spring. It all depends on what's come in and what's been bought. The adventure is in the looking. Aquarius Arteffects is usually open from late June until just past Columbus Day.

Marianne Clark, Fine Antiques

Main St. (Maine Hwy. 102), Southwest Harbor • 244-9247

Tucked in the quiet town of Southwest Harbor, this fine antique store is filled with high-quality 18th- and 19th-century American furniture beginning with Queen Anne. Both country-style pine and formal cherry and mahogany pieces can be found here as well as paintings from past centuries, folk art and appropriate accessories. Most pieces are from Maine estates. Clark is open mid-June through mid-October, or by appointment.

E.L. Higgins Antique Wicker

off Maine Hwy. 102, Bernard • 244-3983

So, you want to refurnish your home to look like a Maine summer cottage? If you have money to spend and want only high-quality, high-end pieces in perfect condition, find your way beyond Southwest Harbor to E.L. Higgins in Bernard. Higgins, the region's preeminent antique wicker emporium, carries furniture from the 1860s to the 1940s, with more than 300 pieces in stock. You won't find as much antique wicker anywhere else, or as good quality wicker. (Higgins says most wicker made today is not nearly as good as the old stuff, which was built on wood and actually does last.) Higgins' shop is open daily from April to October and by appointment other times.

Shaw Antiques and Fine Art

204 Main St., Bar Harbor • 288-9355, 288-0114

For the very finest 19th-century American and British furniture, glassware and silver, stop at Shaw's in downtown Bar Harbor. Shaw has done his research; he knows his pieces and only sells what is "correct." Most of the furniture he stocks is made of mahogany, cherry and good-quality pine. Some pieces are painted — but only if it's correct to the period; most is not, he says. You'll also find paintings and marine art of the past century. Shaw Antiques is open weekends from late April until June 15, then Monday through Saturday until mid-October.

For a year-round glimpse at Shaw's collection, visit his store a few miles outside town at the Chiltern Inn, 3 Cromwell Harbor Road, off Main Street.

Pine Bough

Main St., Northeast Harbor • 276-5079, 244-7060

Associated with Wikhegan Books (see subsequent entry), the Pine Bough offers the objects that might have surrounded a home's fine collection of old books, like early writing devices and nineteenth century decorative arts. Since the store has been enlarged, there's a lot more room for fine antiques, as well as books. It's open mid-May through mid-October, or by appointment.

Book Shops

Serious book lovers could make a tour of Maine antiquarian bookstores and still see some of Maine's most beautiful sights. That's because the towns of Maine's Mid-Coast — Camden, Stockton, Bangor, Castine, Blue Hill, Deer Isle, Ellsworth and those on Mount Desert Island — are spiced with old book shops.

Whether you like an intimate shop or a huge barn, cosmopolitan urbanity or the feel of someone's country library; whether you're looking to add to a serious collection or to settle a question with a quotation from an out-of-print volume, chances are you'll find your source here.

There are so many antiquarian bookstores in the region that we've limited this section to the old shops. Except for a very few special contemporary bookstores that we would go out of our way to visit, we discuss new bookstores in our subsequent "Shopping the Main Streets" section.

Waldoboro to Stockton Springs

Lobster Lane Bookstore
Island Rd., off Maine Hwy. 73, Spruce Head • 594-7520

A surprising number of titles tucked into a shoreside outbuilding make this well worth the trip halfway down the St. George Peninsula (Spruce Head is south of South Thomaston). This place is well-known in the trade for its selection of fiction, nonfiction and Maine-related titles. It's open Thursday through Sunday June to September and weekends throughout May and October. Note that the listed number is the owner's home.

Dooryard Books
436 Main St., Rockland • 594-5080

This charming little shop could be in London; it looks old, comfy and crowded. Fortunately, it's right in the center of Rockland, and it specializes in hunting, fishing and sporting titles. You'll find it open May through October.

ABCdef
23 Bayview St., Camden • 236-3904

This wonderful store sells rare and used books and specializes in maritime, art, New England and history titles. Ask about the rare-book room, with first editions, leather-bound books and 18th- and 19th-century volume sets. ABCdef has one of the most imaginative display windows around, and inside, it has that quiet, intelligent atmosphere book lovers crave.

Hooked rugs and armchairs make it seem downright homey — a blissful place to be on a quiet, rainy afternoon. It's open late March through mid-January.

Stone Soup Books
35 Main St., Camden • 763-3354

This small second-story shop is filled to overflowing. Fortunately, owner Paul Joy knows what he has and can help you find what you're looking for. We see him out around town scouring yard sales and tag sales, and he's amassed an excellent collection of titles.

Penobscot Books
164 W. Main St. (U.S. Hwy. 1), Searsport • 548-6490

While the exterior of Penobscot Books is a startling yellow, the interior has an almost Zen-like elegance. This is a great place for books on fine arts, painting, sculpture, photography and architecture. We also found an strong selection of philosophy/religion titles. In the winter months after Christmas, Penobscot Books is open by chance or appointment.

The Booklover's Attic
U.S. Hwy. 1, Searsport • 338-2450

As the name might suggest, this is not a musty, dusty used-book store. It's fresh and clean — many of the books have dust covers — and owners Peter and Estelle Plumb are meticulous organizers. Look for aviation, military, hunting, fishing, music, Americana and children's titles as well as a fine collection of records plus American first editions behind glass doors. The shop is open mid-April to mid-October.

Inland to Bangor

Lippincott Books
36 Central St., Bangor • 942-4398

Bill Lippincott's 2,000-square-foot shop holds 30,000 titles from as early as 1488 — *Predicabilia Porphirii*, a medieval scholar's commentary on Aristotle — to as recent as last month. Prices range from $1 for paperbacks to $10,000 for rare editions. While carrying a range of subjects, Lippincott has a notably large stock of Maine hunting and fishing titles as well as a number of hard-to-find works on Eastern Woodland Indians.

Bucksport to Gouldsboro

Big Chicken Barn Books and Antiques
U.S. Hwy. 1, Ellsworth • 667-7308

Here stands the proud rooster — the big, fat, crowing rooster in full, puffed plumage — of old bookstores. Above the floor of antiques (see the previous "Antiques" section) in this former chicken barn, you'll find a jam-packed floor of old books — at least 125,000 of them. You'll find books of every kind: Maine books; nautical books; books on religion, Americana, nature and health; mysteries; cookbooks; fictional works; leather-bound classics; autographed books; hand-set and handmade books; old pulp paperbacks; and much, much more.

Owner Annegret Cukierski buys and trades books almost on a daily basis, going into homes to look at large collections and reviewing smaller collections from her crowded office at the barn. You'll find some 430 different magazine titles too. The section of carefully preserved *LIFE*, *The Saturday Evening Post* and *Better Homes and Gardens* magazines is just a starter. You'll find the nautical magazines you drooled over as a child, newspapers from the day you were born and much more.

Just before Christmas one year, we found ourselves climbing the steep stairs to the book level. While hunting through the Maine section for some reference books, we couldn't help overhearing two little boys, neither of whom could have been much older than 6. Somehow, among the hundred-thousand books, they had found their way to a book about the Christmas story. As one boy read aloud to the other, the two got to speculating over the nature of God (whether a He, She, It or Other) and the relationship of Santa Claus to God. We were not alone among the browsers stopping to listen. We could picture returning in 20 years and finding the same two boys as grown men, still pondering the issue among the Big Chicken Barn's aisles of dusty tomes. The shop is open daily June through September; hours vary according to the season.

The Book Shelf
24 State St., Ellsworth • 667-1120

Maite and Pete Johnson's Book Shelf is just a few steps from the Ellsworth Library. It's a small place and has the feel of an older store, perhaps from a time when the building housing the library was a grand mansion. Books are displayed on shelves and tables here, with the more precious works stored away inside cabinets. The mix is great: titles you've been missing (paperbacks from the 1950s and '60s, for instance) as well as true antique books in fine bindings. There's one children's section for browsing (complete with toys) and another, with volumes too delicate and precious for chubby hands, placed high and out of reach.

For older readers, The Book Shelf stocks Maine books, quality cookbooks, nature books and general literature.

If you can't seem to find what you're looking for, the Johnsons can do a book search. They are knowledgeable and genuinely interested people — not only about books, but also many subjects. One lazy summer afternoon, we heard them easily segue from Latin American politics to 1950s culture to speculation on antique children's books, all in a matter of minutes.

Dolphin Books & Prints
Maine Hwy. 166, Castine • 326-0888, 326-4467

Maine Highway 166, the road to Castine, branches into Maine 166 and 166A, and you'll find a bookseller on either route (see the subsequent Barbara Falk entry). The roads rejoin later, so if you like books, make the loop and check out both shops.

Leon and Elizabeth Ballou of Dolphin Books & Prints offer an extensive collection of antiquarian, rare and out-of-print books. The emphasis here is on Maine, nautical themes, modern literature, biography, history, natural history, architecture, art, gardening, cooking, crafts and children's books — in short, almost any topic. Modern first editions are a specialty. You'll also find antique prints and framed art.

Dolphin Books & Prints is open much of the year, but only by chance or appointment in winter, so call ahead (especially if the leaves have already turned color).

Flea markets and craft fairs dot the landscape along Maine's popular coastal highways.

Barbara Falk
Maine Hwy. 166A, Castine • 326-4036

Call ahead to visit Barbara Falk and peruse the select collection of antiquarian books. You'll need both an appointment and directions. Falk carries general books from the 17th to 20th centuries, with an emphasis on literature, women, poetry and better-quality children's books. She also has a growing stock of ephemeral material from around the nation and the world: letters, maps, guides, advertising and miscellaneous literature.

Falk's book shop is connected to her home and is open from May to October by appointment only.

Wayward Books
Maine Hwy. 15, Sargentville • 359-2397

A literary couple from New York retired to Sargentville and opened this excellent bookstore serving some 12,000 "choice used and medium rare books," along with a good selection of Maine books of recent and older vintage. There's an excellent selection of poetry, art and architecture as well as a well-rounded collection of literature, among a more general stock of books. This is a very literary place, almost as if the New York landmark bookstore Gotham Books had taken a vacation and gotten waylaid on the coast of Maine.

Wayward is open May through December, or call for an appointment. Proceed slowly along Maine 15 as you approach the Deer Isle Bridge. The store is on your left behind a tall stand of trees, and it comes upon you unexpectedly.

Mount Desert Island

Port in a Storm
Main St. (Maine Hwy. 102), Somesville
• 244-4114, (800) 694-4114

With it's two-story window overlooking Somes Sound, Port in a Storm is in just about the loveliest location for a bookstore we can imagine. It's not an antique bookstore, but it's so well-suited to the reader, we've included it in this book lover's journey. Painted bright white, with tall ceilings soaring two stories high and a large stairwell to the second floor, Port in a Storm is the kind of place you want to settle in, snuggling by the window with a rocking chair beneath you and a cat in your lap.

It's not impossible. Cats Fred and Ginger have been fixtures at the store since it opened in 1992. And settling in is not frowned upon — that is, if you can tear yourself away from the multitude of titles and fix upon just one book.

Deer Isle's Craftspeople

It's true that craftspeople have long been interested in the hands-on life of rural Maine. That's how Haystack Mountain School of Crafts got started in 1950. As the school slowly grew, many of the summer faculty and students saw the possibilities of a creative community on rather remote Deer Isle. They began to settle in. Other craftspeople followed. Today, a drive through Deer Isle holds both the spectacular scenery of sky and sea and the more earthly adventure of peeking in at numerous local craft studios.

Close-up

What follows is a driving tour of the arts and crafts of the island. Please remember that most of the listings are of working artists, some of them getting on in years. Also, places do come and go frequently. We've tried to limit ourselves to long-standing craftspeople, but don't let this list limit you. If some place looks interesting, stop in and check it out.

You've crossed the bridge onto Deer Isle. Keep going on Maine Highway 15, passing over the long, narrow causeway that connects Little Deer Isle with Deer Isle. Once you've driven onto terra firma again, you'll see a sign for Old Ferry Road. Turn left to visit **Ronald Hayes Pearson Design Studio**, 348-2535, a gallery of fine handcrafted gold and silver jewelry that's open Monday through Saturday in summer and Monday through Friday the rest of the year. Returning back to Maine Highway 15 for about a half-mile, you'll notice the blue Maine highway signs announcing **William Mor** on the Reach Road. Drive 3.3 miles until you get to 409 Reach Road, where you'll find Mor, maker of stoneware and seller of Oriental rugs. Mor has been throwing functional pottery for use on the dining table for 20 years. He also is a connoisseur of fine tribal and village rugs and kilims, and he sells them, along with vegetable-dyed Afghan and Tibetan carpets woven under projects guided by the organization Cultural Survival. (Buyers can rest assured that no children have been detained from school or play to make the rugs.) Like many craftspeople, Mor is open much of the summer, but by appointment only in winter; call 348-2822.

Returning to Maine Highway 15, you might check to see whether **George Hardy** is around. Hardy (no phone listing) is a Deer Isle native who began carving whimsical animals to lessen the loneliness after his wife died. The products of his sadness have brought cheer to many, especially after a local boy created the documentary *George Hardy, Folk Artist* to fulfill graduation requirements at Hampshire College in Massachusetts. The video has been shown on public television and is available at many local stores. If Hardy's studio is open, by all means, stop in. Also try **Hance Pottery**, 348-2883, where Charles Hance produces high-quality stoneware and flatware. Hance Pottery keeps hours in summer, or make an appointment the rest of the year.

Proceed on Maine 15 until you get to Deer Isle Village at the island's minuscule waist. For elegant crafts mixed with fine art, stop by the **Turtle Gallery** (on the left going into town), 348-9977, where Haystack's founding director, Fran Merritt, lived for more than 40 years. Today, Elena Kubler presides over the lovely barn gallery, exhibiting paintings, crafts and sculptural objects — much of it made by Deer Isle artists.

You'll find other stops in the village. Across from the Turtle Gallery, potter **Melissa Green** and blacksmith **Eric Zeiner**, 348-2601, feature garden sculpture, large wheel-thrown vessels and more. Look for their open sign or call for an appointment. Just two houses off Maine 15, at 6 Dow Road, is the **Maine Crafts Association Shop**. The association, a large nonprofit craft resource organization, has about 700 members. The

— continued on next page

Quilt making is part of Maine's summer-long festivals, where craft tables offer these handmade treasures for sale.

shop is open year round, Monday through Friday; call 348-9943 for summer hours. The **Deer Isle Artists Association**, open June through August (no phone), is in the same building. Also on Dow is the home and studio of **Daniel Hodermarsky**, a painter who has created exceptional images based on his experiences as a soldier in World War II. Call 348-6010 to find out if his studio is open.

Back on Maine Highway 15, across from the Bar Harbor Bank in Deer Isle Village, you'll find the **Blue Heron Gallery**, 348-6051. Open June through September, Blue Heron features the work of Haystack faculty.

On Church Street (Maine Highway 15 in town), **Dockside Quilt Gallery**, 348-2849 or 348-7712, sells locally made and custom-made quilts. Nearby, in the Seamark Building, you'll find classic furniture and paintings by **Bruce W. Bulger**, 348-9955, as well as some quilts, rugs, tiles, paintings and sculpture by other artists. Also look here for information on summer workshops, or call 348-9353.

Around the corner, on Main Street, Jenepher Burton has the **Mainstreet Studio + Gallery**. Besides making jewelry (you can watch her work), she also offers art for home and garden. She's usually open Monday through Saturday. **Terrell Lester Photography**, on the corner of Maine Highway 15 and Main Street, features Maine landscape photography. Lester's shop is open Monday through Friday from mid-May through early October and by chance or appointment thereafter; call 348-2676.

Leaving Deer Isle Village, you'll see the Mill Pond Mobil station on your right after about a quarter-mile. Turn left here onto a road known either as the Mountainville Road or the Sunshine Road, leading to Haystack Mountain School as well as several studios. About 2 miles in, turn onto French Camp Road to find **Carol Wainright's** weaving workshop. Scandinavian-trained, her 6-foot-wide rugs are hand-dyed, extremely dense and quite contemporary. Call 348-2580 for directions. Farther down Mountainville Road is **Mountainville Studios**, 348-5681, the workplace of Marcia and Vaino Kola. She is a potter, creating functional stoneware and porcelain pottery. He is a painter, drawer and maker of etchings and lithographs. The studios are in the Mountainville district of the Sunshine Road, on Fire Road 525. Call for precise directions.

Just past Mountainville Studio is **Nervous Nellie's Jams and Jellies** (see the previous "Specialty-food Shops and Stops" section), with its sculpture garden featuring work by Peter Berrits, 348-6182 or (800) 777-6845.

— continued on next page

As you continue down the long and winding road en route to Haystack, you'll cross the Sunshine Causeway onto Stinson Neck. At the Sunshine Advent church, turn right onto Fire Road 570 and go to 570A, the home and studio of **Jutta Graf**, maker of cotton rugs of contemporary design. As of press time she was considering a move off the island, so call in advance, 348-7751.

Back on the Sunshine Road, it's only a bit farther to **Haystack Mountain School of Crafts**. It is well worth the visit if you've never been, but call beforehand — unless you just want to see what's in the gallery at the entrance to the school. Otherwise, the administration asks that you wander only during specific visiting hours. It is a school, after all.

Continue on Maine 15 to Stonington, where you can visit **Emily Muir**, artist, writer, architect, craftsperson — practically an institution unto herself and nearing 94 years old. In the past, she has opened her studio Monday, Wednesday and Friday afternoons. You might try calling ahead, 367-2287, but know that Muir is quite hard of hearing. Look for the intersection marked by St. Mary's Church and Greenlaw Oil on Maine Highway 15 as you get into town. Turn left, and proceed past the lily pond to Fire Road 5, looking for signs for Muir.

There's much to do in Stonington as well, so park, stretch and browse. As you leave, consider taking Maine Highway 15A. Just out of town is **Green Head Forge**, 367-2632, at Old Quarry Road off W. Main Street. Here you'll find blacksmith Jack Hemenway and jewelry maker Harriet Rawle Hemenway. At the forge, he creates functional and sculptural objects of iron while she works on jewelry and small objects.

Returning off-island, if you haven't had your fill of craft, you have one more stop to make. **Harbor Farm**, just before the Deer Isle bridge on Maine Highway 15, 348-7737 or (800) 342-8003, is a large store featuring some Maine crafts — pottery, hooked rugs and etched glass — and plenty from around the world. It has everything from wood-burning stoves to hand-painted tiles on which the stoves may rest.

Owner Linda Lewis loves books, and she and her staff offer personal attention to all who come in. Maine is a featured subject, of course. The section of books by Maine authors and about Maine is one of the most extensive in the state. Art books, poetry collections and books about Mount Desert Island are plentiful. Lewis says she stocks at least 15,000 books year round, but come summer, she adds another 5,000. She also offers a book-club deal. After you've bought 10 books here, you receive a coupon for 10 percent of the cumulative cost of the books you've bought, which generally gets you an 11th book free.

Port in a Storm hosts authors for readings and talks (see our Arts chapter for more information).

Wikhegan Books
Main St., Northeast Harbor • 276-5079,
244-7060
The next best thing to browsing a London

bookseller (remember the one depicted in the film *84 Charing Cross Road*, based on the book by Helene Hanff?) is a stop at Wikhegan Books, dealing in out-of-print books. This bookstore, enlarged from its former intimate nook of a place, is lined with books from floor to ceiling, with a few spaces remaining for decorative antiques sold under the business Pine Bough (see previous "Antiques" section). You could browse for hours here, looking among the nautical titles, collections of Mount Desert Island history, books on the Eastern Woodland Indians, decorative arts, or natural history. Wikhegan is open from mid-May to mid-October, or by appointment.

Specialty-food Shops and Stops

On a glorious Maine summer day, you'd probably enjoy a meal in the warm sun rather than eat indoors; on a cold, misty day, you'd probably prefer to bring hot soup and fresh bread to savor by the warm fire in your cottage or room. To these ends, we include some options for picnics and take-outs as well as a few places offering packaged specialty foods. Here, too, you'll find some steady farmstands that generally are open all summer long; you'll pass others in your travels. For instance, if you're driving out of Bucksport in late June or early July, you can get juicy, fresh-picked strawberries at a stand just before the True Value hardware store. No name, no phone, just the sign: "Strawberries." We've gotten our best corn a bit closer to Bucksport out of the back of someone's truck. Just about anywhere you drive in Maine in summer, you'll find produce purveyors. Frequently, you'll see simply a card table, a few pints of blueberries and a coffee can. Take your pint, deposit your money, make change if you need to and remember the moment: You are trusted.

FYI

Unless otherwise noted, the area code for all phone numbers listed in this guide is 207.

Waldoboro to Stockton Springs

Borealis Breads
1860 Atlantic Hwy. (U.S. Hwy. 1 and Maine Hwy. 220), Waldoboro • 832-0655

Called Bodacious Breads when it started in 1993, this company has grown astronomically. No one would have guessed that plain bread would cause such a stir. But then, there's nothing plain about these hearth-baked rustic breads. Made of a mild sourdough, they come in elegant flavors including Kalamata olive, cardamom-raisin, sun-dried tomato, savory rosemary and orange date. You'll also find unadorned French and Italian breads. Word-of-mouth spurred a distribution network of more than 175 outlets, so check your nearest grocery as well.

Morse's Sauerkraut
3856 Washington Rd. (Maine Hwy. 220), Waldoboro • 832-5569

No preservatives, no additives, just fabu-

lous fresh sauerkraut, the way your grandparents used to make it. Shut down during the summer while the cabbage is growing, Morse's is open from September through May. It also sells beet relish, pickled beets and processed (cooked) sauerkraut, along with other Maine-made food products.

White Oak Farms
1986 Western Rd., Warren • 273-3695

Learning the truth about some farmstands is like learning the truth about Santa Claus. We found out the hard way: As we drove past a local stand early in the morning, we were shocked to see the "farmer" empty net bags of store-bought potatoes into his bins. That's not the case at White Oak Farms, which is why we're such fans. Open from May 1 to Thanksgiving, this family-run business tracks the seasons, with tomatoes from its hothouse, strawberries, blueberries, sweet corn, apples and cider. If you see signs for Beth's berries or Beth's corn, this is the place they're directing you to.

Morgan's Mills
168 Payson Rd. (Old Maine Hwy. 17), East Union • 785-4900

This water-powered flour mill sells a variety of stone-ground whole grains and great pancake, muffin and doughnut mixes in a country-store setting. Specialty foods, especially those made in Maine, are available too. Try the Griffles mix — they're like pancakes, only better.

Kohn's Smokehouse
Maine Hwy. 131 S., St. George • 372-8412

What looks like a converted garage is actually a retail store selling an amazing array of smoked fish, poultry, sausage and imported German delicacies. We've made wonderful picnics from items we've bought here.

Camden Farmer's Market
Colcord Ave., off Union St., Camden • no phone

Friends in-the-know say this is one of

the best farmers markets around. You'll find lots of organic items and lots of smiling people sauntering about. Its hours are 9 AM to noon Saturdays from mid-May through October. During July and August it's also open Wednesday evening from 4:30 to 6:30 PM.

Capt. Andy's
Upper Washington St., Camden • 236-2312

This home-based business is a great place for live or cooked lobsters to go. Best of all, Capt. Andy's delivers, so if your cottage doesn't have a big lobster pot, and you don't relish handling live lobsters (remember that scene in *Annie Hall*?), give 'em a call. The lobsters are caught daily, and cleaned clams are available as well. You can even get cooked, picked lobster meat — a real boon for chowder makers.

French & Brawn
1 Elm St., Camden • 236-3361

Established in 1868, French & Brawn is one of the oldest businesses in town and one of the few remaining independent grocers. In fact, the star that adorns Mount Battie at Christmas used to hang on the side wall of this shop. The much-loved Brawn family put its heart and soul in this business, and while it's changed hands, its call-you-by-name service still makes it the heart of town. Besides that, its meat counter is renowned. Between the meat counter, the deli and the produce department, you can put together a fabulous picnic.

Center General Store
Maine Hwy. 52, Lincolnville Center • 763-3666

The interior of this 1830s general store is right out a movie set: dark wood trim, wooden floors, glass-front display cases. In fact, it's been used as a backdrop in the movies *Man Without a Face* and *Thinner*. It stocks groceries, wine and liquor and sells take-out food, gas and fishing and hunting licenses. You'll also find a nice selection of videos to rent. It's a friendly, fun place to stop if you've had your fill of massive, modern food stores.

Belfast Co-op Store
123 High St., Belfast • 338-2532

Come and marvel at this amazing co-op. Unlike many we've frequented across the country, it's clean, well-organized, well-lighted and stocks a dazzling array of natural and organic selections. Friends on macrobiotic or other limited diets call it a godsend. Look for a deli, cafe and take-out counter as well.

Ducktrap River Fish Farms
57 Little River Dr., Belfast • 338-6280

This stop will take you off U.S. Highway 1 and into Belfast's tidy little industrial park, but it's a one-stop shop for delicious smoked salmon, trout and shellfish. You'll also find a full line of pâtés.

Young's Lobster Pound
Mitchell Ave., Box 4, Belfast • 338-1160

Turn off U.S. Highway 1 onto Mitchell Avenue to find lobsters, clams and corn. Get 'em cooked on site or to go. You can order a shore dinner — lobster, clams, corn, butter and potato chips — and eat it at one of the picnic tables out on the wharf. (Eating a lobster is a messy affair; enjoying it outdoors is the best way.) For dessert: ice cream pie.

Periwinkles Bakery
225 W. Main St. (U.S. Hwy. 1), Searsport • 548-9910

This truly spectacular bakery excels in the art of pastry-making. It's a perfect place to pick up Sunday morning brunch sweets. Periwinkles also has a small cafe. See the entry in our Restaurants chapter for more details.

Bucksport to Gouldsboro

Bah's Bake House
Water St., Castine • 326-9510

In just about five years, Bah's has changed the nature of Castine, elevating the quality of the town's daily food intake and exponentially expanding the level of its gossip. Bah's is the quintessential meeting place, where you may stop in with the best intentions of picking up a muffin, refilling your travel mug and getting to work, but wind up in a discussion of town, state or global politics. In summer, the conversation settles over tables on the expansive outside porch. In winter, folks crowd into the two interior rooms. But you can read about that in our Restaurants chapter.

For now, be aware that Bah's sells food to go — and lots of it at that: hearty soups, sesame noodles and thick sandwiches of liverwurst, roast beef, meat loaf, fish and chicken. It also sells French bread, pâtés and rich, sinful deserts such as pies, cheesecakes and thick chocolate fudge cakes. That's in addition to the morning offerings: coffee, croissants, muffins, coffee cakes, gingerbread, jelly rolls and whatever else Bah feels like making that day. Oh yes, we forgot the chocolate chip cookies, brownies — and the wines.

Bartlett Maine Estate Winery
U.S. Hwy. 1, Gouldsboro • 546-2408

Kathe and Bob Bartlett are food enthusiasts. They'll talk dishes, subtle food combinations and restaurants for hours. No wonder they opened a winery: For them, it's work from the heart. The quality of a wine's texture, the complexity of its blend and the tang it creates on the palate is the source of days, if not years, of consideration. The result of the Bartletts' mulling is a fine array of wines, none of which stems from the vine. Bartlett Maine Estate Winery produces award-winning vintage blends from New England fruits such as apples, pears, raspberries and blueberries. The raspberry wine, a sweet after-dinner affair, is as scrumptious as the raw fruit.

Still, the Bartletts are struggling against vine prejudice. To prove that their wines are not fruity, the winery offers tastings of five or six different kinds of wine (from dry to sweet) Monday through Saturday from Memorial Day weekend through Columbus Day weekend (except holidays). The tastings occur in July and August, may last a half-hour and are conducted by knowledgeable staff who will talk not only about the wines, but also about the food each wine might accompany. If you want a tour of the plant, with its oak and steel barrels and long, tentacle-like gleaming pipes, arrange it in advance.

Blue Hill Farmer's Market
Blue Hill Fairgrounds, Maine Hwy. 172, Blue Hill • no phone

One way to find food direct from the farmer is to go to a farmers market. You'll find local farmers selling produce at the Blue Hill Fairgrounds from 9 to 11:30 AM Saturdays from late June through September. If you're launching a garden, you frequently can pick up herbs and other plants here. You might also find prepared foods such as breads and jams.

Blue Hill Food Co-op
Greene's Hill Place, Main St. (Maine Hwy. 172), Blue Hill • 374-2165

This local food co-op offers a wide selection of organic vegetables, natural foods, bulk flours, seeds and grains, organic lamb, local poultry and alternative medicines, including herbal and homeopathic remedies. The store is well-stocked and popular, and it has recently expanded next door, allowing the public greater access to the grand array of foods, medicines and other products. A special bonus: the smells of the breads from Pain de Famille (see subsequent entry as well as our Restaurants chapter), baked fresh daily right at the co-op. Members of other co-ops may use their co-op cards for a discount here.

Blue Hill Tea and Tobacco
Main St., Blue Hill • 374-2161

For 20 years, William Petry and David Witter have been old-fashioned purveyors of the good things in life from out of this 1885 converted barn. Though the shop's name obscures it, the main offering here is wine. Wines sporting some 500 different labels are sold, including Maine's own Bartlett Estate Wines (see previous entry). Should you be in town the last Saturday of any month, stop by between 2 and 5 PM for a free wine tasting. The store also stocks a range of coffees, including organic varieties, and about 30 different kinds of loose tea from around the world that's sold the age-old way — loose in glass jars. And yes, you'll find premium cigars here as well as pipes and pipe tobacco.

Castine Co-op
Water St., Castine • 326-8760

As you stroll toward Bah's Bake House in

Castine (see previous entries in this section and in our Restaurants chapter), look to your left for the Castine Co-op. If it's summer, you won't be able to miss the expansive array of potted flowers and herbs casually placed outside — all for sale. Inside, there's a small array of locally grown organic produce; natural foods such as flours, nuts and dried fruits; organically raised poultry and lamb; and a delightful assortment of brightly painted, locally made pottery. If you're making a special trip, call ahead; the co-op keeps odd hours, frequently taking a long afternoon siesta.

Darthia Farm
W. Bay Rd. (Maine Hwy. 186), Gouldsboro • 963-7771

Bill and Cindy Thayer have made Darthia into a sort of testament to the possibilities of small, organic farms. The couple grows and sells a variety of produce. Ever eaten a fingerling potato that's literally finger-size? Ever tried a Russian banana potato? Add to this variety of potatoes 30 kinds of tomatoes; many kinds of sweet and hot peppers; squash and cucumbers; carrots and beets; beans and peas; herbs such as basil, cilantro and chives; mixed greens including mustard, kale and head lettuce; fresh and dried flowers; and prepared foods such as chutneys, jams, vinegars and the like. The Thayers also sell organic lamb and free-range poultry, but plan to wait on turkeys — they're sold out a year in advance.

The Thayers work the farm with the help of their daughter-in-law and a handful of summer apprentices. Come at 2 PM on a Tuesday or Thursday in July or August, and Bob or an apprentice will give you a farm tour culminating with a horse-drawn wagon ride ($2 per person). The farmstand is open Monday through Saturday from June through the end of September, sometimes longer.

John Edwards Market
158 Main St., Ellsworth • 667-9377

John Edwards Market is Ellsworth's natural-foods store. About three years ago, the market moved from a tiny space across the street to this expansive store. It's made all the difference. You can browse in comfort without worrying about jostling your fellow shoppers; the selection is vast, and you get the feeling the goods are well watched over. You'll find vitamins, homeopathic medicines, health foods, skin-care products, fresh-baked bread, gourmet coffee and wine as well as organic fruits and vegetables and natural pet supplies. Unlike health-food stores in most other towns, this market is not a cooperative. It is open daily year round.

Ellsworth Farmer's Market
High St. (U.S. Hwy. 1), Ellsworth
• no phone

Ellsworth Farmer's Market is a popular stop on the commercial strip in Ellsworth from July through October. You'll find produce, herbs and prepared foods from regional purveyors. The market is open 2 to 5:30 PM Monday and Thursday and 9:30 AM to 12:30 PM Saturday.

Haight Farm Farmstand
Maine Hwy. 175, South Blue Hill
• 374-2840

Courteney and Woody Haight grow their vegetables hydroponically (in nutrient-rich water). That way, they can raise lettuce, herbs, tomatoes, edible flowers such as nasturtiums, violas and a special variety of very small marigolds from March until December. The farmstand, about 2.5 miles beyond the Blue Hill Falls bridge, is open Memorial Day until the end of October and also sells some gourmet foods like jams and olives. You might also find Haight Farm produce at farmers markets and some local stores.

Herrick Bay Farm
Flye Point Rd., Brooklin • 359-2772

Guess the favorite food sold at this summer farmstand: Berries? (Mmmm, fresh-picked strawberries, blueberries, raspberries.) Nope. Corn? (Ahhh, just off the stalk. Is there anything better?) Wrong again. Tomatoes? No. Give up? It's greens. Patrick Needham, farmer and purveyor, packs his bag o' fresh greens: lettuce, spinach, beet greens, mustard . . . whatever. Customers snap 'em up for soups, stews and, most likely, large summer salads. Needham sells what he grows, which is anything that will come up in Maine's short season. All of Needham's fruits and vegetables are organically grown. The stand is open Memorial Day through Columbus Day.

Photo: Mary (Dysart) Hartt

A pod of whales breaks the surface as they feed in the Atlantic Ocean off Bar Harbor.

Left Bank Cafe
Surry Rd. (Maine Hwy. 172), Blue Hill • 374-2201

When Arnold Greenberg opened up the Left Bank Cafe more than a decade ago, he transformed the region. Greenberg not only placed Blue Hill on the national folk, blues and jazz circuits, but also got folks' mornings started right, serving fresh bagels and breads. Greenberg has since moved on to other projects, but both the bakery and the cafe remain open (see our Restaurants, Nightlife and Arts chapters). Stop by for bagels and hearty fresh-baked breads such as farmer's rye, six-grain, peasant, spinach, French and Italian. The bakery is open year round except Tuesdays, but you'll find the greatest selection in late spring, summer and fall.

Nervous Nellie's Jams and Jellies
Sunshine Rd., Deer Isle • 348-6182, (800) 777-6845

As you drive up Sunshine Road toward Haystack Mountain School of Crafts (see our Education chapter), you'll find Nervous Nellie's Jams and Jellies, the food purveyor with the best name, hands down. And the name is reason enough to stop by, even if the prospect of sampling a host of jams and jellies somehow doesn't draw you in. There's also a little cafe

open in July and August, possibly longer, plus sculptures of knights in armor in an eclectic sculpture garden.

Pain de Famille Bakery and Cafe
Greens Hill Place, Maine Hwy. 176 and Morgan Bay Rd., Blue Hill • 374-3839

The first time we had focaccia bread, it had just come out of the wood-fired oven at Pain de Famille Bakery in South Brooksville. We've been following the bakery around ever since.

Now it adjoins the Blue Hill Co-op. You can also find rustic sourdough bread and an array of sandwiches, salads and soups to go. The price is delightful too.

Penobscot Bay Provisions
W. Main St., Stonington • 367-2920

You've made the long trek down the winding roads, found yourself practically in the waters off Stonington, and now you're starving. It's a beautiful day, and you've no desire to remain cooped up indoors — so stop by Penobscot Bay Provisions. Pick up some fresh-baked bread, cheese, salad, even pâté for a picnic at the docks or among waterlilies of Ames Pond (ask for directions). And if you're really feeling generous, buy a gift basket filled with select foods of Maine and bring it home to those who couldn't come with you. The store is open between June and October, and even then, the hours can change. We suggest you call ahead.

Rooster Brother
18 W. Main St., on U.S. Hwy. 1 at the Union River Bridge, Ellsworth
• 667-8675, (800) 866-0054

Rooster Brother is a two-story cook's emporium, specializing in a full range of delights for the table, from sturdy, bright-colored plates to the bread to put on them; from a good range of coffee makers to the ground coffee to brew in them. For a perfect outing, stop at Rooster Brother in the morning for a crusty loaf of sourdough bread, a chunk of imported cheese, a bottle of good red wine and a bittersweet bar of Swiss chocolate; pack it all into a picnic basket, or better yet, a Maine guide pack basket you wear on your back like a knapsack; drive down the coast to Blue Hill, Schoodic Point, Deer Isle or Mount Desert Island (choosing where might be your biggest problem); take a short walk; then pull out the bread. Then again, perhaps you should buy a cup of their coffee (they roast their own) and a roll, muffin or croissant to eat while you're driving; it might help to keep your hands off the chocolate, cheese and bread until picnic time.

Sow's Ear Winery
Maine Hwy. 176, near Herrick Rd., Brooksville • 326-4649

Tom Hoey has been making his own cider and wines for about 20 years. He's been selling them since 1991. He uses local, organically grown fruit, much of it from his own orchards. Apples, blueberries and rhubarb go into his vintage, making dry and sweet wines and dry ciders. Call ahead if you're visiting in the off-season and see if Tom can arrange a tasting for you. In summer, the tastings are rather routine.

Sullivan Harbor Farm Smokehouse
U.S. Hwy. 1, Sullivan • 422-3735

Just 2 miles beyond the famous Singing Bridge that spans Taunton Bay, you'll find Sullivan Harbor Farm Smokehouse. Owner Joel Frantzman smokes salmon like you've never tasted before — unless you've eaten smoked salmon at Legal Seafood in Boston, the Ritz Carlton in Boston or Phoenix, or any Palm Restaurant nationwide.

Frantzman was trained in Scotland to smoke fish using hickory wood. He sells cured and smoked salmon wholesale to the aforementioned fine restaurants and retail to visitors who stop by the smokehouse. Maybe you'll find some smoked scallops here too. And should you enjoy the view, ask about lodging at Sullivan Harbor Farm (see Accommodations), which Frantzman runs with wife Leslie Harlow.

Mount Desert Island

Alternative Market
16 Mt. Desert St., Bar Harbor • 288-5271, (800) 423-6269

After two years of seeking a location, Bar Harbor's natural-foods and specialty store has finally expanded. Here, besides vitamins, herbs, alternative medicines, health-food supplements, organic produce and natural foods, you'll also find gourmet foods like cheeses, wines and beers, a bakery offering fresh-baked goods, a juice bar and a large deli for take-out. The motto here is "Healthful Foods for Active People." The store has long hours, offering all meals from breakfast to late-night snacks, mostly for takeout. As of presstime, the Alternative Market did not have a phone; the listed numbers are for Benbow's Coffee Roasters (see next listing), the market's "other half." The folks at Benbow's will either answer your questions or direct you to the market.

INSIDERS' TIP

Maine has done well by secretaries of defense in the U.S. Cabinet. Former Secretary of Defense Casper Weinberger lives in Somesville, on Mount Desert Island; his wife, Jane Weinberger, runs a small children's publishing company there known as Windswept House Publishers. William Cohen, the current Secretary of Defense, was born and raised in Bangor.

Benbow's Coffee Roasters
99 Main St., Bar Harbor • 288-5271, (800) 423-6269

Benbow's Coffee Roasters sells sandwiches, salads, bagels and muffins, but mostly coffee. There's an espresso bar here as well as pots of coffees, granitas and teas, among them steamed Himalayan chai, black teas, soy steamers and herbals. The front shop also stocks good-quality wine and beer.

Ben & Bill's Chocolate Emporium
66 Main St., Bar Harbor • 288-3281, (800) 806-3281

OK, here we go. This is Bar Harbor's ice cream store — *the* ice cream store, if you will. And the ice cream is good. You'll find a huge array of flavors, though the long counter displays of chocolates, candies and fudge give the ice cream a run for its money. Those goodies are as hard to resist as the ice cream, even with the knowledge that the fast-disappearing bag of fudge and licorice you bought to bring the kids is going to ruin your meal at that gourmet restaurant where you've finally landed a reservation. If you do go for the ice cream, promise us that you won't succumb to false bravado and taste the lobster ice cream. Yes, you can try a lick of the moose-dropping flavor (moose droppings don't quite clash with ice cream the way lobster does). Go for the mint chocolate chip, the pistachio, cookies and cream, even the moose droppings; but please don't try the lobster ice cream.

Shopping the Main Streets

Waldoboro to Stockton Springs

Waldoboro

As you come into the Mid-Coast region on U.S. Highway 1, you'll see a flag flying on the left side of the road advertising The Well-Tempered Kitchen. This kitchenware shop in the barn of an old Cape might be more at home in Boston or San Francisco, but we're mighty glad it's here. Besides the usual high-end cookware and culinary accoutrements, this shop has a solid selection of cookbooks. It also sells cards and wraps gifts with panache, so if you forgot to bring a hostess gift, stop here.

Farther on, Glockenspiel Imports is on the left side of the road — a small gray building standing alone on the downslope of the hill into Waldoboro. The German woman who runs this shop stocks imported lace, curtains, table cloth and fabric by the yard. She also offers smaller decorative pieces that would be lovely in older homes. She closes down during some winter months, so call ahead, 832-8000, if you're coming during the off-season.

The Roseraie at Bayfields, 670 Bremen Road (Maine Highway 32), is a wonderful stop. Lloyd Brace specializes in old-fashioned and hardy roses, and you are welcome to wander through his garden of more than 300 varieties. He does have a catalog business, so if something seizes your fancy, you might arrange to have it delivered when you get home.

A right turn on Maine 32 takes you to the center of Waldoboro. This little town hugging the shores of the Medomac River is worth poking around. Among its shopping stand-outs is Central Asian Artifacts, at the corner of Main and Jefferson streets. It's crowded with Oriental carpets, handmade artifacts, rosewood craft work and tribal jewelry. Among the rich jewel-tone hues of the textiles are glints of brass accents. This must be the kind of booty Maine's sailing ships brought back from trading expeditions.

The Waldoboro 5 & 10 is in the opposite direction. It advertises itself as "a 5 & 10 like you remember," and that's the truth. It's a time machine: narrow aisles, stuff all over, creaky floors, decent prices, nice folks. What more could you want, except to live in this little town and get to come here all the time?

Hardware stores aren't usually mentioned in this chapter, but we heard such raves, we had to tell you that the RZR Ace Hardware, on U.S. Highway 1 in East Waldoboro, has a reputation for being one of the most helpful and best stocked in the area.

Thomaston

U.S. Highway 1 travels right through the center of Thomaston. On the way into town you'll see the Maine State Prison Showroom Outlet, on the right side of the road next to the prison. This shop sells items made by inmates — mostly wooden furniture and accessories, including coffee tables, cedar chests, stools and desks. A part of the proceeds goes back to the prisoners.

As you continue on, you'll come to the center of town. There you'll find Thomaston Books & Prints, 105 Main Street (U.S. Highway 1). Mainers love bookstores, and this is just the first of many in our area. The sales staff is knowledgeable — Georgia Hansen's been there since it opened in 1989 — and the store has a great children's area. This is a store for readers. You'll find handwritten comments from staff and customers in some of the books — and not just the new ones. The tradition has carried into the children's room, and it's charming for children to find another child's thoughts about a book tucked into its pages. Owner Darrilyn Peters has a winner here. She does a strong mail-order business as well.

Rockland

U.S. 1 takes a sharp turn north in Rockland and traverses its downtown as well. You could easily spend a day here, and maybe you should! We'll just focus on the highlights.

Your first stop is Goodnow's Pharmacy, 300 Main Street, right at the corner as U.S. 1 angles northward. One of the last independently owned pharmacies in the area, Goodnow's has been in the same location and owned by the same family since 1938. Here's a place to hear those lovely but rare native Maine accents as you get your prescription filled, buy the usual array of health and beauty aids, pick up a magazine or get a treat at the authentic soda fountain.

Down the street is the Black Parrot, 328 Main Street. This hip little store carries women's and children's outerwear and some art objects. The store has its own label designed by artist/owner Cheryl Gibson, who's known for using fleece and fabric in unique color combinations. The result is functional but fashionable clothing so cheerful, it makes you smile. Toys and small pieces of furniture are stocked as well.

Another interesting stop is the Farnsworth

Museum Store, 352 Main Street. You'll find prints of many paintings in the museum's collection, especially its fine Wyeths. The shop also stocks art books, postcards and note cards as well as Maine-made jewelry and pottery. It's open daily year round except Mondays between Columbus Day and Memorial Day. Last year it was open on Mondays in December as well.

Huston-Tuttle & Gallery One, 365 Main Street, sells maps and charts; office and art supplies; and prints, posters and original art. If you or the kids need a creative outlet on rainy days, this is the place to get a jump-start.

Kitchenware is the bulk of what you'll find at The Store, 435 Main Street, but it sells cards, bath accessories and toys as well. It's a great place to noodle around (pardon the pun).

Rockport

As you take U.S. 1 through Rockport, look out for Down East Enterprise, on the right side of the road. This classic Maine "cottage" gracefully houses a small publishing empire. *Down East* magazine is edited here, as are a number of sporting magazines and a line of books. The front room is a low-key showroom/store where you can buy Maine-related books and gifts the company sells through its catalog.

Off U.S. 1, at 67 Pascal Avenue, is L.E. Leonard, an intriguing import store full of furniture, decorative accents, clothing and jewelry from Japan, China, India and the Spice Islands.

There's a cluster of little shops in downtown Rockport on Central Street, some of which are mentioned in the "Antiques" and "Specialty-food Shops and Stops" sections of this chapter as well as in the Restaurants chapter.

For your many photo needs, check out Resource, the Maine Photographic Workshops' store for its students and faculty; the public is welcome too. Look for hard-to-find photo and film books, cards, postcards and T-shirts.

Back on U.S. 1, you can't miss Maine Sport Outfitters, on the left side of the road. Called a phenomenon by one travel writer, it sells sporting gear of all kinds: running, swimming, fishing, camping, hiking, climbing, biking, kayaking, canoeing, skating, hockey, tennis, skiing, soccer and snowshoeing. You'll also find sports clothing for men, women and children; books; tapes; shoes/boots; and a nice array of clever games and gifts. The shop also rents sports equipment, and its Outdoor School offers classes, trips and tours (see our Parks and Recreation chapter).

Camden

Camden is a shopper's paradise. You can park near the center of town, walk in any direction and find interesting shops.

But before you do that, look for Reny's, on the left, and Margo Moore, on the right, as you drive into town.

Reny's, a department store, is part of statewide chain offering all manner of bargains and markdowns on brand-name merchandise. This store has a certain homegrown cachet with Mainers, and in its aisles you'll see folks of all ages and all income brackets. Carrying a Reny's bag is the next best thing to a Maine license plate. (There's also a Reny's in Belfast at the corner of U.S. Highway 1 and Maine Highway 3, and one in Ellsworth on U.S. 1.)

Margo Moore, on the other hand, is an upscale homeowner's dream. While Marcy van der Kieft does interior decorating, her shop carries all the ingredients: lamps and home accessories, china, fabrics, wall coverings and area rugs. If that sounds utilitarian, the store is anything but: These are the sort of bright, tasteful accents that make a room sing, and they make great gifts.

As it passes through downtown, U.S. 1 is called Elm Street, Main Street and then High Street in quick succession. Mechanic Street cuts off to the left past French and Brawn, while Bayview Street cuts off to the right.

Down Mechanic Street, you'll find the Camden 5 & 10, another small-town wonder that sells everything but the kitchen sink.

The Foreside Company, 6 Main Street, sells imported gifts and household accessories, while Star Bird, 17 Main Street, specializes in American and country decorative accessories. You'll also find old fishing decoys, porcelain, cut glass, needlepoint and Herend and Limoges pieces. Somewhat in the same vein but with a different style is The Right Stuff, 38 Main Street, with country collectibles, lamp shades, quilts and coverlets. It also sells jewelry and pretty household things — perfect for hostess gifts.

Don't miss the Maine Gathering/Finest Kind Candies, in its new location at 21 Main Street, for Maine crafts, fine Native American baskets and delicious hand-dipped chocolates.

Surroundings, 39 Main Street, offers a selection of items for the kitchen, bath and garden. Whoever does the buying here manages to find really imaginative pieces with color and style.

Planet is all over the map and on both sides of Main Street: One store carries women's clothing, shoes and accessories, while the other carries household items, children's toys and men's clothing. This place is incredibly popular, and the merchandise is both unusual and imaginatively displayed.

If you're still on the hunt for clothing, try the House of Logan, 32 Main Street, and Admiral's Buttons, 36 Bayview Street. Both are upscale, selective shops with traditional fine clothing for men and women. (Both are closed during the winter months.) Admiral's Buttons offers quality sailing gear as well, and it's the local distributor for Thos Moser, Cabinetmakers, an exceptional Maine furniture maker. Moser works mostly in cherry, and his pieces are drop-dead elegant.

Theo B. Camisole and Company, above Surroundings, is a charming lingerie and sleepwear store for women. And The Leather Bench, 34 Main Street, sells high-quality leather goods, including coats, jackets and bags.

Don't miss the Smiling Cow, across the street, a Camden institution since 1940. Meg and Paul Quijano carry on the family tradition of selling souvenirs, gifts, T-shirts, books, cards and crafts in a warm, friendly atmosphere. Help yourself to free coffee and tea on the back porch. The view of Camden Harbor is fabulous, and it's a nice place for weary shoppers to rest their feet.

Bayview Street is its own little shopper's paradise. Look for the Owl & Turtle Bookshop, 8 Bayview Street, a longtime favorite of area book lovers, with a strong selection of nautical and children's books.

At Bay View Landing, off Bayview Street, you'll find another cluster of shops. Wild Birds Unlimited sells everything you need for feeding our feathered friends, and The Oracle is an excessively hip little store with a urbane sense of humor and an environmental conscience. Look for recycled items, housewares, all-natural bath products, sachets, and yes, Voodoo soap, to wash off spells and bring you love and good luck.

Take the next turn to the left off Bayview Street, into Willey's Wharf, and you'll find Fabrics de France, with fabulous imported fabrics, wall coverings and decorative accents. One snowy winter day we stared in the window felt we'd been transported to Paris for a few precious seconds.

Just beyond that turn-in is Ducktrap Trading Co., a fine place for those who love the natural world. Here you'll find decoys, sculpture, painting and prints. Wildlife is the theme, but so is the sea, with a range of nautical items like ship models, half hulls and boat kits.

Farther down the street is Once a Tree, 46 Bayview Street, where you'll find toys, kitchen items, clocks, furniture — everything imaginable made out of wood.

Lincolnville Beach

This little cluster of buildings faces a beach directly across U.S. Highway 1. The Beach Store is a great little convenience store with wonderful pizza, and there's a basket store that sets up shop in a tent next to the post office during the summer months. There's more; see the Lincolnville entries in this chapter's "Antiques" section and in the Restaurants chapter.

As you continue north along U.S. 1, look for Windsor Chairmakers, on the left side of the road. In a showroom on an old farmstead, you'll find handsome handcrafted tables, high

boys, four-poster beds and, of course, classic Windsor chairs.

Farther down the road on the right, you'll see a saltwater farm with a sign for Painted Lady. This is one of a wave of new antique shops that focus more on design and decorative accents than fabulously expensive heirlooms — which is why we're putting it in this section of this chapter. Owner Sherry McGrath collects sophisticated country, American and European antiques, but you'll see her expert work in decorative and faux finishes as well.

Northport

As you pass through Northport on U.S. 1, check out Northport Landing in a barn on the right side of the road. You'll find an eclectic collection of crafts, collectibles and country furniture. We have friends who swear by it and say it consistently surprises them with interesting things.

Belfast

This is another town worth poking around. The downtown area is off U.S. Highway 1; just follow the signs. The Good Table, 68 Main Street, carries all manner of tabletop accessories, cookbooks and kitchenware, including respected brand names such as Calphalon, All-Clad and Wustoff.

Canterbury Tales Books, 52 Main Street, and the Fertile Mind Bookstore, 105 Main Street, are required stops for book lovers, while Coyote Moon, 54 Main Street, has made a name for itself with its funky natural-fiber clothing and jewelry for women. It also carries journals, cards, stationery, incense, bells, music and candles — everything you need for a good pampering.

INSIDERS' TIP

Many a notable soul comes to Maine's Mid-Coast. Look sharp when you buy a cup of coffee, go for that morning croissant or duck out of the rain at the antique emporium. Celebrity spotters know that actor John Travolta has a home on Islesboro. Singers Billy Joel and Don McLean also have homes nearby. Up the coast, newsman Jack Perkins now lives on half of Bar Island, the little island off the coast of Bar Harbor; Martha Stewart has a new home in Seal Harbor (upping the ante in island hospitality), and former newsman Walter Cronkite likes to dock at Northeast Harbor when he sails Maine waters.

If you have children, Away We Grow, 96 Main Street, has a great selection of good toys, and it resells children's clothing.

Searsport

If you love pottery, look for the Monroe Salt Works Outlet and Mainely Pottery. Both are on U.S. Highway 1. While Monroe Salt Works carries its signature patterns, Mainely Pottery features the work of more than a dozen potters from around the state.

In the center of town, toy collectors might like to stop at Dakins Gift and Collectibles Outlet Store, 18 Main Street. It specializes in Steiff, Ertle, Dakin's Plush and Lionel brand items.

Don't miss the Penobscot Marine Museum Store, on Church Street just off U.S. Highway 1, for its reproductions of maritime, China trade and Victorian items. While these aren't exact copies of the museum's collection, some are quite close. The gimbaled candlesticks, for instance, are very similar to the ones on display. The store is open Memorial Day through at least mid-October.

Silkweeds is another gift shop on U.S. Highway 1. It's full of pretty country items and Victoriana.

Just into Stockton Springs is a tiny store called The Rug Rat. It's a little rough on the outside — and maybe a little rough on the inside — but Sarah Nickerson makes hooked rugs like none we've seen. She does custom work for the tony crowd on Islesboro, but there's nothing pretentious or self-conscious about her style. This is the real deal: clear, true colors and lively designs that come from the heart. We still covet the off-balance wolf with its head thrown back, baying at a moon the size of Texas.

Inland to Bangor

Winterport and Hampden

Molly's, on U.S. Highway 1A, is an upscale ladies specialty store, but that's not the half of it. Owners Molly Woodsum and her daughter, Kimberly Pitula, stock clothing from Maine and New England designers, but they also sell paintings, wreaths, children's toys and specialty foods. You won't find this quality in the malls, and Molly's draws customers from Camden, Deer Isle, Blue Hill and Bangor. Gift wrapping is lavish — and free.

Another stop is The Flower Patch, also on U.S. 1A. In addition to plants, flowers and floral arrangements, this store sells lovely 19th-century flower cards and stuffed animals, especially teddy bears and cats.

You wouldn't expect to find a gift store tucked into a hardware store, but that's the story at Schacht's Gift Shop in Schacht's True Value Hardware, on U.S. 1A in Hampden, next to the Hampden Academy. It sells three lines of candles, glassware, china, rubber stamps, afghans and a full line of baby clothing and books.

Bangor Area

We interrupt this shopping tour of small towns to bring you ... Bangor, a city you might enter from any number of directions, not just via U.S. Highway 1!

We focus on some local favorites here, but don't miss the newly renovated Bangor Mall (see the "Major Malls" section). It, and the minimalls that have sprung up around it, might be like the shopping centers you're used to in other cities, but there aren't many malls in Maine, so it's a favorite for locals. Of the shops discussed in this section, assume they're in Bangor unless otherwise indicated.

Let's start with clothing stores. Best Bib & Tucker Clothiers, 30 Main Street, is a stand-out. It stocks better natural-fiber clothing and accessories for men and women, and while the local owners have great taste, what distinguishes this store is its ethic of service. Who else will keep a record of your choices from season to season, along with fabric swatches?

Just up U.S. Highway 2 (Main Street) in Orono, The Pretty Woman, 24 Main Street, has the same dedication to personal service. It's the classic nice ladies dress shop. In business for six years, owner Nancy Paul is the kind of person who'll call you if she sees something you'd love. She's particularly good at tracking down mother-of-the-bride or mother-of-the-groom dresses. The Pretty Woman carries career clothing, sportswear and separates as well as accessories, jewelry and scarves.

Cormier's Men's Clothing, 25 Broad Street,

is another fine choice. In the old Merchant's National Bank building (there's a vault in the store), Cormier's is known for its suits and tailoring. But you'll also find sportswear, robes and underwear.

A new breed of resale shops makes it possible to find first-class clothing at modest prices. Repeat Performances, 60 Main Street, only sells quality labels in perfect or nearly perfect condition. Look for career clothing and coordinate sets by Ann Taylor, Anne Klein and Ralph Lauren. Set up with displays like a full-price dress shop, Repeat Performances offers real bargains. Owner Laurie Bedami tells us a $400 Jones – New York suits might sell here for $80. The merchandise moves quickly so visit often.

The Growing Place, 552 Hammond Street, has the same approach for children's clothing, toys and equipment: Quality labels in mint condition. Look for clothing by Gymboree, Hannah Anderson, Gap and Rothschild, and educational toys by the likes of Little Tikes.

If you're traveling up the coast, these two stores plan to open new outlets next to each other in Ellsworth in the spring.

If books are your bent, look for Betts Bookstore, 26 Main Street. It sells new and used books, with a focus on Maine authors, the Civil War and a huge selection of Stephen King titles. The selection at Bookmarc's, 78 Harlow Street, has a more literary bent. It sells both new and used books as well as quite a few small-press books. Maine titles include a number of self-published works. They can be real finds, as they're written as labors of love and packed with hard-to-find information. The store has a cafe as well, which sells light breakfasts and vegetarian lunches.

For children's books, don't miss the Briar Patch at 27 Central Street. It also sells toys, games and puzzles.

The solution for antsy travelers? The Grasshopper Shop, 1 W. Market Square, is a hip, lively mix of clothing, jewelry, accessories, housewares, games and toys. The staff is notably friendly and happy to recommend restaurants, places to stay and places to go while you're in Bangor — a wonderful backup source to this guide!

Rebecca's, 43 Main Street, is similar in scope but different in style. The atmosphere is muted, the music soft, and the merchandise more conservative. Here you'll find country furniture, Victorian reproductions, candles, wreaths, glassware and prints.

Another stop for gifts and decorative accents is The Gift Gallery, 44 Main Street. You'll find baby gifts such as Beatrix Potter ceramics, picture frames plus a complete line of tabletop furnishings. Royal Doulton, Waterford, Wedgewood and Spode are just some of the names on the china and crystal.

If ethnic wares are more to your taste, try Ingrid's German Gift Shop, 117 Buck Street, for European imports, Scandinavian hand-blown vases and, at Christmastime, German nutcrackers. Owner Ingrid Perkins also has a wonderful selection of imported foods, including all kinds of chocolates, cookies and pâtés.

Many shops have special Christmas offerings. Ingrid's for instance, carries wonderful German nutcrackers. Out in Newburgh, Piper Mountain Christmas Trees sells cut and cut-your-own Christmas trees. A fun place to go, especially with children, it has a seasonal Christmas shop as well with decorations, bird feeders, quilts, baskets and crafts. Piper Mountain also sells trees in Hampden at the Rite-Aid parking lot next to Hampden Academy, and in Belfast, at Reny's Plaza. Both satellite tree lots sell some Christmas wares as well. Want to send a Christmas tree to your mother in Pheonix? Piper Mountain handles mail order as well.

Sanborne's Fine Candies, 849 Stillwater Avenue, carries chocolates and other sweets. It brags about having the best caramel on the planet, and loyal customers agree. Try their turtles, fudge or those wonderful old-fashioned sugar mints.

Maybe you'd like some flowers with your candy. Bangor has a surprising number of excellent florists. Bangor Floral Co., 96 Center Street, is in what used to be the Advent Christian Church. It's worth a visit just to see those beautiful stained-glass windows. The present owners have had the shop for 20 years and offer a wide selection year round. They're known for personalized service.

Lougee & Fredericks, 364 State Street, is right across from Eastern Maine Medical Center, so it's a great place to pick up flowers if you have friends or family in the hospital. While Lougee & Fredericks is a favorite with the professional crowd, most of it's business is residential.

Flowers, 46 Main Street (U.S. Highway 2), in Orono, is not a typical florist shop. It doesn't do wire-service flower arrangements; it doesn't do balloons. It does offer beautiful cut flowers and arrangements, along with gardening gifts. (If you're looking for Maine-made Snow & Neally hand tools, you'll find them here.) Not surprisingly, Flowers is also popular with the college crowd, who come in for single red roses.

Now we take you from the sublime to the mundane. For a taste of local flavor, check out Marden's Surplus and Salvage on Wilson Street in Brewer. It's packed with overstocks and manufacturers' closeouts. The best way to describe what Marden's carries is to quote it's advertising: "We buy anything we don't have to feed."

Bucksport to Gouldsboro

Bucksport

Once plagued with rows of empty storefronts, Bucksport has recently become a charming place to browse, with several locations for the browsing. The first is Main Street. In an old movie theater known as The Alamo, at 377 Main Street, Northeast Historic Film offers an unusual array of movie-oriented gifts, from postcards to posters, from books on the movies to the movies themselves, in video form. There is also a nice array of gifts for children at this organization that works to preserve old New England movies (see our Arts chapter). Across the street is the venerable Rosen's, the kind of longed-for hometown clothing store that, unfortunately, seldom outlasts the malls. Don't miss the bargain basement, but also don't overlook the local specialties like Maine sweat shirts and homey flannels.

Also on Main Street is The Bittersweet, featuring country-style gifts. Nearby is Bucksport's bookstore, BookStacks, at 333 Main Street, with a good selection of nautical, Maine and alternative-health books as well as novels. On Main Street just before the traffic light, you'll find a classic secondhand shop, known as Sebastian's, where you'll find everything from furniture to first-edition Hardy Boys mysteries. Come here to outfit a camp for next-to-nothing, or to buy that elegant rocker you've been longing for. Across the bridge on U.S. Highway 1 as it travels through Verona Island, you'll find Mayari Farm & Gift Shop. It's a curious little place, with goats out back and an array of goat products — softly scented goat's milk soap and goat cheese — as well as items that are not goat's-milk-related, like butterfly houses and feeders. Mayari is open from mid-May through October.

Castine

Main Street cascades practically into the harbor at Castine, and Water Street veers off it to the left, providing an L-shaped browsing opportunity. Compass Rose Books is on Main Street down the hill from Leila Day Antiques and Gallery (see the previous "Antiques" section). Don't let the side entrance mislead you; this is a sizable place with a lot of books inside, including a good selection of hardbacks and paperbacks to satisfy the specific curiosities of visitors and keep locals going through long winters. We've found books on Maine here that we haven't seen elsewhere — some from publishing companies with names we've never even heard. There's also a good children's section and a nice collection of prints.

Across the street is Water Witch, a clothing store featuring dresses, tops and pants made of delightful Javanese batiks. Down the block, at the corner of Main and Water, stands Four Flags, selling an extensive array of nautical-oriented gifts and some necessities for boats, and featuring a small nook filled with well-chosen books for children and older people as well as some great Maine-oriented games and toys.

Blue Hill

Browsing in Blue Hill is an afternoon's affair, with an unexpectedly global array of crafts. You'll find many shops lining Main Street as well as both banks of the cascading Mill Stream as it hurries to Blue Hill Bay. Additional shops are a bit outside town. Blue Hill is the location of one of our favorite craft stores in the state. Handworks Gallery, on Main Street, is up a back stairway on the second floor. We like it for the mix of local and global crafts including quilts, earrings, bright-colored pieces of a carved Noah's Ark set and the funny pottery dishes painted to amuse. The store also features furniture, rugs and blown glass.

Down the block, North Country Textiles offers handwoven home furnishings and other goods. Look here for rugs, baby blankets, throws, place mats and clothing. Carole Ann Larson runs this store with two other weavers. She also has a store in South Penobscot, where she lives with her husband, David Larson, who has an art gallery above the small store (see our Arts chapter). The Blue Hill shop is the larger of the two and features local crafts — pottery, jewelry, toys, candles and chimes — in addition to the softly woven textiles.

Blue Hill must be a town of readers, for it supports two bookstores: Blue Hill Books, 2 Pleasant Street, and North Light Books, Main Street. Both are general, family-run stores. North Light Books features a selection of art, architecture and photography books, perhaps because it is run by artist Allie Saballis and her family.

The Jud Hartmann Gallery has moved around in the past few years, but it always seems to be somewhere in downtown Blue Hill — most recently at the corner of Main Street and Maine Highway 15. Here you'll find cast bronze sculptures of Plains Indian heroes.

In Blue Hill, you'll also want to visit two potteries. Rowentrees has been around for 50 years. While in India, owner Adelaide Pearson became inspired to make functional ware from local clay and glazes as the result of a conversation with Mahatma Gandhi. She returned to Blue Hill and has been making tableware ever since using glazes from local granite and feldspar. Rowentrees is in town on Union Street.

Rackliffe Pottery got its inspiration from Rowentrees. It's on the Ellsworth Road (Maine Highway 172).

When merchant vessels sailed the world, Maine was in the center of commerce. Today, Mainers frequently hop airplanes to maintain global connections. Enter World Marketplace, just a quarter-mile up Maine Highway 15, and you'll feel like you're in an Oriental bazaar. Look up, look down, look around — intriguing

goods from around the world command your attention, as will the story of owner Jeff Kaley who first went to Nepal in 1967 as a Peace Corps volunteer. He never lost contact, and today he sells Nepalese, Thai and Indian goods from this store connected to his home. You'll find nesting boxes, beautiful hand-loomed fibers, journals, jewelry, puppets (both delightful and scary) and much more. There's a fair range of prices: Both you and your children can find affordable gifts here, and if nothing else, you can lust after cherished objects such as the Tibetan mask that you might love to have in your home.

Two miles from the village, Truus Geraets runs another global market — the African Market — on Maine 177, across from the St. Francis Episcopal Church. After working for years in the Black townships of South Africa, Geraets has found herself in Blue Hill selling handcrafted South African dolls, Bushman instruments, jewelry, small sculptures, fabric and baskets.

Stonington

Only in the last few years has Stonington begun to turn the corner from fishing village to tourist center, and that change is tentative. In winter, when the retail shops close their doors, Stonington reverts to the simple, slightly wild fishing village it has always been. Summer tames it, offering a cornucopia of shops, all on Main Street, beginning with a shop by that name. Main Street overflows practically into the street with lobster buoys, antiques and gifts. Nearby, near Eagull Antiques (see the previous "Antiques" section), is the Hoy Gallery, featuring artwork by Jill Hoy. She's an excellent artist, celebrating the glory of Maine summers with porch scenes, flowers and bright interiors. Down the road is a branch of the Grasshopper Shop, the smallest and newest of the four outlets (the others are in Rockland, Bangor and Ellsworth), open late May through early October. The Good Prospect is a small but nice gallery, while Print and Reprint offers what it suggests — prints and books. Dockside Books and Gifts is, as its name implies, a bookstore and gift shop, weighing in heavily with books about Maine written by Maine authors. The selection is quite focused, but what you'll find is generally worthwhile. Expect most of these stores and galleries to be open only from Mother's Day to the end of October.

Ellsworth

Over the past 20 years, Ellsworth has grown from a relatively stately and quiet shire town to a supply center for the entire Down East region, including Mount Desert Island and the Blue Hill Peninsula. There aren't many large stores in those areas, so people tend to make a day of shopping, driving over an hour to get to Ames, Wal-Mart, Reny's, even the large Shop 'n' Save supermarket, all in a couple of strip malls lining the southern edge of U.S. Highway 1. Visitors to Maine needing basics, such as bathing suits or sweaters — pick your season — printer cartridges or a few sets of children's pajamas also might take advantage of Ellsworth as a supply center.

Across from the strip, on the north side of U.S. 1, are some stores you might want to visit on your way to Acadia National Park, especially if you have any rugged plans for your stay. The L.L. Bean Outlet on U.S. 1 is the Freeport store's thrifty cousin (see our Daytrips chapter for more on L.L. Bean). One of us had always meant to buy a kids L.L. Bear sleeping bag, but Bean discontinued the item. Fortunately, we happened by the outlet store, and there it was — at about half the catalog price. You'll find the previous year's jackets and boots as well as over-stocked shirts, long underwear in odd colors, even L.L. Bean's quality bedding, all at a discount. You can't be certain of any item, but we've seen skis, ski boots, tents, bicycles, canoes and kayaks at the outlet store over a number of years and a variety of seasons.

If it's something you absolutely need, however, like a kayak you want to use while in Maine, Cadillac Mountain Sports, down the block, is a surer bet. The store offers products for outdoors and sporting activities, organized by numerous specialty areas within one store. You'll find climbing equipment, camping goods, gear for virtually any sport including baseball and weight-lifting, books and magazines. The store has an unusually expansive footwear section, with quality shoes for every activity. It also sells kayaks and canoes of all kinds. If you're headed to Bar Harbor, you'll find a smaller Cadillac Mountain Sports store

Agamont Park Fountain is in downtown Bar Harbor.

Photo: Bangor Daily News

there; you'll find a store in downtown Bangor as well. Monroe Salt Works, next to L.L. Bean, can't help with your outdoor gear, but it has an outlet for its salt-glaze pottery here, and you'll find a whole line of dishes, mugs and serving pots with ravens (note the abundance of these birds along the roadside) and other animals stenciled on. The pottery is made inland from our Mid-Coast area, in Monroe.

Around the corner from the U.S. Highway 1 strip (and still officially on U.S. 1, though it's called Main Street) are two blocks of stores. The Grasshopper Shop offers multiple treasures: imported clothing, jewelry, some housewares, unusual toys and the kind of crafts that are classified under the broad label "gifts." We find ourselves rummaging through tablecloths, mats and bedspreads whenever we need an unusual piece of fabric. We have annual visitors who make certain to steer toward Ellsworth or Bangor for one outing. They won't admit it, but when they return with big bags filled with clothing, we know they've been stocking up on the specialties from the Grasshopper Shop (also see the previous "Bangor" section).

Down the block at 100 Main Street is Treasure Island, an excellent specialty toy store where you can find a full line of

Playmobil and Brio, and many other toys to engage creative young minds. Owner Betsy Hewlett has a Ph.D. in child development, so you can sound her out on any questions you might have about your kids — or about toys. Union River Gallery, 92 Main Street, sells art, crafts and frames. Our favorite infant outfit and a very dear snowy owl puppet came from Ruth Foster's: The Children's Shop, across the way at 95 Main Street. Foster, a longtime state representative, specializes in young children's clothing and stuffed animals.

Up the block at Wild Bird Station, 163 Main Street, you'll find all you need to lure birds to your home. Bird feeders are the major item, along with bird seed, audio tapes, books and wind chimes. For a true summer delight, pick up a hummingbird feeder that sticks to your window via suction cups and watch the miniature gems flutter as they drink their sugar water. Batman enthusiasts might wish to indulge in a bat house, either pre-assembled or make-your-own. (Queasy about the thought of luring bats? Remember: Bats eat mosquitoes.)

Prospect Harbor

Prospect Harbor, on Schoodic Peninsula, doesn't quite have a main street, but it does have some main drags dotted with intriguing stores. As you wander along Maine Highway 186, don't miss U.S. Bells. Any scruffiness is part of the charm here. You'll find windchimes and doorbells sandcast by hand in bronze. Better yet, you'll be able to watch the casting in action at the shop's year-round foundry. Nearby is the Chickadee Creek Stillroom, where Jeanie and Fred Cook sell a lovely array of herbs and spices.

Mount Desert Island

Ever since the first European met the first Native American on the shores of Mount Desert Island, the pursuits of commerce and adventure have been intertwined here. Back in those days, commerce took place amid the crashing waves, with the goods strung on a line between ship and shore. There wasn't much opportunity for browsing with that setup — the buyers were just as busy keeping their boat from smashing against the rocks as gathering in the wares.

It's gotten a lot easier to shop on Mount Desert Island — a lot easier — though it might help to remember the trials of the early European buyers as you circle slowly, again and again, trying to find a parking spot in Bar Harbor in August. There isn't nearly as much traffic in Northeast Harbor or Southwest Harbor, the island's other significant towns for shopping. Though they are smaller, don't pass them by if you're hankering for an afternoon of plain old town life. The fewer stores are also more select.

FYI

Unless otherwise noted, the area code for all phone numbers listed in this guide is 207.

Bar Harbor

Come summer, Bar Harbor takes on the look of a resort town, with myriad stores and restaurants vying for visitors' attention. On your first swing through the galleries, gift shops, bakeries and book shops, you might not know where to start. Once you settle in, however, you'll find your favorites and return. We'll help you by singling out a few of our favorite stores.

Main, Cottage and Mt. Desert are the big shopping streets. Main Street runs roughly from the park into the harbor, the other streets of downtown Bar Harbor run perpendicular to it, ending at Main. We'll lead you down Cot-

INSIDERS' TIP

Browsing for books? Look around for popular local authors. William Kotzwinkle, author of *ET*, the popular *Fan Man* and the more recent *The Bear Went Over the Mountain*, is a Bar Harbor resident. And Dutch spy-thriller author Jan William van der Vetering has a home in Surry. Oh, and then there's Stephen King . . . .

tage, jog over to West, then travel down Main to Mt. Desert, which parallels the village square.

Two New Age emporiums are on Cottage Street. At 140 Cottage Street you'll find the Bar Harbor Hemporium, featuring all things hemp — clothing, paper, bags and shoes, all made from hemp. Farther down the road, Eden Rising, at 39 Cottage Street, is a place worth settling into for an afternoon. You could certainly spend a good hour just in the bookstore area, reading about Bar Harbor and the rest of Maine, boning up on natural medical cures or planning your next vacation through one of many unusual travel guides. Then move on to shoes and clothing. Here you'll find fine accouterments, accessories and footwear — Birkenstocks, silver jewelry, ethnic vests and dresses. You can liven up your house with mobiles and bells, or calm it with incense and music. Also check out the second store on Main Street. But if it's gear you need — climbing, running, hiking, camping, tennis, whatever — stop by Cadillac Mountain Sports, 26 Cottage Street (also see our previous "Ellsworth" section).

At 47 West Street, Song of the Sea delights the gentle with dulcimers, bowed and plucked psalteries, harps, guitars, mandolins, banjos, concertinas, bagpipes, pipes, drums, penny-whistle flutes, Native American flutes, children's kinder harps and more. Many of the dulcimers are built by owner Edward Damm, who opened the store with his wife, Anne, shortly after moving here in 1979. Go to dream, to buy, to listen or to simply admire these musical works of art.

Maine-made stores are popular in our state. They sell everything from stuffed moose dolls to candied moose droppings. The grandma of them all is The Lone Moose Fine Crafts, 78 West Street, on the waterfront, where you'll find fine furniture, crafts and clothing as well as special summertime shows. Another place to find Maine-made objects and gifts is the Acadia Shop & Bookloft Gallery, 85 Main Street. Downstairs are the Maine gifts and crafts, including a good selection of Liberty Graphics' popular shirts and sweat shirts with silkscreen designs of Maine wildlife, plush moose and lobster toys, balsam wreaths decorated with lobster claws, Maine-focused videos and Maine-

made pottery. Upstairs, there's a selection of books about Maine or written by Maine authors. We were tired when we visited, interested in settling down for a rest. We browsed to our hearts' content among the several rows of Maine travel books and nature books without anyone disturbing us. What a pleasant memory! The same outfit also has three stores within Acadia National Park: a sizable store at the Jordan Pond House and smaller ones at the summit of Cadillac Mountain and near Thunder Hole on the Park Loop Road.

More books can be found at Sherman's Book & Stationery Shop, 56 Main Street. Sherman's is Bar Harbor's largest bookstore. It always seems crowded, if not with people (which is typical, especially in the summer months), then with books. Aisles are narrow, which gives the store a sense of urgency: You might be looking at one book, but down the line, or behind you, many more are grappling for your attention. There is a large selection of Maine-oriented books: guides, histories and photography books. You'll also find a large selection of popular fiction. Gather up your paperbacks here.

Is the ghost of Christmas future haunting you? Stop at Christmas Spirit, 80 Main Street, for old-fashioned Santas carved from lobster buoys. Also check out the seashell wreaths. Speaking of seashells, you might find them used as buttons on handmade children's sweaters across the street at Island Artisans, 99 Main Street. This craft gallery displays the work of a select dozen or so fine Maine craftspeople. Look for thick woven silk scarves, baskets decorated with stones or leaves, embossed paper, traditional-style basketry, hand-wrought jewelry, watercolors and small sculptures.

In the Scrimshaw Workshop, 150 Main Street, Chris Cambridge sells the scrimshaw he carves by hand into fossil ivory. In case you're wondering, fossil ivory comes from Alaska, where the remains of wooly mammoths and walruses are so plentiful, their ancient tusks can be legally sold. Cambridge carves nautical scenes and wildlife images into his ivory. Look here, too, for the work of other scrimshanders, and for other Maine-made gifts.

For fine crafts from around the nation, visit

Eclipse Gallery, around the corner on 12 Mt. Desert Street. Sculptural fountains gurgle while delicate blown glasses reflect rose and azure over the water. You'll find beautifully crafted jewelry, elegant furniture and more. At the lower end of Main (317 Main Street), Burwaldo's has a walk-in cigar humidor as well as an agency liquor store. Out of town a little bit, on Maine Highway 3 as you come into Bar Harbor, stands Mount Desert Island Workshop, where you'll find furniture such as Adirondack lawn chairs, folding chairs and tables, bird houses, note cards and other crafts made by people with developmental disabilities. The work contributes to the independence and self-esteem of the craftspeople; their workmanship will contribute to the beauty of your home.

Northeast Harbor

Jeans and a T-shirt just don't seem right in Northeast Harbor. Wear them, and you'll walk around feeling kinda naked, like you should be wearing a Victorian gown, a morning coat or perhaps — God help us — bloomers. Northeast is classy; the rusticators seem more than just a memory here. Whether you've stopped to peer at the yacht club or decided to wander through the stores on Northeast's Main Street, the ghosts of the rusticators — the Rockefellers, who loathed the noisy, stinky automobile; the Pulitzers, whose industrial fortune now has such a literary ring; the Eliots, of Harvard fame; and others — seem to lurk in the air, ensuring a certain panache to even a run-of-the-mill newspaper stand.

Are you a house guest on the island? Have you been invited to dinner? You'll have no trouble finding that perfect house gift at The Kimball Shop, which spreads over several Main Street storefronts. You'll find fine and hand-painted craft china, coffee pots, striking linens, oilcloth floor coverings, musical toys, fine wine and much more. Beal's Classic also sells beautiful house gifts, hand-painted pottery, painted chairs, mugs and pillows. Be sure to check out its excellent wine cellar.

Down the block, Animal Crackers offers casual clothing for women, glorious clothing for children and gifts like greeting cards, soaps and candles.

The business card of Fourteen Carrots, next door on Main Street, features a delightful little rabbit sniffing away at a carrot. Perhaps the 13 other carrots are the craftspeople of this delightful store filled with handcrafted items. We loved the combination wool-and-silk scarves and the heavy woven shawls with black, gold and purple stripes — they'd go very well with the warm felt hats we coveted. Look for the handcrafted jewelry and the wonderful stick and bottle cap rattles made by Native Americans. Fourteen Carrots is open from late spring to mid-October.

At Main Street's G.E. Redfield Gallery you may find photos of Mount Desert Island, like close-ups of stones and gardens, fine furniture and designer jewelry mixed in with impressionist and contemporary paintings and sculptures.

Shaw Jewelry, across the road on Main Street, is much more than a jewelry store: It's also a store of fine contemporary crafts. You'll find fascinating pull toys that are so delightful, you'd hesitate to give one to a child; jewelry so intricate, it's more like a small sculpture than a pin; and sculpture so beautifully crafted, you'd think it was made by a jeweler — and it is. Owner Sam Shaw creates sculpture of wood, metal and other materials as well as jewelry. Across the road and down the block, but still on Main Street, Local Color really does add color to the streets of Northeast Harbor with its bright, fun, unusual clothing.

At the end of Main Street you'll find the aromatic Romantic Room, with its numerous potpourris, flower-laden fabrics, white wooden furniture, bird houses — the feminine romance of cottage-style home goods. Northeast, as we said, has that quality of lazy luxury that lends itself to the cottage-furniture style of the Romantic Room.

Around the corner, at Rock End and Neighborhood Road, you'll find another Romantic Room outlet, specializing in furniture and other home accessories like quilts, rugs and garden sculptures.

Southwest Harbor

Fifteen years ago, there was hardly a store in Southwest Harbor. Today, the place is booming with specialty shops, cafes and inns, turning a few hours in Southwest Harbor into a delightful browsing experience. A favorite is Lil' Tadpoles, on Main Street, featuring children's wear, flap-doodle hats, well-crafted educational toys, beautiful handmade sweaters you might rather frame than subject to the mud and chocolate sauce that are the fuel of childhood, Polartec fleece outerwear for the chilly days, and other delightful clothing up to size 14, plus some good children's books. Harbor Variety 5 & 10, on Main Street, is a great old-time rummaging place: part variety store and part hardware store. Sawyer's Market, also on Main Street, is another flashback — one of the few remaining old-time grocery stores on the island. Nearby is a small natural foods store, Burdocks Natural Foods. Just off Main Street, on Clark Point Road, is Hot Flash Annie, featuring stained glass, paintings, pottery, crystal, blown glass, crafts and "all sorts of weird things," says Annie. The best part of visiting Annie's studio, however, is watching her work and hearing her explain the process of creating stained glass. During summer 1998, you might find her restoring the gorgeous Tiffany and Armstrong windows of St. Saviour's Church in Bar Harbor.

Next door, Christina's Gallery offers art supplies and prints.

For any boating needs, visit the Hinckley Company's Ship Store, on Manset Shore Road, about a mile from downtown Southwest Harbor. You'll find Hinckley T-shirts, nautical gifts, nonbreakable dishware, charts (the mariner's word for maps) and warm, weatherproof clothing. Even if you don't have a boat and don't have the need for foul-weather gear, the Hinckley Ship Store makes for fascinating browsing, introducing you to high-quality marine items stocked by the Hinckley Co., one of the top yacht builders in the nation. Ask to see a video on the making of a Hinckley boat. (Also see our Attractions chapter.)

A bit off the beaten path, less than a mile out of town, you can pick up a Clarkpoint Croquet set at the Claremont Hotel. Yes, you can buy a generic set at Ames for about $25, a fraction of the $160 to $1,700 a set you'll pay here, but you'll watch your grandchildren play with these — and think of the pedigree. When the Claremont hosts its croquet tournament each summer, you can be a part of it, even if you're halfway across the nation.

Check out the *Bangor Daily News* and other local newspapers as well as the bulletin boards outside post offices and supermarkets for information about special events such as summer musicals, puppet shows, library story hours and festivals.

Kidstuff

Kids, this one's for you. To get on the trail of adventure and fun, we've organized a child-tested journey through Maine's treasures. Follow the trail to towers of stones and towering horses, a pirate cove (or two), lobster babies and a pet pig. You'll also find the more usual things, such as boats, beaches, miniature golf, roller rinks and skating ponds.

When you're in the area, check out the *Bangor Daily News* and other local newspapers as well as the bulletin boards outside post offices and supermarkets for information about special events such as summer musicals, puppet shows, library story hours and festivals. Also, check out our Lighthouses chapter — these beacons are always worth a trip. See also Attractions, Parks and Recreation, and Fairs — virtually every fair has a midway, and midways mean rides.

This chapter offers ideas. To find costs and hours for the kid-centered attractions contained herein, see the cross-referenced chapter (unless we haven't written about an item anywhere else, in which case — *voilà* — it's here).

Waldoboro to Stockton Springs

Maine Watercraft Museum
4 Knox St. Landing, off Main St., U.S. Hwy. 1 and Maine Hwy. 131, Thomaston • 354-0444

Bring a picnic, look at the old boats, then put on a life jacket and get out on the water. Would you rather row, paddle, sail or zoom? The museum rents many of its boats by the hour. It will

also ferry you around on it's classy old Chris Craft. (See our Attractions chapter for details.)

Laura B Mail Boat
at the end of Maine Hwy. 131 S., Port Clyde • 372-8848

Pile onto the *Laura B* for a trip to the cliffy island of Monhegan. It's crowded in summer, emptier on the shoulder seasons. Look for rusted treasures on the rocks by the docks, or go for a walk through Cathedral Woods. You'll find tiny fairy huts with stepping stones leading to their doorsteps. Sometimes, the tables are set for fairy tea. This is a daytrip for summer on a windy boat. When Mom says bring a sweater, listen. Believe us, it can get cold on the windswept seas. Off-season, if you want to visit, you'll most likely have to stay over, because of the ferry schedule. (See our Offshore/Islands chapter for more information about the *Laura B* and trips to Monhegan.)

Owls Head Transportation Museum
Maine Hwy. 73, Owls Head • 594-4418

Come during an air show if you can, and you might see pilots hanging out upside down from their old biplanes, slicing ribbons with the propellers (yes, it's as risky as it sounds!). Even if you can't get there during one of the 16 or so summer air shows, even if you're not that interested in cars, close your eyes and picture yourself flying with the Red Baron, or riding that classic, wood-sided convertible, scarf trailing 3 feet behind. (These cars were no slowpokes!) Don't miss the soapbox derby cars or the old, funny bikes. But most of all, look at the planes. Some are beauties, with fabric wings stretched tightly over polished wood. Others are downright ludicrous. Exhibits vary, but we distinctly remember seeing a plane covered with bird feathers. (No, it didn't fly.)

There's a great store at the museum too. And like the museum, it's open year round. Air shows happen in summer and fall on select weekends. Call to find out when. (See our Attractions chapter for details.)

Rockland Breakwater Light
Marie H. Reed Memorial Park, Samoset Rd., Rockland • no phone

Want to try walking on water? You can step right out to Rockland Breakwater Light, about a mile into the harbor. OK, it's a jetty you're walking across — the breakwater that keeps the harbor calm — but it's built from a narrow jumble of rocks, so it kind of feels like you're walking on water. (See our Lighthouses chapter for more information.)

Rockland Skate Center
299 Park St., Rockland • 236-0815

It's Saturday night, and you're tired of hanging out with your family. What's a kid to do around here? If you're a teenager, glide over to the Skate Center, where you can skate for two hours, then waltz and rap the night away — or at least until the rink closes. The center is heated in winter and air-conditioned in summer, and the regulation-size rink is old-style (made of wood). That means your in-line skates must be inspected to ensure they are rink-safe. If you don't have your own skates, you can rent (or buy) a pair at the center.

Your parents and kid brother probably won't want to break into the Saturday evening crowd; they may want to come weekend afternoons. Schedules change seasonally, so call ahead. (See our Parks and Recreation chapter for details.)

Second Read Bookstore
369 Main St., Rockland • 594-4123

"Is it really OK to, like, just sit and read?" a young girl asked the manager of this bookstore/cafe stocked mostly with used books. Yes, it really is. So, while your parents sip cafe au lait and dream about moving here, you can browse the children's shelves. Or, if you'd like, join them in the cafe for some fancy pastries. (See our Restaurants chapter for more information.)

Shore Village Museum
104 Limerock St., Rockland • 594-0311

Imagine standing inside the glowing lens of a lighthouse light, feeling the thick glass of the powerful prisms that send beacons across the waters, or playing captain inside a pilot house. Visit the Shore Village Museum, and you can do it all. But don't expect a quiet place: You'll hear the foghorns and whistles that make ocean mournfulness such a sweet experience. (See our Attractions chapter for more information.)

FYI

Unless otherwise noted, the area code for all phone numbers listed in this guide is 207.

Maine State Ferry Terminal
off Main St., Rockland • 596-2203

If you haven't gotten off land yet, the Maine State Ferry to Vinalhaven is your ticket to another world. You'll be sailing on a rugged, no-nonsense ferry to this fishing island. Bring bikes or rent them on the island (tell your folks not to bother with the car in summer unless they want to spend half their time waiting in line to debark), don't forget your bathing suits and plan to make a day of it. Swim in the quarries, visit the beaches, and discover the tree that's been carved to look like a Coke bottle in the shape of the Statue of Liberty (you'll know it when you see it). Eat fried fish and chips to your heart's content at any one of a number of take-outs, or stop for dinner or an ice cream sundae beneath old-fashioned tin ceilings at The Islander. A copy of the island's brochure will help you get around (also see our Offshore/Islands chapter for details).

Belted Galloways
Aldermere Farm, off Chestnut St., Rockport

Rockport's famous black cows with a wide white stripe around their midsection have made it to souvenir T-shirt fame. See them for yourself at Aldermere Farm on a back road between Camden and Rockport. Sometimes, the

Photo: Bangor Daily News

Fall pumpkins ripen in the garden just in time for Halloween.

calves trot right up to the fence. The little ones are all black; they've yet to grow into their stripes. (See our Attractions chapter for more information.)

Maine Sport Pond and Hockey Rink
Main St., Rockport • 236-7120,
(800) 244-8799

When the pond freezes, the public emerges, coming to the ice behind the store to skate away any hour of the day or night. There's no admission. If you need to rent skates, go inside Maine Sport. Be sure you check the hours, and get the skates back before the outfitters close. Rental hours are the same as store hours, but the ice stays open longer.

If you prefer snow to ice, you can also rent cross-country skis or snowshoes. By the way, if you need any other kind of outdoor gear, the folks here are friendly and knowledgeable (see our Shopping chapter for details).

There's also a hockey rink next door. It's pretty much taken over by the 100 kids of the local Youth Ice Hockey League, but if there's some empty space in the schedule, you can skate here too for a small fee. The pond is free. (Also see our Parks and Recreation chapter.)

Mini Golf Rockport
U.S. Hwy. 1, Rockport • 594-5211

The bright fencing acts like a pied piper, luring you into this classic miniature golf course. Once inside, you'll find a straightforward, old-fashioned and fun layout. We liked the many-holed lighthouse and the activated lobster buoys best. (See our Attractions chapter).

Miss Plum's Homemade Ice Cream & Yogurt Parlor
U.S. Hwy. 1, Rockport • 596-6946

Look for the long, plum-colored building on the western side of U.S. 1. The delicious ice cream sold here speaks for itself. If your parents want you to eat a meal before dessert, you can do that here too — indoors or out. Miss Plum's open daily for breakfast, lunch and dinner April through October, and just for breakfast, lunch and afternoon tea the rest of the year.

Rockport Waterfront Park
Pascal Ave., Rockport • no phone

Bring a picnic, Frisbee, ball and bat; enjoy the narrow strip of green space that hugs the harbor here for about a half-mile. The last time we played a pickup ball game here, we stretched our lips trying to speak French to the young visitors from overseas who joined us. Soon, everyone got into the action, including a black Labrador who retrieved all balls, except the one our French slugger friend hit into the water. (A fisherman helped us with that one.)

Go exploring — walk the small footbridge beside the harbor; check out the lime kilns and the tiny steam locomotive once used to haul lime from the quarries; and don't forget to give the sculpture of the Andre the Seal a hug. Andre, if you remember, was abandoned by his mom, but befriended by a local man named Harry Goodridge. Andre hung out in the harbor near Harry's home and was honorary Harbormaster until he died in 1986 at age 25. Now he's remembered by a book, a film and this statue. (See our Parks and Recreation chapter for related information.)

Vesper Hill Foundation Children's Chapel
Beauchamp Point, Calderwood Ln., Rockport • no phone

Romance hides in the shadows of this open-air chapel high over Rockport Harbor. If you're of the romantic age, come here and dream. If you're not, come run around the small park below. (See the related Close-up in our Worship chapter for more information.)

Barrett's Cove
Maine Hwy. 52, Camden

Shhh. There's no sign to this lakeside beach. That's because all of Camden knows where it is, and they don't want to broadcast it. Simply follow Maine Highway 52 for no more than 3 miles from downtown Camden. As soon as you see Megunticook Lake, make a left. You can't miss it. Once you get there, make a run for the water. It's shallow and warm! You can swim without ice cubes forming in your veins! While you're here, enjoy the grass, sand, climbing equipment and picnic tables. (See Parks and Recreation for more information.)

Camden Hills State Park
U.S. Hwy. 1, Camden • 236-3109

There are two kinds of families: those with parents who like to climb while the kids organize sit-down strikes at the foot of the trail; and those with kids who run up the mountain, dragging their parents behind. When our 5-year-old first climbed Mount Megunticook, he complained for a third of the way, whined the second third and dashed up the final leg. At the top of the mountain, he danced and shouted, trying to grasp wisps of fog speeding past him. At age 6, he only complained for half the trip (when he thought it might do some good). Now, at age 7, he's back to the sit-down strike, unless his friend who *loves* to hike comes along — then they chase each other up the hill.

Try this hike — it's worth it. You'll see much of Penobscot Bay spread before you, tiny Camden tucked into its pocket of land and Megunticook Lake behind it. (See our Parks and Recreation Centers chapter for more information about the park.)

Camden Public Library
Main St., Camden • 236-3440

You walk into the Camden Public library underground, but this isn't an old, dark, cave-like repository. The children's room is sunny with skylights. If you're a wee one, you can snuggle up to a hamburger pillow or clutch a soft puppet during story hour (get your parents to call for times). If you're a bit older, you might head right for the interactive computer with CD-ROM. If you're older still, maybe the Internet will attract you. (Bring your parents along to sign an Internet agreement.)

The children's collection here is good, the librarians friendly. Sometimes staff organize special events such as doll tea parties or visits with Santa. Outside, the children's garden has stone benches held up by stone books engraved with the names of a few of Maine's many children's authors (see our Maine Experience chapter). Take a look — do you recognize any?

Library hours are 9:30 AM to 5 PM Monday through Saturday (until 8 PM Tuesday and Thursday) and Sunday 1 to 5 PM.

Camden Snow Bowl Ski Area
Hosmer's Pond Rd., Camden • 236-3438

It's not the tallest ski slope in the world, but on top, below and throughout all 950 feet of vertical drop, you'll find it is one of the friendliest. The toboggan run goes straight downhill until it careens you over an icy pond. You'll scream your ears out along all 400 feet. You also can rent skis and buy snacks at the mountain . . . er, hill. Ski season runs from about mid-December to late March, depending on the snow (about 45 percent is machine-made). There's also a 600-foot snow-tubing park.

In summer, the ski trails are turned over to mountain bikers. (See our Parks and Recreation chapter for details.)

Laite Memorial Beach
Bayview St., Camden • 236-3438

It's steamy hot outside, and you're fed up with tourists crowding all the stores. Leave it.

Go up Bayview Street, past the shops and the yacht club, until you find the entrance to this small park. Splash in the waves, dig in the sand, picnic in the sun — and don't tell too many people about it. Laite Beach is one of those spots that Insiders know about and most outsiders don't. If you come Wednesday afternoon in summer (between 1 and 3 PM), you'll also find music, thanks to a summer concert series held here. There's no lifeguard or concession stand, but there is a public bathroom and a set of swings. (See our Parks and Recreation chapter for related information.)

Sea Dog Brewing Company
43 Mechanic St., Camden • 236-6863

Play chess, checkers or Scrabble, draw a picture or mess around while your folks sample the brew and grub. The vats outside are for your parents; the shelves of toys and games are for you. (Parents, see our Restaurants and Nightlife chapters for more information about Camden's Sea Dog.)

Zaddick's Pizza
20 Washington St., Camden • 236-6540

Is it pizza you want? Tacos? Veggie pockets? Yummy food aside, you'll find your own carpet to play on and a couple of shelves of games and toys to play with at this restaurant. (See our Restaurants chapter.)

Kelmscott Farm
Van Cycle Rd., off Maine Hwy. 52, Lincolnville • 763-4088, (800) 545-9363

The 120 Cotswald sheep grazing here are covered, head to hoof, with curly white dreadlocks, and Pete, the Shire horse, stands 6 feet high, not counting his head. You can't know what to expect when you visit. Maybe you'll find easels set up to paint a pair of pigs. Maybe you'll felt a ball from sheep's wool. Most likely you'll be given a passport to the animals, which you can fill with stamps at each animal's home. There's always something at Kelmscott Farm. (See our Attractions chapter and look for special events in the Annual Events chapter.)

Lincolnville Beach
U.S. Hwy. 1, Lincolnville

You can't miss this long stretch of sand, right beside the road, with a parking lot that's packed in summer and empty in winter. The beach is tidal, so if it looks like mud when you get there, you have two choices: Stick your feet into the muck, or wait a few hours and return when the tide is higher. There's four-hour parking in the lot. (See Parks and Recreation for details.)

Tumbleweeds Barbecue Restaurant
235 Northport Ave., Northport • 338-2231

We know few other restaurants as kid-friendly as this place, where you can sit on saddles, imagining you're way out west, about to lasso a cow — or is that a chicken? — for dinner. There's also a large-screen projector playing movies sometimes, sports other times. So even though it might seem odd to eat western in lobster territory, broaden your horizons and give it a try. The atmosphere alone is worth it. Like most every Maine establishment, hours change from season to season, so give a call to make sure it's open.

All About Games
78 Main St., Belfast • 338-9984

Downstairs, you can buy just about any game you've been hankering for — or new ones like Maine's own Stacks.

Upstairs, simply hang out and play under the supervision of responsible high school students. For just $1, you can be there all day (well, you should be about 11 years old to hang out on your own). Play board games, collectible card games, miniatures, role-playing games and family games such as chess and checkers. All About Games is open weekends, afternoons and most evenings, but the schedule changes, so call for hours.

Belfast and Moosehead Lake Rail
11 Water St., Belfast • (800) 392-5500

If you like railroads, don't miss this excursion into the deep, dark woods where train robbers often hang out. Hope a gang doesn't board your train!

You can ride inside or out, first class or coach, or send your parents to the first-class car while you get dusty on the 90-minute ride outside. (See our Attractions chapter for more information.)

Belfast City Park
High St., Belfast • 338-3370

You could spend the whole day here and not get bored. In summer, the local Y often does just that with its day campers. There's a large pool supervised by lifeguards, an extensive creative playground reached via a tiny wooden bridge, picnic tables, tennis courts, a basketball court, a Little League field and an open beachfront where you can beachcomb, rock-hop, even swim if you dare (folks older than 30 generally find it much too cold).

The pool is geared to the school schedule, opening when school lets out for the summer and closing around Labor Day. Call City Hall at the listed number or the pool itself, 338-1661, to check hours. Adults have the pool to themselves for a bit of time each week too.

There's a sign-up sheet for tennis at the courts, although it and the ball field are sometimes filled with local teams and classes.

As for the playground, this one has bridges, boats, sand, climbing rigs and, best of all, a sloping field leading to the shore. But there's no food here, so bring your own treats. (See Parks and Recreation for more about this park.)

Come mid-July, the Belfast Bay Festival (see our Annual Events chapter) takes over the park with rides, food treats, music and games.

Colonial Theatre
High St., Belfast • 338-1930

This is one theater where children are not forgotten. There's almost always a first-run kids' special, and come December, the weekend children's matinees are free. Now that's style. (See our Nightlife chapter for details.)

Skateboard Park
off Lower Main St., behind Dudley's Diner, Belfast • no phone

In fall 1996, the kids on wheels took over. What could the city do but follow their lead? Until further notice, a portion of this parking lot is the place where you take the pyramid, the quarter-pipe, do an air on a vert — enjoy. It's Maine's largest skateboard park without admission charge. Its construction was made possible thanks to donations by hardware and lumber stores at the urging of local expert skateboarder A.J. Dutch, who's also a mason.

Penobscot Marine Museum
Church St., off U.S. Hwy. 1, Searsport • 548-2529

It wasn't only the captains who went to sea; kids did too. They went as stowaways, as young hired hands or as children of the captain.

You can find out about them at this museum, which is really a village of museums, each built in an old home, and each looking at one part of the seafaring memory of Maine. You'll find a diary written by a young girl at sea and a gallery of photographs including some showing men climbing the rigging to take down sails in the midst of a gale. The waves seem to reach high up on the mast, almost to the sailors' toes.

INSIDERS' TIP

If you want to keep beach stones as shiny as they look under the sea, rub them against your nose. The oil on your face will polish the stones. Don't take our word for it: Try it, it works.

Photo: Bangor Daily News

Many communities in Maine hold summer fairs or festivals. Pig-calling contests are frequently a part of the festivities.

There are numerous hands-on activities, and special events happen throughout the year. (See our Attractions chapter for more information.)

Perry's Store
U.S. Hwy. 1, Stockton Springs
• 567-3392

About six years ago, a legend grew up around Rosebud, the pet pig of Mr. Perry, the owner of this otherwise standard general store and gas station (note the large Citgo sign). Rosebud rutted in the hay, rolled in the mud and ate. And ate. She now lies buried next to her home, which was taken over (after an appropriate interval) by Rosie. At a year old (in the summer of 1997), she weighed in at a quarter-ton. Nearby is a small menagerie of mostly large creatures — rabbits, pheasants and the hugest turkey you'd ever want to see.

Fort Knox
**Maine Hwy. 174, off U.S. Hwy. 1,
Prospect • 469-7719**

Kids, this place is for you. This fort is so large, it's almost a palace — and much better than a Playmobil, with secret passageways, circular stairways and parapets looming at dizzying heights over the Penobscot River, which it guards with huge cannons you can crawl on. You can crawl around the entire fort, most likely. Bring a flashlight for the tunnels, and tell your folks to pack a picnic. You'll want to spend a few hours running and climbing off all those miles spent sitting in the back seat of the car.

If you come the last weekend of either July or August, however, you won't be climbing over the cannons, you'll be covering your ears when they boom around the stone walls and echo back from the cliffs below. On these weekends, an encampment of Civil War soldiers takes over the fort. They go through their drills, even fight a bit, and best of all, they might let you touch their guns and swords. Meanwhile, the women — ever watchful — sit beside their tents, tending to the wounded, cooking and crocheting. (See our Annual Events and Attractions chapters for more information.)

Inland to Bangor

Bangor Public Library
145 Harlow St., Bangor • 947-8336

Come see the grand old Bangor Public Library in its 1912 home renovated for the 21st century. You'll find everything you might want in a library, from quiet children's games to a pet hamster to computers with Internet access. And yes, there are books — stacks and stacks of them — as well as very friendly librarians to help you sift through them.

Come summer, look for the library's calendar of daily activities, with special guests. Otherwise, between September and mid-May, expect about nine story hours. Some change, but the following don't: Monday Story Time, 10 to 10:30 AM for ages 3 to 5 (bring a snack); Story/Craft, Tuesday from 9:30 to 10:15 AM for ages 4 and 5 who don't need parental supervision; Time for Two's, Wednesday from 9:15 to 9:35 AM for ages 12 to 24 months with an adult; and Tiny Tot Time, Wednesday from 10 to 10:30 AM or Thursday from 9:30 to 10 AM for ages 2 to 4 with an adult (registration required for this program only).

Library hours are 9 AM to 9 PM Monday through Thursday and until 5 PM Friday and Saturday from after Labor Day through mid-June. From mid-June through Labor Day, it's open 9 AM to 7 PM Monday through Thursday and until 5 PM Fridays; closed weekends.

Blackbeard's Family Fun Park
**339 Odlin Rd., behind the Econo Lodge,
Bangor • 945-0233**

Get your heart pumping on the high-banked 'S' turns of the Indy-style go-cart track. The track is a quarter-mile long, and there are three (count 'em, three) 'S' turns to speed through. Need a hand to hold? Carts are two-seaters.

Then take a turn at the batting cage or one of two miniature golf courses on Treasure Island (see any pirates?). You'll also find video games and a fish pond. (See our Attractions chapter for details.)

Borders Books & Music
**116 Bangor Mall Blvd., Bangor
• 990-3300**

Listen to a story, meet a character from a storybook, maybe make a picture. Borders Books & Music features weekly story hours, generally Wednesday at 10 AM and Saturday at 1 PM. Sometimes activities are attached to the stories. About once a month, the store also holds special events such as visits from character figures like Arthur or Madeline. (See the "Major Malls" section of our Shopping chapter for additional information.)

Broadway Park
**Broadway and Stillwater Ave., Bangor
• 947-1018**

Tired of driving, tired of hanging 'round the mall? You didn't come to Maine to stay inside, did you? Head down Stillwater Avenue and tumble into Broadway Park. There's a bright-colored playground, a picnic table, a covered gazebo, volleyball nets, a walking trail, Dakin Pool (see subsequent entry) and an outdoor skating rink that's flooded over when its cold enough to freeze. It turns to muck about four months later, just in time to greet the robins.

Cole Land Transportation Museum
405 Perry Rd., off the Odlin Rd. exit of I-395, Bangor • 990-3600

Wow! There aren't simply cars here; there are rows and rows of vehicles of all kinds. You'll find just about everything — toy trucks, sleds, soap box derby cars, fire engines, old milk trucks, even a railroad car. You can climb into the railroad car and visit the replicated mail station at which it is stopped. The word at Cole's is that if it ran on land in this century or last, it's here. Roller skates? Skateboards? Doll carriages? You find 'em here. (See our Attractions chapter for details.)

Dakin Pool
Pine St., Bangor • 947-1018

Even Maine gets hot in summer, and if you're in Bangor, then you're about an hour from the coast. Need we say more? Come to the 40-by-60-foot Dakin Pool, between Broadway and Stillwater Avenue, and jump in. Yes, Mom, there are lifeguards. And no, it doesn't cost a penny. (See our Parks and Recreation chapter for details.)

Great Skates
Sylvan Rd., near the Bangor Mall, Bangor • 945-0202

Get rolling at Great Skates, a large, 80-by-240-foot rectangular surface for roller and in-line skates. Numerous sessions are scheduled, each for a different age group. In summer, the hours are limited. During the school year, there are sessions for little kids, families and teenagers, but the schedule changes by the season, so just call ahead. (See our Parks and Recreation chapter for details.)

Hayford Park
13th St., Bangor • 947-1018

If the sun is shining and you're in Bangor, this is a great place to be. With a playground, pool, ball field, skating rink, tennis courts and picnic tables, this is the hub of outdoor, in-city activity. The park is bordered by Union Street, W. Broadway and Hammond Street. Except for access to the Ice Arena, all activities here are free.

Bangor Creative Playground stretches for miles — or so it seems. It's so big that some guardians create signals, a kind of call-and-response, to be sure their charges haven't gotten into trouble on this small city of a playground. For some years, this playground was the largest in the nation, and for good reason: Robert Leathers, the designer of these great wooden creative experiences, is a Bangor boy. (Nothing but the best for his hometown.) Swing on the tires, climb the ropes, slip down the slides, hunt for the pirate ship. Enjoy.

The Ice Arena, 947-0071, has limited public hours; check out the Parks and Recreation chapter for details.

If you've come with rackets, two outdoor tennis courts are available on a first-come, first-served basis (as long as they're not snow-covered). The courts are open the same hours as the park.

Some people call Trevor Mansfield Baseball Field the field of horrors: This is the ball field author Stephen King gave to the children of Bangor. It's a senior Little League field, which means it's regulation size. It also means that league teams occupy the field some of the time. Otherwise, it's open to the public.

Splash down with your peers in Westside Pool (near Union Street). Its usually open to the public afternoons from mid-June to late August.

Sea Dog Brewing Company
26 Front St., Bangor • 947-8004

The food and the games are a lot like those at Camden's Sea Dog (see previous entry), but this one is on the Penobscot River, with a balcony overlooking the docks. Get your folks to sit outside, and you can hobnob with the sailors. (See our Restaurants and Nightlife chapters for additional information.)

Hudson Museum
University of Maine, 5746 Maine Center for the Arts, Orono • 581-1901

The carved whale bowl is big enough for you to crawl into, and the terrifying masks can bring nightmares to the squeamish. There are gold, silver, pottery and weapons galore, including bows and arrows, shields and spears. It's all the real stuff, and there's just enough of it to amaze you and perhaps even get you to make masks of your own from the shells, stones and sticks you gathered on the beach. Each month during the year features a Discovery Day; you might make a mask, or learn ancient games. (See our Arts and Culture chapter for more information.)

Maine Forest and Logging Museum
off Maine Hwy. 178 near the experimental forest, Bradley • 581-2871

Maybe Paul Bunyan started here, chopping down the trees that were processed in this old sawmill, hanging out in the old wooden camp down the line, pounding out Babe's shoes on the anvil at the blacksmith's shop. Special weekend events include winter sleigh rides and summer festivals, when men shear sheep and women card and spin the wool. Or come when it's quiet to experience the solitude of the wilderness. (See our Attractions and Annual Events chapters for details.)

Felt Brook Golf Center
Bar Harbor Rd., Holden • 989-3500

You can putter around for a round and a half (27 holes) at this brand-new, maximum miniature golf center. But keep your ball out of the waterfalls, say the owners, or you might have to chase it all the way to the 18th hole. (See our Attractions chapter for details.)

Bucksport to Gouldsboro

Bucksport Cemetery
U.S. Hwy. 1, across from the Shop 'n' Save, Bucksport

Just before Jonathan "Jake" Buck executed a woman accused of witchery, she swore she would get even. That was about 200 years ago. She may have died, but she has spent eternity dancing on old Jake's grave, her boot print etched into the headstone. You'll find the stone, the boot and a plaque in this tiny cemetery at the corner closest to the traffic light. (Also see Attractions.)

Bucksport Creative Playground
Elm St., Bucksport

From the Dairy Port (see subsequent entry), the walk to Bucksport's fine creative playground is so short, you might not finish your ice cream by the time you get there. Drive the truck, walk the bridges, slip down the slides and jump on the miniature trampoline. This wooden playground is seldom crowded and always fun.

Champion International Paper Mill
River Rd., Bucksport • 469-1482

You won't forget the heat, the infernal noise, the massive vats of blue pulp or the huge rolls of paper taller than Michael Jordan. You might, however, forget the particulars of the papermaking process, which are pretty complex. You have to be 12 or older to take the mill tour. For those of you who are of age, it's well worth the time, if only to begin to understand paper production, one of Maine's backbone industries. (See our Attractions chapter for details.)

FYI

Unless otherwise noted, the area code for all phone numbers listed in this guide is 207.

Dairy Port
Main St., Bucksport • no phone

At 50¢ for a kiddie cone dipped in hard chocolate, we think this ice cream stand is about the best deal around. You'll also find plenty of flavors of hard ice cream and a staff of sweethearts who clearly enjoy children. So tell your parents to turn left when they get to the traffic light in Bucksport (if they're traveling north on U.S. 1). No need to ask which light — it's the only one in 18 miles, any way you drive.

Hours are 11 AM to at least 9 PM in July and August, though it closes earlier in the shoulder seasons, from early spring through early summer and in early fall.

Craig Brook National Fish Hatchery
Alamoosook Lake, Hatchery Rd., Orland • 469-2803

Even people from the coastal town of Castine come here to swim in the lake in summer. Hey, the water is comfortable, unlike the ocean. The park stretches for quite a bit along the pond, which is also a great place to swim

Photo: Bangor Daily News

The winter season in Maine brings a number of recreational activities including ice fishing on the state's thousands of lakes.

or canoe. And Craig Brook is the first salmon hatchery in the nation. Check out the salmon eggs, alevins, parr and smolts, and read about how the relatively petite salmon go through almost as many life stages as humans. (See our Attractions chapter for details.)

The Breeze
Castine Dock, Castine • no phone

You might barely reach the top of the lunch counter, but that shouldn't keep you from eating the hamburgers, hot dogs or veggie burgers that come so deliciously grilled at this outdoor take-out stand. Eat on the docks next door; you'll be hanging with the sea gulls, a group of local dogs and a number of kids ready to play Tag or Follow the Leader around the central tables. (See also our Restaurants chapter.)

Blue Hill
Maine Hwy. 172, off the dirt road opposite the fairgrounds, Blue Hill

It isn't really the one, but we like to think that this is the hill little Sal climbed in the children's book, *Blueberries for Sal,* by Robert McCloskey (see our Maine Experience chapter), when she lost her own mom and found Little Bear's instead. There certainly are

enough blueberries from late July into August, and you can pick them until they're gone (or until your hands turn blue), especially on top of the hill. Atop the fire tower — way up top, round and round and round, up and up and up — your hair will stand on end from its height, its teetering motion, the breeze and the stunning views of Mount Desert Island, Blue Hill and Deer Isle.

Caterpillar Mountain
Maine Hwy. 15, Blue Hill

Be sure to get your folks to stop at the overlook on Caterpillar Mountain (not more than a hill, really), from which you can see Walker Pond, Penobscot Bay and Deer Isle — a grand vista of land and sea. This, folks say, really is the place where Sal and her mother picked blueberries in Robert McCloskey's children's book, *Blueberries for Sal* (see our Maine Experience chapter). For many years, McCloskey lived on Scott Island in Penobscot Bay. Sal was his little girl.

Holbrook Island Sanctuary
Goose Falls Rd., off Maine Hwy. 176, Cape Rosier • 326-4012

Part of it is an island, though part is on the mainland — not hard to find if your parents don't mind driving to a peninsula that's off a peninsula that's off a peninsula (got all that?). The sanctuary came into the public trust by way of Anita Harris, a rich lady who lived nearly alone on Holbrook Island and was used to getting her way. Maybe that's why there are so many rumors about her: She had the inside of her barn varnished; she so hated to look at other people's houses that she bought up their land and destroyed their homes; she painted her cows' toenails red. Park manager Philip Farr, who knew Miss Harris, is left speechless by that last one.

Truth is, none of those rumors is really true, but Harris did have a dream of returning the land to the Maine she once knew — to the wilderness, to the animals. So when a farm came up for sale on the mainland across from her, she bought the land and got rid of its many farm buildings. Some were burned, some were removed, and some were left to crumble in place, which is why you can walk around the sanctuary (or ski or snowshoe in winter), gaze out to Penobscot Bay, explore forest, field — and the foundations of houses that have long since crumbled to the ground. (See our Attractions and Parks and Recreation chapters for related information.)

MERI Community Resource Center
Maine Hwy. 175, Brooklin • 359-8078

Are you longing to go to summer camp in Maine but are here just a week? At MERI, which stands for Marine Environmental Research Institute, you can have a chance at camp for a day. Take a trip to an island, see ocean wildlife and learn how to use field guides to identify marine species. There are outdoor sessions for children ages 7 to 12 and a small indoor program for kids ages 4 to 6. (See our Education chapter for details.)

Round the Island Mini Golf
at Joyce's Cross Rd., between Maine Hwys. 15 and 15A, behind Finest Kind Restaurant, Deer Isle • 348-7714

Putt your ball up the ramp, through a lobster boat (if you can) and around some granite blocks, and learn a bit of local lore while you do. This little miniature golf course has a Deer Isle theme and offers a bit of solid history with its holes. (See our Attractions chapter for details.)

Granite Museum
Main St., Stonington • 367-6331

Everything works here. The little men walk onto the boats in the morning, and the boats cross over to Crotch Island, just across the harbor. The trains move, the rocks move. (Hey, how do rocks move?) This is a model of a quarry about a hundred years ago, when rock by the ton was blasted out of the ground, loaded onto ships and sent out to build streets, bridges and buildings in Boston, New York and elsewhere. (See our Attractions chapter for details.)

The Houses of Stonington
Main St., Stonington

Just as you're getting to the fork in Stonington's Main Street, you'll find a village of doll houses on a small hillside. The wedding couple forever stands just married, and the barn is always half-filled with hay. It looks something like the villages that appear in storefront windows at Christmastime, only this one is larger, and it's up in summer. Look, enjoy and maybe leave a few cents in the box to help with the upkeep of The Houses of Stonington. (See our Attractions chapter for more information.)

Ellsworth Public Library
46 State St., Ellsworth • 667-6363

Three sunlit children's rooms offer delight, comfort and a good deal of games. Take a trip to anywhere in the rowboat docked at one room's bookshelves. Snuggle in beanbags or rocking chairs. Take out a puzzle or head straight for the CD-ROM games. The library also offers Internet access, children's story hours and special events (call for a schedule). It is open Wednesday and Thursday from 10 AM to 8 PM and Monday, Tuesday, Friday and Saturday from 10 AM to 5 PM, though summer hours may differ; call ahead.

The Mex
185 Main St., Ellsworth • 667-4494

Plenty to look at plus a bucket of magic markers and rolls of paper keep you happy while waiting for your mounds of chips and dips. If it's pretty quiet, take a tour of the mosaics in the smoking room. Can you guess which were kid-made and which were made by local artists? The friendly wait staff and the inviting children's menu make this a good place to settle into. (See our Restaurants chapter for food details.)

Stanwood Homestead Museum and Bird Sanctuary
Maine Hwy. 3, Ellsworth • 667-8460

See eye to eye with an owl. Call it by name. At this sanctuary, injured birds are cured and released, but those too hurt to be set free, like the blind owl, are given permanent sanctuary, much to our delight. Bring some bread to feed the ducks by the pond and watch geese, possibly even a swan. (See our Attractions and Parks and Recreation chapters for details.)

Acadia Zoo
Maine Hwy. 3, Trenton • 667-3244

Have you been the subject of animal comparisons lately? You swim like a fish but screech like a monkey? Bone up on their behavior at the Acadia Zoo. Watch gibbons climb, caimans yawn and snap and buffaloes simply loll in the fields (you can see them from the road). It's the area's only zoo, and if you haven't yet seen a moose, here's your chance. The zoo is open the first Saturday in May through December. (See our Attractions chapter for more information.)

Frisbee Golf
Maine Hwy. 3, Trenton • no phone

Challenge your folks to Frisbee golf. You probably already know what it is — an open course in which the object is to get the Frisbee into a succession of metal cages. Most likely you'll have the edge on your folks, whether you're 5 or 15 years old, for the elders are bound to get lost in the giggles. At $2 for them and $1 for you (1997 rates), it's hard to pass up. (See our Attractions chapter for details.)

Great Maine Lumberjack Show
Maine Hwy. 3, Trenton • 667-0067

They're funny and they're good, and you'll go a long way before you see this kind of thing again. We're talking about the lumberjacks who climb smooth poles, throw axes, roll huge logs and also walk them. (See our Attractions chapter for details.)

Odyssey Park
Maine Hwy. 3, Trenton • 667-5841

Have you ever played laser tag? It's like tag grown into war — tag for big kids, if you will — with a laser gun, black lights, fog and a mine sector. Is your vest vibrating? Yikes! You've been hit. Odyssey Park offers laser tag, bumper boats, go-carts for both little kids and big ones and an arcade. (See our Attractions chapter for details.)

Seacoast Fun Park
Maine Hwy. 3, Trenton • 667-3573

Coast down the water slide, play a round of golf, speed around the race track or bounce on a huge trampoline rigged with bungee cords that allow you to launch 24 feet into the air and do flips without fear of falling off the canvas. (See our Attractions chapter for details.)

Whale-in-One Mini-Golf
Maine Hwy. 3, Trenton • 667-4300

Can you putt your ball through the lobster's claw, the legs of a puffin or the spokes of a ship's wheel? You'll fall in love with this straightforward, old-fashioned miniature golf course; your parents will fall in love with the $1.50-per-player rate, any time. (See our Attractions chapter for more information.)

Schoodic Point
Acadia National Park, off Maine Hwy. 186, south of Winter Harbor

Get your parents to drive to the end of Maine Highway 186 to the spot known as Schoodic Point. Get out of the car and walk around — carefully — on the rocks. Can you see Ireland? It's just over the hump of the horizon. You have a better chance of seeing it here than almost anywhere else in the Mid-Coast region, for this is one of the few places in the area where you can look out at the open ocean without seeing a gentling rim of islands. If you come at high tide, the waves crash against the rocks, so don't go down too close to the water. We've come here to watch storms — it's a wild sight — but we pretty much stay in the car. The rocks are definitely slippery when wet, and people have been grabbed by the sea from time to time, so use your head and be safe. (See also our chapter on Acadia National Park.)

Photo: Bangor Daily News

Civil War re-enactments are a favorite summertime program
at Fort Knox in the town of Prospect.

Mount Desert Island

Acadia National Park takes up much of the center of Mount Desert Island. Bar Harbor lies to one side, the "back side" to the other. In the park you can swim, hike, bike, take a carriage ride, eat the best popovers in the world, canoe, see a beaver dam, climb ropes on the same cliffs from which baby hawks learn to fly, kayak in the surf and learn about stars, fish, rocks and raccoons. Outside the park you can chase whales, hit pirates with golf balls, listen to the fizzing of root beer as it's being made, watch a movie in a bowling alley and eat lobster ice cream (if you dare!).

Acadia is pretty much geared to you kids, so you might just as well read up on it in our Acadia National Park chapter. Look there for places to swim, bike, canoe and ski and to find information about outfitters that teach kayaking or rock climbing and rent bikes, skates or cross-country skis.

You also might want to get off the island and onto the high seas. Some folks kayak, others take ferries — to Swan's Island, the Cranberry Isles or smaller Baker Island. See our Attractions and Parks and Recreation chapters for information.

Here we include the absolute kid-oriented highlights of the Mount Desert Island experience.

Acadia National Park

Cadillac Mountain
Park Loop Rd., outside Bar Harbor

Get out and whoop, scream in the breeze, jump on the rocks and tremble in the cold. You are at the very highest coastal spot on the eastern seaboard, and the wind can whip you around like a leaf. Bring your sweater for this journey.

Carriages in the Park
Wildwood Stables, Park Loop Rd., near Seal Harbor • 276-3622

At a park filled with carriage paths, it seems a shame not to take a carriage ride at least once. Try a sunset ride up Day Mountain, or arrive in style for tea and popovers at Jordan Pond House (see subsequent entry) behind a team of horses. (See our Acadia National Park chapter for more information.)

Children's Programs
various sites in Acadia National Park
• 288-5262

Kids, have the park rangers got nature programs for you! Walk around an island, look at tide pools or listen to a story. If you are adventurous, hike up a mountain. If your family lets you stay up late, try a dusk walk to see creatures of the night, or maybe make it a stargazing evening.

Tell your parents that they may need to reserve ahead for some of these programs, so call the listed number or go to the visitors center in Hulls Cove. (See our Acadia National Park chapter for details.)

Junior Ranger Program
various sites in Acadia National Park
• 288-5262

You can leave Maine with your own button or badge to prove you're a Junior Ranger. Just pick up a fun book of activities from one of the park's visitors centers and take part in one ranger program if you're 7 or younger, two if you're 8 or older. After, at a visitors center, the Nature Center or one of the park campgrounds, ask a ranger to go over the book with you, then claim your badge.

Just remember, you may need to reserve ahead for some programs, so have your folks call in advance.

Nature Center
off Park Loop Rd., Sieur de Monts Spring
• no phone

Junior Rangers, this is your spot. Examine rocks under magnifying glasses, identify birds, look over books and figure out the ranger's quizzes. This small nature center is built for kids (though parents are welcome too).

Sand Beach
off Park Loop Rd., outside Bar Harbor

There aren't many broad sand beaches along Maine's Mid-Coast. Come summer, the world flocks to this one to build sand castles, fly kites, even swim, as the water reaches nearly 60 degrees on a warm day. Lifeguards are on duty in summer.

Seawall Beach
off Maine Hwy. 102A, 5 miles southeast of Southwest Harbor

Remember creating a block tower so high you stood on your tiptoes to put the final block on? Try doing it with cobblestones. You won't be alone. Year in and year out, the huge cobblestones that form Seawall Beach prove irresistible for people who love to build; they turn this beach into a garden of minarets.

FYI

Unless otherwise noted, the area code for all phone numbers listed in this guide is 207.

Thunder Hole
off Park Loop Rd., outside Bar Harbor

Come at high tide or during a storm; the cavernous echo of the tide moving the rocks in this unusual geologic formation can sound like thunder. It also can sound . . . well, like a gargling monster, depending on the tide and the force of the ocean. Check the sign at the visitors center the day you plan to go: It will tell you the best time to hear the "thunder." Parents, please watch kids closely!

Wild Gardens of Acadia
Park Loop Rd., Sieur de Monts Spring • 288-3338

Make this into a treasure hunt. See how many plants you have already seen. Can you remember where? This garden replicates all the habitats on the island. How do they do it? With bags and bags and more bags of fertilizer and sand and other additives to each soil plot so the gardens can mimic a dozen different habitats in one location. (See our chapter on Acadia National Park for more information.)

Outside Acadia

Acadia Repertory Children's Theatre
Masonic Hall, Maine Hwy. 102, Somesville • 244-7260

It's time for laughter, delight, excitement and fear — time for a morning at the Acadia Repertory Children's Theatre, with performances of a stage production geared just for you kids. They're offered twice weekly during July and August, Wednesday and Saturday mornings at 10:30 AM. Summer 1997's offering was E.B. White's *Charlotte's Web*. The 1998 show was not determined at press time, so call to find out what it is. Or drop by on a Thursday at 10:30 AM for storyteller Jackson Gillman. In summer 1997, he presented Rudyard Kipling's *Just So Stories*. In 1997, tickets cost $16 for adults, $4 for children. Call the theater for more details.

Ben & Bill's Chocolate Emporium
66 Main St., Bar Harbor • 288-3281, (800) 806-3281

This clean, well-lighted place is filled with rows of chocolates and lollipops shaped liked lobsters and moose on one side and an ice cream counter on the other. Can anything be better? (See our Shopping chapter for details.)

Freddie's Route 66 Restaurant
21 Cottage St., Bar Harbor • 288-3708

"Fill 'er up," said the owner, and someone did, with a decade's worth of highway memories, many in the shape of toys. Toy cars, toy railroads and signs galore hang from the walls, ceilings, behind booths and between tables. You can't play with the old tin toys, but there's a lot of hands-behind-your-back looking to be had. See our Restaurants chapter for details about the food, which includes burgers, taco salad, chili and lobster.

Mount Desert Oceanarium
Maine Hwy. 3, Thomas Bay • 288-5005
Clark Point Rd., Southwest Harbor • 244-7330

Visit harbor seals swimming in a 50,000-gallon tank at the Thomas Bay oceanarium, then take a walk along the marsh to learn about

INSIDERS' TIP
Make a collage journal of your travels with sea glass, pottery shards and stones, words and pictures, leaves and flowers.

the fragile ecosystem between land and sea. Observe just how tiny lobsters are when they begin their lives; look, in particular, at their miniature claws.

At the Southwest Harbor oceanarium, you can explore, touch, hear the songs of whales, climb into a replicated wheelhouse and find out what you weigh under water at this center for hands-on exploration of the ocean.

See our Attractions chapter for more information about MDI's oceanariums.

Natural History Museum
College of the Atlantic, Maine Hwy. 3, Bar Harbor • 288-5015

See muskrats come home to their tunnels, pufflings (baby puffins) in their burrowed nests and ospreys flying with fish in their talons. This place is fun, guaranteed. Every animal on exhibit looks absolutely real. (See our Attractions chapter for details.)

Pirate's Cove Adventure Golf
Maine Hwy. 3, Bar Harbor • 288-2133

You can't miss the waterfall cascading from the cove's mountain, and if you like miniature golf, you won't want to miss this active course, complete with little stories about pirates, male and female. Choose from two different pirate courses, or play both for an afternoon of golfing. If you get a hole in one, you get the chance to win another game. (See our Attractions chapter for details.)

Asticou Terraces and Thuya Lodge and Garden
Maine Hwy. 3, near Maine Hwy. 198, Northeast Harbor • 276-5130

Your parents will revel in the garden, and you'll love the garden stage that's at the top of this short walk. You can also drive, but it's much more exciting to come upon this garden in the woods following a cliffside walk. (See our Attractions chapter for details.)

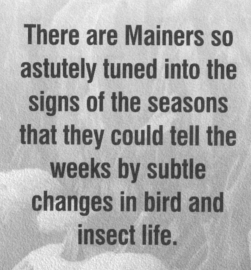

There are Mainers so astutely tuned into the signs of the seasons that they could tell the weeks by subtle changes in bird and insect life.

Annual Events

It's not that the calendar governs Maine entirely, but the seasons certainly mean something here. Sometimes they mean everything.

There are Mainers so astutely tuned into the signs of the seasons that they could tell the weeks by subtle changes in bird and insect life. But sometimes it's more fun to be obvious, as in lawn art. A favorite lawn on a back road in Bucksport is graced by a series of pink flamingos in summer. Come Christmas, the birds sprout antlers and lead a sleigh. In spring, the birds sport bunny ears and trail a wagon filled with ostrich-size eggs. And if the flamingos don't wear witches' caps at Halloween, their neighbors make up for it with a ghost town set up along a long driveway, complete with haunted tones and tombstones.

Maine's winter events center around the snow, the cold and getting away from it all with cabin-fever relievers. Spring events are about waiting for summer, and summer is about celebration. Most every town hosts a fair with children's games, music, food (usually hot dogs and hamburgers or a chicken barbecue), a parade and, finally, fireworks. But each has its own local flavor — one even features egg games and the largest egg scramble in the world.

Fall is for harvest fairs followed by haunted houses at every school and day-care center, not to mention the many private homes wrapped in webs and with skulls peaking out of garret windows.

And then we return to the season of lights.

Some organizations host regularly scheduled weekend events either seasonally or year round. For example, the Maine Audubon Society, at its **Fields Pond Nature Center**, off U.S. Highway 1A in Holden, offers various nature programs — Natural History of Snow and Ice, Animal Tracks in the Snow, Early Signs of Spring for the Winter Weary, Return of the Ducks and an Earth Day celebration, to name a handful. Most events have an admission fee

of about $5; call 989-2591 for details. The **Maine Forest and Logging Museum**, on its grounds at Leonard's Mills, off Maine Highway 178 in Bradley, offers horse-drawn sled rides one Sunday mid-month throughout the winter — provided there's adequate snow cover; call 581-2871 for information. The University of Maine's Just for Kids program, held at the **Hudson Museum** in the Maine Center for the Arts, in Orono, introduces school-age children to the wonders of global culture through various hands-on activities; call 581-1901 for the scoop. And the **Owls Head Transportation Museum**, Maine Highway 73, Owls Head, 594-4418, hosts the Owls Head Antique and Classic Car and Plane Meets almost every weekend from late May to late October. Admission generally is $6 for adults and $4 for children. (Air shows also happen some weekends, weather permitting; look for military aircraft around July 4).

Acadia National Park also hosts guided and unguided nature walks, naturalist programs and other daily or weekly events June through September. Check out the *Beaver Log*, which lists daily events such as "Written on the Rocks," a look at Acadia's geology, and "Forests of Lilliput," which examines the park's mosses, ferns and lichens. Otherwise, ask at the Information Booth, or call 288-5262.

Remember, regularly scheduled events happen throughout the year, particularly late spring through early fall. Keep an eye on local newspapers for announcements and schedules for these and other related programs and activities.

Unless indicated, the following events can be enjoyed for free, though specific portions of a festival or event might carry a price tag. Many of these events are connected with an institution — read more about them in our Attractions or Arts chapters. Before you go to an event, or schedule a visit to the area around one, you should always call to confirm the date. Local calendars can be quixotic — weather and many other factors need be considered. Encampments get changed around all the time, and parade schedules frequently conflict, so if a town's fire trucks are already booked for an out-of-town parade, the local parade may simply switch weekends.

Please note that we've bypassed our typical geographic breakdown in this chapter in deference to a loose chronological (early, mid- or late month) pattern of organization. We willingly drive from one end of the region to the other for many of these events, and we figured you would too. But even if you'd prefer to stick close to home base, chances are you'll find something happening nearby. Read on.

FYI

Unless otherwise noted, the area code for all phone numbers listed in this guide is 207.

January

Robert Burns Dinner and Performance

St. Andrew Lutheran Church, U.S. Hwy. 1, Ellsworth • 244-7193

The West Eden Highlanders Pipes and Drums sponsor a cold-weather retreat to highland cheer on a Sunday evening in mid-January. Come for a traditional Scottish dinner and listen as the pipe band plays, dancers dance and an emcee treats diners to the words of Robert Burns. There's a lot of laughter and joy, but when the pipe organ commences the strains of "Amazing Grace" accompanied by a bagpipe, awed silence ensues. In 1998, the cost was $12 for adults, $6 for children.

Winterfest

Kathy's Catering, 1606 Hammond St., Bangor • 941-2903

Celebrate a winter's eve in late January and help out the American Red Cross Pine Tree Chapter in northern and eastern Maine at the same time. This winter festival includes dancing, a casino and great munchies. The cost for the evening is $20 a person.

Gala Performance of Dance, Poetry and Music

Camden Opera House, Main St., Camden • 338-5380

Mid-Coast dancers, poets and musicians come together in late January for an evening celebration of the arts, including drumming, dancing, singing and poetry-reading. The event is sponsored by the Belfast Dance Studio and the Community Multi-Cultural Arts Project. Admission in 1998 was $8 for adults and teens, $4 for children ages 5 through 12.

February

U.S. National Toboggan Championship

Camden Snow Bowl, Hosmer Pond Rd., Camden • 236-3438

The Snow Bowl's toboggan run is a one-of-a-kind place — the only traditional wooden toboggan chute in the nation. Calling it the "nationals" was a tongue-in-cheek designation when the championships began in 1990, but there's truly nothing like it, anywhere. Participants dress up in zany costumes, decorating their toboggans as well, and zoom down the hill and over the ice with bloodcurdling screams. Prizes are given for best times overall and in the following divisions: oldest, all-female and family — but no longer for costumes. Registration forms are available in November, so sign up early. Only 280 can participate. Fees are $24 for a two-person team, $36 for a three-person team and $48 for a four-person team. There's also a children's division. But many people come simply to watch.

Camden Conference

Camden Opera House, U.S. Hwy. 1, Camden • 236-1034

Looking for a way to explore global issues, folks in Camden decided to devote the first full weekend in February to intense discussion of

INSIDERS' TIP

A tour of the sugar bush is simply a visit to the grove of sap-producing maple trees.

one major topic. This "community forum for rational discussion and exchange of ideas," originated in 1988 as a Rotary project focused on the Iran-Contra affair. It is now an independent organization with an advisory council that includes former policymaker Lawrence Eagleburger. Each year's conference has a focus such as Islam, Russia, China, the global environment or the new world order. (At press time, the 1999 topic was still undecided.) The conference is open to all, with a free session Friday evening, a $75 Saturday program (cost includes lunch; reservations are necessary) and a free Sunday program. Moving to the Camden Opera House in 1998 has allowed the audience to increase to 500, but still, the conference usually sells out, so reserve early.

Winter Carnival
H.O.M.E., Maine Hwy. 15, Orland
• 469-7961

The good folks at the H.O.M.E. cooperative, a small village of an organization, have organized this mid-February event to give rural Mainers a cure for cabin fever. In 1998, they scheduled it to coincide with Valentine's Day, a good time for a hearty lift. Come for sleigh rides and snow sculpting, an outdoor barbecue, large flea market, games for children, crafts and snow softball.

Games Day
University of Maine, Hudson Museum, Orono • 581-1901

At least three different versions of hopscotch might be taught, Go from Japan, or games from Africa or from the Inuit Eskimos. Games Day, focused on children, is held one day only in mid-February, usually around school vacation week. Nearby exhibits display the glaring masks of the Northwest Coast Tlingit and the glittering gold of pre-Columbian America in Maine's beautifully spacious ethnological museum. Admission is $2 a person.

Seafarer's Tavern Annual Toboggan Challenge: Slide for Scholars
Camden Snow Bowl, Hosmer Pond Rd., Camden • 548-2465

The Seafarer's Tavern sponsors toboggan races in late February or early March to benefit local scholarship funds. A fee of $25 per four-person team allows each squad two runs down the chute. The lowest score wins bragging rights plus an engraved pitcher. Team spirit is the order of the day; some teams dress up, though no prizes are awarded for costumes.

March

Children's Poetry Festival
Camden Opera House, U.S. Hwy. 1, Camden • 236-3440

Who is not amazed by the writings of young children? The Live Poets Society and Camden Public Library sponsor an afternoon of children's words in mid-March at the elegant Camden Opera House. Between kids reading their own work, children's choral groups perform choral poetry. The choir and many of the poets have been trained by George Vandeventer, a poet who works in area schools and who founded the Live Poets Society in 1993. Admission is $4; the anthology is extra.

Saints & Spirits Weekend
various pubs in Camden • 236-4404

Knowing March can be a dispiriting time in Maine, the local chamber of commerce has organized a celebratory weekend featuring Camden pubs. Crawl the pubs of town and enjoy the live music that's in most every area pub and microbrewery — then walk back to your local accommodation.

Stitch-Inn
Camden Room, Camden Opera House, Main St., Camden • 236-9636

Eight years ago, the Camden Maine Stay began sponsoring a weekend of stitching in mid-March inside its small bed and breakfast inn. The weekend was so successful, classes are now held in a large room above the Camden Opera House. A different instructor teaches a different project each year, such as making pendants or linen samplers. Participants pay a fee of around $150, depending on the cost of materials. The price includes lunch for the two days, but neither lodging nor other meals.

Cultural Connection
various locations, Camden • 236-4404

The local chamber of commerce can't quite hurry spring, but it can bring a taste of summer in late March by orchestrating a summer weekend's round of cultural activities. Expect demonstrations at area studios, special exhibits, performances at the Camden and Rockport opera houses and music as well. The weekend is usually planned to coincide with Maine Maple Sunday (see next entry), when the Conway House/Cramer Museum welcome visitors to its sugar house.

See this and many other **Insiders' Guide®** destinations online — in their entirety.

Maine Maple Sunday
various locations statewide • 289-3491

Warm days and cool nights make the maple sap flow. By the end of February, growers always worry that the optimal weather combination will never happen, but it always clicks in — just in time for the annual celebration of the sap, which you can see dripping into oak barrels, plastic milk bottles and ungainly plastic tubes that run into sugar houses. On the third Sunday in March, sugar houses open their doors and pour their boiled syrup onto pancakes, pie, ice cream or, best of all, snow. Visit the Cramer Museum at the Conway Homestead in Camden, 594-8047, which also offers candle-making and blacksmithing demonstrations, or call the listed number for a rundown of locations in the area.

Harlequins of Isle au Haut
Maine Audubon Society, Isle au Haut Ferry Pier, Stonington • 781-2330

Come winter, harlequin ducks, named for their beautiful facial plumage, flock to the remote island of Isle au Haut. The Maine Audubon Society finds just the right time — after the weather has warmed up, but before the harlequins head off to their summer grounds — to visit the island. Expect to spend about four hours on the boat with a naturalist on a mid-March Sunday. You'll be on board the entire time, cruising around looking at the ducks. Dress warmly and bring food (there's a head but no galley on board). You might also want to pack a thermos of hot chocolate. Cost for the trip is $30 a person.

YWCA Bangor Spring Fair
Bass Park Complex, 100 Dutton St., Bangor • 941-2808

Slogging in ice or mud? Get inside the Bangor Civic Center in late March. Folks welcome spring with a Ferris wheel, merry-go-round and other rides as well as games, food and gifts. Although 1998 admission had not been set at press time, 1997 rates were $2 for adults and 75¢ for kids ages 12 through 17.

Feel Good About Yourself
various locations, Camden • 236-4404

This weekend is intended to encourage visitors to spruce up for the coming spring and summer. Area inns and bed and breakfasts, along with area teachers and studios, have found all sorts of way to help you feel good about yourself, just in case you need some help. Fitness studios offer special deals, some inns host masseuses and beauticians, and others teach knitting or bread baking. Maybe you want a yoga class? You can mix and match from the year's offering, or simply spend the weekend in a hot cribbage tournament — a gaming weekend is planned as part of the deal.

St. George River Race
Belfast area • 338-4598

A few miles west of the coast, the St. George River offers lots of whitewater in spring, when it's the site of a popular 6-mile, late March paddling race. In 1997, 225 people entered at $10 a paddler. The race begins in Searsmont and ends in Appleton. Spectators can follow Maine Highway 131 south from outside Belfast, then turn off at the Robbins Lumber Road.

April

Bangor Garden Show
Bass Park Complex, 100 Dutton St., Bangor • 990-1201

After five months of winter — shoveling

Migrant workers find employment in Maine
during the annual blueberry harvest.

snow by moon, sun and blizzard light —
Bangor's garden show in early April is beyond therapy: It's necessity. Landscapers
and nurseries go all-out, turning the gray
concrete floors of the combined Auditorium
and Civic Center into a lush and flowery
springtime scene. Admission is $5 for adults
and $2 for children.

Passagassawaukeag Stream Race
Belfast area • 338-4598

The river that runs just north of Belfast is
called the Passagassawaukeag (pa-SAG-as-
a-wa-kag), meaning "sturgeons fly at night,"
for this is the river the region's Native Americans fished at night. Locals bypass the pro-
nunciation and affectionately call it the
"Passy." Come spring, many get deep into
it — literally — paddling the annual river
race in early April. This is not a competition
for the wary. It begins at a farm in Waldo
and ends 8 miles and several rapids later,
before the river cuts over a dam north of
Belfast.

Registration is $10 a paddler.

Spectators: Follow Maine Highway 137 to
Marsh Road and proceed to Poors Mill Road.
You'll find a bridge traversing the Passy near
a three-way junction.

Kenduskeag Stream Race
Bangor area • 947-1018

This mid-April canoe race is for the social set. With more than a thousand participants and numerous swarming television
cameras, it's known as the largest canoe
race in the country. It is also easy to find —
some 20,000 come to view it. The race begins at the grange hall in the middle of
Kenduskeag Village, right off Maine Highway 15, and ends just after the Bangor ca-
nals. Registration in 1997 was $15 in ad-
vance, $25 at the race.

A good viewing spot is Six Mile Falls Bridge,
6 miles from downtown Bangor on Maine Highway 15. Or try Kenduskeag Stream Park at the
outer end of Harlow Street.

Fisherman's Festival
**Maine Hwy. 127, Boothbay Harbor
• 633-2353**

OK, this one is a little out of the area, but
it's too famous and fun to pass up. Don your
fishing boots and foul-weather gear, and join
the race through town — holding a codfish by
its tail. Run from harbor to cove across lobster
traps strung in a line, or watch the coronation
of Miss Shrimp (no, her crown does not have
even one little crustacean on it). The 1998

event, which takes place the third weekend in April, is a gala 25th celebration.

Lambing Time
Kelmscott Farm, Maine Hwy. 52,
Lincolnville • 763-4088, (800) 545-9363

There's nothing like the sweet beauty of a newborn lamb. Kelmscott Farm is committed to raising and preserving rare breeds, including five kinds of sheep: Cotswald, Jacob, Merino, Shetland and Katahdin. You'll be able to stroke the lambs, maybe even hold one in your lap, then engage in whatever activities the creative people at the farm cook up — and they always come up with something different. Admission is $3 for children, $5 for adults.

Earth Day Celebration and Environmental Fair
Merryspring Park, end of Conway Rd.,
off U.S. Hwy. 1, Camden • 236-2239

Merryspring's free Earth Day celebration is different each year, but it's always held on Earth Day, April 22. If it falls on a weekend, more events are scheduled — African dancing, perhaps some rain or sun dances, depending on what the earth needs that year. The celebration always features tables with information about ecological activities in the region.

Woodsman and Log-hauler Day
Maine Forest and Logging Museum,
Leonard's Mill, off Maine Hwy. 178,
Bradley • 581-2871

Teams of woodsmen demonstrate traditional lumbering practices such as hand felling, broad-axe work, skidding logs and using a lumbard (a onetime popular and very noisy Maine-made machine with tractor treads used to haul logs from the woods). Activities change each year, so call if you want specifics. Admission to this late April

event is $3 for adults and teens, $1 for children 12 and younger. A traditional logger's meal of beanhole beans (cooked underground overnight) and reflector-oven biscuits costs an extra $5.

May

Maypole Celebration
Merryspring Park, end of Conway Rd.,
off U.S. Hwy. 1, Camden • 236-2239

Stand three men, one on top of the other, and they probably wouldn't reach to the top of Merryspring's Maypole. It's a tall one, festooned with colored wool ribbons that dangle until the Highland Merry Morris Dancers start playing and the children start dancing. Then, suddenly, the ribbons are braided around the pole. The whole thing might be undone and done again and again, depending on how many children come to dance. Many wear crowns of bittersweet — the weekend before, Merryspring Park hosts a workshop at which participants learn to make crowns from the blossoming vine. If there's time, more crowns may be made at the May Day celebration, always held May 1 at Merryspring. Expect refreshments, dancing and lots of music.

Marsh Stream Race
Loggin Rd. to Marsh Stream Rd., West
Winterport to Frankfort • 338-4598

By early May, the Marsh Stream flowing from West Winterport to Frankfort has become Class II and III rapids. This 8-mile race is exciting and challenging, offering plenty of chances to watch folks known as river vultures, who swim in the icy waters to aid racers ejected from capsized canoes. Registration to participate is $10. Good vantage points for spectators include Loggin Road and the area around the railroad trestle on Marsh Stream Road — the spot where everyone "takes a swim."

INSIDERS' TIP

A great annual event that just about every Mainer engages in is lawn-ogling. You don't need to wait for Christmas to see decorations — look for hanging eggs at Easter, hanging ghosts at Halloween, flags on the Fourth of July and entire trailer homes outlined in lights before the winter holidays.

Spring Festival
H.O.M.E., Maine Hwy. 15, Orland
• 469-7961

Hanging plants and seedlings are sold at the opening of H.O.M.E. cooperative's greenhouse around Mother's Day. The festival celebrates new growth, with hay rides, an outdoor barbecue, a large flea market, crafters and games.

Warbler Wave Weekend
Pilgrim's Inn, Sunset Rd., Deer Isle
• 348-6615
Goose Cove Lodge, off Sunset Rd., Deer Isle • 348-2508

For two weekends in mid-May, Pilgrim's Inn and Goose Cove Lodge, both famous for their food (see our Restaurants chapter), are for the birds. Listen to talks about the jewel-like migrating warblers, look at bird art by local artists, take walks with naturalists, hop on a boat to see pelagic birds and puffins, and enjoy the fine surroundings. The lectures are free, but expect to pay to stay at either of the inns (see Accommodations for rates and other details about these lodgings). Call for current information.

Cultural Heritage Festival
Pickering Sq., Bangor • 945-4400 Ext. 409

Celebrate Bangor's internationalism in mid-May with food, crafts, music, song and dance from Greece, the Philippines, China, Korea, India and elsewhere.

Memorial Day Parade
Brewer to Bangor • 947-0307

The parade of the Air National Guard, fire engines, the Sheriff's Department and other public servants begins on the Brewer side of the Penobscot River and marches to Main Street or Exchange Street in Bangor.

Annual Plant Sale
Merryspring Park, end of Conway Rd., off U.S. Hwy. 1, Camden • 236-2239

Each spring, the volunteers at Merryspring Park are faced with a problem: The gardens have grown wild, and there are too many plants. What to do? Share the excess. That's when folks around Merryspring get lucky. For

$3.50 a shovelful (sometimes a large shovelful, sometimes a small one, depending on the plant), the public can buy the garden's extra parsley, sage, rosemary and thyme as well as lily, marjoram and many other plants. You take a number, then walk around the gardens and make your list while enjoying the emerging green as well as minstrels, refreshments and children's activities. When your number comes up, a volunteer gardener begins digging your plants right out of the ground. This annual sale happens the weekend after Memorial Day.

June

National Trails Day
Acadia National Park, Mount Desert Island • 288-3338, 288-5262

Help out the park for a morning during National Trails Day in early June. Pick up winter debris and get the park ready for visitors. Bring a picnic and water to enjoy in the park afterward. (If you're lucky, there will be a barbecue.) This volunteer event is sponsored by Friends of Acadia and Acadia National Park.

Coastal Arts & Heritage Week
various locations, Rockport and Camden • 236-4404, 236-4885

The region between Rockport and Belfast wakes up for summer and celebrates its heritage with a week of culture and history. This is the time when many institutions open for the summer. To celebrate, nearly everyone offers something special. At the Conway Homestead, for instance, you might find demonstrations of traditional activities like candle dipping, blacksmithing and spinning. Look for plays at the local opera houses as well as concerts and special lectures at museums and galleries. Admission and activities vary, so call the listed numbers to find out exactly what's happening.

Fleece Festival
Kelmscott Farm, Maine Hwy. 52, Lincolnville • 763-4088, (800) 545-9363

What does a llama, a sheep and an alpaca have in common? Say "fleece" (not fleas, please, and definitely not wool — only the sheep has wool), then visit Kelmscott Farm's annual fleece festival. Llama and alpaca fiber are not technically wool, because the fiber of these camelids is hollow-cored, but it's all wonderful for knitting, felting and weaving. First, however, it must be carded and spun. You can watch it all at the annual Kelmscott Farm Fleece Festival held in early June. Admission is $3 for children, $5 for adults.

Trek Across Maine
Bethel to Rockport • 622-6394, (800) 458-6472

While you get in shape for summer by biking west to east across Maine, your pledges benefit the Maine chapter of the American Lung Association. In three days you'll pedal 180 miles from Sunday River to the sea with as many as 1,400 others. The trek ends on Father's Day with a band, a great meal at the Samoset (see Restaurants and Accommodations) and a medal hung around your neck. Registration is $50 a person plus a minimum $350 in pledges.

Hiking the Hills of Isle au Haut
Maine Audubon Society, Stonington • 781-2330

Spend a Sunday in mid-June hiking the hills of Isle au Haut at that precious moment between spring and summer, when migrating birds, some quite rare for these parts, are likely to flock to local islands en route to their nesting grounds. Some 20 people are divided among three Audubon Society leaders, who talk about the wildflowers encountered on the island and help search for warblers and other birds in breeding plumage. Bring your own lunch. The cost for the day, frequently Father's Day, is $45.

Maine Special Olympics Summer Games
University of Maine, Orono • 879-0489, (800) 639-2401

More than 1,500 mentally challenged Maine athletes of all ages come to the playing fields of the University of Maine for three days in mid-June. These folks have been training all year. There is a parade and a grand dance as well as competitions in gymnastics, aquatics, bowling, track and field and other events. Everyone is welcome to cheer and help.

NORBA Mountain Bike Spring Run-off
Camden Snow Bowl, Hosmer Pond Rd., Camden • 236-7120

The North American Off-Road Bicycle Association (NORBA) sponsors this mid-June event. It's an unusual race in the NORBA series — mud and sizable rocks pose hazards — though beginners can enter in a different category from professionals. Registration in 1997 was $15 in advance, $20 on race day. Spectators enjoy watching from the main lodge, or walking the course in reverse.

Opening of the Center for the Wyeth Family in Maine
Farnsworth Museum, 19 Elm St., Rockland • 596-6457

When the Wyeths decided to offer the Farnsworth their personal collection of works, a revolution of sorts started at the museum. It acquired a church, dug up part of the grounds for a library and expanded greatly. Mid-June is Victory Day, when the Wyeth Center, along with its first show, opens in a former grand old church that's now part of the Farnsworth Museum. Details of the day were not finalized at press time, but expect a public celebration with Jamie Wyeth, the extroverted artist son of famous introvert Andrew Wyeth (himself the son of illustrator and painter N.C. Wyeth), in attendance; also expect free admission to the museum (ordinarily $9).

Celebrate Bar Harbor Festival
various locations, Bar Harbor 288-5103

The musical whale-watches, calliope, parade, tours of town and bed and breakfast inns, even the tastes of Bar Harbor's restaurants, all pale beside the centerpiece of this mid-June festival — the Bar Harbor Lobster Race. Bet on Clawed Camper or Lobsterzilla (bets top out at 50¢), then urge your "horse" to race — eh, undulate — to the finish line. The race track is measured by the foot (no longer than 3) and set inside a specially built tank. If that seems too slow, you can watch the wait staff race — and see how many glasses get broken. The festival features myriad events, including a Blessing of the Boats in the harbor. Bring your own boat to ensure fair sailing this summer, or simply enjoy the parade of rigs.

Maine Soapbox Derby Finals
Washington St. (Maine Hwy. 105), Camden • 236-8087

The cars come in kits and are assembled by youngsters throughout the state, many of whom then gather on Washington Street, one of Camden's steeper hills, for a hell-raising plummet to the bottom. These soapbox racers are a bit different from those actually built from old crates and boxes: These are made of fiberglass. That means the new derbies are a skill-only event, since the cars are exactly the same except for surface decals. The winner of this mid-June race goes to Akron, Ohio, for the national finals in August.

Children ages 9 through 16 who live in Knox, Lincoln, Sagadahoc and Waldo counties are eligible to race. Registration is $20; participants must also buy their own kits, which cost as much as $400. To watch, just go to Washington Street (Maine Highway 105).

Eastern Maine Soapbox Derby
State St., Brewer • 989-5199

The starting line for this mid-June race is at the top of State Street in Brewer, near Dunkin' Donuts. The kids, some 125 of them, plummet down the hill through the center of town, finishing near Brooks Street. As in the Camden finals (see previous entry), the winners go to Akron, Ohio. Registration in 1997 was $20; the car kit costs about $400. It costs nothing to stand on the sidelines and cheer your heart out with some 3,500 other spectators.

Castine Village Fair
downtown Castine • 326-4884

Castine might look too elegant to host this funky village fair, held at the end of June, but inside all the white clapboards are folks who love food, live music, crafts and games, just as anywhere else. Look for fine crafts, ethnic food, a farmers market, excellent local music and a strong sense of community.

Windjammer Days
Maine Hwy. 27, Boothbay Harbor • 633-2353

Maine's windjammer fleet arrives in Boothbay en masse, and the town comes out to greet it with music, food contests, fireworks, a street parade, antique boat parade of as many as 50 nautical beauties, waterfront concerts, nautical exhibits and tours of Navy and Coast Guard vessels for two days in late June.

Rare Breeds Weekend
Kelmscott Farm, Maine Hwy. 52, Lincolnville • 763-4088, (800) 545-9363

Celebrate the work of the folks at Kelmscott Farm to preserve rare breeds. Look for pigs, cows, chickens and rare animals plus a myriad of activities for children and adults. Admission is $3 for children, $5 for adults.

Juried Arts and Crafts Show
Harbor Park, Atlantic Ave., Camden • 236-4404

New England artists, jewelers and craftspeople line the head of the harbor with their work in late June. Shop and browse to the strains of fiddlers and a barbershop chorus.

July

Fourth of July Events
towns throughout Mid-Coast Maine

Maine celebrates the Fourth of July the old-fashioned way: with parades of children, antique cars, streams of fire engines (whose drivers get a kick out of blasting onlookers' eardrums), high school bands and the Anah Temple's gloriously ridiculous lawn mower brigades. Fireworks boom at night. The largest regional celebrations are in Bar Harbor (with a seafood festival), 288-5102, and in Thomaston, 596-0376. Downtown Thomaston features a parade and a chicken barbecue, and Montpelier, 354-8062, the mansion and onetime home of Revolutionary War hero Gen. Henry Knox, hosts a celebration to carry on Knox's tradition of opening his house to the public every July 4. If you love a parade, you'll find one marching from Brewer to Bangor, 945-4400, featuring a celebrity grand marshal. Expect fireworks in Thomaston, Rockport, Searsport, Stonington and Bar Harbor.

Close to the region are the Wiscasset Parade, which ties up U.S. Highway 1 traffic for hours, and Eastport's seaside festival.

The tiny but picturesque village of Orland holds its River Day Raft Race on the Narramissic

Pick Your Own

Maine might not be the agricultural giant it once was, but you wouldn't know it from the many farms offering baskets and bushels for you to fill with a handpicked bounty from June through October. There's nothing like picking your own for understanding how, where and when fruits grow. Don't worry about the "why" — your tastebuds will know that from the first bite. There is simply nothing like the taste of fruit just off the bush, vine or tree, and it's not your imagination, but rather the action of the sun and soil.

Close-up

Before you go, however, we have two bits of advice. The first concerns your clothing. You'll get red from the juices of strawberries and raspberries and blue from the blueberries. (Remember, berry juice is an age-old dye.) Apples won't stain, but if you or your children plan to get the elusive top-of-the-tree fruits, you'll want to do some climbing—and who can resist? Dress down.

The other reminder: Don't expect to make a morning (or an afternoon) of it unless you're heading to a very big party or plan to do lots of baking or canning. Pick-your-own places are professional farms. Picking at these places is not like picking blueberries in a field or raspberries on a trail. You won't be playing hide-and-seek with the berries — in a half-hour, you'll have more fruit than needed to satiate a large family.

Photo: Bangor Daily News

A young strawberry picker takes a break to sample the fruits of her labor.

We can offer approximate seasons for finding fruits, but the beginning and ending dates vary according to weather conditions. Also, the cost varies according to the bounty of the season. Call ahead for times, directions and prices.

Strawberries come first, ripening at the end of June and lasting through mid-July. These juicy red berries are nothing like the packaged ones at the supermarket. They are plumper, sweeter, juicier — even better than the local berries sold at market or the heavenly ones sold by the side of the road. These berries are warm off the vine. We suggest you check out Spear Farm & Greenhouse, U.S. Highway 1, Warren, 273-3818; Route 97 Strawberries, Maine Highway 97, off U.S. Highway 1, Warren, 273-3226; What-A-View Farm, Coggin Hill Road (take N. Union Road from Maine Highway 17), Union, 785-4866; Silveridge Farm, MacDonald Street, off Main Street, Bucksport, 469-2405; and C & G Growers, Maine Highway 175, South Penobscot, 326-9311.

Next comes raspberries, from about the third week of July to mid-August. Again, there's nothing like the taste of a juicy, sun-warmed raspberry fresh off the bush. The taste is heavenly — there hasn't been time to crush it. To pick some for yourself, try Sue

— continued on next page

Wright, Maine Highway 97, off U.S. Highway 1, Warren, 273-3778. In Rockport, Stony Lonesome Farm, 188 Main, 236-2009, follows raspberries with blackberries — our idea of heaven. Ask about picking veggies at the farm too. Look in your local newspaper for other farms. Raspberries are a sensitive crop, so some growers decide right at harvest time whether or not to open up their fields.

Blueberries frequently grow beside trails and on mountainsides from the last week in July (or the first of August) to the first week in September. But to ensure you'll find some, stop by the historic barn and farm of Staples Homestead, Old County Road, off U.S. Highway 1A, Stockton Springs, 567-3393.

You'll find apples in September and October. Some apple orchards allow you to climb a tree and pick a bag or a bushel, and some also offer cider fresh from the press. Try Hope Orchards, Maine Highway 105, Hope Corner, Union, 763-4080; Wight's Orchards, Maine Highway 46, Bucksport, 469-3773; and Merrill Farms, Bangor Road, U.S. Highway 1A, Ellsworth, 667-9750.

Last but not least come pumpkins. The folks at Simons Hancock Farm, on U.S. Highway 1 in Hancock (across from the White Birches Motel), 667-1359, make an event out of picking your own pumpkin. Ask about hay rides to the pumpkin field, pumpkin weight guessing and, dare we say it, pumpkin smashing.

River on a Saturday near July 4 as well as a village fair; call 469-2581.

But many folks head for Jonesport, where there's a new tradition to the season: lobster-boat races. From a vantage point on the Jonesport-Beal's Bridge, you can watch two boats speeding toward you, then veering off, vying for the title World's Fastest Lobster Boat. Ask a native which boats to watch. Call 497-2804 for more information.

A Weekend With Henry Knox
Montpelier – Gen. Henry Knox Museum, U.S. Hwy. 1 and Maine Hwy. 131, Thomaston • 354-8062

Gen. Henry Knox, the man who built Thomaston's mansion, Montpelier, orchestrated moving 59 cannons from New York to Boston, Massachusetts, to win Boston from the British. He gained and lost more than one fortune in his life — in short, he was a colorful guy, a man worth getting to know. Bud Jenkins' historical impersonation makes him feel like an old friend. In 1998, other personalities may join him, such as an aide to Gen. George Washington. Admission is $5 for adults, $4 for seniors and $3 for children; no more than $12 a family.

Schooner Days
on the waterfront, Rockland • 596-0376

When the great ghostly shapes of Maine's two dozen-strong schooner fleet enter the Rockland harbor about a week after the Fourth of July, you get a vision of a world long gone, when trade and travel passed on the water, and Maine was a major player in the world's commerce. The festival begins with a parade of schooners in full sail, followed by open houses on many of the vessels. During the day, there are tents of arts and crafts, marine demonstrations and food vendors of all kinds. On Friday night, fireworks.

Admission charges are somewhat complex. The craft tent is free, but because the North Atlantic Blues Festival (see next entry) takes over the same grounds Saturday and Sunday nights, a gate is erected, which means access to a portion of the grounds requires paid admission to the blues festival.

North Atlantic Blues Festival
on the waterfront, Rockland • 596-6055

The North Atlantic Blues Festival follows Schooner Days. The great Koko Taylor headlined the first event; Clarence Gatemouth Brown, the third. That is to say, "getting down" by the downtown waterfront is the real thing. Admission from noon Saturday is $30 for the entire musical weekend, including a club crawl. Daily admission costs $20 a person at the gate.

Downeast Dulcimer and Folk Harp Festival

Agamont Park, near Town Pier, Bar Harbor • 288-5653

Song of the Sea, a Bar Harbor store (see our Shopping chapter), builds and sells hammered dulcimers, psalteries, mountain dulcimers and folk harps. The store also sponsors this free festival in early July, instructing people on how to play exquisite musical instruments like mountain dulcimers and harps. Instructors perform in the evening at St. Saviour's Episcopal Church on Mt. Desert Street. Admission to these concerts is $7 a person.

Harbor House Days

Harbor House, Main St., Southwest Harbor • 244-3713

The local nursery school joins the parade, which lasts all of four minutes — it's a small community, after all. This mid-July parade is followed by a craft fair, an 8K foot race, a 10K bike race, a 1K fun-run and the all-important crab-picking demonstration. This is the kind of close-knit community event that's rare in this day and age.

Gardens in the Watershed

various locations along the St. George River • 594-5166

The Georges River Land Trust is a non-profit organization that helps people preserve their land through conservation easements. Each annual tour of gardens and some homes covers only a third of the watershed that extends from Port Clyde to the tip of Lake St. George in Liberty, encompassing 15 towns and 225 square miles. There's a lot of distance to cover, so each year the trust offers a tour of gardens in just a third of the region. In 1998, the watershed tour features the lower watershed — the coastal area, St. George, Thomaston and Cushing. Visit about five or six gardens. A few locations will host gardening workshops. Bring a picnic lunch, and plan to make a day of it. The $12 tour takes place on a Sunday in mid-July.

Stonington Lobster-boat Races

Commercial Fisheries Pier, Stonington Harbor, Stonington • 367-2396

The waters boil when *Lil' Josh, Lil' Jan* and the *Love Beat* vie for the Jimmy Stevens Cup, awarded to the fastest working lobster boat. This Sunday race in mid-July is part of a series of lobster-boat races brought to the public by *Commercial Fisheries News*. There are numerous classes, ranked by size and engine type (gas or diesel). Between boats you can look over the Coast Guard vessels brought to Stonington for the events, or wander the pier looking at exhibits.

Antique Show

Camden-Rockport High School, Milton St., Camden • 236-2257

This mid-July antique show, sponsored by the Camden-Rockport Historical Society (which oversees the Conway Homestead; see Attractions), offers wares from several dozen New England dealers. Admission is $3 a person.

Salad Days

Watershed Center for the Ceramic Arts, Cochran Rd., off U.S. Hwy. 1, Newcastle • 882-6075

Maybe you wouldn't travel out of the area for a salad — but for these pots, who wouldn't travel? Get all the salad you can eat for the cost of a ceramic plate from one of the center's potters (from about $10 to $20). Watershed is a residency program for some excellent potters and artists. Visit them in their studios, or simply stroll the luscious gardens during this mid-July event.

WERU Full Circle Summer Fair

Union Fairgrounds, off Maine Hwy. 17, Union • 469-6600

Celebrate the eclectic, all in support of WERU, Maine's most unusual, wide-ranging

Photo: Bangor Daily News

The annual soap box derby in several Maine communities pits youngsters against each other for the right to compete in national races.

community radio station. It began in the basement of Noel Paul Stookey's barn (Stookey is the Paul in Peter, Paul and Mary) and has never diminished. Expect lots of music, fun children's activities, poetry readings and a bone-vibrating drumming circle at this two-day, mid-July event, along with plenty of information booths, craft booths and representatives from all walks of alternative Maine. Admission is $5 for adults and teens, $1 for children 12 and younger.

Arts in the Park
Belfast City Park, High St., Belfast
• 338-9764

To encourage the cultural use of this lovely seaside park, a local jury asks some 72 artists to show their art and crafts on a mid-July Saturday. You'll also find strolling musicians, a bagpiper, stilt walker, chorus and band.

Belfast Celebration of the Arts
Heritage Park, Front St., Belfast
• 338-5900

On the same weekend as Belfast's Arts in the Park (see previous entry), downtown Belfast features a festival of art, music and crafts, with many children's art events in its Heritage Park, near the pier on Front Street.

Belfast Bay Festival
Belfast City Park, High St., Belfast
• 338-4910, 338-5719

Saturday morning's parade features a bicycle brigade of area kids, and prizes are awarded for the best-decorated bike. Rides, cotton candy, more rides, sack races, even more rides, fried dough and music round out the events of this five-day festival toward the end of July that manages to remain a community event even as Belfast grows. Belfast City Park, the festival site, also has a pool, an elaborate creative playground and a lovely beach for walking.

Admission varies, but in 1997 it was $1 for anyone older than 12. Individual rides cost extra but can be covered by purchasing a bracelet. Please call to find out how much the 1998 bracelet will cost.

Penobscot Marine Museum Benefit Auction
Penobscot Marine Museum, Church St., Searsport • 548-2529

Under a tent on its grounds, the Penobscot Marine Museum offers a mid-July luncheon plus live and silent auctions. The museum concentrates on the water — and so does its auction. In 1998, a sail boat is up for bid as are other boats, Windjammer packages and nautical items. Admission in 1997 was $20 a person. Expect a slightly higher rate in 1998.

House and Garden Tour
various locations, Camden and Rockport
• 236-4502

Have you been ogling the houses of Camden and Rockport? Longing to sneak into their secret gardens? Here's your chance. From eight to 10 houses and/or gardens — shingled cottages, board and batten and contemporary homes — have agreed to be part of the 51st annual tour. Buy tickets on event day — the third Thursday in July — at Whitehall Inn on U.S. Highway 1, or at the homes themselves. Proceeds go to the Camden Garden Club for scholarships and local horticultural and conservation activities. Admission is $20.

Central Maine Egg Festival
various locations, Pittsfield • 487-5416

It's hard to ignore a festival featuring egg races and the world's largest scrambled egg, even if it's slightly out of the Mid-Coast area. Maine used to be a major poultry producer. This festival in late July, along with rural Maine's prevalent chicken barns — and numerous chicken barbecues held throughout the summer — are what's left of the industry.

Friendship Sloop Days
Rockland Harbor, Rockland • 596-0376

The focus of this three-day event in late July is the sea and the lovely class of boats known as Friendship sloops that were built more than a century ago by folks on Bremen Long Island, which lies west of Friendship across Muscongus Bay. The sloop is a safe, responsive, well-balanced and fast boat created after the railroad came through Maine, expanding the shellfish and agricultural markets. It's also beautiful, which is why it's such a coveted pleasure craft today. There are several races, a parade of sloops, tours of the ships, a barbecue and entertainment. At the end of the week, the sloops depart Rockland for the home port of Friendship.

Friendship Day
various locations, Friendship • 354-8036

As at many town festivals, Friendship Day features a children's art show, pet show, town parade, music on the grass and an auction and variety show. Friendship Day, held the Saturday following Rockland's Friendship Sloop Days (see previous entry), also offers a parade of the dreamy Friendship sloops.

Bar Harbor Antiques Market
Mount Desert Island High School, Eagle Lake Rd. (Maine Hwy. 233), Bar Harbor
• 563-1013

This midweek event in late July features approximately 50 dealers, most of whom offer 19th-century antiques. Look for Victoriana, folk art and other wares. Admission is $5.

Civil War Encampments
Fort Knox, Maine Hwy. 174, off U.S. Hwy. 1, Prospect • 469-7719

When British ships chased U.S. fleets up the Penobscot River in the 18th century (see History), Fort Knox — not to be confused with the U.S. gold bullion depository in Kentucky — had not yet been built. In the 1830s, fearing yet another war against the British, the young U.S. government decided to build a fort to guard Bangor, the queen city of the lumber industry. The war never happened — a good thing since the fort's construction lasted 20 years. Fort Knox has never been part of a battle, but it did become a training ground for Civil War soldiers, hence the presence of Civil War soldiers for encampments, which feature gun battles, cannons and a period fashion show.

This event generally takes place the last full weekend of July. Admission to the fort is $2 for folks ages 12 through 64, $1.50 for kids ages 5 through 11 and free for the rest.

Silver Tea
Montpelier – Gen. Henry Knox Museum, U.S. Hwy. 1 and Maine Hwy. 131, Thomaston • 354-8062

War hero Gen. Henry Knox was born in late July. To celebrate, the museum at Montpelier, the reconstruction of the home he built, hosts a party for all. Speakers talk about the Revolutionary War hero. Perhaps a military general or a member of congress will be on hand. There also will be singing, a luncheon (hence the event's name, Silver Tea) and birthday cake for all. Donations are accepted.

Hancock Days
various locations, Hancock • 422-2310

Celebrate the little town of Hancock with a homegrown festival in late July. It's one of Maine's great little festivals. It starts out with a road race, then continues with an auto show, chicken barbecue, bingo tournament and family fun games. Following the traditional bean supper, join the locals in a street dance.

Shakespeare on the River
Penobscot Theatre Company, along the Penobscot River, Bangor • 942-3333

Sword fights accompany Shakespearean verse spoken beside the gently rolling Penobscot River. Nightly performances of Shakespeare's plays begin in late July and continue into August. Additional entertainment is provided by Renaissance dancers and madrigal singers. For the 1998 festival, *A Midsummer Night's Dream*, *Romeo and Juliet* and *The Merry Wives of Windsor* are scheduled in rotating repertoire Wednesday through Sunday, with 26 total performances. Admission ranges from $5 for children in bleacher seats to $15 for regular adult seats.

Open Farm Day
various locations statewide • 287-3219

Maine is swiftly losing its farms, but you wouldn't know it on this exuberant day in late July, when farmers open their barns for the rest of us to see. It's a great time to pet goats, stroke llamas, nuzzle horses and learn the working reality behind such romantic roadside signs as Horsepower Farm, Happy Town Farm and the Anniversary Farm.

Conway Day Celebration
Conway Complex and Camden Historical Society, off U.S. Hwy. 1, Camden • 236-2257, 594-8047

Celebrate Maine's history at this historic cape in late July when a Civil War encampment group usually arrives with tent and costume. You'll also find various craft demonstrations like broom making, chair caning, shingle making, spinning, weaving and basketmaking — some done by volunteers, some the result of visitors' hands-on activities. Expect music — everything from solo harmonica performances to a high school

jazz band. Since the shop contains all Maine-made products, you'll also find many vendors demonstrating their wares. All buildings of the Conway Complex are open to the public for free.

State of the Art Auction
Maine Coast Artists, 162 Russell Ave., Rockport • 236-2875

Some of Maine's top artists offer prints and paintings for the annual fund-raising auction of this nonprofit gallery. Items are previewed for about a week at the end of July, and the auction occurs in early August. Admission is $30 a couple for dinner and the opportunity to bid.

Castine House and Garden Tour
various locations, Castine • 326-8786

Castine is a historic village, as anyone who wanders its streets can tell. It's also quite a contemporary one, as this late July tour makes apparent. From Castine's earliest house, built in 1760, to a home that's nearing completion, the tour could also be a history of Castine architecture. Why not? The $25 it costs to view the seven homes and three gardens on the 1998 tour goes to the Castine Historical Society. Register early, and you can peruse the brochure before the tour.

Maine Lobster Festival
on the waterfront, Rockland • 596-0376, (800) LOB CLAW

Maine's sea goddess is crowned, little girls dressed in their best summer cool jump on floats, and rugged individuals race across lobster crates. Lobsters are everywhere: on T-shirts, posters, coins, key rings, nutcrackers, caps — and plates. This is an immensely popular festival: 75,000 from around the nation attended in 1997. Held between the end of July and early August, this festival includes all kinds of food vendors, lots of art and crafts, a marine tent and literally tons of lobsters. In 1998, to keep up with the crowds, the festival is scheduled for five days. Details weren't settled by press time, but expect a grand parade, great entertainment (the Temptations performed in 1997) and plenty of fun. Admission in 1997 was $5 per adult, which does not include rides.

Bangor State Fair
Bass Park Complex, 100 Dutton St., Bangor • 942-9000

This 10-day fair, beginning the last day of July and extending into August, is the big summer event in Bangor. There's a little something for everyone: a midway, rides, agricultural exhibits and horse racing. Nightly entertainment features well-known rock, country and gospel musicians. Admission is $5 for adults and teens, $3 for seniors and $1 for kids 12 and younger; rides cost extra. See our Fairs chapter for more information.

August

Maine Festival
Thomas Point Beach, Thomas Point Rd., off Maine Hwy. 24, Brunswick • 772-9012, (800) 639-4212

Fly a kite, listen to a story, dance, paint, browse Maine books, crafts, arts and ideas at Maine's premier arts festival, held in early August. Brunswick is not in our Mid-Coast area, but this event is definitely worth the drive. Some of the best artists in the state drive hours to attend this hands-on fair, with music of all kinds, art installations, craft sales and more. In the past, Thursday has been artist's day, Friday children's day, and the weekend for the multitudes. But there's something for everyone each day. Admission to the festival is $12 for adults, $9 for seniors and teens age 13 through 17 and $6 for kids 12 and younger. Or get advance tickets at Shop 'n' Save for $10, $8 and $4.50 respectively. Bring additional cash for food and on-site purchases.

Revolutionary War Encampment
Montpelier, U.S. Hwy. 1 and Maine Hwy. 131, Thomaston • 354-8835

Gen. Henry Knox, owner of the stately Montpelier, was second in command during the Revolutionary War. To commemorate his work, a band of Revolutionary War soldiers, dressed in period garb, camp out on the grounds and remember the struggle for three days in early August. Yes, they actually "fight" a band of British soldiers. In addition to the staged battle, expect to see the soldier's tents, fire pits and various period activities: the men make weapons and ammunition; the women spin wool and cook over open fires. There may also be a period doll exhibit. Also expect a drawing for the Tree of Life quilt, made by local quilters — a yearlong fund-raising effort for the museum. There's no admission to the grounds, but tours of the museum cost $5 for adults, $4 for seniors and $3 for children, with a family cap of $12.

Maine Indian Basketmakers Alliance Summer Sale
College of the Atlantic, Maine Hwy. 3, Bar Harbor • 827-7776

Maine's native tribes used to spend their summers on Mount Desert Island, offering visitors canoe rides and canoes, beaded bags and baskets ranging from the size of a thimble to great ash laundry baskets. A joint effort of the Maine Indian Basketmakers Alliance and the Abbe Museum, this event ensures that members of Maine's tribes return each summer to Bar Harbor for at least one day in early August to sell baskets. Look for demonstrations of basketmaking — from pounding the ash wood to weaving strips — as well as demonstrations of quillwork (decorating with the dyed quills of porcupines) and other crafts. Specific events vary from year to year.

Kitchen Tour
Merryspring Park, end of Conway Rd., off U.S. Hwy. 1, Camden • 236-2239

Area homeowners open their kitchens in early August as a fund-raiser for Merryspring Park, a lovely 66-acre preserve filled with equally lovely gardens. Don't expect squeaky-clean facilities — they'll be buzzing with various local caterers, perhaps even a winemaker or bread baker — but do expect something delectable to taste. And because the tour is sponsored by Merryspring Park, itself a large garden, there's almost always a lovely garden associated with the kitchen. The cost of the tour, generally including about nine gardens in the Rockport, Camden and Lincolnville area, was $20 in 1997. Expect a similar if slightly higher rate in '98.

Claremont Croquet Classic

**Claremont Hotel, Claremont Rd.,
Southwest Harbor • 244-5036**

Come enjoy a week of croquet — singles, doubles and mixed doubles. Rumor has it that folks come from everywhere to play, some dressed in their croquet best. On the final day, there's a jazz band and a lobster buffet beside this elegant Old World hotel. The tournament takes place the first full week of August. Participation is open to qualified players; contact the hotel by the end of July. It costs $5 a person to play.

Maine Antiques Festival

**Union Fairgrounds, off Maine Hwy. 17,
Union • 563-1013**

With more than 350 dealers, there's no larger antique show in northern New England. Wares run the gamut from fine antiques to 20th-century collectibles. You'll find Irish and Scottish antiquities and works by New England folk artists. Dealers at this early August event truck in items from as far away as California, New Mexico, across the Midwest and Canada — some stuff even comes from Europe. General admission is $5 a person each day ($25 for a three-day pass). Friday night is the early-bird special - it costs a bit more but how else can you get first pick?

Fisherman's Days

**Commercial Fisheries Pier, Stonington
Harbor, Stonington • 367-5959**

The second Sunday in August heralds Fisherman's Day here, with local crafts, children's games and some Maine signature waterside games, including Wacky Rowboat Races, Codfish Relays and Survival Suit-ups.

Winter Harbor Lobster Festival and Lobster-boat Races

Main St., Winter Harbor • 963-7774

Because the wind comes up from the southwest, this is a tricky race for lobster-boat captains. The fastest boat doesn't always win. Winter Harbor has a long-standing tradition of races on the second Saturday of August, held in conjunction with its lobster festival. Some 1,800 lobsters are prepared for the crowd that descends upon the little town of Winter Harbor for this event. Expect games for children

and adults, art and craft displays, live music and an evening parade.

Directions: Maine Crafts Guild Craft Show

**Mount Desert Island High School, Eagle
Lake Rd. (Maine Hwy. 233), Mount
Desert Island • 763-3433, 897-4261**

The Directions show proves how much creative energy bursts out of Maine's granite bedrock. Weavers, jewelers, sculptors, papermakers, potters, carvers and leather workers show their year's work at this mid-August weekend event. This is a juried show, so expect excellent quality from the 90 craftspeople represented. In fact, some people come to the Bar Harbor area specifically in mid-August, just to be around when the show is happening. Admission is $2 for adults.

Community Festival

**Farnsworth Museum, 19 Elm St.,
Rockland • 596-6457**

One year, 22 members of an African dance troupe and the drummers of the Atlantic Clarion Steel Band plus an enthusiastic core of visitors got everybody jumping at this community day sponsored by the Farnsworth Museum. You never know what's going to happen at this truly hands-on art festival. But you will have the chance to make puppets or paintings. The festival takes place on a Sunday in mid-August. In 1998, the Farnsworth is celebrating its 50th anniversary and will be flush from the opening of the Wyeth Center (see previous "June" section), so expect a truly grand community celebration.

Sankofa Festival and Street Dance

**corner of Church and Spring Sts., Belfast
• 338-5380**

The Belfast Dance Studio has exposed the region to African-inspired dance, and everybody celebrates that for a few hours on a Saturday in mid-August. Performers display ethnic dance and music from around the world with a focus on Afro-Caribbean culture, ending with a large street dance to live music.

Summer Fair

H.O.M.E., U.S. Hwy. 1, Orland • 469-7961

Crafters from around the state cover the

grounds here during the third weekend in August. You'll also find musicians and storytellers. Enjoy the outdoor barbecue, hay rides, pony rides, children's games, music, a flea market, farmer's market and a huge harvest sale. Admission is $1 per adult; children and seniors get in free.

Antique, Classic and Special-Interest Automobile Auction
Owls Head Transportation Museum, Maine Hwy. 73 Owls Head • 594-4418

Here's your chance to own — or even just dream about owning — an early Model T, a classic Pontiac, you name it. These cars are handpicked by museum officials, and only the finest 200 make it into this consignment auction. Director Charles Chiarchiaro is a licensed auctioneer and does the honors, fetching from $1,200 to $175,000 a vehicle at this large museum fund-raiser held the third weekend in August. Bring your checkbook, but make sure it's healthy!

Union Fair and State of Maine Blueberry Festival
Union Fairgrounds, off Maine Hwy. 17, Union • 236-4859, 785-4180

This late August event is small enough to seem human, not larger-than-life. Stand on the midway and you can see to the outskirts of this fair, along with all the events you might enjoy. Come Friday for the State of Maine Blueberry Festival, when the Blueberry Queen is crowned and plenty of berry fun events happen. You can visit the Matthews Museum of Maine Heritage, then watch harness racing, a farm parade and fireworks. Admission to the fair is $5; rides are extra. (See our Fairs chapter for more details.)

Searsport Lobster Boat Race
Mossman Park, off U.S. Hwy. 1, Searsport • 548-6114, 548-6302

These late August lobster-boat races, held on a Saturday, bring participants money, jackets and plaques — and bragging rights. They are equally meaningful to the lobster-boat builders, since lobstermen like fast vessels to speed themselves to distant lobstering grounds. On land, there are arts, crafts, food, games and a view of the races with the islands of Penobscot Bay in the background.

Civil War Encampments
Fort Knox, Maine Hwy. 174, Prospect • 469-7719

On a promontory just below the town of Bucksport, where the stately Penobscot River rounds the bend, a fort was built of local granite. Stroll through Fort Knox during the encampment, generally held the last full weekend in August. When you walk past costumed soldiers languishing in canvas tents and playing soulful tunes on violins and mouth harps, you'll swear they haven't been home in years. Admission is $2 for folks ages 12 through 64 and 50¢ for kids ages 5 through 11; everyone else gets in free.

Renaissance Festival at Kelmscott Farm
Kelmscott Farm, Maine Hwy. 52, Lincolnville • 763-4088, (800) 545-9363

For three days at the end of August, this farm of rare breeds becomes transformed into a world unseen for hundreds of years. Watch jousters perform, see the Queen parade through the grounds every morning, and enjoy fencing and all sorts of period booths. A preliminary list of demonstrations include spinners, weavers, felters, lace makers, potters, carvers of stone and wood, makers of paper, dyers, calligraphers and printers. Admission is $10 for adults, $6 for children.

Blue Hill Fair
Blue Hill Fairgrounds, Maine Hwy. 172, Blue Hill • 374-9976, 374-5092

This late August event is a real country fair, with lots of room for livestock, a midway, cotton candy and country music. Watch for races or the monster truck exhibition. Admission to the fair is $5 for adults and teens, $3 for seniors and free for children 12 and younger. (See the related entry in our Fairs chapter for details.)

September

Windjammer Weekend
Camden Public Landing, on the waterfront, Camden • 236-4404

As many as 25 multi-masted sailing vessels line up with sails unfurled to enter the harbor in style during the opening parade on the first evening of this Labor Day weekend fest. The weekend includes sailing events, a contra dance, lobster-crate races, nautical workshops, fireworks and a boat-building contest. At night, listen for raucous sea shanties as the crews put on a Schooner Bum Talent Show at the public landing. Stay at a local inn, or ask about Berth and Breakfast options when you call the listed chamber of commerce number.

Maine Healing Arts Festival
Hidden Valley Camp, Maine Hwy. 220, Montville • 336-2065

Walk on coals or bask in a hot tub while you learn to heal with herbs or hands and get focused on inner, future and past lives with the help of an array of regional healers. Bring the kids to this Labor Day weekend event for children's and teen programs, or come alone for the adult programs. The 1997 weekend cost $265 for adults, $70 for kids ages 6 to 14 and $60 for youngsters ages 3 to 5, and included cabin or tent lodging and vegetarian meals.

Penobscot River Festival
on the waterfront, off Main St., Bucksport • 469-7300, 469-2803

The lovely riverside town of Bucksport hosts this early September festival to celebrate and learn about the mighty Penobscot's geology, biology, industry and culture through musicians, storytellers, boat trips and exhibitors. Look for guided river tours and music across the river at Fort Knox (see our Attractions chapter). Peek into the lives of salmon, or learn an unusual paper craft. Storytellers and musicians recount tales of river drives, tugs hang out in the harbor, and exhibitors reveal the work going on in and around the river. There's no admission to the festival, though specific events may carry costs.

Archeology Field School
Abbe Museum, Acadia National Park, Sieur du Monts Spring, Mount Desert Island • 288-3519

Dig and sift at a prehistoric site along the Maine coast during one week in early September, side by side with anthropologists willing to train. One year, the field school came back with remnants of a 4,000-year-old dog. Another year, while excavating a hearth, archaeologists found seeds, mostly from berries. The workshop costs $200 a person plus $175 for room and board.

Bald Eagles of Merrymeeting Bay
trips depart from the harbor off Maine Hwy. 27, Boothbay Harbor • 781-2330

In early September, Maine's Audubon Society takes bird-watchers on a daytrip from Merrymeeting Bay up the Kennebec River to observe as many as 27 eagles nesting in the region. Bring lunch, or buy a snack from the boat's snack bar. The all-day trip costs $32 a person.

Common Ground Fair
Maine Hwy. 220 and Crosby Brook Rd., Unity • 623-5115

Maine's organic country fair, held the third weekend in September, has some of the best food in the state as well as some of the best crafts. There's no midway, but children love the drumming circles and the multitude of animals. Go to the 1998 event, and you'll make history. This is the first time the fair is held on its own grounds. Then keep coming to see how the grounds grow with the years. Admission is $6 for adults, $2 for children and seniors. (See our Fairs chapter for more information.)

Windfall Fair and Apple Festival
Conway Homestead and Merryspring Park, end of Conway Rd., off U.S. Hwy. 1, Camden • 236-2239

The Windfall Fair, held annually either in late September or early October, has been equated with the early days of the Common Ground Fair — no small compliment. After you wander among the flowers of this horticultural park and learning center, you can check out the vendors, listen to the Quasimodal Chorus or learn the arts of the season: pruning, preserving and drying flowers and making wreathes. This is a hands-on event. You might even be invited to learn to spin and weave at the Conway Homestead.

The Wings of Autumn: Migration on Monhegan Island
trips depart from the harbor off Maine Hwy. 32, New Harbor • 781-2330

If birds get blown off-course during their annual fall migration, they are likely to land on Monhegan Island, just far enough offshore to act as a haven for warblers, peregrines and other birds. Join Maine Audubon Society naturalists on a visit to the island during the last weekend in September. You'll see migrating raptors and other passerines, like warblers, as well as pelagic birds like Northern gannets. We think there might be no better reason to go to this distant island after the crowds have gone.

The weekend trip (Friday through Monday) costs around $325, including accommodations, breakfast and lunch, the boat trip and a guide.

The Second 50: Senior Lifestyle Exposition
Bangor Civic Center, 100 Dutton St., Bangor • 942-9000

Maturing baby boomers take note: This late September exposition covers the needs, activities and desires of those who are moving into their second 50 years. Exhibits and workshops include healthcare, Medicare, nutrition, fitness, education and legal and financial matters. Admission is $2 a person.

October

Church Street Festival
Church St., Belfast • 338-5777

Children aren't the only ones who love this community harvest festival on the first Saturday in October. Waldo County's spirit gets celebrated in a zany festival parade featuring wild local costumes as well as those made by Mary Weaver, creator of MythWeaver Theater and the Playhouse (see our Arts chapter for more information). There's also crafts, activities, performances, stands, food and plenty of input from the folks of Belfast, a burgeoning alternative, arts and banking community.

FYI

Unless otherwise noted, the area code for all phone numbers listed in this guide is 207.

Fall Festival Arts & Crafts Show
Harbor Park and Camden Amphitheater, Atlantic Ave., Camden • 236-4404

As many as 80 New England crafters and artists line the head of Camden harbor for this juried show in early October, held close to the height of the fall foliage season. At the same time, the stately Camden library offers a book sale.

Scottish Performing Arts Weekend of Workshops
St. Saviour's Church, Mt. Desert St., Bar Harbor • 244-7193

Come Saturday for a day of bagpiping and Highland dancing with some of the top instructors in the nation. A practical workshop happens during the day and a concert at night during this Columbus Day weekend event. Admission to the workshop, geared to musicians, costs $35; the evening concert is $5 for adults, $3 for children.

Bar Harbor Chowder Festival and Great War Canoe Race
downtown Bar Harbor • 288-5103, 288-3519

On the Sunday of Columbus Day weekend, the Bar Harbor Chamber of Commerce presents its third annual chowder cook-off. Sample chowders from throughout the town, choose the best, and be sure to stop by the Town Pier where the Abbe Museum presents Man-Es-Ayd'lk, the great war canoe race. Watch two war canoes (they're the very large ones) race against each other as well as other canoes and sea kayaks. Or race yourself, at $10 a registration slip. There is a fee for the Chowder Festival, but it hadn't been determined by press time, so call the first listed number (the local chamber of commerce) for details. Oh, by the way, Man-Es-Ayd'lk is the old name for Bar Harbor. It means clam gathering place.

Kelmscott Farm Fall Festival
Kelmscott Farm, Maine Hwy. 52, Lincolnville • 763-4088, (800) 545-9363

Watch out for the goblins, scarecrows and dangling spiderwebs haunting the path to

Kelmscott Farm on a Saturday in early October. Wear a costume and you may win a prize — for the silliest, scariest or most unusual. There are haunted goings-on throughout the pastures — but beware the horse barn. Who knows what lurks there after the horses are put out to pasture? Admission is $5 for adults, $3 for children.

Gulf of Maine Pelagic Birding
Maine Audubon Society, Bar Harbor
Whale Watch Pier, Bar Harbor
• 781-2330

On Columbus Day weekend, the Maine Audubon Society charters a whale-watch vessel to scoot bird watchers out 30 miles around Mount Desert Rock. You'll be looking for great skua, jaegers, shearwaters, northern fulmar and other pelagic or ocean-living birds that hang out far from shore and sometimes follow the fishing vessels. The trip lasts from six to eight hours, leaving early in the morning. There's a full galley on board. Note: The $70 tickets do not include food.

United Maine Craftsmen Show
Bass Park Complex, 100 Dutton St.,
Bangor • 621-2818

Some 75 exhibitors fill the civic center with folk art, pottery, jewelry, leather, dolls and stuffed animals. The show takes place in mid-October. Admission in 1997 was $1.

October Fest
Hinckley Great Harbor Marina, off Maine
Hwy. 102, Southwest Harbor • 244-9264

Under tents set up at the marina, 20 microbreweries offer tastes of the many new drafts they've created — representative examples of the multitude of breweries that have sprouted across the state. But what's a party without food and music? Rest assured this event, held the Saturday of Columbus Day weekend, has it all. Sets of tickets are sold, with each set allowing a certain amount of tastes. But it's not only the beer that attracts people. Some folks buy the nondrinkers ticket, allowing them access to the International Food Court, music, children's activities, etc., without drinking. Admission to the 1997 event was $3 for adults and teens; children 12 and younger got in free. To drink, it

cost $15 for 10 samples (4 ounces each). Additional samples cost $1 each.

Festival of Scarecrows
Farnsworth Museum and other locations,
Rockland • 596-6457

Scarecrows sneak across the street and hang out in doorways, on lampposts, in parks and in windows. Merchants put them up, artists conjure them up, children dress them up — everyone gets into the action. The scarecrows hang for the last three weeks in October. The middle weekend features a harvest festival with children's activities, games and contests such as foot races and tug of war. Visit the farmers market or museum, or buy a ticket to tour local inns, where artists display their work. But before you travel, call the museum — construction may make it difficult to host the festival in 1998.

The house tour cost $10 in 1997; all other events were free.

Great Fall Auction
Owls Head Transportation Museum,
Maine Hwy. 73, Owls Head • 594-4418

Take a chance on a ride that just can't be bought: a trip in one of the museum's vintage biplanes. Everything from a used plow truck, a truckload of gravel and health-club memberships has been sold at this late October auction.

Spooky Doings at Harbor House
Harbor House, Main St., Southwest
Harbor • 244-3713

Harbor House, the neighborhood community center of Southwest Harbor, becomes a ghostly home in late October for a week of free after-school activities during the season of spooks.

Ghostly Gatherings at Fort Knox
Maine Hwy. 174, off U.S. Hwy. 1,
Prospect • 469-7719

It doesn't take much to turn the shadowy alcoves and dark tunnels of Fort Knox into a haunted fort. It can be pretty spooky even on a bright summer day, in fact. For a real thrill, come the weekend before Halloween (call for times) and you'll encounter Civil War soldiers, faces painted a ghostly white, telling old ghost stories.

November

Take Pride in Acadia Day
Acadia National Park, Mount Desert Island • 288-3340

If the leaf pile on your own lawn seems daunting, imagine having to rake an entire park! Help the Friends of Acadia at Acadia National Park in early November by clearing the leaves from drainage ditches and culverts along the park's stately carriage paths. Your "thank you" is a barbecue lunch.

United Maine Craftsmen Show
Brewer Auditorium, Wilson St., Brewer • 621-2818

Start your holiday shopping with true Maine-made gifts. On Thanksgiving weekend, United Maine Craftsmen offers a three-day sale with 60 craftspeople selling wood, wool, fabric and fancies of all kinds. (See our "October" entry as well.) Admission is $1.

December

Christmas By The Sea
various locations in Camden, Rockport and Lincolnville • 236-4404, (800) 223-5459

During the first full weekend in December, Santa's lobster boat is decked with pine boughs and wreaths and trimmed in red and green as he makes his way by lobster boat — destination Rockport and Camden. From there, he rides a fire engine to Lincolnville. With him come a host of family things to do, such as a tree lighting on the beach at Lincolnville accompanied by a bonfire and caroling, and a community Christmas party at the historical society. In Camden, carollers are joined by bands playing on town balconies and in passing vehicles. There's also a holiday tour of Camden's and Rockport's classic homes, decorated for the season, sponsored by the Camden Women's Club, 236-0935. Santa will be there, so after you listen to him read from the wish lists he's received, you can help him out by taking advantage of sales at Camden stores. But if you've already taken care of that part of the season, forget the shopping and enjoy the several concerts offered during the day

plus a holiday theater performance at the Camden Opera House at night.

At Merryspring, look for the tree of lights outside and lovely holiday crafts inside. Children can make a bird tree. At Kelmscott Farm, there's cookie decorating. In Rockport, Maine Coast Artists usually has workshops for parents and children.

Most events associated with this festival are free.

Christmas at Montpelier
Montpelier, U.S. Hwy. 1 and Maine Hwy. 131, Thomaston • 354-8835

Montpelier, the stately Thomaston mansion, is decorated in flowers, boxwood and berries for an early December holiday celebration. Expect holiday music and carolling. Late Sunday afternoon, the lights in the mansion are turned off for a candlelight tour. In 1794, when the mansion was built, candle light was the standard means of illumination. Today, the unexpected scene is spine-tingling.

Penobscot Marine Museum Victorian Christmas
Penobscot Marine Museum, Church St., off U.S. Hwy. 1, Searsport • 548-2529

Holiday visitors to the Fowler-True-Ross home of the Penobscot Marine Museum will see banisters and mantels decorated with a variety of holiday evergreen boughs set off by bows of red flocking. The kitchen bustles as preparations are made. Perhaps a family will greet you at the door. Perhaps you can play a game from the 19th century. Nearby, Santa Claus greets kids with carved toys. While most of the museum already has closed for the season prior to this event, it reopens for this Victorian Christmas celebration the second weekend in December. Santa brings children's entertainment, refreshments and song. While admission is free, some parts of the event might carry charges.

Colonel Black Mansion Christmas Tea and Tour
Maine Hwy. 172, Ellsworth • 667-8671

The stately Black Mansion is laden with boughs and bows for its annual Christmas celebration, generally held the first two Saturdays of December. See how folks in the 19th century celebrated the darkest part of the year

Photo: Bangor Daily News

Hundreds line the shores of the Kenduskeag Stream in Bangor to watch the annual Kenduskeag Canoe Race, held each spring.

and the coming of light while enjoying a spot of tea and a Christmas cookie or cake. The cost for both tea and tour is $10. Otherwise, the tea is $6; the tour, $5.

Basket Makers Sale and Demonstration
Hudson Museum, University of Maine, Orono • 581-1901

Maine's majestic multi-cultural museum hosts the state's Native American basketmakers for a pre-holiday sale in mid-December. Watch as sections of trees are pounded into delicate wooden strips and woven into elegant baskets. Listen to Native American storytellers and musicians. You'll find baskets and possibly Native American food such as Navajo fry bread, stew and soup. Don't miss the books and gifts from the excellent museum store.

Farnsworth Homestead Holiday Open House
Farnsworth Homestead, 19 Elm St., Rockland • 596-6457

The Farnsworth Homestead still looks much like it did when Lucy Farnsworth, the last owner of the house built by her father, was a child. The decorations remain Victorian, with garland draped on the stairs and candles hung on trees. During weekends in December, look for the elaborate doll house, the boughs of green and as many antique toys as the museum can fit. (See our Attractions chapter for details on the homestead.)

Christmas Lights Contest
throughout Belfast • 338-5900

In mid-December the post office, with its wrought-iron balcony, lights up the head of Main Street. The rest of the town rises to the occasion, vying for attention with elaborate window decorations.

New Year's by the Bay
various locations, Belfast • 338-4501

When Jennifer Hall went to Portland's elaborate New Year's arts event in 1996, she was so excited and had so much fun, she decided to take it home. An organizer by trade, she set out to create New Year's by the Bay for New Year's Eve 1997. It must have been an idea whose time had come, for an impressive number of musicians, entertainers, creators and actors joined in to create an overwhelming success the first year. The festival runs from 3 PM to midnight, when fireworks greet the new year. Expect to hear musicians like Paul Sullivan and Glen Jenks, see dance and theater, maybe even participate in a tournament at All About Games (see our Kidstuff chapter). There will be children's shows, perhaps a session of cowboy singing, or circle dancing and much, much more. Admission is $10 a person.

The 179-year-old Skowhegan Fair is the oldest continuously running fair in the United States.

Fairs

When they pulled into the Fair Grounds, they could hear music and see the Ferris wheel turning in the sky. They could smell the dust of the race track where the sprinkling cart had moistened it; and they could smell hamburgers frying and see balloons aloft. They could hear sheep blatting in their pens. . . .

"Let's let the children go off by themselves," suggested Mr. Arable. "The Fair only comes once a year." Mr. Arable gave Fern two quarters and two dimes. He gave Avery five dimes and four nickels. "Now run along!" he said. "And remember, the money has to last all day. Don't spend it all the first few minutes. And be back here at the truck at noontime so we can all have lunch together. And don't eat a lot of stuff that's going to make you sick to your stomachs." . . .

The children grabbed each other by the hand and danced off in the direction of the merry-go-round, toward the wonderful music and the wonderful adventure and the wonderful excitement, into the wonderful midway where there would be no parents to guard them and guide them, and where they could be happy and free and do as they pleased.

The magic of fairs has not abated since 1952, when E.B. White wrote about the Blue Hill Fair, the site of "some pig" Wilbur's glory in *Charlotte's Web*. That magic, garnered not only from the rides and the honky tonk, but also from the gathering of so many people from near and far, hasn't changed since then (though it has gotten a bit more expensive), and it is about the same at any one of the agricultural fairs in the state.

Maine has many festivals and fairs, but only 25 can call themselves true agricultural fairs. Of those 25, three are state fairs, drawing exhibitors from across Maine. Agricultural fairs have specific criteria — basically, they must promote agriculture. Some of the rules are pretty detailed, such as if a fair wants to have pulling events, it has to have a minimum

of three different kinds of animals. Whoa, have we jumped ahead?

Pulling events are popular strength competitions for animals. Shackle the horse to a load of logs. Shackle the oxen to a load of stones. See how far these animals can drag a load twice their weight. Frequently, you'll find farmers raising animals just for the pulls. The reward might be a $100 cash prize; primarily, it's a matter of continuing a tradition that has since been updated to include tractor pulls.

Agricultural fairs must also have specific agricultural exhibits, such as a grange exhibit, an exhibition hall, a 4-H component and livestock. Moreover, they must fulfill a probationary period that lasts three years. Finally, they are continually observed for safety and health by the Maine Association of Agricultural Fairs, part of the Maine Department of Agriculture, Food and Rural Resources. The state supports the fairs with funds from harness racing, a big draw at many of these events.

Maine fairs are almost as old as the nation. The 179-year-old Skowhegan Fair is the oldest continuously running fair in the United States. The newest, a relative baby, is the 21-year-old Common Ground Fair. Some fairs, such as Skowhegan and the Bangor State Fair, are honky-tonk affairs — heavy on midway activities, big on big-name entertainment. Others, such as the Monmouth Fair, near Augusta, are so small, you could almost hug them. All the fairs in or near the Mid-Coast offer harness racing, though there is no wagering at the Blue Hill Fair.

In Fern's time, the family picnic was a big event at fair time, for there were few, if any, food booths. Today, however, the food is a big draw. At virtually every fair, you can fill yourself with cotton candy and fried dough — with one exception. The Common Ground Fair, sponsored by the Maine Organic Farmer's and Gardener's Association, allows no sugar — you won't be able to get cotton candy. Nor can you buy a cup of coffee or put your child on a ride.

Except for the Common Ground Fair, fairs are very similar to each other, and yet each has its glory, its claim to fame — each its connection to community and land. And Mainers — whether from away or here, whether massage therapists or mill trainees — flock to the fairs.

Of Maine's 25 fairs, only three are in our Mid-Coast region; we've included a few nearby options as well.

Bangor State Fair
Bass Park Complex, 100 Dutton St., Bangor • 942-9000

State fairs, as the name may imply, bring in exhibits from around the state. Other regional fairs draw from a more narrow geographic area. The Bangor State Fair, held for 10 days from the last day in July through early August, gets people from all over Maine. It's one of the larger fairs, with an almost overwhelming amount of things to do: a large midway, games of chance, baubles, bangles, beads and seemingly acres of activity.

Held on the cusp of summer, the fair is the place to be in Bangor. How could it not be, with floodlights illuminating an alluring playground of Ferris wheels and topsy-turvy rides visible from the highway?

Because the fairgrounds are adjacent to the Bangor Civic Center, the Bangor State Fair can offer indoor entertainment in unusually classy surroundings for a state fair. But the fair also offers a full contingent of agricultural exhibits, including Old McDonald's Farm, a children's petting zoo, sections devoted to Maine's outdoor traditions and even to ecology. The fly-fishing demonstration comes complete with a stocked stream so visitors can learn about the ecosystem of the Penobscot River. And get this: In 1997 the blueberry pie-eating contest came with an exhibit about blueberry barrens, so those gorging themselves with pie at least knew from whence came their berries.

Admission is $5 for adults and teens, $3 for seniors and $1 for kids 12 and younger. Rides cost extra, performances do not.

FYI

Unless otherwise noted, the area code for all phone numbers listed in this guide is 207.

Blue Hill Fair
Maine Hwy. 172, Blue Hill • 374-3701, 374-5092 (during the fair)

Under E.B. White's pen, Blue Hill became the quintessential, classic agricultural fair. And it is. There is a sense of wonderment at the midway — the large space of it, the corn dogs, hot dogs and chili dogs.

"That fair," says Muriel Bonin, executive secretary of the Maine Fair Association (see this chapter's Close-up), about the Blue Hill Fair, "has so much local interest, the independent midway is so large, that it allows many of your local groups to come in and do fund-raising projects at the fair."

She's right. We remember book sales, possibly even yard sales, as if the fair were a community project. We also remember flying cars, flaming cars, for there's always an automobile thrill show. Entertainment is a big part of the fair. In 1997, Johnny Paycheck performed.

Held for five days around Labor Day weekend, Blue Hill's is a fair classic enough to sustain a booth of oddities: "See the two-headed snake," someone hawks on the way past booths of crafts from Mexico and Guatemala to the agricultural demonstrations behind. Much is for sale: sheep, rabbits, lambs, skins, wool. It's hard not to leave with a piglet under one arm — a pink pet to take home and name Wilbur.

Admission is $5 for adults and teens, $3 for seniors and free for children 12 and younger. Rides and the auto thrill show cost extra, but musical entertainment does not.

Common Ground Country Fair
Maine Hwy. 220 and Crosby Brook Rd., Unity • 623-5115

The Common Ground Fair is unique. There's no midway, no sugar, even no coffee sold on the grounds (though who's to say what's in thermoses). As a showpiece of the Maine Organic Farmer's and Gardener's Association (MOFGA), the Common Ground Fair features a way life that is healthy, wholesome, creative and (except for the stilt-walkers who dance their way through the fair) so down-to-earth that not even a Ferris wheel dare cycle

Muriel Bonin: Grande Dame of Maine's Fairs

As a child, Muriel Bonin used to bring her ponies to the Litchfield Fair, not too far from the state capital of Augusta. She'd put up a ring and sell pony rides. "That's how I made money for clothes."

Now in her late 60s, Bonin spends time every summer at each of Maine's 25 state fairs, traveling from southern York to northern Aroostook. She's not selling pony rides anymore, but rather she's in charge of inspecting them. For the last 20 years, Bonin has been the Maine Fair Association's Executive Secretary.

Fairs, she says, "started out as a place where farmers and people in agriculture would share ideas and show off what they have been able to grow. From there, it has just expanded. As the focus of agriculture has changed and modernized, so have the fairs."

Still, she says, "most of your fairs try to retain the semblance, at least, of old-time fairs. Livestock are very carefully washed and scrubbed and combed and brought to fairs looking their very best.

"It's the most wonderful place in the world to show people and educate them about agriculture."

As for some of the sleazier aspects of fairs, Bonin says, "I like to think I had a part in getting rid of them. I felt girlie shows added absolutely nothing to the fairs, it didn't enhance the agricultural emphasis — and besides, children get enough sex education in schools, they don't need anything else."

Like a loving, indulgent mother, Bonin can't choose a favorite fair. "Big, little — I enjoy them all. They are all different, all have something unique," she continues,

Muriel Bonin is the grande dame of Maine fairs.

adding, "Have you heard of Holman Day?" (Day was a literary voice — poet, novelist, playwright and editor — from the turn of the century.) "Have you heard his poem about the fairs?"

Without waiting for an answer, she recites:
'Hurray for the Season of Fairs
This is the season for fairs, by gosh,
Oh, this is the season for fairs;
They're thicker than spatter, but what does it matter?
They scoop up the cash, but who cares? . . .'
"I don't know enough to shut up about fairs," adds Bonin.

---

its way in. Speaking of cycling, most things are recycled: There are separate bins for paper and cans. Most plastic throwables simply are not allowed (though organizers haven't quite found a good substitute for forks, spoons and knives).

The 1998 event will be a grand celebration: It marks the first fair of MOFGA's own land — twice the space and half the traffic hassles of the previous Windsor location. The grounds will be a work-in-progress, with a couple of buildings completed and designs for an affordable, energy-efficient, off-the-utility-grid building underway.

Additional activities are planned: Want to learn how to build a stone wall? One will be built on the fairgrounds. (In five years, maybe you can return to learn how to repair a stone wall!)

Food booths will still take up about half the fair. There might be no sugar, but there is no lack of sweetness in the waffles topped with blueberries, whipped cream and maple syrup. There might be no preservatives, but there are delicious smoked foods. There's corn, roasted chicken, stir fry, baked potatoes, soups, stews, chili . . . you'll just have to go.

A favorite activity is watching the children show their animals. There are sheep dog trials, judging of lambs and goats, and more rabbits of more kinds than most of us ever knew existed. Another favorite activity is watching women who calmly, gently brush angora rabbits, then proceed to spin the delicate tufts into the softest, silkiest of fibers. These women have such patience — as if time stopped for them.

Look for the seed booths and the seed potato booths, the cider presses and the booths that display a mind-boggling array of apples — more kinds than you'll find at any modern nursery, for sure. Among organic farmers, there's a big movement to preserve vegetable varieties. Look for ecology centers and folk art booths featuring felting, beading or canoe-building demonstrations.

Even if there are no rides, children forget about them. They love the palpable presence of the real — watching blacksmiths and stone carvers at work, dodging stilt dancers and parading around in vegetable costumes. There's truly nothing like it.

Admission is $6 for adults, $2 for children and seniors.

Skowhegan State Fair
Skowhegan Fairgrounds, U.S. Hwy. 201, Skowhegan • 474-2947

"The Skowhegan Fair is so old that the atmosphere is that of its old buildings, its history," according to Maine Fair Association Executive Secretary Muriel Bonin (see this chapter's Close-up). We echo the sense of age in a different way.

Some years ago, Chuck Berry, still twisting away after 30 years, entertained the crowd. From the old stands, we saw him surrounded by a group of artists from the Skowhegan School of Art. These young artists, the cream of the crop of the nation's art majors who had come to Maine for a lakeside summer intensive, seemed so urban, so urbane in punk hairdos and dark makeup, that they seemed to be from another era beside the Mainers in flannels and functionals. It was an odd juxtaposition, but everyone — the punkers, the Mainers, even the reporters — had a great time at the fair.

The Skowhegan Fair, held for 10 days in mid-August, offers headline entertainment, stage shows, a long midway, races and plenty of agricultural exhibits and shows.

Admission to the 1997 fair was $5; rides cost extra.

Topsham Fair
Elm St., Topsham • 725-2735

The Topsham Fair used to be held in fall — the very last fair in Maine each year. But organizers eventually decided it was more practical to go with the tourist season; it's currently held the first full week of August. Still, according to Muriel Bonin, executive secretary of the Maine Fair Association, Topsham is a very traditional fair, with a delightful old grandstand and a built-in museum beneath the benches. (See this chapter's Close-up about Bonin for more information about the grande dame of Maine's fairs.)

For those who like their fairs more manageable, Topsham is a more midsize fair, not quite as large as those in Skowhegan, Bangor and Blue Hill. Like most Maine fairs, there's a mixture of honky tonk and horticulture, horse racing and demolition derbies, but the solid agricultural demonstrations are the favorite of those in the know.

Admission is $4 for anyone 12 and older; rides cost extra.

Union Fair and State of Maine Blueberry Festival
off Maine Hwy. 17, Union • 785-4180

We remember dusk at the fairgrounds,

Photo: Bangor Daily News

A good look at the outcome of the annual lobster boat races requires a good vantage point. Several races are held in summer as part of fairs and festivals.

watching clouds come in as the sun set until the sun was squeezed to an impossible red rose line across the horizon. Sitting on a glowing white park bench, there seemed to be a moment of almost surreal silence, a moment of intimacy quite unusual in a fair. But Union, held for seven days in late August, is just small enough to attain that quiet quality, just small enough for the ride tenders to take mercy on the stubborn will of a small child and let him ride the miniature train over and over and over again.

Like other fairs, there are 4-H programs and daily parimutuel harness racing. The Union Fair stands alone, however, in having Matthew's Museum of Maine Heritage, a museum of old tools (and old ways), right on the grounds, and the official State of Maine Blueberry Festival where the state's Blueberry Queen is crowned. The festival is always on a Friday. Come then to get your fill of blueberry bubble gum-blowing contests and free blueberry pies.

Admission to the fair is $5 per person; rides cost extra.

Windsor Fair
Maine Hwy. 32, Windsor • 549-7121

Windsor may not be a huge fair, but it is the second-largest agricultural fair in the state (after Fryeburg, which is several hours from the Mid-Coast region, near the border with New Hampshire). That it's an agricultural fair means that it specializes in the nitty-gritty farm events, like oxen, horse, even pony pulls. There's a draft horse show, lots of vegetable exhibits and harness racing on one of the best tracks in the state.

Recently, the fair has branched into other traditional activities. New in 1997 was a Woodsman's Day, celebrating the work of the woods. Look for competitions in felling trees, sawing logs (with hand or chain saws) and loading them — all tasks of the old-time lumberman.

The Windsor Fair is a nine-day event, ending on Labor Day. Admission is $4 during the week for anyone 16 and older, free for kids 15 and younger. Weekend admission is $5. Rides cost extra, but the country western performances sprinkled through the week do not.

Mainers don't feast on
natural beauty alone,
and you won't want
to either.

Attractions

The main attraction in Maine is Maine — the rocks, the coast, the hills, the misty fog over a harbor, brilliant red and gold autumn leaves, and silver moonlight shining on the winter snow.

But we don't feast on natural beauty alone, and you won't want to either. You'll want to get out of the car . . . see something, do something. There are plenty of options: Paddle down a river in a classic canoe; soar above one in a hot-air balloon; or let a vintage plane do the soaring while you watch its acrobatic display from the ground. Or be the acrobat yourself on a powerful trampoline fitted with bungee cords.

Of course, there are also more staid activities: strolling through acres of gardens; examining old tools; tasting new beers.

We have arranged this chapter according to our U.S. Highway 1 corridor. We move up the coast from Waldoboro to Prospect (just beyond Stockton Springs), loop inland to Bangor, then follow the coast again from Bucksport to Castine, Blue Hill, Deer Isle, Ellsworth and farther Down East toward Gouldsboro. Finally, we examine Mount Desert Island and the attractions that surround Acadia National Park. (For attractions inside the park, see our Acadia National Park chapter.)

Now for a word on what you'll find in this chapter — and what you won't.

Maine's Mid-Coast region has numerous lighthouses, so many, in fact, that we've included them in a separate Lighthouses chapter.

Parks, too, are great attractions, whether your inclination is to drive up the Camden Hills, ski through Holbrook Island Sanctuary or picnic by the Penobscot River. Except for a few that we just can't resist writing about again, we've left the parks out of this chapter; you'll find them in Parks and Recreation. And then there's Acadia National Park, an attraction so big that, as we mentioned, we've given it its own chapter.

The region also has a multitude of historical societies, many with small museums of local artifacts. These offer wonderfully eclectic details of life in Maine with nothing excluded, not even the chamber pots. But except for those that have substantial and regular hours, we've left historical societies out of this chapter (see our History chapter instead). Plan to visit at least one during your stay, especially if you've grown attached to a particular town.

We can't stress enough the glory of going offshore. Early settlers chose Maine because of its coast, and its geography — its very history, really — is tied to water. Chances are you also have come here, at least in part, because of the tales of its coastal beauty. So take advantage of the waters; take a ferry or an excursion boat, whether it be a 40-foot lobster boat or an 80-foot schooner. Our Offshore/Islands chapter includes strategies for spending some time visiting the islands of Penobscot Bay and beyond. At the end of this chapter, you'll find information on the swifter trips, the boat excursions of an hour or a day, as well as a section outlining whale watches and nature cruises.

Finally, don't forget to look at our Annual Events chapter, where you'll find information about special celebrations and festivals. Many are organized in conjunction with some of the specific attractions listed subsequently.

Waldoboro to Stockton Springs

Old German Church
Maine Hwy. 32, Waldoboro • 832-5100

This 1772 peach-colored church stands beside a cemetery that is marked by one of the most bitter arrival announcements possible:

This town was settled in 1718 by Germans who emigrated to this place with the promise and expectation of finding a populous city, instead of which they found nothing but a wilder-

ness; for the first few years they suffered to a great extent by Indian wars and starvation.

These were the people who eventually built Waldoboro; but first they built this spare church with its straight, unpainted pews. It was here that Andrew Wyeth set his well-known painting "Maidenhair," frequently displayed at the Farnsworth Museum of Art in Rockland (see our Arts chapter). The church gallery looks onto a handmade communion table and a cabinet containing a collection of German mementos.

The church is open from 1 to 4 PM daily during July and August.

Olson House
Hathorn Point Rd., Cushing • 354-0102 (in-season), 596-6457 (year round)

You can't miss the Olson House as you drive down Hathorn Point Road. Looming large and gray, the home has become more than just the house Christina Olson was reaching toward in Andrew Wyeth's painting "Christina's World." It is the symbol of 19th-century endurance, the proud independence and self-sufficiency of the rural farm. Thanks to Wyeth's many paintings of the house — especially "Christina's World" — people flock to this home as if it were a shrine.

And it is a shrine — not only to its last inhabitants, but also to much of Maine's history. The home was built in the late 1700s as a saltwater farm by the Hathorne family, who had first settled the area in 1743. It remained in this family of sea captains (distant relations to writer Nathaniel Hawthorn), until Capt. Samuel Hathorne IV, Christina Olson's grandfather, added a row of bedrooms to the third story. This was in 1871, and Capt. Hathorne was cashing in on the influx of urban visitors looking for a farmhouse to lodge in for the summer. Then in 1892, an early freeze on the St. George River forced ashore Swedish sailor John Olson. He fell in love with Kate Hathorne, the captain's daughter, and the two were married. Christina was born the next year. Alvaro came a year later, in 1894.

As a child, Christina spent many happy years playing on her family farm, but her falls

were worrisome. She most likely suffered from Still's disease, a progressive form of arthritis. By the end of her life, she was so crippled that she could not walk; still, she refused a wheelchair.

There were other children, but the farm passed to Christina and Alvaro, the unmarried brother and sister. Wyeth met them as a young man, and he was captivated by her wit and their straightforward lives. He practically moved in with them, taking a floor of their home as a studio and painting the siblings until they died within a month of each other. Alvaro passed away Christmas Eve 1967; Christina, 34 days later. After both had died, their household effects were auctioned off, but the house itself was bought by movie producer Joseph E. Levine. Briefly, Levine ran a museum at the house, complete with his own collection of Wyeths — only he forgot to add facilities and a parking lot. Neighbors were not happy, and Levine closed the museum. When the house came up for sale 20 years later, it was bought by Lee Adams and her husband, John Sculley, former chairman of Apple Computers. They donated it to the Farnsworth Museum in Rockland in 1991 (see our Arts chapter).

The house is now empty of objects but filled with spirits — of the Maine farmhouse; of Christina, bright, stubborn and taciturn; and of her brother, Alvaro, painted by Wyeth as the quintessential Maine farmer. And then there's the spirit of Wyeth, who worked there for years. Reprints of paintings Wyeth created here hang on the walls, along with notes about their creation. A museum to a vision is an uncommon place — and uncommonly fulfilling.

Admission to the Olson House is $3 for adults and $1 for children ages 8 to 18. Or buy a comprehensive ticket — $9 for adults, $8 for senior citizens and $5 for students 12 and older — allowing entry into the extensive Farnsworth Museum complex in Rockland. The house is open daily from Memorial Day through Columbus Day, 11 AM to 4 PM. If you're visiting off-season, you can still wander around outside the house.

FYI

Unless otherwise noted, the area code for all phone numbers listed in this guide is 207.

Photo: Bangor Daily News

The Thomas Hill Standpipe, part of the Bangor water district, rises above the trees in this fall scene.

Maine Watercraft Museum
4 Knox St. Landing, off Main St., U.S. Hwy. 1 and Maine Hwy. 131, Thomaston • 354-0444

On a small peninsula in South Thomaston, right beside the St. George River, you'll find a collection of boats to stir the heart of even the staunchest landlubber. You'll find boats with pedigrees and histories among the 130 fine examples of a craft in which undeniable beauty emerges from a form that simply follows function. As museum director John Shelley says, "Violate the shape and you end up getting wet. It just won't work." Each boat here has a story; scare up Shelley and you'll hear of fabulous boating adventures.

Or start one yourself. This is a hands-on museum. For as little as $10 an hour, you can row a Rangeley guide boat, paddle a double-end canoe or hoist the canvas on a little sailboat, steer it downriver and go poking into coves. In the quiet of the river, with banks overhung by trees, visitors can find a taste of the way life used to be. Those interested in a swifter life can join an excursion on the museum's vintage Chris Craft, the classic mahogany mail boat that delivered the mail in the movie *On Golden Pond*.

The museum is open from Memorial Day weekend through October 1, 10 AM to 5 PM Wednesday through Sunday, or by appointment. Admission is $4 for adults and $2 for students and senior citizens.

Montpelier – Gen. Henry Knox Museum
U.S. Hwy. 1 and Maine Hwy. 131, Thomaston • 354-8062

Montpelier is the name given to the 1794 mansion built by Gen. Henry Knox using design elements popularized by Charles Bullfinch. Knox was a self-taught lad who learned through his work — first as apprentice, then as owner of a Boston bookstore. He was a Bunker Hill veteran and the nation's first Secretary of War, but he was best known for moving 59 canons from Fort Ticonderoga, just north of New York's Lake George, to Dorchester Heights in Boston, thus helping win back Boston from the British. After the war, Knox married Lucy Flucker, a granddaughter of Brig. Gen. Samuel Waldo (the man who enticed a boatload of Germans to journey to the wilderness that was Waldoboro at the time — see the previous Old German Church entry — and a local land baron). As a result of his marriage, Knox and his wife inherited the Waldo patent, acquiring all the land from Newcastle to beyond Belfast and inland as far as Warren, Appleton and Hope. He was the sort of man, apparently, who would try anything — and do so with passion. He got involved with lumbering, with lime kilns, with brick making. He built up the maritime trade in the region. He was said to have been generous, hard-working and a good supervisor — but not the best money manager. He certainly made enough to build his mansion on a bluff in Thomaston, but he also lost a lot, which bears upon the saga of his home.

Nothing in the Mid-Coast region today rivals Montpelier's large, white and imposing grandeur. Nathaniel Hawthorne wrote in his journals about coming to this house. So did French nobleman François Alexandre Frederic, Duc de la Rochefoucauld-Liancourt, who came to Maine in 1795 and 1796 as a guest of Gen. Knox. Only Frederic was none too pleased; in fact, this odd man found it the worst accommodation in America. (See our History chapter for details of the duke's displeasure — and another side of the story.)

Knox spent only 11 years in his mansion, dying with his fortunes in ebb. His descendants could not keep up the mansion, which quickly fell into disrepair. In 1871 it was torn down — and furniture put in storage — to make room for the railroad. But a half-century later, the deed was repented. The current structure is a reconstruction, meticulously rebuilt beginning in 1926. Note the arched flying staircase and the bookcase (supposedly from Marie Antoinette). Look here for Knox family furnishings of the Colonial and Federal eras and for a sense of the impact the early landholders in Maine had over the development of the state. Special programs are planned throughout the summer and fall. Many are listed in the Annual Events chapter; more may come about.

Admission to the museum is $5 for adults, $4 for seniors and $3 for children, with a family cap of $12. The museum is open Tuesday through Saturday from 10 AM to 4 PM and Sunday from 1 to 4 PM, Memorial Day weekend until mid-October.

www.insiders.com

See this and many other **Insiders' Guide®** destinations online — in their entirety.

Visit us today!

Matthews Museum of Maine Heritage
Union Fairgrounds, off Maine Hwy. 17, Union • 785-3281, 594-7113

Maine's farms generated a host of tools over the centuries, and some 5,000 of them, from hoes to wagons, are displayed at Matthews Museum of Maine Heritage. But that's not nearly all. There's a full kitchen, household furniture, toys, clothing, quilts, weaving, even an entire school building. The museum is housed in a barn that's in itself worth a visit — dark, old and filled with enveloping shadows that seem to hold the mystery of the ages. The museum is at the Union Fairgrounds, site of one of the sweetest of Maine's agricultural fairs (see our Fairs chapter). Admission is $2 for adults, $1 for seniors and 50¢ for children. Hours are noon to 5 PM Tuesday through Sunday from July 1 to Labor Day, or by appointment in June and the rest of September.

Morgan's Mills
168 Payson Rd., East Union • 785-4900

Long before Shop 'n' Save and Shaw's, most bread flour was processed locally at water-powered mills. But Morgan's Mills is a far cry from its predecessors. Morgan's is a restored mill, yes, but not a museum piece: It is powered via turbine — not via water wheel — which makes the electricity that creates stone-ground whole wheat flours. The mill has been grinding flour since 1978 and has been open to the public since 1980. Some of the operations take place beneath the floorboards, but others are visible, and visitors are most welcome to watch. Call, however, if you're coming as a large group. The mill is open Monday through Friday from 9 AM to 5 PM and Saturday from 10 AM to 4 PM, May until Christmas. Sundays, it's open by chance or appointment.

A store at the mill sells flour and bulk natural and regional foods. (See our Shopping chapter for related information.)

Owls Head Transportation Museum
Maine Hwy. 73, Owls Head • 594-4418

Owls Head Transportation Museum is a

glorious place to marvel at the vehicular craft of yesteryear. On summer weekends, weather permitting, it turns into a circus of vintage transportation. Cars and motorcycles surround you, and biplanes, flying aces from World War I and Navy trainers from World War II soar overhead, their sheer beauty capturing the hearts of onlookers. Weaving through the crowd are tandem bikes, with riders pedaling side-by-side, and high wheelers. And then there are the wood-sided and gossamer-winged planes. You can't help but love the detail and energy that went into these classic early cars and aircraft.

Along with air shows come car meets. For one weekend the museum's outdoor lot is filled with 1950s fins, the next weekend with Model T Fords. Come winter, the museum focus turns inside, where visitors find a concentrated look at the history of modern transportation.

The museum is open year round; air shows happen in summer and fall on selected weekends. Weekday admission is $6 for adults and teens, $5 for seniors, $4 for children 12 and younger and $16 for families. Summer weekends, it's $7 for adults and teens, and $5 for children 12 and younger, with a $20 cap for families. During aerobatic shows, the admission goes up to $8 for adults and $6 for children, with a $23 cap for families. Hours are 10 AM to 5 PM daily from April through October, 10 AM to 4 PM daily from November through March.

Farnsworth Homestead
19 Elm St., Rockland • 596-6457

Lucy Farnsworth's house had hot and cold running water before most homes had indoor plumbing. Her father owned a lot of real estate in town, which she inherited. In her later years, when she was the only one remaining in the family, she sat at the window dressed in black, collecting her rents. When she died at age 96, the rent money and whatever she saved from her father's long-standing lime trade went into founding the Farnsworth Museum and Library, now known as the Farnsworth Museum (see our Arts chapter).

Because of her endowment, the Greek Revival townhouse she lived in her entire life has been turned into a period museum. Visit in summer, or come around the holidays, when the old toys are displayed and the home is decorated in Victorian Christmas style. Admission to the homestead includes the Farnsworth Museum. It's $9 for adults, $8 for senior citizens and $5 for students 12 and older; everyone pays $1 less, respectively, in winter. The Homestead is open 10 AM to 5 PM Monday through Saturday from June through September and generally on weekends in December. Call for December hours and activities (also see our Annual Events chapter).

Shore Village Museum
104 Limerock St., Rockland • 594-0311

Enter the Shore Village (the old name for Rockland) Museum for a whirlwind "tour" of lighthouse lore. You'll learn more than you ever knew existed about the essential, separate world of lighthouses and their keepers, who raised families on the most desolate of coastal rocks. The museum houses the largest collection of lighthouse and coast guard artifacts in the country. Just an examination of the powerful lighthouse lens — magnifying simple oil lights to shine through the stormy darkness — will make the experience memorable. The museum is open 10 AM to 4 PM daily from June 1 through mid-October and by chance or appointment the rest of the year. Donations are appreciated.

Rockport Lime Kilns
Pascal Ave., Rockport • no phone

At one time, this elegant little town exported canned sardines, pickled herring, frozen blueberries and sails. In the 1880s and '90s, when Maine led the world in limestone production, kilns here and in Rockland produced 2 million casks of the powder. A few old kilns still stand near slips lined with lovely wooden dories in the expansive waterfront park. Walk or drive to the park — bring a snack or a Frisbee — and enjoy the quiet elegance of Rockport's harbor. (See our Kidstuff chapter for related information.)

Mini Golf Rockport
U.S. Hwy. 1, Rockport • 594-5211

Give the kids a break — they've been driving long enough. The bright-colored fencing around this charming miniature golf course is like a beacon for youngsters. They skip around gleefully from hole to hole at this old-fashioned, easily manageable 18-hole course featuring minimalist representations of Maine's coast. Putt through a lighthouse, between lobster buoys and around bumps and stones.

Mini Golf Rockport is open from May to mid-October. It's open daily 10 AM to 9:30 PM (the last "tee time"), weather permitting, from the beginning of school vacation in June to Labor Day. In May, early June, September and October, it's open weekends only. The cost per round is $3.50 for adults and teens, $2.75 for children 12 and younger.

Vesper Hill Foundation Children's Chapel
Calderwood Ln., Rockport • no phone

This open-air chapel, perched on the rocks over Rockport Harbor, has long been a haven for locals and visitors alike. Adults may stroll in the gardens down the hill from the chapel while children play hide-and-seek. The children's chapel is a nice conclusion to a drive down the back roads of Rockport to view the Belted Galloways (see next entry). See the related Close-up in our Worship chapter for additional details about the Children's Chapel.

Belted Galloways
Aldermere Farm, just off Chestnut St., Rockport • no phone

They're just cows, but they are stunning — and they're a local landmark. As anyone in the area will say, "you can't miss 'em:" With a broad white band around the middle of their otherwise black bodies, you really can not. The ancestors of this herd (the oldest continuous herd of Belties in the United States) were brought to this country from Scotland about 45 years ago, albeit not for their appearance — they are very good beef cattle. Since then, a few other farmers have raised Galloways in Maine, but these striped beasts are still an unusual sight. Stop to admire them in their pastures, and perhaps one will amble up to the gate to admire you too. When you get back to Camden, you can pick up a postcard of the Galloways, even a T-shirt, and be able to say, "Been there, seen that."

Camden Hills State Park
U.S. Hwy. 1, Camden • 236-3109

You can climb for hours among the "three long mountains and a wood" of Camden Hills, but if you're pressed for time, you can still see the wondrous view of the islands spread out in Penobscot Bay. Just drive to the summit of Mt. Battie and look out to see the view young Edna St. Vincent Millay (see our Maine Experience chapter) memorialized as "three islands in a bay" in her poem "Renascence," after scrambling the rocks of her home hills as a girl. The access road is open from May 1 until the end of October. If you decide to walk up the road on a snowy winter day, bring a sled for the return trip. Admission to the park is $2 for adults, 50¢ for children; seniors get in free. (For details, see our Parks and Recreation chapter.)

Knox Mill Museum
MBNA, Washington St., Camden • 236-1400

MBNA moved into Camden with a whirlwind of activity and largesse in the early 1990s, building its headquarters around the Knox Woolen Mill, which supplied felts for paper mills. Lovers of old movies might recall the site as the Harrington Mill from the 1957 movie *Peyton Place*, starring Lana Turner. Inside the plant, one room is set aside as a museum on the history of the old woolen mill, with photographs and some machinery on display. It's open weekdays year round from 9 AM to 5 PM. There's no fee to enter.

Merryspring Park
end of Conway Rd., off U.S. Hwy. 1, Camden • 236-2239

Drive beneath overhanging branches to a bountiful nature and horticultural center focused on education as well as beauty. Trails take you through extensive perennial, herb, lily and rose plots, a woodland garden and an arboretum as well as undeveloped woods and fields — 66 acres in all. Seasonal activities, including wagon rides in winter and a May Day dance in spring, frequently are scheduled. (See our chapters on Parks and Recreation and on Annual Events for more details.) Admission is free.

This is a busy horticultural center, with many activities going on throughout the year at different hours. You'll find the park open daily during daylight hours and the office open from 9 AM to 5 AM Tuesday through

Friday and until noon Saturdays. Call for a list of summertime talks, children's activities and other events.

Conway Homestead – Cramer Museum
Conway Rd., off U.S. Hwy. 1, Camden
• 236-2257

Not very many houses were built in Maine in the 18th century, and still fewer survive today, but Robert Thorndike moved here before the American Revolution, and his son may have been the first European child born in the region. The Conway Homestead is all the more valued because it harkens back to 1770. The farmhouse is a wood-frame building with a brick oven and hand-hewn beams. Additions were built in 1815 and 1835. The house is but one part of a complex that includes a barn, blacksmith shop, sugar house, museum and gardens. Room furnishings represent several periods, revealing the changing ages. The barn holds collections of carriages, sleighs and farm tools, including a saw used to cut ice from local ponds. Look for the Victorian privy. The house is open in July and August, 10 AM to 4 PM daily. Admission is $2 for adults, $1 for students and 50¢ for children. Call for June and September appointments.

Kelmscott Farm
Van Cycle Rd., off Maine Hwy. 52,
Lincolnville • 763-4088, (800) 545-9363

A member of one of our families has placed a picture of winsome Charlotte on his office wall, with hair curling right into her longing eyes.

Charlotte is a Cotswald sheep, one of 120 that Kelmscott Farm has imported from Britain to be raised here in hopes of preserving the variety of domestic animal breeds. Kelmscott also has Shetland, Katahdin, Merino and beautifully horned Jacob sheep, a quartet of rare ducks and one rare breed each of goat, pig, cattle and horse.

The farm began in 1834 and has been farmed continuously. The Metcalfes took ownership in 1993 and soon after established the Kelmscott Rare Breeds Foundation in the hopes of extending animal bio-diversity. You can adopt one of Kelmscott sheep (except for Charlotte, please — she is already spoken for)

and place its picture in your office. When you visit, you'll probably want to wander the farm and get a "passport" stamped as you stop to visit each animal. Special events happen frequently, with art activities joining agricultural ones. See our Annual Events chapter for details about special happenings at the farm, or come simply to pet the animals, watch spinning demonstrations (most weekends), browse in the Wool Shed (the foundation's museum and store), or walk the nature trail. Sometimes, Pete the Shire horse offers wagon rides at 50¢ a spin. The public is invited to look at the rare breeds daily. The hours are 10 AM to 3 PM from November 1 through April 30 and 10 AM to 4 PM from May 1 through October 31. Admission is $8 for adults, $3 for children.

Belfast & Moosehead Lake Railroad
11 Water St., Belfast • (800) 392-5500

Chug into the woods with this 1940s-era diesel for an hourlong excursion to Waldo Station and back. Ride in a passenger coach, parlor car, dining car or open-air car, or take first-class accommodations, depending upon what's on the line the day you travel. Light lunches are served in the dining car (reservations are advised), and snacks are available.

The railroad was praised in 1996 for being "a business with a soul of its own," when it won the Blue Chip Enterprise Award for facing adversity and emerging stronger.

While riding the rails, a narrator relates the history of the region and talks about the rail line that never quite made it to its namesake, Moosehead Lake, but which continues to serve as a freight line. But beware of Waldo Station, where the train turns around. We've heard that train robbers lurk in the woods. . . .

The schedule is complicated, so we advise that you call ahead. Ask about special theme trains, such as Easter and Mother's Day dinner excursions. With the exception of these special trains, the railroading season is June to October, with trains running daily throughout July and August. Tickets are $14 for adults, $10 for teens ages 13 through 17 and $7 for children ages 2 through 12. See the subsequent "Boat Excursions" section for information about the railroad's Penobscot River cruises. The rail also has another train — a steam engine that blows the smoke that forms the stuff of children's dreams — that runs north from Unity Station to Burnham Junction. Unity is about 40 minutes inland from Belfast. Call for that schedule.

Penobscot Marine Museum
Church St., off U.S. Hwy. 1, Searsport
• 548-2529

A hundred years ago, Searsport sent more captains to sea than any other town in the nation. In ports around the globe, the quality of Searsport leadership and the captains' navigational abilities were legendary. On their return voyage, these men carried cabins-full of Oriental goods. Then they built homes along Main Street to hold their exotic furnishings.

Searsport's captains' expertise on the waves is remembered in this village-like museum on a side street in town, marked by a large sign at the site of its own sea-captain's home: a yellow, two-story building facing U.S. Highway 1. (Soon, the museum will extend to Main Street, following the purchase of some land on U.S. 1, though the new building might not be ready for the 1998 season.)

Inside the museum's one home, known as the Fowler-True-Ross home for its many owners, you'll find poignant diary entries from the captain's daughters, who also traveled the seas, and exotic inlaid cabinetry brought home from the Far East. Another building houses a well-crafted exhibit of the Down Easters and an explanation of the special construction of these ships whose designs brought Maine maritime fame.

Across the narrow road you'll find a display of ship models from around the world, including delightful Chinese junks. Wait, there's more. There are galleries focusing on local history; a diorama of the disastrous Penobscot Expedition of the American Revolution (see our History chapter); galleries focusing on the local economy and the various boats used to fish in and transport goods around Penobscot Bay; and an art gallery with paintings by noted 19th-century father and son maritime painters Thomas and James Buttersworth. (Note the fascinating blow-by-blow painting of the dismasting of two vessels during the War of 1812.) New for 1998 is an exhibit called *Trav-*

els to the Pacific Rim, featuring the childhood sea voyages of a local family.

The museum is open Memorial Day weekend until October 15 from 10 AM to 5 PM daily except Sunday (noon to 5 PM). Admission is $5 for adults, $4 for seniors and $2 for children ages 7 to 15. The Stephen Phillips Memorial Library has its own hours: 9 AM to 4 PM Monday through Friday from April through November and Tuesday through Friday from December through March. (See our entry in the Annual Events chapter for special Christmas events at the museum.)

Fort Point Light
Cape Jellison, off U.S. Hwy. 1, Stockton
Springs • no phone

In 1759, a group of 150 men sailed up the Penobscot River, charged with building a fort at the tip of Cape Jellison, known then by its Indian name, Wassaumkeag. These builders were among the first European settlers along the Penobscot. Gen. Samuel Waldo, the man for whom Waldo County is named, was in charge of the group; later he left most of the men at the fort while he sailed upriver on an expedition to what is now Bangor. (Waldo died beside the Bangor falls and was returned first to Fort Pownal, then to Boston.)

The earthwork the other men erected can still be seen, looking like a big mounded star at the water's edge. The wooden blockhouse, however, was burnt by the British in 1778. The fort now shares space with the Fort Point lighthouse.

The keeper's house is private property, but you're welcome to walk through Fort Point Park, which has some picnic tables in the woods, a nice shoreline path and an old, long dock that once served the coastal trade.

Perry's
Exxon Station, U.S. Hwy. 1, Stockton
Springs • 567-3392

Behind this gas station and country store (where a changing group of locals hold court daily with Styrofoam cups of coffee), owner Perry has built a small zoo. There are partridges, rabbits, a goat, chickens and a pig named Rosie. Rosie is the baby (or rather was; she'll be grown by the time you read this). She replaces — but can never take the place of —

Photo: Bangor Daily News

Horse farms with riding stables offer an inland alternative to the attractions found along Maine's rocky coast.

Rosebud, herself something of a local heroine. Rosebud was the much-beloved pig that began Perry's informal menagerie, only Rosebud grew so huge that she could no longer support her own weight. Her grave lies beside the mud pen she loved to root in.

Fort Knox
Maine Hwy. 174, off U.S. Hwy. 1,
Prospect • 469-7719

Built on a promontory over the Penobscot River, Fort Knox recalls the early 19th century when Bangor was the lumber capital of the world and essential to protect.

The fort was commissioned in 1839, during the northern turmoil known as the Aroostook War, when Maine and Canada squabbled over their boundaries. No one ever fired a shot in this war, but there was enough concern over yet another attack by the British to commission this massive fort. It was built between 1844 and 1869, the first of many granite forts built in Maine. (See our History chapter for more details on the Aroostook War.)

The fort was never actually needed to defend the river, or Bangor for that matter, but it was used to train Civil War volunteers between 1863 and 1865. In 1898, during the Spanish-American War, about 500 Connecticut troops were stationed here.

Today, the fort stands as an architectural and engineering delight, extending 252 by 146 feet over several levels. With walls thick enough to walk on, dark tunnels and blackberry-lined paths, the fort is also a child's paradise of intrigue and discovery. Bring a flashlight to explore the pitch-black tunnels; wear climbing shoes to best enjoy the beauty of the river from the Fort's heights; and marvel at the engineering, which nearly came to grief when well-meaning repairers replaced the original sod roof with blacktop. (The sod had worked well, draining water away from the walls; the blacktop channelled the water into the vaulted brick ceilings.) Much of the sod was replaced in 1996 and 1997. In 1998, crews are expected to repoint the masonry in Two-Step Alley, a narrow passageway around the fort that was very popular with kids before it had to be closed for fear of falling bricks. Look for it to be open in summer 1998, thanks to Friends of Fort Knox and community devotion.

The fort is open 9 AM to sunset daily from May 1 to November 1. There are daily guided tours from June through September. There's also a Civil War encampment at the fort on the last weekends of July and August. (See our Annual Events chapter for more on the encampments.) Admission, which includes the tour, is $2 for anyone ages 12 through 64 and 50¢ for kids ages 5 through 11; everyone else gets in free.

Inland to Bangor

Bangor Historical Society
Thomas A. Hill House, 159 Union St., Bangor • 942-5766

The Hill House, which Bangor's historical society calls home, is a Greek Revival structure from 1834 (1836 by some records), designed by Richard Upjohn during the height of Bangor's prominence as a lumber city. Upjohn was a noted architect of the time (he designed New York City's Trinity Church as well as St. John's Episcopal Church in Bangor) and the first president of the American Institute of Architects. The large double parlor furnished with Victorian antiques serves as a symbol of the era's grandeur. The upstairs bedrooms were visited by many a luminary, including Daniel Webster and President Ulysses S. Grant. The society offers temporary exhibits in the front hall and a collection of photographs and paintings by Jeremiah Pierson Hardy.

The museum is open for tours from noon to 4 PM Tuesday through Friday between April and December and Saturdays from June through September. A $5 donation is requested of each adult; children get in free.

Best of Bangor Bus Tours
Bangor Chamber of Commerce, 519 Main St., Bangor • 942-5766

With its extensive red-light district — now razed — Bangor has had quite a history. The Best of Bangor Bus Tours don't miss much of it. Run by volunteers from the Bangor Historical Society, the hourlong tours feature everything from the Queen City's fine architecture to the site of the shooting of Al Brady, who was Public Enemy No. 1 in 1937 before FBI agents gunned him down at a Bangor gun shop. Stephen King's house, gargoyles and all, is also featured. Tours ($5 per adult) leave the chamber at 10:30 AM Thursdays and the first Saturday of the month from July through September.

Blackbeard's Family Fun Park
339 Odlin Rd., across from Howard Johnson's, Bangor • 945-0233

Bangor's pirate-oriented fun park advertises New England's fastest and most modern go-cart track, with features such as three major high-banked S-turns. The park also has 10 batting cages for both softball and baseball. Each cage offers adjustable pitching speeds.

The third and fourth items in this quartet of excitement: two 18-hole miniature golf courses. Expect a pirate theme — this is Blackbeard's park, after all, and the golf courses are on Treasure Island.

Has it started to rain? Don't worry, you'll also find video games at Blackbeard's.

Blackbeard's is open in July and August. Hours in 1997 were 9 AM to 11 PM Monday through Friday, 8 AM to midnight Saturdays and 10 AM to 8 PM Sundays. In June and September, it's open 3 to 9 PM Tuesday through Thursday, 10 AM to 10 PM Saturdays and 10 AM to 6 PM Sundays. Call for current hours and prices.

Cole Land Transportation Museum
405 Perry Rd., off the Odlin Rd. exit of I-395, Bangor • 990-3600

The Coles owned a trucking company since the days of the horse and wagon. Before Gaylen Cole retired from running his fleet of 18-wheelers, he decided to preserve some of his family's history. The large warehouse that contains the museum holds a massive number of vehicles: aisles of fire engines, logging sleds, snowplows, tractors, trucks, trains, toys, wagons, even old soapbox derby cars and antique automobiles. The vehicles are piled high and thick: You'll get the feeling of exuberance in numbers here.

Don't miss the photographs. The museum has enlarged and captioned some 2,000 images, and it displays many of them in panels under the name of the town where they were taken. If you have Maine ancestors, you might find Grandma Jean leading her town's Memorial Day parade or Uncle Joe hanging out at the local barber shop. In October 1997, the museum also became the site of Maine's World War II Veteran's Memorial, with the addition of a bronzed replica of a Jeep. The man sitting at the wheel has the likeness of Cole's best friend, a soldier who didn't make it back from the war.

Cole Land Transportation Museum is open 9 AM to 5 PM daily from May Day through Veteran's Day. Admission is $3 for adults, $2 for seniors and free for anyone younger than 19. Are you traveling via RV? There's ample parking here.

Stephen King House
W. Broadway, Bangor

Do you want to see the bat house yourself? First, promise you won't tell anyone where you found this information, then drive south on W. Broadway (the airport side) and look to your right. See the house with the big bats on the iron gate, their wings spread wide? See the spider webs? Now keep on going. We certainly don't want to disturb the prince of horrors.

Mount Hope Cemetery
State St., Bangor • no phone

Landscaped with ponds, Victorian monuments and tree-lined paths, Mount Hope is the nation's second-oldest garden cemetery. The grave of Hannibal Hamlin, Lincoln's first vice president, is here, as is a cannon marking the Grand Army Lot, where veterans of the Civil War are buried. If you like cemeteries, you can stroll through this one by yourself; or for $5, you can join the Bangor Historical Society's tour. You won't just find out about the heroes — there were lots of characters in Bangor in the days when sea captains, sailors, lumber barons and lumberjacks strode the streets. The tour departs from the cemetery's lone building at 10 AM on the first Saturday of the month from May through September.

Paul Bunyan Statue
Lower Main St., Bangor

As the land that provided the masts for the king's ships — way back before America was a nation — Maine claims Paul Bunyan as a native-born son and commemorates his birth with a 31-foot-tall, 2.5-ton statue of the man. The statue is hard to miss as you drive down Main Street: It's just in front of the Bangor Civic Center (home of the Bangor State Fair; see our Fairs chapter) and not far from the offices of the *Bangor Daily News*.

Thomas Hill Standpipe
Thomas Hill, off Ohio St., Bangor
• 947-4516

This famous Bangor landmark — a 110-foot-tall water tower affording a bird's-eye view of Bangor and environs — is open only four days each year, but it offers the panorama of a lifetime from the top. So give a call, or look in the *Bangor Daily News* to find out when it's open and then climb, climb, climb up the 96 stairs for a vista that reaches to both Mount Katahdin and Cadillac Mountain. See our Architecture chapter for more details.

Hudson Museum
5746 Maine Center for the Arts,
University of Maine, Orono • 581-1901

Masks from Africa and the Northwest Coast of North America, shields from New Guinea and ceramic figurines from ancient Mexico are on display at this anthropological museum, the only such global museum in the state. Look for exhibits by Maine's Native Americans, including an engrossing computerized "primer" of the Passamaquoddy language as well as some hands-on exhibits for children. This summer, there's another local exhibit: *Brilliantly Beaded: Northeastern Native American Beadwork*, showing all kinds of beads, including findings from Maine archaeological sites as well as contemporary work. The museum is open Tuesday through Friday from 9 AM to 4 PM and Saturday and Sunday from 11 AM to 4 PM. Admission is free, but donations are appreciated.

Maynard F. Jordan Planetarium and Maynard F. Jordan Observatory
Wingate Hall, University of Maine, Orono
• 581-1341, 581-1348 (observatory hotline)

The planetarium is our place in space — a circular room, seating up to 45 people, where public shows geared to different age groups are presented. Shows feature various astronomy topics. A show during the December holidays, for instance, focuses on the legends that arose around the star of Bethlehem. And a children's show about constellations is called *Where is Little Bear?* The hourlong programs are offered at 1:30 and 3 PM one weekend a month. Friday evenings, expect to see *Worlds of Wonder*, a tour of the solar system. The planetarium offers more weekend programs when staff are available. Check to see what's happening when you visit. Friday evenings at 7 PM, expect to see one of a few possible programs about space, astronomy and related subjects.

The nearby observatory is open some weekend evenings, depending on staffing. Hours change from semester to semester, so it's best to call ahead. There is no charge to tour the observatory. The planetarium shows cost $4 for adults and $3 for folks older than 62 or younger than 18.

Page Farm & Home Museum
University of Maine, Belgrade Rd., near Maine Center for the Arts, Orono
• 581-4100

The campus of the University of Maine was once a farm, and the Page Farm & Home Museum offers historic proof. The 1865 barn is the last original agricultural building on the campus. The barn houses a variety of exhibits. There's a large collection of field and agricultural implements, including those used in clearing the land; a blacksmith shop; a dairy; and tools for seasonal jobs such as ice harvesting. There's also a domestic exhibit featuring Brownie's Kitchen (dedicated to Mildred Brown Schrumpf), a parlor and a bedroom with mid-19th-century furnishings.

We once overheard two kids speaking who had just been to the museum. By their adjectives — "awesome" and "way cool" — you would have thought they were talking about the latest *Star Wars* movie. But no, it was the Page Farm & Home Museum they were talking about. The museum has its own gift shop — it's displayed like a general store — and a one-room schoolhouse that was moved to the site. The nearby Heritage Gardens are also part of the museum.

The Page Farm & Home Museum is open 9 AM to 4 PM daily from May 15 to September 15 and 9 AM to 4 PM Tuesday through Saturday the rest of the year. Admission is free.

Maine Forest and Logging Museum
off Maine Hwy. 178, Bradley • 581-2871

At the site of a sawmill that was active in the 1790s, a living-history museum of the era has arisen. Beside the sawmill, there's a blacksmith shop, a trapper's line camp, a hovel for animals, a dam and a reconstructed log cabin. Here is a rare chance to see the world of the forest pioneer, with some updated machinery to see how life in the woods changed over the past 200 years.

Most days, it's a self-guided experience — a place for a quiet and historic nature hike in summer where you'll find signs explaining forest life in the 1790s. Come on special days, however, and the museum will be filled with volunteers. In winter you'll find sled rides; in spring, a lumberjack demonstration; in fall, a celebration of blacksmithing. Or come in July or October for the museum's grand Living History Days, when the grounds swarm with activities of 200 years past (see our Annual Events chapter).

The site is open daily during daylight hours, and except for event days, no admission is charged (though donations are greatly appreciated).

INSIDERS' TIP

If you're spending the day on the coast, remember to bring a sweat shirt or windbreaker. Winds come up, fog settles down, and the coast can get mighty cool, even on a scorcher inland.

Penobscot Nation Museum
off Maine Hwy. 43, Indian Island
• 827-4153

Across the bridge from Old Town is Indian Island, home to the Penobscot Nation. Today, the Penobscots are renowned for their sturdy brown ash baskets. You can see examples of traditional pack and potato baskets here, along with more delicate sweetgrass baskets, carved walking sticks, beaded moccasins and jewelry. The museum is open Monday through Friday from 1 to 5 PM. Donations are appreciated.

Felt Brook Golf Center
Bar Harbor Rd. (U.S. Hwy. 1A), Holden
• 989-3500

We're talking challenge here, not child's play. This brand-new miniature golf place is so elaborate, it calls itself a golf center. Twenty-seven lighted holes are available for daytime or nighttime play. There's also a lighted driving range and a brand-new nine-hole, par 33 regulation golf course. But mostly this is a minigolf center.

You'll be putting through Mt. Katahdin at this course; do try to keep your ball out of the waterfalls and sink holes — and be careful not to break any windows in the Victorian houses there. Miniature golf costs vary according to your age and the number of holes you play: $6 for 18 holes and $8.50 for 27 holes for adults and teens; ask about discounts for seniors and children. The miniature golf area is open from mid-May to mid-October, 10 AM to 10 PM daily. The driving range is open from 6 AM to 11 PM daily and stays open from when the snow leaves to when it arrives again.

Fields Pond Nature Center
216 Fields Pond Rd., Holden • 989-2591

A new and environmentally sound visitors center, designed by Holland and Foley Building and Design (see the "Maine Sustainable Building Network" Close-up in the Real Estate chapter), welcomes visitors to this 192-acre nature center. This northern branch of the Maine Audubon Society opened in late 1997, but it's taken off running, with talks and walks scheduled nearly every weekend. There are some exhibits in the nature center, some lovely art and a warm place to see slides before set-

ting off on a walk through the center's fields and wetlands, or beside Fields Pond. There's no admission charge to the center, but programs do have fees (see Annual Events). Expect the grounds to be open daily during daylight hours; the center is staffed mostly on weekends, but that arrangement may change in summer.

Bucksport to Gouldsboro

Bucksport Cemetery
U.S. Hwy. 1, across from the Shop 'n' Save, Bucksport • no phone

There's a faint black outline of a boot on the tall obelisk that marks the grave of Col. Jonathan Buck. His family tried everything to get it off, they say, even carving a new stone, but the boot print always returns. It's not the stone's fault, according to legend, but Col. Buck's, who was called upon to execute a woman for sorcery before he moved to Maine. She vowed she would curse him ever after. When he died, it seems she got her revenge. Does the boot print over his tomb mean she actually was a witch?

The stone has become a stopping point in Bucksport, with a plaque explaining the "witch's curse" right next to the stone in the small cemetery. Park at either the Shop 'n' Save across the street or the gas station beside the cemetery, then walk over.

Champion International Paper Mill
River Rd., Bucksport • 469-1700

Thin glossy paper is Champion International Paper Mill's staple product — the paper that forms the background for the news in *Time*, *Newsweek*, *People* and other magazines.

The shiny paper is created from piles of lumber. How do they do it? Take a tour of the mill to learn all about it. It's an uncommonly fascinating experience, filled with a sense of magnitude that's virtually unmatched. There's fierce noise (you'll be given earplugs for that), some heat, huge vats of stirred and whitened pulp and enormous coils of lightweight, coated paper. The mill produces enough paper in a year to wrap a 12-inch-wide sheet around the globe 670 times.

You must be 12 or older to tour the mill.

Remember to wear closed shoes (no clogs or sandals), and leave your cameras in the car. Tours are offered Monday, Wednesday and Friday on the hour from 9 AM to 3 PM with a break at noon for lunch. You'll report to the security office at the mill gate on River Road. The season for tours is June 17 through August 23. Admission is free.

Craig Brook National Fish Hatchery
Alamoosook Lake, off U.S. Hwy. 1, Orland • 469-2803

The oldest salmon hatchery in the nation stands at the edge of Alamoosook Lake. Craig Brook began in 1871 in an effort to augment the natural production of Atlantic salmon. Since then, it has aided in preserving the gene pool of the wild species. At the brand-new visitors center, you'll find information about the life cycle of the fish and the process of working a hatchery. Most summers, you also can check out samples of the hatchery's miniature fish. Also new since 1997 is the Atlantic Salmon Museum, in an old icehouse, the oldest house on the hatchery grounds. In the pine-paneled room, you'll find information about the history of salmon fishing, antique salmon fishing equipment, flies, rods, reels and a discussion of fishing as interpreted by the volunteers — fishing enthusiasts all — who built the museum. Bring your bathing suit if you visit in summer, and wear walking shoes whatever time of year. The hatchery is beside a lovely lakeside park, site of a favorite regional swimming hole. There are also trails through the woods and up Great Pond Mountain. The visitors center is open 8 AM to 5 PM daily, and the park is open 6 AM to sunset daily. Admission is free.

H.O.M.E.
U.S. Hwy. 1, Orland • 469-7961

When Sister Lucy came to Orland as a young activist nun, she and her fellow sisters took a look at the poverty of the population and realized that people needed more self-employment opportunities. Together, they set up H.O.M.E.: Homemakers Organized for More Employment. Begun as a small crafts cooperative, today you'll find more than a home's worth of activities here as well as a craft shop, greenhouse, schools, a chapel, history mu-seum, thrift shop, craft studios, pens for large draft horses and more. In summer, a sea of bright-colored tents shelter college students who come to participate in the carpentry program. This program helps local people build homes they can afford to live in. The craft store is open daily from 9 AM to 4 PM during the "winter" half of the year and 9 AM to 5 PM during the "summer" half.

Castine Historical Society
Abbott School, Town Common, off Court St., Castine • 326-8786

To celebrate its bicentennial in 1996, the Castine Historical Society renovated the 1859 Italianate Abbott School in the town common and hung a grand quilt of modern design displaying four centuries of area history. The quilt itself makes a visit to the society worth the trip. Designed by a local artist (the former owner of the Castine Inn), it was pieced together over the winter by members of the community — old and young, male and female, experienced quilters and novices.

Each year, the historical society mounts a new exhibit. In 1998, the society will focus on the early 20th-century rusticator experience through memorabilia of an old Castine hotel and general store.

The society is open 10 AM to 4 PM Tuesday through Saturday and 1 to 4 PM Sunday from July 1 to Labor Day. Admission is free.

Fort George
Battle Ave. and Wadsworth Cove Rd., Castine • no phone

You wouldn't know it today, but the sedate, elegant community of Castine was a hotly contested region for centuries at a time. Look on a map and you'll see why: The peninsula commands a powerful view over a wide expanse of Penobscot Bay, both up the Penobscot River to the west and toward Eggemoggin Reach to the east. Whoever controlled Castine could control shipping down east. So, throughout history, the French, British, Dutch and Americans have all vied for it.

This site, which featured a fort as early as 1626, is best remembered as the site of the fort the British were beginning to erect in 1779 when the Americans surrounded Castine, then lost their nerve to attack — the start of the disastrous Penobscot Expedition (see our History chapter). At the end of the war, Fort George was the last fort the British abandoned. They captured it again in 1812 — indeed, they held all of Castine until they were forced to give it all up in 1815. What happened to the fort? The British blew it up.

Today, visitors enjoy the green space and the grassy mounds which once were the fort's granite foundation. There is no admission fee.

Wilson Museum
Perkins St., Castine • 326-8753

After the Revolutionary War, many homes in Castine were lifted and pushed on barges and sailed farther down east to St. Andrews, New Brunswick, Canada. The rest of the homes didn't survive subsequent battles during the War of 1812 . . . except one: The 1763 John Perkins House, framed with hand-hewn timbers and held together by hand-forged nails, is the only remaining pre-Revolutionary home in historic Castine. The Perkins House, part of the Wilson Museum complex, is a place to glimpse late 18th-century life. But this quiet repository is also a natural history museum — one of the first anthropological museums established in the nation. It houses the collection amassed by anthropologist John Howard, who summered in Castine. There are prehistoric artifacts from around the world, with a focus on the toolmaking process. You'll find Ethiopian carvings and Balinese masks, along with Maine Native American artifacts. There's also a blacksmith shop on the grounds.

The Perkins House is open during July and August, Wednesdays and Sundays from 2 to 4:45 PM. The Wilson Museum is open from Memorial Day through September, Tuesday through Sunday from 2 to 5 PM. Admission to the Perkins House is $4. Donations are appreciated for the Wilson Museum.

Caterpillar Hill
Maine Hwy. 15, Blue Hill • no phone

As you climb the hill up Maine Highway 15, just past the junction with Maine Highway 175 (which enters from Brooksville), slow down and be sure to stop at the turnoff on Caterpillar Hill. If it's not too foggy, you will have an amazing view of Walker Pond, Deer Isle and Penobscot Bay — a most magnificent vista of

land and sea, laid out almost in stripes. Closest to you are the blueberry barrens of Caterpillar Hill. Beyond are Walker Pond, a section of Brooksville, Eggemoggin Reach, Little Deer Isle and Penobscot Bay. Word has it that this is the hill where Sal and her mother picked blueberries in Robert McCloskey's charming children's book *Blueberries for Sal* (see our Maine Experience chapter). Look, breathe, stretch, then continue on your way.

Jonathan Fisher Memorial
Main St. (Maine Hwy. 15), Blue Hill
• 374-2161

Parson Jonathan Fisher was probably a typical turn-of-the-19th-century, fire-and-brimstone kind of preacher, insisting on a straight-and-narrow adherence to Christianity. But you won't see that side of him during a visit to the home he built in Blue Hill in 1814 — only his prolific creativity. Fisher altered the typical post-and-beam construction in such a way that when the beams of the Federal-style, hip-roofed home eventually began deteriorating, the exterior planks held it up. The clock he made remains in the chimney he set. The natural history books he wrote, along with the illustrations he created in block prints, are in his library. Missing, however, is his "Morning in Blue Hill," the classic pioneer painting of that town on display at the Farnsworth Museum, down U.S. 1 in Rockland (see our Arts chapter). But you will find other Fisher paintings in this monument to an extraordinary man. The home is open from Monday through Saturday from 2 to 5 PM, July through September. Admission is $2.

Holbrook Island Sanctuary
Goose Falls Rd., off Maine Hwy. 176, Harborside • 326-4012

Anita Harris didn't like looking at other houses. Living on Holbrook Island across from Castine Harbor, she bought all the houses built around her, then razed them. When it was her time to go, she deeded her land to the state — provided the state destroy her own home. Her gift to the state remains one of the loveliest and least crowded parks on the coast. Holbrook Island Sanctuary's 1,230 acres partially encompass both a peninsula off the Cape Rosier Peninsula of Blue Hill and the island that Harris lived on, just inside a cove. You'll need a boat to visit the island, but the mainland part of the park includes a beautiful stretch of coastal woods extending to a sandbar known as Indian Bar. Frequently, the waters inside the sandbar are warmer than the generally frigid ocean. Bring your mosquito repellent if you plan to spend any time on Indian Bar in summer. If you're visiting in winter, you can forget the bug dope, but do remember your skis or snowshoes.

But there's more to the sanctuary than coastal wilderness; it's also something of a mansion graveyard. Every so often you'll come across the foundation of an old summer cottage — one of Harris' purchases lying in rubble in the park. The sanctuary is open during daylight hours year round. Admission is free. (See Parks and Recreation for related information.)

The Good Life Center
Forest Farm, Goose Falls Rd., off Maine Hwy. 176 at Orrs Cove, Harborside • 326-8211

Helen and Scott Nearing moved to this site in Harborside in the early 1950s seeking "the good life," which they defined in several books, most notably *Living The Good Life: How to Live Simply and Sanely in a Troubled World*. According to Helen Nearing, the good life means "being able to take care of yourself, fulfill your own needs, live according to your own principles, adapt to the world only where it helps the world, not where you can benefit from it."

Together, the Nearings built a home from the stones that they cleared off their land and adopted a lifestyle based on self-sufficiency, work and study. Through their books and their integrity to their vision, they helped to launch the back-to-the-land movement of the 1970s that lured so many young urban refugees to Maine.

Scott died in 1983; Helen, in 1995. Their home, which was always open to visitors, and their gardens, whose bounty provided sustenance, is now a public trust. The house, its library and the outside meditation yurt, organic flower and vegetable gardens and greenhouse are well-maintained. Expected hours for public tours are Wednesday through Sunday 1 to 5 PM from Memorial Day through Labor Day. Call to check on more extensive hours and to

find out about weekly meetings with speakers on aspects of "the good life."

Round the Island Mini Golf
Joyce's Cross Rd., between Maine Hwys. 15 and 15A, Deer Isle • 348-7714

New in 1997, Round the Island Mini Golf features bits of Deer Isle and Stonington history and lore. Putt your ball over the causeway or the bridge — but watch out for the lobster boat. Ever tried to catch a lobster with your bare hands? It's about that hard to sink your ball through the lobster boat. The 18-hole course costs $5 for adults, $4 for children and seniors. A second round is $1 more.

Crockett Cove Woods Preserve
Sunset Rd., near Burnt Cove, Stonington • no phone

The amount of rain falling in this 100-acre woodland has turned Crockett Cove into a temperate rain forest, otherwise known as a coastal "fog forest." There's a fairyland appeal to it, with thick moss underfoot, especially on the granite boulders, and old man's beard lichens hanging like ribbons from the trees. Some folks recommend visiting this preserve on a rainy day, when the moisture heightens the colors. We've never walked in the rain here, but it's very possible that the overhanging branches of red spruce, tamarack and white cedar will keep you relatively dry. Other folks recommend you bring a hand lens and get on your hands and knees to look at the dozens of species of moss, lichen and liverwort growing here, including black, white, pink and yellow slime molds — part fungi, part protozoa. Another spot for close inspection is the small bog near the center of the preserve, where round-leaf sundews and pitcher plants grow. This preserve, donated by artist and architect Emily Muir, is owned and maintained by The Nature Conservancy. Admission is free. (See Parks and Recreation for related information.)

Granite Museum
Main St., Stonington • 367-6331

The animated model of this brand-new museum takes 16 minutes to run. The 7-by-15-foot centerpiece model depicts the life of the granite quarry workers on Crotch Island

Photo: Bangor Daily News

Thunder Hole, where the constant action of the sea has cut a hole deep into the rock, is a popular tourist attraction as the tide rises at Bar Harbor.

at the turn of the century. The detail is delightful. You can see the men leaving Stonington in the morning and crossing the harbor to the island. On the island, the trains move, as do the rocks. There are also a few storyboards on the wall with turn-of-the-century photos of Stonington and some references to places where stones from Crotch Island were used, such as New York City's Rockefeller Center, the Triboro Bridge and John F. Kennedy's tombstone in Arlington Cemetery.

The museum is open Memorial Day through Labor Day. Admission in 1997 was $2 for adults and teens and free for kids 12 and younger. Hours were 10 AM to 5 PM, Tuesday through Saturday and 1 to 5 PM Sundays.

The Houses of Stonington
Main St., Stonington

A miniature village has settled on a small slope on the western edge of Main Street. A wedding couple emerges from the church; hay is stored in a nearby barn; there are houses, a store, even the Sail Inn, with multiple bedrooms. Some houses are empty, others occupied. This village stands as a tribute to its creator, the late Everett Knowlton, who built it for fun at the rate of about one house per year. Thanks to the care of people in town (who shelter the miniatures in their own homes from Columbus Day through Memorial Day), this replica of Stonington has become a small park. All that's missing are the sturdy granite foundations that shore up so many of Stonington's homes. Walk through the park, scootch down to look inside the homes and, if you'd like, leave a quarter or two in the box as you leave.

Colonel Black Mansion
Maine Hwy. 172, Ellsworth • 667-8671

John Black came to Maine from England as a teenager in 1799 to serve as clerk of the large Bingham estate and as assistant to Gen. David Cobb. He attained the high position of general agent to the estate, married Gen. Cobb's daughter and built a Georgian mansion in 1824 unlike any other in the riverside mill town of Ellsworth. When he retired in 1850, he was able to turn over his position to his son.

The mansion, with its red bricks imported from Philadelphia, survives along with some of Cobb's furniture dating back to the 1700s. The house remained in the Black family until 1928, when it was given to the public to be preserved as a historic building. The integrity of the house remains strong. The Black estate, also known as Woodlawn, includes a barn of old carriages and sleighs and about 150 acres of grounds. Visitors enjoy the architecture, period furniture, collections of porcelain and glass, a small gift shop and the extensive formal gardens filled with lilacs and roses. Admission costs $5 for adults and teens and $2 for children 12 and younger, and the fee includes a guided tour. The house is open 10 AM to 5 PM Monday through Saturday from June 1 to October 15, with the last tour departing at 4:30 PM. Tea is served in the lovely gardens Wednesdays at 2 and 3 PM, but don't forget to make a reservation, preferably by Monday.

Stanwood Wildlife Sanctuary (Birdsacre)
Maine Hwy. 3, Ellsworth • 667-8460

More than a hundred bird species can be found at Birdsacre, the birthplace of pioneer ornithologist, nature photographer and writer Cornelia Stanwood. The resident owls have their own names. They perch on trees, wide-eyed and blinking at the passersby who come to visit them from outside their large enclosures. The birds are taken in when injured. Those that can't be sent back into the wild — such as a blind owl and a hawk with a badly broken wing — regale visitors with their sheer presence.

The sanctuary also offers trails through 130 acres of forest. The longest trail stretches 2 miles, and the shortest is but a half-mile path flanking a pond that's home to ducks and geese.

A gift shop on the premises is open 10 AM to 4 PM daily from early June to mid-October. Here you'll also find a collection of stuffed birds and eggs. The 1850 homestead on Maine 3 is open by appointment. Inside, you'll find family furnishings, 19th-century clothing and old photos. Touring the home costs $2.50 for adults, $1.50 for seniors and 50¢ for children. The bird sanctuary is open year round, from dawn to dusk, and there's no admission fee.

Acadia Air Inc.
Bar Harbor Airport, Maine Hwy. 3,
Trenton • 667-5534

Does the complicated coast of Maine, with its multitude of islands and peninsulas, have you bewitched and confused? Are you entranced by the idea of soaring vistas? Do you want to get above it all?

Fly higher than Cadillac Mountain, soar over Frenchman Bay or cruise down past the islands of Merchant Row on one of Acadia Air's scenic flights, which depart from Bar Harbor Airport. The seven different tours last from 10 to 40 minutes. Costs range from $17 for a 10-minute bird's-eye view of Mount Desert Island, known as "Acadia Aerial," to $39 for the 45-minute "Penobscot Panorama," which flies you over some of Maine's most glorious coast — west over Blue Hill Bay to Castine on Penobscot Bay, turning north, then east to the western shore of Mount Desert Island. All fares are based on a two-person minimum. Scenic tours generally run between 9:30 AM and about 6:30 PM daily from Memorial Day to Labor Day, unless special arrangements are made. Flights are booked by reservation during the rest of the year. Acadia Air has fair-weather flights only — there's just not much to an aerial view of fog.

Acadia Zoo
Maine Hwy. 3, Trenton • 667-3244

You can see the buffalo from the road — always a surprising sight on the coast of Maine, especially when you're looking for moose. The moose are visible as well, but only after you enter Acadia Zoo, the area's only animal park. To visitors, the moose seem to be the greatest attraction. To locals, the rarer species are more exciting. Once inside the gates of the zoo, you'll find separate rain forest and savannah (plains) areas. Other animals at this zoo include wolves, monkeys, reindeer, pronghorns, antelopes, cougars and camels. This is a popular place come summer, with tours of more

than 200 descending upon the animals. Admission is $6 for adults and teens, $5 for children ages 3 to 12. July and August hours are 9:30 AM to 8 PM daily. From May through June and September into December, the zoo is open 9:30 AM to at least 5 PM daily.

Frisbee Golf
Maine Hwy. 3, Trenton • no phone

Think you're good at throwing Frisbees? Try your hand at Frisbee golf. You probably already know what it is, but just in case you're new to the sport, as we were, it's an open course in which the object is to get the Frisbee into a succession of metal cages. The rules are simple: "relax." At $2 for adults and $1 for kids, including the loan of the Frisbee (1997 rates), it's hard to pass up.

Great Maine Lumberjack Show
Maine Hwy. 3, Trenton • 667-0067

Lumberjacks have been exaggerating their prowess for as long as Paul Bunyan has been leaving his pond-size footprints in the North Woods soil. The Great Maine Lumberjack Show is your chance to see the lumberjacks put their money where their axes are. But since today's loggers are technicians, operating an array of elaborate machinery, these lumberjacks are college students who have created an art out of what was work. The logging team members are mostly from the University of Maine in Orono, Colby College in Waterville and Unity College in Unity. The show features competitions and a bit of lore from the 125-year history of what are now called woodsmen's athletics. Here's one tidbit: The competitions started as a way of settling fights, since fights could mean injury and an injured worker couldn't do his share of the work. Besides, logging was dangerous enough as it was. In this humor-laced show of 75 minutes, you'll see sawing races between a chain saw and a hand-powered crosscut saw, pole climbing, log rolling and ax throwing. Expect to find

---

INSIDERS' TIP

One of the great attractions anywhere is people-watching. Check out the town square in Camden or Bar Harbor, or can hang out at those towns' waterfronts, where Mainers stock up on a year's worth of spectating.

eight shows a week, both matinees and evenings, from Memorial Day through Columbus Day. Check out the STIHL Timbersports Series, which has chosen the Lumberjack Show as a venue for part of its annual championship — you might already have seen it on ESPN. Specific hours were not yet set at press time, so call ahead. Admission in 1997 was $6.50 for adults and teens, $4.50 for kids 12 and younger; ask about a seniors discount.

Island Soaring Glider Rides
Bar Harbor Airport, Maine Hwy. 3, Trenton • 667-7627

The glider takes off, pulled by a tow plane. Below you is Cadillac Mountain, Frenchman Bay or Blue Hill Bay, depending on your choice of vistas and the direction the wind is blowing. The higher you rise, from 2,500 feet to a full mile, the longer you stay in the air as the silent glider softly coasts back to Bar Harbor Airport. And the longer you stay up, the more you will spend. Rides begin at $44.50 a person. As many as three passengers can fly in one glider. Flights leave Bar Harbor Airport daily from about 10 AM until sunset, mid-May through Columbus Day. Reservations are suggested.

Odyssey Park
Maine Hwy. 3, Trenton • 667-5841

At Odyssey Park, you don't have to be a kid to play tag — Lazar Tag, that is.

Lazar Tag is something between traditional tag and all-out war. You don a vest, wield a lazar gun, enter a maze of black lights and fog, and stalk the other participants. Yup, it's every person for themselves. Watch out for the mines! As many as to 12 people can play at one time. The park also offers bumper boats and go-carts for kids young and old. Expect to pay $4 for Lazar Tag, $5 for regular go-carts and $3 for kiddie go-carts and bumper boats. In the arcade, you pay as you play — 25¢ or 50¢ a game.

The park is open 10 AM to 9 PM daily from mid-June until Labor Day. For about a month before and after, the park is also open on warm weekends; call for hours.

Seacoast Fun Park
Maine Hwy. 3, Trenton • 667-3573

Slip down a water slide or two, play a round of miniature golf, speed around the race track in miniature Indy-race cars, or bounce as high as 24 feet into the air on a huge trampoline rigged with bungee cords. They call it the slingshot. Drop by the park for a quick ride, or spend the afternoon moving from one adventure to another. You'll find an arcade and snack bar on the premises.

Rates for 1997 were $5 for the Indy-cars, $3 kiddie cart rides and $5.50 for the adventure golf course ($4.50 for children younger than 12 and seniors older than 60), $10 for a one-day water-slide pass ($7 after 4 PM). Or go for the $16.95 pass — unlimited water slides, golf, and two rides on the go-cart or trampoline, with additional rides half-price. Daily hours are 10 AM to 10 PM, Memorial Day to Labor Day. In May and September, assuming the weather is good, the park is open Fridays from about 1 to 8 PM and Saturdays and Sundays from 10 AM to 9 PM. Call to confirm hours and prices.

Whale-in-One Mini-Golf
Maine Hwy. 3, Trenton • 667-4300

Old-fashioned miniature golf courses are one of the joys of childhood — and a favorite memory in adulthood. You'll putt your ball through lighthouses, water wheels or, here at Whale-in-One, a lobster's claws. The friendly folk at this course are open 9 AM to 9 PM daily from Memorial Day weekend through Labor Day. The $1.50-a-round cost is proof positive of their kindness.

Schoodic Point
Acadia National Park, off Maine Hwy. 186, south of Winter Harbor • no phone

Many people think of Maine's coast as a place of crashing waves and foamy surf — images garnered from Winslow Homer's paintings of southern Maine, or George Bellows' paintings from Monhegan Island, but not from the Mid-Coast area. In fact, most of Maine's Mid-Coast is shielded from the ocean by a row of offshore islands that keeps the coast in this region relatively serene. But drive down to Schoodic Point, on a peninsula across Frenchman Bay from Mount Desert Island, and you'll see waves crashing against massive boulders, especially at high tide or during a storm. Schoodic is a nice destination for a lazy drive followed by a short stroll along the rocks, or you can get more active and bike the circular drive around the peninsula. (See our Acadia National Park chapter for more information.)

Mount Desert Island

Abbe Museum
Sieur de Monts Spring, Maine Hwy. 3, Bar Harbor • 288-3519

The Abbe Museum, housed in a delightful but nearly miniature octagonal building, is charged with presenting the history and continuity of Maine's Native American people. The curators are immensely innovative in creating in-depth, focused exhibits that work well in the small museum building. In 1998, the museum celebrates its 70th anniversary with an unusual exhibit: Various folks — a teacher, a museum director, a poet, a writer — have been asked to chose favorite objects — and to explain why they're favorites. The display consists not only of the object, but also the rationale. According to the curator, the choosing has been hardest on the professionals, who can't quite bring themselves to say, "I like this because I like it — because it's beautiful"; they need justification. The layfolk are freer with their answers. One object was chosen because it felt good in the chooser's hands, another because it reminded her of her mother's kitchen and the baskets that hung there. The museum ultimately will move to a recently acquired space in town; for the 1998 season, however, the old building, next to the Wild Gardens of Acadia will be the site of the exhibition.

A gift shop sells books, contemporary baskets and other Native American crafts. Admission to the museum is $2 for adults, 50¢ for children.

You, too, can get involved in Maine history by signing up for the museum's annual Archeology Field School, usually in September, but sometimes in June. One year, the participants discovered a 4,000-year-old dog. Another year, while excavating a hearth, archaeologists found seeds they could identify — most were berries.

Park Loop Road
Acadia National Park, Bar Harbor • 288-3338

When we ask Mount Desert Island locals where they take their guests, they shrug and say, "the Park Loop," then look down, almost embarrassed, and add, "We never get to see it otherwise." Yes, the Park Loop Road is Maine's Statue of Liberty or Empire State Building — locals need visitors to see it. So thanks, guys, we're glad you've come because the Park Loop Road is a treat. Along it you'll find some of Acadia's most breathtaking offerings: Thunder Hole, the water-carved rock formation that emits "tidal thunder"; Otter Cliffs, towering high above the ocean; and the imperious Cadillac Mountain, with its windblown heights, huge glacial boulders and astounding views. (See our Acadia National Park chapter for a rundown of the park's history, geology, activities and attractions.)

Access to the loop road costs $10 for a seven-day pass.

Bar Harbor Brewing Co. & Sodaworks
Otter Creek Rd. (Maine Hwy. 3), Bar Harbor • 288-4592

Tour and taste the delights of this brewing company, either the hard stuff or the soft kind. The Bar Harbor Brewing Co. & Sodaworks brews five beers, including award-winning Cadillac Stout and Thunder Hole Ale as well as Bar Harbor Root Beer Syrup. Tours and tastings happen between 3:30 and 5 PM Monday through Friday in summer. Visitors meet in a log cabin adjacent to the brewery for beer or root beer tastings, then head over to the brewery, where owner/brewer Tod Foster explains the brewing and bottling process. Kids can come along or enjoy the yard out back. If you plan to come in June, September or October, call ahead for tour hours; at other times, call for an appointment. Tours are free.

Bar Harbor Historical Society
33 Ledgelawn Ave., Bar Harbor • 288-3807

The historical society's large room beneath the town library is filled with archives, books and surprising photos of the elegant old town. The large scrapbook of photos and newspaper accounts of the glowing (literally!) island during the 1947 fire is in itself worth a visit. (The fire blazed out of control for more than two weeks, cutting off access to the island and destroying a third it, burning 14,000 acres in only eight hours.) This summer, the society opens in a new location — its own building, the former St. Edward's Convent built in 1918. Check out the new displays in the larger space, complete with lovely stained-glass windows. The society is open year round (by appointment only in winter). From June to October, hours are 1 to 4 PM Monday through Saturday. Admission is free, but donations are appreciated.

Carriages in the Park
Wildwood Stables, Park Loop Rd., Bar Harbor • 276-3622

What better way to ride the park's carriage roads than in a carriage? Wildwood Stables offers six carriage rides throughout the day — each lasting one or two hours. We particularly like the romance of the two-hour sunset ride up Day Mountain, leaving between 5 and 6:30 PM, depending on the month. At 1:15 PM, ride in style to the Jordan Pond House (see our Acadia National Parks and Restaurants chapters), arriving in time for tea and popovers. Other rides include a two-hour tour (leaving at 9:30 AM) through the woods to the park's cobblestone bridge, and three hourlong tours (leaving at 11 AM, 2 and 3:45 PM) that circle Day Mountain and feature views of Frenchman Bay and the Cranberry Isles.

The stables are open from mid-June to Columbus Day. Hour-long rides cost $13 a person. The Jordan Pond House tea trip is $14.50, and two-hour rides are $16.50. There are reduced rates for children and seniors. Reservations are recommended.

Jackson Laboratory
Maine Hwy. 3, Bar Harbor • 288-6087

The genetic research done at Jackson Laboratory has had worldwide import in battling cancer, diabetes and birth defects. Though tours are no longer offered, you can visit the labs through free audiovisual tours, which in 1997 were scheduled Mondays and Wednesdays at 3 PM from mid-June through September. You'll spend about an hour watching the video, then listen to a staff member speak about various aspects of the lab's work.

Mount Desert Oceanarium/ Oceanarium Bar Harbor and Lobster Hatchery
Thomas Bay, Maine Hwy. 3, Bar Harbor • 288-5005

The Mount Desert Oceanarium has two locations: this one in Bar Harbor and another in Southwest Harbor (see subsequent entry in this chapter; also see the Acadia National Park chapter). The Bar Harbor location is divided into a few sections with an attached lobster hatchery where you can see baby lobsters, mama lobsters and the process of raising lobsters. There's also a lobster museum, complete with a lobster boat, where you can learn about the lobstering industry. Frequently, retired lobstermen stop by, so you may hear about harrowing days on the high seas, learn to band a lobster claw, or watch how the lobster nets inside the traps are knit. There's more. The oceanarium is beside a marsh, and you can take a guided tour to learn about the fragile ecosystem between land and sea. You may also be able to attend a live seal program at the 50,000-gallon seal tank. The oceanarium takes in seals in need of rehabilitation. If there's a seal inside, you can visit and learn about it; if not, be glad, for that means another injured seal as been released into the wild.

The Oceanarium is open 9 AM to 5 PM Monday through Saturday from mid-May through mid-October. There are a number of rate schedules, so you can choose just what you want to do. The following are 1997 rates, which are likely to remain the same in 1998: Admission to just the hatchery was $3.95 for adults and $2.75 for children; to the rest of the oceanarium, with seal, $6 for adults and $4.50 for children; without a seal, $5.25 for adults and $3.95 for children. If lobsters are your interest, you can get the Lobster Packet, including the hatchery and lobster museum, for $7.95 for adults and $5.50 for children. Or buy a combination ticket, which gets you into the

INSIDERS' TIP

Even a summer of rain yields to the crisp cool of autumn. Visit Maine in the fall for a feeling of quiet and balance.

hatchery, the Bar Harbor site and the Southwest Harbor site for $11.95 for adults and $8.95 for children (less if there's no seal).

Natural History Museum
College of the Atlantic, Maine Hwy. 3, Bar Harbor • 288-5015

Using road kill, students and faculty of this environmentally focused college have created dioramas depicting animals going about their typical day. See baby muskrats return to their tunnels, pufflings snuggled in their burrowed nests and an owl fighting with a skunk. The focus in each scene is the animal and its interaction with its environment. There's also a hands-on interactive room with self-discovery puzzles and other exploratory ways to learn about the natural world. Come October, the museum will be in its own building on campus, an original ranger station that Acadia National Park donated to the museum.

While at the college, take some time to tour the campus, walk through the restored Beatrix Farrand gardens, wander the self-guided Shoreline Nature Trail, view the immense exhibit of a whale's skull and enjoy the Blum art gallery (see our Arts chapter).

The museum is open daily from mid-June to Columbus Day. Until Labor Day, hours are 9 AM to 5 PM, then they're reduced to 10 AM to 4 PM until Columbus Day. From then until June, the museum is open Monday through Friday, generally from 10 AM to 4 PM, but the hours can be more casual, so call ahead if you don't want to be disappointed. Admission to the Natural History Museum is $2.50 for adults and $1.50 for seniors and children.

Pirate's Cove Adventure Golf
Maine Hwy. 3, Bar Harbor • 288-2133

Seen from the road, Pirate's Cove is a mass of waterfalls plunging past cliffs toward the street and the large pirate's head above the sign. This is adventure golf, not miniature golf; instead of obstacles, the difficulties of the course are terrain-oriented, with balls journeying around mounds, through caves and down a waterfall. Two courses are offered: The original is fairly straightforward; Blackbeard's Challenge is slightly more difficult.

Beware of the dangers: The cave at No. 3 emits scary noises, and another hole threatens you with showers. But get a hole-in-1 and the manager will spin a roulette wheel offering you a chance at a free game.

Spring (April and May) and fall (September and October) hours vary, so call ahead. In June, July and August, the course is open 9 AM to 11 PM daily, but it's all weather-permitting. The original course costs $5.50 for adults and teens, $5 for children ages 5 through 12 and younger; Blackbeard's Challenge costs $6 for adults and teens and $5.50 for children. Or try both courses — $9.50 for adults and teens, $8.50 for children. Children 4 and younger play for free here.

Jolly Roger's Trolley
Testa's Restaurant, 53 Main St., Bar Harbor • 288-3327

Jolly Roger's Trolley, with its blue sides and wood trim, offers a one-hour "Mansions and Mountains" tour that takes you past the old mansions of Bar Harbor (enjoy the gossip-filled narrative history), into Acadia National Park and up Cadillac Mountain for a 10-minute stop. Tours leave at 10 and 11:30 AM, 2, 3:30 and 6 PM. Tickets are available at Testa's Restaurant. Reservations are suggested. Tickets are $10 for adults and teens and $5 for children 12 and younger.

Oli's Trolley
Town Pier, One Harbor Pl., Bar Harbor • 288-9899

Leave the driving to someone else as you travel the Park Loop Road and enjoy a narrated tour. Oli's Trolley, with its red body and green roof, travels the loop on a 2½-hour tour, with 15 minute stops at Thunder Hole, Sieur de Monts Spring and the summit of Cadillac Mountain. In July and August, the trolley adds a one-hour tour, focusing on Bar Harbor and its history, that also includes a run to Cadillac Mountain's summit. All tours leave downtown Bar Harbor on Cottage Street, right across from the post office. The one-hour tours depart at 10 and 11:30 AM, 12:30, 2, 3:30 and 6 PM. The park tours, which run May through October, leave at 10 AM and 2 PM. Tickets are also available at the Acadia Restaurant at 62 Main Street, or at the town pier (see the listed address). Tickets for the park tours are $15 for adults and teens and $6 for children 12 and younger; the shorter tours cost $10 for adults, $6 for children. Reservations are suggested.

Wild Gardens of Acadia
Sieur de Monts Spring, Bar Harbor • 288-3338

Wondering about the name of that purple flower you see by the roadside? Curious about the tiny white blossoms atop Cadillac Mountain? The Wild Gardens of Acadia offer a dozen habitats filled with the flowers and foliage typically found in the national park's ecosystem: mixed woods, roadside, meadow, mountain, heath, seaside, brookside, bird thicket, coniferous woods, bog, marsh, pond. Each plant and tree is labelled. Visit the gardens on the way to the Abbe Museum (see previous entry). The park's entry fee covers your admission. The gardens are open from dawn to dusk.

Azalea Garden
Asticou Way (Maine Hwys. 3 and 198), Northeast Harbor • no phone

June, when the azaleas are in bloom, is the best time to stroll this spare, Oriental-style garden. You'll find azaleas of all colors and sizes, some looking like roses, plus irises blooming by the water. The heather comes in August. Between the times when the azaleas have withered and the heather are not yet in bloom, the Azalea Garden is still an elegant, quiet respite from a busy travel schedule. When you walk through the beautifully detailed gates of twisted twigs and across a sea of stones, you'll find yourself in another world. Bring a book and settle on a bench overlooking the pond or beside a raked Oriental rock garden. Admission is free. Hours are dawn 'til dusk.

Asticou Terraces/Thuja Lodge
Maine Hwy. 3, near intersection with Maine Hwy. 198, Northeast Harbor • 276-5130

The walk up Asticou Terraces may be steep to some, but it's worth it — a miniature pilgrimage through woods and terraces offering increasingly broader vistas of the harbor. At the top are a lodge and garden that pay homage to the designers of Mount Desert Island.

FYI

Unless otherwise noted, the area code for all phone numbers listed in this guide is 207.

The terraces and Thuja Lodge (named for the stands of northern white cedar in the woods) were created by Boston landscape architect Joseph Henry Curtis, who summered in Asticou. Landscape architect Charles Savage took over after Curtis passed on, adding the formal gardens using material from the gardens of famed Maine coastal landscape architect Beatrix Farrand (who also designed Dumbarton Oaks in Washington, D.C.). The formal garden is structured as a long lane bordered by perennials and surrounded by forest, offering visitors a sense of the expansiveness of cottage life on the island amid the beauty of the woods, hills and rocks.

On cool days, the lodge is filled with the fragrance of cedar burning in its fireplace. You'll find a host of botanical and horticultural lore in the lodge's library, which has nooks for reading and research.

The gardens are open 7 AM to 7 PM daily, but you'll find them most colorful between July and September. The lodge is open 10 AM to 4:30 PM Monday through Saturday and noon to 4 PM Sundays from July 1 to Labor Day. A donation of $2 is requested of each adult visitor.

Great Harbor Maritime Museum
Main St., Northeast Harbor • 276-5262

Though the Great Harbor museum is in a fire house, it has always had a maritime focus. In 1997, the museum reflected that focus by changing its name from the Old Firehouse Museum. Downstairs, you'll find a maritime collection; upstairs, a show of objects offering unusual insights on the region's past. You'll find an elegant Old Town Canoe with dark wooden planks and dark-green canvas, a V-hulled racing sailboat and a great collection of old marine photographs. Travel up stairs bordered with old photos to view a collection of clothing and tools as well as some dental equipment that terrifies oldsters probably more than youngsters. Perhaps you'll be treated to John Philip Sousa's "Stars and Stripes Forever" played on an old windup Victrola, or to a blast from the old fog horn.

The museum is open 10 AM to 5 PM Mon-

Photo: Bangor Daily News

Tourists line up to board *The Acadian*, a sightseeing boat docked at Bar Harbor.

day through Saturday between June and Columbus Day. Admission is $2 for adults, free for children.

Rockefeller Gardens
Rockefeller Estate, off Maine Hwy. 3, Seal Harbor • 276-3330

The house, which had been known as The Eyrie, was razed in 1963, but one morning a week the Rockefellers open their extensive gardens to a limited number of visitors. Abby Aldrich Rockefeller started these gardens, designed by Beatrix Farrand, after a trip to the Orient. The perennial borders rise four feet high and are arranged to provide lovely views from all sides. The Rockefellers traveled extensively in the Far East, and apparently Abby was quite taken with the figures of the Buddha. The formal gardens are inside gates. Visitors who walk through the round moon gate will find a stunning natural woodland setting dotted with ancient stone Buddhas. Call in advance to find out when reservations are being taken. There is no charge to visit the gardens.

The Hinckley Company
Shore Rd., Manset • 244-5531

Visitors love to wander through the boatyard and onto the docks, eyeing the fine work and expansive digs of Hinckley boats. (You can tell a Hinckley by its distinctive hand-like symbol at the bow.) The yard isn't actually open for tours, and the boats are all owned, so you can't board them. But for many a boat lover, just looking at a Hinckley is an experience. When you're done looking at the real thing, learn more about it by making your way across the street to the Hinckley Ship Store. Ask to see the video of the making of a Hinckley.

Mount Desert Oceanarium/ Oceanarium Southwest Harbor
Clark Point Rd., Southwest Harbor • 244-7330

Hear the songs of whales, feel the tiny suction cups of starfish, chart your course for an overseas adventure and find out what you weigh under water — all at this Southwest site of the Mount Desert Oceanarium. (See our previous entry for information about the Bar Harbor site.) Twenty-two tanks holding more than 2,000 gallons of sea water display resident Maine sea life, while a replica of a wheelhouse brings the fishing life of Maine right up to land. Through interactive exhibits, visitors learn about the ocean, Maine's famous fog and the lives of a shrimp dragger, sea urchin diver and other Maine fishermen.

The oceanarium is open 9 AM to 5 PM daily except Sunday, mid-May through mid-October. Rates for 1997 were $6 for adults and teens and $4.50 for children ages 4 through 12; combination tickets, offering admission to the Bar Harbor site as well, were $11.40 and $8.35, respectively. Rates are likely to be the same in 1998.

Nancy Neale Typecraft Museum
Steamboat Wharf Rd., Bernard
• 244-5192

Irving Silverman has a few passions. Lighthouses is one; old type is another. His collection of old letterpress type and antique printing artifacts includes the type — the old letters, that is — of *The New York Times* before it upgraded. His collection is housed in a "lighthouse" he had built for himself by some of the best boat builders on the island. Hanging outside is one lobster buoy of every lobster family from Bernard and nearby Bass Harbor. Does the place look vaguely familiar? It's been photographed by *Vogue* and a few other magazines. Inside, the type items are for sale, and many an old *Times* employee has stopped by to reclaim a piece of the old ways. Hours are by chance or appointment between June and October; call Nancy and Irving Silverman for an appointment. Admission is free.

Seal Cove Auto Museum
Maine Hwy. 102, just past Pretty Marsh Rd., Seal Cove • 244-9242

Delight in the romance of early automobiles at the Seal Cove Auto Museum, the work of one collector. Antique automobiles, from an 1899 DeDion Bouton to a 1934 Packard, are displayed, with an emphasis on rare breeds from the elegant brass era that lasted from 1905 to 1917. See early motorcycles, woodsided sedans and elegantly polished vehicles resting as if in anticipation of a drive to a picnic on Cadillac Mountain or a yachting party in Southwest Harbor.

The museum is open 10 AM to 5 PM daily from June 1 through September 15. Admission is $5 for adults and teens, $2 for children 12 and younger.

Seawall
Seawall Rd., Southwest Harbor

This little beach of surf and cobblestones becomes the annual site of an ever-changing sea of sculptures. Visitors pile the round stones into little towers, like miniature minarets. The towers brave the snows, winds and crowds, and should they fall down, they are rebuilt. Year after year, these wonderland sculptures are always standing.

Wendell Gilley Museum of Bird Carving
Main St. and Herrick Rd., Southwest Harbor • 244-7555

Birds flourish here any time of year, though most are made of carved wood, not feathers. The museum features a collection of carvings by Wendell Gilley (1904-1983), a famous native Maine carver. It also features the carvings of and demonstrations by carver-in-residence Steven Valleau, of Orono. You'll also find wildlife art exhibits, natural history video programs and a museum shop.

Hours are 10 AM to 4 PM Tuesday through Sunday from June to October (until 5 PM in July and August). In May and from November through Christmas, the museum is open 10 AM to 4 PM Friday through Sunday. From January through April, it might be open by appointment. Admission is $3 for adults and teens, $1 for children ages 5 to 12.

Islesford Historical Museum
off Islesford Dock, Little Cranberry Island • 244-9224

This historic museum is part of Acadia National Park. It displays memorabilia about the social life of the five islands that make up the town of Cranberry Isles as well as the maritime life that most of the 19th-century population here engaged in.

Associated with the museum is the Blue Duck, a simple 19th-century building of a kind common to the islands. Once a maritime store, the Blue Duck was bought by historian William Sawtelle in 1917. He found a number of wooden duck decoys inside, painted them Prussian blue and put them around the yard, hence the name.

The museum is accessible via ferry from Northeast Harbor and Southwest Harbor. It is open daily — 10:45 AM to noon and 12:30 to 4:40 PM — from mid-June through September. Call Beal and Bunker Mail Boat Service at 244-3575 (or see the subsequent entry in the "Ferries" section) for a schedule. Admission is free.

While you're on Little Cranberry Island, take a walk through town and visit the Little Cranberry Store, which houses the island's post office. Plan to buy stamps from here throughout the year, by mail. You'll not only get the stamps, but also know you've helped keep another island post office — and town center — in business. As thanks, you'll also get a newsletter about the island written by Postmaster Joy Sprague.

Boat Excursions

When we first came to Maine, all our trips eventually ended up on the water. Whether we were hiking, biking, skiing, picnicking or camping, water was somehow involved, even if only as our last sight before we lay our heads down at night. Then we figured out how to get on the water, and the fun really started. We hope you can enjoy water-bound excursions too. To that end, we've compiled this special section with information about some local tour boats.

Boats do tend to come and go, however, so while we've made this rundown of excursions as up-to-date as possible, we won't swear by it. And neither should you.

The following information is just that: information, not recommendations. It's up to you to eye the boat for seaworthiness and to give it at least a quick once-over to be sure there are life jackets, lifeboats and a visible captain's permit authorizing the boat to accept paying guests. Reservations are always a good idea.

By Motorboat

Waldoboro to Stockton Springs

Lively Lady
Lively Lady Two
Sharp's Wharf, Camden Harbor, Camden • 236-6672

Watch Capt. Philbrick pull lobster traps, hear him talk about the lobster industry, and learn about how seals fight, love and lounge as you take the *Lively Lady's* nature-lobster excursion. The *Lively Lady* fishing-type vessels provide three two-hour cruises during the day, or join a lobster bake at night. Adult passage is $15, $5 for children. Trips run between June and September.

Balmy Days
Belfast City Dock, Belfast • 338-4652, 596-9041

Hop aboard the *Balmy Days* in either Belfast or in Castine. Go one-way across Penobscot Bay (90 minutes), or make it a day with round trip from either point of departure. The layover in Castine or Belfast is 90 minutes — enough time to get a bite to eat or tour the town. Then there's more sea breeze and joyous waves on the return trip.

Capt. Stephen Olson also makes a bread run, bringing along loaves from the Belfast Co-op, on the Belfast-to-Castine trip. He'll gladly take along bicycles, kayaks and almost anything else as well, and he'll provide you with plenty of tales. "I consider myself to be a limitless source of useless information," Olson says. Having worked on oceanographic research vessels and being something of a Colonial-history buff, his information might not be entirely useless to either his position or your questions.

Olson's *Balmy Days* was built in 1932 to perform the mail-boat run between Boothbay and Monhegan. The current mail boat, *Balmy Days II*, holds many more than the 49 passengers *Balmy Days* accommodates but has nothing more to do with this tour operation.

Balmy Days makes special Saturday trips, either to Holbrook Island or up the Penobscot River to the stately stone blocks of Fort Knox (see this chapter's previous entries). Ask about other special excursions such as a foliage trip down the Penobscot River in autumn. Generally, voyages leave Belfast at 9:30 AM daily. Tuesdays and Thursdays, a second trip leaves at 4 PM, allowing time for dinner in Castine (make your own reservations), then returning to Belfast at 8:15 PM. Adult and teen fare is $18 round trip; children 12 and younger travel for $9.

Belfast & Moosehead Lake Railroad Cruise Boat
Railroad Pier, Belfast • (800) 392-5500

The Belfast & Moosehead Lake Railroad offers a 90-minute Penobscot Bay boat excursion around the famed island of Islesboro and back up the coast to Belfast. The boat is a classic, a turn-of-the-century vintage ferry, new to the railroad in 1998.

Excursions run between June and October, with twice-daily trips scheduled for July and August. Call for the complete schedule, and when you do, ask about special events. Rates are $14 for adults, $10 for teens ages 13 to 17 and $7 for children. Reservations are suggested.

Bucksport to Gouldsboro

Balmy Days
Castine Town Pier, Castine • 338-4652, 596-9041

Travel Maine the old-fashioned way on the closest thing to a coastal steamer. *Balmy Days* crosses Penobscot Bay a few times daily between Castine and Belfast. (See the previous entry in the "Waldoboro to Stockton Springs" section for details.)

Palmer Day IV
Stonington Harbor, Stonington • 367-2207

Capt. Reginald Greenlaw has been sailing these waters for much of his 88 years. He still goes out daily, leaving at 2 PM from Stonington and cruising 16 miles around the pink stones of Crotch Island and the Deer Isle Thorofare without retracing a wave. He also travels Thursday mornings to Vinalhaven (see our Offshore/Islands chapter) and North Haven, stopping on both is-

lands. The cost for the Vinalhaven trip is $12 for folks 10 and older and $7.50 for children younger than 10; the afternoon trip is $10 and $5 respectively.

Mount Desert Island

Chippewa
Bar Harbor Inn Pier, Bar Harbor • 288-4585, 288-2373, 546-2927 (in winter)

The 1923 motor vessel *Chippewa* offers an elegant 90-minute journey among the lighthouses and islands around Frenchman Bay. Bring a picnic. Sunset and moonlight cruises also are available. A professional naturalist is frequently aboard to answer questions. Sometimes, however, storyteller and former Shakespearean actor Jason Dylan Hooper is on board to regale passengers with stories of days of old in Frenchman Bay. One tale tells of a lighthouse keeper whose lonely wife played the same song over and over again until he was driven insane. The *Chippewa* generally has morning, afternoon and sunset runs from mid-May to mid-October, but there's no precise schedule; call for dates and departure times. Excursions cost $16 for adults and teens, $10 for children 12 and younger.

Katharine
1 West St., Bar Harbor • 288-3322, (800) 508-1499

You've been eating lobsters for the past five days that you've been in Maine. Now's your time to try your hand at hauling them. For sure, going out with a commercial excursion lobstering boat isn't quite the same as leaving before dawn with your local lobsterman or lobsterwoman. But let's face it, the will to rise at 4 AM while on vacation is probably even harder to come by than a lobster boat ready to carry passengers. So take a ride on the *Katherine*, a modified lobster boat holding 40 passengers. You'll learn how lobstering is done, visit seals and enjoy spending 1½ hours on the water. The cost is $16.75 for adults, $12.75 for those 15 and younger. From three to five trips depart daily between May and mid-October, but call for hours as they vary according to season.

R.L. Gott
Little Island Marina, Bass Harbor
• 244-5785

Leaving from Bass Harbor, this 40-foot lobster boat/passenger boat goes out to Frenchboro, a remote island with a stalwart year-round population that harkens back to a time when many of Maine's islands hosted a family or a town. A four-hour lunch cruise leaves at 11 AM: Visit the Frenchboro Museum, have a dockside lunch and return among the islands of Blue Hill Bay. The cost for the trip is $17 for adults and $8 for children.

A two-hour nature cruise, departing at 3 PM, travels among Great and Little Gott islands and the Green Islands, but does not land at Frenchboro. On this trip, you'll hear stories about the wildlife and history as well as tall tales best classified as "yarns." Tickets are $14 for adults and teens, $8 for children ages 4 through 12.

By Sailboat

Waldoboro to Stockton Springs

Many of the following schooners were once part of the windjammer fleet, taking passengers on excursions into Penobscot Bay for five days at a time. Such voyages allow visitors to not only experience the glory of the bay with its multitude of islands, but also savor the energy and expertise of the 19th-century sailor. However, not every would-be romantic sailor can spare five days, so a few schooners have decided to offer short excursions lasting from a few hours to a day, weather permitting. For more information about windjammer excursions, see the related Close-up in our Accommodations chapter.

Surprise
The East Wind Inn, Mechanic St.,
Tenants Harbor • 372-6366,
(800) 241-VIEW

Friendship sloops were built to make lobstering easy under sail, but they are now among the most romantic and lovely of all sailing vessels. The 33-foot *Surprise* takes six people at a time for three trips daily at 9 AM, 1 and 5 PM. Voyages into Muscongus Bay last two or three hours. The cost is $25 to $30 a person.

Appledore
Sharp's Wharf, Camden Harbor, Camden
• 236-8353, (800) 233-PIER

An 86-foot schooner is a rare, large beast. Yet *Appledore* sails in and out of Camden Harbor like there was nothing to it. She departs for two-hour cruises daily between June and October with a maximum of 49 passengers on board. A trip might include a look at lobstermen working their traps, glimpses of seals and ospreys, or simply a panorama of the Camden Hills. The cost is $20 a person. Cocktails are available for passengers "of age." From June to mid-September, sailing times are 10 AM to noon, 12:30 to 2:30 PM and 3 to 5 PM. There's also an hourlong sunset cruise that departs around 5 PM; cocktails are available. After mid-September the schedule changes; call for specific hours.

Olad
Northwind
Town Landing, Camden Harbor, Camden
• 236-2323

The *Olad* (55 feet) and the *Northwind* (75 feet) are two early 20th-century wooden schooners. Both vessels offer family-oriented cruises. The *Olad* takes only 21 people at a time; the *Northwind* takes 49. Between Memorial Day and mid-October, depending on the weather, one boat leaves each hour for a two-hour voyage ending with a sunset cruise. (The *Northwind* is undergoing reconstruction, so cruises on that might be delayed.) You'll get a glimpse of Penobscot Bay and its islands whenever you go. Where you'll go, however, will be determined by wind and sail. Adults and teens can expect to pay $15 for a cruise on the *Olad*, $20 on the *Northwind*. Children ages 6 through 12 pay $10 each, and children 5 and younger pay $5, for cruises on either vessel.

Shantih II
Rockport Harbor, Rockport • 236-8605,
(800) 599-8605

This 40-foot wooden sloop keeps its excursions intimate, taking only six people for lobster roll lunch cruises between noon and 4 PM. Trips cost $50 a person (adults and teens) in June and September, $75 in July and August; children 12 and younger sail for half-price. Or take a sunset cruise between 5:30 and 7:30 PM for $25 a person in June and September, $35 in July and August; children sail for half-price in each instance. Also ask about full-day charters, which will allow some flexibility, maybe a stop on an island or two.

Mount Desert Island

Bay Lady
1 West St., Bar Harbor • 288-3322, (800) 508-1499

This massive, 85-foot schooner was fashioned after the *Joann*, designed by the famous Herreshoff family of boat builders. Visit the Porcupines and see the mountains and cliffs of Acadia National Park from the same vantage point as the first explorers. Rest assured, however, they had nothing like the luxury of this watercraft, padded with soft cushions and shining with varnished mahogany. Two or three 1½-hour cruises depart during the day; a two-hour sunset cruise leaves in the evening. The daytime trips cost $12 a person, and the sunset cruise costs $15. Call for departure times as they change according to season. Refreshments are available.

Margaret Todd
Bar Harbor Inn Pier, Bar Harbor • 288-4585, 546-2927 (in winter)

New in 1998, this 151-foot, four-masted schooner with brick-red sails looks quite astonishing in Frenchman Bay. Modeled after a turn-of-the-century vessel, the *Margaret Todd* claims to be the only four-masted schooner in New England. She will take 150 passengers at a time on three to four trips daily. Expect to be on the water for between 1½ and two hours. There is no specific schedule, so call for information and reservations.

We like the idea of the sunset sail, which frequently features a musician. Bring a snack. Tickets are $22 for adults and teens and $14 for children 12 and younger.

Resolute
Golden Anchor Pier, 52 West St., Bar Harbor • 288-9505

This 31-foot traditional Friendship sloop was built in 1976 and holds a maximum 15 passengers. In 1997, excursions departed daily between mid-May and mid-October from the Golden Anchor Pier at 10:30 AM, 1 and 3:30 PM and at sunset. Call for current times and costs.

By Ferry

Ferries are the work boats of the coast. They traffic in people, groceries and mail. We can remember squeezing in among a week's supply of groceries for the entire island when taking the mail boat to Islesford one fall day. We had traveled on the same day as the store owner, who was stocking up. When the boat arrived, the entire boat — island people, visitors and tourists — formed a chain of hands to pass the goods up the ramp to her truck.

While ferries are often the best way of getting to an island — whether it's to walk around for a day or to stay awhile — they are also a way of taking an excursion cruise on a budget. The motor may be loud, the cushions few, but the view is spectacular.

FYI

Unless otherwise noted, the area code for all phone numbers listed in this guide is 207.

Laura B Mail Boat
Port Clyde Dock, Port Clyde • 372-8848

The *Laura B*, crowded with passengers, is the way to visit Monhegan (see our Offshore/Islands chapter). The cost for the round-trip journey is $24 for adults, $12 for children. Parking at the dock costs $4. The schedule changes throughout the year; call for current departure times.

Maine State Ferry
Rockland Ferry Terminal, Rockland • 596-2202, 734-6935

Maine State ferries serve Vinalhaven and North Haven. Six ferries depart daily from the ferry terminal in Rockland bound for Vinalhaven. It's a glorious passage of about 75 minutes, ending with an island trail through Hurricane Sound.

The *North Haven* ferry leaves three times daily, and the trip also takes about 75 minutes. The round-trip cost is $9 for adults, $4 for children. A car costs $26 more. Call for a current schedule.

Photo: Bangor Daily News

The Asticou Azalea Gardens in Northeast Harbor draw many visitors each year.

Islesboro Ferry
Maine State Ferry Dock, Lincolnville Beach • 789-5611, 734-6935

The *Margaret Chase Smith* ferry leaves from Lincolnville seven times daily in summer, arriving in Islesboro 20 minutes later. The cost is $4.50 round trip for adults, slightly less for kids and $13 for a car. Call for a current schedule.

Isle au Haut Company
Seabreeze Ave., Stonington • 367-5193

Take the 40-minute mail boat from Stonington to Isle au Haut, passing the lovely Merchant Row. The schedule is complicated; see our Acadia National Park chapter for details. Round-trip fare is $24 for adults and teens, $10 children 12 and younger, Monday through Saturday.

The company also offers one-hour narrated island tours at 2 PM daily. These cost $10 for adults, less for children. Schedules do change, especially off-season, so call ahead.

Beal & Bunker Inc.
Municipal Pier, Northeast Harbor • 244-3575

This small mail boat is the lifeline of the five islands known as the Cranberry Isles: Bear, Sutton, Great Cranberry, Islesford (also known as Little Cranberry) and Baker Island. The mail boat stops year round at Islesford and Great Cranberry, with a summer hailing stop at Sutton Island. The boat leaves six times a day between mid-June and early September, but only three times a day between October and early May. (Four boats depart daily on the shoulder seasons.) Take a bike, or simply hike, and soak in the decidedly different atmosphere of Maine islands.

Swans Island Ferry
Maine State Ferry Dock, Bass Harbor • 244-3254

The Swans Island Ferry leaves the ferry terminal in Bass Harbor and arrives at Swans Island 40 minutes later. Round-trip passage costs $6 for adults, $3 for children and $18 for a car.

Whale-watching Cruises

Four boats leave Bar Harbor on as many as three daily cruises to visit the whales' feeding grounds near Mount Desert Rock. This is a distant outpost of an island, so if you go, expect to spend an hour or more getting there, an hour or more watching the whales and then an hour or more returning, for a total time commitment of three to four hours. Frequently, the same boats also offer early morning and sunset nature visits to Petit Manan to see puffins (see this chapter's subsequent "Puffin Cruises" section). Tour boat captains keep in close touch with fishermen within a wide radius of Bar Harbor to monitor whale activity, so sightings are virtually guaranteed. But since boats speed out to the whales' feeding grounds at speeds as great as 40 knots, you'll be more comfortable traveling on a day when waters are relatively calm; otherwise, the trip might be a bumpy one. The one major difference among the boats is that the *Friendship V*, used by The Bar Harbor Whale Watch Co., is a catamaran. It's rare not to see a whale, but you might inquire about the guarantee policy, just in case.

Costs average $25 to $30 per adult (less for seniors, sometimes) and about $19 per child. The season generally runs when the whales are in the region — from May through October. In midsummer, each boat leaves about three times a day for the feeding grounds, tapering off to once a day at either end of the season. Call for hours. Reservations are recommended.

We suggest any of the following companies:

Acadian Whale Watcher, Golden Anchor Inn and Pier, 52 West Street, Bar Harbor, 288-9794 or (800) 421-3307

Bar Harbor Whale Watch Co., 39 Cottage Street, Bar Harbor, 288-2386 or (800) WHALES-4. (Its catamaran leaves from Holiday Inn Regency next to ferry.)

Sea Bird Watcher Co., Golden Anchor Inn and Pier, 52 West Street, Bar Harbor, 288-2025 or (800) 247-3794

Whale Watcher Inc., 1 West Street, Bar Harbor, 288-3322 or (800) 508-1499

INSIDERS' TIP

If you see a notice for a bean supper — *go*! Afterward, you'll understand Mainers a lot better.

Puffin Cruises

Puffins are seabirds with huge orange beaks and black and white coats. You know them when you see them, but you can't see them unless you have a boat — they are shy and don't venture far from their babies, known as pufflings. We have listed some excursions subsequently. Depending on the time of year and the island you're traveling to, you might be able to get off the boat (Machias Seal Island has blinds from which you can watch puffins, and you can get on Matinicus Rock once the pufflings have hatched, usually in mid-July). Most trips cost about $20 for adults and $16 for children.

Trips to Eastern Egg Rock, off Muscongus Bay, are accessed southwest of our Mid-Coast region. Try any of the following:

Hardy Boat Cruises, New Harbor, (800) 278-3346

Cap'n Fish, Pier One, Boothbay Harbor, 633-3244 or 633-2626

Maine Audubon Society, Falmouth, 781-2330 (offering at least one field trip in June and July)

Matinicus Rock is farther east. For these trips, try Hardy Boat Cruises or the Maine Audubon Society (see previous addresses and phone numbers) as well as **Atlantic Expeditions**, St. George, 372-8621.

Petit Manan is even farther east. For voyages this island, call the **Acadian Sea Bird Watcher**, 288-9794 or (800) 421-3307, which offers both whale and puffin cruises via a regular boat. Trips to Petit Manan, lasting two to three hours, leave each morning from the Golden Anchor Pier, 52 West Street, Bar Harbor. Some additional trips leave afternoons. Or try the whale and puffin combo cruise — a five-hour journey. Call for hours. The cost for the puffin trip ranges from $20 to $24 per adult, and the combination trip, $33 to $35. Children pay about $18.

For trips to Machias Seal Island, try **Capt. Barna B. Norton**, Jonesport (a bit east of our Mid-Coast area), 497-5933.

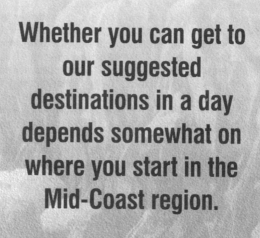

Whether you can get to our suggested destinations in a day depends somewhat on where you start in the Mid-Coast region.

Daytrips and Weekend Getaways

The Mid-Coast area — the coverage area of this book — by itself might encompass several daytrips when you consider the distance between its farthest points. Still, there are plenty of interesting destinations outside its borders, and we've chosen four that offer a variety of experiences. We chose Freeport for its factory-outlet stores, Portland for a taste of city life, Nova Scotia for a great ferry ride and a bit of Canada, and finally, Campobello Island in New Brunswick, Canada, for President Franklin Delano Roosevelt's summer home. Whether you can get to these destinations in a day depends somewhat on where you start in the Mid-Coast region. Do a little calculating with a map to make sure you can make the trip in the time you have. We suggest some attractions, shopping destinations, restaurants and accommodations (in case you decide to spend the night).

Freeport

It's hard to believe Freeport was once a quiet little town not unlike many of the communities that line Maine's coast. Now, there's one reason, and one reason only, why the town boasts 3.5 million visitors a year: shopping. L.L. Bean started it all, with a catalog mail-order business that began to draw visitors to its factory showroom. The showroom turned into a retail store, and since 1951, it's been open 24 hours a day, 365 days a year. It's one of the top three tourist destinations in Maine. That's some anchor tenant, as they say in the mall business.

Still, the very success of Freeport might be that it doesn't look or feel like a mall town.

The strip of factory-outlet stores is about a half-mile long, but it lines U.S. Highway 1 as if it was the center of a small town. Granted, the stores are much larger and more imposing that most small-town downtown stores, and there aren't the barber shops and grocery stores; but you are outside, walking along a sidewalk, smiling at fellow passersby. Behind the facade of shops are huge parking lots crisscrossed by side streets sprinkled with more shops. And there are still more shops in little clusters as you drive south on U.S. 1. All in all, there are more than 100 stores, so leave early and stay late!

Getting There

To reach Freeport, follow U.S. 1 south. We can't help but mention that if you're hungry on the way, check out **Red's Eats**, on U.S. 1, a little red take-out spot on the right after you cross the bridge on your way into Wiscasset. It has the biggest, best crab rolls we've eaten anywhere. Be sure to look around as U.S. 1 makes an S-curve at the end of Wiscasset's downtown strip: The huge old houses are a feast for the eyes.

After you go through Brunswick, U.S. 1 splits to the left, but you want to take Interstate 95 south and follow the signs to Freeport. Freeport's strip of outlets is on U.S. 1 between exits 20 and 19 — take either one. The parking lots behind the stores are free, so find a good spot, leave your car there and start walking.

We suggest finding the **Hose Tower Information Center** on Depot Street, on the east side of Main Street, and parking nearby.

It has a large three-dimensional map of the area posted outside, public restrooms (a rarity here), an ATM and a pay phone as well as reams of material on businesses in the area. The Freeport Merchants Association (FMA) headquarters is on the second floor, and the first floor is staffed seven days a week, mid-May to Columbus Day. During the rest of the year, help yourself to the free brochures piled in racks.

Attractions

We exaggerated earlier. There are more things to do here than shop. The **Desert of Maine**, 95 Desert Road, 865-6962, is 2.5 miles from town and a favorite with kids. This 40-acre sand dune is a glacial wash plain left at the end of the ice age. Poor farming practices in the late 1800s and early 1900s eroded the topsoil, leaving a vast expanse of sand.

The Desert is open early May to mid-October. During June, July and August, it's open 9 AM to 6 PM daily, with tours every half-hour. Off-season, it closes at 4:30 PM. Admission is $6 for seniors 65 and older, $6.50 for adults, $4.50 for folks ages 13 to 16 and $3.50 for ages 6 to 12; kids 5 and younger are admitted free. The tours and admission to the museum are included in the entry fee.

Wolfe's Neck Woods State Park, Wolfe's Neck Road, 865-4465, is another option for visitors allergic to shopping. This 244-acre park offers well-marked nature trails for hiking and bird watching on a peninsula in Casco Bay. Bring a lunch to enjoy at one of the picnic tables.

Visitors are welcome year round, but the park road is open from early May into October depending on weather conditions. The day-use fee is $2 a person for folks 12 and older and 50¢ for children ages 5 through 11. Children 4 and younger and seniors older than 65 are admitted free. Take Bow Street, which runs perpendicular to U.S. 1 and intersects it at L.L. Bean. Turn right at Wolfe's Neck Road. The entrance road is about 2 miles down and marked by a sign.

FYI

Unless otherwise noted, the area code for all phone numbers listed in this guide is 207.

Shopping

As we said, shopping is Freeport's calling card. The **L.L. Bean** store, on U.S. 1, is the major attraction and a kind of congregation point. We've sat on the benches in front and seen old friends we last heard were reporting from the Philippines.

The company began in 1912 when Leon Leonwood Bean started selling The Maine Hunting Shoe by mail. It still has a gumshoe sole that curves up around the foot and leather uppers that laced up the front. From a distance the uppers look a little like spats. It was a natural for hunters and outdoorsmen, giving them some protection from moisture. The first shipment of boots didn't perform as well as intended, but Leon Leonwood managed to land on his feet. He started offering a satisfaction-or-your-money-back guarantee that eased the concerns of customers buying from a distance and made Bean a retail legend. For years, the company repaired and resoled the boots without charge. That's changed, of course, but it helped foster the company's reputation for service and reliability.

The store itself is a modern multilevel wonder complete with indoor trout pond. (It wasn't always thus. Look for a model of the old building in the lobby of the new one.) The company sells gear for every conceivable outdoor activity, some home furnishings (originally intended for camps) and Maine foodstuffs. The sales staff is excellent, friendly and knowledgeable. When buying our first pair of Bean boots, we were urged to buy a larger size than we thought looked well. "Do you want to look nice, or do you want to be warm," said the saleswoman, a classic outdoorsy type. She was too young to look over the top of a pair of bifocals, but we felt she would have if she had been wearing them. We were a little ashamed of being so vain, and her good sense paid off.

Around Maine's retail icon swirls a changing array of factory-outlet stores, so use your map or call the **Freeport Merchants Association**, (800) 865-1994, to ensure your favorite store is among the present tenants. The **Polo/Ralph Lauren Factory Store** has been a fixture for ages, but **Cuddledown of Maine**, 231 U.S. 1, for instance, a manufacturer of down bedding, has moved more than a mile south, just past Exit 19. Here are a few of the brand-name retailers you can look for: **Banana Republic**, 39 Main Street; **Donna Karan Company Store**, 42 Main Street; **Brooks Brothers Factory Store**, 24 Bow Street; **J. Crew**, 10 Bow Street; **Patagonia**, 9 Bow Street; **Burberry's**, 42 Main Street; **Samsonite**, 20 Bow Street; **Coach**, 48 West Street; **Crabtree & Evelyn**, 100 Main Street; **Cannon Sheets, Towels and More**, 5 Depot Street; **Villeroy & Boch**, 5 Bow Street; **Johnston & Murphy**, 100 Main Street; **Reebok/Rockport Factory Direct**, 200 Lower Main Street; **Timberland**, 42 Main Street; and **Cole-Haan**, 66 Main Street. Also, for a real deal on Bean's goods, skip the main store all together and wend your way to the **L.L. Bean Factory Store**, Depot Street, in the parking lot between Bow Street and Mill Street. Here you'll find imperfects and factory seconds as well as first-quality discontinued items at savings of as much as 60 percent. While you'll find discounts and markdowns all over town, they go particularly deep on Memorial Day weekend, President's Day, Labor Day, Thanksgiving and the third weekend in July, which according to *Down East* magazine is when many parents visit their kids at summer camp. One year we happened to hit the outlets on the Thursday before Memorial Day weekend, and we had the best of all possible worlds. The place was deserted, but the weekend's discounts were already in place. We made out like bandits.

There are a number of stores that aren't outlets and don't offer discounted goods, but the variety and selection might tempt you. Check out **Abacus American Crafts**, 36 Main Street, for one-of-a-kind jewelry, pottery and housewares. We are partial to **Bridgham & Cook British Gifts & Groceries**, 6 Bow Street, for its range of English cookies, jams, jellies and other foodstuffs. This is the place to get genuine English Christmas pudding! You can find wool sweaters, after-shave lotion and an incredibly extensive selection of Barbour clothing. Unlike many Barbour dealers, owner Bob Bussey carries many of the smaller sizes that best fit women.

Another interesting stop is **Harrington House**, 45 Main Street, a Greek Revival townhouse turned into a museum store by the Freeport Historical Society. You'll find lots of antique-reproduction furniture as well as pottery, glass, textiles and crafts.

Restaurants

Who has time to eat? Grab an ice cream at **Ben & Jerry's**, 83 Main Street, in front of Bean's, and keep moving. No, seriously, there are a number of restaurants where it's worth taking the time to actually sit down and enjoy your food. **The Corsican**, 9 Mechanic Street, close to the center of town, is a great place for lunch, but it also serves dinner. The menu includes soups, sandwiches and salads. While **Gritty McDuff's**, 183 Lower Main Street, is a bit of a walk (about a mile from L.L. Bean; just drive), it's the town's only brewpub.

Accommodations

Sleep? Sleep you say? OK, so maybe you've shopped and you want to drop rather than drive back up the coast. We suggest you check out the **Harraseeket Inn**, 162 Main Street, 865-9377. This handsome country inn is built around two historic properties, one built in 1798 and the other in 1850. Recently expanded, it includes an indoor pool, a new ballroom and a larger tavern. Many have fireplaces, and there are a number of suites as well. Most are decorated with antiques and reproductions, and the atmosphere is classy. Breakfast and afternoon tea are included in your stay.

You might also try **181 Main Street Bed & Breakfast**, 181 Main Street, 865-1226, an 1840s Cape Cod-style inn that was featured in *Country Home* magazine. Its seven guest rooms have private baths and are decorated with antiques. Your stay includes a full breakfast. Gardens and an in-ground swimming pool top off the package.

Portland

Portland is where we go for a dose of the city — for museums, great shopping and fabulous restaurants. If you squint, parts of the Old Port look just like parts of Boston, with narrow cobblestone streets, brick buildings and interesting shops. The city proper, the largest in Maine and at one time its capital, has a population of 62,000; Greater Portland boasts 243,000 residents, almost a fifth of the state's population.

The peninsula that forms Portland was first settled by the British in 1632, who joined a Native American population that called the land Machigonne, or "Great Neck." The area was leveled by the Great Fire of 1866, so many of the buildings are brick and built in 19th-century style. Attempts to preserve these gems started in 1961, and the long-derelict Old Port began attracting artists and crafters in the 1970s. Small retail specialty shops and restaurants soon followed, as did a boom in real estate prices and rental rates.

Getting There

Portland is 15 miles beyond Freeport (see the previous "Freeport, Getting There" section). Take Exit 15 off I-95 onto I-295. Get off on Exit 7, which leads toward the waterfront on Franklin Street. Keep going until you hit Commercial Street, then find a place to park. That's your best bet for poking around the Old Port. Other destinations require parking arrangements that you can find as you go.

Attractions

Founded in 1882, the **Portland Museum of Art**, 7 Congress Square, 775-6148, is a real calling card for the city. The modern building was designed by I.M. Pei & Partners, and houses works by Van Gogh, Picasso, Degas, Winslow Homer, John Singer Sergeant, George Bellows, Edward Hopper, Rockwell Kent and the Wyeths. Free guided tours are given daily at 2 PM, and Thursday and Friday evenings at 6 PM. There's a museum shop and cafe as well.

The museum is open 10 AM to 5 PM Tuesday, Wednesday and Saturday; until 9 PM Thursday and Friday; and noon to 5 PM Sunday. From July to Columbus Day, it's open on Monday from 10 AM to 5 PM as well. Admis-

sion is free from 5 to 9 PM Friday; the rest of the time it's $6 for adults and teens, $5 for seniors and $1 for kids ages 6 through 12.

Right next door is the **Children's Museum of Maine**, 142 Free Street, 828-1234, which offers kids a hands-on, learn-by-doing experience of art and science topics. While you can bring a book and let your child play in the computer room (no Internet connection, just interactive CDs), the exhibits are aimed at family involvement. There's a craft center, a space shuttle replica and a huge globe. Other displays explore Maine's heritage and culture. The newest exhibit, *Flurry of Feathers*, is an international traveling exhibit on the world of birds.

From Memorial Day to Labor Day, the museum is open 10 AM to 5 PM Monday through Saturday and noon to 5 PM Sunday. Admission is $5 for anyone older than 1. The rest of the year the museum closes on Monday and Tuesday, and admission is $4. Also, admission is free from 5 to 8 PM on the first Friday of every month except June through August.

While there are a number of historic houses to see in the city, the **Wadsworth-Longfellow House**, 487 Congress Street, 879-0427, is the oldest brick home you'll find and the boyhood home of poet Henry Wadsworth Longfellow. Built in 1785 in the Georgian style, it was later converted to the Federal style. The interior is filled with three generations of family furnishings but frozen in the late Victorian era, when the last generation of Longfellows passed on.

The museum is open June through October, and admission is limited to 40-minute guided tours that run on the hour and half-hour; the last begins at 4 PM. In 1997, the cost of the tour was $4 for adults and teens, $1 for children 12 and younger. The adjacent Maine History Gallery is open to tour at will, and its exhibits change periodically.

Shopping

And you thought Freeport was shopper's heaven! Downtown Portland is awash in stores, especially the Old Port area along the waterfront. Here are a few of our favorites. The **Stein**

www.insiders.com

See this and many other
Insiders' Guide® destinations
online — in their entirety.

Visit us today!

Thousands of miles of well-groomed snowmobile trails cut through the Maine wilderness.

Gallery of Contemporary Glass, 20 Milk Street, 772-9072, feels like a museum. More than 75 artists are represented, and their work is simply smashing — bold, direct and beautifully fluid.

Geraldine Wolf, 26 Milk Street, 774-8994, is small but filled with lovely things — an 1875 hand-engraved, five-piece sterling tea set, for instance. We weren't sure we could live without it. Wolf is an expert on antique and estate jewelry, and it shows in her display cases. An 1860 necklace and earring set — black and white stone cameos in a heavy gold Victorian setting — was stunning. Check out the collection of antique brooches. Dating from 1830 to 1930, they're made of precious and semiprecious stones set in gold or platinum.

Looking for an interesting souvenir of Maine? Try something made out of tourmaline, a gemstone native to these parts that ranges in color from green to pink, sometimes in the same piece. **Cross Jewelers**, 570 Congress Street, 773-3107, is the place to go. It boasts the world's largest collection Maine tourmaline jewelry.

Joseph's, 410 Fore Street, 773-1274 (men's) and 773-4454 (women's), is one of the top clothing stores in the city, with fine European and American brands for both sexes.

Amaryllis Clothing Co., 41 Exchange Street, 772-4439, is another choice for women, particularly for those sharp, unusual pieces that add spice to your wardrobe.

If interior design is your passion, check out **Penelope Daborn Ltd.**, 2 Milk Street, 761-2711. We amateurs are well aware that those in the trade see an entirely different selection of fabrics and wallpaper. Well, here's a shop that opens that world to those of us who don't do decorators. The choices are dazzling, and the staff is helpful and friendly.

F.O. Bailey Antiquarians, 141 Middle Street, 774-1479, handles auctions and appraisals, but it also operates a showroom of antique furniture, paintings, rugs, lamp shades and other furnishings. Interesting to see that those low rectangular couches of the 1960s (in tangerine and avocado, of course) are now worth something.

J. Nelson Collection, 425 Fore Street, 772-7200, is an elegant little place that houses an impressive selection of dinnerware, crystal, flatware and furnishings. This is one of the few places in the state where you can find Herend and Mottahedeh china, with its handsome reproduction patterns. **The Resourceful Home**, 111 Commercial Street, 780-1314, features all manner of environmentally friendly clothing and housewares, including sheets, blankets and towels. Some of these items are hard to find, and it's nice to see a store dedicated to such a range of goods. **The Whip and Spoon**, 161 Commercial Street, 774-4020, is a wildly popular place. It always seems crowded. Here you'll find professional-quality cookware, imported knives and all manner of kitchen gadgets. The emphasis is on quality and selection — we can't imagine a better place for hard-core cooks to browse. Wine and specialty foods are tucked in the back corner.

Restaurants

Cafe Always, 47 Middle Street, 774-9399, is recommended by everyone and their brother, including media heavyweights such as *The New York Times* and *The Los Angeles Times*. It's small — just a dozen tables — but the food is spectacular. Maine foods are highlighted, and the menu changes weekly; we've seen pan-roasted farm-raised venison with juniper demi-glace and red-onion cream sauce, and a rich North Atlantic monkfish bouillabaisse. Cafe Always is known for its desserts, and choices might include an awesome Panna Cotta Cafe with Cointreau chocolate sauce or a sun-dried cranberry and pear tart. The atmosphere is elegant, as gentle Victorian wallpaper designs ghost across pale yellow walls. The lighting is dim, brightened by candles and white linen tablecloths.

Walter's Cafe, 15 Exchange Street, 871-9258, is another good choice. Chef Jack Neal makes a great Crazy Chicken, sauteed with prosciutto, scallions, sweet peas and garlic in a red-wine cream sauce and served over angel hair pasta. Try the mocha truffle torte or white chocolate cashew cheesecake for desert. This is a sophisticated little place with an open kitchen, lots of wood and brick and a faux painting on the back wall with peas worked into the filigree design. We liked this place the minute we walked in the door.

Our personal favorite is **Uncle Billy's**, 69 Newbury Street, 871-5631, so forgive us while we rattle on about it. This was once a diner in South Portland with a pig motif, a great jukebox and a smoker behind the building. Oh yes, and it had the best barbecue we'd ever eaten in Maine — or anywhere else for that matter. Then it moved uptown, to Forest Avenue. Now it's at the foot of Munjoy Hill. Go for lunch or dinner. Order ribs, jambalaya or any entree on the menu; we think you'll be happy regardless. Then order Death by Chocolate for dessert and die happy.

Accommodations

Staying in Portland? We have a couple suggestions for you to check out. First, **The Pomegranate Inn**, 49 Neal Street, 772-1006, is a small, remarkable bed and breakfast in the middle of the city's West End. We don't know exactly how many magazines have commented on its striking interior, but we've seen quite a few. The walls were hand-painted by local artists in repeating patterns of flowers or urns — they look wallpapered only better. Antiques fill the eight rooms, each of which has a private bath. The breakfasts of cheese puffs, French toast and quiches are highly praised.

We don't usually recommend chain hotels because their strong suits are consistency and predictability; you pretty much know what you're getting. However, we're making an exception with the **Holiday Inn by the Bay**, 88 Spring Street, 775-2311, because of its location. You'll find a fitness center, large indoor pool, sauna and 239 standard rooms, much like you'd find at almost any Holiday Inn. But what you don't expect are the fabulous views from rooms on the upper floors, especially of the harbor.

Yarmouth, Nova Scotia

Incorporated in 1890, Yarmouth is a small fishing village with a population of nearly 8,000. Half the appeal of a trip here is the ferry ride, especially on a sunny summer day. We made the trip on the old ferry, which took six hours, but a new high-speed ferry launched in spring 1998 cuts that in half. In the past it was best to stay overnight, but with new, shorter travel times, this can be a daytrip after all. In any case, the evening ferry back to Maine is glorious. The boat travels in velvety darkness, broken only by the intermittent flash from a lighthouse and a scattering of lights in the distance as you approach Bar Harbor. The sea smells wonderful, and you see stars you haven't seen before.

Getting There

A company called Marine Atlantic ran the 412-foot *Bluenose* ferry between Bar Harbor and Yarmouth for years, but the ferry was sold recently and the Canadian-based Bay Ferries Ltd. is launching a new 300-foot, high-speed ferry. Instead of being powered by propellers, it has four water jets that enable it to cut through waves, reaching speeds of up to 60 mph on open water.

A one-way trip now takes 2½ hours, which means you can make a round trip in a day, depending on the schedule. Off-season (May 28 through June 15 and October 4 through October 30) the ferry leaves Bar Harbor at 10 AM and returns in the afternoon, leaving Yarmouth at 3 PM AST. That schedule makes for an impossibly tight daytrip, but day-cruise fares are available: $34.95 for adults and teens, $29.95 for seniors, $14.95 for children and $179 for a car with two passengers. One-way fares are $27.25 for adults and teens, $24.50 for seniors 65 and older, $13.75 for children ages 5 through 12 and $55 for vehicles.

In high season (June 16 through October 3) the ferry leaves Bar Harbor at 8 AM and 3 PM; it leaves Yarmouth at 12:30 and 7:30 PM. Day-cruise fares are $44.95 for adults and teens, $39.95 for seniors, $19.95 for children and $199 for a car with two passengers. One-way fares are $45 for adults and teens, $40 for seniors 65 and older, $20 for children ages 5 through 12 and $55 for vehicles.

A $3 U.S. Custom tax is added to the fare for each person traveling, including children of any age. A $25 charge is required to make reservations, billed to your credit card; all but $5 of that is refundable. Call (888) 249-7245 for the latest on schedules, and to make reservations.

The ferry departs from the Bar Harbor International Ferry Terminal, at the only flashing yellow light on Maine Highway 3 in Bar Harbor. Follow the signs, and plan to arrive at the ferry at least an hour ahead of time. There's an abundance of tourist information at the terminal, so make sure you look around and snag what looks interesting; you can read it on the boat.

There's plenty of parking if you want to leave your car behind in Bar Harbor. Many people we traveled with did not take their cars, and they were happy sitting on deck in the sun on the way over and walking around town once they arrived. A number of us bought a package deal that included meals and lodging at a motel near the ferry terminal. This worked out well; it was convenient and gave us lots of time to explore Yarmouth.

Once on the boat, we're told you'll find two passenger decks, four lounges, a cafeteria, a duty-free souvenir shop and a sun deck. The old ferry had a gambling casino on board; the new one retains the arcade, gaming tables and slot machines.

As we've said, we haven't traveled on the new ferry, but here are some tips that may smooth your way. As we boarded the old ferry, we watched the more experienced travelers make a beeline for two choice spots. Some headed to the sun deck, grabbed deck chairs and positioned themselves for the best views. Others gravitated to any seating area where a person might spread out and actually lie down. The wisdom of this move became evident as half the passengers on the boat seemed to fall asleep by mid-morning. Those who'd scouted comfortable berths were able to stretch out.

If you're traveling with kids, or even if you aren't, you might want to pack a small bag with a light blanket, books, cards, a game or two and some snacks. The families who did this seemed to travel with the least fuss and muss.

Reservations are suggested for your return trip as well, and you must be present for loading an hour early. A final reminder: You'll go through Canadian customs on the way over and U.S. customs on the way back. You'll be asked whether you're carrying alcohol, tobacco or firearms, and you'll be asked to declare your purchases.

Attractions

Arriving in Nova Scotia, you'll feel the locals are delighted you've arrived. A big banner hung across the street in front of the ferry terminal welcomes you. Right next to the terminal, your first stop should be the

Nova Scotia Visitor Information Center, 228 Main Street, (902) 742-6639. *Abbondanza!* This modern architectural marvel is a gold mine of information, brochures, advice and friendly smiles.

Second stop: the **Yarmouth County Museum**, 22 Collins Street, (902) 742-5539. It's housed in an 1893 granite building that was once the Congregational Tabernacle. Inside you'll find one of the largest collection of ship paintings in Canada as well as wonderful room tableaus, displays and a huge lighthouse lens. The place seems to be the repository of the community's treasures. Evidence of local participation and pride abounds.

FYI

Unless otherwise noted, the area code for all phone numbers listed in this guide is 207.

The **Firefighters Museum of Nova Scotia**, 451 Main Street, (902) 742-5525, is another must-visit. There are fire wagons from all time periods, including an 1880 Silsby Steam Pumper. Small children are allowed on a 1935 fire engine, but only with parent or teacher supervision. The two floors of displays captured our attention for more than an hour. While the items themselves were interesting, we were most impressed by documentation of local firefighters battling local fires.

Folks we met on the ferry raved about a tour of the area given by the **Rodd Colony Harbour Inn** (see the subsequent "Accommodations" section). It leaves at 11 each morning; tickets are $10 plus tax (Canadian), and they go on sale at 4:30 PM the previous day. Admission is not restricted to guests, but they are given first priority. We discovered some of the same sights as we drove around, but if time is limited and you didn't bring a car, take the tour.

Some of our happiest discoveries were the historic houses in the area beyond Main Street. The **Yarmouth County Tourist Association**, (902) 742-5355, has a brochure that describes a walking tour of the town, and it highlights some properties we discovered plus many more. For just a taste of what's out there, walk straight up Forest Street, take a right on Highland, a right on William and a right again on Fore Street. It's a nice stroll, and the houses are impressive. Most are private residences,

of course, but you can enjoy the exteriors. We spotted a number of architectural styles: English cottage, Georgian and Second Empire. Our favorite was at 57 William Street. Called Yarmouth's finest example of the Gothic Revival style, it had a sharp peaked roof and pointed-arch openings above the doors and windows.

If you did bring your car, drive out to the **Yarmouth Light**, (902) 742-1433, in Cape Forchu. First lit in 1840, it's the tall, slender lighthouse with red and white vertical stripes you see from the ferry as you approach Yarmouth Harbor. To get there, drive north on Main Street and take a left at the horse fountain. (Trust us, you can't miss it.) Drive past the hospital and take another left on Grove Road, then follow the signs. The drive takes you through a range of neighborhoods and ends at the rocky point where you'll see the light. Bring a picnic; we were sorry we didn't.

Shopping

The shopping area of Yarmouth is basically either side of Main Street. Just walk up Forest Street from the ferry terminal, turn left on Main Street and start nosing around. This is a real working town with a healthy year-round economy, so while there are some tourist shops, there aren't as many as you might find in, say, Bar Harbor.

Uptown Antiques, 300 Main Street, is on the second floor. It has an interesting array of old pieces and also offers an appraisal service.

We couldn't resist **The Yarmouth Wool Shoppe Limited**, 352 Main Street, with its incredible selection of Scottish woolens. You'll find tartans, tams and throws plus fisherman sweaters, Viyella shirts, Burberry coats and Hudson Bay blankets. If full price is too rich for your blood, go upstairs, where seconds are sold at discounts.

For cards, gifts and knickknacks, try **R.H. Davis & Co. Ltd.**, 361 Main Street. It has a number of Nova Scotia-made items. Upstairs is **Samuel B's**, a year-round Christmas store.

Photo: Bangor Daily News

Chesuncook Village, a small village on the west branch of the Penobscot River, offers sporting camps for freshwater fishing.

Restaurants

Dinner and breakfast at **The Colony Restaurant** in the Rodd Colony Harbour Inn (see the subsequent "Accommodations" section) were part of our package deal with the ferry ride, and we weren't disappointed. The halibut at dinner was fresh and perfectly cooked, and breakfast was great, especially the sausage and home fries. Local patronage is often the best recommendation for a restaurant, and we weren't surprised to see local fishermen come in for breakfast and take over one of the long tables in the middle of the room.

For lunch, we found **Joshua's Fine Coffee and Ice Cream Ltd.**, 95 Water Street, (902) 742-6566, at the corner of Jenkins and Water streets on the waterfront. The lunch counter looked adequate, with the focus on coffee and sweets, but it proved to be better than that. On a whim, we ordered a local favorite called "rappie pie," and it knocked our socks off. The lush, comforting combination of potato and chicken sent us scouring the town for a recipe.

Accommodations

Since few people seem to bring cars to Yarmouth, we limit our selection of lodgings to those closest to the ferry terminal. The **Rodd Colony Harbour Inn**, 6 Forest Street, (902) 742-9194, is across from the ferry and is a good choice. You'll find 65 clean, fresh rooms — some have views of the dock — and a concierge who can't seem to do enough for guests. It's a level of attention that's as refreshing as it is rare.

You might also try **Murray Manor**, 225 Main Street, (902) 742-9625, a bed and breakfast just a block or two from the ferry on Main Street. Built in the early 1800s, the house looks like an English cottage, with Gothic-style windows on the first floor. Owners George and Joan Semple let three rooms, and guests are treated to a full breakfast. Afternoon tea is available by reservation.

Campobello Area

While the point of this trip is to see the Roosevelt Campobello International Park and Nature Area, in New Brunswick, Canada, the drive to get there takes you through what some say is the real Maine. In practical terms, that means a Maine that's not entirely preoccupied catering to visitors. That also means a struggling economy, few gas stations, few stores, few ostensible tourist attractions, few gourmet restaurants and few luxury accommodations. It also means relatively low prices, light traffic, open roads, beautiful bays and inlets and wide-open blueberry fields that turn shades of scarlet in the fall. That, we feel, should attract any tourist worth their salt. And, of course, Campobello Island is lovely.

Getting There

From anywhere along the Mid-Coast, just get on U.S. Highway 1 and drive north to Whiting. Turn right onto Maine Highway 189 and continue until you reach Canadian customs in Lubec. Cross the bridge to Campobello Island and follow the signs.

Attractions

The 2,800-acre **Roosevelt Campobello International Park**, (506) 752-2922, is the main draw on Campobello Island. The 34-room Roosevelt cottage is fascinating, but there are also numerous drives and walks open to the public, and they are well mapped in the park's brochure. Look for **Liberty Point**, where there are observation decks, lovely views and occasional whale sightings. **Friar's Head** is a great place for a picnic. It has fields and trails as well as picnic tables, grills, a hand-pump well and an outdoor toilet. But, wait, we're getting ahead of ourselves.

Start at the **Edmund S. Muskie Visitor Centre** for the film *Beloved Island*, which describes the island and its hold on President

---

INSIDERS' TIP

A word of advice: Summer really is the best time to take the ferry from Bar Harbor to Yarmouth, Nova Scotia. The seas get rougher in the fall, and it's too cold to enjoy the open decks.

Roosevelt and his family. From there, it's a short walk past a massive hedge of beach roses to the main cottage. Franklin's parents, James and Sara Delano, first owned a cottage to the north of the present Roosevelt cottage, where the family spent its summers as Franklin grew up. Then in 1910, Sara bought the Roosevelt cottage, which she later gave to Franklin and Eleanor. For years the Roosevelts spent July, August and part of September hiking, sailing and picnicking there. F.D.R. contracted polio during a trip to the island in 1921, and while his later visits were few and far between, his wife and children continued the tradition for many years.

The house itself speaks volumes. Yes, it's huge, but the furnishings, either originals or reproductions, are notably informal: plain, ruffled sheers on the windows; traditional green shades; lots of wicker; and lots of chintz. Not every room is wallpapered, and some floors are bare but for a rag rug next to the bed. These furnishings, while harmonious and tasteful, leave the wonderful impression that although the Roosevelts were well-to-do, they were also unpretentious, coming here for the fun of romping outdoors and being together.

It's unlikely the family had much to do in the kitchen, but the period furnishings and arrangements there are worth a good look.

As we mentioned earlier, the vast grounds are open to visitors as well. You could spend days exploring, and the wildlife alone would make it worthwhile. The last time we visited, we walked the broad back lawn that rolls down to the water and saw two bald eagles fly off over the trees.

The park opens the Saturday before Memorial Day and closes 20 weeks later on Columbus Day. It's open 9 AM to 5 PM (EST), seven days a week, and there's no admission fee. The last tour of the cottage is at 4:45 PM (EST) each day.

On the way back to the Mid-Coast, you might want to stop at **Quoddy Head State Park** in **Lubec**. Follow the signs off Maine 189. You'll find a handsome little fireplug of a lighthouse with broad red and white horizontal stripes that marks the easternmost tip of the United States. Visitors can drive to a parking lot adjacent to a picnic area, with benches, a toilet and fabulous views. A 2-mile hiking trail

offers a taste of all that Maine's coastal landscape has to offer: pebbly beaches, high cliffs and fields with wild irises.

The park is open May 15 through October 15. Day-use fees are $1 per person 12 and older, 50¢ for kids ages 5 through 11; kids younger than 5 and seniors older than 65 get in free.

Shopping

Your best bet for any shopping is in the town of **Machias**, on the way back from Campobello (so you know you have time!). One of the University of Maine's campuses is here, and the downtown area seems on the upswing. Two large brick buildings in the center of town were recently renovated as part of Machias Savings Bank. They seem to anchor the area and announce an intention to care for the town's assets. (Within a two- or three-block area are some beautiful churches, and the Washington County Courthouse is handsome . . . we know, we know, get to the shopping!)

Try **The Sow's Ear**, 7 Water Street, Machias, 255-4066, for jewelry, clothing, gifts, toys, books, cards and kitchen items. The selection is varied and imaginative. We don't know who does the buying, but they excel in finding stylish, clever items.

For a real taste of Maine, go to the **Downeast 5&10**, Main Street, 255-8850. This isn't a gift boutique; it's a time machine. This two-story Ben Franklin is reminiscent of the old general stores, with everything a person might need for everyday life, from household goods to sewing supplies to underwear.

Restaurants

Eastport is about an hour's drive from Lubec, but you might try the **Waco Diner**, on Bank Square in Eastport, 853-4046, for lunch or dinner. It's a small, funky old place, but you'll find standard diner fare done right; it's cheap too. Look for deep-fried seafood, meat loaf, roast beef and comfort-food desserts such as bread pudding, mince squares and cheesecake. **Uncle Kippy's**, U.S. Highway 1, Lubec, 733-2400, is highly recommended — an ordinary-looking place, but inexpensive and an

Fly fishermen are shrouded by fog on an early morning outing in Maine.

obvious favorite with locals. The menu is large and varied, but seafood is the local specialty. Try the scallop or shrimp rolls. You might want to wait for Helen's (see subsequent information) for pie, but **Grandma's Pantry**, a mile east of Maine Highway 191 on U.S. Highway 1 in East Machias, 259-3656, caught our eye, and it might catch yours. One member of our group had a sweet tooth and stocked up on snacks, but meals are available as well. The maple nut fudge drew rave reviews.

For dinner, consider **Micmac Farm Restaurant**, off Maine 92 in **Machiasport**, 255-3008. And don't be put off by the dirt road. This country inn dining room has been called one of the best in the state. Built in the late 1700s, its low beams and candle-lit tables add atmosphere to the splendid fare. For $16 to $18 you get a four-course dinner with entrees such as filet mignon with bordelaise sauce and fillet of sole stuffed with shrimp and crabmeat.

We've been to **Helen's Restaurant**, 32 Main Street, Machias, 255-8423, only in the fall. We hear it can be overrun by bus tours in the summer, but who cares? Helen's is legendary for pies. The pumpkin wouldn't have been our first choice, but it will be the next time we go. Spectacular! Crisp, flaky crust we'd swear was made with lard, and spicy, sweet filling that took an old standard to a new level. We arrived in late afternoon to find the booths filled with senior citizens having early dinners. That's a very good sign. The menu includes steak, pot roast and excellent haddock, each served with a potato, a choice of two vegetables and homemade dinner rolls.

Accommodations

The **Owen House**, Welshpool, Campobello, New Brunswick, (506) 752-2977, run by Joyce Morrell, has a shining reputation. Built in the 1835, it's near the Welshpool dock on a point that overlooks Passamaquoddy Bay. Almost all the rooms have views of the water. Ms. Morrel lets nine rooms from Memorial Day to Columbus Day. Choose from double-occupancy rooms with private or shared baths. Each morning, guests are treated to a full breakfast including items such as fruit juice, coffee, blueberry pancakes and sausage, or eggs, bacon and muffins.

Ah, and then there's **Tootsie's**, in Jonesport, (207) 497-5414. **Jonesport** might be a daytrip in itself, but this place is one of our favorites. Not because it's fancy or luxurious. It isn't. We like it because it feels real. None of the smoke and mirrors and kitsch so common to the tourist trade. Charlotte Beal and her lobsterman husband raised a handful of children in this house. Now the children have grown up, become or married lobstermen, and she's running the family home as a bed and breakfast. It's sparkling clean, and we slept happily under a sloping roof, with that peaceful feeling you have when you sleep at your grandmother's. Mrs. Beal rents three rooms: one with two double beds, one with one double bed and one with two twin beds. Jonesport is a coastal town, and you can see the water from all three rooms. Breakfast includes your choice of bacon and eggs, pancakes and sausage or French toast and sausage, served with juice and coffee.

Perhaps Maine's greatest asset is that time seems to move more slowly here — people do too. This has served to preserve architectural integrity and historic interiors.

Architecture

This chapter has one modest aim: to celebrate the architectural gems scattered throughout Maine's Mid-Coast region.

We've tried not to get bogged down by terms of art — the pediments and pilasters of professionals in the field. Rather, we've sketched some time frames and illustrated them with strong examples that can be seen from a car or on foot.

Perhaps Maine's greatest asset is that time seems to move more slowly here — people do too. This has served to preserve architectural integrity and historic interiors. Even today, people are able to find houses that have been relatively untouched since the early part of this century. We went to a yard sale at a house in Lincolnville and were staggered by the array of 1880s farm implements stored in the barn. The house had been a summer home, left vacant since the 1940s and lived in before that for just a few weeks at a time during the summer by a maiden aunt. She lived lightly, leaving the detritus of everyday life from decades before her arrival, and we saw much of it at that yard sale. The new owner was moving just as lightly in his renovation, rebuilding what had decayed as faithfully as he could to the original design.

Friends who own an early 1800s house in Friendship can't seem to bring themselves to tear down the ancient landscape wallpaper in the dining room. They too have left the house's floor plan intact, working around old plaster walls and scarred wide pine floorboards.

Stepping into these old homes, particularly ones that have not been made into museums, can make the hair on the back of your neck stand up; you feel the aura of all the families that lived, loved, laughed and labored there. While right angles are hard to find, you see evidence of a respect for harmony, precision and balance that outstrips the easy regularity of tract homes.

That holds true for the exterior architecture as well. As historians describe architectural styles, they focus on the physical expression in shape and form, but it's worth remembering that people planned and built those buildings, and that architectural styles grew out of their highest ideals. That means as you drive down U.S. Highway 1, you see something about the thinking of the people who once lived here. It's fascinating! Greek Revival, for instance, was a celebration of the nation's democratic heritage.

Now, what will you see?

First let's focus on the big differentiators: shape and size. The early farmhouses are described as Cape Cod-style houses, or capes. These are single-story structures with a central entrance and windows on either side. The roof slants forward over the facade. Older houses have central chimneys, but in some cases you'll see chimneys rising from either end of the house as well. The windows have many panes — nine over six is common; and look for windows (called lights) around the door. Side lights and fan lights over the entrance can be a cape's most elegant feature. Once you've nailed down the cape style, you can start detecting details that might help you get a sense of a house's age. Our favorite capes are wide and squat, with low roofs. They look so broad and capable, so sheltering and strong.

Start looking as you drive. Look for ornamentation around entrances. Look at windows — how big they are, how many panes they have, whether the glass has rippled with age. Notice roof shapes and whether the shingles are made of asphalt, cedar shakes or elegant gray-blue slate. Soon you'll notice the narrower clapboards of older houses — called "three inches to the weather" — and the differing proportions. You'll feel as if you're looking back in time. (Be sure to see our Attractions chapter for additional perspectives on many of the places we discuss here.)

Architectural Styles

Design ideas are dynamic, constantly in motion, but we freeze-frame them for the purposes of analysis. The result is that the definition of architectural styles is approximate at best. We've used the parameters set forth in *Maine Forms of American Architecture*, a collection of authoritative essays on the subject, edited by Deborah Thompson. The examples — from the Colonial period to the turn of the century — noted subsequently are open to the public. If hours and admission charges are not listed here, check our Attractions chapter for details.

Of course, architecture in Maine didn't stop at the turn of the century, even though we end our inspection at that era. But much of what's been built since then bears styles frequently seen in other areas of the country. Maine's claim to fame is that buildings of earlier vintages still stand and can be enjoyed.

FYI

Unless otherwise noted, the area code for all phone numbers listed in this guide is 207.

Colonial Style
1725 to 1790

The elements of later styles are present in buildings of this era, but their execution is always understated. Arches are wide and rounded; pilasters are often Roman Doric; roofs are gambrel, gable or hipped. The overall effect is plain, even spare, but it has great dignity.

The German Lutheran Church
Maine Hwy. 32, Waldoboro • 832-5100

First built in 1772, then moved and reconstructed in 1795, The German Lutheran Church (a.k.a. Old German Church) sits amid a fascinating cemetery, where a tombstone attests to the fact that German settlers were lured to the region by descriptions of a "prosperous city" but found "nothing but wilderness." While the clapboards are narrow, and the style unadorned, almost severe, the real indicator of age here is the proportions. Look carefully, and your eye, trained by modern building standards, will tell you there's something slightly

"off" here, something almost primitive. That's the late 1700s calling to you.

John Perkins House
Wilson Museum, Perkins St., Castine
• 326-8545

The John Perkins House at the Wilson Museum is the oldest house in town and has been restored with furnishings in the period style. As with the German Lutheran Church (see previous entry), the age indicators here are the shingled roof, the clapboards and the overall proportions.

The Conway House
Conway Rd., off U.S. Hwy. 1, Camden
• 236-2257

This is an excellent example of the Cape Cod-style home so favored from 1750 to 1850. Believed to have been built in the 1770s, it's the centerpiece of the Old Conway House Complex.

Federal Style
1790 to 1825

This period brings slightly more ornamentation but an abiding interest in balance, proportion and symmetry. Look for columns and arches, or the imitation of them.

Federal-style houses are usually large, rectangular buildings of two or three stories, with two to five chimneys and hipped or gabled roofs. Smaller capes were built during this period, and they show its influence in a fine sense of symmetry ornamented by a more detailed front entrance.

Montpelier – Gen. Henry
Knox Museum
U.S. Hwy. 1 and Maine Hwy. 131,
Thomaston • 354-8062

This faithful reproduction of a 30-room mansion built by Maj. Gen. Henry Knox in the 1790s is an over-the-top example of the Federal style, with it's rectangular shape and symetrical ornamentation.

Knox was a Revolutionary War hero and President Washington's Secretary of War. An

Photo: Bangor Daily News

Stephen King's home on West Broadway in Bangor is surrounded by a fence adorned with bat wings on the front gate, making it one of the most photographed homes in the city.

advantageous marriage gave him the wherewithal for what was at the time the largest home in Maine and one of the largest in New England. Its design was inspired by the famous Charles Bulfinch (1763-1844), architect of the U.S. Capitol. Montpelier is massive, with high ceilings, tall windows and a semi-flying staircase. Inside is a fascinating collection of Colonial- and Federal-period furnishings, some of which were in the original mansion.

Commentators say this massive house is in no way characteristic of the time in which it was built, but it paints in bold strokes some of the stylistic devices of the late 18th century.

Jonathan Fisher Memorial
Main St. (Maine Hwy. 15), Blue Hill
• 374-2161

Harvard-educated Rev. Jonathan Fisher built this two-story, four-room house in 1814,

and it still contains his furniture, paintings, books and journals. Fisher was the first settled parson in the area.

The First Church (United Church of Christ)
104 Church St., Belfast • 338-2282

This magnificent structure was designed by Samuel French and completed in 1818. It's a classic example of the Federal style: a massive two-story, white clapboard building crowned by a striking tower, with clock faces on each side, a belfry, dome, spire and weather vane. The congregation recently repaired that tower and has been working on other repair projects.

The Colonel Black House
Maine Hwy. 172, Ellsworth • 667-8671

The Colonel Black house was built between 1824 and 1827, at the end of the Federal era. Note the balance, the symmetry, the hipped roof and the railing around it. Red brick with white trim, the central part of the house has two stories flanked by one-story wings on either side. A porch with five handsome columns graces the front of the house. The railing, or balustrade, above the porch matches that on the two wings, but a different pattern crowns the house, almost hiding the low, almost flat, hipped roof. Four tall brick chimneys rise like sentinels in perfect symmetry, and their height is repeated in the first floor windows, which appear to extend from floor to ceiling. Inside, the house has an elliptical flying staircase that must have been the pride of its era.

Greek Revival 1835 to 1850

This style incorporates columns, porticos and pediments from Greek temples, and in practice, it was fairly easy to do. "All a country carpenter-builder needed to produce an up-to-date look was to replace his more delicate federal trim with heavier Greek Revival details," writes Denys Peter Myers in his essay on the subject in *Maine Forms of American Architecture*.

The number of examples of Greek Revival architecture in Maine is staggering. Even tiny capes were built to look as if they had Greek columns supporting their corners.

Farnsworth Homestead
19 Elm St., Rockland • 596-6457
Listed on the National Register of Historic Places, the house is thought to have been built by a Rockland firm in about 1850. You can't miss the heavy imitation-Greek columns, called entablatures, on the exterior.

Inside, it has it's original fittings and period furnishings, so you can see exactly what life was like in 1871.

Winterport Union Meetinghouse
U.S. Hwy. 1A, Winterport • no phone
It's said that there's some Gothic influence in the Winterport Union Meetinghouse, seen perhaps in the peaked arches. Calvin A. Ryder (1810-1890) was the contracting builder on that structure, which was first built as a church and is now used as a community hall. Ryder designed other structures in Belfast and later set up practice in Massachusetts.

The First Congregational Church
Church St., Ellsworth • 667-8321
The style here is straight, solid Greek Revival, and when you see its columns and the temple-like triangular gable (called a pediment) above it, the name "Greek Revival" suddenly makes sense. Its soaring clock tower, cupola and spire give it a pristine elegance. Built in 1847 by noted architect Thomas Lord, this church is said to be the most photographed in New England.

The Thomas A. Hill House
159 Union St., Bangor • 942-5776
The Thomas A Hill House is now the headquarters and museum of the Bangor Historical Society. Designed in 1834 by the renowned Richard Upjohn, it contains period furnishings. The main block of the house is brick, surrounded on three sides by a flat-roofed porch supported by fluted Ionic columns.

The Isaac Farrar House
17 Second St., Bangor • 941-2808
The Isaac Farrar House was designed in 1833 by Richard Upjohn but not finished until

---

INSIDERS' TIP

Folks at The Whitehall Inn, in Camden, still celebrate the warm evening in August 1912 when the young poet Edna St. Vincent Millay first recited *Renascence* to guests. It was to become her most famous work.

Evolution of the Cottage on Mount Desert Island

When artist Thomas Cole returned from his 1844 summer visit to Mount Desert Island with paintings of the majestic mountains plummeting to the ocean, he amazed his fellow artists. More artists, including Frederick Church and Fitz Hugh Lane arrived, creating more paintings of the glories of the island. They were like pied pipers carrying along the movers, thinkers and dreamers of the day who came seeking a more natural life. Known as "rusticators," these city folk, seeking a wilderness experience, boarded with local farmers or set up rough cabins.

Close-up

More and more rusticators of less and less rustic ilk came to the island. It wasn't long before some enterprising folk put up hotels. By 1880, less than 40 years after the first artist came to the unspoiled lands of Mount Desert Island, a visitor could choose from accommodations at 30 hotels.

And then a typhoid epidemic struck. Instead of staying in hotels, which were replete with guests of uncertain health, wealthy summer visitors — the Astors, Carnegies, Fords, Morgans, Rockefellers and Vanderbilts — built homes. In line with the rusticator ethic, these homes featured wood and stone, materials from the land nearby. The

— continued on next page

Photo: Bangor Daily News

Mount Desert Island's summer "cottages" have evolved into majestic structures that are anything but most folks' idea of a vacation house.

cottages, however, were anything but primitive. Many had upward of 30 rooms, yet they exuded earthiness — Martha Stewart does rustic, if you will. (And she does — she recently moved into a granite "cottage" in Seal Harbor.) Remember, of course, that the members of the social register were building in Maine not only to keep up with the Vanderbilts, but also to partake in the romance of the back-to-nature movement that prevailed at the time.

Why these homes were called cottages, however, is uncertain. Folk derivations attribute the name to that era's romance with nature — or it just might be classic Yankee understatement. But many summer hotels also had cottages built on their grounds to handle overflow crowds. So it could be simply that the name stuck: A summer home remained a cottage. The architecture frequently followed the bungalow style that was gaining popularity. Exterior shingles and large overhanging roofs that acted as one large shingle, protecting the building beneath it, characterized the popular regional version of the bungalow.

Bar Harbor soon rivaled Newport, Rhode Island, as the queen of summer resorts. Parties of every kind were *de rigueur* from the Gay Nineties to the Roaring '20s, and these soirees left stories that still flood the island with gossip.

Disaster struck in 1947 when a fire swept across the island, burning for three weeks and destroying a good portion of the cottages and hotels, not to mention numerous residences. The gilded era melted. But the era of country inns and bed and breakfast establishments serving oceanfront lovers and visitors to Acadia National Park was on the horizon.

Today, many of the inns open to visitors were once the cottages closed to all but the giants of high society.

1845. Renovations in the late 1890s altered the appearance of the house, but it did not change the impressive circular library finished in Santo Domingan mahogany. The carpenter on the project was Joseph Bigelow, also known for building the imposing Governor Abner Coburn House in 1849 in his home town of Skowhegan. The Farrar House is on the National Register of Historic Places and owned by the YWCA next door, which opens it to the public free of charge on Thursday afternoons from June to mid-September. The times change from year to year, so call ahead. Often referred to around town as the Farrar Mansion, this handsome structure may be reserved for private functions.

James P. White House
Church and High Sts., Belfast
• private listing

The James P. White House is another prime example of the Greek Revival style. It's a privately owned house on a triangle of land bordered by Church and High streets. De-

signed by Calvin Ryder and built in 1840, it is massive, frosted with Greek elements — Doric porches and Ionic columns — and crowned with a cupola. Myers calls this one of the nation's irreplaceable assets.

Belfast National Bank Building
Custom House Sq., Belfast • no phone

We mentioned earlier that styles other than Greek Revival grew up between 1835 and 1850. While you're in Belfast, drive past the old Belfast National Bank building at Custom House Square, and see how the delicate Victorian trim, which we're so used to see crafted in wood on clapboard houses, is translated into brick and stone.

Turn-of-the-century
1880 to 1920

In this era, Maine became a vacation destination, and no one made more of an impact than John Calvin Stevens, with his shingle-style cottages (see this chapter's related Close-up). Look for sloping shingled roofs that seem to shelter the whole house but are interrupted by second-floor windows and balconies that open to the outdoors and let in light. Exterior walls were shingled as well, and stone terraces were common. Many of these houses are huge, but the overall effect is casual and seems to suit the natural surroundings.

The Standpipe
Thomas Hill, off Ohio St., Bangor
• 947-4516

While the best examples of turn-of-the-century architecture in the Mid-Coast area are private homes in Camden and on Mount Desert Island, the Bangor Standpipe (see Attractions), done in that style, allows closer examination. This round, 110-foot-tall water tower with observation deck and shingled sides is a city landmark. Designed by Ashley B. Tower of Holyoke, Massachusetts, the circular structure was built in 1897. It's operated by the Bangor Water District and is open to the public four times a year. The dates and times are announced in radio and newspaper ads.

Areas to Explore

Having pointed out particular examples of the architectural styles, we'd like to suggest some areas for you to explore. All are privately owned houses or commercial properties.

First, drive through the center of Thomaston on U.S. Highway 1 and marvel at its splendid sea captains houses in the Federal and Greek Revival styles.

Continue on U.S. 1 through Rockland, where Main Street has been recorded in the National Register of Historic Places. You'll see examples of Italianate, Mansard, Greek Revival and Colonial Revival styles.

North of the center of Camden, but also on U.S. 1, you'll find more sea captains houses — those imposing two-story, two-chimney mansions. These have been called Colonial Revival, but all we see are Greek Revival elements. The Whitehall Inn, for instance, has a wraparound porch supported by columns in the Ionic style.

A part of Searsport's main business block was built around 1840, and dozens of sea captains homes dot either side of U.S. 1. Many of them have been turned into bed and breakfast inns.

Winterport, on U.S. Highway 1 after it turns north toward Bangor, also boasts an abundance of 18th-century ship captains' houses. And if you stay on U.S. 1 and turn down Maine Highway 175 to Maine 166, you'll find Castine, with a proud assembly of white clapboard Federal houses, all in mint condition. Continuing on U.S. 1 will take you to a block of three-story buildings in Ellsworth that was built in 1845.

If this chapter has piqued your interest, you might take one of the architectural tours of Rockland and Bangor. Contact School Superintendent Don Kanicki, of Rockland Share the Pride, at his office, 596-6620; or the Bangor Historical Society, 942-5766.

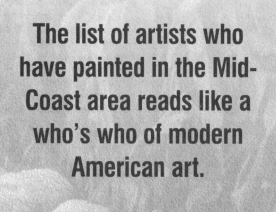

The list of artists who have painted in the Mid-Coast area reads like a who's who of modern American art.

The Arts

That Maine long has been an inspiration to artists is no secret. The paintings Thomas Cole brought back to Boston from Mount Desert Island in the 1840s were so idyllic to cityfolk hungering for a taste of the wild that an entire tourism industry sprang up to house, feed and entertain rusticators who had come for the liberating experience of communing with nature. Art and tourism have been walking hand-in-hand ever since.

The list of artists who have painted in the Mid-Coast area reads like a who's who of modern American art: from the painters of the 1840s and '50s, such as Cole, Frederic Church and Fitz Hugh Lane, to those of the early 20th century, such as George Bellows, Marsden Hartley, Edward Hopper, John Marin and Fairfield Porter, to artists known nationally today, such as Richard Estes, Robert Indiana, Alex Katz, Alan Magee, Neil Welliver and Andrew Wyeth.

Maine's Mid-Coast and Downeast regions long have been havens for musicians as well. The summer music school at Kneisel Hall lured many, while the contemplative opportunities of Zen brought others (led by a Zen-practicing pianist). One amazing result of this influx: A Maine amateur opera group was once invited to tour the Soviet Union. Other examples abound. For instance, at last count the tiny town of Brooksville had three homes with double grand pianos. And conductors from around the world come to the Monteux School, in Hancock, to hone the skills of their trade.

Connections forged beneath Maine's tall spruce are not forgotten. Werner Torkanowsky trained under the renowned Pierre Monteux, retired to Hancock and for 11 years transformed the Bangor Symphony Orchestra into a community orchestra with a professional reputation. And a former Kneisel Hall student has led the Bar Harbor Music Festival (see subsequent entry) for more than 30 years.

Today, the region's wealth of musical of-ferings for all ages is astounding — choral groups, the Bagaduce Music Library, schools and at least five steel-drum ensembles, one of which encompasses professionals and amateurs ages 10 to 72.

Many of the old institutions remain as well: Waldoboro, Rockport, Camden, Belfast, Stonington and Ellsworth each have distinctive, historic performance spaces — many of them vintage opera houses, some of them restored. On their stages you might see musicians, actors or a smattering of dance groups.

This chapter has a summer focus; expect some places to be closed in winter. Galleries are free unless otherwise noted; we'll tell you how much other events cost.

Waldoboro to Stockton Springs

Art Galleries

Gallery House
U.S. Hwy. 1, Nobleboro • 563-8598

Perched on a hill, barely 2 miles south of Waldoboro via U.S. Highway 1, stands the Holly Hill empire, a nursery, gift shop and gallery. Gallery House, run by Marcia Stewart, is a well-lighted, cheerful place to see some very good art from Maine. Stewart focuses on interesting innovators and delightful folk artists. While most her artists are from Maine, a choice few come from Europe and Canada. Look for work by engaging abstractionists Natasha Mayers and Alice Spencer; the soulful, dream-like works of Ann Gresinger; landscapes by Elena Jahn; and playful "spiritscapes" by Heidi Daub. And then there's the ever-popular, glorious work of Eric Hopkins, who paints soaring aerial images of the offshore islands. Gallery House is open year round.

Eliza Sweet Gallery
Maine Hwy. 32, Waldoboro • 832-4969

The sculpture gardens at this gallery, within a bed and breakfast inn of the same name (see our Accommodations chapter), weave foliage and sculpture as if the garden were playing hide-and-seek with the art; the foliage actually becomes part of the art. The galleries are more straightforward, exhibiting fine local, abstract art in a professional setting. A recent beauty of an exhibit was the alter-like installations by Meg Brown Payson. The gallery is open from June through October.

The Drawing Room
Wiley's Corner, Maine Hwy. 131 S., just north of Maine Hwy. 73, St. George • 372-6242

Artist Barbara Anderson has a gallery in two rooms of her house, on one of the major routes to Port Clyde. Her focus is on talented local artists. Hours are limited, so call ahead. In June, you'll find sculpture inside and out; in July, photographs of the town of St. George; and in August, husband Philip Anderson's editorial illustrations. He'll also have a week of an open studio, where he'll demonstrate his gouache and collage methods. You might also ask to see Anderson's own spare sculptures of found art — made from bits of glass, rusted metal and pottery shards collected on the beach.

Between the Muse
8 Elm St., Rockland • 596-6868

This ambitious gallery is elegant and extremely professional. Two large spaces plus a garden gallery offer visitors the option of various combinations of shows, featuring the quirky, the thoughtful and the abstract. Art works range from Robert Shetterly's images of human relationships to Alice Spencer's abstractions to David Little's excellent local landscapes. In 1998, gallery directors expect to show more individual artists, but don't miss the holiday show of small works from a host of local artists. "Art is up to you," is the gallery's motto.

The gallery is open from May through December. Call for hours.

FYI

Unless otherwise noted, the area code for all phone numbers listed in this guide is 207.

Caldbeck Gallery
12 Elm St., Rockland • 594-5935

Some of Maine's finest contemporary artists show at this two-story gallery created in a small home off Main Street. In the spare old rooms of the gallery, you may find Lois Dodd's landscape paintings, Richard Saltonstall's abstracted visions, Yvonne Jacquette's aerial images of city and wood, Abby Shahn's painted pottery and lush canvases, photographer Patricia McLean's musing portraits of children and other fine work. Owner Cynthia Hyde, an artist herself, has an eye for high quality. The gallery is open daily in summer. Call for current hours.

Harbor Square Gallery
374 Main St., Rockland • 594-8700

Good art mixes with fine crafts in this large gallery in a former bank down the block from the Farnsworth Museum. The setting is nothing if not elegant, with large windows, marble floors and a special bank-vault gallery. Look for two- and three-dimensional work by Amero Gobbato, Christine York, Sharon Larkin, Daniel Hodermarsky and Robert Shetterly, among others, as well as jewelry and fine crafts. The gallery is open daily from around May 1 to mid-October, and Tuesday through Saturday the rest of the year. Call ahead, however, to be sure.

Eric Hopkins Gallery
Hopkins Wharf, North Haven • 867-2229

Eric Hopkins gets his inspiration by flying small planes with video camera in hand. He returns to his studio and transforms his videos into large oil paintings — soaring moments of land, sea and sky. He looks through his videos to find the vision he wants to paint, then approaches the image in a slightly abstracted, simplified way, creating large paintings and smaller watercolors that emphasize with dizzying effect the curve of the earth.

Hopkins, a native of North Haven, an island reached by ferry from Rockland, originally made a name for himself as a glassblower making glass shells. His gallery is in an old frame building right on the North Haven waterfront, overlooking the Fox Island

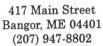

Thorofare (not far from the ferry terminal) and close to the soaring source of his work. The gallery is open daily in summer, or by appointment the rest of the year.

Maine Coast Artists
162 Russell Ave., Rockport • 236-2875

This old fire house, overhung with a great bird carved by Maine sculptor Bernard Langlais, welcomes visitors into two large, barn-like open spaces, one upstairs and one down. As an institution, Maine Coast Artists has been around since 1952; it's been in this building since 1967 (when it was purchased for all of $1,650). As a gallery, this nonprofit organization shows work that is generally thoughtful and sometimes experimental, whether photographs, paintings, sculptures, major installations or innovative collaborative efforts. It is one of the few places in the state that we can depend on to come up with cutting-edge, innovative shows.

It's also a place to see major installations, such as photographer Tilman Crane's, created in homage to an elderly neighbor; Karen Gilg's impressions of India, complete with floating body-like forms; or multimedia artist Katarina Weslien's work on dreams. The gallery also hosts an annual sculpture show — a medium that's sometimes hard to find in Maine. This show begins in the gallery and wends its way through the small waterfront town of Rockport. Come early summer, a yearly juried show offers a glimpse at the work of artists who might be new to the Maine scene.

Following renovations to modernize the building in 1997, the gallery is now open year round. While it's open daily in summer, winter hours are more limited — Tuesday through Saturday, with some special events on Sunday. Look here, too, for a nice gift shop and for unusual workshops on weekends. Admission is $2.

Maine Photographic Workshops
2 Central St., Rockport • 236-8581

Some of the best photographers in the world come to Rockport to teach at week-long workshops that run throughout the summer (see our Education chapter). They show their work, rather informally, in a large room that is sometimes a classroom and sometimes a gallery. There also are public presentations and lectures at night, usually Wednesdays, sometimes on additional days. Call ahead to find out who is showing, who is lecturing and when the gallery is open to the public.

Pine Tree Shop and Bay View Gallery
33 Bayview St., Camden • 236-4534

Part frame shop and part gallery, the Pine Tree Shop and Bay View Gallery overflows with local landscapes and seascapes. Among the work you might find on display are paintings of local artists David Little, Nancy Glassman, Scott Moore and Stephen Pastuhov; but that's just the tip of the iceberg. The gallery is open year round.

Studio at Saturday Cove
608 Atlantic Hwy. (U.S. Hwy. 1), Northport • 338-3654

This studio-gallery in a former gas station on U.S. Highway 1 features work by contemporary Maine artists, among them Philip Barter and Holly Berry. The work frequently is bright and joyful. Look also for whirligigs — wooden sculptures that whirl and twirl in the wind — by Joe Mulkhey and others. A summer 1998 addition is expected to expand the gallery to about twice its size.

Artfellows Gallery
no address at press time • 338-5390

This cooperative, year-round gallery lost its space in downtown Belfast at the end of 1997. Look for it elsewhere — as of press time, the members were considering space upstairs in Rockland, or downtown in Bucksport. Artfellows has been a mainstay of the local arts scene, exhibiting some very good artists, sculptors and photographers who for many different reasons are not plugged into local galleries. Their holiday show of photographs, jewelry, pottery, prints and ornaments has been not only affordable, but also extremely desirable. Belfast will miss it.

Spring Street Gallery
28 Spring St., Belfast • 338-5315

After two very fine Belfast galleries closed in 1995, local Realtor/art collector Sam Mitchell opened the Spring Street Gallery in 1996. Apparently, Belfast had developed too strong an arts community, and to go without galleries seemed impossible. Mitchell has had a great success with Spring Street. Look here for a large group of sometimes innovative paintings by local artists, and some innovative shows like "The Clay Kimono," a collaboration between painter Harald Garde and sculptor Mark Kuzio, and work by Daphne Cummings, Stu Henderson, Tom Higgens, Dennis and Megan Pinette and Michael Reece. Off-season hours are limited or by appointment.

Forest Hart
Back Brooks Rd., Monroe • 525-4437

Call Forest, make an appointment and go see his studio, which is just about 30 minutes inland from the Mid-Coast area. You'll find an engaging man and an amazing menagerie-like world filled with life-size cast sculptures of animals and birds. Hart creates everything from miniatures to monuments and has done so for museums across the nation.

Literary Arts

Thomaston Books & Prints
105 Main St. (U.S. Hwy. 1), Thomaston • 354-0001, (800) 300-3008

This classic small bookstore with an involved staff brings in writers for readings and book signings on a fairly regular basis.

Live Poets Society
Camden Public Library or Camden Opera House, Main St., Camden • 594-6319, 845-2476, 236-3440

When George VanDeventer took on the Live Poets Society in 1993, it was just an informal Rockland poetry group. By the time he left it four years later (he wanted to focus on his own work and on teaching in local schools), the society had a statewide reputation for its gatherings and slams.

The society continues with all its strength. Each month, the Camden Public Library hosts Live Poets Society gatherings. Usually, there's one featured reader, two local poets, a time for readings of "dead" poets plus performances of music or dance. The suggested donation is generally $5 for adults and $2 for students, depending on the event. Sometimes there's a student poet, sometimes there are groups of poets. Kate Barnes, the state's poet laureate, recently joined two other women poets for a notable evening. Meetings are usually held at 7 PM on the first Wednesday of the month.

Museums

Farnsworth Art Museum
19 Elm St., Rockland • 596-6457

The Farnsworth Museum is now the showcase art museum in the state, and soon it will be the largest art museum north of Boston. This year marks the opening of the Wyeth Center, built inside the former Pratt Memorial Methodist Church, just behind the museum, to hold and display the Wyeths' personal collection of 4,000 objects. The summer 1998 opening show at the museum, *Wondrous Strange: The Pursuit of the Marvelous in the Art of the Wyeth Family*, shows work by three generations of Wyeths — Jamie, Andrew and N.C. — plus N.C.'s famous teacher, illustrator Howard Pyle. That's not all. The museum recently has been offered funding to turn its next-door neighbor, a former Newberry's Department Store, into a contemporary art museum. Architectural plans are in the works, and construction will begin as soon as funding (beyond the initial million-or-so ante by an anonymous donor) is in place.

The Farnsworth houses the classic Maine works donated by the late Elizabeth Noyce, who amassed an excellent Maine art collection after her divorce from Intel founder Robert Noyce. Elizabeth Noyce gave a lot to many Maine institutions while alive and willed her extensive collection to be divided between the Portland Museum of Art (in Portland) and the Farnsworth. (The Farnsworth has done well by the computer age. The Olson House, mentioned in our Attractions chapter and part of the Farnsworth campus, was a gift from John and Lee Sculley of IBM.)

Such gifts couldn't happen to a better institution. With grace and determination, the museum has committed itself to showcasing Maine's place in the world of art, focusing its permanent collection on the numerous artists who have worked in Maine and steadily displaying the best of Maine's many contemporary artists. Beyond the Wyeth work, you'll find work painted in Maine by George Bellows, Marsden Hartley, Winslow Homer, Edward Hopper, John Marin, Louise Nevelson, Maurice Prendergast, Neil Welliver and Marguerite and William Zorach.

The museum also offers an extensive educational program run by artist Deb Vendetti and taught by a host of other Maine artists. Children and adults, alike, can learn to draw; paint in watercolor, oil or egg tempera; or join other special classes linked to current exhibits. Classes change frequently; sometimes they are simple evening lectures, sometimes daylong workshops. Call the museum at the listed number, or try Vendetti at 596-0949 to find out what's happening.

The Farnsworth is open year round, unless construction forces it closed, as has happened in winter and early spring 1998. Admission is $9 for adults, $8 for senior citizens, $7 per person for tour groups and $5 for students ages 8 through 18. Admission includes The Olson House, painted so frequently by Wyeth, and the Farnsworth Homestead — also part of the Farnsworth campus and open seasonally (see our Attractions chapter). A ticket to the Olson House also can be purchased separately.

Performing Arts

Venues

Waldo Theatre
Main St., Waldoboro • 832-6060
The art deco touches of the Waldo Theatre got it dubbed "Maine's Little Radio City" when it opened in 1936. The acoustics were (and are) so good, its built-in hearing aids were hardly necessary. The Waldo closed in the late 1950s and reopened in the 1990s after extensive renovations. Call for the schedule of movies, theater for children and adults, and concerts of jazz, folk and classical music. Admission varies.

Rockport Opera House
6 Central St., Rockport • 236-2514
The Rockport Opera house was built in the late 1890s as an opera house, but it has sometimes strayed from the purpose, being used as a library and a gym. Recent renovations even revealed a bowling alley floor hidden beneath the regular floor. Current uses of the renovated opera house also vary, though not as drastically as in the past. It has been the home of Bay Chamber Concerts for 20 years. In addition to jazz, classical and folk concerts, lectures and an occasional play, the opera house is also where Rockport's annual town meeting is held, and where the selectmen meet throughout the year. Want to get married on the coast? You could rent the opera house for that too. If no one answers at the listed number, try the Bay Chamber Concert office, 236-2823, to learn about current opera house happenings.

Camden Opera House
U.S. Hwy. 1, Camden • 236-3353
Built in 1877, leveled in 1892, rebuilt in 1895 and renovated in 1994, the opera house has seen its share of history. It is now so beautifully restored — note the gleaming cream-and gold-colored walls and gold paint covering the molded ceiling plaster — you'd swear the opera house was layered in gold leaf. Watch the schedule for theater, dance, vaudeville, concerts, poetry readings and other special events; prices vary. For a schedule, contact the Camden town office, which rents out the opera house, at the listed number; the Camden Civic Theatre, a principal tenant (see

subsequent entry); or the local chamber of commerce, 236-4404.

Abbott Room
Belfast Free Library, 45 High St., Belfast • 338-3884

Dance and music concerts, foreign films and puppet shows and storytelling for children are among the offerings in this library auditorium. Call the library for a schedule, or keep an eye on the local newspaper for event announcements.

Music

Down East Singers
various locations throughout Thomaston • 354-2262

Choral director Anthony Antolini is a busy man. He directs the Bowdoin Chorus and the Bowdoin Alumni Chorus, offers educational programs for children and adults at some winter Bay Chamber Concerts in Rockport (see the following entry) and has recently issued a beautiful version of Sergei Rachmaninoff's *1910 Liturgy of St. John Chrysostom*. Among the 101 members of the chorus are some 80 to 90 members of Down East Singers, which Antolini conducts in his spare time, offering local performances of classic choral works. The group itself is busy too. It has a spring concert in Rockport, tours with the liturgy in May, and presents holiday concerts in Rockport and Thomaston come December.

Second Read Bookstore
369 Main St., Rockland • 594-4123

About twice a month, this cafe/bookstore with broad windows facing Main Street offers live music in addition to food for the belly and for thought (i.e., books). Jazz and folk concerts are scheduled once a month. Jam sessions of traditional Irish music also occur once a month year round, usually on the third Friday of the month. Admission ranges from free to $10, depending on the performance.

Music in Blue Hill

It's late August. Asters are blooming on the roadside, and a branch of maple leaves has already turned radiant. With the hint of fall in the air, thoughts turn to the cold . . . to winter.

Suddenly, those thoughts are twisted around.

Where's that calypso music coming from? This is Maine, not Trinidad.

In the past 10 years, five Blue Hill steel drum groups have sprouted like feathers at Trinidad carnivale with the help of musician Carl Chase. In a town with a population of less than 2,000, that's one band for every 400 people.

Maybe it's the long winters that keep people in Maine hungering for the tropical beat. Maybe it's simply that Mainers know a good time when they see one.

Chase lives in Brooksville, the western nub of the Blue Hill Peninsula and home to many musicians. When Mary Cheyney Gould, founder of the Bagaduce Music Lending Library (see this chapter's entry), first came here, she found three homes with twin grand pianos — and that's before she moved in with two of her own.

Some of the responsibility for this musical harmony lies at the feet of Franz Kneisel, who brought many musicians to Blue Hill over many summers, developing a lifelong love for the region within the music community.

Some responsibility lies at the feet of Gould and Marcia Chapman. Within six months of Gould's arrival in Blue Hill in 1975, she launched the Bagaduce Chorale (see this chapter's entry), a community group that's been singing and giving concerts ever since. Mu-

Photo: Donna Gold

The Flash in the Pan Community Steel Band performs in Blue Hill and elsewhere along Maine's Mid-Coast.

sic advocate Chapman joined in, and together they started the Bagaduce Music Lending Library, focusing worldwide attention on little Blue Hill.

Enter Carl Chase. In the early 1970s, shortly after he settled in the area, Chase got his head turned by steel drumming during a sail in the Caribbean. He started studying steel drums, muddling along for 10 years on self-made pans and forming a steel drum band. According to Chase, the group sounded pretty good, and people liked the danceable music. Then frustration set in as the group stagnated; so Chase suggested a trip to Trinidad.

Chase and the members of his Atlantic Clarion Steel Band returned fully energized. That was when Chase and his band started playing at local schools and other community venues.

— continued on next page

It wasn't long before Flash in the Pan, Bagaduce Steel, Planet Pan and Rhythm Rockets began. Rhythm Rockets, the kids' version, is composed of members as young as 10. Bagaduce Steel is Marcia Chapman's baby — a small group of musicians ages 10 to 72 that performs with cellos and flutes. The repertoire includes calypso, soca, jazz, classical and pop. Planet Pan, the George Stevens Academy band, presents concerts as well as school performances geared to education.

Flash in the Pan is a larger community group, with as many as 30 members. Every Monday in summer, Flash in the Pan plays for free at a fund-raiser for whoever asks. Performances have been held at the fire department in Winter Harbor, at the library in East Blue Hill and at the hospital in Ellsworth.

Bay Chamber Concerts
Rockport Opera House, 6 Central St., Rockport • 236-2823, (888) 707-2770

This well-established series offers concerts twice weekly during summer and once a month during the rest of the year. Concerts are held in the lovely Rockport Opera House, a few steps above the harbor. The 1998 summer series runs Thursday and Friday nights from early July through late August and includes four performances by the Vermeer Quartet, which is celebrating its 25th anniversary with the series. The opening concert is an all-piano affair, featuring Leonard Hokanson and Edmund Battersby. It's followed by a jazz concert July 10 with Butch Thompson, a tuba player and a bass player. The final two concerts feature contemporary music: the world premiere of a piece by David Baker for clarinet, jazz trio and string quartet in late August; and a violin piece written by Ephraim Zimbalist Jr. for his father.

In winter, Sunday afternoon concerts are preceded by a talk at the Sail Loft (see our Restaurants chapter). Pre-concert talks begin at 7 PM; concerts begin at 8 PM. Tickets are $16 for adults and $7 for students in summer, $12 and $5 respectively during the rest of the year.

Theater

Chamber Theatre of Maine
Watts Hall, Main St., Thomaston
• 354-8807

In residence in Thomaston since 1992, Chamber Theatre of Maine offers three productions between October and May plus a holiday performance of *A Child's Christmas in Wales*. Admission for all performances is $10. The focus of director Erika Pfander is on the literary; productions are kept spare to emphasize language. The 1997-98 season included *Happy Days* by Samuel Beckett, the music-centered play *Old Wicked Songs* by Jon Marans, and *On Golden Pond* by Ernest Thompson.

Pfander's great pride, however, resides in presenting the world premieres for two plays by poet and journal writer May Sarton: *The Music Box Bird* was shown in 1993 before Sarton's death; *The Underground River* premiered in 1995 during a season dedicated to Sarton's memory.

Outlore Theatre Co.
275 Main St., Rockland • 594-2522

Outlore has been both a buffet restaurant and a theater offering drama atypical of the dinner- and lunch-theater fare. No wonder it has called itself the region's "one-stop entertainment center" — $25 a person for dinner, $12 for lunch. As of press time, the theater is in the throws of change. Call to be sure it is continuing as a dinner theater for summer 1998.

Camden Civic Theatre
Camden Opera House, U.S. Hwy. 1, Camden • 236-2281

Since 1968, the Camden Civic Theatre has been gathering massive casts of local talent and offering good-quality live theater to the public. The 1998 schedule includes *The Night of January 16th,* Amy Rand's comedic courtroom drama, in June; *A Funny Thing Happened on the Way to the Forum*, in August; and *My Three Angels*, in December. Tickets are usually $8 for adults and $6 for students. Call for the exact schedule.

Belfast Maskers
Railroad Theater, 43 Front St., Belfast
• 338-9668

The Maskers have been around only since 1987, but they proved so popular so quickly, they were able to build their own stage inside the old Belfast and Moosehead Lake Railroad storage barn in 1993. Currently under the direction of Gardner Howes or Robert Hicks (founding director Basil Burwell passed away in 1997 after performing for 65 years), the theater offers striking, sometimes controversial contemporary drama year round. This summer's offerings include *A Perfect Ganesh* by Terrance McNally, in June; *Pump Boys and Dinettes* by John Foley and other original cast members, in July; the comedy *Beau Jest* by James Sherman, in August; and George Bernard Shaw's *The Devil's Disciple*, in September.

Tickets are $10 for adults, $6 for students.

The Playhouse
beneath the Belfast Opera House,
Church St., Belfast • 338-5777

Run by puppeteer, actress and teacher Mary Weaver, The Playhouse teaches theater and hosts traveling performances for children and adults. It offers from three to a dozen productions each year, depending on Weaver's ability to free herself from other activities. Past productions include *Winnie The Pooh* and *Dragons! Dragons!,* a *commedia della arte* performance. For the most part, Weaver works out of her studio beneath the lovely old Belfast Opera House. She also offers after-school theater classes, studio per-

formances and a varied "Make-It" class for children. Admission varies.

Inland to Bangor

Art Galleries

Clark House Gallery
128 Hammond St., Bangor • 942-9162

In a small space behind a high-end craft gallery, Clark House has launched an art gallery. Exhibits range from the wild expressionist work of Harald Garde to the delicate landscapes of Nina Jerome. Call for current schedule.

Intown Arts Center & Gallery
42 Columbia St., Bangor • 990-2990

This nonprofit, membership gallery shows the work of nearly 50 local artists from eastern Maine. The gallery is open year round, Monday through Saturday, but the staff is all volunteers, so things can go awry; it's best to call ahead. Ask also about art classes and workshops.

Three Sisters Cafe
Brewer Shopping Center, 415 Wilson St.,
Brewer • 989-3133

As it says in its advertising, this old-style cafe is "located (of all places!) in the Brewer Shopping Center." Since even Maine's more metropolitan areas such as Bangor and Brewer are still packed with old Victorian homes, it seems odd to have a romantic arts cafe in a shopping center. But here it is, right in the thick of things, down the line from the local Shop 'n' Save. And many in the Bangor/Brewer area are grateful for it, wherever it might be. Three Sisters offers art shows, music, good coffee and books.

FYI

Unless otherwise noted, the area code for all phone numbers listed in this guide is 207.

INSIDERS' TIP

As you drive through Maine, watch the roadsides for the people's art: lawn sculptures made from old bicycles, chain-saw carvings, mailboxes built in the shape of fire engines and small bridges and lighthouses directing traffic in the tiniest of ponds.

Photo: Bangor Daily News

Quilt-making is one of the demonstrations provided at Leonard's Mills in Bradley, a re-created turn-of-the-century community in central Maine.

Literary Arts

Borders Bookstore
116 Bangor Mall Blvd., Bangor
• 990-3300

Look here for lectures, poetry and literature readings, discussion groups or simple book signings, nearly every day. There's also chess Tuesdays at 7 PM.

Maine Folklife Center
University of Maine, 5773 S. Stevens Hall, Orono • 581-1891

The history of Maine's people is the central focus of the Folklife Center's Northeast Archives of Folklore and Oral History. In this archive of history and lore you can sift through previously conducted research on the songs of Maine's lumbermen, sailors and river drivers, and learn about the traditions of the North Woods or Maine's native tribes. Look through photographs of vernacular architecture, or learn about textile arts or women in the Depression.

Museums

Hudson Museum
5746 Maine Center for the Arts, University of Maine, Orono • 581-1901

Art from around the world, including an unusually comprehensive pre-Columbian collection, can be found at the Hudson Museum. This summer, look for *Brilliantly Beaded: Northeastern Native American Beadwork* (see our Attractions chapter for details). The museum is open Tuesday through Friday from 9 AM to 4 PM and Saturday and Sunday from 11 AM to 4 PM. Admission is free, but donations are appreciated.

University of Maine Museum of Art
Carnegie Hall, University of Maine, Orono • 581-3255

Wally Mason, director here since 1996, has made some great changes in the university's museum, breaking out from more traditional, Maine-only art, keeping the museum open into the weekend and raising money for greater flexibility. The space includes an extensive collection of paintings and prints, including works by Jim Dine, Winslow Homer, George Inness, Pablo Picasso and Diego Rivera. While there's currently no room to display a permanent collection, the museum mounts a series of temporary exhibitions, sometimes showing work by artists of the university, such as a painting show by Michael Lewis and drawing shows by Susan Gross and MaJo Keleshian. Call for current exhibition schedule.

Performing Arts

Venues

Hutchins Concert Hall
5746 Maine Center for the Arts, University of Maine, Orono • 581-1755, (800) 622-8499

Some call the 1,629-seat Hutchins Concert Hall at Maine Center for the Arts the state's finest music hall based on its acoustics and comfort. It hosts a wide variety of performances, including opera, dance, jazz and children's events. Past performances have featured appearances by cellist Yo-Yo Ma, violinists Midori and Isaac Stern, dancer Rudolph Nureyev, The Peking Acrobats, singers Bob Dylan, Arlo Guthrie and Johnny Cash, and mime artist Marcel Marceau. Best of all, you get to walk through the Hudson Museum (see our Attractions chapter for more information) before performances and during intermissions. Call for a schedule and ticket prices.

Dance

Robinson Ballet Company
107 Union St., Bangor • 942-1990

The Robinson Ballet Company links up with the Bangor Symphony Orchestra (see the following "Music" section) each year for a memorable winter holiday performance of the *Nutcracker* at the Hutchins Concert Hall. It performs elsewhere during the year and sometimes brings out its innovative modern-dance arm. Ticket prices vary by performance; call ahead.

Music

Arcady Music Society
locations to be determined, Bangor
• 288-2141, 288-3151

Arcady performs seven programs of classical music at three locations — Bangor, Bar Harbor and Dover-Foxcroft — throughout the summer, all directed by nationally-known pianist Masanobu Ikemiya. The 1998 summer series runs from mid-July through late August and includes such delights as a Carol Wincenc playing with Japanese Court Musicians, the New York Ragtime Orchestra, Virtuosi Wind Quartet and Arcady Festival Orchestra. Tickets for adults are $12 in advance, $15 at the door; a series pass is $72. Children 18 and younger can attend for free.

Borders
116 Bangor Mall Blvd., Bangor
• 990-3300

Check out the cafe at Borders for jazz and folk music by a host of local artists. Friday night is jazz night, when you might find The Lidral Trio, John Cooper Trio or Memphis Belles. You may also find music Saturday night and Sunday afternoon, anything from local groups like Women with Wings to the Bangor Symphony Orchestra. These are informal, cafe-style concerts. The cafe frequently fills up, but you can stand at the cafe's edge and browse through the store's magazines and books while listening to the live music.

Bangor Symphony Orchestra
Maine Center for the Arts, University of Maine, Orono • 942-5555

Since 1896, members of the community have been performing with the Bangor Symphony Orchestra, making it the oldest community orchestra in the country offering continuous concerts. Some musicians make their living as such, others as lobstermen, pharmacists and secretaries.

The orchestra got a large boost when conductor Werner Torkanowsky, who had retired to his home in nearby Hancock Point, took the post of BSO conductor from 1981 until his death in 1992. Torkanowsky brought the orchestra to new heights of performance. Currently, Christopher Zimmerman, assistant conductor at the

Cincinnati College Conservatory of Music, commutes to Bangor for the symphony's five classical concerts offered Sundays at 3 PM each season plus a performance of the *Nutcracker* with Bangor's Robinson Ballet Company (see the previous "Dance" section). Sometimes the symphony holds an outdoor pops concert in summer. Family casual concerts are held at 7 PM Saturdays, the night before the regular concert. These concerts feature a relaxed atmosphere in which excerpts from Sunday's program are performed. Sunday ticket prices range from $10 to $30. Saturday concerts cost $10 for adults, $5 for youths. Advance tickets can be bought at 44 Central Street in Bangor, or by calling the listed number.

If you're traveling from afar, call to find out about bus service organized expressly for BSO events. Passage costs about $12 a person, and the service runs from Camden, Belfast, Stockton Springs, Blue Hill, Surry, Ellsworth, Houlton and Medway.

Three Sisters Cafe
Brewer Shopping Center, 415 Wilson St., Brewer • 989-3133

This small cafe offers live entertainment about every other week on Friday nights; check your local paper for details.

Theater

Winterport Open Stage
Samuel Wagner Middle School, Mountainview Dr., Winterport • 223-2501

In its fifth year of performances, Winterport Open Stage is a steady, ambitious group offering three to four productions each year. The complete 1998 schedule is uncertain, but early season performances include *Grace and Glory* by Tom Ziegler, an area premier and *Sylvia* by A.R. Guerney. There are sometimes productions for adults or children in summer. Read your local newspaper or call the listed number. Tickets are $4 for adults, $2 for students and seniors.

Mystery Cafe
Kathy's Catering, 1606 Hammond St., Bangor • 941-8700, (800) 297-8707

Like clockwork, once a month between October and June, a murder happens at Kathy's Catering in Bangor. It's the job of the diners to find the culprit. Sometimes the murder takes place at a king's coronation, sometimes at a talk show or a detective school. Mystery Cafe's wait staff will help you figure it out — they're also the actors. The cafe offers about eight different shows, all of them comedies as well as mysteries. The $32.95-a-person ticket includes dinner and the show.

Penobscot Theatre Co.
183 Main St., Bangor • 942-3333

Under the direction of Mark Torres, the 24-year-old Penobscot Theatre Company has become a professional and popular repertory theater. During the school year, the company performs about six dramatic plays in its renovated Victorian building or the Bangor Opera House a few blocks down Main Street. Performances in the 1997-98 season include *Harvey* by Mary Chase, *Glengarry Glen Ross* by David Mamet, *A Christmas Carol* by Charles Dickens, *A Streetcar Named Desire* by Tennessee Williams and *Angels in America* by Tony Kushner. Performances are 7 PM Thursday, 8 PM Friday, 5 and 8:30 PM Saturday and 2 PM Sunday. Tickets range from $10 to $15. Student rush tickets are available at the door.

In summer, the theater offers a Shakespeare festival, known as Shakespeare on the Penobscot River (see our Annual Events chapter). The event was an instant hit when it began in 1994. It since has developed into a community gathering with Renaissance dancers, medieval societies, madrigal singers and local food vendors. This summer's plays are *A Midsummer Night's Dream*, *Romeo and Juliet* and *The Merry Wives of Windsor*. They will be presented in a rotating repertoire Wednesday through Sunday for a total of 26 performances. Admission ranges from $5 for bleacher seats for children to $15 for reserved adult seats.

Maine Masque Theatre
Hauck Auditorium and Pavilion Theater, 5788 Class of 1944 Hall, at the School of Performing Arts, University of Maine, Orono • 581-4702

Maine Masque is the college theater group, offering a new show every other week in Hauck Auditorium. You'll find classics like *On Baile's Strand* by William Butler Yeats, *Arcadia* by Tom

Stoppard and *The Baltimore Waltz* by Paula Vogel as well as various student-written productions; admission is $7 a person. Generally, faculty direct and students perform. Check out more experimental works in the Pavilion Theater; admission is free.

Bucksport to Gouldsboro

Art Galleries

McGrath Dunham Gallery
Main St., Castine • 326-9175

Paintings of landscapes and seascapes are displayed in the window of this Main Street gallery, luring visitors inside for a look at the large collection of mostly Maine art. Paintings, drawings and a few sculptures by artists such as MaJo Keleshian, Stephen Pastuhov, Allie Sabalis and McGrath himself are displayed in this jam-packed street-level gallery, with more work downstairs. Most of it is realistic landscapes and seascapes, but the gallery also offers abstracts and a touch of the surreal.

While the McGrath-Dunham's official season runs from May through Columbus Day, it also offers a holiday show. Since both owners live in town, the gallery is almost always open by appointment.

Ellsworth Public Library
46 State St., Ellsworth • 667-6363

Ellsworth Public Library offers monthly art exhibits year round in the ground-floor gallery and the second-floor reading area. Half the exhibits are curated by artists from the local chapter of the Union of Visual Artists, half by the library or other interested people. The thematic shows are lively and unusual.

Jud Hartmann Gallery
Main St., Blue Hill • 374-9917, 359-2544

Years ago, Jud Hartmann and family happened upon Blue Hill. They felt they just had to stay. Perhaps, like many, it was the clear northern light; perhaps it was the shell middens of the ancient Red Paint people, precursors to the four Native American tribes that inhabit Maine today. Hartmann makes cast-metal sculptures of mostly Plains Indians. The hu-

man faces are strong; the horses and buffalos are muscular and active. The gallery is open in summer only.

Larson Gallery
Maine Hwys. 175 and 177, South Penobscot • 326-8222

In the small town of South Penobscot, at the junction of Maine highways 175 and 177, David Larson has opened a studio/gallery to the public. Larson's wife is a weaver and has a small shop at street level called North Country Textiles (see our Shopping chapter for details on her larger Blue Hill store). Climb the stairs to view Larson's bucolic work of large naked women in lush surroundings — something like Edouard Manet meets Maxfield Parish. The gallery is open June through mid-October, seven days a week (though the textile store below is open only six days a week).

Judith Leighton Gallery
Parker Point Rd., Blue Hill • 374-5001

Three floors of an old barn have been gracefully remodeled for an unencumbered display of as many as seven artists at a time plus the work of artist/owner Judith Leighton. Her tastes range from bright-colored, light-hearted paintings of Maine to some complicated, dark, symbolic paintings. Few of the paintings are representational landscapes; Leighton specializes in mythical landscapes that may begin in Maine but lead to dreams, desires and the duality of relationships.

Artists represented here include Philip Barter, Alfred Chadbourn, Doug Frati, William Irvine, MaJo Keleshian, Wendy Kindred, Sandy Olson, Meg Brown Payson and Robert Shetterly. Out back, the yard is a maze of sculptures. Leighton's sculpture garden is one of the most interesting in the state, a place both large and private enough to allow visitors to fully connect with the work of Squidge Davis, Judith Ingram, Cabot Lyford, Sharon Townshend and many more sculptors. There's also a room devoted to craft work by local artisans.

Liros Gallery
Main St., Blue Hill • 374-5370, (800) 287-5370

This small place bursts with fine 19th- and early 20th-century classic, representational art.

But the most exceptional offerings here are the 17th-, 18th- and 19th-century gilded Russian icons, the owner's family passion.

Blue Heron Gallery
Maine Hwy. 15, Deer Isle • 348-6051

The Haystack Mountain School of Crafts brings some of the finest craftspeople to Maine during the summer. Blue Heron showcases glass, pottery, forged ironware and more created by the school's faculty. (See our Education chapter and the "Deer Isle's Craftspeople" Close-up in our Shopping chapter for related information.) The gallery is open June through September.

Haystack Mountain School of Crafts
Stinson Neck, Deer Isle • 348-2306

Craftspeople come here from all over the world to learn from some of the finest potters, weavers, jewelers, blacksmiths, papermakers and rush-weavers during two- and three-week sessions offered each summer. Since sessions are short and the work intense, visitors are requested to refrain from walking around the school on their own. But gallery shows, some lectures and poetry readings, and infrequent tours are open to the public. Call to see what's happening. If you go, relish the architecture and the view off the school's granite cliffs. (See our Education chapter for details about the school.)

Seamark Gallery and Workshops
Maine Hwy. 15, Deer Isle • 348-9955, 348-2577

When local artists hung their drawings of nude models in a Seamark exhibition, a local woodworker installed a bed in the middle of the show. Expect a similar amount of wicked daring in all shows by this loose cooperative organization. Look here, too, for summer classes for children and adults in a variety of arts and sciences such as cartooning, journal writing, papermaking, poetry, science of the sea and sculpture. Call for a summer schedule.

Turtle Gallery
The Old Centennial House Barn, Maine Hwy. 15, Deer Isle • 348-9977

In 1996, Elena Kubler renovated this gallery that artist and former Haystack School director Fran Merritt ran years ago. Kubler's artists fill the space with crafts and excellent art from around the region. Her first summer featured Merritt's unusual prints made with, of all things, gelatin. Expect to find lovely woven rugs, Kubler's silver jewelry and cups, blown glass and other varied works by an array of local painters and printers. The gallery is open at least from Memorial Day into September, and sometimes longer.

Hoy Gallery
E. Main St., Stonington • 367-2368

Owner Jill Hoy hangs her large, realistic paintings of area houses and gardens bathed in brilliant, clear sunshine in this overflowing gallery at the end of Main Street. Visit her in summer only.

Barter Family Galleries
Hog Bay Rd., North Sullivan • 422-3190

Nothing holds back the Barter family. Papa Philip Barter is an artist of extensive capacities, always working, always producing. His art is part of the decor of The Mex in Ellsworth (see our Restaurants chapter) and is shown at the Judith Leighton Gallery, The Studio at Saturday Cove (see previous entries) and here. His colors are bright; his subject-matter, frequently the Maine woods; his approach, a seemingly innocent shorthand with trees painted in distinctive triangular points and lakes created as blue amoebic figures.

His seven children (plus friends who move right in) seem to be following in Barter's steps. Like Barter, a self-taught artist, they make an art out of making do. Son Matthew is a fine painter; others paint furniture, create sculpture and find their way through other crafts. Priscilla Barter, mother to the clan, makes one-of-a-kind hooked and braided rugs. The work is visible in the gallery, which was separated from the private space by a mere curtain when we last visited; the aroma of baking brownies could not be contained.

This place is tricky to find; turn left off U.S. Highway 1 after you cross the bridge over Taunton Bay, and take the Hog Bay Road for about 2.5 miles, following signs. The gallery is open 9 AM to 5 PM Monday through Saturday from about mid-May to mid-November and by appointment at other times.

Spring Woods Gallery
Maine Hwy. 200, Sullivan • 422-3007

Another local family gallery, Spring Woods features work by Paul and Ann Breeden and son Robert. The Breedens retired to Maine after Paul's full career as an illustrator for the U.S. Post Office (remember the Pine Cone stamp?) and *Smithsonian* magazine, among others. Ann's work reveals Southwestern influences. Robert makes functional art including household wares of wrought iron and other materials.

New for 1998 is a sculpture garden with work by area artists. The gallery is open five days a week from mid-May through the end of October. Call to find out which days. It's also open by appointment at other times.

Cinema

Northeast Historic Film
The Alamo, 379 Main St., Bucksport • 469-0924

Wondering about an old film you saw years back? Wondering whether it was about Maine or filmed in Maine? Northeast Historic Film can help. This archive of regional film and video has done a great service to Maine by reissuing documentaries of lumber mills and river drives and storing old home movies deemed culturally valuable. The administrators also show movies sporadically at The Alamo, the old movie theater currently being restored in downtown Bucksport. Annual membership ($25 a person) includes free video rentals.

The Grand Auditorium of Hancock County
Main St., Ellsworth • 667-9500, 667-5911

Thursday through Sunday nights year round, The Grand is likely to have a good foreign or domestic movie. They may take a while in coming, so expect to find that great Chinese movie you missed in Boston some time ago, or that Spike Lee film you never quite got

to. Movies start at 7:30 PM, but call ahead. Sometimes there's a concert or local play instead of a movie.

Literary Arts

Left Bank Bakery & Cafe
Maine Hwy. 172, Blue Hill • 374-2201

Poetry readings by local poets such as Stuart Kestenbaum (who also directs Haystack Mountain School of Crafts; see previous entry), Jackie Michaud, Sylvester Pollet, Pat Ranzoni and Martin Steingesser are sometimes scheduled for an afternoon. Other weeks, the afternoon is left open for whoever wants to get up and read.

Performing Arts

The Grand Auditorium of Hancock County
Main St., Ellsworth • 667-9500, 667-5911

The Grand is both a theater and a community arts organization as well as the only Maine arts organization both run and funded by a city. Housed in a well-worn and much-loved art deco building, The Grand offers art exhibits in its lobby and foreign-movie weekends in its auditorium, unless there are special events scheduled; this is also the large performance place for the region. Stop by and pick up a copy of the schedule, or call to see what's on the bill. It could be a community theater performance of *Oliver* or a session of Native American storytellers; come summer, musical performances — the Arcady Music Society, Clarence Gatemouth Brown, Cajun music or a Gilbert and Sullivan operetta — are more frequently found. Expect live events — local or national — as much as once each week, between showings of that great foreign film you always wanted to check out (see the previous "Cinema" section).

INSIDERS' TIP

Don't forget your own sketch pad and colored pencils, watercolors or pastels as you pack for a trip to Maine. The land and the sea will astonish you, and there's nothing like looking, drawing and looking again to really see Maine's beauty.

Photo: Bangor Daily News

Colorful artwork adorns the front of Ellsworth's City Hall. The city is on U.S. 1 and is considered a gateway to tourist-popular Bar Harbor.

Hancock Country Friends of the Arts
Farmstead Barn, U.S. Hwy. 1, Sullivan
• 422-3615

For years, Ginia Wexler has been offering summer productions of theater, puppetry, music, magic and mime for local children. Finally, with the help of grants, it's not all out of her own pocket. Call to find out the summer schedule of great children's events from this large, old barn overflowing with art.

Music

Atlantic Clarion Steel Band
various locations in Brooksville
• 326-9324

Carl Chase's six-member professional steel drum group has its own recordings and has performed across New England, New York and New Jersey. (See this chapter's related Close-up.)

Bagaduce Chorale
Maine Hwy. 172, Brooksville • 326-8532

Run by the irrepressible Mary Cheyney Gould, this community chorale has performed annually throughout the region since 1975, when it was organized. The 80-member community chorus, composed of singers from

Brewer to Bar Harbor, offers three performances a year, usually at the Blue Hill Congregational Church. The program includes a range of material, from pops concerts to "heavy stuff," such as Brahms and Faure. Donations are appreciated.

Bagaduce Music Lending Library
Maine Hwy. 172, Blue Hill • 374-5454

Twenty years ago, musician Mary Cheyney Gould and her friend Marcia Chapman were traveling in a motor home. One afternoon, while parked in a friend's garage at a funeral home, they invited musician Fritz Jahoda in for tea. Perhaps it was the lugubrious setting, for Jahoda began agonizing over the future of his enormous collection of scores. Chapman suggested starting a music library; Gould and Jahoda took her up on it.

The library started in Gould's garage in Brooksville. Within two months, it outgrew the space. Today the more than 620,000 items of The Bagaduce Music Lending Library are housed in a building on Maine Highway 172, just outside Blue Hill. Scores are lent to schools and orchestras from Bar Harbor to Brazil. Membership costs $10 per year. The minimal fee for borrowing items varies: Books are $1; scores range from 50¢ for individual sheets of music to $5 for a conductor's score (plus shipping and handling if the items are being mailed). The library is open year round, Tuesdays 10 AM to 6 PM and Wednesdays and Fridays 10 AM to 3 PM. There's no fee to simply sit and do research.

Blue Hill Chamber Music Concerts
Blue Hill Congregational Church, Main St., Blue Hill • 374-2161

People drive through ice and snow to attend the five concerts of this winter-long series of chamber music by such performers as the Paris Piano Trio, Parisii Quartet, Lark Quartet, Artemis Quartet and the New England Piano Quartet. Concerts are held in the spare and elegant Blue Hill Congregational Church on Sunday afternoons — you could hardly find a lovelier location. Tickets are $10 for adults; children get in free.

Flash in the Pan
South Brooksville and other locations around Blue Hill • 374-2840

Every other Monday night between Memorial Day and Labor Day, the crossroad town of South Brooksville is transformed into a Caribbean mecca by Flash in the Pan's street dances. On the other Monday nights, other towns — from Bucksport to Stonington to Winter Harbor — are transformed. A donation to these events usually serves as a benefit for some local enterprise — a hospital, library or fire house.

Curious about how steel bands got to Brooksville? See this chapter's related Close-up for details.

Kneisel Hall Chamber Music Festival
Maine Hwy. 15, Blue Hill • 374-2811

An old rustic lodge surrounded by trees becomes the perfect setting for weekly chamber concerts performed by faculty and/or students of the renowned Kneisel Hall Chamber Music School. The current artistic director is Seymour Lipkin. Faculty includes Roman Totenberg and Barbara Stein-Mallow. Programs can be heard inside the lodge from seating beneath the wise gaze of an old moose head hanging on the wall; otherwise, you can

sit outside the hall on the porch. The sound is fine outside, but visibility is poor; tickets can be reserved for indoor seats. Faculty concerts are held Friday nights at 8:15 PM and Sunday afternoons at 4 PM; there also are numerous student concerts from the end of June until mid-August. Ticket prices vary.

Left Bank Bakery & Cafe
Maine Hwy. 172, Blue Hill • 374-2201

Artists look forward to their dates at the Left Bank Bakery & Cafe — which is modern, but so filled with wood that it will remind you of the coffeehouses of the old days. Listen to nationally known folk, blues and jazz artists nearly every night in summer and frequently in winter. Though the 1998 schedule was just beginning to be worked out by press time, expect to hear Dave Mallet, Tom Rush, Peter Rowan, Dave McKenna and Deborah Henson-Conant perform. And comic Judith Sloan appears Thursday nights in August. If you call, the staff will gladly send you a copy of the two-month schedule. Tickets are generally $15.50, with dinner additional. Concerts start 8:30 PM, and reservations are suggested.

Surry Opera Company
Morgan Bay Rd., Surry • 667-9551

The company might be amateur, but it works hard enough — and sings well enough — to have been invited to the former Soviet Union to initiate an active exchange of musicians at a time when such Soviet-American exchanges were quite rare.

Surry Opera Company also has made a name for itself nationally. In 1985, for instance, the group performed at the acclaimed Wolftrap Farm Park in Vienna, Virginia.

The company's leader is well-known pianist and Zen Master Walter Nowick. The company has always been an informal but dedicated group of singers — most from within a 40-mile radius of Surry — who generally offer a few concerts each summer, either at the large Concert Barn at Nowick's home on Morgan Bay Road or at the Grand Theater in Ellsworth. Not infrequently, the Maine singers are joined by singers from Russia. Call to find out about 1998 plans.

FYI

Unless otherwise noted, the area code for all phone numbers listed in this guide is 207.

Pierre Monteux Conducting School
99 Bay View (U.S. Hwy. 1), Steuben
• 422-3931

The late Pierre Monteux first came to the United States from his native France in 1916 as conductor of Diaghileff's Ballet Russe. When the outbreak of World War II forced him to close his French school, he and wife Doris Hodgkins, of Salisbury Cove, decided to move home. It wasn't long before a Monteux school of conducting opened in Maine; it continues today under the direction of Michael Jinbo. Young conductors from around the world come to the school to seek perfection (even if they can never attain it) in a summer of practice and performance. Participants conduct each other in a small orchestra and offer performances in July on Sunday afternoons at 5 PM, with more informal chamber music concerts held Wednesday nights.

Theater

Cold Comfort Productions
Maine Maritime Academy, Delano Auditorium and Emerson Hall, Water St., Castine • 326-8830

Lively producer Aynne Ames, a school teacher who's let loose in summer, has been offering a wide range of summertime performances since 1975, ranging from large-cast musicals to Shakespeare. Directors are culled from the state's prolific acting community. One year, Daniel Elihu Kramer, head of Bowdoin College's theater program, directed Shakespeare's *Measure for Measure* in an open-air performance at Castine's Fort George (he later repeated the performance in Camden). Tickets have been $10 for adults and $8 for students and seniors.

Mount Desert Island

Art Galleries

Blum Gallery
College of the Atlantic, 105 Eden St., Bar Harbor • 288-5015

The architecture of the College of the Atlantic is an art exhibit in itself. But inside, in the Blum Gallery, you'll find year-round exhibits of a wide range of art. Planned for 1998 are an exhibit of paintings by modernist John Marin, who lived farther Downeast; a look at botanical and ornithological drawings; a Mount Desert Island artists' invitational; an exhibit of book bindings; and a fascinating pairing of photographs of a yoga practitioner with Chinese calligraphic drawings.

Shows are frequently lively, such as the recent interactive dialogue exhibit of painted and constructed panels known as *Mother Tongue*, in which viewers were invited to participate. The liveliest of shows, however, might be the late spring exhibit of the exuberant and thoughtful work of the students themselves. Call for hours, which change in summer.

The Wingspread Gallery
Main St., Northeast Harbor • 276-3910

Northeast Harbor is classy, but you still don't expect to see the kind of art casually hung at the Wingspread in your typical small town gallery. In a large open room you'll find temporary exhibits of recent artists. But it's the back rooms that will stun you with work by Marsden Hartley, Rockwell Kent, John Marin, Charles Woodbury and the Zorachs. Call for hours.

A.J. Bueche Gallery
95 Clark Point Rd., Southwest Harbor • 244-5353

At the end of a dusty dirt drive, you'll find A.J. Bueche Gallery. Bueche, himself a painter, features his work and that of other contemporary Maine artists like George Daniell and Rebecca Cummings as well as some Maine Coast classic artists like Edward Hopper, Carroll Tyson, Milton Avery and John Marin. But you're also likely to find surprises here, like a Marc Chagall or an 18th-century drawing show. The gallery is open July through mid-September, Wednesday through Saturday from 11 AM to 5 PM, or by appointment.

Literary Arts

Port in a Storm
Main St. (Maine Hwy. 102), Somesville • 244-4114, (800) 694-4114

Enjoy one of many scheduled readings, signings or lectures in this comprehensive bookstore set beside a pond near Somes Sound.

We've come to listen to Maine poet laureate Kate Barnes read (see our Maine Experience chapter for more about Barnes) and to view and listen to a slide presentation by local painter Richard Estes. In 1998, expect to find Roxanna Robinson read from her new novel (her short stories have been *The New York Times* hot picks); Eleanor Dwight speak about her new biography of Diana Vreeland (her last biography of writer Edith Wharton was highly acclaimed); and Carl Little give a talk, perhaps with slides, from his new anthology of paintings of Maine islands. There are more readings planned from the many writers who visit or live on the island.

Harbor House
Herrick Rd., Southwest Harbor • 244-3713

When Oz Books closed in 1997, it left more than a gap of a bookstore: It left a void of readings. Then an anonymous donor offered former owner Sheila Wilensky-Lanford some money to continue her series of readings and book signings from popular children's authors like Vera Williams and Ashley Bryan and local poets like William (Kit) Hathaway. Call for a current schedule.

Museums

Abbe Museum
Sieur de Monts Spring, Maine Hwy. 3, Bar Harbor • 288-3519

The Abbe Museum is spending its last summer in its a delightful but nearly miniature octagonal building near the Sieur de Monts entrance to Acadia National Park. In 1999, the museum will move into larger quarters in downtown Bar Harbor. Come see the current exhibit of favorites from the museums extensive collection of art and artifact of Maine's Native Americans. (For details, see our Attractions chapter.)

A gift shop sells books, contemporary baskets and other Native American crafts. Admission is $2 for adults, 50¢ for children.

Wendell Gilley Museum
Maine Hwy. 102, Bass Harbor 244-7555

From a 2-inch woodcock to a life-size bald eagle created by resident artist Steven Valleau, this museum, open year round, features wooden bird art, a special genre. There are more than 200 carvings here created by Gilley and others. (See our Attractions chapter for more information.)

Performing Arts

Music

Arcady Music Festival
College of the Atlantic, 105 Eden Dr., Bar Harbor • 288-2141, 288-3151

Thursdays in Bar Harbor and Mondays in Bangor is the mantra of the Arcady Music Festival. (Those going inland can add Tuesdays in Dover-Foxcroft). For 18 summers, the festival has been offering classical concerts in the region. Bar Harbor's are held on the College of the Atlantic campus. The series has recently expanded its season and offers a more sporadic year-round set of concerts. To encourage community participation in the arts, the music festival also offers student competitions throughout the year.

The 1998 summer series runs from mid-July through late August and includes such delights as Carol Wincenc playing with Japanese court musicians, the New York Ragtime Orchestra, the Virtuosi Wind Quartet and the Arcady Festival Orchestra. Tickets are $12 in advance, $15 at the door; a series pass is $72. Children 18 and younger can attend for free.

Bar Harbor Music Festival
Rodick Building, 59 Cottage St., Bar Harbor • 288-5744 (in-season), (212) 222-1026 (off-season)

As a student at Kneisel Hall (see previous entry), Francis Fortier knew the beauty of Maine; he also knew its musical heritage. Before the summer music festival at Tanglewood, Massachusetts, was created, the Boston Symphony used to play on the Bar Harbor Town Green; Leopold Stokowski, Sergei Rachmaninoff and Enrique Caruso all performed on the island. But by the mid-20th century, the musical traditions of Bar Harbor had dried up. Fortier decided to revive the tradition in 1966, launching the Bar Harbor Music Fes-

Noel Paul Stookey, who once performed regularly with Peter, Paul and Mary, makes his home in Blue Hill.

tival with the idea of offering beautiful music in a beautiful place. The festival promotes young instrumentalists, singers and composers in as many as 10 performances held from early July to early August.

The 1998 series includes performances of piano, song, violin and jazz plus a night devoted to new composers and a series of concerts by the Bar Harbor Festival String Orchestra. Concert locations vary but include the Bar Harbor Congregational Church, Kebo Valley Golf Club and Blackwoods Campground Amphitheater in Acadia National Park. Concert tickets in 1997 cost $15 per adult and $10 for seniors and students, except for the Blackwoods concert, which is free. To reserve tickets in July and August, call the listed in-season number; otherwise, use the off-season number.

West Eden Highlanders Pipes & Drums

West Eden Common, Maine Hwy. 102 and Crooked Rd., Town Hill near Somesville • 244-7193

The West Eden Highlanders Pipes & Drums gather in the commons each Monday evening from June through August to practice and perform traditional Scottish Highland music and dance. Come between 7 and 8 PM to listen and watch this group headed by Rebecca Edmondson, a Scottish lass and local music teacher who serves as pipe major. Her 14-year-old daughter is the dance teacher.

Theater

Acadia Repertory Theater

Masonic Hall, Maine Hwy. 102, Somesville • 244-7260

Set in a rustic, barn-like hall, Acadia Repertory is into its 26th season this summer. Artistic directors have changed remarkably few times over the years, so the theater has remained consistent. Though this book went to press before the year's schedule was nailed down, 1997 offerings included an original production about Abraham Lincoln, Henry James' *Turn of the Screw* and Oliver Goldsmith's *She Stoops to Conquer*. Expect to find a choice Agatha Christie mystery in August. Perfor-

mances run Tuesday through Sunday from the Fourth of July to mid-September. Admission is $15 for adults, $12 for seniors and older students and $10 for folks younger than 16. A children's theater program accompanies the adult program, with performances Wednesday and Saturday at 10:30 AM. (See our Kidstuff chapter.)

Support Organizations

Maine Alliance for Arts Education

P.O. Box 746, Rockport, ME 04856 • 338-1225

This organization focuses on arts in education for all Maine schools, offering a newsletter, networking, professional development, information and encouragement about innovative projects that, for instance, incorporate the arts into a classroom curriculum.

Maine Arts Commission

55 Capital St., State House Station No. 25, Augusta, ME 04333 • 287-2724

This state-run organization administers grants, fosters arts in the schools and assists with the continuity of traditional arts by funding a mentoring program of artists and apprentices. It also helps insure the inclusion of art in state-funded buildings by managing the state's percent-for-art program, in which 1 percent of building costs go toward commissioned art for the building — a sculpture, mural, mobile, stained glass or any other form of public art.

Maine Arts Sponsors Association

P.O. Box 2352, Augusta, ME 04338 • 626-3277

This association supports the performing arts and presenters through yearly conferences at which artists and art promoters gather for discussions and performances. It also offers continual arts advocacy.

Maine Community Cultural Alliance

P.O. Box 2154, Augusta, ME 04338 • 626-3277

This group advocates for Maine's cultural resources, including arts organizations, libraries, museums, historic institutions and archives.

Maine Crafts Association
6 Dow Rd., Deer Isle, Maine 04627
• 348-9943

The Maine Crafts Association supports and advocates for Maine craftspeople. It maintains a resource center with a slide registry, sponsors a yearly show and produces the *Maine Cultural Guide*, a comprehensive membership publication.

Maine Writers and Publishers Alliance
12 Pleasant St., Brunswick, ME 04011
• 729-6333

This affiliation of writers and small-press publishers offers lectures and workshops, publishes a newsletter, sponsors an annual chapbook contest and stocks a large collection of Maine books for sale in its Brunswick building.

Union of Maine Visual Artists
P.O. Box 485, Mount Desert Island, ME 04660 • 244-5746
HC 62, Box 224, Bristol, ME 04539
• 677-2534

This member-run organization monitors the fair treatment of artists, offers a yearly sale in Portland and issues a newsletter. The Downeast chapter is among the most active, running art shows at the Ellsworth Library and offering an ongoing presentation of artists' work. For membership information, contact Polly Cote at the first listed number.

Very Special Arts Maine – Arts for All
P.O. Box 4002, Portland, ME 04101
• 761-3861

This advocacy group provides opportunities for all individuals, especially people with disabilities, to access and connect with the arts through workshops and advocacy.

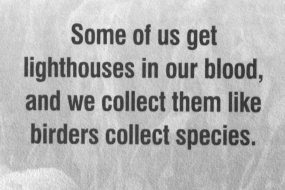

**Some of us get
lighthouses in our blood,
and we collect them like
birders collect species.**

Lighthouses

Coming into a harbor by boat at night, there is nothing more reassuring than the beacon of a lighthouse shining through the dark. For more than a century, these sentinels have stood along the nation's coast, guiding seafarers to safety. White or black- or red-striped, the towers rise from rocks and are topped by glass cupolas holding huge reflective lenses that magnify the lights within. Their shapes are varied but elemental — etched in our minds as children. When we see the real thing, we feel we've come home. When we hear stories of the selfless heroics of the keepers, we are reminded of a time when we as a people truly cared about the well-being of strangers.

Some of us get lighthouses in our blood, and we collect them like birders collect species. There are some 70 lighthouses along the entire coast of Maine, and you can drive to many of them. A few are in private hands and on private property, but 64 are working lighthouses owned by the U.S. Coast Guard.

Actually, Coast Guard ownership has been a problem over the years, as the USCG doesn't have the budget to properly maintain the historic structures. In 1994, the Island Institute, a nonprofit organization based in Rockland, Maine, suggested that 36 lighthouses be transferred to government entities or nonprofit organizations that were ready to maintain them, while the Coast Guard would continue to own and maintain only the light, fog signal and other necessary navigational equipment. The proposal, called the Maine Lights Program, was translated into legislation and signed by President Clinton in 1996, ensuring that the lighthouses continue to be maintained and accessible to the public.

Most working lighthouses are automated and unmanned, so you won't find guided tours of their interiors. What you can do is enjoy their settings — and their silhouettes against the skyline. If that's not enough, check out The Keeper's House on Isle au Haut (see our Accommoda-tions chapter), where you can actually stay inside a lighthouse keeper's house.

A number of the lights have small museums attached, but the mother of lighthouse paraphernalia is Rockland's Shore Village Museum, 104 Limerock Street, 594-0311, open 10 AM to 4 PM daily from June to mid-October, or by chance or appointment. (See our Attractions chapter for details.)

We found a good deal of discrepancies in published material on the number of lighthouses along Maine's coast (Are there 71? 67?) as well as their locations and dates of construction. We relied here on *The Lighthouses of Maine* by Wally Welch, *Maine Lighthouses: A Pictorial Guide* by Courtney Thompson and a one-page guide put together by Ted and Jo Panayotoff at the Elms Bed & Breakfast in Camden. The books are available at the Shore Village Museum; the handout can be picked up at the Rockport-Camden-Lincolnville Chamber of Commerce, Public Landing, Camden.

If you're really driven to research the subject, call the Lighthouse Preservation Society, (508) 281-6336, in Rockport, Massachusetts, or write to the United States Lighthouse Society, 244 Kearny Street, 5th Floor, San Francisco, CA 94108.

To the Lighthouses . . .

Six of the 10 lights discussed in this chapter can be visited by car in a day: Fort Point, Indian Island, Rockland Breakwater, Owls Head, Marshall Point and Pemaquid Point.

Pemaquid Point Light
end of Maine Hwy. 130, Pemaquid

This white conical lighthouse, built in 1827, is just too handsome to miss. The ledges angling down to the sea are dramatic, and visitors of all ages love to clamber over them. Bring a picnic.

Although the light's been automated since 1934, the former keeper's house is now the Fishermen's Museum, 677-2494, which displays fishing and navigational equipment. There are traps, nets, old charts, a map depicting all the lighthouses on Maine's coast and the lens assembly from a lighthouse. It's open late May to mid-October, 10 AM to 5 PM Monday to Saturday and 11 AM to 5 PM Sunday.

The light and museum (and restrooms!) are in a town park, which is open during the same months but from 9 AM to 5 PM daily. Admission is $1 per adult or teen and 50¢ for seniors older than 55 and children 12 and younger.

From U.S. Highway 1 in Waldoboro, take Maine Highway 32 about 26 miles to Pemaquid Point at the end of the peninsula.

Marshall Point Light
Port Clyde Harbor entrance, St. George

Another lighthouse you can reach by car, the Marshall Point Light, built in 1832 and rebuilt in 1858, marks the south entrance to Port Clyde Harbor and the western entrance to Two Bush Channel. This cylindrical light tower stands on a reef running out from Marshall Point, and since its base might be submerged at high tide, a bridge provides access to the tower entrance from the front yard of the former keeper's house.

The Marshall Point Lighthouse Museum, 372-6450, in the keeper's house, displays historic artifacts from the town of St. George. It's open June to September, 1 to 5 PM Sunday through Friday and 10 AM to 5 PM Saturdays. In May and October, it's open on weekends — 10 AM to 5 PM Saturdays and 1 to 5 PM Sundays. Admission is free.

To get there, take Maine Highway 131 south from U.S. Highway 1 in Thomaston. Follow the road to Port Clyde. Turn left onto Duck Cliff Road, then take a right at the first intersection onto Marshall Point Road. The lighthouse is a half-mile away at the end of the road.

Owls Head Light
off Maine Hwy. 73, Owls Head

The Owls Head Light was built in 1826 of white granite, and it marks the south entrance to Rockland Harbor. Today the automated lighthouse and foghorn are part of a state park. While the conical tower is just 26 feet high, it's built on a hill and can be seen 16 miles offshore. You can climb a wooden staircase to the tower, but read the sign: The foghorn might go off, and it can be hazardous to your hearing! In the park you'll find picnic spots, restrooms, hiking paths and tide pools to explore along the shore.

Take Maine Highway 73 south off U.S. 1 in Rockland. About 2 miles down, turn left on North Shore Drive. It's about 2.5 miles to the Owls Head Post office, where you'll turn left onto Main Street, and left again almost immediately on Lighthouse Road. There's a parking lot about a half-mile down, and you can walk to the light from there.

> **FYI**
>
> Unless otherwise noted, the area code for all phone numbers listed in this guide is 207.

Rockland Breakwater Light
off Samoset Rd., Rockland

Just 20 minutes from Owls Head Light (see previous entry) is another lighthouse you can reach by car.

Take U.S. 1 though Rockland and turn right on Waldo Avenue. Turn right again on Samoset Road and drive to the end, where there's a small parking area.

You'll see a mile-long granite breakwater reaching out into Rockland Harbor. At the end is the Rockland Breakwater Light, a square, white tower built in 1888 as part of a fog signal house. It's a working light, but it's automated and unmanned. We've walked this breakwater in all kinds of weather; it can be hazardous at high tide and in the winter, so be careful. In the summer, it's a wonderful place to bring a blanket and stretch out like salamanders in the sun on the warm, flat granite slabs.

Indian Island Light
Indian Island, at the mouth of Rockport Harbor, Rockport

This light was built in 1850, rebuilt in 1874, and is now privately owned. Near the island is its modern-day substitute, a 25-foot-tall automated beacon on Lowell Rock that flashes red every six seconds.

On the south end of Indian Island, at the

Photo: Bangor Daily News

Lighthouses like this one at Port Clyde are scattered along Maine's rocky coast.

east side of the harbor entrance, this lighthouse can be seen from Marine Park, off Pascal Avenue (see Parks and Recreation chapter).

Curtis Island Light
Camden Harbor entrance, Camden

The lighthouse on Curtis Island is part of a town park, and the caretakers who live in the keeper's house during the summer are used to visitors exploring the paths around the island. The light was built in 1832 and rebuilt in 1896. It shines green and can be seen from shore, from Bayview Street just past Beacon Avenue or part way up Beacon Avenue. This is a residential neighborhood, so be considerate.

If you want a closer look, a canoe or kayak will get you there in a snap. It's an easy paddle through Camden Harbor (see our Parks and Recreation chapter for suggestions on where to rent canoes or kayaks), although you do have to dodge boat traffic. We've spent days out there among the wild roses, with picnics, books and lawn chairs.

Grindel Point Light
Gilkey Harbor, Islesboro

Grindel Point Light on Islesboro, a white-painted square tower, can be seen from shore, across from Lincolnville Beach, but you'll have to take a ferry (see our Offshore/Islands chapter) to get there. Built in 1850 and rebuilt in 1874, it marks the north entrance to Gilkey Harbor and is adjacent to the ferry landing. The light is no longer operating; a solar-powered light mounted on a metal skeleton near the original lighthouse provides the necessary illumination.

The building now houses the Sailors' Memorial Museum, 734-2253, run by the town of Islesboro "to preserve the memory of the seafaring men of Islesboro." The island memorabilia displayed was collected by The Islesboro Historical Society in the 1970s. It's open 10 AM to 4 PM every day but Monday from Independence Day to Labor Day. We're told there are times when you might be allowed to climb the lighthouse tower. Ask the volunteer at the museum.

Fort Point Light
east end of Cape Jellison, Stockton Springs

Fort Point Light was built in 1836 at the

www.insiders.com

See this and many other **Insiders' Guide®** destinations online — in their entirety.

Visit us today!

Photo: Bangor Daily News

Once manned to alert ship captains to Maine's dangerous rockbound coast, some of today's lighthouses still shine their beacons.

mouth of the Penobscot River. The closest town is Stockton Springs. Follow the signs to Fort Point State Park. You'll cross an open field and pass the earthworks of Fort Pownal, built in 1759 to protect English settlers. The rectangular lighthouse tower, with its fixed white light, rises from the point. It was automated in 1988 and is adjacent to the Fort Point State Park. The park ranger lives in the keeper's house, so tread respectfully.

Dice Head Light
Castine Harbor entrance, Castine

This light, also called Dyce Head in some reference materials, was built in 1829 and enlarged in 1858. It's been unattended since 1953; a 27-foot-tall tower built nearby flashes white every six seconds. Dice Head is just 5 miles down the bay from the Fort Point Light.

Isle au Haut Light
Robinson Point, Isle au Haut

Built in 1907 and unmanned since 1934, the Isle au Haut Light's been called "the youngest and prettiest along the coast." It's still a navigational aid for fishing and cruising boats traveling the Isle au Haut Bay Thorofare. A bridge links the lighthouse to shore and The Keeper's House, a bed and breakfast (see Accommodations). The light's massive lens is on display at the Shore Village Museum in Rockland (see the chapter introduction). If you'd like to get out to the island, see the Offshore/Islands chapter for more detail.

For centuries, images of Maine's natural beauty have lured people to visit its wild coastal cliffs and islands.

Our Natural World

Maine is a land of astounding beauty, a place of rocky islands with tall, craggy spruce trees bristling like the quills on a porcupine's back; of land tentacles extending into the ocean; of small, sweet coves where tree, water and sky abide in perfect balance. The beauty comes from the state's great natural contrasts: textures of granite and ocean; tall spruce and scrubby blueberry barren; huge, lumbering moose and delicately fluttering hummingbirds; a cloudless sky at one moment, stormy and fog-laden the next.

For centuries, such images have lured people to visit Maine's wild coastal cliffs and islands. But this wildness, along with the state's relative remoteness and the sheer difficulty of living here — with rock-laden soil, scouring winters and inordinately short summers — has kept Maine sparsely populated. What Maine lacks in people, however, is more than made up for in its natural world. Osprey and eagle nest here in summer. Loons call through the stillness of saltwater coves and freshwater lakes. Seals poke their heads up in harbors, while porpoises frolic nearby. Farther off the coast, whales breach the sea's surface with near violence.

Maine's residents and visitors, alike, relish its beauty — always in flux because of the constantly changing sky, sea and light. Ultimately, the source of Maine's great beauty lies in astronomical extremes: the sun, or its absence; the earth, or rather, its rocks; and its complex geological history — much of which occurred millions of years ago — of gouged river valleys, clashing continents and massive glaciers.

Geology

Look at a relief map of Maine's Mid-Coast, with its numerous islands and peninsulas dangling into the water. It looks positively ragged, as if torn from the motherland by a toddler's hand. This ragged coast is Maine's hallmark — the result of several different geologic epochs. This remote and isolated state has really been places — and we're not talking about the great seafaring age when Maine captains and sailors went traveling all over the globe on schooners, clippers and Down-easters. The land itself has traveled.

About 250 million years ago, at the time of the great continental drift, Avalonia (now Europe) drifted westward to North America; Africa later joined it. When all the continents came together, Maine was at the very center of one great continent. Mount Desert Island was located approximately where Ghana is now — latitude, 5 degrees north; longitude, about 0 degrees. At that time, some rock was actually melted by pressure. Great masses of molten magma intruded into the surrounding crust, then cooled and crystallized, becoming the granite now infused throughout Maine's mountains and coast. When the continents were torn apart, some of the European coast stayed behind, wedged onto Maine. (Fossils found in limestone quarries near Thomaston are of European, not North American, creatures.)

But the rocks that form Maine's distinctive fingerlike peninsulas were already in place, even before the continents joined and separated. These peninsulas and islands are the result of an uplifting of the surface about 400 million years ago. As written in David L. Kendall's *Glaciers & Granite: A Guide to Maine's Landscape & Geology* (Down East Books: Camden, Maine: 1987), "immense forces deep inside the earth pushed westward, rumpling layers of sediment on the ocean floor into vertical folds, much as would happen if you slid your hand over the dinner table, pushing the tablecloth ahead." At the time, masses of molten granite were injected into the crumpled layers. Later, these formations were carved by rivers such as the St. George that accentuated the peninsulas.

After the continents were pulled apart, and Maine rotated to its present-day orientation, the climate became about 5 degrees colder. Snow remained year round at high altitudes, accumulating still more snow and cooling the climate even more. An ice pack developed; soon after came the Ice Age. The weight of the ice literally pushed down the land to below sea level; thus, Maine is known as having a drowned coast. As the ice crept southward, it flowed up mountains, dumping its load downward at their pinnacles and frequently slicing off layers of rock. This activity left many Maine mountains with gentle northerly slopes and steep south-facing cliffs where the ice had fallen off. The Porcupines, off Bar Harbor, are good examples of this geological dynamic — reminders that islands are but the tops of submerged mountains.

As glaciers carved the land, they formed U-shaped valleys such as Somes Sound (on Mount Desert Island), which ultimately filled with seawater after the glaciers receded. Sometimes the ice left deposits of churned-up gravel and sand, hence Maine's many gravel pits; sometimes it created moraines (large, ridge-like deposits of rock) 10 to 50 feet wide and as much as 100 feet high and a mile long. Then the ice melted, pouring into the sea. Since the land had been pushed down by as much as 400 feet, the water covered much of today's coast, flowing even farther inland than I-95 runs today.

As the ice continued to recede, the land gradually rose. A blanket of rock debris covered the ground. This debris, or till (a mixture of sand, silt, clay and rock fragments, some as large as boulders), remained in little coves between rocky headlands on what is now Maine's coast, leaving several tiny pocket beaches that, contrary to assumption, are seldom the result of erosion. As the ice scratched northward, it smoothed stones, deposited glacial till and caused million-year-old valleys to flood. The result was long, narrow bays separated by narrow peninsulas. The glacier also scraped off most of the sandy soil covering of the rocks and, especially in Downeast Maine, deposited masses of huge granite boulders.

The islands of the region — Vinalhaven, Deer Isle, Swans Island and Isle Au Haut — are mostly granite, at times contrasted by dull gray lava flows. Some flows also had minerals, hence the copper, lead, silver and zinc mines that once operated on the islands and the Blue Hill peninsula. (By 1997, all mines had closed.) Farther Downeast, on Schoodic Peninsula, rough rocks of greenish black basalt rise through the red granite. Because basalt is less resistant to erosion than granite, these rocks have worn down, leaving trenches. The sea surges into the trenches causing the spectacular surf for which the region is famous. (For a discussion of the geology of Mount Desert Island, see our Acadia National Park chapter.)

Coastal Weather

The old line about Maine weather just has to be told: If you don't like it, just wait — it will change soon enough.

The weather changes drastically from morning to afternoon — and just as drastically from inland to coast. In winter 1996, a heavy snowstorm left 6 inches of snow inland in the state capital of Augusta; at the coast we had driving rain and 40-degree temperatures. But that night, the thermometer plummeted to 0, then hovered around minus-10 the next day.

Summer weather isn't any less variable. A bright summer morning's cloudless sky can turn into a green squall by mid-afternoon. As long as you're comfortably situated, you can frequently spend a cozy summer afternoon

watching a thunderstorm approach, drench and leave.

This is only of aesthetic interest if you've come to Maine to drive, shop or simply wind down in an inn. If you've come for the outdoors — and especially if you're planning to be out on the water, whether inland or ocean — you must be prepared and aware. Lightning comes with thunder. A squall on a large lake can send high waves over your canoe before you reach shore; the danger is even greater in coastal waters. Follow weather forecasts and use your eyes and common sense. We make a daily obeisance to our weather radio each morning — and we obey the forecast, even though it can be wrong.

If you don't have a radio offering the official, endless National Oceanic and Atmospheric Administration (or NOAA) weather forecasts (on channel 2), both the Thomaston and Searsport classical stations — WAVX-FM 106.9 and WBYA-FM 101.7, respectively — give excellent forecasts every hour on the hour. And prepare yourself accordingly. Don't go on the water if you hear small-craft advisories. And if you're traveling offshore, climbing a mountain or taking a long bike ride, bring a sweater and a windbreaker.

Coastal winds moderate the weather along Maine's Mid-Coast. An August day can be a scorching 90 degrees in Augusta but a moderate 70 along the shore. According to Acadia National Park records, Mount Desert Island temperatures average 23 degrees in January and 67 degrees in July. But the extremes are not so moderate. Temperatures on the coast frequently hover around 0 to 10 degrees for a few weeks in January, and we do get a few 90 degree days, even along the coast.

In spring and summer, also expect rain and haunting coastal fog. In winter we usually get snow — about 60 inches each year, with as much as 30 inches on the ground at any one time in January and February. And then there are the astoundingly beautiful — though treacherous — ice storms that cause trees, weeds and bushes to shimmer like Christmas trees. In winter 1997-98, such an ice storm devastated the state, cutting off power to more than half the population for several days. The outage lasted two weeks for some. Entire forests in the Mid-Coast area looked as if a giant had walked along, picking off the tops of trees.

The Coast

From Penobscot to Sagadahock, the Coast is all Mountainous and Iles of huge rocks, but over growen with all sorts of excellent good woodes for building houses, boats, barks or shippes; with an incredible abundance of most sorts of fish, much fowle, and sundry sorts of

Foliage Tours

As summer winds down, flaming-red branches begin to appear — one per tree per mile perhaps, but quite visible nonetheless. These first heralds of autumn are met by some Mainers with shock and sadness signalling, as they do, the year's last days of summer warmth. But as September routines begin, the changing leaves are an awaited event. Come early October, the autumn woods positively dance. Brilliant yellow beech and birch set off the blazing red-orange maples, and Maine's roads begin to buzz again

with visitors coming to see the foliage. Fall foliage is an accelerating event. Beginning in September, the leaves gradually turn until mid-October, when they peak (that is to say, just about all leaves that will change have changed). After that, usually a good windy rain will send them from limb to land.

Autumn in Maine is delightful. The weather is warm, the sun frequently brilliant, and the air unusually crisp and clear. We can think of numerous glorious drives that mingle the blue of the water with the brightness of the wood. Following are a few suggestions.

St. George Peninsula

Trip 1: The St. George Peninsula is a great destination for its small fishing villages and large coastal views. Begin in Thomaston. For a loop trip that's actually a figure-8, take Maine Highway 131 south through the fishing towns of St. George, Tenants Harbor and Martinsville to Port Clyde. Pull off the road to walk, admire and visit whenever you desire. Walk the beach of Mosquito Harbor, after Martinsville, or drive out to Marshall Point Light (see our Lighthouses chapter) just before you get to Port Clyde. To loop back up to U.S. Highway 1, take a series of smaller roads up the western (St. George) side of the peninsula. You'll be following Glenmere Road for a little more than 3 miles until Turkey Road merges from the east, then the route becomes Turkey Road. After

— continued on next page

Photo: Bangor Daily News

In fall, colorful leaves draw thousands of "leaf-peepers" to Maine to view the foliage.

another 3 or so miles, turn left onto Wallston Road and continue until it hits Maine 131. (Don't worry if you miss the turn; you'll simply be directed back onto Maine 131 to Tenants Harbor, just remember to turn left onto Maine 131 north when you reach the town.) In St. George, turn right and take Maine Highway 73 across the peninsula to Spruce Head. Follow that road up through South Thomaston to U.S. 1.

Blue Hill Peninsula

Trip 2: On Blue Hill Peninsula, it's not only the trees that turn in the autumn, but also the blueberry barrens, which change color into what poet Robert Lowell called a "red fox stain." Drive the circuit of Blue Hill. The roads change numbers, and the directions get confused (north roads move south and south move north for instance), so take a map along. From Blue Hill, we suggest taking Maine Highway 177 to South Penobscot, then turning left onto Maine Highway 175 (which turns into Maine 176 before becoming Maine 175 again), continuing past Caterpillar Hill to Sargentville; then, follow Maine 175, the coastal route, past Sedgwick, Brooklin and Blue Hill Falls back to Blue Hill.

Acadia National Park

Trip 3: The roads of Acadia National Park are quiet during autumn, despite the glorious foliage that lines them. Bring a bicycle and ride the carriage roads; drive the Park Loop Road; or take the Pretty Marsh Road (Maine Highway 102) loop from Somesville to Southwest Harbor and back around.

good fruits for man's use. . . . And of all the foure parts of the world that I have yet seen not inhabited, could I have but means to transport a Colonie, I would rather live here than any where; and if it did not maintain it selfe, were wee but once indifferently well fitted, let us starve. — Capt. John Smith in *A Description of New England, 1614.*

It was summer when Capt. John Smith visited the coast of Maine and found a shoreline dominated by forests of massive, tall, straight white pine. Had Smith arrived a few months later or come ashore to try a hoe on the "Iles of huge rocks," he likely would not have expected a "Colonie" to thrive. Still, following Smith's challenge, colonists arrived and cleared the land, eventually removing almost every last white pine for ship masts, floorboards and other building and shipbuilding uses.

A dozen species of softwood — among them pine, balsam, red spruce, hemlock, hackmatack (known outside Maine as tamarack), fir and cedar — have replaced the original white pines. Also in Maine's forests are white and red oak, white or paper birch, sugar and silver maple, elm and ash.

Native Americans made good use of these trees: Sugar maples have been tapped for centuries for their annual yield of syrup; birch has been used for baskets and canoes, which a century ago were known simply as birches; and brown ash is still pounded along its annual rings to form pliant, reed-like strips for weaving traditional baskets. Today, in addition to the aforementioned uses, balsam and other evergreens are wound into wreaths that are shipped all over the nation, frequently along with Maine Christmas trees. And pine logs are carted off in two- and three-story-high piles and stored for eventual use as pulp for paper mills.

Given the abundance of the forest, imagine the colonists' surprise when they discovered that the soil in which the massive pines grew was thin, acidic and almost inevitably stony. It was well-suited to evergreens, but not much more. And still, the land was cleared: Trees were chopped and stones rolled from the fields. The wood framed houses, the stones became walls, and the fields grew corn and cabbage or became simple pasture (since grown over). Ask any longtime resident of just about any coastal town where the pastures used to be, and they'll point to a stand of pines.

Fifty or so years ago, a surprising amount of Maine's forest was field. Even so, many of us imagine that the forest represents the land's natural state. But we don't know for sure. Native Americans also altered the forests, at times by setting fires to flush game and clear the land.

The closer to the coast you get, the more limiting the conditions. The vegetation tells the tale. Fog, salt spray, shallow soil and moderate temperatures often affect growth, resulting in stunted, salt-tolerant trees. Many Maine forests are laden with lichens and mosses that turn the woods into fairylands. A forest on Deer Isle, known as Crockett Cove Woods, is known for its wide variety of mosses (see our Attractions chapter). The moss grows moist after rain but becomes brittle in dry summer months, especially during the region's characteristic August droughts.

Blueberry bushes frequently grow in the acidic soil of forests that open to the sun. Climb a mountain — Cadillac will do — and it's not hard to find refreshing berries at the top. Common on roadsides are raspberry and blackberry bushes, which unfortunately seem to make a happy pair with poison ivy, so watch where you pick. Also growing beside roads, and more frequently tumbling into old gardens and over broken fences, are wild pink roses, molting into rose hips the size of a jacks' ball come late summer. In the woods are trillium, wild lily of the valley, lady-slippers, jack-in-the-pulpits and the more common shad bush. Beside the road are lupines, loosestrife, tiger-lilies, springtime lilacs and autumn asters and apples. Rare orchids are found in some bogs, such as Seawall Bog along Maine Highway 102A on Mount Desert Island. Other bogs, some of them human-made, yield cranberries, a growing business.

The Sea

Maine's seacoast is a world unto itself. Tides affect river flows, turning peninsulas into islands as waters rise over sandbars, then leaving tide pools behind at low ebb. Rachel Carson, Maine's poet of the sea, speaks about Maine's tidal shores in her book *The Edge of the Sea* (Houghton Mifflin Co.: Boston, Massachusetts: 1955):

When the tide is high on a rocky shore,

when its brimming fullness creeps up almost to the bayberry and the junipers where they come down from the land, one might easily suppose that nothing at all lived in or on or under these waters of the sea's edge. For nothing is visible. Nothing except here and there a little group of herring gulls. . . .

The shore is a place of unrest during the rising tide. Surging waters leap high over jutting rocks and run in lacy cascades of foam over the landward side of massive boulders. Conversely, it is more peaceful on the ebb, the waves flowing without the push of the tide. Look for life in tide pools — snails, whelks, periwinkles, barnacles and seaweed.

In Smith's day, fishermen sought cod, working the deep ocean waters from open boats using hand lines. Since then, conditions have gotten better — for the humans, not the cod. Overfishing for groundfish, such as cod and haddock, has been a long-standing problem. Fishermen trawling for groundfish — dragging a large net across the ocean floor from behind the boat — easily can catch thousands of pounds of fish. But such landings seriously deplete fish stocks, hence the $25 million buyout campaign launched by the U.S. government to buy back some 70 ground-fishing vessels in New England.

Cod is no longer Maine's major fishery — lobster is. Lobster boats are prevalent off Maine's coast between May and October, when lobstermen travel from lobster buoy to lobster buoy (each of the 6,300 lobstermen have different color markings on their buoys, so they know which trap is theirs), checking traps they've set for the bluish-red, shelled creatures.

The second-largest fishery is farm-raised Atlantic salmon harvested from Swan's Island eastward. Third on the list are sea urchins, which comprise a new and popular — though somewhat dangerous — industry. Nearly 19,000 divers ply coastal waters for the shellfish in spring, when the urchins are filled with roe, or eggs — a prized delicacy in Japan. The danger is that divers can get entangled in lines, pulled by currents or simply run out of air, sometimes in as shallow as 10 feet of water.

The endangered groundfish fishery — cod and haddock and other bottom-dwelling spe-

Photo: Bangor Daily News

After collecting shells, a young man picks his way back to dry land through a "sea" of seaweed that has been deposited on the rocks by high tide.

cies — is next in importance, followed by the small Arctic shrimp that migrate close to Maine's shore between December and May, and then by soft-shell clams, dug in Maine's ample mudflats by a multitude of independently licensed clam diggers.

Mainers used to be able to dig for clams whenever they needed a meal, but two kinds of pollution have tainted the beds: Simple waterborne pollution has closed many Mid-Coast flats — a problem being remedied by better septic tanks; and, every so often (more frequently in summer), red tide hits. Red tide is the name for an invasion of single-cell plankton-like microorganisms that grow in coastal waters around the globe, multiplying rapidly and sometimes tinting the tide red. It first began hitting Maine's coast in the 1970s. Humans can become ill if they eat a clam or mussel tainted by red tide, so the state monitors shellfish beds weekly year round and more frequently in summer. Bed closings are posted and announced over the NOAA weather radio (see the previous "Coastal Weather" section).

Other coastal fisheries include scallops (commercial) and striped bass and bluefish (recreational).

Inland, common species found in lakes and rivers are landlocked and Atlantic salmon, trout, bass, white perch, yellow perch and pickerel. But some inland waters have traces of mercury, so heed warnings on freshwater fish.

Marine Mammals

There are much larger "fish" in Maine's seas — a host of marine mammals actually. Perhaps most popular among them are seals. We remember a school picnic of kindergartners and 1st-graders at Moose Point, just off U.S. Highway 1 between Belfast and Searsport. For at least 10 minutes, two lines of children stood transfixed, staring into the eyes of a mother seal who had come to a nearby rock. She seemed equally transfixed by this brood of human children. Then the tide came in, and the seal slithered off the rock and disappeared into the ocean.

Seals swim up the Penobscot River and have been seen with whales in Bucksport. They visit Maine harbors and, during almost any offshore cruise, can be seen peering up at boats. Porpoises are less common but are sometimes seen rhythmically diving and rising, luring people to the water with their grace. Whales sometimes come close to shore, but visitors are more likely to see them in deeper waters, especially around Mount Desert Rock, about 25 miles offshore. On whale-watch cruises (see our Attractions chapter), it is common to see humpback and finback whales; less-common sightings include minkes, right whales, orcas and pilot whales.

Birds

We remember when a family member visiting from the Midwest exclaimed, "Look, there's a sea gull — look at that one, sitting on a car!" It must have been perplexing that we didn't share the same enthusiasm. In coastal Maine, it's fair to say that there are more gulls than cars. Lots of ravens winter in Maine too, as do diminutive chickadees and nuthatches.

Ospreys return annually to the same site to nest and frequently have at least two broods a summer. Famous nesting areas in the region include: Pulpit Harbor on North Haven, a sailor's rest; Sandy Point Beach (turn right off of U.S. 1 north of Stockton Springs, just across from the Rocky Ridge Motel); Waldo-Hancock Bridge between Stockton Springs and Verona Island; Bucksport, at the old piers on the Penobscot River just downriver from Champion International's paper mill; and Porcupine Island, off Bar Harbor.

Eagles often are found year round at the same locations as ospreys. A few live on or near the Penobscot River, near Bucksport. Others live on the Porcupine Islands, off Bar Harbor. Coastal bird feeders are visited by downy woodpeckers, rose-breasted grosbeaks and goldfinches. Hummingbird feeders are oft-visited as well, and these tiny flying gems will astound you. Did you know that hummingbirds are the only birds capable of flying backward? Watch one at a feeder or flower, dipping in its exquisitely long, thin beak, hovering, retreating, then dipping again. Did you see a flash of red at the neck? Then it's a male ruby-throated hummingbird.

Folks living near fields have joined in local efforts to bring back the bluebird. In coastal marshes you'll see wood-duck boxes placed in an attempt to nurture duck populations. At harbors you'll find the angular, black-robed cormorants, looking like medieval witches as they stretch out their gaunt wings to dry. You might also see a multitude of ducks, loons and assorted traveling species. (Read on for details.)

Speaking of traveling, every so often a grouse will cross the road. Puffins, clown-faced penguin-like birds, are described by Hank and Jan Taft, authors of the second edition of *A Cruising Guide to the Maine Coast*, as looking like clergymen on a binge. These birds can be seen offshore only: at Eastern Egg Rock, off Muscongus Bay; at Matinicus Rock, off Matinicus; at Petit Manan Island, east of Corea; or at Machias Seal Island, off Machias. (See our Attractions chapter for details about puffin cruises.)

According to the Maine Audubon Society, "access to good birding is seldom a problem." Back roads and logging roads are viable birding sites, and a canoe or a kayak opens up additional possibilities. The Mid-Coast forest shelters northern species such as Swainson's thrushes, red-breasted nuthatches, winter wrens, golden-crowned kinglets, dark-eyed juncos and white-winged crossbills. Just offshore are black guillemots, razorbills and other water birds. Bring binoculars and gaze from the shore.

Acadia National Park has a nesting ground for peregrine falcons at Precipice Mountain. You can't get close to the nestlings, but a ranger with good binoculars is frequently stationed at the trailhead parking area. The ranger will keep you away until the birds are well-grown, but will offer you a few glimpses of them through a pair of high-powered binoculars. Come fall, you might also see them from just about any near-coast hike on the island. The mountain peaks also are good places from which to view migrating hawks.

A few other specific sites are known as bird-watching hotspots. We've relied upon *A Birder's Guide to the Coast of Maine*, by Elizabeth Cary Pierson, Jan Erik Pierson and Peter D. Vickery. We'll direct you to some within our geographic areas of coverage, from Waldoboro north to Bangor and east to Gouldsboro.

In South Thomaston, check out Weskeag Marsh, also known as R. Waldo Tyler Wildlife Preserve. From the south, take U.S. 1 north to Thomaston, turning south onto Buttermilk Lane just after the cement plant. The marsh is across from a culvert, a mile after the turn. On this 300-acre preserve, you'll find a range of nesting freshwater marsh birds, wading birds, migrant shorebirds and some ducks. Look for great blue herons, snowy egrets, glossy ibises, ospreys, common terns and sharp-tailed and swamp sparrows. Near the cattail ponds, you might see American bitterns and marsh and sedge wrens. Migrating shorebirds in spring and fall include semipalmated and black-bellied plovers, greater and lesser yellowlegs, killdeers, sandpipers, Canada geese, blue- and green-winged teals, ring-necked ducks and mallards. In winter, look for rough-legged hawks as well as barred and snowy owls. You might also see a bald eagle.

This is a good spot for a canoe, but don't go as far as the bridge in South Thomaston, where there's a riptide. It's best to come between March and midsummer at high tide. Wear boots and bring your favorite mosquito repellant — this is a marsh after all.

U.S. 1 in Rockland Harbor is the place to look for gulls — greater black-backed, herring, ring-billed and the diminutive Bonaparte's varieties. From November to March you might find glaucous and Iceland gulls. Also look for loons, grebes, great cormorants, old-squaws, common and Barrow's goldeneye ducks as well as buffleheads, red-breasted mergansers and possibly a king eider.

In Belfast, wind your way down Pierce Street to the old bridge across the Passagassawakeag River for a glimpse of red-breasted mergansers or Barrow's goldeneyes, both of which can be found here in winter. The Barrow's goldeneye is a beautiful duck with a sleek, black head accentuated by a bright, white crescent near the eye. It's an uncommon migrant but is frequently seen here in flocks of 15 or more.

On Mount Desert Island, look for waterfowl and water birds, such as old-squaws, and shorebirds on migration in winter at Mount Desert Narrows, Maine Highway 3, on the causeway between the island and the mainland.

The Bar Island bar, off Bridge Street in Bar Harbor, is accessible at low tide only. On the bar you sometimes can find black-bellied plovers, ruddy turnstones, semipalmated sandpipers, Bonaparte's and laughing gulls and common terns.

Off Maine Highway 3 in Acadia National Park, look for signs to Sieur de Monts Spring, one of the best places to see a wide variety of species. Among the more unusual are yellow-throated and golden-winged warblers. You also might find American woodcocks, black-billed cuckoos, great crested flycatchers and Eastern peewees in spring and summer.

At the north side of Seawall Bog, Maine Highway 102A, near Wonderland parking lot, look for nesting yellow-bellied flycatchers, palm warblers and Lincoln's sparrows in early June in this lovely, fragile bog. And keep an eye out for pitcher plants and bog orchids.

Also try Schoodic Point in Winter Harbor. On this headland, with its spruce forest, you might find loons, common eiders, red-breasted mergansers, great black-backed and herring gulls and black guillemots in winter. In summer look for double-crested cormorants, ospreys, Bonaparte's and laughing gulls and common terns. In winter you might see red-throated loons, horned and red-necked grebes, buffleheads, old-squaws, common goldeneyes and purple sandpipers. A bald eagle nests on Schoodic Island to the east.

Other good spots to see birds are the offshore islands, especially Monhegan and Isle au Haut (see our Offshore/Islands chapter for details about these and other Mid-Coast islands). Monhegan, especially, is known as a migrant trap, where an unusual variety of rare and uncommon species such as magnificent frigate birds, ivory gulls, bridled terns, gyrfalcons, American swallow-tailed kites, band-tailed pigeons, white-winged doves and rufous hummingbirds occasionally have been observed.

Mammals

Maine has its share of mammals, both small and large. Some of the smaller furry creatures you might encounter include squirrels, chipmunks, skunks, woodchucks, beavers, otters, fox and personable raccoons — just about anyone who lives in Maine has a story about these masked bandits. (Note that a rabies epidemic that began in the mid-Atlantic states is creeping northward, creating a bit of concern about small wild animals.) For the fleet-of-eye, fox can sometimes be spotted at

Camden Hills State Park in Camden. You'll see beavers, or at least their prodigious work, at Acadia National Park (see our Acadia National Park chapter for specifics). Otters are not uncommon sights if you canoe, especially in slow-moving rivers.

Of the larger mammals, deer and moose are common enough to worry drivers with continual reports of car collisions. Keep an eye on the side of the road as well as in front of you. We've seen moose and deer at all times of day and night, frequently on midsize back roads, such as Maine Highway 166 leading out to Castine from U.S. Highway 1. We've also seen a moose right on U.S. 1, just outside Ellsworth.

To find a moose in May, you might not need to look farther than the side of a road. Moose come to roadside ditches where the first greens of spring can be found. To find a moose in June, you might have to seek out a quiet pond or bog filled with greenery. Though more moose live in the woods north and west of the Mid-Coast, one moose was a daily visitor to a pond on U.S. 1 in Searsport during a recent summer. Another pond on U.S. 1A in Winterport was visited weekly by a different moose. With any luck, you, too, might find a moose munching away at the water plants, night or day, at some pond. They are after salt in spring, for their sodium is depleted over the long winter; bog food is a sure antidote. In summer, you'll need to venture farther into the woods. There are native Mainers who have never seen a moose, so don't despair if you don't either.

Insects

And what about those barely mentionable members of the natural world — the bugs? They weren't overlooked by the very first naturalist who published natural histories of the area. John Josselyn, whose *An Account of Two Voyages to New-England* was published in 1674, wrote:

The Country is strangely incommodated with flyes, which the English call Musketaes, they are like our gnats, they will sting so fiercely in summer as to make the faces of the English swell'd and scabby, as if the small pox for the first year. Likewise there is a small black fly no bigger than a flea, so numerous up in the Country, that a man cannot draw his breath, but he will suck of them in: they continue about Thirty dayes say some but I say three moneths, and are not only a pesterment but a plague to the Country.

Cruelly, black flies visit just when it's finally warm enough for us Mainers to venture out into our gardens: They force us back inside. Black flies are only supposed to be here until

Moose sightings are frequent in the wooded areas of central Maine.

Photo: Bangor Daily News

the end of June, but sometimes they take a liking to the summer weather and stay longer. Josselyn's description of the flies' voracity is not exaggerated. Children and adults not accustomed to black flies can get huge welts from the bites. They are usually not dangerous and go away quickly, but consult a physician if you have any concerns.

Mosquitoes are even more tenacious than black flies. In summer, they are most prevalent near swamps and are most active the hour following sunset. What to do? People put screens on their porches (and sometimes their hats) and experiment with a variety of repellents, from rubbing orange peels over their skin to lathering on serious over-the-counter bug dope. When the cold weather comes, the parasitic villains simply come inside our homes, but by then they're blessedly impotent.

Finally there are the no-see-ums. Forget it. They live up to their name and seep through screens. Your only antidote is to keep out of the woods where they like it best.

Maine Mysteries

Like its weather, Maine's natural world changes year by year, season by season — by the day and by locale. And we Mainers are subject to nature's whim. On summer days, when lupines and delphinium have overtaken our gardens or when an eagle flies overhead, spurred on by a warm breeze, we sometimes try to imagine winter: snow as high as third step to our porch. But winter cannot be summoned. And in the dead of winter, when we're cozily settled by the stove with our morning cup of coffee, watching downy woodpeckers, knowing that by afternoon we might find a snowy owl sitting like a sentinel beside the woodpile, we can't ever imagine the frivolity and color of the summer hummingbirds.

Maine is a world both mysterious and known; it is a world in which there is always something to be discovered. And yet most of the players — the forest and its deer, the sky and its birds, the night and its stars, the sea and its whales — can be named.

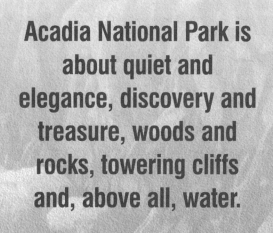

Acadia National Park is about quiet and elegance, discovery and treasure, woods and rocks, towering cliffs and, above all, water.

Acadia National Park

Drive slowly over the Maine Highway 3 causeway onto Mount Desert Island. Look around. You 're approaching Acadia National Park.

The waters of Mount Desert Narrows stretch to either side of you. Perhaps they are covered by cotton wisps of mist, perhaps they shimmer in the sun. Look to the southwest toward Western Bay. If the fog hasn't settled, you might spot Alley Island, perhaps Black Island and Bartlett, as well as the larger Mount Desert to which you're headed. Beyond are the mountains that bring Mount Desert its fame — bareheaded and rounded, ancient and gentle in the mist.

It's not just visitors who take in the view; commuters long accustomed to this causeway pull off the road to watch the sun set in a blaze of glory or the moon rise quietly over the waters.

Though Acadia does have its significant attractions, like the thunderous Thunder Hole and breathtaking vistas from Cadillac Mountain — conveniently served by the 27-mile-long Park Loop Road — if you ask park superintendent Paul Haertel what is special about this national park, he will speak of its small pleasures.

Acadia National Park is about quiet and elegance, discovery and treasure, woods and rocks, towering cliffs and, above all, water. Of all the national parks, Acadia is the only one in the East where hills tumble into the sea.

It is true that most visitors see Acadia by car — a fact that worries Haertel above all else, since auto emissions damage the island's fragile ecosystem. And, as we have said, sight-seeing by auto certainly is one way to see the park.

You'll want to feel Acadia too, and for that, you'll want to take a walk. It needn't be far: Wander to an inland pond to see beaver architecture; climb a hill — or a rock face — for the conquering sense of reaching the summit and savoring the view over land and sea; join a ranger walk to discover tide pools; visit park gardens or seashore trails. At the very least, walk to Otter Cliffs, or pile another stone on the sculpture of towers that each summer turn Seawall Beach into an otherworldly art gallery.

Don't limit your explorations to mere walks. Hop on a bike and travel the carriage roads or skirt the soaring hills of Schoodic Peninsula. Come in winter with cross-country skis, and relish the frozen air against your warming skin — not to mention the views over snow to the ice-blue water. Most of all, get out on the water, whatever the season. Rent, borrow, board or bring something to float on, whether it be a canoe, kayak, sailboat, rowboat or motorboat. This is the nation's island park after all; it's about water.

Getting Your Bearings

Acadia National Park is mostly situated on Mount Desert Island — Maine's largest island — a large, claw-like island off the Down East coast that is almost divided in half by the East Coast's only fjord, Somes Sound. The 74,000-acre island, roughly 16 miles by 13 miles, is 20 miles from Ellsworth via Maine Highway 3.

About half the island (more specifically, about 34,000 acres) is comprised of the national park, but the 40,000-acre Acadia reaches beyond Mount Desert. Most of the park's remaining 6,000 or so acres are on wild and windswept Isle au Haut (pronounced "I'll a hoe"), 15 miles southwest of MDI (the local abbreviation for Mount Desert Island). To get to this offshore island, you must take a ferry from Stonington, on Deer Isle, off the Blue Hill Peninsula west of MDI. (To reach Stonington, take Maine Highway 15 from outside Bucksport, or Maine Highway 172 from outside Ellsworth to Maine 15).

Just 6 miles across Frenchman Bay from Thunder Hole (as the crow flies; it's an hour's drive) is Schoodic Point, a 2,000-acre peninsula due east of MDI (take U.S. Highway 1 to Maine Highway 186 out of Ellsworth). At Schoodic, the coast loses its sheltering line of offshore islands, and the open ocean beats ceaselessly against the rocky shore, crashing boulder against boulder and sending plumes of salt spray skyward.

Other smaller islands also are part of the park. Bar Island off Bar Harbor is accessible on foot during low tide via sandbar (hence Bar Harbor's name). Nearby are the Porcupine Islands. On Eastern Way, off Northeast Harbor, is tiny Bear Island with its lighthouse; farther out, on Little Cranberry Island, stands the Islesford Historical Museum (only the museum is part of the park); and still farther out to sea is Baker Island, also with a lighthouse. Thompson Island, on the causeway to MDI, is also park territory, as are Pond, Little Moose and Schoodic islands, off Schoodic Point. Some of these islands shelter nesting birds, and visitors are not permitted; a mail boat takes visitors to Little Cranberry; and guided ranger trips lead to other islands, such as Baker Island. Pick up a copy of the ranger station's newspaper, *Beaver Log*, for more on ranger-guided trips. (There are more islands off MDI, Schoodic and Isle au Haut, many of which are public but not part of the park.)

Look at a map of the park — it forms a crazy quilt-like pattern over about two-thirds of Mount Desert Island. Park roads, and even park trails, weave in and out Acadia. MDI and the park share history as well as geography; it's almost impossible to experience the park without getting involved in its towns. But first, a word about the rock it all lies on.

FYI

Unless otherwise noted, the area code for all phone numbers listed in this guide is 207.

Geology

About 500 million years ago, Mount Desert Island was merely a collection of silt, sand, mud and volcanic ash on the ocean floor. Gradually, at the rate of an inch every hundred years, these deposits grew to be thousands of feet deep. Affected by heat and pressure over millions of years, the eroded substances of the continental plate began hardening, becoming the island's bedrock. Then, seismic forces erupted, lifting the rocks into a mountain range that might have been as large as the Rockies had it not been ground by the forces of nature — wind, water, gravity and pressure — to leave only the crystalline schists and metamorphic gneisses that comprise the Ellsworth formation.

Millions more years passed. Under repeated pressure during this time, gravel became conglomerate, silt became siltstone, and the Bar Harbor formation was created atop the more ancient Ellsworth formation.

About 400 million years ago, when seaweed ruled the oceans, volcanoes spewed molten lava over the earlier sediments, sinking the Bar Harbor formation into sediments that heat and pressure changed into the Cranberry Island formation.

More time passed, and molten rock again reshaped the Ellsworth, Bar Harbor and Cranberry Island formations — known to geologists as "weak" formations because they were so vulnerable to natural forces, as compared to the extremely hard granite, the most common rock in Acadia. The first time the molten rock, or magma, invaded these formations, relatively rare diorite was formed. Molten rock invaded three more times, creating three kinds of granite.

According to information offered by the National Park Service:

Each of the intrusions altered the overhead bedrock . . . but the most dramatic change occurred when the coarse-grained granite formed.

Far below the earth's surface, a huge molasses-like plug of magma [molten rock] at least eight miles in diameter moved upward. As it undermined the overlying bedrock, the heavy

Acadia
National Park

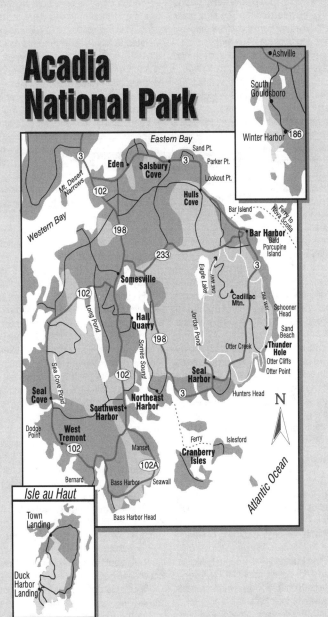

Ashville

South
Gouldsboro

Winter Harbor (186)

Eastern Bay

Sand Pt.

Eden • Salsbury
Cove

(3)

Parker Pt.

Lookout Pt.

(3)

Mt. Desert
Narrows

(102)

Hulis
Cove

Western Bay

Bar Island

Ferry to Nova Scotia

(198)

Bar Harbor

Bald
Porcupine
Island

(233)

(3)

Somesville

Eagle Lake

ONE WAY

Cadillac
Mtn.

Schooner
Head

(102)

Long Pond

Hall
Quarry

Jordan Pond

Sand
Beach

(198)

Somes Sound

Otter Creek

Thunder
Hole

(102)

Otter Cliffs

Sea Cove Pond

Seal
Harbor

Otter Point

Seal
Cove

(3)

Hunters Head

N

Southwest
Harbor

Northeast
Harbor

Dodge
Point

West
Tremont

Ferry

Islesford

(102)

Manset

Cranberry
Isles

Bernard

(102A)

Bass Harbor Seawall

Isle au Haut

Bass Harbor Head

Town
Landing

Duck
Harbor
Landing

roof bedrock began to sag, eventually sinking and melting into the magma. The fiery mass incorporated material from the earlier granites, from diorite, and from the weak rocks.

When this plug reached the surface and cooled, coarse-grained granite was formed.

The hard granite did not permit much further intrusion, but if you go to Schoodic Peninsula, you'll see black basalt dikes coursing through open fractures in older rocks. You'll also see a good example of "weak" rock: The black dikes have eroded to several feet below the hard, pink granite.

We are still at the time that dinosaurs roamed the earth. While they did, the mountains weathered, but the granite remained as a long solid ridge.

Then came the Ice Age, with glaciers possibly as thick as 9,000 feet spreading as far as 150 miles out to sea. The glaciers covered the hard granite of the mountains, smoothing their tops, wearing down the heights and gouging deep valleys that now separate the island's 17 mountains. Jordan and Long ponds, Echo and Eagle lakes and Somes Sound were carved at this time. Each runs north-south and roughly parallel to the others, indicating the direction of glacial movement. Then, as the ice began to retreat, it dragged along boulders, losing some along the way; those atop Cadillac Mountain are examples of these stranded rocks.

History

Among Acadia National Park's many gifts is the fact that the park itself was a gift. Much of it was donated by its former owners — industrialists with names that still ring of wealth and power: Rockefeller, Morgan, Astor, Ford, Vanderbilt and Pulitzer — who came to Mount Desert Island (for details about MDI's history, see our History chapter) for a rustic retreat from the bustle of their lives, molding it for a brief while into an elegant summer playground. These men were spurred on to create the park by members of some well-educated, well-established New England families, such as the Eliots and the Dorrs.

The inertia that ultimately, albeit indirectly, led to the creation of Acadia National Park was set in motion in the early to mid-19th century. In the 1830s, artist Thomas Doughty traveled to Maine, exhibiting his paintings in an 1836 exposition. That same year, Ralph Waldo Emerson published "Nature," his ode to the spiritual force of the landscape. Seeking to articulate a national identity, artists and philosophers of the fledgling nation looked to connect with the land, especially with its rugged wildness. While Henry David Thoreau traveled inland through Maine's North Woods, artists such as Thomas Cole (leader of the Hudson River School), Alvan Fisher and Doughty looked to the special light of the coast to complete their Emersonian voyage into solitude.

Cole, among the most famous artists of his day, was the most influential of the painters. He came to Mount Desert Island in 1844, liked what he saw, painted it and returned, opening the way for Frederick Church, Fitz Hugh Lane, Thomas Birch, Charles Dix and William Morris Hunt. They also liked what they saw and painted it. The paintings became magnets for the intelligentsia of the day. Soon, biologists were coming, and behind them the romantics known as "rusticators," city folks seeking a wilderness experience (sound familiar?).

The rusticators boarded with island residents in rough-hewn cabins, until the villagers' cabins overflowed and enterprising folk began building hotels. By 1880, Bar Harbor alone had 30 hotels.

Then, Harvard University president Charles W. Eliot, at his son's urging, decided to build a summer cottage at Asticou, near Northeast Harbor. William Croswell Doane, Bishop of Albany, also built there, as did landscape architect Joseph H. Curtis, whose Asticou Terraces and Thuya Gardens remain another gift to the island. The "rustic" in rusticating was forgotten as the Vanderbilts, Pulitzers, Morgans, Fords and Auchinclosses built their mansion-size "cottages." Centered around Northeast Harbor, Seal Harbor and Bar Harbor, Mount Desert Island had become one of society's prime summer resorts.

We're talking big-time society here. The coast was lined with mansions whose inhabitants engaged in a summer whirl of mountaintop picnics, tea-house teas, sunset paddles on Frenchman Bay and, of course, balls. One socialite, Mrs. Edward Statesbury, ordered her champagne glasses in lots of 50 dozen. At such a party, young women might not eat supper until 1 AM, after having danced their finest dresses to rags.

Perhaps most influential was the family of John D. Rockefeller Sr., who came, so legend has it, only because the obstetrician of Abby Rockefeller — pregnant with son Nelson — decided to spend the summer on the island.

That was in 1900. The Rockefellers fell in love with the place and built. They built mansions and gardens, gatehouses and trails. More than anything, they built roads — Acadia's famous series of carriage roads hidden from the public throughways.

In the meantime, Eliot feared for the wilderness. It wasn't the carriage roads that concerned him. Rather, Eliot worried that men with portable sawmills would come to harvest Mount Desert's timber and forever ruin the character of the island. He launched a campaign to preserve and protect the island, electing George Bucknam Dorr as chief crusader. Dorr tracked down owners of choice island land and begged them to donate it to the Hancock County Trustees of Public Reservations preservation society. He bought some land himself to preserve it; some land came from the Rockefellers, who donated the coastal stretch between Thunder Hole and Otter Cliffs.

The hope was to create a national park, but the timing was not good. In 1916, Congress was thinking of war, not wilderness. But through influence and persuasion, Dorr got President Woodrow Wilson to proclaim the preserved lands of Acadia a national monument on July 8, 1916, thereby circumventing Congress.

For a few more decades, Society and the park coexisted. Then a trio of tragedies — at least for the industrial class — brought down the summer colony. The income tax was the first blow. The stock market crash of 1929 was the second. Still, Society came to the island. Then, during the dry October of 1947, a fire raged for three weeks, consuming five Bar Harbor hotels, 67 of the 222 large summer cottages, and 170 of the 667 permanent homes. Island society was never again the same, but the park had already been established. It remains our gift.

Birds, Bees and Blueberries

Mount Desert Island offers many habitats for plants, animals, birds and humans: Sand Beach, composed of crushed shells and sand; forests, including dense stands of spruce, fir and mixed deciduous woods; meadows, fields, heaths, bogs and marshes (both freshwater and saltwater); glacier-gouged lakes; and 17 mountains ranging from 200-foot cliffs to 1,530-foot Cadillac Mountain. Flowers include varieties from northern and temperate zones; bird life includes Arctic, Subarctic and Hudsonian species.

Fauna

Birding is quite popular here, with more than 300 species of sea, shore and land birds. Listen for the eerie cry of the loon and the high-pitched peep-peep-peep of the osprey. Eagles and ospreys frequently nest on the Porcupine Islands, off the coast of MDI near Bar Harbor. On MDI, peregrine falcons have nested along the Precipice cliff of Champlain Mountain for the past six years, causing the trail there to be closed during most of the summer.

Rock climbers daring the south face of the mountain reap the rewards. "I've had days on the south wall of Champlain with peregrines dive-bombing around us," said Fred Champlain, who works at a local climbing school. "It's wild; the peregrines are literally screaming above your head. You can get pretty close to the peregrines when you're up there."

In March and April, you can observe falcon courtship from the trailhead to Champlain Mountain — just be sure to heed any trail closings.

At the shore, look for buffleheads, red-breasted mergansers, common eiders and black, surf and white-winged scoters. Find numerous woodpeckers and warblers in the woods, and loons on the lakes.

Seals and porpoises dive in the harbors. If you're beside Frenchman Bay late at night, listen for the frightening sounds of snorting and arguing. It's not a barroom brawl, but rather the talk of the seals on their local rock.

Whales can be seen farther offshore through a host of whale-watch cruises. To understand the size of the whale, look for the whale's skull at College of the Atlantic in nearby Bar Harbor. (See the Attractions chapter for related information.)

At the other size extreme, check out tide pool life — the miniature world of seaweed, periwinkles, snails and barnacles that live in the warmed pools of displaced ocean spray.

Inland, beavers almost have become park pets. You'll find their lodges at a pond known as the Tarn, along the Park Loop Road (see the subsequent "Things To See" section for details). Dawn and dusk are the best times to see these industrious builders.

Also look for various salamanders, toads, frogs, turtles, a number of snakes (all nonpoisonous), minks, otters, muskrats, raccoons and weasels. Red foxes, Eastern coyotes, snowshoe hares and whitetail deer are also common in the park.

Flora

Acadia's forests offer a good lesson in impact. The 1947 fire altered the nature of the island's forests, replacing old-growth white pine stands with a more diverse crop. The white pine forests that remain are unmistakable — tall, clear and powerful. If you don't mind travelling back roads, you can find a 200-year-old stand off Norway Drive, which in turn is off Maine Highway 3 in Salisbury Cove.

While you also can find some dense spruce-fir forests, for the most part you'll see a mixture of spruce, balsam fir and deciduous trees such as paper birch, sugar maple and quaking aspen.

Common wildflowers include bluets (a.k.a. Quaker ladies), a lovely field flower (in spring), the showy lupines (in June) and rosa rugosa (in summer), growing anywhere near the shore. In late May and June, look for ladyslippers in wet woods. (Most are endangered,

so enjoy your flowers in the wild, without picking.) Come June, nonnative lilacs are so common, they seem indigenous. Wherever you see lilacs, a house likely once stood.

Bog flora, such as you'll find at Seawall Bog on the north side of Maine Highway 102A, include black spruce, black chokecherry, sheep laurel, sphagnum moss, pitcher plants, blueflag iris and bog orchids.

Along dry, rocky places — in the mountains and at shoreside woods — you can find bush-honeysuckle, jack and pitch pine, lichen and moss. At windswept spots, such as Schoodic Point, pitch pine is a common sight.

In meadows and along the roadside, you'll see a changing array of colors by season, perhaps beginning with bluets in the spring, progressing to tall, buttercup-colored meadow rue, pearly everlasting, brilliant purple common evening primrose and fireweed through the summer, and changing to golden black-eyed Susans, asters and goldenrod in the fall.

Along marshes and ponds, you might see northern white cedar, water lobelia, wild calla, common cattail, American waterlily, bog laurel and shadbush among other plants.

A great introduction to the park's flora can be found at the wildflower garden, Wild Gardens of Acadia at Sieur de Monts Spring, off the Park Loop Road, 5.6 miles from Hulls Cove Visitor Center. The garden replicates a dozen zonal conditions you're likely to see in the park. If you think caring for your own garden is hard, consider what it's like to reproduce the range of conditions, from sandy shore to a rain-for-est–like mountain. The upkeep takes about 100 volunteer hours each week between June and August — and a lot of additives. Keeping the soil habitats rich requires nearly a half-ton of compost each summer, while the beach habitat soaks in a mixture of 105 pounds of seaweed, 30 gallons of seawater and 50 gallons of sand.

Almost anywhere you go, especially in August, keep a sharp look out for blueberries, raspberries and blackberries. Find them, and you've got yourself a trailside feast.

Getting Around

Accommodations and services such as equipment rentals, restaurants and stores

A coin-operated telescope offers a scenic view from the deck of the Jordan Pond House.

can be found in several MDI towns. The largest of these is Bar Harbor, on the eastern portion of the island. The towns on the other side of Somes Sound (a.k.a. "the quiet side") are Southwest Harbor, Bass Harbor and Bernard, and the hamlets of Somesville and Town Hill. Facing Southwest Harbor across Somes Sound is Northeast Harbor, which got its name from being northeast of Southwest.

As for guiding you through both park and towns, you'll find general maps to the park at Hulls Cove Visitor Center. DeLorme's *Maine Atlas & Gazetteer* (see our Getting Around chapter) is almost indispensable for driving excursions. But for hiking or serious use of the carriage roads, we recommend picking up a U.S. Geological Survey topographical map and/or a map of the carriage roads at Hulls Cove Visitor Center, or in winter, at the Winter Visitor Center. (See the subsequent "Visitors Centers" section for details.)

National park fees have increased nationwide in 1998. Current fees are $10 for a seven-day vehicle pass, $5 for pedestrians or cyclists. For $20, you can enter for a year. A $50 Golden Eagle pass allows the bearer and family into all federal fee areas for a year. A $10 Golden Age pass allows U.S. citizens older than 62 park visitation rights to all national parks for life. And a Golden Access pass is free to anyone with disabilities.

That said, you can also enjoy parts of the park without passing through an entrance gate. Currently, the park has one gate, just before you get to Sand Beach. (Two more gates are slated to go into place — one at Jordan Pond and the other near the visitors center.) Still, local roads wind in and out of the park, passing trails and beaches. That's the way the park is set up: You're not cheating if you don't pay. But to drive most of the Park Loop Road, you will have to pay.

Visitors Centers

Acadia Information Center
Maine Hwy. 3, Trenton • 667-8550, (800) 358-8550

You'll find Acadia Information Center on the mainland just before you reach the causeway to Mount Desert Island. This center offers plenty of brochures, information on the area and an interactive video screen with referrals for dining, lodging, camping and cruising — aided by nine courtesy phones.

Acadia Information Center is open 10 AM to 8 PM daily from May through mid-October.

Hulls Cove Visitor Center
off Maine Hwy. 3, Hulls Cove • 288-3338, 288-5262 (event registration)

A wanderer needs bearings, and the park's visitors center at Hulls Cove, just off Maine Highway 3 and clearly indicated with signs, is Acadia's main orientation center. There's a 15-minute audiovisual presentation depicting what you can expect to find in Acadia; a large stash of free brochures about the park's hiking trails and roads; and a nice selection of books. Hiking guides are sold here, as are field guides and guides to the carriage roads. Pick up a copy of the *Beaver Log*, which offers the extensive schedule of ranger walks, discussions and trips.

Round-the-island–tour audio tapes are available too. These cost $8.95 to rent, $11.95 to buy or to rent with a cassette deck.

The center is open 8 AM to 6 PM daily in July and August and 8 AM to 4:30 PM during May, June, September and October; it's closed the rest of the year.

Nature Center at Sieur de Monts Spring
off Park Loop Rd., 5.6 miles from Hulls Cove, Sieur de Monts Spring • no phone

This is not actually a visitors center, but it does provide an excellent orientation to Acadia National Park. The Nature Center's purpose is to introduce parents and children to the park's natural world: the animals, birds and flowers. Since the experience of Acadia is based on entering the realm of animal, vegetable and mineral, the Nature Center is an excellent place to get your bearings, even if you don't have kids. Here you'll find general information, books and educational discovery activities for children.

The Nature Center is open 9 AM to 5 PM daily from mid-June through mid-September.

Thompson Island Information Center
off Maine Hwy. 3, Thompson Island • 288-3411

Thompson Island is near the midpoint of the causeway to Mount Desert Island. Here you'll find an information center owned by the National Park Service but run by the local MDI chamber of commerce. It provides information about lodging options as well as the park.

The center is open 10 AM to 8 PM daily from late May to mid-October.

Winter Visitor Center
Park Headquarters, off Maine Hwy. 233, north of Eagle Lake • 288-3338

The winter visitors center — essentially a small room staffed by a ranger — offers information, free maps and guides and a personal slide show to orient visitors to winter in the park. The small sales area has more maps, histories of the region, geology books and field guides.

This center stays open from the end of October to about mid-April. Daily hours are 8 AM to 4:30 PM.

Campgrounds

There are two campgrounds on the Mount Desert Island portion of the park — Blackwoods and Seawall. A third campground serves visitors to Isle au Haut. None has utility hookups.

Outside the park, you'll find campgrounds and numerous hotels, many of which also fill up quickly during summer. It's a good idea to plan ahead when you are coming to Mount Desert Island in summer.

Because of the fragile nature of the park's ecosystem, no overnight backpacking is permitted.

See our Campgrounds chapter for additional options and related information.

Blackwoods
off Maine Hwy. 3, 5 miles south of Bar Harbor • 288-3338, (800) 365-2267

South of Bar Harbor on the eastern portion of the island, Blackwoods offers 300 campsites (50 are open year round) with picnic tables and fire rings. Sites cost $16 nightly (credit cards are accepted), except from December to mid-April, when facilities are reduced to hand-pumped water and pit toilets, and camping is free. Site limitations include one vehicle, six people and two small (or one large) tents. There are no utility hookups.

From mid-June to mid-September you must reserve in advance. Beginning April 15, you can make reservations for mid-June to mid-July; beginning May 15, you can make reservations for mid-July to mid-August; and beginning in mid-June, you can make reservations for mid-August to mid-September.

Duck Harbor Campground
Duck Harbor, Isle au Haut • 288-3338

Duck Harbor has five lean-to shelters, each accommodating up to six people. Reservations, postmarked on or after April 1 only, are required for the sites, which cost $25 each.

The campground is open mid-May through mid-October.

Seawall
off Maine Hwy. 102A, 5 mi. from Southwest Harbor • 288-3338

Seawall, on the western portion, not far from Southwest Harbor, has more than 200 sites. They are offered on a first-come, first-served basis; lines of hopeful campers form each morning in July and August. Sites cost $14 per night, $10 without a vehicle. Group sites also are available. If you have a choice, chose high ground. Drainage is not always the best at Seawall.

The grounds are open from Memorial Day through September.

Things To See

Park Loop Road
off Maine Hwy. 3, Bar Harbor
off Maine Hwy. 233, Bar Harbor
off Maine Hwy. 3, Seal Harbor

The Park Loop Road, a 20-mile loop with a 3-mile extension from the visitors center, passes the major sights of the island. It is the standard introduction to the park. You can get there from the visitors center, Bar Harbor or several other entrances. The loop costs $10 for a seven-day pass. (See the previous "Getting Around" section for additional fee information.)

The Loop is well worth traveling. It cascades down hills and circles the ocean, passing crescent-shaped Sand Beach and Thunder Hole, where, when the tide is full and the wind is up, the flowing water creates a thunderous boom within the eroded rock. (In sum-

mer, a sign is posted at the Hulls Cove Visitor Center, indicating the best hour to visit Thunder Hole.) The Loop also passes Otter Cliffs, pink and soaring 100 feet from the sea, and the Jordan Pond House, Acadia's in-park restaurant (see subsequent entry). Park Loop Road also leads to Cadillac Mountain (see next entry).

There are three ways to access the Loop: from Maine Highway 3 as you come onto Mount Desert Island (signs for the visitors center lead you onto it); from Maine Highway 233 outside Bar Harbor; or, at Stanley Brook, off Maine 3 in Seal Harbor.

Cadillac Mountain
west of Park Loop Rd., 5 mi. from Hulls Cove Visitor Center

For at least some of the year, Cadillac Mountain (elevation 1,530 feet) greets the day with the first sunrise on U.S. territory. You'll see sunrise visitors frequently — in summer, on the solstices and equinoxes.

It's also spectacular for sunsets, when the panorama of water spreading out from islands below reflects pink above an azure blue. As the wind blows, exhilaration heightens. Run over the rocks or sit quietly, contemplating grandeur.

Some of the boulders here are known as erratics. They are the deposits of glacial-borne rocks left by retreating ice about 18,000 years ago.

Check out the subsequent "Things To Do, Bicycling" section for information about a sunrise bike tour down the mountain. Please note that the road to Cadillac stays open until about the first snow; then it closes for the winter.

Carriage Roads
throughout Acadia on the eastern side of Mount Desert Island

Though the Rockefellers made their fortune in oil, they feared the automobile would ruin Mount Desert Island. John D. Jr. tried to keep cars off the island, but lost the battle in 1915. Rockefeller's roads were for carriages only. He had workers line the road edges with granite, lay cobblestones for bridges, create special passageways and lookouts — all concealed from the public. The 50 miles of park carriage roads with 17 stone bridges and stately gatehouses remain some of Acadia's most charming assets; today, these roads are used for walking, biking, cross-country skiing, horseback riding and, yes, carriage rides.

Rockefeller spent 27 years having these roads built; they're considered the nation's finest remaining example of "broken stone" roads, popular at the turn of the century. The oil magnate followed the road-building closely, walking the areas, calling workers by name, going over plans to be certain the roads were aligned with the contours of the land and swept near special views. Roadsides were landscaped with blueberries and sweet fern, and landscape architect Beatrix Farrand, whose hand is present in the finest MDI gardens, was consulted on the framing of vistas and bridges.

FYI

Unless otherwise noted, the area code for all phone numbers listed in this guide is 207.

Over the years, many of these vistas became overgrown, and the roads themselves began to deteriorate. The park conducted an extensive rehabilitation of the roads between 1992 and 1996.

Marked by posts and guarded by two large gatehouses, Rockefeller's roads prove an ironic legacy to a fortune born in oil. For the most part, the roads remain separate from the public highway. You can travel a full day on the carriage roads and barely notice the park's intense automobile traffic.

But do notice the details — the granite edging, cobblestone bridges and glorious vistas framed by the arch of a bridge or the sweep of a rock face.   •

Wild Gardens of Acadia
Sieur de Monts Spring, off Maine Hwy. 3

The Wild Gardens of Acadia will help orient you to the many flora zones you'll pass as you walk and drive through the park. In just a small space, a dozen habitats are recreated, showing the flowers and foliage typically found in the park's many ecosystems: mixed woods, roadside, meadow, mountain, heath, seaside, brookside, bird thicket, coniferous woods, bog, marsh and pond. With plants and trees labeled, you can answer many a question you've been harboring about what's what in the park. See our Attractions chapter for details.

Jordan Pond House
Park Loop Rd., between Cadillac Mountain and Stanley Brook entrances
• 276-3316

Acadia's in-park restaurant is most noted for its location, across a field from Jordan Pond — and for its popovers. Don't laugh — these popovers, pulled steaming from the oven, are themselves worth a trip to the park.

Tea, which includes two popovers, jam and tea or another beverage, costs $5.50 plus tax and is served from 11:30 AM to 6 PM daily from mid-May through mid-October.

Lunch is served outdoors on the lawn or indoors on a screened-in porch. Dinner is served as well. Popovers are available with any meal. (See our Restaurants chapter for details.)

Islesford Historical Museum
off Islesford Dock, Little Cranberry Island • 244-9224

Take a ferry from Northeast or Southwest Harbor to Islesford and learn about the coastal culture of early fishing folk on Maine's islands. You'll find information about life on all five islands of the Cranberry Isles as well as the maritime life that most of its 19th-century population engaged in.

Associated with the museum is the Blue Duck, a simple 19th-century general ship's store. Once a maritime store, the Blue Duck was bought by historian William Sawtelle in 1917. He found a number of wooden duck decoys inside, painted them Prussian blue and put them around the yard, hence the name. Admission is free once you get to the island. For information about ferry service, check out the park's *Beaver Log*, or call Beal and Bunker Mail Boat Service at 244-3575. Also see our Attractions chapter for more information.

Schoodic Peninsula
off Maine Hwy. 186

Schoodic Peninsula, Acadia National Park's only mainland section, juts into the open ocean east of Mount Desert Island. It might be attached to the land, but sea winds make it a wild place in any season — and one of the best places to witness the rage of the open ocean.

The tip of the peninsula had been donated to the public as a park before Acadia was organized as a national monument (and then as a national park), so it was only natural that the peninsula became part of Acadia.

A one-way road circumnavigates the peninsula, with pull-offs for scenic vistas, hikes and the Frazier Point picnic area (at its start). The major destination here is Schoodic Point, where massive waves slap the rocks at high tide and during storms. Walk around, but don't get too close to the ocean if it's stormy, especially if you are small. Waves knock around the huge granite boulders at the ocean's edge: Be especially aware of the danger they pose to children.

This is a relatively quiet part of Acadia National Park — a place to get away from crowds or enjoy a bike ride. Just east of the parking area, you'll find trails winding through stunted jack pines. From the parking lot, little Moose Island is accessible at low tide (time your return carefully). You'll find Arctic plants on this windswept island.

A short drive from Schoodic Point is Blueberry Hill, with an ample parking lot. It offers a nice, easy climb. Before you get to the point of Schoodic Point, there's a road leading to Schoodic Head (another short, moderate hike) at an unmarked left turn about 2 miles after the picnic area at Frazier Point.

Isle au Haut
off Stonington

Isle au Haut is one of a series of barrier islands that shelters much of Maine. About half of the 18-square-mile island is part of Acadia. On the other half is a small summer community and an even smaller year-round community. There is one store on the island, one romantic inn (see our Accommodations chapter) and one summer-season campground (see this chapter's previous "Camp-

grounds" section). A visit to Isle au Haut is a trip for adventurers, who will be extraordinarily rewarded by the island's wild, remote quality.

From Duck Harbor, where you'll find the campground, there are 18 miles of moderate hiking trails around the southern tip or across the breadth of the island, just about all of which offer frequent vistas over Penobscot Bay. Hike to the beaches where, each year, driftwood constructions as big as a house take form — begun by one family and added to by just about every hiker who passes (who can resist?). A more distant walk takes you to a mile-long freshwater lake, where islanders enjoy taking a dip in summer.

The ferry, also known as the Isle au Haut mail boat, leaves from the Old Sardine Cannery Dock, on Seabreeze Avenue in Stonington, bound for the town wharf on Isle au Haut. Ferries dock at Duck Harbor on the park section of the island in summer only; they also travel Sundays, summer only. Schedules and rates for the 45-minute trip are as follows.

From April 6 through June 13, boats leave Stonington at 7 AM and 4 PM and leave Isle au Haut at 8 AM and 5 PM Monday through Saturday.

From June 15 through September 12, ferries leave Stonington at 7 and 11:30 AM and 4:30 PM. They leave Isle au Haut at 8 AM, 12:30 and 6:30 PM Monday through Saturday. Sundays and holidays, boats leave Stonington at 11:30 AM and Isle au Haut at 12:30 PM.

Also, from June 15 through September 12 only, ferries travel to Duck Harbor, the Acadia National Park dock on the island. They leave Stonington at 10 AM and 4:30 PM and leave Duck Harbor at 11:15 AM and 6 PM. Fares follow the summer schedule.

From September 14 through October 17, boats leave Stonington at 7 and 11:30 AM and 4 PM Monday and Saturday. They leave Isle au Haut at 8 AM, 12:30 and 5 PM.

These trips costs $12 one way for adults

INSIDERS' TIP

To feel like a real Insider, spend a half-day at Hunter's Beach, where the locals go to wander the coast. The entrance is .8-mile past the Blackwoods Campground, off Maine Highway 3. The beach is a half-mile down the trail.

and teens and $5 for children 12 and younger. (All ferry rides are free for infants and toddlers).

In winter 1997-98, vessels were scheduled to leave Stonington at 7 AM and 2:30 PM and leave Isle au Haut at 8 AM and 3:30 PM Monday through Saturday at a one-way cost of $7 for adults and teens, $4 for children 12 and younger.

In addition, bikes cost $7; pets, $3.

Things To Do

Bicycling

John D. Rockefeller's Carriage Roads (see the previous "Things To See" section) have become favorite biking routes. Thick-wheeled mountain bikes are best suited for these gravel roads. The visitors center offers a list of suggested trips, as do places that rent bikes. No bikes are allowed on park trails — the bikes damage small trees' delicate root systems.

Always stay to your right. If you approach horses, *do not* use bells, but *do* use caution. Yield to both hikers and horses. For families with younger children, try renting what's known as a trailer bike, a tandem bike for an adult and young child. The adult ends up working a little harder, but it's a great solution if you're traveling with children who aren't quite strong enough to go solo on a real biking excursion; it keeps the child riding with you — and even helps teach the child about balance.

A favorite loop is the 6-mile circle around Eagle Lake.

Another favorite is the 3.4-mile loop that passes around Witch Hole Pond. Both of these are popular in summer, but that only means you'll pass a dozen or so other bikers — plus a handful who have stopped to snack on the blueberries. Both the Eagle Lake and Witch Hole roads are blanketed in fine-grained gravel, a suitable surface for slender tires. Try going up Paradise Hill for a slightly more difficult 1.2-mile trek that offers glorious views of Frenchman Bay.

Bicycling around Schoodic Point is fun, but exercise caution; shoulders are not always present, and there can be extensive automobile traffic.

Cadillac Mountain itself is a bike destination, especially for the sunrise. Early risers with a touch of laziness might want to get in on Acadia Bike & Coastal Kayaking's sunrise trip on Cadillac (see subsequent entry). The staff takes you up the mountain; the bike takes you down.

Possible excursions are numerous, with directions according to carriage road posts and paved road routes.

There are trips around Day Mountain, near Jordan Pond House, around Jordan Pond and beside Bubble Pond. Check with the following bike shops or at the visitors center, or pick up a copy of *Biking on Mount Desert Island*, a pocket guide ($7.95) published in 1996 by Down East Books. It's written by Audrey Minutolo, whose family owns the Bar Harbor Bicycle Shop.

Acadia Bike & Coastal Kayaking
48 Cottage St., Bar Harbor • 288-9605, (800) 526-8615

You can buy or rent bikes at Acadia Bike & Coastal Kayaking, or book a $34 sunrise trip down Cadillac Mountain. Everyone meets at 4:30 AM. You get a lift up the mountain, eat a brief continental breakfast while watching the first sunrise of the day in the United States, then take part in a guided tour on a specially equipped bike with drum brakes and no gears to get you safely to the foot of the mountain.

Acadia rents Raleigh and Giant mountain bikes: $16 for a full day, $11 for a half-day and $12 a day for multiple days (up to $75 a week). This outfitter also rents high-performance Cannondales for $30 a day, for hard-core mountain bikers. Staff will agree, however, that there are few trails to challenge the qualities of this lightweight, $3,000 bike.

Rentals include locks, route maps, rear bike racks, a water bottle cage and helmet.

Acadia also rents bicycles built for two. Half-day rentals are $20, a full day costs $30, and multiple days are $20 a day (up to $120 a week).

Also available are children's trailers at $10 a day ($8 a day for multiple days) and a child seat at $4 a day. A car rack is $5. Acadia also rents bikes for children ($10 a day). Reservations are suggested.

Acadia Bike & Coastal Kayaking is open year round. Summer hours are 8 AM to 9 PM

Photo: Bangor Daily News

Bicycle trails are popular in summer throughout Acadia National Park — many of them leading to the summit of Cadillac Mountain.

daily, and spring and fall hours are 8 AM to 6 PM daily; call for winter hours.

Acadia Outfitters
106 Cottage St., Bar Harbor • 288-8118

Acadia Outfitters works in loose association with Acadia Bike & Coastal Kayaking (see previous entry). At this Cottage Street outfitter, you can rent bikes as well as canoes (see subsequent "Kayaking and Canoeing" section), generally at rates equivalent to Acadia Bike & Coastal Kayaking's. Twenty-one–speed Giant mountain bikes are $15 a day for adults, $10 a half-day, $11 daily for multiple days; kids bikes rent for $8 daily.

Bicycles built for two cost $20 a day, up to $120 a week.

Rentals include locks, route maps, rear bike racks, a cage for a water bottle and a helmet.

The daily cost for children's trailers is $10 ($8 a day for multiple days). A child seat is $4 a day, and a car rack is $5.

Bar Harbor Bicycle Shop
National Park Outdoor Activity Center, 141 Cottage St., Bar Harbor • 288-3886

The Minutolos, who own this shop, are multi-generation islanders. They rent bikes of all kinds: mountain, road, high-performance, children's and tandem.

Recreational mountain bikes and road bikes are $10 a half-day, $15 a full day. The recreational bikes are more upright, while road bikes are thin-wheeled. Front-suspension bikes are $15 a half-day, $20 a full day. Tandem bikes are $20 a half-day, $25 a full day. Children's bike rentals are available for the same cost as adult bikes. Tag-along bikes, in which a child rides tandem with an adult, are also available; call to find out the cost.

Rentals include helmets, locks, trail advice and maps of access and carriage roads.

This outfitter also rents various accessories, including car racks, L.L. Bean baby backpacks, Kiddie Kart trailers and jog strollers. Call for rates. Child bike seats are provided free, if desired. You can also buy Audrey Minutolo's guidebook to biking in Acadia for $7.95.

Bar Harbor Bicycle Shop is open March through December for rentals, sales, service and repairs. Daily hours from June to September are 8 AM to 8 PM; 9 AM to 6 PM in the fringe season. In summer, try to arrive before 9 AM to beat the rush on rentals. For off-season hours, call ahead.

Southwest Cycle
Main St., Southwest Harbor • 244-5856, (800) 649-5856 (instate only)

This bike shop rents and sells bicycles year round. For rentals, Southwest's standard issue is a mountain bike, though it has a few hybrids as well. Mountain bikes cost $16 a day, $70 a week. Tandem bikes are $25 a day. Children's bikes cost $10 to $12 for a day, $55 for a week. Jog Strollers and trailer bikes are $10 a day. Bikes come with helmets, locks and trail maps. Car racks and baby seats are $5 for as long as needed.

The store is open 8:30 AM to 5:30 PM daily between June and September, decreasing to 9:30 AM to 5 PM, Monday through Saturday in October. Hours shorten thereafter, so it's best to call for winter hours.

Carriage Rides

Wildwood Stables
Park Loop Rd., Seal Harbor • 276-3622, (606) 356-7139 winter reservations

Wildwood Stables offers six carriage rides daily — three lasting two hours and three lasting an hour — including a 1:15 PM tea run to the Jordan Pond House and a sunset ride up Day Mountain. The stables are open mid-June to Columbus Day.

Hour-long trips cost $13, with reduced rates for children and seniors. The Jordan

Pond House tea trip is $14.50, and two-hour rides are $16.50.

If you've brought your own horse, or horse and carriage, Wildwood Stables provides box stalls for about $20 a night. Owners must care for and feed their horses. Reservations are necessary for stables.

Should you come with a horse, feel free to camp at the stables. There's a $7 fee for Wildwood campsites (available to equestrians only).

Climbing

Acadia Mountain Guides
198 Main St., Bar Harbor • 288-8186, 866-7562 (winter)

Only a handful of climbing schools across the nation are accredited by the American Mountain Guides Association, and Acadia Mountain Guides is among them. Owner Jon Tierney, a certified rock-climbing and Alpine guide, and his staff of up to eight guides offer classes for families, camps, schools and groups.

Participants climb one of several sites — perhaps Mount Desert Island's Otter Cliffs, where the rock face rises directly from the ocean, or along the south wall of Champlain Mountain — that might include a 25-foot cliff for beginners or a 200-foot climb for more experienced students.

Rates listed are for 1997 (the only ones available at press time), but they are not expected to change much. A private half-day lesson cost $90. Half-day group lessons for two cost $60 a person; for three, $55 a person. A solo beginner lesson cost $75 during July and August (the school will find a small group to include you in, or offer you a private lesson). Full-day private lessons cost $140. The small-group cost per individual is $110 (again, that's for a beginner lesson only during July and August, and the school will find a group for you). For a group of two, it's $95 a person; for three, $85 each.

The whole family can jump right into climbing: The half-day family program, especially, is geared to children as young as 4, who are sometimes the best climbers because they are without fear. A half-day family lesson costs $159 for up to four people; $230 for a full day. This is technical climbing with gear included.

Multi-day custom lessons are available and are priced accordingly. You can even hire a guide to accompany you to South America.

Acadia Mountain Guides sells climbing and backpacking gear and rents climbing shoes ($6 for a half-day, $10 for full day).

Generally, classes are offered mid-May through mid-October.

Atlantic Climbing School Inc.
Cadillac Mountain Sports, 24 Cottage St., Bar Harbor • 288-2521

Rock-climbing instruction for the unexperienced to the well-experienced as well as guides are available at this school accredited by the American Mountain Guides Association.

The half-day exposure course lasts up to four hours. You get a primer on climbing and the use of basic equipment, then you climb.

Popular spots are Acadia's seaside cliffs, so expect to climb Otter Cliffs or the south wall of Champlain Mountain. The Otter Cliffs climb offers the opportunity to learn rappelling because it's approached from above.

Individual rates for 1998 are $100 to $150 a day, depending on the number of people participating; half-day rates are $65 to $95.

Special group rates also are available, so a family of four can learn for $160 a half-day, $230 a full day.

Fishing

Freshwater fishing is permitted in all Acadia lakes and ponds, except the Tarn, where it's limited to folks older than 60 and younger than 16. You'll find bass, perch and pickerel in most freshwaters, and landlocked salmon and brook trout in larger lakes.

The park includes both cold- and warm-water lakes.

Cold-water lakes include Echo Lake, with brook trout; the deeper waters of Long Pond, with landlocked salmon early in the season and smallmouth bass in summer; Bubble Pond, with brook trout; Eagle Lake, with landlocked salmon, brook trout and lake trout; Jordan Pond, with landlocked salmon and lake

trout; Upper Hadlock Pond, with brook trout; and Lower Hadlock Pond, with brook trout, brown trout and white perch. Park rangers recommend special fishing gear, such as downriggers, to catch trout and salmon — species that prefer the deep, cold waters of these lakes and ponds.

The shallower areas of Long Pond — considered a warm-water fishery — are inhabited by smallmouth bass and pickerel. Other warm-water lakes include Hamilton Pond, with pickerel and largemouth bass, and Seal Cove Pond, with chain pickerel, smallmouth bass, white perch and yellow perch.

Maine residents 16 and older and nonresidents 12 and older must have licenses to fish in freshwaters. Resident fishing licenses cost $20 for the season. These licenses must be bought at the resident's town office; otherwise, residents can buy a one- or three-day license at nonresident rates that can then be upgraded to a season's pass for the difference plus $1. Out-of-state licenses cost $51 for the season, $39 for 15 days, $35 for seven days, $22 for three days and $10 for one day. For nonresident youths ages 12 to 15, licenses are $8.

Licenses are available at numerous MDI locations. In Bar Harbor, try Paradis True Value Hardware, 31 Holland Avenue, 288-4995; Rite Aid, 38 Cottage Street, 288-2223; or Bar Harbor Municipal Building, Cottage Street, 288-4098. In Northeast Harbor, you can purchase a license at the Northeast Harbor Municipal Building, Sea Street, 276-5531. And in Southwest Harbor, stop by the Southwest Harbor Municipal Building, Main Street, 244-5404; or National Park Canoe Rentals, Pretty Marsh Road (Maine Highway 102), 244-5854, which also rents fishing canoes with gear for two for $40 a day (see the subsequent "Kayaking and Canoeing" section).

There are some notable saltwater fishing spots in Acadia. In Northeast Harbor you can try the picnic area off Sargent Drive, where mackerel, bluefish and striped bass have been caught, or the public docks of Asticou just below the terraces leading to the Thuja Gardens, where striped bass have been caught.

At Schoodic Point, people fish for mackerel in the spring at Frazier Point. In recent summers, striped bass action has boiled off the coast, but the 36-inch–minimum length for keepers is hard to reach. That size limit might change, so ask around.

Hiking

Within Acadia National Park there's a spider's web of trails — 120 miles in all. Many interconnect. While most trails wander among the island's 17 mountains, we concentrate primarily on the gentle and flat hikes. Stronger hikers can take our suggestions for moderate or difficult hikes, but you may also wish to speak with rangers at the visitors center and browse through the many hiking guides sold there. Some paths are wheelchair-accessible.

Most any hike on the island follows a hand-hewn trail lovingly built by the many creators of Acadia National Park. Recently, park staff have been working on keeping up the signposts, which are hand-carved with designs as well as directions. Whether your hike includes a vista of Frenchman Bay, or of rocks within a mossy glade, the beautiful views will remain among the most cherished memories of your trip.

One very easy hike is the Ocean Trail, a smooth path along the ocean paralleling the Park Loop Road between Sand Beach and Otter Point. It's a 3-mile round trip.

Jordan Pond Nature Trail, a mile-long loop through the forest near Jordan Pond, is a short and easy leg-stretcher. There's also a 3-mile walk around Jordan Pond. It's still easy and takes you across a marsh on some large, flat stepping stones toward the mountains known as the Bubbles.

Witch Hole Pond takes you from the north end of the Hulls Cove Visitor Center through woods and marsh. You'll encounter birds, a beaver pond and a view of Frenchman Bay.

Bar Island is a 10-minute walk across the sandbar of Bar Harbor. Allow time to explore the half of the island that is park property and to look at the shells, sea creatures and other goodies left on the bar, which is ocean floor half the day. Just be sure to leave one to two hours after low tide. Don't even consider swimming across: The strong, swift currents are perilous.

On the "quiet side," near Southwest Har-

FYI

Unless otherwise noted, the area code for all phone numbers listed in this guide is 207.

bor, you'll find two easy trails side by side. Wonderland is a lovely trail a mile south of Seawall Campground that takes you through woods and across moss-covered rock to a short shore path. Ship Harbor Nature Trail is about a mile beyond Wonderland and is about a mile longer. It wanders near a harbor and offers nature-trail markings for part of the walk.

For a moderate hike, try the 2.5-mile Gorham Mountain Trail; park at the base of Gorham Mountain, about a quarter-mile beyond Thunder Hole. There's a crossroads at the trail; take the Cadillac Cliffs Trail (on your right) to climb over and under the mountain's massive boulders. Look for marks of the ancient shoreline, when the coast was a good deal higher. About a half-mile later, you'll rejoin the path you split from. After about a mile of sometimes steep climbs, you'll see Sand Beach, Otter Cliffs and Cadillac, Dorr and Champlain mountains.

Another moderate hike takes you to Bubble Rock, which perches on the mountain known as the South Bubble. Allow about an hour for the mile-long round-trip climb. The trailhead intersects Park Loop Road after the Cadillac Mountain entrance (look for the Bubble Rock sign). Be sure to take the detour to see the house-size "bubble." Follow signs for the South Bubble.

Huguenot Head offers another experience in which you'll appreciate the trail-building care of the park's founders. Much of the trail to Huguenot, known as the Beachcroft Trail, is carved into winding stone steps. The trail ends up on the summit of Champlain Mountain. Reach it from the west side of Maine Highway 3, just south of the Sieur de Monts entrance to the park. This is a moderate hike, but the sun will bake you in summer: Don't forget your drinking water.

Scramble up to the footpaths of the quiet side's Flying Mountain Trail for a view of Somes Sound, Southwest Harbor, Northeast Harbor and the farther islands. To get to the trailhead, take Maine Highway 102 to Fernald Point Road (turn when you see signs for the Causeway Club Golf Course). At the end of the cove, park at the gated road on your left. This is not the trailhead. Walk 200 yards; the trail is on the right. It's a steep, quick rise: 284 feet in a half-mile. The trail to the north offers a loop return to your car.

The hike up 1,194-foot Penobscot Mountain is labeled difficult. It offers the reward of a swim in Frog Pond and Sargent Mountain Pond (.2-mile beyond the summit, on the Sargent Pond Trail), also known as Lake of the Clouds. The trail leaves from the Jordan Pond House overflow-parking area. Notice the number of steps laid by the original trail builders, island rusticators who sometimes went as far as *adding* boulders to improve the aesthetics of the walk. On this hike, you'll find thrills of beauty and chills of daring as you negotiate a trail about 5 feet wide between a smooth cliff rising 20 feet above to one side and a 30- to 40-foot drop to the other side. Allow for at least four hours of walking.

Sargent Mountain is far from paved roads and considered the wildest and most Alpine-like peak in the park. If you go in spring, or after a rainfall, you'll see the added attraction of a powerful cascade on Hadlock Brook. At any time of year, this 4-mile trail is considered difficult but grand, with its summit vista, waterfalls and great views of the elegant carriage-road bridges. Take Maine Highway 198 toward Northeast Harbor from Bar Harbor. On the east side of the road, at the top of the hill, about a mile north of Northeast, is the trailhead for Parkman Mountain. Registered Maine Guide Earl Brechlin, editor of the *Bar Harbor Times*, offers the following route in his nice companion hiking book *Hiking on Mount Desert Island* (Down East Books: 1996):

Take the carriage road here, turning right, then left, winding with it for almost a mile. At the second granite bridge, turn left onto Hadlock Brook Trail. You'll be passing the waterfalls here, and crisscrossing over the brook. The trail rises steeply to granite ledges and about a half-mile walk over blueberry barrens to the summit. The cairn you see on top once held a wooden fire tower.

Remember: Hike with a friend; keep your pet on a leash; stay on the trails; bring a map and compass; carry a jacket (or better, rain gear) for Maine's variable weather; carry water; and plan your hike so you have some daylight left for your descent. It's also a good idea to let someone — even your innkeeper — know where you're going.

Kayaking and Canoeing

The first visitors to the land that became Acadia National Park came by foot and then by canoe. The first Europeans came by sailing ship. Folks have been coming by canoe, sail, kayak and motorboat almost ever since.

Look at a park map for the dozen boat ramps on MDI, and obey signs if you're boating in one of the reservoirs.

Recently, kayaking has churned Maine's salt water — with a fervor. Van after van can be seen traveling U.S. Highway 1, pulling a load of yellow, red and green kayaks so colorful, you'd think there was a party at the end. It's not a party exactly, but it's fun. Kayaking is very easy to learn. And once you're comfortable, the paddling stroke is even easier to execute than canoeing or rowing. But be sure you know what you're doing if you head out into the ocean; Maine's weather is notoriously unpredictable.

Numerous other excursion boats ply the waters around Mount Desert Island. See our Attractions chapter for more information.

Acadia Bike & Coastal Kayaking
48 Cottage St., Bar Harbor • 288-9605, (800) 526-8615

These folks offer several tour and rental options. We're listing 1997 rates because no changes had been established at press time. Basic tours cost $43 for a half-day or $65 for a full day. Four two-seat kayaks (eight people) go out with one guide for half-day tours.

Solo tours in single-seat kayaks (up to eight guests) cost $55 per person and last five hours. At the short end, there are the popular two-hour harbor tours and sunset tours (imagine paddling the sunset-pink and heavenly blue waters of Frenchman Bay) for $34. Multi-day island camping tours are available for a minimum of four guests — $199 per person for two days and $359 per person for three days.

Typical short tours go out to the Porcupine Islands, Cranberry Islands or Bartlett's Island. A guide initiates guests in the ways of the kayak and keeps talking as you paddle — about the natural world, the history, the gossip of the island. In each instance, you'll stop halfway for a 15-minute island jaunt to stretch your legs and relieve yourself. You might be paddling with the porpoises around the Porcupines, or with the seals near Bartlett's Island. Custom packages — created according to your needs — are also available.

Standard kayak rentals are $45 a day for a single boat, $55 for a tandem; both have rudders. Lake kayaks are $30 a day. All kayak rentals include paddles, life vests and car-top carriers.

Canoe rentals are $25 for a full day, $15 for multiple days and $75 for a week. Rental includes a car rack, maps, life vests and paddles.

The shop is open year round. From May to October, daily hours are generally 8 AM to 8 PM. Off-season hours are approximate: In March, April and November, the shop is usually open six days a week from 9 AM to 6 PM; from December through February, it's open four days a week from 9 AM to 5 PM. The weather affects hours, however, so it is best to call ahead.

Acadia Outfitters
106 Cottage St., Bar Harbor • 288-8118

The folks at Acadia Outfitters are like kissing cousins with the folks at Acadia Bike & Coastal Kayaking. While each is a separate organization, there is a connection. Both offer some very similar but complementary sea kayaking excursions, including morning and sunset harbor tours (also offered at Acadia Bike & Coastal Kayaking); no multi-day tours are offered. In 1997, half-day tours cost $43; full-day tours, $65.

Acadia Outfitters also rents kayaks and canoes. In 1997, single-seat kayak rentals cost $45 for a full-day, and tandem kayaks cost $55 (both have rudders). Lake kayaks cost $30 for the day. Rentals included paddles, life vests and car-top carriers.

For daily canoe rentals: $25 for a full day, $15 a day for multiple days and $75 for the week. Rentals included a car rack, maps, life vests and paddles.

The store is open daily from Mother's Day to Columbus Day. July and August hours are 8 AM to 9 PM daily. Spring and fall hours are 8 AM to 6 PM daily.

National Park Sea Kayaking Tours
National Park Outdoor Activity Center, 137 Cottage St. and Maine Hwy. 3, Bar Harbor • 288-0342, (800) 347-0940

Six tandem kayaks go out for each of National Park's sea kayak tours. A half-day excursion, morning or afternoon, costs $45 per person; all necessary gear is included. Two tours leave each morning and afternoon and last four hours each. Sunset trips are available Tuesday through Friday.

You don't need experience, gear or even tremendous upper-body strength for kayaking. Just spend about 10 minutes learning the strokes and how to raise and lower the rudder, and you'll be ready for an exploratory trip of 5 to 7 miles. Children are allowed, but unless they're about 4-foot-8 or taller, they probably won't be able to get their arms high enough off the water to paddle.

A guide will lead you through Frenchman Bay to the Porcupines, just around the corner. Bartlett Landing, at a pretty harbor near the Rockefeller's Bartlett Island, is on the other side of the island — reached by first taking a 15-minute drive from the center. Maybe you'll start in Pretty Marsh, stop on Black Island and look at Green Island, where there's a seal nursery. Maybe you'll glide past porpoises.

Guides keep a running commentary going about the wildlife, history of the land and each island — perhaps even some gossip.

Rental kayaks are available for experienced paddlers. Call for rates.

The Outdoor Activity Center is open for sea kayak tours and rentals from Memorial Day weekend until the end of September. From late June through August, it is open 8 AM to 8 PM daily. In the shoulder seasons, it's sometimes open only until 6 PM.

National Park Canoe Rentals
Pretty Marsh Rd. (Maine Hwy. 102), Somesville • 244-5854

This outfitter is on the western side of Acadia National Park, on Long Pond. It stocks 30 canoes. The supply runs out frequently, so make reservations. Half-day rentals are $20 for the morning, $22 for the afternoon; all-day rentals are $30; and weekly rentals are $125 for Old Town canoes, paddles and life jackets as well as straps and cushions for car-top carriers if you wish to canoe another lake beside Long Pond). Uncertain about your stroke? Lessons are free.

National Park Canoe Rental also rents five fishing canoes with an anchor and fishing gear for two for $40 a day or $32 for a half-day. Or try a rowing canoe, with oar locks — $25 for a half-day, $50 for a full day.

The romantic — or playful — might consider a three-hour guided sunset and moonlight cruise with a Maine guide. You bring dinner, they bring you and as many as nine other canoes to a swimming spot. Cost in 1997 was $24. Departure time, 5:30 PM. Call for particulars.

National Park Canoe is open 8 AM to 5 PM daily from mid-May through mid-October.

Rainy-day Activities

Rain ought not to dampen your visit to Acadia National Park.

First of all, from woods to water, Acadia is simply more mysterious and beautiful in its wet moods. A drizzle needn't keep you off the trails. Have the heavens unleashed a downpour? There's plenty of family indoor explorations in and around the park. Following are some ideas, each of which is covered in detail elsewhere in this book:

• Spend an hour in the Abbe Museum, Maine Highway 3, Sieur de Monts Spring, 288-3519, Maine's only museum devoted solely to the archeology and history of its Native Americans, with pottery, bone, stone tools and recent artifacts. (See our Attractions chapter.)

• Stop at the Nature Center down the hill from the Abbe Museum for a sheltered introduction to the area's flora and fauna.

• Take a slow sight-seeing drive around the island, favoring small roads to view the cottages of the past and the gardens of the present. Or take your sight-seeing with a guide, joining Jolly Roger's or Oli's Trolley, both charming, bus-like, wood-sided excursion vehicles that drive through Bar Harbor. They each offer an hour-long tour of the mansion history of the island. It ends with a trip up Cadillac Mountain, not great in the rain, we know, but we think the rest of the narration makes it worth it. You can get tickets for Jolly Roger's at Testa's, at Bayside Landing, 53 Main Street, Bar Harbor, 288-3327; for Oli's, at the Town Pier, 288-9899, or the Acadia Restaurant. (See our Attractions chapter.)

• Stop at the Mount Desert Oceanarium, a hands-on museum of the ocean in one or both of its two locations: at Thomas Bay, Maine Highway 3, Bar Harbor, 288-5005, and Clark Point Road, Southwest Harbor, 244-7330. (See our Attractions chapter for details.)

• Ship out through fog and drizzle on the mail boat from Northeast Harbor to the Cranberry Islands. We know it's damp out, that's why we suggest the trip. The water is quite beautiful in the fog. Good times to take the boat from Northeast Harbor are 10 AM, noon and 2 and 4 PM.

• Stop at Little Cranberry for a visit to the Islesford Historical Museum, where you can find artifacts from the area's early history, including the era of tall ships when the island was known as New France.

• Go to a bookstore — Port in a Storm sounds right. It's on Main Street (Maine Highway 102) in Somesville, 244-4114 or (800) 694-4114. (See our Shopping chapter.)

• Visit the College of the Atlantic's Natural History Museum, where fascinating dioramas show animals in the heat of life experience. The museum is on the college campus on Eden Street (Maine Highway 3), Bar Harbor, 288-5015. (See our Attractions chapter for details.) While you're there, visit the college's Blum Art Gallery (see our Arts and Culture chapter).

• A rainy day isn't a bad time to Explore any one of the towns on Mount Desert Island: Bar Harbor, Northeast Harbor, Southwest Harbor or even tiny Town Hill, near Somesville. Sifting through the world goods at Aquarius Antiques, Maine Highway 102, Town Hill, 288-4143 (see our Shopping chapter), can involve an entire morning.

Browsing on Main Street in Northeast Harbor can be a pleasure too. Don't miss the excellent Wingspread Gallery, 276-3910 (see Arts and Culture), and Samuel Shaw's Fine Contemporary Jewelry, 276-5000 (see Shopping), if you're a person who appreciates visual aesthetics. If you're in Southwest Harbor, don't miss the Wendell Gilley Museum of bird art at Maine Highway 102 and Herrick Road, 244-7555 (see our Attractions chapter), or Hot Flash Annie on Clark Point Road, 244-7323.

Bar Harbor is full of browsing opportunities. Get lost at the New Age emporium Eden Rising, 39 Cottage Street, 288-9081, with its soothing music, excellent books and delightful clothing. Or cross the street and dream of exploits at Cadillac Mountain Sports, 26 Cottage Street, 288-4532, outdoor outfitters for the region (see our Shopping chapter). Or simply settle down at the Lompoc Cafe and Brew Pub, 36 Rodick Street, 288-9392, over a brew, a cup of java or a bowl of warm soup (see our Restaurants and Nightlife chapters).

•Speaking of settling down, why not simply retire to your inn and curl up with a good book beside the fire that's invariably lit. You've paid for a beautiful room, haven't you? Relax.

Ranger Programs

From bird-watching to boating, rangers offer more than 30 programs — many of them daily. Some special events are geared for children, others for folks in wheelchairs. Some activities are strenuous and long, such as the three-hour early morning hike up Acadia Mountain. Others are simple, such as talks at the visitors center. You'll find many activities geared for adults to experience with their children. Pick up a copy of the *Beaver Log* for the schedule. Most activities are free, though boat tours include passage and cost up to $16 a person.

Swimming

There's a lot of water in Acadia National Park, but unlike the old saying about "water, water everywhere," so much of it here is for drinking that much is restricted for swimming. Nonetheless we include some places where you are permitted to take a dip. The ocean temperature usually stays in the mid-50s. One hot summer, ocean temperatures topped off at 61 degrees, which is what lakes reach in June. Lake temperatures climb to about 70 degrees in July.

Sand Beach
Park Loop Rd.

Children plunge into the ocean from Sand Beach, which gets as warm as 60 degrees (if you are lucky). More sensible (read older) folk prefer the lakes. There is a lifeguard on duty daily in summer from 9 AM to 5 PM.

Echo Lake
Maine Hwy. 3

The water won't take your breath away here, but the view might. The sparkling waters of this mountain lake afford views of the cliffs of Beech Mountain rising sheer above the lake. There's a roped-off, guarded (9 AM to 5 PM daily in summer) area for swimming. A bathroom and changing rooms also are available.

Lake Wood
off Crooked Rd., approx. 2 mi. from Hulls Cove

The license plates are distinctly local at this small lake's swimming hole, with a marsh full of tadpoles on either side. That's because Lake Wood is not on any park map, and the sign is one you can't miss . . . *after* you turn. From Maine Highway 3 at Hulls Cove, drive down Crooked Road, taking the second left after the gravel pit, not quite 2 miles from Hulls Cove. Proceed to the second parking lot for bathing suits and beach; the first lot leads to a bare rock jump — along with bare bodies on occasion.

Winter Sports

There are few experiences more beautiful than skiing by moonlight. Imagine the white expanse of snow, the pale light of the moon, the dull sheen of a frozen Eagle Lake (on Maine Highway 233).

Snow doesn't always last on Mount Desert Island; coastal areas are funny that way. But when the snow does last, the carriage roads, and sometimes even the park access roads, seem to have been constructed for winter sports. The carriage roads are the best for skiing when there's at least 4 inches of snow on the ground; many of them are even groomed. The Park Loop Road, which is closed in winter, is given over to the snowmobiles, though many folks also ski those roads, keeping their ears peeled for motors. Brave souls hike with skis up Cadillac Mountain, then telemark down, despite the fact that the top third of the mountain is sheathed in ice most winters. Snowshoers sometimes walk the carriage roads and oceanside trails. Hikers relish sites of deer and snowshoe hares amid leafless hardwoods. Jordan Pond and Ship Harbor nature trails (each about a mile long — see previous "Things To Do, Hiking" section) are good options for short winter visits to

Acadia. But don't expect to do any horseback riding; the trails are groomed for skiers, not horses.

Be prepared for drastic changes in the weather; dress in layers, and bring extra dry clothing. Remember, some automobile roads are closed in winter, which means even emergency vehicles have limited access. Bring a first-aid kit, water, food, a blanket and matches. Also remember, in December the sun sets before 4 PM.

Cadillac Mountain Sports
26 Cottage St., Bar Harbor • 288-4532

Bless this expansive store. It not only remains open in winter, but also serves outdoor enthusiasts' winter as well as summer sports needs. Rent cross-country skis (plus boots and poles) at $12 a day; or for $19 a day, rent shorter, faster tracking skis, known as skate skis; or wider backcountry skis.

If you'd rather be on Eagle Lake than around it, you can rent ice skates — hockey or figure — for $5 a day. (Remember, while the ponds might be frozen, they frequently are blanketed by snow. Ask about conditions.)

Do you have a hankering for deep-woods exploration? Snowshoes will carry you above the trails without sinking beneath the snow. Rent aluminum snowshoes with walking crampons for $9 a day.

Weekly rates — seven days for the price of five — are available for all gear. For an early morning departure, pick up your rentals after 4 PM the day before.

Cadillac Mountain Sports is open 9 AM to 11 PM daily from late June through September and 10 AM to 6 PM the rest of the year.

For the Kids . . .

The *Beaver Log*, available at Hulls Cove Visitor Center, has a schedule of daily walks and ranger talks. A good third of the hikes, boat trips and talks are geared for children.

Actually, there isn't much that children won't enjoy in Acadia National Park. Peruse this chapter (including the previous "Rainy-day Activities" section) and consider the following ideas:

• Visit a beaver lodge: On the one-way portion of the Park Loop Road, just after Sieur de Monts park entrance, you can see a lodge at Beaver Dam Pond. There's another lodge on Paradise Hill Pond. Take the access trail to the carriage road at the far side of the Hulls Cove Visitor Center parking lot. After about 200 yards, turn right on what the park calls a "social trail" to find the beaver lodge.

• Explore the tide pools among the rocks along the ocean shore.

• Walk the beach or any number of trails. Kids seem to get a special charge out of climbing — try the relatively short trail up Gorham Mountain. Kids also enjoy the amazement of walking "through the water" across the sandbar to Bar Island — just make sure you have enough time to get back before the tide begins to rush in. It comes on swiftly. (See our previous discussion under "Hiking.")

• Go to the beach — try Sand, Seawall or Hunter's Beach (see this chapter's "Things To Do, Swimming" section), or swim at a lake.

• Visit the kids' brewery, Bar Harbor Brewing Co. & Sodaworks, in Otter Creek, 3 miles past Jackson Lab on Maine Highway 3, 288-4592 (see our Attractions chapter), where root beer also is made.

• Look for tadpoles in the ponds, birds in the pines.

• Eat some ice cream at Ben and Bill's Choco Emporium, 66 Main Street, Bar Harbor, 288-3281.

• Go biking (see "Things To Do, Bicycling"). Some bike rentals offer trailer bikes, letting you and your child can ride in tandem.

• Learn a new skill — even rock climbing (see "Things To Do, Climbing").

• Create a collage of shells or a mobile of sticks, or build a tower on a beach.

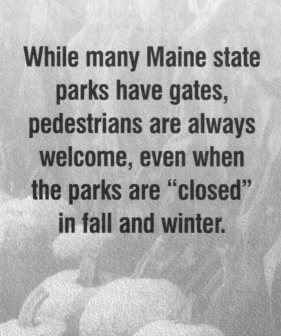

While many Maine state parks have gates, pedestrians are always welcome, even when the parks are "closed" in fall and winter.

Parks and Recreation

This is why we came to Maine. This is why we stayed. The mountains, sea and woods are close enough to be part of daily life. Friends in Camden, for instance, can ski, fish, bike and hike during lunch hour. Others swim before work, kayak or canoe on the way home. Garages and barns are cluttered with gear, and car racks to carry the stuff are everywhere.

There's a strong sentiment in the state to preserve public access to the natural wonders described in this chapter, and that accounts for the number of opportunities to explore some of the most beautiful spots on earth.

The great appeal of Maine's Mid-Coast area in particular is the range of activities available, from mountain climbing to sea kayaking. This chapter was designed to get visitors started. First we describe the parks and nature preserves, then we offer sections on specific sports — where to go, where to rent equipment and some guides and tours.

Perhaps the biggest attraction in the area is Acadia National Park, so we've dedicated a separate chapter to it. Most of the recreation opportunities on Mount Desert Island are related to Acadia, which should explain why some of the MDI listings here may seem a bit slim.

This book was going to press just as the state's outdoor-sports industry was setting its rates for 1998, and when unable to get '98 figures, we've listed 1997 rates. Also, most of the distances described are estimates, so don't be surprised if a ride or a hike is a little longer or shorter than expected.

Finally, a word of caution. If you're ambitious and have dreams of outdoor adventures, plan ahead. The retailers we include are generous with advice. Follow it. Hire a guide if you don't have a lot of experience in a particular sport. Whatever you do, make sure you have a good map with you, and assume the weather will change. As the saying goes, "If you don't like Maine weather, just wait a minute." We've been soaked by sudden showers, threatened by thunderstorms, and pelted by golf ball-size hail. It's always colder on or near the water, so bring pants and an extra sweater or jacket no matter what the forecast. Do we sound like your mother? Good. She was right. And so is our fishing pal Jack, who continually cites the Eleventh Commandment: "The stupid shall be punished."

Parks

Most Maine state parks are open from 9 AM to sunset. While many have gates, pedestrians are always welcome, even when the parks are "closed" in fall and winter. Pets are not allowed on beaches. (See our Attractions chapter for related information about many of the following parks.)

Waldoboro to Stockton Springs

Marine Park
off Pascal Ave., Rockport • 236-0676

This little pocket park along Rockport Harbor has picnic tables and easy parking. It's flat, grassy and features a statue of Andre the Seal, who used to frequent the harbor. The park is run by the town and contains the remains of lime kilns from the early days when Rockport was a busy limestone processing center. The road to the park is a steep curving drive, so be careful when it's icy. There's no admission fee. The listed number is the harbormaster's phone. In the off-season, try the town office at 236-9648.

Camden Hills State Park
U.S. Hwy. 1, north of Camden • 236-3109

This splendid park of some 5,500 acres is the pride of the town. Old-timers still tell of buying up the land to prevent development and of raising money for the asphalt auto road to the top of Mount Battie. That road is a boon to visitors who aren't up to the climb. A handsome stone circular tower adorns the top of Mount Battie, and it's here the Lion's Club hangs an enormous five-pointed star during the December holiday season.

The park has an extensive hiking trail network that leads to many scenic overlooks throughout the park. Maiden Cliff, at 800 feet, looks out over Lake Megunticook to the west, while Mount Battie, at 790 feet, and Bald Rock Mountain, at 1,200 feet, offer panoramic views of the shoreline, Penobscot Bay and the islands. Pick up trail maps at the entrance. U.S. 1 actually bisects Camden Hills, so don't miss the park's rocky shoreline. Just cross the road and enter through the gate. Camping is available as well (see our Campgrounds chapter). Although there are no facilities, cross-country skiing is allowed in winter.

The park is open from May 15 to October 15. The day-use fee is $2 a person, 50¢ for children ages 5 through 12. (Children younger than 5 and adults older than 65 are admitted free.)

Warren Island State Park
Warren Island in Penobscot Bay • 236-3106

This 70-acre spruce-covered island south of Islesboro is a jewel, but the only access is by private boat. You'll find protected docking and mooring facilities, camping, fishing, picnicking and walking.

Warren Island is open Memorial Day to mid-September, and the day-use fee is $2 a person, 50¢ for children ages 5 through 12. (Children younger than 5 and adults older than 65 are admitted free.)

Belfast City Park
87 Northport Ave., Belfast • 338-3370

This 17.5-acre park has a pool, tennis courts, picnic facilities and a rocky beach. The pool is open from late June to Labor Day; hours vary and are posted. There's no fee for admission; the park is open from 8 AM to 10 PM daily.

Moose Point State Park
U.S. Hwy. 1, Searsport • 548-2882

Had your fill of busy U.S. 1 traffic? Pull off for a picnic at Moose Point. You can stretch your legs by walking the rocky shore of Penobscot Bay or by hiking a trail through the woods. Let the kids run around the open fields or through the grove of evergreens.

Moose Point is open Memorial Day to September 30, and day-use fees are $1 a person, 50¢ for children ages 5 through 12. (Children younger than 5 and adults older than 65 are admitted free.)

Swan Lake State Park
Maine Hwy. 141, Swanville • 525-4404, 941-4014 off-season

This 67-acre park at the head of Swan Lake is great for family outings. There's an excellent sand beach, a lifeguard on duty, barbecue pits and picnic tables under the trees. It's open Memorial Day to Labor Day, and day-use fees are $2 a person, 50¢ for children ages 5 through 12. (Children younger than 5 and adults older than 65 are admitted free.)

Fort Point State Park
Fort Point Rd., off U.S. Hwy. 1 on marked access road, Stockton Springs • 941-4014

On the tip of a peninsula near the mouth of the Penobscot River as it flows into the bay, this 154-acre park is the site of Fort Pownall, built in 1759 by the British to defend their claim to Maine. It was burned twice to prevent it from being taken by American patriots, and the earthworks remain.

This is a wonderful spot for picnics, and you can walk along the shore. Swimming is not recommended; the waters can be uncom-

FYI

Unless otherwise noted, the area code for all phone numbers listed in this guide is 207.

Kebo Valley Golf Club

8th Oldest Course in the Nation   **Est. 1888**

Restaurant and Lounge
Facility Serving Great
Lunches Daily!

Complete meeting, banquet, and reception planning

Accommodations for up to 225 people.

Kebo Valley G.C.
Rte. 233 • P.O. Box 583
Bar Harbor, ME 04609

Public Welcome!

Telephone:
Clubhouse: (207) 288-5000
Golf Shop: (207) 288-3000

---

fortably cold, and the current can be fierce in spots. A 200-foot-long pier welcomes those arriving by boat. It's a favorite place for mackerel fishing.

The park is open Memorial Day through Labor Day; admission is $1 a person for adults and teens, and children younger than 12 are free.

Inland to Bangor

Dorothea Dix Park
U.S. Hwy. 1A, Hampden • 862-3034

Established at the birthplace of Dorothea Dix, the Civil War-era advocate of prison reform, this town-owned 23-acre park is marked by a handsome stone arch. Beyond the arch, you'll find picnic tables, swings, outside toilets and some trails that lead to the Penobscot River. Some of the land behind the park is private property, and it may be posted against trespassing, so respect the signs. The park is open from spring to fall — the exact dates vary — but pedestrians are always welcome. You're asked to be out of the park by 10 PM, but there's no official opening time.

Grotto Cascade Park
State St., near Eastern Maine Medical Center, Bangor • 947-1018

An original WPA project in the 1930s, this lovely riverside park has benches, picnic tables, nature paths and a small gazebo — the site of many weddings during the summer. The park itself is a little more than 6 acres, and its centerpiece is a striking 45-foot-high man-made cascade of water.

Bucksport to Gouldsboro

Holbrook Island Sanctuary
Cape Rosier Rd., off Maine Hwy. 176, Brooksville • 326-4012

The bulk of this 1,345-acre state park was donated in 1971 by a longtime area resident who wanted to preserve the unspoiled Maine she used to know. It borders Penobscot Bay and is a wonderful place for hiking, birding and picnicking. Clearly marked trails guide visitors through forests, along the shores, around a beaver flowage and along a pond. It's open year round dawn to dusk. (See our Attractions chapter for additional information.)

Lamoine State Park
off Maine Hwy. 184, Lamoine • 667-4778

There are times on Mount Desert Island when you feel you can't see the forests for the trees — or the tourists! It gets busy, crowded, even exhausting. Lamoine State Park is the answer. It's across Eastern Bay from MDI and offers spectacular views of that island. There's camping (see our Campgrounds chapter), a picnic area and a boat launch.

Lamoine State Park is open from mid-May to mid-October, and day-use fees are $2 per adult or teen, 50¢ for children ages 5 through 12. (Children younger than 5 and adults older than 65 are admitted free.)

Mount Desert Island

Of the parks in the Mid-Coast region, Acadia National Park on Mount Desert Island is the jewel in the crown, and we've dedicated a whole chapter to it. Within its 34,370 acres are hiking trails, 50 miles of carriage roads, and opportunities for swimming, climbing, biking and cross-country skiing. Just driving the Park Loop Road is a pleasure. Cadillac Mountain, at 1,530 feet, dominates the landscape and provides spectacular views of the surrounding area.

Nature Preserves

All of the following preserves can be enjoyed for free. See our Attractions chapter for additional details on these preserves.

Waldoboro to Stockton Springs

Merryspring
Conway Rd., off U.S. Hwy. 1, Camden
• 236-2239

This 66-acre nature park, managed by a nonprofit foundation, is open year round sunrise to sunset. You'll find herb, lily and rose gardens, a 10-acre arboretum, wildflower fields and miles of trails. It also offers classes, sleigh rides in winter and a wonderful fall fair, the Windfall Fair.

Fernald's Neck
off Maine Hwy. 52, near Youngtown Rd., Lincolnville • no phone

Managed by The Nature Conservancy, Fernald's Neck is a 315-acre preserve on a heavily wooded peninsula that juts out into Lake Megunticook. It's open year round, dawn to dusk.

Take the first left (onto Fire Road 50) off

Maine 52 just after it doglegs at the Youngtown Inn, 5 miles from U.S. 1 in Camden. FR 50 passes Lake Megunticook on the left and eventually heads up a short slope. There's an old cape-style farmhouse on the right, so close you feel you're driving into its dooryard. The road crosses an open field then curves to the right. The access road to Fernald's Neck is on your left and marked with a sign. Follow it to a parking area near the trail registry.

Fernald's Neck is great for walking, snow-shoeing and cross-country skiing. Its 4 miles of trails are so wide, clear and well-marked, a child could navigate them. Different trails are marked in different colors, and they traverse different terrain: thick woods, bogs and along high cliffs above Lake Megunticook. Those cliffs are favorite jumping-off spots for high school kids. We don't know how they muster the courage; we prefer paddling around in secluded coves along the shore.

Be sure to sign in at the trail registry, and pick up a map of the trails. Leave dogs at home — they aren't allowed.

Bucksport to Gouldsboro

Crockett Cove Woods Preserve
off Whitman Rd., Stonington
• no phone

This 100-acre preserve managed by The Nature Conservancy borders Crockett Cove and offers a self-guided nature trail winding through a spruce fir forest. It's open year round, dawn to dusk.

Stanwood Wildlife Sanctuary
Maine Hwy. 3, Ellsworth • 667-8460

Commonly referred to as Birdsacre, this 130-acre sanctuary is open to the public. Its nature trails are a favorite destination for bird watchers as well as cross-country skiers during winter. A museum, the former home of pioneer ornithologist Cordelia Stanwood (1865-1958), is open 10 AM to 4 PM daily from mid-June to mid-October. The grounds are open year round.

Ice fishing is a favorite winter pasttime.

Mount Desert Island

Blagden Preserve
Indian Point, off Indian Point Rd., Mount Desert Island • no phone

Managed by The Nature Conservancy, the 110-acre Blagden Preserve on the northwestern corner of Mount Desert Island is one of the few forested sections of the island that survived the 1947 fire. It has 1,000 feet of shorefront and winding paths through red spruce, balsam and white cedar forests. You'll find great views of Blue Hill Bay; also look for seals sunning themselves on the rocks. Be sure to pick up a map and guide at the caretaker's house. It's open year round, dawn to dusk.

Recreation

Biking

If you find yourself near a quiet country road, get on your bike and go for it. Several chambers of commerce offer bike-tour maps, and you might want to write the state for information: Maine Department of Transportation, State House 16, Augusta, ME 04333. Also,

check out DeLorme's *Biking in Maine*, a $4.95 paperback of biking trail maps.

There are few, if any, bike trails per se, but here are a number of routes that are favorites with bicyclists. Distances are approximate. Le Va Tout, a bed and breakfast in Waldoboro, has maps of good rides in the area around the inn, and the owner will happily lead trips when she has the time. You might also check out our Acadia National Park chapter for information on bike trails and rentals in that area.

Road Biking

Waldoboro to Stockton Springs

Waldoboro to Friendship
Park in Waldoboro and bike Maine Highway 220 south to Friendship and back. This 20-mile trip takes you along the Medomak River and down the peninsula to the little town of Friendship. Maine 220 is a somewhat narrow country road, so traffic is moderate — but you do want to keep your wits about you. You'll pass forests, water views and lots of wonderful old houses.

Lake Megunticook
Park in Camden and bike Maine Highway 52 inland (it cuts off U.S. 1 across from the

Camden Public Library, at the head of the harbor). There's a tough hill just before Lake Megunticook, but a public landing off to your left at the bottom of the hill makes a nice rest stop. Maine Highway 52 literally hugs the shoreline, then curves inland away from the lake and takes a sharp left in front of Youngtown Inn. Follow the road to its intersection with Maine Highway 173, where you'll take another left and head into Lincolnville Center. Turn left again on Maine Highway 235 and follow it along the far shore of Lake Megunticook. At Maine Highway 105, turn left and head back to U.S. 1 in Camden.

This popular 15-mile ride offers spectacular views of Lake Megunticook and the Megunticook River. Take care though — in some sections the roads have very narrow shoulders.

Bucksport to Gouldsboro

Ellsworth to Aurora

Park in Ellsworth and take Maine Highway 179 off U.S. Highway 1A. Follow it along the east side of Graham Lake. The road ends at Maine Highway 9, where you'll turn left, heading west. Take another left on Maine Highway 181 and head down the east side of the lake back toward Ellsworth.

This 61-mile ride offers lake views, woods and marshes at the north end of the lake.

Schoodic Point

Park in Winter Harbor and head east on Maine Highway 186. Take a right on Schoodic Point Road, which hugs the shoreline of the peninsula as it extends into the ocean. You'll be riding south, east, then north. Head back to Winter Harbor on Maine 186 by taking a left at the T-intersection. This rolling 12-mile ride traverses a beautiful section of Acadia National Park. Forested areas open up to fabulous views of open ocean. There are plenty of places to stop and rest or picnic.

Mount Desert Island

Southwest Harbor Loop

Park in Southwest Harbor and head south on Maine Highway 102. At the first fork in the road, Maine Highway 102A will cut east (to

your left), through Manset and Seawall, then back to Maine 102 as it curves around Bass Harbor. Follow Maine 102 as it heads west and north along Seal Cove Pond. The road bends east again (to your right), and you'll come to a T-intersection. Turn right and follow Maine 102 south again, back to Southwest Harbor.

This is about a 25-mile ride, looping around the "quiet side" of Mount Desert Island. It offers intermittent water views of all kinds — open ocean, harbors, coves, lakes and ponds.

Mountain Biking

Waldoboro to Stockton Springs

Ragged Mountain

Park at the Camden Snow Bowl lot and look for the trailhead off to your right as you look up at the mountain from the base lodge. The trail leads up the mountain, curves to the left about a third of the way up the slope and crosses the front of the mountain toward the smaller T-bar. The trail follows the last ski trail going up the left side of the mountain and cuts left into the woods, following snowmobile trails and tote roads.

When asked why this sounded a little vague, a friend who mountain-bikes said, "Hey, half the fun of mountain biking is exploring!" He said the route was about 3.5 miles long, but don't hold him to it.

It's not a trail for novices, so take care.

Camden Hills State Park

This is a trail for novices. There are two access points. The first is the front entrance on U.S. Highway 1, about 2 miles north of Camden. The second is off Youngtown Road as it meets Maine Highway 173. You can pick up a map of the park's trail system at either point.

If you're starting from the front entrance, you'll follow the 2-mile-long Snowmobile Trail. If you're starting from Youngtown Road, you'll follow the 3-mile-long Ski Shelter Trail.

Those two trails meet, so you can ride the 5 miles from entrance to entrance if you like. Of the two trails, the Ski Shelter Trail has a more gradual, less frustrating start. If it gets steeper than you like, you can just turn around and ride back down.

There are a number of hiking trails in this park, but these are the only two open for mountain bikers.

Mount Desert Island

Many of the trails in Acadia National Park are best suited for mountain bikes. Check out suggested routes in our Acadia chapter.

Bike Rentals

To rent bikes, try the following shops. The real center for bike rentals in the Mid-Coast area is Mount Desert Island, so you'll have more options there. Remember to tell the shop where you plan to ride so its staff can suggest the most appropriate bike — some carriage paths in Acadia National Park, for instance, are best traveled on mountain bikes. Prices range from $14 to $16 a day, $8 to $11 a half-day. Many shops include free locks, helmets and maps, so ask about that when you call.

Waldoboro to Stockton Springs

Maine Sport
U.S. Hwy. 1, Rockport • 236-7120,
(888) 236-8797

Maine Sport's bike shop rents road bikes, mountain bikes, bike trailers and car racks. Rates are $15 a day. The rate drops for longer rental periods, so you'll pay $12 a day for a three- to four-day period and $10 a day for five or more days.

Brown Dog Bikes
53 Chestnut St., Camden • 236-6664

Once called Fred's Bikes, Brown Dog rents a range of bikes including mountain, road, hybrid, tandem and children's styles. It also rents trailers, carriages, seats and strollers. Rentals are $9 a half-day, $15 for a full day. Monthly and weekly rates are available as well.

Birgfeld's Bicycle Shop
U.S. Hwy. 1, Searsport • 548-2916

Birgfeld's rents mostly mountain bikes, although it also offers trailers and rear racks. Rentals are $3 an hour, $8 a half-day and $15 a day.

Inland to Bangor

Bangor Ski Rack Bike Shop
24 Longview Dr., Bangor • 945-6474
(800) 698-6474

This shop rents mountain bikes, Cannondale M500s to be precise, as well as full-suspension bikes, which make a rough ride less rough on your body, and a tandem. Rates are by the day: $15 for the M500s, $40 for the full-suspension bikes and the tandem.

Bucksport to Gouldsboro

Moose Look Guide Service
Maine Hwy. 186, Gouldsboro • 963-7720

Danny Mitchell rents mountain bikes for $15 a day. He has 10-, 12-, 15- and 18-speed bikes, including Huffy brand.

Mount Desert Island

Acadia Bike & Canoe Company
48 Cottage St., Bar Harbor • 288-9605,
(800) 660-8615

This outfitter has a full line of rentals. See our Acadia National Park chapter for details.

Bar Harbor Bicycle Shop
141 Cottage St., Bar Harbor • 288-3886

You can rent various types of bikes from this shop. See our Acadia National Park chapter.

Southwest Cycle
Main St., Southwest Harbor • 244-5856

Southwest Cycle rents mountain, hybrid and children's bikes as well as kiddie seats and car racks. Rates are $16 per day, $70 per week and include locks and helmets. It's open year round, except for a hiatus in the dead of winter. See our Acadia National Park chapter for more information.

Bowling

The bowling crowd is split between those who prefer candlepins and those who prefer tenpins. They are completely different games, so be prepared. In candlepins you throw a 2-pound 6-ounce ball and play around the fallen pins. Most lanes don't have automatic scoring. In tenpins, you throw a 10- to 17-pound ball at larger pins in an automatic setup where the deadwood is cleared out between throws.

Waldoboro to Stockton Springs

Oakland Park Bowling Lanes
U.S. Hwy. 1, Rockport • 594-7525

Oakland Park has 18 candlepin lanes. Games here are $1.90; shoe rentals are $1. A snack bar sells pizza, hot dogs and chips, while pool tables and an arcade might amuse the non-bowlers in your party.

Inland to Bangor

Bangor-Brewer Bowling Lanes
534 Wilson St., Brewer • 989-3798

With 24 lanes, Bangor-Brewer is the biggest facility in the area. Candlepin is played here at $2 a game and $1 for shoes, but there are all kinds of special rates available. All-you-can-bowl specials run for $5 from 9 AM to noon and from 3 to 5 PM. On Friday nights, you can bowl from 8:30 to 11:30 for $6, and drinks are half-price. Other diversions include a snack bar, lounge, arcade and pool tables.

FYI

Unless otherwise noted, the area code for all phone numbers listed in this guide is 207.

Family Fun Bowling Center
15 Hildreth St., Bangor • 942-6701

An outlet for tenpins fans in the area, this 20-lane bowling alley charges $1.50 a game on weekdays, $2.50 a game on weeknights, $2 during the day on weekends and $2.50 weekend nights. Shoe rentals are $1.

Moonlight bowling is offered Saturday night from 9 PM to midnight. Games are $2.50 and played in complete darkness, except for spotlights on the pins. The party atmosphere is encouraged by a zany guy on a microphone giving away free games and other prizes.

There's a snack bar and lounge as well as an arcade and pool tables.

Bucksport to Gouldsboro

Bucksport Bowling Center
Maine Hwy. 46, Orland • 469-7902

Bucksport has 12 candlepin lanes. Games are $1.50 weekdays ($2 after 5 PM) and $2 on

weekends; shoe rentals are $1. You'll also find a snack bar, pool table, pinball and video games.

Eastwood Bowling Lanes
Eastwood Plaza, 20 Eastwood Ln., off U.S. Hwy. 1, Ellsworth • 667-9228

Eastwood has 12 candlepin lanes, a snack bar and a restaurant. Games are $1.75 weekdays, $2.25 weeknights and weekends. Shoe rentals will cost you $1.

Canoeing and Kayaking

Maine has an embarrassment of riches when it comes to kayaking and canoeing. There's water around every corner. DeLorme's *Maine Atlas and Gazetteer* (see our Getting Around chapter) is a great resource — it shows boat launches right on the detail maps. You also can contact the Maine Bureau of Parks and Lands, 22 Statehouse Station, Augusta, ME 04333, 287-3821, for a list.

First we'll discuss a few lake and river (read calm-water) destinations, followed by whitewater opportunities. Sea kayaking and canoeing is best undertaken with a guide. Coastal weather conditions can change in a flash, making navigation difficult, even treacherous at times. Experienced paddlers may be fine on their own, but the rest of us might best book trips with one of the subsequently listed outfitters.

Inland waters are far more hospitable, and we mention a few worth exploring. You'll notice that some are called ponds, but don't be put off. It's just another instance of Yankee understatement. A pond in Maine would be a lake anywhere else. And don't forget Acadia National Park — check that chapter for tours and rentals if you plan to be on Mount Desert Island.

In Lakes and Ponds

Waldoboro to Stockton Springs

Sennebec Pond
off Maine Hwy. 131, Union

Sennebec Pond is part of the St. George River chain and is surrounded by rolling hills dotted with farms and houses. The boat launch is off Maine 131 on the southern end of the pond, but do paddle to the river's inflow at the northern end. You'll find a lovely meandering wetland that's home to hundreds of waterfowl including wood ducks, mallards, black ducks and great blue herons.

Lake Megunticook
off Maine Hwy. 52, in Camden and Lincolnville

At 1,108 acres, Lake Megunticook is one of the largest lakes in the Mid-Coast area. It's ringed with hills, including a stretch of Camden Hills State Park and its 800-foot Maiden Cliff. The water rambles around a large peninsula (see Fernald's Neck Preserve, mentioned earlier in this chapter) and is dotted by islands, making it an interesting and beautiful place to explore. While there are two public access points, the biggest and easiest to use is off Maine 52, about 3 miles from Camden.

Bucksport to Gouldsboro

Silver Lake
Silver Lake Rd., off Maine Hwy. 15, Bucksport

This 630-acre lake is a rough right triangle dotted with islands on its northern end. Its wooded shoreline seems to reach out in all directions, so there are lots of little coves to explore. There's little development, so it's not surprising that bald eagles and ospreys have been spotted soaring overhead, and Maine's famous loons are summer residents. The public boat launch is on the southwestern side, off Silver Lake Road.

Wight Pond
off Maine Hwy. 177, South Penobscot

Another undeveloped gem, Wight looks like the boot shape of Italy, only thinner. It's small — 135 acres — and has little development. The public boat launch is on the southwestern end of the lake, off Maine 177. The marshes on this end give way to deeper water and a rocky shoreline in the main part of the lake. At the northern end, on the western side, is a rounded peninsula with a picnic area. The northeast corner disappears into more marshlands at the inflow of McCaslin Stream.

In Rivers

St. George River

This is a beautiful river — and a blessing for canoeists of all skill levels. Whitewater aficionados willing to do their homework and time their trip for early spring can have some exciting paddling in the stretch from Searsmont village to Appleton village. We'd suggest two kinder, gentler trips.

First, you might put in at the northwest corner of Seven Tree Pond, south of Union village off Maine Highway 235, and take out a quarter-mile or so before Maine Highway 90. Keep a sharp eye out for the takeout because just beyond it is a sharp drop called Powder Mill Dam. You shouldn't run that without some scouting. This 9-mile stretch is all flatwater, meandering through rural countryside.

You might also launch just below Warren village. This stretch is a lovely, undeveloped tidal marsh, home to all sorts of waterfowl. We've seen bald eagles, ospreys and herons. It's also tidal, so an outgoing tide will take you the 6 miles to Thomaston Harbor. All you have to do is steer.

Penobscot River

The Penobscot's not the mighty Mississippi, but it's the biggest river in these parts. Try paddling the 21-mile stretch from Bangor to Bucksport, which winds past Hampden, Winterport, the beautiful marshes around Frankfort, and forests and farms. There are a couple of boat launches on the east bank of the river above Brewer, and there's one in downtown Bucksport.

The river is wide, and this stretch is tidal, which can make it challenging. If at all possible, time your trip on the outgoing tide. There's plenty of water, so it can be run year round, but watch the currents and the weather.

In Whitewater

This sport is an acquired taste for those looking for greater challenges in their watercraft. The following are reversing falls caused by the incoming tide meeting the outgoing river, and they're a treat for experienced kayakers and canoeists. (Please note: We do not recommend this activity for novices; negotiating this kind of whitewater requires a good deal of skill and composure.) The rapids run inland (upriver) as high tide approaches and run out to sea (downriver) as the tide ebbs, so get a tide chart when you arrive in the area — try convenience stores — and time your trip accordingly.

Bucksport to Gouldsboro

Blue Hills Falls
Maine Hwy. 175, beneath bridge to Blue Hill Neck over Salt Pond outlet, South Blue Hill

As the tide flows into this narrow channel, the pressure builds, gradually creating Class V rapids. The best time to run them is about two hours before high tide. An incoming tide will empty into a pool, so if you overturn, you can easily swim ashore. Don't run this on an outgoing tide; the hydraulics will pin a boat, and if you overturn, the current will take you out to sea.

The beauty of this spot is that you can use the big eddy on the right to turn around and float to the top of the run with no effort at all. Since the water is some 30 feet deep under the rapids and there are no underlying obstructions, it's quite safe. The biggest hazard here may be the traffic: There's limited parking, and people park along the side of the road. Use caution going to and from your car.

Bagaduce Falls
Maine Hwys. 175 and 176, beneath the bridge over the Bagaduce River, North Brooksville

We're told there are two sets of rapids between the Bagaduce estuary and Snow Cove: one under the bridge and another about a mile or so down, which is somewhat more lively. Access is easy, making it a favorite practice run for kayakers and canoeists. This is a beautiful stretch, but there is a slight current. If you're going in a canoe, it's good to have at least one strong paddler.

Outfitters

If you want to rent a canoe or kayak, or arrange for a guided tour, try the following sources.

Waldoboro to Stockton Springs

Ducktrap Sea Kayak Tours
U.S. Hwy. 1, Lincolnville • 236-8608

Two-hour harbor tours cost $25 to $30, while half-day tours are $50. Both include all the equipment you'll need plus some preliminary instruction to ensure your safety. Special group or family tours can be arranged. Ducktrap has added rentals this year. Prices range from $15 to $30 for half-day, $20 to $40 depending on the kayak style. Weekly rates are available as well.

Maine Sport
U.S. Hwy. 1, Rockport • 236-8797, (888) 236-8797

Maine Sport's Outdoor School is making a name for itself in kayaking on the East Coast. Two-hour ($30) and half-day tours ($60) are available as are a range of other options including daylong and multi-day tours. In some, you camp at night; in others, you stay at the school's facility on Gay Island in Muscongus Bay. Family trips, instruction and rentals are available as well.

Single plastic sea kayaks rent for $40 a day, including paddles, PFDs, wet suits, spray skirts, paddle floats, bilge pumps, foam car-top carriers and straps. Lake kayaks rent for $20 a day, including paddles, PFDs, foam car-top carriers and straps. Whitewater kayaks rent for $35 a day, including paddles, spray skirts, PFDs, wet suits, helmets, foam car-top carri-

---

INSIDERS' TIP

The Maine Island Trail Association offers a guidebook for low-impact use of a string of islands. This is a particularly popular resource for experienced sea kayakers who want to paddle and camp their way up the coast. Contact: MITA, P.O. Box C, Rockland, ME 04841, 596-6456.

ers and straps. Sea and whitewater kayak rentals require previous paddling experience. Canoes rent for $25 and $30 a day, including paddles, PFDs, foam car-top carriers and straps. Longer rentals cost less for all boats.

Inland to Bangor

Maine Bound
University of Maine, Center for Students and Community Life, 5748 Memorial Union, Orono • 581-1794

Maine Bound offers scheduled whitewater canoe and kayak courses on a first-come, first-served basis. The three-day courses cost $75 and $130 respectively. Other related courses, instruction and teen programs are available as well. Call for specifics.

Kayaking packages, including boat, PFD, paddle, spray skirt and helmet, rent for $18.50 a day. Canoes rent for $15.50 and $12.50, including paddles and PFDs. Equipment may be rented on a per-piece basis — $5 a day for a spray skirt and $4 a day for a Farmer John wet suit, for instance.

Bucksport to Gouldsboro

The Phoenix Center
Maine Hwy. 175, Blue Hill Falls • 374-2113

The outdoor education center offers half-day kayak trips (9:30 AM to 2:30 PM) for $50, including all equipment, spring water and a snack; you'll need to bring a bag lunch. Weekend trips are available as well ($100 a person a day), but we were most intrigued by the overnight "Fantasy Island" trip. You start at 9:30 AM on Saturday, put in a full day of paddling and end up on an island, where a luxurious camp has already been set up for you. The guide feeds you a gourmet dinner, leaves you alone there for the night, picks you up the next morning, and you paddle back. The trip is done with one or two couples at a time ($200 a person for 1½ days). "We spoil you rotten," the staff say. Sounds great.

The Phoenix Center also rents canoes for freshwater use at $25 a day, including paddles and life jackets. Check out the new junior guide program for kids ages 12 through 18. It's $300 for a five-day course in kayaking and outdoor

education, including orienteering, navigation and CPR.

Moose Look Guide Service
Maine Hwy. 186, Gouldsboro • 963-7720

Danny Mitchell rents Old Town canoes for $24 a day (a full 24 hours) and kayaks for $25 to $40 a day, including racks, paddles, life jackets, and spray skirts. He guides trips in both craft: canoe trips in the Pleasant and Machias Rivers, and morning and evening kayak tours along the coast. The kayak tours sound great: $35 for three hours, and the sunset tour offers lovely views of Cadillac Mountain.

Mount Desert Island

Acadia Bike & Canoe Company
48 Cottage St., Bar Harbor • 288-9605, (800) 526-8615

This outfitter can set you up with canoes or kayaks. See our Acadia National Park chapter for details.

Climbing

Climbers come from all over New England to test their skills on Maine's ledges. We describe their favorite areas, but specific climbs are beyond our scope. We wouldn't dream of suggesting you can get started mountaineering with directions from a travel guide. As any climber knows, this is a sport where setting off on your own in an unfamiliar area can get you killed. Just looking at the sheer drop off the cliffs in Camden make it clear that a fall could be fatal; there's nothing but more rocks at the foot of the climb. Ice climbing can be particularly treacherous because of changing, unpredictable weather conditions. We've seen stories of tragic accidents in the newspaper, some involving experienced climbers, so proceed with caution.

Waldoboro to Stockton Springs

Camden Hills State Park
The main cliffs here are above Barrett's Cove and at Maiden Cliff, two areas about a half-mile apart on Maine Highway 52, about 3 miles inland from U.S. Highway 1 in Camden.

Most climbers park on the shoulder of the road below the sheer face at Barrett's Cove or at the parking area up off the road to the right at the Maiden Cliff trailhead.

Many rock climbers prefer Clifton or Acadia to Camden Hills, but the tables turn in ice climbing. In the *Ice Climber's Guide to Northern New England*, author Rick Wilcox says Camden "hosts some of the scarier ice climbs in the East."

The best source of info on Camden Hills is a small but informative paperback called *Rock and Ice Climbs in the Camden Hills* by Ben Townsend, published by Georgetown Press, Augusta, Maine. It details the climbs and precautions you should take. You can pick up a copy at Maine Sport on U.S. 1 on your way through Rockport.

Inland to Bangor

Clifton, Maine

Clifton, about 20 minutes east of Bangor on Maine Highway 9, may be one of the largest climbing areas in the state. It has 10 bluffs ranging from 40 or 50 feet to almost 400 feet. Chick Hill, Eagle Bluff, Parks Pond Bluff and Fletcher Bluff are the major climbs. There are a number of access roads where you might park. DeLorme's *Maine Atlas and Gazetteer* or a topographical map will detail the area for you so you can find your way around.

Mount Desert Island

Acadia National Park

Otter Cliffs, one of the climbing areas here, has granite rock that rises straight out of the ocean, offering the rare opportunity to climb sea cliffs. See our chapter on Acadia National Park for more on the climbs and tours available there. You might also consult *The Climber's Guide to Mount Desert Island* by Geoffrey Childs. It's out of print, but Cadillac Mountain Sports, 288-4532, in Bar Harbor has laminated pages available to help customers get oriented. Another new book, *The Pocket Guide to Climbing in Acadia National Park*, by Pete Warner, has much of the same information. You can get that at Cadillac Mountain Sports as well.

Rentals/Tours/Classes

Unfortunately, while climbing is growing in popularity, we found few outfitters operating outside Acadia. We list them here. See the Acadia National Park for outfitters operating in that area.

Inland to Bangor

Maine Bound
University of Maine, Center for Students and Community Life, 5748 Memorial Union, Orono • 581-1794

This facility is open to university students, staff and faculty as well as the community at large. It rents some climbing gear and offers group-based trips that are scheduled like classes. Sign up for trips to Clifton, Acadia, Camden, even the legendary Mount Washington in New Hampshire. Daytrips to Acadia or Clifton, for instance, cost $45 for UM students, $55 for others. A skill-level self-assessment will help you pick appropriate courses.

Daily rental rates are $7.25 for rock-climbing shoes, $2.50 for a snow ax, $15 for double boots and $5.25 for hinged crampons. The last three items come in a package for $18 a day. Longer rentals — for a weekend or a week — are discounted.

Alpenglow Adventure Sports
36 Main St., Orono • 866-7562

This outdoor retail store specializes in rock climbing, mountaineering, backpacking and camping. It's open year round while its sister store in Bar Harbor, 137 Cottage Street, 288-8186, is open May through September. (At press time the Bar Harbor store knew it was moving to Main Street but didn't have an address yet.) The owners run Acadia Mountain Guides Climbing School, described in the Acadia National Park chapter, but you can book them for instruction or guided trips in Clifton or Camden as well.

Fishing

The Mid-Coast is not among Maine's more famous angling destinations, but it's definitely worth bringing your gear.

From June through September, the har-

Thousands of freshwater lakes dot Maine.

bors and estuaries are apt to be full of mackerel; they're a great quarry for the kids, since they're a schooling fish that bite any lure they see. There are no bag or length limits on mackerel, and midsize freshwater spinning or fly-fishing gear will do the trick.

In June, July and August, striped bass attract more serious anglers. Stripers are big fish, running 18 to 40 inches, so bring appropriate gear. Spin-casters need 8- to 10-foot rods and a good saltwater reel loaded with 12- to 20-pound test line. Fly-casters use 8- to 10-weight rods and sturdy reels holding a minimum of 150 yards of backing; leaders should be at least 12- to 20-pound test. If you don't want to buy gear for a day of fishing, hire a guide for a day and use their gear.

As this book went to press new state regulations governing striped bass had yet to be announced. The best source for the new rules is the Maine State Department of Marine Resources, 624-6550.

Bluefish are also occasional visitors to Maine's coastal waters in summer, but they're caught much less frequently than stripers. The bag limit is 10 fish.

There's an abundance of freshwater fishing as well. You'll find small- and largemouth bass and Atlantic salmon on the Penobscot River, brook and brown trout in Maine's lakes and ponds. Other species (pickerel, white and yellow perch, lake trout) are out there, of course, but those are the ones we brag about.

Now, how to get started? Maine isn't like Florida, for instance, where you go to a pier, drop your line in the water and catch a fish. Much like climbing, you'd best go out with a friend or guide who knows the area and has been fishing recently. Fly shops or the fishing departments of outdoor sports stores are another source of information on what's biting where, and it does change from week to week. Conditions do change from week to week; water conditions vary widely, and so do the hot spots.

The state offers freshwater licenses for one, three, seven and 15 days and for the season. They range from $8 to $51, and you can buy them at fly shops, outdoor sports stores and town offices. No license is required for saltwater fishing.

Some freshwater areas are fly-fishing only, while others are open to all methods, so when you buy your license, ask for a law book that will help you stay legal. There's nothing like the wrath of a fly-caster or warden who finds you using worms in the wrong section of a river.

Waldoboro to Stockton Springs

St. George River

This river has a nice variety of fish. It's tidal from its mouth in Cushing upstream as far as Payson Park at the Maine Highway 90 bridge. From late May through July and August, this stretch offers very good striper fishing. The U.S. Highway 1 bridge has a nice access spot where it crosses the river, as does the next bridge upstream in Warren village. Fly-casters, try Clouser minnows and deceivers, especially white and olive. Spin-casters prefer Kastmasters Atom Poppers.

Upstream, beyond Payson Park is good brown trout water. Fish are in all sections of the river, but the bridge in Appleton village is a good spot. Fly-casters might try the catch-and-release section (artificial lures only, no natural bait allowed) from the next bridge upstream, where Maine 105 crosses the river, to the Ghent (say gent) Road bridge. After that stretch, try the next bridge upstream in Searsmont village. There's a nice stretch of quick water below the bridge and some nice pools above the bridge. Some flies to try: Adams, Caddis dry flies and streamers (natural-bait imitations). Spin-casters, use Mepps spinners.

Once trout fishing slows down in mid-July, these same sections offer some good smallmouth bass fishing. Use poppers or woolly buggers.

Rockland Breakwater

Make a family outing to this mile-long stretch on Jamieson Point at the end of Samoset Road. Anglers of all ages can try for the little rock bass that swim between the crevices in the structure, for mackerel, even stripers and bluefish, while the rest of the family has a picnic and takes a walk on the huge granite boulders that make up the breakwater. Spinning gear's what you'll want here: 8- to 12-pound test for mackerel and a little heavier for stripers or bluefish. Use mackerel jigs, Kastmasters and big Rapalas, or bait such as cut fish or sea worms.

Inland to Bangor

Penobscot River

For the last 20 years, this river has been the flagship for Atlantic salmon restoration on the East Coast. The pools in Bangor are the most famous, but there are other popular spots in the towns of Veazie and Eddington. Salmon fishing is quirky: The gear is specialized, the flies are traditional, and the protocol at the pools is somewhat precise. Check with Eddie's (see subsequent listing in "Outfitters & Guides") for more specifics.

While Maine is not particularly known as a bass-fishing mecca, it has some of the best waters on the East Coast. There's a fabulous 40-mile stretch from Old Town upstream to where Interstate 95 crosses the river in Medway — inland from our Mid-Coast region. The best access is off Maine Highway 2, which parallels the east bank of the river. There are at least six boat launches in the first 30 miles upriver from Old Town, and you can wade-fish at most of those. (See DeLorme's *Maine Atlas and Gazetteer*, or call the state — see this chapter's introduction for contact information — for boat launch locations.) Fly-casters might try white Clouser minnows, poppers, woolly buggers and muddler minnows, while Rapalas work well for spin-casters. In deeper sections, try a rubber lead-headed jig like Gitzits.

Bucksport to Gouldsboro

Graham Lake

Graham Lake is one of the best bass lakes in the state. (Maine Bass Federation held a tournament there a few years back.) Conveniently situated north of Ellsworth, it was cre-

FYI

Unless otherwise noted, the area code for all phone numbers listed in this guide is 207.

ated by a dam that pools the flowage from the east and west branches of the Union River. It's big too — 16 miles long — with at least four public boat launches.

Other fish include pickerel, white and yellow perch, bullheads and even brook trout, salmon and brown trout. Fly anglers will want to try this lake in the early morning in the spring, using flies that match what's on the surface. Spin-casters, try bass plugs or rubber worms.

Mount Desert Island

Acadia National Park
See Acadia National Park chapter.

Outfitters & Guides

Waldoboro to Stockton Springs

Johnson's Sporting Goods
15 Walnut St., Rockland • 594-2916
The fishing department here sells gear for fly-fishing and spin fishing in salt- and freshwater. It may also be able to hook you up with fly- and spin-fishing guides and charter boat captains in the area for guided trips.

Georges River Outfitters
1384 Atlantic Hwy. (U.S. Hwy. 1), Warren • 273-3818
Jeff Bellmore is a Maine native, a Master Maine Guide, a U.S. Coast Guard captain, and an all-round prince of a guy. He's been in the business for 10 years and can take you almost anywhere for almost any species, freshwater or salt. He also guides hunting, snowmobiling, canoeing and nature trips for those who shoot with a camera.

Bellmore charges $175 for three hours of fishing, $275 for six hours. Longer trips to Northern Maine are also available. If you have your heart set on booking a trip with Jeff, call ahead. Like any good guide, he's developed a stable of regular customers who book year after year.

Maine Sport
U.S. Hwy. 1, Rockport • 236-8797, (888) 236-8797
Maine Sport's fishing department focuses mostly on fly-fishing but does carry some salt-water spin-fishing gear. Brands include Orvis, St. Croix and Ross. It also offers fly-casting clinics, fly-tying lessons and one-day fly-fishing schools. If you'd like to fish with a guide, the store has a guide on staff, and also books fresh- and saltwater trips with a handful of local guides. Prices range from $90 to $175 for a half-day and $160 to $300 for a full day. Longer trips are available for destinations all over the state.

Catch 22 Sport Fishing Charters
RR 1, Box 3265, Appleton • 785-2408
Capt. Russell Troy will take you on the hunt for stripers and blues in the inlets of the Kennebec or Sheepscot rivers, just south of our Mid-Coast region. He's on the pro staff for Fin-Nor and G. Loomis and is a member of the Yamaha Motors national fishing team. Troy says he hasn't been skunked in five years; in 1997 one of his customers landed a 46.5-pound striper.

Call early for the best dates. Russell says many of his regular customers book a year in advance, but he still has some good August and fall openings. The full-day rate for a party of one to four people is $375 and includes G. Loomis fly-fishing or spin-fishing gear, tackle and bait. His cruiser, *Catch 22*, has live wells, downriggers, and yes, ladies and gentlemen, a private porta-potty. He keeps ice and coolers on board as well.

Ken Bailey's Wilderness Ways
15 Knowlton St., Camden • 236-4243
Guides don't get any more local than Ken Bailey. His family has lived here for generations, and he's fished the area for more than 30 years. He's a great guy to fish with, especially for children old enough to enjoy the trip. He offers half-day ($90) and full-day ($160) spin-fishing trips that include bass boat and related equipment, fishing gear, bait and lunch (if you're out for the whole day). A 10- to 12-hour trip to the Penobscot River for smallmouth bass will cost $200 for one or two people, including transportation, boat, bait, gear and lunch.

Clyde Cook Fishing Company
Maine Hwy. 52, Lincolnville • 763-3005
Paul McGurren's been fishing since he was a child, but it was his college roommate who

turned him into a fly-fisher in the early '70s. Now he writes for a national fly-fishing magazine, buys for the fishing department at Maine Sport and teaches fly-casting and fly-tying. While he'll happily organize trips to Maine's North Woods, the St. George and the Penobscot are specialties as well. He offers half day ($100) and full-day ($175, includes lunch) fly-fishing trips — either wade-fishing or from a canoe.

The Outdoor Sportsman
U.S. Hwy. 1, Northport • 338-4141

You can get everything from bait to fly-fishing gear at The Outdoor Sportsman. While it does not offer guided trips, it does have classes in fly-fishing, fly-tying and fly casting. The store is a Cortland Pro Shop and a FinNor dealer, and handles many other lines, including Penn, Shimano, Berkeley and Fenwick.

Inland to Bangor

Eddie's Flies and Tackle
303 Broadway, Bangor • 947-1648

If you're out to get the scoop on fishing in the Bangor area, there's no better place to start than Eddie's. You can book trips with Eddie as well through the Mainely Fishing Guide Service. He'll take you spin- or fly-fishing for smallmouth bass on the lower Penobscot River and for brook trout and land-locked salmon on the west branch of the Penobscot. The trips run $220 a day for one person, $240 for two, and include use of his boat, all fishing gear and lunch.

Bucksport to Gouldsboro

Willey's
137 High St., Ellsworth • 667-2511

This store started 75 years ago as a clothing store, but it's developed a solid sporting goods department in the basement. Here you'll find good advice and all kinds of gear: fly-fishing, spin-fishing and bait-casting, for fresh- and saltwater.

The owner tells us there aren't many guides operating in his area; most fishermen set out on their own with DeLorme's *Fishing Depth Maps*, a $5.95 paperback that details depth and species information on the lakes and ponds in the area.

Moose Look Guide Service
Maine Hwy. 186, Gouldsboro • 963-7720

Master Guide Danny Mitchell is game for almost any kind of freshwater salmon or trout fishing: spring trolling, fly-fishing on the west branch of the Penobscot and brook trout fishing on inland ponds. He charges $200 a day, $220 with a second person, $235 with a third. Longer trips may cost a bit more, depending on where you're going and how long you plan to be gone. He also sells nonresident fishing licenses.

Golf

There's a surprising number of courses in the Mid-Coast area, and most have enviable views. You don't even have to bring your clubs. Many course pro shops offer club and cart rentals, and we've indicated them in the following entries. Yardages provided for 18-hole courses are primarily from the back tees. The prime golf season runs from Memorial Day through Columbus Day, but Samoset Resort (see subsequent entry), for instance, is open from mid-April through late November. Of course, it's made a name for itself as a golf resort and caters to the staunchest golf enthusiasts. Your best bet is to call the course you plan to visit in advance if you're traveling in the off-season.

Waldoboro to Stockton Springs

Rockland Golf Club
Old County Rd., Rockland • 594-9322

At the Rockland Golf Club, the back nine overlooks Chickawaukee Lake and Dodge Mountain. It's an 18-hole, par 70, 6017-yard course, with a pro shop, a clubhouse and cart and club rentals; lessons are available. Greens fees are $30 for 18 holes, $18 for nine.

Samoset Resort
Warrenton St., Rockport • 594-1431

With seven holes right on the water and an ocean view from 14 holes, it's no surprise that in 1995 *Golf Digest* named the Samoset the seventh most beautiful course in the country. This 18-hole, 6548-yard, par 70 course has a pro shop and cart and club rentals, and lessons are available. Greens fees include a cart.

State parks along Maine's coast offer beaches for family fun, barbecues and swimming.

While rates depend on when you play, they range from $55 to $100 for 18 holes, $30 to $60 for nine. Resort guests get a discount.

Goose River Golf Course
50 Park St., Rockport • 236-8488

The rolling nine-hole, par 35 Goose River course has a total yardage of 3049. Watch for the par 5 No. 5; it's a tough 495 yards. You drive uphill, then play to a small green at the top of a knoll. You're rewarded with spectacular views of the Camden Hills.

The course offers cart and club rentals, and it has a pro shop and clubhouse. Greens fees are $25 for 18 holes (you play the course twice), $15 for nine.

Northport Golf Club
Bluff Rd., Northport • 338-2270

This nine-hole, par 36 course dates back to 1916 and has a total yardage of 3047. Its greens are well-maintained, and you can get a glimpse of the ocean on the 2nd green by the 3rd tee.

The course opens April 1, weather permitting. Greens fees are $18 for 18 holes (you play the course twice), $12 for nine through June 1 and after Labor Day. From June 1 to Labor Day, the high season, fees are $20 for 18 holes, $14 for nine holes.

Northport has a clubhouse and a pro shop, and it offers cart and club rentals and lessons.

Country View Golf Club
Maine Hwy. 7, Brooks • 722-3161

The name fits. This nine-hole course is designed so you play around the top of a hill with panoramic views of surrounding farms and fields at each hole. It's 2856 yards, par 36. You'll find a pro shop, snack bar, clubhouse and cart and club rentals. Greens fees in 1997 were $16 for 18 holes (you play the course twice), $10 for nine.

Inland to Bangor

Bangor Municipal Golf Course
Webster Ave., Bangor • 941-0232

Past host of the United States Golf Association Public Links Championship, the Bangor 18-hole course satisfies players of all skill levels. Because the tees and greens are so large, the course can play differently from day to day. Watch for a tough stretch between the 6th and 12th holes.

Another newer nine-hole course, called the New 9, is operated separately. Traps, trees and small greens make accuracy all the more important; the tees are relatively smaller too.

The main course plays 6350 yards, par 71. Amenities include club and cart rentals, a pro shop, clubhouse, lounge and restaurant; lessons are available. Greens fees on the 18-hole course are $19 weekdays ($14 after 4 PM) and $20 on weekends ($15 after 4 PM). Fees on the New 9 are $12 weekdays, $13 weekends; if you play through twice for a total of 18 holes, it's $18 weekdays, $20 weekends.

Bucksport to Gouldsboro

Bucksport Golf Club
Duckcove Rd. (Maine Hwy. 46), Bucksport • 469-7612

At 3864 yards, par 36, this is the largest nine-hole course in Maine and one of the finest in New England. This club offers cart and club rentals, a pro shop, clubhouse, snack bar and lessons. Greens fees in 1997 were $20 for 18 holes (all-day rate), $15 for nine. Call for more details.

Castine Golf Club
Battle Ave., Castine • 326-8844

This venerable club celebrated its centennial in 1996, and its nine-hole course boasts of having been redesigned in 1921 by British Open champion Willy Perke Jr. The par 35 course plays 2977 yards. The club offers pull-cart rentals and lessons, and there's a pro shop on site. Greens fees are $20 for all-day play, $10 after 4 PM.

Island Country Club
Maine Hwy. 15A, Sunset • 348-2379

Look for a challenge on the final hole of this nine-hole course — an uphill, 323-yard par 4 with trees lining the right side. Island Country Club is a relatively short 1930-yard, par 31 course offering cart and club rentals, a pro shop, clubhouse and lessons. Greens fees are $15 for all-day play weekdays, $20 weekends.

White Birches Golf Course
Thorsen Rd., Ellsworth • 667-3621

This nine-hole course takes pride in its high-quality greens and water views (the first green is almost entirely surrounded by water). White Birches is a par 34 that measures 2622 yards. It offers cart and club rentals, a pro

shop and restaurant. Fees are $15 for all-day play, $10 after 4 PM.

Bar Harbor Golf Course
Maine Hwys. 3 and 204, Trenton • 667-7505

Views of Cadillac Mountain make this a dazzling place to play. The 18-hole, par 71 course measures 6667 yards and offers cart and club rentals, a pro shop, clubhouse and lessons. Greens fees are $24 for 18 holes, $15 for nine.

Grindstone Neck Golf Course
Grindstone Ave., Winter Harbor • 963-7760

Boasting fabulous scenery and well-manicured grounds, Grindstone is a par 36, nine-hole track that measures 3095 yards and offers cart and club rentals, a pro shop and lessons. Greens fees are $16 weekdays, $18 weekends for nine holes; $22 weekdays and $25 weekends for 18 holes.

Mount Desert Island

Kebo Valley Golf Club
Eagle Lake Rd., Bar Harbor • 288-3000

Established in 1888, Kebo is the eighth-oldest golf course in the nation. This 18-hole course has a large membership, but visitors may reserve tee times three days in advance. This par 70 layout measures 6131 yards and is soft-spike only.

Kebo Valley offers cart and club rentals, a pro shop, clubhouse (available for private functions), lessons and a full restaurant serving lunch. Greens fees are $30 for 18 holes from opening day through May; $35 throughout June; $60 from July through mid-September; and $40 for 18 and $18 for nine after mid-September until season's end. (Opening and closing dates are weather-dependent, of course.)

Northeast Harbor Golf Club
Sargent Dr., Northeast Harbor • 276-5335

Call ahead because this scenic 18-hole course is popular. Since it's connected to the Hadlock Pond trail system, you might bring along traveling companions who would rather take a hike. A par 69, the Northeast Harbor course stretches 5800 yards. It offers a pro shop, cart and club rentals and lessons. Greens fees in 1997 were $30 from opening until mid-June, $40 in high-season and $30 after Labor Day until season's end.

Causeway Club
Fernald Point Rd., Southwest Harbor
• 244-3780

Golfers here have great views of mountains and a cove. It's a nine-hole, 2302-yard, par 32 course with cart and club rentals, a pro shop and lessons. The course is set up so you can play it twice. The "back" nine is 2416 yards (par 33), making 18 holes a total 4718 yards and par 65.

During May, June, September and October, greens fees are $15 for 18 holes. During July and August, fees are $18 for nine holes and $24 for all-day play.

Hiking

In our area, the question is not where can you hike, but where can't you hike? Start by scanning the parks and nature preserves listed previously in this chapter. Find the nearest one and get out your hiking boots. You'll want to stay off private property, and since the boundaries aren't always well-marked, stick to the trails. Most are marked. There are spectacular hikes in Acadia National Park as well, so do check listings in that chapter if you plan to be nearby.

The following hikes are some of our favorites.

Waldoboro to Stockton Springs

Rockland Breakwater
Try this mile-long walk over the Rockland breakwater on Jamieson Point at the end of Samoset Road. Children love to scramble over the boulders, and you'll enjoy views of the lighthouse, the islands, the Camden Hills and passing sailboats.

Camden Hills State Park
The park has nearly 20 trails, many of which connect, so you can plot a course that suits your time and abilities. Start by picking up a

trail map at the main entrance to the park on U.S. Highway 1, about 2 miles north of Camden, to get your bearings.

We suggest taking the mile-long Megunticook Trail from the park campgrounds at the main entrance to Ocean Lookout, where it connects with the 2.5-mile Megunticook Mountain Ridge Trail. The Ridge Trail connects to the 1-mile Maiden Cliff Trail, which takes you to Maiden Cliff and then down to a parking lot on Maine Highway 52, about 3 miles inland from U.S. 1 in Camden.

This is a moderately difficult hike, but it offers unparalleled views of the ocean, the islands and Lake Megunticook. Logistically, it means bringing two cars, parking one at the Maiden Cliff parking lot and leaving the other at the main entrance to the park. You hike from one car to the other. Just make sure you bring both sets of keys with you. (Oh, the stories we could tell. . . .)

Bucksport to Gouldsboro

Holbrook Island Sanctuary
There are a number of hiking trails here, but try the Backshore Trail. Take Maine Highway 176 south from West Brooksville, turn right on Horseshoe Creek Road and follow it 1.5 miles to Lawrence Hill Road. Turn right, then take a right again onto Indian Bar Road. Park in a lot on the left. The Backshore Trail starts here. Almost a mile long, it winds through old estate fields, passes a cemetery and ends at the shore. You'll have lovely views of Penobscot Bay and its islands.

If you continue on Indian Bar Road, you'll find the sanctuary headquarters and a picnic and parking area with toilets.

Blue Hill
From its summit, this rounded mountain offers views of Blue Hill Harbor and Mount Desert Island. To get there, take Maine Highway 172 northeast from the town of Blue Hill for about 1.5 miles. Then, take a left on Mountain Road, across from the Blue Hill Fairgrounds. The unmarked trailhead will be on your right; the trail itself is about a mile long.

Schoodic Mountain
Already hiked Blue Hill? You might try

Schoodic Mountain as well, off Maine Highway 183, north of Sullivan. From the summit, you'll have spectacular views of Frenchman Bay and Cadillac Mountain on Mount Desert Island. Parking is easy, the trails are well-marked, and you can take a dip in nearby Donnell Pond.

Horseback Riding

For people who love horses, no vacation is complete without riding. Here are some opportunities, including some nice options for children.

Hill-N-Dale Farm
626 Western Rd., Warren • 273-2511

Hill-N-Dale offers trail rides, lessons and a children's day-camp program. Rides for those who already know how to guide and control a horse cost $20 an hour. If you and the kids would be more comfortable taking one, a group lesson can be had for $20 an hour. The stable also offers a day camp for children at $35 a child a day, $22 a half-day.

Apple Blossom Acres
Box 35, Douglas Hwy. (Maine Hwy. 184), Lamoine • 667-9214

If you want to bring your horse with you on vacation, you can board it here for $10 a day and trailer it to Acadia National Park to ride the trails there (see our Acadia chapter). A feed and tack shop can provide supplies. Owner Bonnie Moretto offers private and group lessons. She also runs a weeklong children's camp. This is not a babysitting service. Your child has to be ready for hard work, sweat and bugs; but if he or she loves horses, you could offer no better vacation. For $250 they'll get two lessons a day and lots of training in caring for horses.

Wildwood Stables
Acadia National Park, Park Loop Rd., Seal Harbor • 276-3622

Wildwood Stables offers horseback riding on Acadia National Park's carriage roads as well as daily carriage rides to points of interest in the park (see our Acadia National Park chapter for related information). If you've brought your own horse, or horse and carriage, Wild-

wood Stables provides box stalls for about $20 per night. Owners must care for and feed their own horses. The stables are open mid-June to Columbus Day.

Roller and In-line Skating

This sport has moved well beyond the metal contraptions we strapped on as children. We include indoor facilities here, but you can rent in-line skates and take them out on the road. We'd advise caution if you decide to do that. Maine Sport in Rockport, for instance, used to rent in-line skates, but people had no convenient place to use them. Many of our country roads have narrow, rough shoulders, and the main roads can be quite busy. Ask for advice on where to skate when you rent.

Outfitters

Bucksport to Gouldsboro/ Mount Desert Island

Cadillac Mountain Sports
34 High St., Ellsworth • 667-7819
26 Cottage St., Bar Harbor • 288-4532

In-line skate rentals at both stores are $16 a day, $12 a half-day, including a helmet, elbow and knee pads and wrist guards. The Bar Harbor store is open until 11 PM in the summer, so the half-day rate, which begins at 1 PM, actually gives you 10 hours to skate. Such a deal. The Bangor store, 6 Central Street, 941-5670, may be renting in-line skates by the time you read this, so give them a call if you're interested.

Indoor Venues

Waldoboro to Stockton Springs

Rockland Skate Center
299 Upper Park St., Rockland • 594-1023

This wooden rink is one of the largest in Maine, with a light system, lots of speakers and a snack bar. The key here is to call ahead and listen to the recorded information about upcoming sessions. The recording will indicate the admission fee, but $3 a session and

75¢ to rent skates is about average. Afternoons are great family skating times; the 11- to 15-year-old crowd pretty much takes over in the evening. Saturday evenings used to be targeted to teens, but now it's called Christian Music Night and is open to everyone.

Inland to Bangor

Great Skates Entertainment Center
82 Sylvan Rd., Bangor • 945-0202

The rink here is a concrete floor covered with a urethane coating. Great Skates features a snack bar, video arcade and light shows. Admission ranges from $3 to $4.50, depending on when you skate. You can bring your own skates or Rollerblades, or rent them for $1 or $3 respectively. Older children would be comfortable skating by themselves, so you might want to slip across to the Bangor Mall and get in some shopping.

Running

Once you get onto the country roads off U.S. Highway 1, your running options multiply exponentially. Your best bet is to time your runs: Just start out from where you're staying, run for half the time you have, then turn around and run back. We've picked a few good routes to get you started.

Routes

Waldoboro to Stockton Springs

Beauchamp Point

Our favorite is a 2.5-mile loop around Beauchamp Point in Rockport. From Russell Avenue (known as Chestnut Street, if you're coming from Camden), take Calderwood Lane past the private golf course, onto a dirt road that loops around the point, along Rockport Harbor and onto Mechanic Street. Return by way of a right turn back onto Russell Avenue.

Inland to Bangor

University of Maine Trails

If you're in the Bangor area, try what has been called a mecca for local runners: the University of Maine trails in Orono. Park in front of Alfond Arena and start next to the track; follow the dirt path past the Mahaney baseball diamond, through the woods and around an open field. One loop around the field and back to the track is 3 miles; every extra loop around the field adds 1.5 miles to your run.

Bucksport to Gouldsboro

Schoodic Point

Distance runners might enjoy the 11-mile loop we outlined in the previous "Biking" section. From Maine Highway 186, take a right on Schoodic Point Road, which loops around the point. Head back to Winter Harbor via Maine 186 by taking a left at the T-intersection.

Races

There are a number of road races in the area you might want to participate in. The Schoodic Point 15K Road Race has been called one of the nation's five best. It's part of the Winter Harbor Lobster Festival (see our Annual Events chapter). Call Tom Severance, 963-7580, for more information.

Others area races include the Camden 10K organized by Maine Sport, 236-7120, in early June; the Spring 5K and Fun Run in June, and the Bar Harbor Half-marathon in September, both of which are organized by the Mount Desert Island YMCA, 288-3511; and the Maine Lobster Festival 10K Road Race and Fun Run in Rockland in August, organized by Mark Lincoln, 785-2391 or 785-4706. The first is his work number; the latter, his home number (please don't call after 8 PM).

Ice Skating

When the weather's good and the ice is thick, you'll see skating on ponds and lakes all over the region. (Pickup ice hockey games were all the rage during a cold snap a few years back.) Still, rinks are the best bet for visitors unfamiliar with the underwater springs that can make some sections of those ponds downright dangerous.

There are a number of small neighborhood rinks sprinkled throughout Bangor. All are free, some have lights, but none have warming huts, toilets, skate rentals or concession stands. They're open only when weather permits and are run by the Bangor Parks and Recreation Department, 947-1018.

Look for skating at Bangor Gardens Park on Sherman Avenue; Broadway Park at Broadway and Stillwater Avenue; Chapin Park on Forest Avenue; Fairmount Park on Norway Road; and at an unnamed rink on Davis Road.

More serious skaters may try the following.

Skating Rinks

Waldoboro to Stockton Springs

Hosmer Pond
Camden Snow Bowl Ski Area, Hosmer Pond Rd., Camden • 236-3438

A section of this pond about the size of a hockey rink is kept cleared of snow for ice skating from late December to March, weather permitting. There's a little warming hut and an overhead light nearby for nighttime use. The skating is free, and you can grab something to eat at the Snow Bowl lodge nearby. Rentals are not available.

Inland to Bangor

Sawyer Arena
107 13th St., Bangor • 947-0071

This regulation-size indoor rink is run by the city of Bangor and is used mostly for youth hockey. There are public ice times, however: 4 to 5:30 PM Saturday and 6:30 to 8 PM Sunday, with an admission charge of $3; and 12:30 to 2 PM weekdays, with an admission charge of $2. Children younger than 5 skate for free. Public ice times are flexible, so call ahead. Skate rentals are not

available. There's a snack bar in the arena if you want a bite to eat.

Alfond Ice Arena
University of Maine, College Ave., Orono • 581-1103

This arena is used for college hockey and basketball practice and games, but public skating is allowed during certain times. The open-skating schedule generally is noon to 1 PM Monday through Friday for $1 a person and 2 PM to 3:30 PM weekends for $3, but those hours will vary from week to week, depending on the needs of the Athletic Department. Call the listed number for the latest information. Skate rentals are $1. No concessions are available, but you can walk over to the Student Union if you want a snack.

Bucksport to Gouldsboro

Town of Bucksport Skating Rink
off Miles Ln. (to the right), Bucksport • 467-3372

This 200-by-85-foot hockey rink is open during the winter when weather permits. Warming hut hours are 1 to 9 PM Monday to Friday and 9 AM to 9 PM weekends. The rink is reserved some nights for hockey games, but most of the time it's divided so free skaters have one half and younger skaters have the other half. A warm-up hut has toilets and concessions, and there are about 20 pairs of skates on hand that are lent free of charge to kids who don't have their own. If there's no answer at the listed warming-hut number, try calling Bucksport's recreation department at 469-3518.

Ice-skate Rentals

Pickin's are slim in the Mid-Coast region,

INSIDERS' TIP

Hypothermia can be a real threat in cold weather. Dress properly — in wool or fleece, not cotton. Wear a hat. Bring an extra pair of socks. Stay dry and rested; getting sweaty can be almost as bad as getting wet. Eat high-energy foods. Know your limits, and turn back before you're totally spent.

primarily because most kids have their own skates or can buy them cheaply at yard sales. We can point you in the direction of two outfitters that rent ice skates.

Waldoboro to Stockton Springs

Maine Sport
U.S. Hwy. 1, Rockport • 236-8797, (888) 236-8797

Maine Sport rents ice skates — both hockey and figure-skating styles — for $5 a day. Hourly rates are available. Children and adults may use the store's pond or take them to nearby Hosmer Pond.

Bucksport to Gouldsboro/ Mount Desert Island

Cadillac Mountain Sports
34 High St., Ellsworth 667-7819
26 Cottage St., Bar Harbor 288-4532

Ice skate rentals are $5 a day, $4 after 1 PM and until 6 PM at both stores. The Bangor store, at 6 Central Street, 941-5670, may be renting ice skates in 1998 so call to check if you're interested.

Skiing

The bad news is that the coast of Maine can be unreliable for any sports requiring snow. The ocean has a warming effect that can make our area feel positively balmy. But when the weather's right, there's nothing like skiing within sight of the Atlantic Ocean. We've included various places to downhill and cross-country ski, followed by a few outfitters.

Downhill Skiing

Waldoboro to Stockton Springs

Camden Snow Bowl
Hosmer Pond Rd., Camden • 236-3438

When it's cold and snowy, this place is a dream. Skiers are treated to breathtaking views from Ragged Mountain. The hill has a vertical drop of about 950 feet, 11 trails, two T-bars (one is 4,100 feet long!), a double chairlift and snow-making facilities. There's also a lodge,

snack bar, ski shop, certified ski school and rental equipment. Lift tickets are a bargain at $10 to $16 weekdays for adults, $25 Saturdays, Sundays and holidays. Cross-country ski trails (not groomed), an ice skating pond, tube-sliding area (rent a tube for $3 an hour) and the fabulous toboggan chute ($1 a ride with the Snow Bowl's toboggan, 50¢ a ride if you bring your own) make this a great place to bring the family.

Cross-country Skiing

Waldoboro to Stockton Springs

Tanglewood 4-H Camp
Tanglewood Rd., off U.S. Hwy. 1, Lincolnville • 789-5233, 789-5868

This lovely, undeveloped area operated by the University of Maine Cooperative Extension is bordered by Black Brook and the Ducktrap River. The cross-country trails are not difficult, and since they range from a third-mile to 3.5 miles and interconnect, you can plan a trip that suits your strength and stamina.

Park on the right side of the road as you drive into the area, and make sure you sign the register at the main gate. The trails are neither groomed nor patrolled, so you do ski at your own risk. There's no admission fee.

Camden Hills State Park
U.S. Hwy. 1, north of Camden • 236-3109

Cross-country skiers may use the park's groomed snowmobile trails, which include a 3-mile entry-level stretch, a 3-mile intermediate stretch and a 4-mile difficult stretch. See the previous "Parks" section for additional information on the area.

Samoset Ski Touring Center
Warrenton Rd., Rockport • 594-1431

The Samoset Resort (see our Accommodations chapter) grooms 10 kilometers of cross-country trails, half of which are entry-level and half more difficult. The views of Penobscot Bay are spectacular. Check in at the golf clubhouse, which does double-duty as the ski-touring headquarters during the winter. You can rent boots, skis and poles as well. The cost is $12 a half-day (four hours) and

$15 a full day (seven hours) for adults and teens; $10 and $12, respectively, for children 12 and younger. Staff can outfit 4- and 5-year-olds, depending on the size of the child. When the snow is deep and the trails have been groomed, you'll pay $3 a day to ski. We're told you can ski free if the trails haven't been groomed.

Bucksport to Gouldsboro

Holbrook Island Sanctuary
Indian Bar Rd., off Maine Hwy. 176, Brooksville • 326-4012

Here you'll find 7 kilometers of trails along wooded roads and through upland forests and fields. You'll find great views of Penobscot Bay. See our previous entry in the "Nature Preserves" section for more information about this area.

Mount Desert Island

Acadia National Park
Mount Desert Island • 288-3338

The 50 miles of carriage roads and trails in this national park are a winter wonderland for cross-country skiers. Pick up a trail map from the park's headquarters on Maine Highway 233, about 3 miles west of Bar Harbor.

Ski Rentals

Waldoboro to Stockton Springs

Maine Sport
U.S. Hwy. 1, Rockport • 236-8797, (888) 236-8797

Cross-country ski rentals cost $9 for a half-day (from 1 to 5:30 PM) and $15 for one to two days, including skis, books and poles. Youth packages are available at $6 for a half-day and $10 a full day. Long-term rental rates are available on both packages.

Inland to Bangor

Cadillac Mountain Sports
6 Central St., Bangor • 941-5670

This store rents regular cross-country skis, skate skis and backcountry skis both daily

and half-day. All rentals include poles and boots. See the subsequent "Bucksport to Gouldsboro/Mount Desert Island" listing for rates.

Maine Bound
University of Maine, Center for Student and Community Life, 5748 Memorial Union, Orono • 581-1794

Maine Bound offers cross-country ski clinics, trips and rentals. The "Full Moon" trip to ski from 7 PM to midnight in Acadia, scheduled in winter 1996-97, sounded fabulous. For $20 you got hot drinks, transportation and a discount on ski rentals. Call to see what's currently planned.

Ski rentals cost $8.50 a day, $18.50 a weekend and $42.50 a week, and include skis, poles and boots.

Bucksport to Gouldsboro/ Mount Desert Island

Cadillac Mountain Sports
34 High St., Ellsworth • 667-7819
26 Cottage St., Bar Harbor • 288-4532

Three types of ski rentals are available at these stores. Regular cross-country skis rent for $12 a day, $9 a half-day; skate skis rent for $19 a day, $15 a half-day; and back country skis rent for $19 a day, $15 a half-day. All rentals include skis, poles and boots. Call ahead for conditions.

Snowmobiling

Snowmobiling in the Mid-Coast region is not an activity you can plan on. Local fanatics say it's good when the weather is snowy and cold, but in many areas, that's infrequent and a matter of chance. While Camden Hills State Park and Acadia National Park have groomed trails, there are no local outlets that rent snowmobiles.

If this sport is your passion, northern Maine is the place to go. Its 1,500 miles of snowmobile trails are considered the best in New England. The entire state has some 12,500 miles of trails, most of which are groomed by volunteers from local snowmobile clubs. December to March is the prime season.

For more information, contact the Maine

Photo: Bangor Daily News

Numerous golf courses dot the landscape along Maine's Mid-Coast.

Snowmobile Association, 622-6983, the umbrella organization for the more than 280 local clubs, or the Snowmobile Program, Maine Bureau of Parks and Lands, 287-4957.

Maine has had its share of snowmobiling accidents, most due to alcohol and/or excessive speed. Operating a snowmobile under the influence of alcohol is illegal. In most cases, you can't operate snowmobiles on plowed roads. Riders must be older than 10 unless accompanied by an adult. They must be at least age 14 to cross a public way. For questions about snowmobile registration, law enforcement or safety, contact the Maine Department of Inland Fisheries and Wildlife, 287-5209 or 287-2871. Most nonresidents must pay a registration fee of $35 to $60 to ride in Maine; residents pay $25.

Snowshoeing

Here's our theory: Snowshoeing is the winter version of kayaking. In kayaking, you buy expensive new gear, but it's relatively simple to use and opens a whole new world — the coast of Maine seen from a duck's-eye view. In snowshoeing, you buy the new- (or old-) style snowshoes, slip them on over your boots and start walking. It too opens a whole new world — snowy woods and fields that would have been impossible to navigate without something to keep you from falling through the snow or ice crust. Like a duck's feet, snowshoes have webbing or a span of fabric that keeps the frame and your foot on the surface of the snow. You simply walk, and if you're still worried about losing your balance, bring some ski poles. Now, as in kayaking, the experienced gain skills the newbie doesn't have, but the great thing is, you can go out and have fun without those skills.

Showshoe Rentals

The old-style snowshoes are elegant: wooden frames, leather webbing, usually a teardrop shape. The new style by Atlas and Tubbs have metal frames, a synthetic fabric webbing and cleats on the bottom to keep you from sliding on icy patches. The old style is far less

INSIDERS' TIP

Maine has 6,000 lakes, 32,000 miles of rivers and streams and more than a half-million acres in state and national parks.

popular with the adventure sports crowd, and only the new style is available to rent from the stores listed here. On the plus side, new-style snowshoes are lighter, require less maintenance and are easier to get on and off.

Waldoboro to Stockton Springs

Maine Sport
U.S. Hwy. 1, Rockport • 236-8797, (888) 236-8797

Maine Sport rents showshoes — the new Tubbs and Atlas styles — for $9 a half-day (from 1 to 5:30 PM) and $15 for one to two days. Youth packages are available at $6 for a half-day and $10 a day. Long-term rental rates are available as well.

Inland to Bangor/ Bucksport to Gouldsboro/ Mount Desert Island

Cadillac Mountain Sports
6 Central St., Bangor • 941-5670
34 High St., Ellsworth • 667-7819
26 Cottage St., Bar Harbor • 288-4532

All three stores rent Tubbs snowshoes for $9 a full day, $7 a half-day.

Swimming

Hankering to take a dip? We've dug up a range of options including the warm, shallow waters of Megunticook River, the icy waters of the Atlantic and the pools of the Camden and Ellsworth YMCAs. The outdoor swimming season varies according to the weather and your preference. All but the most hardy find ocean swimming too cold, but on a hot day in a shallow spot, it might be just the ticket. The subsequently noted lake and river spots are far more comfortable. Still, July and August are your best bets. Most of these swimming spots don't have toilets, lifeguards or fees for use, so assume they don't unless we indicate otherwise.

Waldoboro to Stockton Springs

Lucia Beach
Birch Point Beach State Park, Owls Head • 941-4014

This is a lovely sandy beach — a rarity on Maine's rocky shoreline — with some flat rock areas that are nice for picnics. It overlooks the islands that dot Mussel Ridge Channel and the Atlantic Ocean beyond. The 20-acre undeveloped park has outhouses and lots of parking but no lifeguards. It does get crowded on sunny summer Saturdays, so get there early for a good parking spot.

Johnson Memorial Park
Chickawaukee Lake, Maine Hwy. 17, Rockland

Owned by the town of Rockland, this sandy, sloping warm-water beach has a boat launch, plenty of parking in a lot off the road and a bathhouse with toilets, changing rooms and cold showers. It can be very crowded, but it's convenient for families, and there's a lifeguard on duty 10 AM to 6 PM seven days a week from late June to Labor Day. Tables and grills make it a nice spot for picnics.

Laite Memorial Park and Beach
Upper Bayview St., Camden

This is a real find. Imagine, low-key no-fee access to upscale Camden Harbor! As you approach on Upper Bayview Street, you'll see swings and picnic tables. You'll also find cooking grills, restrooms, an outdoor shower and, down the slope, a sweeping pebbled beach with a floating platform offshore. It's a wonderful place to take children who have had their fill of driving and shopping.

Walker Park
Elm St., Rockport

This tiny pebbly beach has picnic tables, an adjacent playground and views of Rockport Harbor and Indian Island Lighthouse.

Barrett's Cove Memorial Park and Beach
off Maine Hwy. 52, about 3 miles northwest of Camden

A town-owned park on Lake Megunticook, Barrett's Cove is a favorite cooling-off spot in summer, with dramatic views of Maiden Cliff and Mount Megunticook. Parking is easy and plentiful, and the roped-off swimming area has a floating platform offshore. You'll also find grills, a picnic area, a playground and restrooms nearby. If you come for the day, as many do, bring snacks and cool drinks — there's no place nearby to buy refreshments.

Shirttail Point
Maine Hwy. 105, Camden

This town-owned park is on a point of land jutting into the Megunticook River. The water is shallow and warm — perfect for toddlers — and there's a playground, picnic tables and restrooms nearby.

Camden YMCA
Chestnut St., Camden • 236-3375

This indoor pool is Olympic-size — great for lap swimming. Hours are set aside for open, family and lap swims. The schedule varies, so call ahead. Nonmember use fees are $3 for adults and children.

Lincolnville Beach
U.S. Hwy. 1, Lincolnville Beach

You can't miss this sandy ocean beach, a stone's throw from U.S. Highway 1. Just pull off and park in the town landing lot. There's no bathhouse, but the town has placed a bright blue Porta-john nearby. Directly across the street is a string of shops, including a convenience store with fabulous pizza. You'll also find a cluster of two or three restaurants, so it's easy to spend the day here, enjoying the water and views of Penobscot Bay and the islands.

Sandy Point Beach
off U.S. Hwy. 1, north of Stockton Springs

Popular with windsurfers, this beach at the mouth of the Penobscot River is about a mile long but has no facilities and relatively little parking. Still, it's a little bit of heaven.

Inland to Bangor

Dakin Pool
Pine St., Bangor • 947-1018

Come to the 40-by-60-foot Dakin Pool, between Broadway and Stillwater Avenue, and jump in. There are swimming lessons in the morning and public swims from about noon to 4:30 PM. See our Kidstuff chapter for details.

Nickerson Municipal Pool
Goodridge Dr., Orono • 866-3093, 866-5065 off-season

This outdoor 75-foot-long, six-lane pool is L-shaped, with a diving area on the short leg. It's a popular summer attraction. The facility is equipped with poolside lounge chairs, a bathhouse, wading pool, playground and picnic tables. You can enjoy it seven days a week from mid-June through August for just $1 for adults, 50¢ for children. Hours are posted for general-swim, adult lap-swim and family-swim times.

Bucksport to Gouldsboro

James Russell Wiggins Downeast Family YMCA
State St., Ellsworth • 667-3086

This 25-yard indoor pool is open to visitors, and the nonmember use fees are $5 for youths or senior citizens, $8 for adults and $10 a family. Call ahead for open-swim or lap times; the schedule varies.

Lamoine Beach
Lamoine State Park, off Maine Hwy. 184, Lamoine • 667-4778

The swimming at this park is said to be the best in the area. Actually, the beach is leased to the town of Lamoine. While there's no fee, bathhouse or lifeguard, you swim in Eastern Bay with a panoramic view of Mount Desert Island. (See the previous entry in our "Parks" section for more information about the park.)

Mount Desert Island

Sand Beach
Acadia National Park, Park Loop Rd., Mount Desert Island • 288-3338

This crescent beach of ground shells, not sand, is bordered by two rocky points and supervised by lifeguards 9 AM to 5 PM daily from late June through August. It's 4 miles south of Bar Harbor near Cadillac Cliffs. There's a parking lot nearby, and you can park along the side of the Park Loop Road as well. See our Acadia National Park chapter for more information.

Tennis

Casual players will find a sprinkling of

Photo: Bangor Daily News

A small park in Camden gives a great vantage point from which to watch pleasure craft of all sizes visit the coastal community.

outdoor courts in the area — some with lights. The Camden Snow Bowl and Belfast City Park have two courts each, and the latter has lights (see our previous "Parks" section for more information). In Bangor, there are two courts each at Bangor High School, 885 Broadway; Hayford Park, 13th Street (lighted); and Little City Park, Lynden Street. You'll also find a court at Williams Park, Newbury Street.

For more serious players, there are more serious facilities. Read on.

Waldoboro to Stockton Springs

Samoset Resort
Warrenton St., Rockport • 594-1431

Two of these four outdoor painted asphalt courts are lighted. They are available 6 AM to 10 PM daily from April through November, depending on the weather. Nonmembers pay $8 an hour from October 18 through May 7 and $10 an hour from May 8 through October 17. You must pay at the Fitness Center, which closes at 9:30 PM, so plan accordingly. You may use the resort's Fitness Center locker rooms and showers as well. Call to reserve a court.

Inland to Bangor

Bangor Tennis Club
Mecaw Rd., Hampden • 942-4836

Four indoor courts are open 6 AM to 10 PM Monday through Friday and 9 AM to 9 PM Saturdays and Sundays. Rates are $26 to $36 an hour, and you're welcome to use the lounge, locker rooms and showers.

Bucksport to Gouldsboro

Fitness East Health & Racquet Club
Maine Hwy. 3, Trenton • 667-3341, (800) 838-3341

This full-facility health club has three indoor courts with Plexi-cushion surfaces (a rubberized synthetic over asphalt). You'll pay $9 to $12 an hour to use them, and a guest fee of $10 entitles you to use the rest of the facility, including the lounge, locker rooms and showers. The courts are open 6 AM to 9 PM Monday through Friday and 7 AM to 5 PM Saturdays and Sundays, except from June through August, when the hours are 7 AM to noon weekends. A pro is available for private lessons, and clinics are offered during the winter.

Mount Desert Island

Atlantic Oakes
**119 Eden St. (Maine Hwy. 3), Bar Harbor
• 288-5801**

This hotel allows visitors to use its four outdoor courts for $6 an hour. All have painted asphalt surfaces, and two are lighted. Check in at the hotel office. Hours are morning to evening — the desk clerk we spoke with could be no more specific.

Tobogganing

Although there's only one place to do this, it's fabulous — built by volunteers and loved by nearly everyone who tries it.

Waldoboro to Stockton Springs

Camden Snow Bowl
Hosmer Pond Rd., 3 miles from U.S. Hwy. 1, Camden • 236-3438

Home of the U.S. National Toboggan Championship, this 400-foot-long chute is a blast. You can use your own toboggan (50¢ a run), or use toboggans provided at the hill ($1 a run). Don't think it's just for kids. The run is far more exciting than it looks, and since it extends onto the frozen surface of Hosmer Pond, you'll find yourself skidding halfway across the lake before you know it. An attendant is posted at the top of the run to load you in your toboggan and warn you about keeping your hands away from the chute!

The chute is open weekends and holidays, and it's weather-sensitive, so call ahead to be sure it's operating.

Visitors aren't always prepared for island life. They may find themselves living the life of a century ago: no cars, electricity, flush toilets or running water.

Offshore/Islands

Islands are Maine distilled. Something about the water and the wildlife, the wind and the weather, sums up the best of life here. The sense of community is unmistakable, but so is a sense of independence and self-reliance.

The state's coastal island registry lists 4,617 islands, including ledges that remain exposed at high tide. Of that number, an estimated 1,150 islands encompass more than 10 acres each. Most island acreage is privately owned, but even publicly held land is not necessarily open to the public. Only 14 islands have year-round communities. And while those communities are struggling, lately they've been seeing an increase in short-term visitors — a mixed blessing. Tourists bring business, but they also strain limited resources. Sewage, solid-waste disposal and adequate drinking-water supplies are just some of the issues vexing planners.

For their part, visitors aren't always prepared for island life. They may find themselves living the life of a century ago: no cars, electricity, flush toilets or running water. But while this spartan existence might be an acquired taste, once sampled, it's hard to shake.

We've spent week-long vacations on a privately owned island, and it's a bit of heaven. We had no running water or electricity, but we had deer in the dooryard and could see the bay from our pillows. We had miles of paths to walk plus three or four beaches. We bought lobster and baked goods from our hosts. We raked clams, picked apples and read piles of books on rainy days. Just staring at the water was soul-restoring, but we were happiest mindlessly combing the shoreline for beach glass. It was October, it was bitter cold some days, and the handful of regular summer visitors had gone. Only one couple wintered there, and we saw little of them. There was nothing and nobody, and we loved it.

Not all islands are like that, of course. We've chosen to highlight four here that are roughly representative of island life. Isle au Haut (say "I'll a hoe") is the least developed, while Islesboro is almost a part of the mainland. Vinalhaven has a healthy year-round community; and Monhegan, while smaller, is starkly beautiful and, like Vinalhaven, has a vibrant artists community.

You can take a state-run ferry to either Vinalhaven (from Rockland) or Islesboro (from Lincolnville), but the latter is just a 20-minute ride and might be best for those with limited time, queasy stomachs or antsy children. Private mail boats make runs to Isle au Haut and Monhegan. (Read on for more information.)

How long should you stay? One Vinalhaven native told us there were beautiful places to hike and beachcomb that wouldn't be immediately obvious to the daytripper. The key, he said, was to come and stay for a while. He's right, of course. That's true of every place we've explored, but it is especially true of the islands, which tend to be both more intimate and more insular.

When to go? Summer is the most active season, but the rest of the year can be enchanting. Many places shut down in the winter, and their "season" can be somewhat irregular, so be sure to call ahead if you're traveling in the spring, fall or winter.

Getting Out On the Water

If you're coming to Maine with a boat in tow and want to explore the islands, we suggest you pick up one of the nautical guides. *A Cruising Guide to the Maine Coast* by Hank and Jan Taft and Curtis Rindlaub (Diamond Pass Publishing) is especially good. If you'd just like to get out on the water, you can take a tour by boat or kayak. Tour operators are described in our Attractions chapter, and coastal kayak tours are covered in the Parks and Recreation chapter.

Ferries and Mail Boats

A few words of advice: Bad weather can cause a rough trip, delays or even cancellations. Summer brings crowds of visitors, and that means long lines, particularly if you're intending to bring your car. Call ahead for advice from the mail boat or ferry office, as traffic patterns vary from day to day and from week to week.

The Maine State Ferry Service has a number of offices along the coast. The ones pertinent to the trips mentioned here are the following: 517A Main Street, Rockland, 596-2202; P.O. Box 191, Vinalhaven, ME 04863, 863-4421; and P.O. Box 214, Lincolnville, ME 04849, 789-5611 or 734-6935. Reservations cost an extra $5, and they must be made well in advance, but they can be a tourist's best friend. When you make the reservation, ask how early you need to be in line. We've seen ferries load 20 minutes early and leave five minutes early. God help the unsuspecting soul who thought his reservation was a guarantee! You simply must plan ahead.

Another option is to take a plane. Penobscot Air Service, P.O. Box 1286, Rockland, ME 04841, 596-6211, flies out of Knox County Airport (see our Getting Here, Getting Around chapter) to Islesboro, Vinalhaven, North Haven and Matinicus on a regular basis. The cost ranges from $25 to $70, depending on when you go and whether you share the flight with other travelers. Penobscot Air also flies charters and will take you to any island on demand.

What To Pack

Start with sweaters and jackets or windbreakers no matter how warm it is on shore. It always gets chillier out on the water. Rain gear is essential, as are good rubber-soled shoes or hiking boots. Flashlights are a good idea too. Be ready to entertain yourself, so bring a good book or two and maybe a deck of cards. And don't assume you'll find a bank or an ATM; bring cash or traveler's checks. If you're staying overnight, ask for advice from your hosts about how best to prepare for the weather and what other items you might wish to bring.

Islesboro

This lovely, friendly island, just 3 miles off Lincolnville Beach, has 600 year-round residents scattered across its woods, fields and rocky shoreline. We've visited on bicycles and in cars, and every time we've been amazed at the number of people who waved to us. Most often it's just an easy two-finger salute off the top of the steering wheel, but it's a wave nonetheless, so be ready to return it. You'll get the hang of it in no time.

FYI

Unless otherwise noted, the area code for all phone numbers listed in this guide is 207.

The first question you might ask yourself is whether to travel the island on foot, on a bike or in a car. We suggest you bring your car, even if it means waiting in line for the ferry. A long, narrow island, Islesboro is 11 miles long and 5 miles wide. It's 2 miles from the ferry to the post office and almost 7 miles from the ferry to the town beach. Those distances are too long for all but the hardiest hikers. We found them too long to bike comfortably, and quite apart from the distances involved, the roads themselves are winding, hilly and sometimes quite narrow. While many have spectacular vistas, they can be downright unsafe at times, especially during the busy summer season. On one occasion, we nearly were bumped off the road as two trucks going in opposite directions passed on a curve.

Because Islesboro is just 3 miles off Lincolnville Beach, the ferry ride is quite short. It leaves nine times a day Monday through Saturday from early May to mid-October, with fewer runs on Sunday and during the rest of the year. Round-trip fares are $4.50 for adults and $2 for children. Call the Maine State Ferry Service (see previous "Ferries and Mail Boats" section) for a schedule. To find your way on the island, grab a copy of the brochure/map available at the ticket booth in Lincolnville Beach.

Seasoned travelers stay in their cars during the ferry trip to Islesboro, but we like to get out and enjoy the views. We've traveled with children, and there's nothing like the wonder on their faces as they stand on deck and watch the shore recede.

As you come off the boat, you might want to stop at the Sailor's Memorial Museum at Grindle Point (see our Lighthouses chapter), immediately to your left. Park in the lot ahead of you. If you arrive hungry, grab something to eat at The Islander, 734-2270, a take-out restaurant operated out of a trailer at the end of the parking lot. It serves great fried onion rings. And you can flop down with your snack under the fragrant wild roses along the shore.

Moving along from Grindle Point, take the first left, the next right, then the road dead-ends at Main Street. You can head north (left) toward Pripet or south (right) to Dark Harbor. The road north takes you past the post office, the town office and The Island Market, 734-6672, a great little general store/grocery. The lemon bars we bought there were worth the price of the ferry, and the patrons vary from rough-clad handymen to well-coiffed be-pearled matrons.

As you continue north on Main Street, you'll pass the library, the Islesboro Historical Society and the Masonic Hall. The road forks just past Durkee's General Store, and cleared fields open spectacular vistas of Penobscot Bay and Cape Rosier on the Blue Hill Peninsula. The road curves and cuts in close to Turtle Head Cove, with more views, this time of the mainland in the distance.

The road south takes you through Dark Harbor to the town beach and picnic area at Pendleton Point. You'll pass a blacktop driveway to Islesboro Central School, which really is remarkable. It's a turn-of-the-century stone mansion with a tasteful addition and a great playground. This would be worth a detour if you have kids — they might enjoy the play area when school's out.

As you drive on, you're bound to find yourself rubbernecking the huge, elegant "cottages" of the well-to-do summer folk. You can be sure a sign reading "Service" at the entrance to a drive does not denote the family's name.

The small cluster of shops around Derby Street should encourage you to slow down and pull over. The Dark Harbor Shop, 734-8878, is the place to go for sandwiches, gifts or just an ice cream cone. Oliver's, right around the corner, 734-6543, is a good choice for dinner. Upstairs is a bar and eating area with a menu of burgers and pizza, while downstairs is more upscale with elegant entrees such as pan-blackened tuna with roasted fennel and citrus vinaigrette, and roasted pepper polenta with wild mushrooms and bitter greens.

You'll pass the splendid Dark Harbor House (see our Accommodations chapter), with it's summery yellow clapboard siding, proud white columns and huge rolling lawns. But for all its grandeur, and the grandeur of the houses around it, nothing can beat the natural beauty of Pendleton Point, with its views of the bay and the islands. This town-owned public area has a parking lot and picnic sites, each with a barbecue cooker. It's one of the few places on the island where you can get out of your car and noodle around without trespassing.

That's a quick roundup of some destinations, but if you're like us, you'll be happy exploring the back roads to see the countryside, horses, gardens and the way folks live. Just make sure you don't miss your ferry. We did and had to wait a full two hours for the next one! Then again, we were first in line, first on the ferry and the only car with a real view of the island as we pulled away. That made up for the delay. The lobster boats bobbed in the bay, the lawns of the grand houses rolled to the shore, the fir trees stood tall on neighboring islands, the sun shimmered on the water . . . a great end to a great day.

Vinalhaven

This island is a good 13 miles from Rockland, and its vital year-round economy relies primarily on commercial fishing. That gives Vinalhaven a definite sense of place even when it isn't catering to an abundant summer population. We've visited in November — well off-season — and found the downtown area alive and well.

Vinalhaven is 7 miles long and 5 miles wide with a varied landscape of spruce woods, moorlands and granite outcrops. Incorporated in 1789, it reached its peak population of nearly 3,000 in the 1880s, when farming, fishing, ship building and granite quarrying were more profitable pursuits. Summer visitors started arriving about that time, and now they swell the year-round population of about 1,100 to at least three times that number.

That brings us to the question of whether you should bring your car with you on the ferry. We think you'll regret it during the summer. Ferry transportation is first-come, first-served, so cars line up as early as a day in advance(!) and must be moved as the line moves. When we visited in November, we arrived at the Rockland terminal at 7:10 in the morning for an 8:45 AM ferry, and even then we weren't sure we'd make it. The Rockland ferry office advised us to check with the Vinalhaven office for a ballpark waiting time for our return trip. After an unnerving flat tire, we cut our visit short just to be sure we'd lined up in time. (Face it, sitting in a car just ain't the way to spend a vacation.)

Bikes would work fine as long as you're in shape and have the proper gear. You can rent them at the Tidewater Motel, 863-4618, in the center of town, if you like. Otherwise, it's less than a half-mile walk from the ferry docks. (Frankly, you can easily explore a nice portion of Vinalhaven on foot.) The Tidewater is a great place to stay, by the way. Some of its 12 rooms have decks as well as huge windows facing the water. We envied the couples happily reading the paper in the warm sunshine. While the motel is open year round, a double room starts at $85 in high-season — July 1 through Labor Day.

The ferry leaves Rockland (on the mainland) for Vinalhaven six times a day every day from April through October, with fewer runs during the rest of the year. Round-trip fares are $9 for adults, $4 for children. Call the Maine State Ferry Service (see the previous "Ferries and Mail Boats" section) for a schedule.

The downtown area of Carver's Harbor is a short walk from the ferry landing. The main street curves around the harbor, with shops on either side, and it crosses over the inlet to Carver's Pond so the Tidewater Motel, for instance, is actually built on a bridge directly over the water. Many of the buildings date back to the late 1800s, adding grace to the downtown and back roads alike. We liked start-

ing at one end of Main Street and exploring our way to the other end. We liked Port o' Call, 863-2525, with its old-fashioned hardware store-like variety. We found canning supplies we'd been at a loss to locate on the mainland. The Island Home, 863-2020, at the far end was a real stand-out as well, with interesting items for kitchens and all around the house.

The Haven, 245 Main Street, 863-4969, is an excellent choice for dinner, but you must make reservations. "Truly gourmet," said the native who recommended it. For lunch we liked the Harbor Gawker, 863-9365, a carry-out place in the center of town. The scallops in our scallop rolls were fresh that day, and while they were deep-fried, there was not the slightest sign of oil.

Vinalhaven is home to a number of artists, including well-known Robert Indiana. Look for their work at The Fogg Gallery, 863-2182, at Harbor Wharf (on the right as you walk from the ferry to downtown). Also look for Indiana's home and studio next to the U.S. Post Office in the heart of downtown; you can't miss it. The first-floor windows of the massive mansard-roofed, ornately painted building display his signature "Love" design — the letters forming a square, the "O" tilted outward.

If you walk to the far end of Main Street, the road to the right will take you to Armbrust Hill Town Park and Lane's Island Nature Conservancy Preserve. Armbrust Hill Town Park is a 30-acre site reclaimed from an abandoned quarry. Lane's Island Nature Conservancy Preserve is a 40-acre natural area with tide pools, a beach and wonderful views.

Monhegan

Monhegan is some 10 miles off Port Clyde on the St. George Peninsula south of Rockland. The 700-acre island is rocky, with dramatic cliffs, pine forests, open meadows and fewer than 100 year-round residents. Most make their living in commercial fishing, particularly lobstering.

Native Americans already occupied the island when the English arrived in the 1600s. Some accounts say the Englishman John

The captain of a coastal cruise boat checks his direction as he heads into the open ocean off Maine's rocky coast.

Smith, of Pocahontas fame, first spotted the island in 1614, but others indicate explorers visited as early as 1605. No matter the nationality, fishing has always been the island's mainstay.

There is a time-machine quality to Monhegan. The community generally shunned electricity until the past decade or so; the roads aren't paved; and cars aren't allowed. But a 17-mile network of trails makes this a great hiking destination. Trail maps are available at island shops. Two favorite hikes are the Cliff Trail around the perimeter of the island, and the Cathedral Woods Trail, which winds through magnificent spruce forests. The trail maps don't specify trail lengths, but the island is 1.5 miles long and .75 miles wide. Our best advice is to ask for advice when you pick up a map.

If you're interested in the island's history, check out the Monhegan Museum, 596-7003, in the former keeper's house at the Monhegan Island Lighthouse. Some documents stored there date back to the 17th century, and there's information on the island's flora and fauna as well. Registered as a national historic site, it's open 11:30 AM to 3:30 PM daily from July 1 through Labor Day. The lighthouse itself is worth the trip. Built in 1824, rebuilt in 1850 and automated in 1959, it

stands atop a hill in the center of the island overlooking the village.

Monhegan's stark beauty has attracted artists for more than a century. It's been called the most famous Maine island in American art, having played a prominent part in the careers of Robert Henri, George Bellows and Rockwell Kent. Jamie Wyeth still summers and paints on the island, as do a number of other names in contemporary art. Some have open studio hours during the summer; a list is available at most businesses and posted on bulletin boards around town.

The mail boat stops at the harbor on the eastern end of the island — a convenient destination because the island's community is clustered there, and you'll find yourself getting around on foot. As you get off the ferry, walk up the hill, turn right and look for the rope shed, a covered box with flyers and signs about events and businesses on the island. It's the community bulletin board — a great place to find out what's going on. (Look for the list of open-studio hours.) While you're poking around Main Street, check out The Lupine Gallery, 594-8131, a great place to explore — and buy — the work of the island's artists. If you must hit a gift shop, The Black Duck, 596-7672, sells pottery, jewelry, T-shirts and cards.

Overnight visitors have their choice of three inns and a few bed and breakfasts. If the locations seem vague, you'll easily get your bearings once on the island, and if you expect you'll need help with luggage, ask someone to meet you at the ferry dock. The Island Inn, 596-0371, on the harbor, has 36 rooms, most with shared baths. It's open Memorial Day to Columbus Day and offers breakfast, lunch and dinner in its public dining room. Rates start at $90 for a double room with shared bath and include a full breakfast.

Built in the late 1880s as an inn, the Monhegan House, 594-7983, across from the church, has 32 rooms — all with shared baths, many with the original furnishings — and a cozy fireplace in the downstairs lobby. It's open late May to mid-October, and rates for a double are $85 plus tax. Rates don't include meals, but the inn's public dining room serves three meals a day.

The Trailing Yew, 596-0440 or (800) 592-2520, on Lobster Cove Road, is actually a compound of four white-clapboard buildings that house 37 simple rooms. It's open mid-May to mid-October, and all the rooms share baths. One of the buildings has electricity in all the rooms; one has no electricity; and two have electricity in the bathrooms. Rates in 1997 were $56 a person per night and included dinner, breakfast, tax and tips for your waitress and chambermaid.

You might also consider the Shining Sails Guest House, 596-0041, up Wharf Hill. The year-round accommodation has three rooms and four efficiencies. Rates in 1997 range from $72 to $115 and include breakfast.

To get to Monhegan, take the *Elizabeth Ann* or the *Laura B*, 372-8848, from Port Clyde on the mainland. It runs one route daily in May, two routes from late May through June, three daily through Labor Day, two daily until the end of October, and one on Monday, Wednesday and Friday in winter. The trip takes about an hour and costs $24 (round trip) for adults, $12 for children. Parking in Port Clyde near the dock costs another $4 per day. If that's full, you take your chances parking on the side of the road.

Isle au Haut

Isle au Haut, 6 miles south of Stonington off the Blue Hill Peninsula, is a lovely example of the many unspoiled, undeveloped islands that dot Maine's coast. It's 6 miles long and 3 miles wide, with a small year-round fishing/lobstering community of approximately 70 residents.

Named the French equivalent of "high island" in 1604 by Samuel de Champlain, about half the island is privately owned, while the remaining 2,800 acres are part of Acadia National Park (see our Acadia National Park chapter.) You'll see fir and spruce forests growing up from a rocky shoreline.

The town of Isle au Haut is tiny. You never know what will be open from summer to summer, but the regular spots include the general store (with a very friendly staff), the post office and the Union Congregational Church. There are no restaurants, and the only places to stay are The Keeper's House, which affords an extravagant opportunity to stay in a lighthouse keeper's house (see our Accommodations chapter), and five Adirondack-style lean-tos at Duck Harbor maintained by the park staff for campers. That's the only place camping is permitted, and reservations are required. Call 288-3338 for information about reservations, which must be requested by mail and postmarked on or after April 1.

That being the case, most visitors just spend the day — and they spend it hiking. You can get maps and hiking information from the Acadia Park ranger, who usually meets the ferry. The ranger station is nearby. Just make sure you take an early boat, so you'll have plenty of time to explore before the last

---

INSIDERS' TIP

Trails on any of the islands flanking Maine's Mid-Coast are rugged. Expect rough paths, steep climbs and forest glens. On Monhegan especially: DO NOT expect sandy beaches, smooth paths for strollers, restrooms or comfort stations.

boat leaves. And take the boat to Duck Harbor if you can; the other boat drops you at the Isle au Haut town landing, 5 miles away.

The Isle-au-Haut Company, 367-5193 (days) and 367-2355 (evenings), runs a mail boat year round from the Seabreeze Avenue Dock in Stonington to the town of Isle au Haut. The trip takes 45 minutes, but the travel and fee schedules are a little complicated because departure times and fares depend on the season. In 1998, the highest fare is $12 with discounts for children 12 and younger.

From mid-June to early September, the Isle-au-Haut Company also makes runs to Duck Harbor, the entrance to Acadia National Park's land. (See our Acadia chapter for details.)

34th Annual CITGO Paul Bunyan Amateur Golf Tournament

New England's Largest Golf Tournament
June 19-20-21, 1998

OVER $8,000 IN Gross & Net PRIZES

$500 Champion Plus Division Gross & Net Prizes

500 golfers playing on three of Maine's finest golf courses - two along Maine's coast:
- **Bangor Municipal Golf Course •**
- **• Kebo Valley Golf Course, Bar Harbor •**
- **• Rockland Municipal Golf Course •**

CITGO
Junior Bunyan
June 23, 1998
Kebo Valley Course
207-288-3000

NEW ENGLAND'S LARGEST
GOLF TOURNAMENT
CITGO
BUNYAN

For more
information call
207-941-9549

Bangor Daily News
ENTERPRISES

Spectator Sports

Contradictions abound in Maine's love of sports. Here's a state that nearly grinds to a halt during high school basketball tournaments but has no professional basketball team — just the Boston Celtics, two states away. The fact is, this sparsely populated state simply can't support major pro teams, so Maine's passion for sports tends toward the amateur arenas of high school and college competitions.

This penchant for the local, for the amateur, can be seen in other more offbeat spectator sports as well. Check out our Annual Events chapter for descriptions of The Rockland Schooner Race, the Stonington Lobster Boat Race and the much-loved Kenduskeag Stream Canoe Race just after ice-out in the spring. While much of the state's auto and harness racing are done by local mom-and-pop garages and stables, Maine does have two minor-league baseball teams, a minor-league hockey team and an auto-racing track that seats 20,000 fans.

Auto Racing

The auto-racing scene in the area is a homegrown affair. The racers are local, for the most part, and most of the tracks are relatively small. Still, there is a strong base of loyal support and a lot of enthusiasm for the sport.

Oxford Plains Speedway
877 Main St., Oxford • 539-8865

Oxford Plains means business. Its three-eighths–mile track is the largest in the state, and its open bleachers accommodate some 20,000 spectators. (Sixty-five acres are dedicated to parking alone!) That's the largest seating capacity for any sporting event we've found in the state of Maine. The season runs from the third week in April to mid-October, with races on Sunday afternoons until the third week in May, when they move to Saturday nights. Ticket prices vary by event — $8.50 to $50. Call or write for a schedule of races. Most popular are the July 3rd race (with a fireworks show) and the Oxford 250 on July 6th, one of the major short-track events in the country. A full-service concession is available, but you're welcome to bring your own food. (Anything but alcohol, say organizers.)

Wiscasset Raceway
W. Alna Rd., 1 mile off Maine Hwy. 218, Wiscasset • 589-4780, 882-4271 (on race day)

Wiscasset's one-third–mile track draws racers from all over the state. It runs six classes, from amateurs in the cars they drive every day to professionals in eight-cylinder race cars. Two to three heats qualify racers for the main event in each class, so there's lots of action. Fans are seated in open bleachers with a capacity of about 6,000. Look for ample parking and a full concession stand. The season runs from April through September, with races on Saturday at 2 or 6 PM. Tickets are $8 for adults; $6, senior citizens and students 12 and older; $3, children ages 6 through 11.

Speedway 95
Odlin Rd., off Exit 44 of I-95, Hermon • 945-9595

This one-third–mile asphalt track features local racers in six divisions, from street-legal cars to sportsman classes. It also offers occasional Northeast Pro Stock Association tour races. The season runs from May to September, Sundays at 2 PM until June, when the start time changes to Saturday at 6:30 PM. Tickets are $8 for adults; $6, seniors and teens; $3, children ages 6 through 12. You'll have no trouble buying tickets at the gate, but you can call ahead and have a schedule of races sent to you. In the off-season, contact owner Del Merritt at 989-1226.

Unity Raceway
Maine Hwy. 139, about a half-mile from Maine Hwy. 9, Unity • 948-5232

Built in the late 1940s, this one-third–mile oval is one of the oldest tracks in Maine. Its current claim to fame is that Winston Cup driver Ricky Craven got his start here. While local racers compete every Saturday from late April to mid-October, the track also occasionally hosts tours of the Northeast Pro Stock Association. Races match up drivers in six different classes of cars, from "bombers" to pro stock. Spectators watch from covered and uncovered bleachers. The gate opens at 6 PM, and races start at 7 PM. In 1997 tickets were $8 for adults, $6 for college students and seniors and $3 for children ages 6 through 17. Prices might be higher for special events. If you're calling off-season, try the home and office number for track manager Ralph Nason Jr., 948-3404.

Winterport Dragway
Maine Hwy. 139, a mile south of Maine Hwy. 69, Winterport • 827-3014

This is your Mid-Coast destination for drag racing. Contestants from all over Maine race on this one-eighth–mile straightaway every Sunday from early May to early October. Time trials run from 9 AM to noon; eliminations run from 1:30 to about 5 PM. There is one set of bleachers, but most people back their pickup trucks up to the chain-link safety fence and tailgate. The pit areas are open, and while you have to use caution, you can go through them and get a good look at the cars. Admission is $10 for anyone 12 and older; children younger than 12 are admitted free.

Baseball

Portland Sea Dogs
271 Park Ave., Portland • 879-9500

In Portland since 1994, the Sea Dogs play Double-A ball in the Eastern League. The team is a link in the minor-league farm system of Major League Baseball's Florida Marlins and competes against teams such as the Trenton (N.J.) Thunder, an affiliate of the major-league Boston Red Sox. The players are young and hungry, and the fans are focused and knowledgeable.

While the team sponsors some promotions and contests — it's not above the occasional greased watermelon race, for instance — surveys indicate that Sea Dog fans are pretty conservative. They come for the baseball. Most games in the second half of the season are sellouts, so if you are buying tickets after mid-June, you have little chance of anything but general-admission seats. A good portion of the tickets for weekend games are sold by April, and most box seats are sold out by the time the season begins. The stadium seats 6,800, which makes those sellouts all the more impressive. Advice? Buy early by telephone.

The Sea Dogs play home games at Hadlock Field, next to the Portland Expo on Park Street. The 1998 season runs from April 9 through September 7. Afternoon games start at noon, 1 or 4 PM; night games, at 6 or 7 PM. Tickets are $4 for general admission; $5, reserved; $6, box seats. (They drop to $2, $4 and $5 respectively for children and seniors.) Buy tickets at Hadlock Field box office or call the listed number.

Harness Racing

Harness racing, in which Standardbred horses pull jockeys in two-wheeled carriages, has a long tradition in Maine; one track in Bangor dates back to the mid-1800s. Most of the racing is done by mom-and-pop stables, and while there's a fairly clear circuit of races, the dates change from year to year. Horses start at the Bangor Raceway (see subsequent entry), and then go on to race in the state fair circuit. The Union and Blue Hill fairs, in the Mid-Coast area, are part of that circuit (see our Fairs chapter). Scarborough Downs runs the most races, and since it has higher purses, it attracts a higher class of horse. The Maine Harness Racing Commission, State House Station 28, Augusta, ME 04333, 287-3221, has approved dates for the 1998 season, and it can send you a schedule. Betting is allowed on all races except the two run at the Blue Hill Fair.

FYI

Unless otherwise noted, the area code for all phone numbers listed in this guide is 207.

Bangor Raceway Historic Track at Bass Park
100 Dutton St., Bangor • 866-7650

This track is one of the oldest in the country, having been around since 1849 and in its present location since 1883. Avid fans call its races a bellwether for the season, since horses make their showing here first and then move on to the fair circuit or to Scarborough Downs. Races run from early June to late July; 27 are scheduled for the 1998 season. Organizers cultivate an outdoor carnival-type atmosphere including balloons and a small petting zoo for the kids, contests and giveaways for adults and a Dixieland band most Sundays. The paddock is open, so fans can get quite close to the horses and drivers. While most of the seating is in covered bleachers, some box seats are available. The track sponsors a North American Drivers Championship in June that attracts top drivers from all over the Northeast. Many of them got their start in Bangor, so it's like a homecoming. In mid-July the Anah Temple Shrine sponsors a parade before a race, and the last race of the season is sponsored by the Penobscot Indians — its $10,000 purse attracts horses and drivers from Canada and the Northeast. Ten to 12 races run nightly, starting at 7 PM Tuesdays, Fridays and Saturdays and 1:30 PM Sundays. Admission is free.

Scarborough Downs
U.S. Hwy. 1, off Exit 6 of I-95, Scarborough • 883-4331

Live or simulcast, you can always watch (and bet) on the horses at Scarborough Downs, just 10 minutes south of Portland. This track has 206 races scheduled for the 1998 season, far and away the most races run anywhere in the state. Live harness racing runs at various times from April to November, but the grandstand is open year round from 11 AM until midnight for simulcast racing. Banks of televisions broadcast races from tracks all over the country, and you can bet on any of the races as they happen. One bettor won nearly $40,000. Tickets are $2.50 for admission to the clubhouse and $2 for grandstand seats. The clubhouse is newer — lots of brass and glass and a full-service dining room where you can see the track from your seat or watch simulcast races on a small TV at your table. The grandstand is more rustic, with a country fair atmosphere. It was built in the 1950s, and it looks it. But it's especially nice in warm weather when you want to be outside. Bring a camera.

Hockey

Portland Pirates
85 Free St., Portland • 828-4665

The Pirates are a developmental team, the American Hockey League affiliate of the National Hockey League's Washington Capitals. There's a good tradition for hockey in Portland. From 1977 to 1992, the city reveled in the Mariners. When that team left town, the Skipjacks moved from Baltimore and changed their name to the Pirates.

In 1993-94, their first season in Portland, the Pirates won the Calder Cup, symbolic of playoff supremacy in the AHL. In their second season, the Pirates set a North American professional hockey record for the best start, going undefeated in their first 17 games (14-0-3). The Pirates had a rough start in their third season, but went to the seventh game of the Calder Cup finals.

Not surprisingly, crowds are large and enthusiastic. The team is near the top of the AHL in attendance, and it led the league in sellouts in its second season. In 1996-97, attendance averaged about 5,700, about 1,000 shy of capacity. Organizers work to make the games a family event, with frequent premium giveaways and entertainment on the ice between periods (bowling frozen turkeys around Thanksgiving time, for instance).

The team plays at Cumberland County Civic Center, 1 Civic Center Square, between

---

INSIDERS' TIP

If you plan to be in Bangor during the high school basketball tournament the third week of February, make your hotel reservations early and be prepared for crowded restaurants.

Pride of the Black Bears

University of Maine senior (at press time) Cindy Blodgett is a paradox in Maine sports. On the basketball court she's fleet-footed, flashy and aggressive; off the court she's a little awkward, soft-spoken and self-effacing. This, of course, endears her to Mainers all over the state. Not surprisingly, attendance at Black Bears women's basketball home games jumped dramatically since she started as a freshman during the 1994-95 season.

Close-up

The 5-foot-9 point guard from Clinton, Maine, attended Lawrence High School in Fairfield, which won four straight Class-A state basketball titles during her four-year career there. Called the most highly publicized high school athlete in the history of the state, Blodgett's college career has been even more closely covered. No less than *Sports Illustrated*, *The New York Times* and the *Boston Globe* have reported her successes. But all this attention has less to do with personality than it does with performance.

Blodgett grew up emulating the Boston Celtics' Larry Bird, she's been compared to Magic Johnson, and she breaks records year after year. She finished the 1995-96 season as the NCAA Division I scoring champion, averaging 27.8 points a game to lead the nation. She led the nation again as a junior with 27 points per game, the second woman to lead the NCAA in scoring for two consecutive seasons.

In 1996-97 she was AMERICA EAST Player of the Year and AMERICA EAST Most Outstanding Player. She combined for 128 points in the AMERICA EAST Conference (AEC) Tournament, breaking the record for total points and points in a single game.

Blodgett scored her 2,000 career points in 83

Photo: Bangor Daily News

Cindy Blodgett

games, faster than any player in conference history. She was the first female to reach that point total in her junior year.

During the 1995-96 regular season, her league totals included the most points (550), field goals (191), field-goal attempts (362), free throws (137) and free-throw attempts (161). During the AEC tournament that year, she had the most total points (102), points in a single game (44), total three-pointers (8) and three-pointers in a game (5). In the 1996-97 AEC tournament quarter-final, she scored 52 points — the most scored in an AMERICA EAST women's basketball game.

This level of play has inspired teammates, attracted talented recruits and propelled the Black Bears to the NCAA tournament year after year. Where it will propel Cindy is anybody's guess, but many hope to see her in the pros.

Photo: Bangor Daily News

Blodgett dribbles past a foe.

Spring and Free streets. Its season runs from early October to mid-April, followed by the play-offs, which can push play into mid-June. Game times are 7 PM weekdays, 7:30 PM Fridays, 2 PM Saturdays and 2 or 5 PM Sundays. Tickets run $9 to $13 ($7 and $5 for seniors and children respectively); drop by or call the Civic Center Box Office, 775-3458.

College Sports

University of Maine is the only NCAA Division I school in the state, so its teams play some big-time schools and compete for a berth in the NCAA tournament.

In the early 1990s, when Paul Kariya, now of the National Hockey League's Anaheim Mighty Ducks, was playing hockey at University of Maine, the crowds were overwhelming. While the hockey program is still popular, women's basketball dominates the headlines as senior Cindy Blodgett burns up the court (see this chapter's Close-up). Indeed, we saw a plaintive plug for the men's basketball games in the local newspaper, as attendance at the women's games was outstripping them nearly three to one. Actually, both men's hockey and women's basketball draw almost 5,000 spectators per game, sometimes more.

U-Maine women's basketball games are held at Alfond Arena, on the Orono campus. The season runs from November to mid-February, with post-season play through March. Game times are usually 1 or 7:35 PM. Tickets range from $4 to $12. Tournament prices may be more. Children younger than 2 are admitted free.

Men's hockey games are held at the Alfond Arena as well. The season runs from early October to early March, with post-season play through March. Game times are usually Friday or Saturday night at 7 PM, although there are occasional Sunday games at 2 PM and Tuesday games at 7 PM. Tickets are $12 for everyone; all seating is reserved.

The box office number is 581-2327, and tickets may be purchased ahead of time with a Visa or MasterCard.

High School Sports

The big draw in high school sports is the statewide basketball tournament in February. Maine is a close-knit state of small communities, and people like to see kids they know play ball. Besides that, basketball has a long season, it's played indoors during the winter, and teams from all over the state are focused on winning in this competition.

The Maine Principal's Association, (800) 244-0217, oversees the event, and it divides the schools by location (Eastern or Western) and size (Class A, B, C and D, with Class A being the largest schools). Augusta is the site for Western-team play, while Bangor hosts the Eastern teams. Most of the games are scheduled during the third week in February, which is vacation week for the public schools. Playoffs between Eastern and Western division teams are scheduled during subsequent weekends, and the locations of those games alternate between Augusta and Bangor from year to year.

The week-long Eastern tournament in Bangor is a big event. Total attendance has reached as high as 50,000, and many people plan their work schedules around the games. Some take the whole week off and spend it in bleacher seats.

The Bangor games are played at the Bangor Auditorium in the Bass Park Complex, 100 Dutton Street, 990-4444. Tickets are $5 for adults and $2 for students, and you can get them at the door.

While you're in Bangor for the tournament, don't miss Hoop Town in the Civic Center. While it's set up like a trade show with booths around the perimeter, there are baskets at different levels, different size basketballs and organized passing and dribbling events. Fans can try their hand at some of those great shots they just witnessed. Also displayed is the R. H. Foster/Mobil Tournament Hall of Fame board listing 51 years of Eastern Maine's all-tournament players. Yes, the William Cohen you see on the board is now U.S. Secretary of Defense.

Real Estate

Walk down any street in a Mid-Coast town in summer and you'll see tourists eyeing pictures on the windows of real estate companies, dreaming.

Moving to Maine. . . . Even the sound of it has momentum.

If you've decided you want to live here, retire here or buy a summer place, we hope this chapter will smooth the way. We'll take you on a tour of the areas in the Mid-Coast region, and then detail some of the real estate companies doing business here. But first, some general information and advice.

Good news! We've interviewed more than 50 real estate agents, and they all say it's a buyer's market. Those with some history here remind us that there have been slow periods before. We remember when 1989 rang like a funeral bell for anyone in the business. "For Sale" signs dotted the landscape, and nothing was moving. It was particularly painful because previous years had been a time of explosive growth — some say 20 percent a year — the kind that induced speculation.

No one wanted to call what followed a recession, but in retrospect, that's exactly what it was. While the market has made a slow climb, houses have not regained the value they once were thought to have. That means owners who bought in the go-go '80s might have to bring money to the table when they sell.

What can you expect in the way of prices now? That is wildly difficult to predict. Give us a moment to explain. Most real estate agents we spoke with resisted using statistical averages as a way of characterizing an area. It finally dawned on us why. The answer is in the nature of the towns themselves. Most are an amalgam of properties, from high-value waterfront to rundown trailers on quarter-acre lots. Averaging those extremes tells very little. It always comes down to what you're looking for and how badly you want it. In the material that follows, we include ballpark averages

where available, but we offer them with the aforementioned caveat.

That said, many buyers come to the state dazzled at how reasonable the prices are, while others come wondering why they are so high. A lot depends on where you come from and what you're willing to do to move here. We spoke with one broker who said many buyers just don't want to spend the time, money or energy fixing up a property. We might be biased, but we're enchanted by the old houses here. To us, they're like children; constant care is just part of loving them.

Real estate contracts here might include all sorts of conditions to ensure the sale depends on a satisfactory building inspection, septic inspection, water test, radon test, lead test, etc. Avail yourself of every one you can. One old hand in the real estate business said he resisted these conditions when they first came on the scene, but he's come to see the wisdom in them. If you aren't used to rural properties, get advice. Read the disclosure form carefully. There are a million questions to ask. Ask them. How deep is the well? Where's the septic field? When was it built? Ask if there's anything the seller wishes you wouldn't ask.

Also, don't assume your new hometown has a police department and a full-time paid fire department. Yours might be one of many towns covered by volunteer firefighters and the county sheriff's department. The town office will have the lowdown on all this.

Actually, the town office is a wonderful resource for home buyers. The tax assessor can give you a list of house sales in the last year or so, and you can check out the properties in the town records. That will give you a good firsthand understanding of the market in the area. Check out the town's valuation of the property you want to buy; most real estate agents don't think much of it as an indicator of a fair purchase price because they've seen selling prices both well more and less than the town's assessments, but it might get you in the ballpark. Ask about taxes and zoning. Talk to the code-enforcement officer. This might sound alarming, but ask if the U.S. Environmental Protection Agency has any Superfund (federally designated toxic waste cleanup) sites in town. There's one in Union and one in Lincolnville that came off the list but still needs a cleanup. No one likes to talk about that sort of thing, but potential buyers ought to know.

You certainly don't have to do all this work yourself. A good buyer's broker can and should do it for you. The traditional real estate agent represents the seller, but in a relatively new arrangement, buyers can hire brokers to represent them during the sale. The feeling was not universal, but most agents we spoke with advocated a buyer's broker for people coming to Maine from another state.

While the larger real estate firms generally do business in a large area, many advise buyers to pick where they want to live and find an agent who really knows that area. That's not always possible, but it sounds like good advice.

As we talked with real estate agents about the areas we review subsequently, we asked where they thought there were good buys. You'll be glad to know that most said the whole region was a good buy!

Waldoboro to Stockton Springs

This stretch is a string of pretty, small towns. You can see them pinpointed on a map, but since the area is mostly rural, they tend to blend into one another. Most commercial development borders U.S. Highway 1, but there are lively town centers off that beaten track.

Waldoboro, with a population of about 4,000, is at the mouth of the Medomak River on Muscongus Bay. It was first settled in 1740 and incorporated in 1773. It's handsome town center is off U.S. 1, a cluster of buildings at the intersection of Maine highways 32 and 220.

Between Waldoboro and Rockland hang

FYI

Unless otherwise noted, the area code for all phone numbers listed in this guide is 207.

peninsulas with **Friendship**, **Cushing** and **Port Clyde** at their tips. These are wonderful areas, with rolling hills and water views. The population is relatively sparse, and the traffic is too. While homes here feel deliciously remote, it wasn't always this way. Before motorized transport, sailing ships were the main mode of transportation; the peninsulas were bustling, while the inland areas seemed isolated. That accounts for the nice supply of old Cape Cod-style homes (a.k.a. Capes) on the water at the ends of the roads. The average price of a three-bedroom home in the area is $125,000, but we think that figure is skewed by the high prices of miles and miles of shorefront.

Speaking of shorefront, a specialist in that market says the least expensive tidal frontage sells for about $40,000 for a half-acre, while bold deepwater frontage might go for $100,000 to $200,000 an acre. We spoke with another broker who said she'd seen river frontage go for much, much less. Most communities provide public access to the ocean or waterfront, so you won't feel locked out if you settle away from the shore.

The town of **Warren** is inland from U.S. 1. Realtors refer to it as a family town and say there are good buys here. Its population is a little more than 3,000, and some of its properties border the St. George River. We have friends who love it and don't mind the 20-minute commute to Camden.

Thomaston will dazzle you. You drive though the center of town on U.S. 1, and while you'll pass a state prison on the way in, you'll be amazed at the housing stock: big white clapboard Federal-era and Victorian mansions that seem to go on forever; they are positively noble. The town center is a block of attached brick buildings with great character. Thomaston has a population of 3,360, and the average three-bedroom home sells for $79,000, but we've seen a handsome 10-room Federal with four- to five-bedrooms, two baths and an extra kitchen list for $179,000. We've also seen a three- to four-bedroom home with hardwood floors, marble fireplace and attached barn with loft list for $89,500.

Owls Head juts into Penobscot Bay south of Rockland. This is another town with fiercely loyal residents. There's no through traffic, except to the Knox County Airport, and there's a strong sense of community in the neighborhoods. Again, friends who live here say they wouldn't live anywhere else. House styles include farmhouses, cottages, colonials and contemporary ranches. A turn-of-the-century shingled cottage near Crescent Beach with a master suite, sauna and some ocean views lists for $199,000. A modern home with two-car garage and 150 feet of protected shore frontage with harbor and lighthouse views lists for $250,000.

Recently named one of the best small towns in America, **Rockland**, population 8,000, is enjoying a surge in popularity. Its harbor has a growing reputation with sailors, and it's home to the ever-expanding Farnsworth Museum. Hip coffeehouses, art galleries and great restaurants already draw customers from miles away. Those in the know predict further growth and say the town will become a cultural center, a notion that amazes many longtime residents.

The average three-bedroom home here sells for $65,000. We find that too inexpensive to believe, but that's what the Chamber of Commerce says. What we don't find hard to believe is the statement from a number of brokers that the town is underpriced. We're also told that commercial properties are moving faster than residences.

It seems a shame to lump the inland towns together as if they are all of a piece, but in many ways they are alike. **Union**, **Hope** and **Appleton** are part of the Mid-Coast's lovely inland areas. These are the towns most frequently mentioned when real estate agents talk about best buys, and properties are changing hands. You'll find lots of houses from the 1800s, large acreages and panoramic views from the hills. A three-bedroom cape with large kitchen and garage on 7 acres lists for $76,000.

While the town centers of Hope and Appleton seem little more than bends in the road, Union has a town green and a bustling circle of businesses and restaurants. If you know anything about small towns, you'll know that the size of the town does not necessarily speak of its character (in fact, less of the former often means more or the latter). Just attend the town meetings of these places and you'll see what we mean.

Camden and **Rockport** are anomalies any way you cut it. One real estate agent put the average house price in these towns at $125,000 to $150,000, almost double that of their neighbors. There's a variety of reasons, some of which can be chalked up to sheer attitude. The market here is very strong.

Camden weighs in with a population of roughly 5,000; Rockport at nearly 3,000. Both have great public libraries, and the two towns share a great school. Rockport has Penobscot Bay Medical Center; Camden boasts a YMCA. Both towns have lovely town centers with equally lovely harbors; Camden's is bustling and sprawls along U.S. 1, while Rockport's is quiet, concentrated and well off the highway. Both have attracted wealthy homeowners, many of whom use their properties as vacation homes.

Properties and prices in Camden/Rockport span the gamut. In Camden, a three-bedroom Victorian with fireplace, hardwood floors and dining room lists for $125,000. An architect-designed three-bedroom, 2½-bath home with two-car garage and large barn on 12 lakeside acres lists for $695,000.

Lincolnville Center is inland; you'll pass Lincolnville Beach as you travel up the coast. Those designations name a cluster of houses and shops, but the town of **Lincolnville** spreads over a much larger area. The Ducktrap River flows through it and spills into the bay north of the beach. A three- to four-bedroom farmhouse on 1 acre in Lincolnville lists for $89,900. Seventy acres of fields and woods lists for $159,000.

As we talked with real estate agents about this area, MBNA kept coming up, so we should note that this financial institution moved into the area a few years ago. With centers in Camden and Belfast, MBNA has become the largest employer around, purchasing properties as a corporate investment

and relocating employees to the area, who buy houses when they arrive.

Real estate agents say this activity has sent ripples through the market, boosting values and fostering second- and third-generation sales. What rental markets exist are tightening fast.

On the coast between Lincolnville and Belfast, **Northport** is appealing for its long, rambling coastline. It boasts a nine-hole golf course and the Blue Goose Hall, home of antique auctions and some great dances. A log camp on an acre lot with 300 feet of ocean frontage lists for $150,000. A two-story, two-season Victorian cottage with wraparound porch and ocean views lists for $110,000.

Belfast, the county seat of Waldo County, has a population of 6,335. Incorporated in 1773, it has a handsome downtown with a harbor, a 45-bed community hospital, two newspapers and a lively community life. The housing stock is impressive. There are some massive, old colonial-, Federal- and Victorian-style homes. This town has been a best buy for years, but real estate agents say it's getting downright hot as MBNA's presence prods the economy into an upswing. The average selling price of a single-family home in Waldo County is $87,000; brokers say the average in Belfast is closer to $75,000. This masks a wide range of housing options. A four-bedroom suburban split-level lists for $119,000. An antique cape in the historic district lists for $134,000. An 1862 Italianate with cupola, hardwood floors and a large barn lists at $198,500.

On the way north along U.S. 1, **Searsport**, population 2,603, is the next town. Incorporated in 1845, it played a proud role in Maine's maritime history and has the Penobscot Marine Museum and ship captains' homes to prove it. Now it's a center for antiques and flea markets, and Realtors say it's undervalued. A beat-up, fixer-upper cape lists for $45,000. A surveyed, soils-tested, 1-acre subdivision lot with splendid ocean views lists for $35,000. A three-bedroom modern home with cathedral ceiling, open floorplan and wraparound deck on 11 acres lists for $150,000.

Tiny **Stockton Springs** is next along the coastal highway, but you must detour off the highway to find its center. Many of the homes were built in the 1800s, and with a population of 1,300, this town's residents generally know one another. At least that's what they told us at a local restaurant. One real estate broker told us the area was a sleeper, about to wake up. Another said it was well on its way. A modest two-bedroom cape just minutes from Sandy Point Beach lists at $69,000, while an older home with new kitchen, bathrooms and heating system lists at $89,000.

Real Estate Companies

Betty Lou's Real Estate
U.S. Hwy. 1, Waldoboro • 832-6331, (800) 490-6331

The owner's name is indeed Betty Lou, and while hers is a relatively young company, you'll see its signs on properties as far south

as Bristol and as far north as Rockland. The company handles residential properties, but some commercial as well.

Mahan Properties
P.O. Box 608, Waldoboro, ME 04572 • 832-5361

Gail and Jim Mahan, a husband-and-wife team, are the brokers in this 7-year-old company. They operate in Lincoln and Knox counties, with listings in Waldoboro, Friendship, Cushing, Union and Thomaston. Their specialties are antique and waterfront properties.

Parker Spofford Real Estate
U.S. Hwy. 1, Waldoboro • 832-5270, (800) 734-MAIN

This company has been in business for more than 50 years; and the husband-and-wife team who run it are real old-timers in the area. They used to cover a larger area, as far as Tenants Harbor, but as more real estate firms moved in, they narrowed their scope to Nobleboro, Waldoboro, Warren and down to

Sitting Right With the Land

Many in Maine seek to put their money where their ideas are. When building a house in a place so beautiful and fragile, you want your home to sit firmly on its land — but you also want to tread lightly, right?

Energy efficiency has gotten more sophisticated since the alternative building movement of the 1970s hit Maine with windmills flying. (You know, "Hey the wind's up; we can watch TV!") Energy-efficient homes now grapple with quality-of-life issues as well, like healthy indoor air, which means good ventilation. Our souls need light, and sometimes that light must come from the frigid north. And while we want rich fabrics and beautiful tiles in our home, we don't want them to be of materials that outgas poisons.

Enter the Maine Sustainable Building Network, a loosely organized group of individuals and companies looking for ways to make our homes and workplaces environmentally sustainable while conserving energy, water and other materials. Most of the following companies have joined together to form the network.

Neal Carter & SUN Inc., RR 1, Box 1670, Charleston, ME 04422, 285-3138, was an early promoter of fully energy-efficient building (the kind with no northern exposure and little ventilation). That was then. Now Carter generally designs and builds more subtle, super-insulated, solar-assisted homes using the latest technology and a sensitivity to his crews and clients that extends to daily on-the-job meditation sessions and careful consideration of client needs.

Another company focusing on incorporating environmentally friendly architecture with good design is David Foley and Sarah Holland's **Holland and Foley Building Design**, 232 Beech Hill Road, Northport, ME 04849, 338-9869. They also do some construction management. Foley has recently returned from Europe, where he studied energy-efficient homes in northern Germany.

Homes that sit right with the land are implicit to the work of **Northern Log Homes**, 300 Bomarc Road, Bangor, ME 04401,

Photo: Bangor Daily News

Architects and homeowners in Maine's Mid-Coast region have adapted home designs to coexist with the land's rugged features.

942-6869 or (800) 553-7311. Whether you're building a first home, retirement home or a getaway camp, the folks at Northern Log Homes can help you design a home that fits your land, needs and budget. They also can hook you up with builders, masons and electricians between Maine and Arizona to help you assemble a pre-cut and shipped home of white pine, white cedar or Western red cedar.

When moving into an older house, it's diagnostics you may need. James Shea of **Applied Solar Concepts**, 108 Third Street, Bangor, 942-8036, will diagnose your

— continued on next page

house for energy efficiency, find all the leaks and put you on the road to good environmental design.

Two other members of the network deal with what goes into the home. Mark Letizia of **Osprey Healthy Homes**, in Orland, 469-3409, distributes nontoxic, plant-based paints and varnishes.

Upholsterer **Barbara Meyer**, P.O. Box 64, Whitefield, ME 04353, 549-5741, focuses on fabric. She's been scouring the market in search of fabric and stuffings created from nontoxic, sustainable materials.

Speaking of sustainability, many folks worry how much simply building a home depletes the environment.

In Warren, mill owners Julia and Paul Sampson of **A.E. Sampson**, 273-4000, found customers were coming to them wondering about the consequences of building with wood. Three years ago, they entered into a binding agreement with the owners of Seven Islands Land Co., in northern Maine, which owns one of only three forests in the United States that are independently certified as well-managed (the others are in Texas and Oregon). Through Seven Islands, A.E. Sampson can mill and produce flooring and trim that is certified to be environmentally sound.

Indeed, builders are re-examining every aspect of construction. Says Foley, "Everyone has their own take on the issue. They're concerned with conserving energy, conserving resources, healthy materials, less toxic materials, good design, building natural places into homes, increasing daylight. None of us has the final answer, we all have parts of it."

If you're still wondering about resources for green construction — or looking for efficient water heaters, refrigerators, freezers or toilets — stop by the **Green Store**, 67 Main Street, Belfast, 338-4045. The staff might not have all the answers, but they are good at directing you to those who do.

Friendship. The company handles farmland, farms, village and coastal properties.

Rubenstein Realtors
99 Main St., Thomaston • 354-6654

Another old hand in the business, Rubenstein Realtors has been in operation for more than 30 years. Its two brokers and four licensed agents work in an area ranging from Bristol to Rockland, and specializes in land, waterfront and residential properties.

SoundVest Properties
101 Main St., Thomaston • 354-0233

This 11-broker company has been in business since 1991, operating in an area from Damariscotta to Belfast. While it specializes in residential properties, SoundVest

has a commercial division based in Rockland. It also handles rentals and residential property management.

ERA Cousens Realty
310 Main St., Rockland • 596-6433

While this company ranges all over the state, most of its work is done within 30 miles of Rockland. With 10 brokers, it is a relatively large office. Ask about ERA's home-warranty program. The company's listings are mostly residential, but it does handle some commercial properties and land sales.

Charles and Mary Jordan Real Estate
99 Camden St., Rockland • 594-5503

Here are two experienced hands in the

INSIDERS' TIP

Most rural property has no municipal water or sewage service; you must dig your own well and septic tank.

Rockland market. This husband-and-wife team have been in business as Charles and Mary Jordan Real Estate since 1977. Both are brokers, and they specialize in primary residences within about a 15-mile radius of Rockland.

E. Kinney Coastal Realty
147 Park St., Ste. 1A, Rockland
• 596-6095

While Eleanor Kinney's company is quite new, we've seen its signs on some wonderful properties, and we're seeing it with more and more frequency. She is an expatriate from one of the largest real estate firms in the area, and has three brokers in her office. Kinney has the advantage of being a native, and while she lives in St. George, we've seen her listings as far north as Camden. While the company handles all kinds of sales, it specializes in waterfront and peninsula properties.

C.R. de Rochemont, Realtor
104 Pleasant St., Rockland • 594-8124

Cap de Rochemont is a character, a wonderful character, and if we could afford the splendid waterfront pieces he specializes in, we'd work with him in a heartbeat. He's a native of the area, he's been in business for 35 years, and he has a reputation for integrity and a sense of humor. (He did a slide show on the history of real estate in Camden and Rockport at a chamber of commerce event a few years ago; we saw grown men cry, they were laughing so hard.) There are three brokers in his office, and they work an area from Waldoboro to Lincolnville, inland to Union and out to the islands.

Allen Agency
23 Main St., Camden • 236-4393,
(800) 328-1631

Allen Agency says it's the oldest real estate firm in the area; the owner's grandfather bought it in 1930, and now it has nine full-time brokers. Residential sales are the bulk of its business, and its listings generally lie within 30 miles of Camden.

Camden Hills Realty
U.S. Hwy. 1, Camden • 338-3266,
(800) 763-3266

This company specializes in retirement and second homes as well as vacation rentals.

Since it's connected with The Lodge at Camden Hills (see our Accommodations chapter), John Burgess can put you up while he helps you look for a home. The company has three brokers and works primarily in Camden and surrounding towns.

Camden Real Estate
77 Elm St., Camden • 236-6171,
(800) 236-1920

Scott Horty is an expatriate from a large local real estate firm. In business since 1995, he runs a three-broker office that specializes in personalized service. He works in Camden, Rockport and inland to Hope, Appleton and Lincolnville. Horty was one of the early advocates of buyer's broker arrangements, a real boon to area newcomers. One of us has worked with him and found him to be straightforward, smart, good-humored and refreshingly low-key. His company Camden Accommodations handles long- and short-term rentals as well.

Green-Keefe Real Estate
66 Elm St., Camden • 236-4777,
(800) 233-7250

A merger brought these two firms together in 1995, and it seems to be a happy partnership. Green-Keefe employs 21 brokers and specializes in land and residential properties. Offices in Rockland and Belfast expand the scope of its business well beyond Camden.

Jaret & Cohn
75 Elm St., Camden • 236-9626

Jaret & Cohn started in 1980 and is now the largest real estate company in the area, with 35 brokers in four offices: Rockland, Camden, Belfast and Vinalhaven. That growth should come as no surprise, as the firm is the exclusive agent for MBNA's corporate purchases (see this chapter's introduction) and handles rentals and purchases for many MBNA employees. The firm is also the exclusive agent for Sotheby's International Realty. Listings range from Friendship to Stockton Springs, and include all manner of properties.

LandVest
9 Elm St., Camden • 236-3543

LandVest is a New England real estate company headquartered in Boston. It focuses on finding and marketing high-quality second and third homes. Terry Sortwell is LandVest's regional manager for the Camden and Northeast Harbor offices. He has an excellent reputation and recently handled the sale of Fisherman Island in Boothbay Harbor. The 68-acre island has a recently renovated 1928 stone house and listed for $2.75 million.

Eagle Real Estate
651 Atlantic Hwy., Northport • 338-4848

Jim Nealy's firm has been in business about 10 years and employs seven sales people. You'll see its bright yellow and orange signs throughout Waldo and Knox counties, mostly on residential properties.

Field & Quimby
58 High St., Belfast • 338-2700

Sales manager and vice-president Larry Fogle says Field & Quimby is 150 years old, "although the agents are younger than that." Started in 1838 as an insurance company, it moved into real estate in the 1950s and now has 12 brokers handling all manner of properties throughout the Waldo County area.

Rollerson Realty
185 W. Main St., Searsport • 548-2280

This company has been in business since 1990, but owner Mary Rollerson has a track record in real estate going back at least 15 years. She and her husband have their home above the office, and she makes herself available night and day, seven days a week. She's knowledgeable, dedicated and a real advocate for the area. The company has eight brokers, and its listings range through Waldo County all the way to Trenton, Cherryfield and Rockwood.

Inland to Bangor

As you travel inland to Bangor along U.S. Highway 1A, you'll fly by the tiny towns of **Prospect** and **Frankfort**. Prospect's population is around 500; Frankfort's is just twice that. The towns are perched on the Penobscot River as it flows toward the bay. The property taxes are low here, and while the towns are an easy commute to Bangor, brokers say most Bangor residents don't see them as legitimate housing opportunities. Why make the drive when there's plenty of affordable housing in Bangor?

Winterport has a little more heft, with a population of 3,300. It split off from Frankfort and incorporated in 1860. Once home to sea captains, the entire downtown area is listed on the National Register of Historic Places, and the houses on U.S. 1A cause newcomers to rubberneck in amazement. They are old, but most are in fine condition, clearly treasured by their owners. For instance, we've seen a handsome 1839 Greek Revival home on 2 acres and with four bedrooms, a modern kitchen, original detail and a two-car garage listed for $135,000.

Hampden, Bangor, Veazie and Orono seem to meld into one large metropolitan area.

Hampden, on the road north to Bangor, has a wonderful public library, a strong middle school and a new public swimming pool.

With a population of 33,000, **Bangor**, the third-largest city in the state, was rated the best small town (less than 100,000 population) in Macmillan Travel's *Places Rated Almanac 1997*. It boasts an international airport, a great high school, a noteworthy theater company and malls galore. The Eastern Maine Medical Center is the largest employer in the area.

The market here seems soft. Brokers say buyers these days are tough-minded; they don't fall in love with properties the way they used to. While the number of sales is increasing, prices are actually declining. Some owners are losing money in the process, needing to bring money to the table when they sell. Only where the house is new construction does the advantage tilt to the seller. There's a dearth of new construction in Bangor though Realtors say it's just a matter of time until that's rectified.

There are roughly 1,200 homes on the market within a 40-mile radius. The average

FYI

Unless otherwise noted, the area code for all phone numbers listed in this guide is 207.

sale price in the greater Bangor area is $86,000; newer construction is generally more expensive. The average days on market is 119; the average turnaround time is four to five months. Usually you can close in 45 days. Bangor has a range of housing stock available, from a three-bedroom colonial for $38,900 to an 11-room modern home with custom kitchen, Jacuzzi and indoor lap pool for $391,000.

Real estate agents say there are a lot of rental units available. One- and two-bedroom apartments run from $350 to $500 monthly, while two- and three-bedroom townhouses average $650 per month. Rental homes are fairly scarce, and they run $500 to $800, primarily because of property taxes and high maintenance costs. The supply of low-end houses in the $60,000 to $70,000 range is growing, making it cheaper to buy one of those than to rent. Maine has a number of programs for first-time buyers to help ease the way.

Some brokers say the city doesn't really have "bad" neighborhoods, and the crime rate is relatively low. They speak favorably of areas such as Laurel Circle, the Yankee Avenue subdivision, and Little City, several streets on the east side of Bangor lined with older colonial and Victorian homes.

If you're looking for new construction, Laurel Circle is a new subdivision off Kenduskeag Avenue. The homes are all single-family, built in the last five years, and they range from $115,000 to $185,000.

Yankee Avenue is another newer subdivision with three- and four-bedroom homes selling for $85,000 to $120,000. It's hard to find new construction for $100,000 or less in Bangor, which makes this area attractive.

Little City is an older historic neighborhood between St. Joseph's Hospital and Kenduskeag Avenue. One section was built in the early 1900s and encompasses a mixture of single- and multifamily dwellings that sell for $85,000 to $150,000. The other section, built in the late 1950s and early '60s by well-respected builder Johnnie Russell, features three- to five-bedroom homes selling for $150,000 to $175,000.

Veazie, between Bangor and Orono, is tiny, with 1,500 residents. Brokers say it's long been thought to be a little rough around the edges, but that's changed. It's building a brand-new school (grades K through 8) and is a growing community. Real estate agents recommend Silver Ridge development and Buck Hill Estates. Silver Ridge was the first subdivision in Veazie, and it took off like a scalded dog. Begun in the late '80s, all the lots (quarter- to half-acre) sold in six months, and it's now a well-established, well-landscaped neighborhood of primarily four-bedroom, two-story homes ranging from $140,000 to $225,000. Resale is excellent — high demand and little availability.

Buck Hill Estates abuts Silver Ridge, and its lots are larger (1 to 2 acres). The mostly four-bedroom homes are more expensive as well, ranging in price from $170,000 to $350,000. All were custom homes, so styles vary from contemporary to colonial. Again, demand is high for these houses. A Realtor told us a $287,000 house in Buck Hill Estates sold in two days last year. This year he listed it again for $40,000 more and it sold in four days.

A new subdivision called Oak Grove recently opened in **Brewer**, and phase one is nearly sold out and built. Some 30 to 40 homes in the $130,000 to $285,000 range have been built. The majority are two-bedroom homes in the 2,500- to 3,500-square-foot range, which is fairly large for this area. Oak Grove's softened the existing home market, but it may prod additional new construction.

Orono, on the Stillwater and Penobscot rivers, has a population of 10,000, including the students at University of Maine. The university brings a liveliness to the town, and its art and athletic events are a real draw to people from all over the state. The town boasts of more than 200 acres of green space, threaded with walking, skiing and biking trails. The housing stock includes fine examples of colonial and Victorian architecture. For $89,900, you can pick up a three-bedroom cape with a fireplace, hardwood floors and a two-car garage. A three-story, four-bedroom contemporary with two baths and a two-car garage lists for $165,000.

Real Estate Companies

Century 21 At River Town
Main Rd., Hampden • 862-5611, (800) 750-5611

Started in the late '80s, this firm has more than a dozen brokers. While it once concentrated on the Hampden/Winterport/Newburg area, it has since expanded its scope to include greater Bangor and beyond. Its 15 sales people handle all kinds of properties.

Century 21 Queen City
416 Hammond St., Bangor • 942-4618

The Mullins family has been in real estate in the area for four generations. The company's 15 brokers handle commercial and residential properties from Bucksport to Charleston and from Newport to Greenbush. Its Century 21 affiliation connects the company to an international network of offices, and Mullins says 10 percent to 15 percent of its business comes from referrals.

ERA Dawson-Bradford Co.
417 Main St., Bangor • 947-3363, (800) 649-4178
50 Main St., Orono • 866-5571, (800) 564-5571

Dawson and Bradford merged in 1989, and while the resulting ERA Dawson-Bradford Co. focuses on greater Bangor, its listings include all manner of properties in Bar Harbor, Newport and Dover-Foxcroft. With 60 brokers, it's one of the largest real estate firms in the area and claims to be a leader in unit sales and volume for the last 15 years.

INSIDERS' TIP

High-dollar real estate listings can drop by as much as $100,000 without notice, so don't despair: While the listing price of the property you love might not approach your ideal of the Maine dream, the selling price just might.

Quinn Real Estate
292 Hammond St., Bangor • 942-4864

Quinn has been in business since 1961, and its 12 brokers handle all manner of real estate transactions in the greater Bangor area. This is not a franchised agency, and it prides itself on personalized service. Broker David Brown is former president of the Bangor Board of Realtors and has a keen grasp of the market.

Realty Executives
139 State St., Bangor • 942-6310

Realty Execs has a total of more than 40 brokers working from its State Street location and a branch office in Old Town. The company handles residential, commercial, multifamily and land listings throughout the greater Bangor area. The company is opening a Belfast office in spring '98.

Mark Stimson Real Estate Network, Town & Country
760 Union St., Bangor • 942-6711

The Town & Country name has been bouncing around since the 1950s, but it's current incarnation is about 4 or 5 years old. That's not to say its 50 brokers are new at this business. Some have logged 20 years or more, and owner Earl Black is a highly respected old hand. Town & Country's listings range within 100 miles of Bangor, and the company has offices in Dover, Ellsworth, Blue Hill, and Unity.

Bucksport to Gouldsboro

Prominently situated on a hill leading down to a bend in the Penobscot River, **Bucksport** could hardly have a more lovely location. The main street and many houses above it face the river, the stately Waldo-Hancock Bridge and the ancient-looking fortress of Fort Knox on a point directly across the river. If you arrive on Maine Highway 15 from the north, Bucksport seems dominated by Champion International Paper Mill; if you arrive from U.S. Highway 1 from the south, it becomes the quintessential New England village. Both forces characterize the town. In the past, there's been a lot of commercial space for rent in Bucksport — less so now, thanks to an active mayor and a very community-oriented town government that's working hard to fill the storefronts.

The town's population is just shy of 5,000. Folks who live in town have classic sea captain's houses or modern ranches. Farther from town, you'll find farmhouses. A remodeled two-story, three-bedroom Cape in town can go for $69,000.

Keep going down Maine Highway 1 to reach the pretty river town of **Orland** (pop. 1,800), on the western edge of the Blue Hill Peninsula. You can find a four-bedroom fixer-upper on 5 acres for $60,000. A five-bedroom Victorian with views of the Narramissic River, or a small 19th-century Cape with deepwater frontage on the Penobscot River, lists for around $190,000. In nearby **Penobscot** (pop. 1,100), it's harder to find the low-end properties, but it's still possible. A 7-acre waterfront parcel lists for $130,000; 100 feet of lake frontage with a contemporary three-bedroom Cape, $175,000. Inland, a farmhouse with a small barn on 5 acres costs $110,000. On the level of a "find," we saw a three-bedroom, 19th-century Cape for $80,000.

Follow the road from Orland down the long peninsula that ends in **Castine**. The region's powerful history has left many fine buildings of many eras: Colonial, Victorian, 20th-century summer mansions, even some contemporary homes. Many properties here are noteworthy because of the town's historical and architectural traditions.

Not too long ago, Castine's reputation was as a retirement community and a summer community. It seemed no one worked year round in Castine. The long, winding peninsula, a good 20-minute drive from the nearest supermarket, was just too off-the-beaten-path for most younger families. Maybe that's why it has been favored by writers. Robert Lowell lived here, as did Mary McCarthy. Elizabeth Hardwick still has a home on the shore. Poet Philip Booth's ancestral home is on Main Street. Singer/songwriter Don McLean ("Bye, Bye, Miss American Pie") also owns a home in town, though he and his family spend most of the year outside Camden.

Recently — perhaps because the computer allows for so many home offices, perhaps because people are just more accepting of the commute — Castine has become a year-round community, cherished for being the kind of place where you'd be comfortable letting your

Photo: Bangor Daily News

Many celebrities visit Maine, and some have chosen to buy homes along Maine's coast. Former U.S. Secretary of State Casper Weinberger purchased a home and settled in Somesville, a small coastal town in Hancock County.

kids bike to the corner store. It still doesn't have a supermarket, though the small Tarratine market can accommodate many needs, augmented by a natural foods cooperative and a delicious bakery. As Realtor Jean Cass explains, "Castine has retained its character because it's not convenient. It's a wonderful place to raise children; all the children belong to all the grownups." Particular kinds of grownups, we might add. Because housing costs are high in Castine, the ongoing complaint at the coffee shop is that no worker can afford to be among the 1,100 who live in town. We recall one morning's conversation: Someone needed a ditch dug that day, but there was no one left in town to dig it.

There's another element added to the Castine mix, the Maine Maritime Academy, which holds a prominent place on the shore of the harbor. MMA is a college devoted to maritime and oceanographic skills (see Education). Faculty members have homes in town, the lights on the playing fields burn bright into fall evenings, and students have been known to march through town as part of their academy drills.

Prices here, as elsewhere, vary according to water frontage, condition and size. A 1.5-acre coveside homesite might go for $150,000,

and we saw a three-bedroom, newly constructed classic Cape with deeded water access for $180,000.

The rolling hills and craggy ocean inlets of the Blue Hill Peninsula make for many snug homes and spectacular views over ocean, river or meadow. The Blue Hill Peninsula is sometimes compared to Mount Desert Island (which is now so anchored to the mainland, it is more a peninsula than an island). Separated by Blue Hill Bay, these bodies of land jut southward next to one another off U.S. Highway 1. But because Acadia National Park is so enticing — and takes up so much land — Mount Desert Island values tend to be a notch higher. (See this chapter's subsequent "Mount Desert Island" section for details.)

The **Blue Hill Peninsula** — which real estate agents expand to encompass everything from Orland to Surry, including Deer Isle, offshore — is the quiet, refined cousin. It's also extremely desirable. While Mount Desert Island is home to some wealthy names — the Rockefellers and Fords are two — Blue Hill has an equivalent amount of wealth, but without broadcasting the names. Many artists, craftspeople, sailors, writers and musicians, not to mention a group of Zen practitioners

Ready for Retirement?

If you're older than 55 and plan a move to Maine, think before you buy or build your dream home. You may not be ready for retirement, but you may be ready for a congregate retirement community. The name is awkward, but the facilities can be fabulous. You may also want to think ahead about where you might live as you grow older. Finding a place that can meet a range of needs can be a real comfort; familiar faces and familiar routines will ease your way.

Close-up

Penobscot Shores, 338-2332, in Belfast is an elegant example of what's available. As the name implies, it's right on the shore of Penobscot Bay, and many of its apartments and cottage units have fabulous views of the water. Amenities include a library, a walking trail, a wood shop and housekeeping services so extensive you may not need to leave the grounds — ever. It's an affiliate of the Waldo County General Hospital.

Depending on where you might want to settle, check out similar apartments at **Camden Gardens**, 236-0154, in Camden, or **Park East Retirement Villa**, 947-7992, in Bangor. Each community governs itself a little differently; they have different clienteles and different policies, so it's worth some exploring before you commit to one.

Like Penobscot Shores, **Parker Ridge**, 374-5789, in Blue Hill offers apartments and cottages, but it also offers assisted-living units. That means you can settle here, but be provided for should you or your partner's health deteriorate in the years to come. It's also an affiliate of Blue Hill Memorial Hospital.

If you are retiring in Maine, and you or your partner need more care, places like **Harbor Hill**, (800) 228-3811, in Belfast are available. It offers a range of facilities on one campus. The Assisted Living Residence rents rooms or suites by the day or the month to those who wish to remain independent, but may need help doing so. The Health Center rents semiprivate and private rooms by the day to those needing subacute care,

— continued on next page

Photo: Parker Ridge

Mid-Coast retirement communities offer a wide variety of services —
not to mention the breathtaking views and natural settings.

rehabilitation and extended care. The Harbor House is a more secure unit for patients with Alzheimer's and other related memory disorders. Its private and semiprivate rooms rent by the day. Comfort Care is offered for patients with terminal illnesses.

Windward Gardens, 236-4197 or (800) 236-4197, in Camden offers assisted living, skilled care and rehabilitation as well as extended nursing care and an adult day-care program. The **Camden Health Care Center**, 230-6100, offers short- and long-term care for older adults, and **The Knox Center for Long-Term Care**, 594-6800, in Rockland, also offers levels of care, including a specialized program for residents with Alzheimer's.

Forgive us if it seems there's a preponderance of retirement options in Belfast and Camden; that part of the Mid-Coast has been a magnet for retirees for years.

---

who have taken root around Surry, also call this area home.

The schools on the peninsula are reputable, including the well-regarded Bay School, a Waldorf school, in the town of Blue Hill. The high school for Blue Hill, George Stevens Academy, is also notable. It's both private and public, so students from outside the district can tuition in. (See our Education chapter for details.)

Blue Hill, the town, is centered among the many villages that comprise the peninsula. Here is where you'll find the supermarket, well-regarded hospital, natural foods co-op, most of the restaurants and some 3,000 people.

While the real estate market in the region had been fairly flat over the last few years, it has recently become more of a seller's market. By Maine standards, prices are getting steep. In the town of Blue Hill, $300,000 might get you one of the following: a four-bedroom farmhouse on 48 acres of fields and woods with shorefront on Salt Pond, but not on the ocean; a four-bedroom Victorian in town; or a former bed and breakfast with four bedrooms, four baths and water views, set on a hillside on 4 acres.

A half-million dollars will get you a contemporary home on 46 acres with 750 feet of shore frontage and your own beach.

Waterfront property is most expensive — it's the Maine dream, after all. But not all waterfront property is alike. A 63-acre lot on a stream with waterfalls might cost only $60,000. Then, again, if you want to do your own work, you can still find bargains almost anywhere on the peninsula.

Cape Rosier, literally on a peninsula off a peninsula off Blue Hill Peninsula, is a remote high bluff overlooking all of Penobscot Bay. Views from the shore extend to the islands, the Camden Hills and the eastern and western horizons — great sunrises and sunsets.

When Helen and Scott Nearing, credited with creating the back-to-the-land movement, moved here in the 1950s, Cape Rosier was a place of blueberry fields, farms and summer camps (Maine-speak for small summer homes). Now, the bold head of the cape has been divided and turned into something you might find off Big Sur. On these remote cliffs, off roads scarred by construction crews, summer mansions costing as much as $2 million are being built on parcels going for about $200,000 for 400 feet of shoreline.

On the more gentler slopes of the cape, you can still find typical old farms. We saw a charming four-bedroom farmhouse with two barns and a two-car garage on 20 acres selling for $190,000.

Nearby **Brooksville** (pop. 760), which encompasses North Brooksville, West Brooksville, South Brooksville and Brooksville proper, is also a summer colony, though it's now populated by retired musicians who have added immeasurable character to the place. Just look at all the signs for steel band concerts!

South Brooksville, also known as Bucks Harbor for the harbor it fronts, is the choice area here. A year-round, white-clapboard house with three bedrooms and wraparound porches, and within walking distance of the harbor, can cost $150,000. Here, as elsewhere, everything changes away from the water. An inland, three-bedroom, 19th-century farmhouse on a small lot was recently on the market for $62,000.

You can also find some relative deals on other parts of the peninsula, especially if you're willing to wield a hammer and paint-brush. In **Brooklin** (pop. 785) and nearby **Sedgwick** (pop. 905), there is everything from moderately priced inland homes to modern ranch homes to classic storybook farmhouses complete with rambling roses and white picket fences. Examples include a new three-bedroom, Cape Cod-style home on 1 acre in Brooklin for $100,000 and a two-bedroom ranch home on 3 acres in Sedgwick with a view of Eggemoggin Reach for $115,000. Actual shore front-age will cost more, though not as much as on Cape Rosier. A half-acre lot with 530 feet of shore frontage costs $115,000 here. The value of the classic farm-house, once quite modest, has escalated commensurate with the value of it's view.

Surry (pop. 1,000), on the eastern edge of the Blue Hill Peninsula, has some of the most reasonably priced properties on the peninsula, such as a two-story Cape with a modern kitchen, barn and garage and limited water views for $140,000.

Across from the mainland lies Deer Isle, which has three areas of note: Little Deer Isle and Deer Isle, two separate islands connected by a causeway; and Stonington, a town at the end of Deer Isle. Between mainland and is-lands lies Eggemoggin Reach, the watery thor-oughfare that joins Penobscot and Jericho bays; it's named a reach because it can be sailed in either direction on just one tack, or set of the sail. Until 1939, a ferry took traffic to Deer Isle, but the glorious, narrow span of the Deer Isle Bridge now crosses the reach be-tween Sargentville and Little Deer Isle.

On **Deer Isle** (pop. 1,900), you can find your-self paying for isolation and beauty. In Deer Isle Village, a six-bedroom farmhouse with a three-story attached barn on the water costs $400,000. On **Little Deer Isle**, a contemporary four-bed-room home with views of Penobscot Bay lists for nearly $500,000. A smallish 19th-century Cape with views of the bay costs $250,000, while a 5,000-square-foot contemporary home on 14 acres with 2,000 feet of shoreline frontage was recently on the market for $825,000.

FYI

Unless otherwise noted, the area code for all phone numbers listed in this guide is 207.

Over the past decades, Deer Isle has been influenced by Haystack Mountain School of Crafts (see our Arts and Education chapters), an internationally known craft school in a lo-cation so gorgeous that, were it not for the powerful draw of the art at Haystack, people could be accused of applying to the school just for the view of Jericho Bay. Many craftspeople and artists of all kinds have since fallen in love with the island, and they add significantly to the population.

Stonington has also expe-rienced a boom in recent years. Once a forgotten fishing village, it is now "The Forgotten Fish-ing Village," with galleries, res-taurants and tourist-oriented establishments climbing over themselves on the waterfront streets. The number of real estate brokers as well as property prices have risen accordingly. But Stonington, with 1,300 residents, is still the working village of the island, and prices around town can still be relatively low. A three-bedroom Victorian in the village and with har-bor views costs $90,000. Shorefront property out of town is more like the rest of the island: a 20-acre parcel can cost as much as $200,000, but there's still more moderately priced prop-erty inland.

Everyone on the Blue Hill Peninsula, on Mount Desert Island and farther Down East treats **Ellsworth** as "town." Once elegant and stately, Ellsworth (pop. 6,000) has truly been altered by modern strip development. But take a look beyond U.S. 1. The old Ellsworth re-mains. Those familiar with the region under-stand its reputation as a nice place to live, especially for families with children. The schools are solid (the high school consistently so), there's an active YMCA, good after-school activities, a city-supported performing arts cen-ter (The Grand; see our Arts chapter), a fabu-lous library and a river to fish in. What more could a growing family want?

As the county seat, Ellsworth is a year-round market, though the area certainly in-cludes many desirable coastal properties as well. In-town, three-bedroom homes list for $78,000 to $98,000; $120,000 in more mod-ern subdivisions.

Shorefront properties, such as those on

Bayside Road (leading to Oak Point) in **Trenton** (pop. 1,000), range from $72,000 to $350,000. But the average vacant shorefront lot is closer to $100,000, and a contemporary five-bedroom home on an acre beside Union Bay, also in Trenton, can go for as much as $300,000.

According to one agent, younger folks tend to want acreage wrapped around their homes, while older folks want to live in town. As is the case throughout most of Maine, Ellsworth does not have a strong rental market. There are some apartment buildings, but generally speaking, most apartments are above garages in people's homes. There are also a couple of condominium complexes.

Outlying areas vary. Where there's waterfront, as in Lamoine or Hancock, prices rise.

As is true on Blue Hill Peninsula and Mount Desert Island, in **Lamoine** (pop. 1,300), Trenton and Surry, the market has finally recovered from the recession after the late 1980s. While in 1997 we reported a buyer's market, Realtors see 1998's as more a seller's market.

Then there's lakefront property. A recreational buyer need not worry about year-round access, but a year-round buyer might have to put in a road — and think about plowing it. There's a local market for recreational land, which goes for less than land with easy year-round access. But now, lakefront property is being sold as year-round housing, keeping prices up. On Green Lake north of Ellsworth, for instance, a three-bedroom contemporary costs $125,000.

The farther Down East you go, the more possible it is to find the Maine dream — a simple shorefront Cape — and still have money left to fix it up. Schoodic Peninsula, close as it is to Acadia National Park and the astounding vistas of Mount Desert Island, is quite desirable despite its distance from the population centers. **Gouldsboro** (pop. 2,000) property is still a good buy. Most properties are built for year-round use, though investment buying is not uncommon.

This area hasn't quite recovered from the land recession of the early 1990s, so there are bargains here, especially since the military base in nearby Winter Harbor is due to be closed. A post-and-beam farmhouse with an attached barn on 16 acres recently sold for $110,000, while an 1826 renovated, center-chimney Cape on 5 acres with a brook didn't sell at $140,000. In nearby **Hancock** (pop. 1,800), a modest two-bedroom home with decks, right across Frenchman Bay from Bar Harbor, sold for $90,000. As one agent explained, "homes that are well-priced for the market do sell."

Many real estate agents in Ellsworth and Blue Hill cover the Gouldsboro area.

Real Estate Companies

Landmark Properties
128 S. Main St., Bucksport • 469-2275

David and Alice Grant have run this medium-size office of six agents since 1989, and Alice has been in business since 1981. The focus here is both sides of the Penobscot River, inland lakes and town properties throughout Waldo, Hancock and Penobscot counties. Landmark's specialties are properties on the many lakes in the region, farms and some saltwater properties. Because of the paper mill in Bucksport and the changing of the guard at the Maine Maritime Academy in nearby Castine, Landmark also finds itself handling many employee relocations. It also handles summer cottage rentals.

Castine Realty
Main St., Castine • 326-9392, 326-4041

The focus here is on the Blue Hill Peninsula in general and Castine in particular, though there are also properties in the quiet hamlets of nearby Orland and Penobscot. Though many home prices tend toward the high-end, Castine Realty's three brokers, two associates and one sales rep cover properties that range from $75,000 to more than $500,000. The agency began in 1986 and is run by two natives, Scott and Robin Vogell.

Saltmeadow Properties
Main St., Castine • 326-9116
Main St., Blue Hill • 374-5010

Marcia Kropp and Karen Koos opened Saltmeadow in 1992 after gaining considerable experience with other agencies. It's headquartered in Castine with another office in Blue Hill and has five active brokers. Saltmeadow deals in coastal properties throughout the Blue Hill Peninsula and Deer Isle. Properties range from modest to grand and include saltwater farms, antique Capes, academic-year homes for Maine Maritime Academy faculty and whatever else is available. Generally, the first order of business for people unfamiliar with the area is getting acquainted with the region and the varied natures of its many communities. Saltmeadow actively co-brokers.

Compass Point
Main St., Blue Hill • 374-5300

Compass Point's staffers have been in the business for years, but the agency only began in 1994. With five active brokers, Compass Point has done extremely well handling the region's high-end real estate. It is now the area affiliate for Sotheby's International Real Estate. It is also affiliated with The Coastal Connection, an association of coastal real estate agencies from York to Bar Harbor, committed to assisting buyers of waterfront properties. Owners Carol Beaven and Tad Goodale say they do focus primarily on waterfront properties, frequently as summer homes for people with discretionary income looking for a potential retirement home. But like most Maine agencies, Compass Point handles what's around, whether it be a $75,000 parcel of land or a large waterfront home.

Downeast Properties
Main St., Blue Hill • 374-2321, 374-5033

Vance Gray has been a broker for 26 years, personally overseeing a wide range of waterfront, waterview, oceanfront and island properties. Gray essentially works alone, assisted by an office manager. Downeast Properties' listings include a motel in Bar Harbor, an island off Deer Isle and a steady base of new and classic homes in Castine and Blue Hill.

Madeline Mattson Realty Inc.
Main St., Blue Hill • 374-2766

This small agency, consisting of three brokers, covers a wide range of properties from Stonington on Deer Isle to the Blue Hill Peninsula and Ellsworth. Madeline Mattson has done business in Blue Hill for 22 years, and before that in the Washington, D.C., area. She is a community-oriented broker, caring deeply about the nature of the towns

she sells in, though her focus is on summer homes and second homes.

Shepard's
Main St., Blue Hill • 374-5464
Main St., Deer Isle • 348-6105
Main St., Stonington • 367-2790

This company's three offices — Blue Hill, Deer Isle and Stonington — work in partnership. Nine agents staff the offices (three at each). Shepherd's specializes in coastal properties, from 2 acres in Stonington for $22,000 to a small island for $1.5 million. The company is also handling the landmark Opera House in Stonington.

Mark Stimson Real Estate Network Town & Country
144 High St., Ellsworth • 667-7557
Main St., Blue Hill • 374-2000

In 1997, Mark Stimson Real Estate Network, Town & Country Realtors and Coldwell Banker Full Sail Realty merged. The company is now the largest agency in the region. With a new office just opened in Blue Hill, it now has two offices in the Mid-Coast area and 22 licensed brokers on staff. The agency deals with all manner of commercial and residential properties, has a relocation department, a construction specialist, property-search computers and a 24-hour hotline for access to all listings. Agents frequently have specialties, whether shorefront, commercial, residential, restaurants, cottages or motels.

Katsiaficas
125 Main St., Ellsworth • 667-9333

This family-owned company has been in business since 1960, and three of the five current agents are related. Owner Steve Joy has been around since 1985. The focus here is on property in Ellsworth, surrounding towns (Trenton, Lamoine, Franklin, Hancock, Surry, Blue Hill) and island properties. The business runs the gamut of real estate enterprises, including land development, and also covers Mount Desert Island, other areas of Hancock County and Washington County.

Knowles Real Estate
105 High St., Ellsworth • 667-4604

The 16 brokers at Knowles Real Estate pride

themselves on their community activism and on their traditional approach to the market backed up by modern technology. Knowles, a full-service agency, has been working in Hancock and Washington counties for more than a century, specializing in shorefront and in-town residential property and representing both sellers and buyers. The agency handles local, vacation and retirement buyers.

Sargent Real Estate
125 High St., Ellsworth • 667-2144, 667-3255

There are four people who actively sell real estate at this family-run, 25-year-old agency led by Dan Sargent. Sargent deals with all of Hancock County and some of Washington County, including residential and commercial properties, land and cottages.

Rocky Shore Realty
U.S. Hwy. 1, Gouldsboro • 963-2945, (800) 244-2945

Betty Lou Sawyer's Rocky Shore Realty is the only realty office along the Gouldsboro segment of U.S. 1. She's been in business for more than 20 years, covering summer and year-round coastal residential properties in Gouldsboro, Winter Harbor, Petit Manan and inland.

Mount Desert Island

Mount Desert Island (a.k.a. MDI) is the big Mid-Coast market, where coastal properties can rent for $30,000 a month and sell for as much as $5 million.

We're talking big houses, big names and big money. Homes that were once the property of the Rockefellers or the Vanderbilts — or perhaps guest cottages from large estates — are now being sold or offered as summer rentals. We're also talking limited space: The park takes up about half the island, making the other half even more desirable. And yet, MDI is also a year-round community with its share of workers.

In a tip of the hat to first-time Maine home buyers on the island, the Maine State Housing Authority has recognized the relative expense of property on Mount Desert Island and has altered their funding arrangements accordingly.

For the most part, Realtors find that Mount Desert Island is hot again. After all, Martha Stewart just bought here — a granite home in the posh community of Seal Harbor that Edsel Ford built in the late 1920s. Stewart's price? Not quite $5 million. Her home is three stories, built of huge granite blocks, making it different from most island cottages and more like homes found in Rhode Island or Connecticut. Perhaps you've already seen it on her television show?

Realtors say MDI is a seller's market for residences valued up to $300,000. There's a lot of demand but not a lot of property on the island, especially if you're seeking something for less than $125,000. Good waterfront property is also a seller's market. And whereas mid-range homes languished on the market a few years ago, they too are selling again. A year or so ago, a waterfront home on the quiet, western side could be found for from $200,000 to $300,000; now it seems all such homes have been bought. It's homes in the next higher price range — the $300,000 to $600,000 market — that are still sluggish sellers, but even that market has gotten tighter since the early 1990s. Indeed, even high-range properties in Bar Harbor, once relegated to the tourist market, are starting to sell. Waterfront homes that had been boarded up for years are starting to go on the market, with prices upward of $1 million.

Inland, the volatility of the early 1990s has now settled. Land close to the trails of Acadia National Park but lacking water views is going for $30,000 to $40,000 an acre. You might find property in this price range in some innovative developments, like one that is basically encircled by land deeded "forever wild" thanks to the developer.

To many out-of-staters, the cost of land on the island is relatively low, but it depends on what you're used to. Realtors note that people used to New York and New Jersey real estate prices are amazed at how affordable gorgeous water frontage can be; Californians think we're giving our land away; but folks from the Midwest or South suffer sticker-shock here.

As for specifics, we saw a five-bedroom farmhouse in Bar Harbor listed at $150,000. Abutting the park, a five-bedroom modern Cape costs $250,000. But inland, near Salisbury Cove (on the Bar Harbor Road), we found a three-bedroom contemporary home for only $82,000.

If you look on the island, remember that Bar Harbor and Mount Desert both have broad property lines. **Bar Harbor** (pop. 4,600) extends from Thunder Hole in Acadia National Park to Blagden Preserve at Indian Point, including Thompson Island on the causeway from the mainland to MDI. The town of **Mount Desert** (pop. 2,000) includes high-price areas such as Seal Harbor, Northeast Harbor and Somesville. What is known as "the quiet side" of the island is divided almost evenly between **Southwest Harbor** (pop. 2,000), of growing value, and **Tremont** (pop. 1,000).

Within these boundaries, there's a lot of fine tuning. It's almost impossible to find something for less than $100,000 in the exclusive and posh Northeast Harbor, for instance, where an in-town home with four bedrooms goes for about $245,000. But in **Bass Harbor**, part of Tremont, you'll find homes for right around $100,000. A three-bedroom, secluded contemporary home on a private road in Bass Harbor was on the market recently for $128,000, while across the harbor in **Bernard**, a modified cottage with three bedrooms and mountain views was listed for $115,000.

As elsewhere, you need to know where to look. If you want a small house, you'll have a hard time finding it where multi-guest-roomed summer cottages have been built. Southwest Harbor does have smaller offerings, including condominiums overlooking the harbor, but these modern affairs can be pricey. A two-bedroom contemporary condo goes for $175,000.

Indeed, in each locale on MDI, there are pockets of high-value property as well as pockets of lower-end.

Somesville is a special place. There is no zoning law requiring buildings in Somesville to be painted white with black or dark green trim, it just looks that way. Even though it's smack in the middle of MDI, Somesville seems to have been forgotten by time. Appearances are deceptive, however; people in Somesville are very private about their community. After all, among the rich, powerful, famous and semi-retired locals are the Weinbergers and the Roosevelts. When George Mitchell rented a home there, his neighbors were so concerned

for his privacy that they practically shunned him. Again, we're talking larger prices for Somesville homes. A relatively small, three-bedroom modified bungalow was recently listed at $165,000.

Real Estate Companies

The Swan Agency
43 Cottage St., Bar Harbor • 288-5818

Four years ago, Kim Swan-Bennett took over the Swan Agency from her father, who ran it for more than 20 years. It's a full-service agency, with 10 associates handling everything from first-time to high-end buyers. A mark of this company's success with high-dollar properties: Swan is included in the *Who's Who in Luxury Real Estate* and is a representative for Estate's Club.

The agency also has a division for bed and breakfast inns statewide, from Kittery to Eastport. In fact, they've just sold a classic cottage that had been renovated as a bed and breakfast back into a private home. The asking price, $2.9 million, reached the top of anything sold in Bar Harbor. There is excitement in selling a property like that, says Swan-Bennett, but an $80,000 sale might be more thrilling if it's the first home for a young couple.

Swan agents are frequently involved in community organizations, including Habitat for Humanity. They've recently launched a program called Sharing our Success, in which buyers are asked to choose a favorite community organization from a list Swan offers. After the sale, the agency will make a donation to that organization in that buyer's name.

Mike Woodard Realty
61 Cottage St., Bar Harbor • 288-8181

Mike Woodard's specialty is going to bat for buyers to try to save them money (a.k.a. buyers brokerage). This company offers a market analysis to determine what a property is really worth and thoroughly investigates a property's design specs (to be sure the septic designs, for instance, are appropriate for the numbers of bathrooms). It also does home searches to help potential buyers find what they're looking for.

E. Pat Foster Real Estate
Maine Hwy. 102, Mount Desert
• 244-9251

Working alone in the center of Somesville, Pat Foster attributes her success during the last 21 years to her hands-on, personal, local approach. Currently, she has more than 20 exclusive listings. Foster's listings are focused on Mount Desert Island. She also rents her own properties — Acadia Pines Chalets — as weekly vacation cottages.

Knowles Co.
One Summit Rd., Northeast Harbor
• 276-3322

In summer 1997, Knowles Co. reached its century mark. Begun in 1897 by Belle Smalidge Knowles, it was the first agency on the island. Today, Knowles Co. prides itself on luring those who wish to step back to the island's Golden Age (read high-dollar) era, selling homes from $1 to $5 million.

But Knowles is also happy to sell everyday, run-of-the-mill homes. It also offers summer rentals from $500 a week to $30,000 a month. (See our Summer Rentals chapter for related information.)

Knowles' extensive listings are focused on Mount Desert Island and The Cranberries. There are six full-time real estate brokers, two part-time brokers and two full-time rental agents.

Train Properties
3 Summit Rd., Northeast Harbor
• 276-5108

Train's logo features a set of building blocks that depicts what it's about. In addition to brokerage, which comes out on top, there's rental, property management and construction. Train offerings feature the high end of Mount Desert Island property. While they may have some lesser-priced properties off the island, at presstime their range was from

A dairy farm in central Maine seems like the pot of gold at the end of a rainbow during a spring shower.

$200,000 to more than $2 million for a classic shorefront cottage in Seal Harbor.

Hinckley Real Estate
Mansell Ln., Southwest Harbor
• 244-7011
E. Blue Hill Rd., Blue Hill • 374-5785

In 1986 Bob Hinckley, builder of the famous Hinckley sailboat, realized an increasing number of people chartering boats from him also were curious about buying land. Hinckley approached Realtor Jane Pooler, and together they set up Hinckley Real Estate. More than a decade later, Pooler is still at it; the company staffs six brokers. Hinckley's real estate, like its yachts, rests on the high end of the market. Listings feature waterfront and island land as well as homes that can go for more than $2 million.

Hinckley also does seasonal rentals on the island (see our Summer Rentals chapter).

Maine as a whole has 600 official child-care centers and about 2,700 family day-care homes.

Child Care

When it comes to caring for our children, people in Maine's Mid-Coast region like to think in terms of home, though not necessarily our own homes — nannies, au pairs and steady babysitters are uncommon in rural Maine. So are day-care centers. Maine as a whole has 600 official child-care centers and about 2,700 family day-care homes. These are programs set up in people's basements or family rooms, usually with no more than a dozen children. One of our kids grew up with a woman who launched a licensed day care when her best friend had a baby. She found about six to eight more children of similar age, got registered and licensed, and put all her energy into caring for the children — so much that when the group reached school age, she couldn't bear the separation and changed careers. We like that intense involvement. Many another parent goes into the day-care business to tide them over their own children's preschool years. They'll stay at home for eight or nine years until the last child starts school, then move on. In other words, these home-based centers do come and go, but they're not at all fly-by-night.

They also don't advertise. But they do have some publicity — through a publicly funded child-care referral system that is organized by county. As a parent looking for child care, you can call up the county office, explain your needs (maybe you're looking for someone to watch your toddler three mornings and one afternoon a week), and the referral center will get back to you in a few days with as many as three providers that might be able to accommodate your requirements. If nothing pans out, they'll try again. (If your need is immediate, let them know — they might be able to speed things up.) For the traveling parent or occasional worker, the referral service will also let you know who in the area offers a drop-in service for children on an irregular basis.

This referral service is free, but it does not provide recommendations. It's more like a clearinghouse of state certified day-care centers.

While in the past there were two tiers of home care, registered homes and a more rigorous tier of licenced home care, by July 1998 all family day-care homes — homes in which from three to 12 children are cared for — will have to be certified by the Department of Human Services (Child and Family Services, 221 State Street, Augusta, ME 04330, 287-5060). If there are 13 or more children, the home becomes a day-care center and must follow those regulations.

As of press time, the rules for certification of family day-care homes had not been determined. The Department of Human Services will, however, oversee such issues as the provider's knowledge of CPR; health and safety of children, staff and premises; and background checks of providers to be sure that there have been no run-ins with child protective services. In addition to initial inspections by a fire marshal and the human services department, all providers will be subject to ongoing safety inspections.

Providers at day-care centers caring for 13 or more children have still stricter rules, including experience and training. And if the child-care center has more than 20 children, the director must have even more training and/or child-care experience. For facilities with more than 50 children, the director must have satisfactorily completed at least two years of college-level child-development courses.

Whether in a home or a large center, limits to the amount of children who can be cared for vary by age: For instance, one person can care for only four children younger than 2 but as many as 10 children 2 or older (as long as two of the 10 children are school-age). Even in larger centers, infants can never be cared for in groups larger than 12, and the maximum-size group for toddlers up to 3 years old is 15 (with one staff member for every five children). But a group of children ages 3 to 6 can be as large as 30, as long as there are three helpers (one for every 10 children).

Those are the legal parameters, but as parents you may also want to make your own inspections. Drop by unannounced and survey the scene. Check the safety of the place the way you'd check your own house: Are there sharp objects around, or pointed table edges that kids could crack their heads on? Is there an unguarded heater or stove? Are electrical outlets covered? Does the food area look clean? What about the changing area and toilets? Are all children supervised at all times? Is there an outdoor play area? Is it sheltered from the road or other dangers? Are there hidden corners inside or out that your child could escape to? Talk to the other parents: Do their expectations seem similar to yours? Do you detect any misgivings? Also ask about staff turnover: Young children don't make allegiances to places but to people, and there's nothing more distressing to your child, whether infant or kindergartner, than to adjust to a staff member, have that person leave, finally make an adjustment to a new person and then find that person's leaving too.

Check also on the philosophy of the place, and on its ambience. Do the children look happy? Are there books around? Do children have free access to them? Are there blocks? Art supplies? Musical instruments? Is the television on whenever you come in? Is it given altar-like prominence? Is there bedlam whenever you stop by? Or is it quiet . . . too quiet.

Most importantly, do you feel comfortable with the provider? Here you must trust your instincts. As parents, you have your styles, your expectations, your values. You and your child will be best served when you find a sympathetic provider, someone you can talk to about Johnny's nightmares and Sally's current rebellion, someone who understands both you and the child. But also remember your day-care provider is not a parent, not your child's total influence, so this is a good time for balance. Your child might grow up more well-rounded and more accepting if given the opportunity to have varied experiences.

As for specific child-care needs, you will find some home-based centers amenable to drop-in care, depending upon how full they are, but it might be easiest to go through the referral organizations to find them. Expect to pay between $75 and $110 weekly for 40 to 50 hours of child care. Of course you'll pay less for shorter hours, but it won't always be prorated. Some centers have subsidized care and can offer rates on a sliding scale.

Sick-child centers have not yet come to Maine. If you need that service, see the subsequent sections for a rundown of people who will come to your home or hotel.

We did find one general clearinghouse for many child-care needs in the form of Family Connections Inc. (see subsequent entry), Simon Road, Waldoboro, 832-2248. This non-profit organization is run by Marcia O'Reilly.

> **FYI**
>
> Unless otherwise noted, the area code for all phone numbers listed in this guide is 207.

Are you interested in a nanny? Family Connections will place nannies in homes throughout the state and will provide continued support for them, assuring the happiness of child and child-care worker. Because rates vary so greatly, generally parents come to O'Reilly with an idea of what they can afford, and she tries to accommodate their budget.

Do you need a very reliable babysitter immediately? For a week? Family Connections also offers an "In a Pinch" service that has found sitters for from a day to a week — or even just a marriage-saving weekend. Though 90 percent of the business of "In a Pinch" has been in southern Maine — O'Reilly generally works only as far north as Winterport — she assures us that her statewide connections with qualified sitters are so good that she may be of use to people needing good sitters anywhere in the Mid-Coast region (though the earlier you contact her, the better). Family Connections charges no fee for referrals to child-care centers but does charge for nanny-finding and "In a Pinch."

Referral Services

Referral services are organized by county. The following services cover Maine's Mid-Coast. Each is a state-certified agency, and each will refer you to centers in the county it covers.

Waldoboro to Stockton Springs

Child Care Resource Development Center
32 Hennessey Ave., Brunswick
• 725-2413, (800) 675-2413

This center is open 9 AM to 3 PM Monday through Friday. It covers Sagadahoc and Lincoln counties and the Brunswick portion of Cumberland County. (If you're looking in Waldoboro, call here first; Waldoboro is just over the line into Lincoln County.)

Child Care Resources of Waldo County
Maine Hwy. 137, Waldo • 342-5535

This center is open 8 AM to 4:30 PM Monday through Friday. It covers Waldo County, which is where Belfast and Searsport are located.

Coastal Community Action Program
7 High St., Rockland • 594-5342

This center is open 7:30 AM to 4 PM Monday through Friday. It covers Knox County, where Rockland, Rockport and Camden are located.

Family Connections Inc.
Simon Rd., Waldoboro • 832-2248

Marcia O'Reilly runs this nonprofit agency that takes care of all kinds of child-care needs as well as the needs of child-care providers (see previous section). She also offers referrals for family day-care homes and child-care centers from southern Maine to Waldo County.

Inland to Bangor

Child Care Services Division of Penquis CAP (Community Access Program)
120 Cleveland Ave., Bangor • 941-2840, 941-2853

This center is open 9 AM to 1 PM Monday through Friday. It covers Penobscot County, where Bangor is located.

Bucksport to Gouldsboro/ Mount Desert Island

Child Care Opportunities in Hancock County
Cross St., Ellsworth • 667-2467

This center is open 8:30 AM to 4:30 PM from Monday through Friday. It covers Hancock County, which includes Mount Desert Island, and also offers counseling to parents on how to look for child care.

Babysitting Services

Want to go out for a night? Word of mouth is the best source for babysitters. If you're visiting or new to the region, it's hard to get into the loop. If you're traveling, for instance, you might ask at your hotel. Does it offer babysitting services? Do staff members at the hotel have kids? If so, who watches their children? Or are they young folks themselves? Would they like to moonlight? If all else fails, go for the tried-and-true methods: Go to a local playground, select a few exemplary parents and see if they can recommend a sitter; call the local school, if it's in session; or try the local YMCA. Bulletin boards sometimes advertise babysitters — not as reliable as a personal referral, but you can always ask for references.

Child-care Centers

The previously mentioned referral services will help direct you to child-care centers if that's your desire. So will we. Following are some of the major centers in the area. Remember, these are referrals, not recommendations. All are open Monday through Friday only. Many centers offer sliding-scale fees or have subsidized slots. Be sure to ask.

Waldoboro to Stockton Springs

Coastal Child Care Center
64 Summer St., Rockland • 594-2591

Children ages 2½ to 5 are cared for at

the Coastal Child Care Center in Rockland. The program is open from 6:30 AM to 5:30 PM Monday through Friday. A head teacher and a staff of three take care of as many as 25 children (though generally only 18 are at the center at any given time). Together, the four care providers have been at the center for about 25 years.

The program is center-based, meaning there are several things for children to focus on during free play, including blocks, books, music, dramatic play, a water table and a sand table. Each week the center chooses a theme of focus, which might be as simple as a color, one color per week. Play, crafts and science experiments are centered around the theme.

The playground is large, with a shady and a sunny side. There's a barn-like old garage outside offering shelter but fresh air in bad weather.

The center is housed in an old duplex with two large rooms on each floor. Children can float through the rooms; staff members follow.

There is sometimes a waiting list here.

Penobscot Bay Medical Center Child Care Center
U.S. Hwy. 1, Glen Cove • 596-8700, 596-8702

Penobscot Bay Medical Center has a large center providing care for as many as 73 children, ranging in age from 6 weeks to 5 years, from 6:30 AM to 5:30 PM Monday through Friday. Priority goes to children of hospital staff members.

The children are divided by age; the day, divided by structured and unstructured activities. This center's staff emphasizes learning through hands-on activities.

There is one infant room, a room for 1-year-olds, a room for 2-year-olds and a pre-school program for children ages 3 to 5. A staff of 20 full- and part-time employees care for the children, with three consistent primary-care people in each room. These folks have been at the center for at least six years. The others work part of the day or on a per-diem basis.

The older groups have weekly lesson plans organized by teachers, with daily activities such as circle time, art projects and cooking. The philosophy is to expose the children to as many experiences as possible and to educate through play while providing a warm, nurturing environment.

The center's large playground is divided between younger and older children, with age-appropriate apparatus in each area. Rooms are divided into learning centers, with a block area, library, dramatic-play area, housekeeping area, science and discovery area and art area.

There is often a waiting list, and reservations for infants are taken a year in advance. There are some drop-in slots, depending on the day.

Y-Care
YMCA, 50 Chestnut St., Camden • 236-3375

At Camden's YMCA, 25 children ages $2\frac{1}{2}$ to 6 can be cared for from 7 AM to 5:30 PM Monday to Friday. There's a staff of three, some of whom change frequently. Because the Y does not have outdoor space, children take advantage of local playgrounds, including those at nearby Elm Street School. The Y offers a focus on independence, gender-neutral play and a choice of "centers," including art, blocks, pretend and discovery, as well as some pre-academics. Part-time slots sometimes open up.

Belfast Area Children's Center
Maine Hwy. 137, Belfast • 342-5535

Recently built facilities — with high ceilings, large windows and innovative play areas — and a well-trained, caring staff mark the Belfast Area Children's Center. On any given day, about 47 children from infants through age 5 are cared for by 14 full-time and about four part-time workers from 7 AM to 5 PM Monday through Friday.

The facility here is tremendous, with tree house-like hideouts inside and a large play area set back in the woods outside.

The philosophy is to provide child-oriented, developmentally appropriate child care with a lot of hands-on experience for the kids. Children are helped to help themselves. In addition to the four classrooms, there is a one-on-

one resource room for therapy, especially for developmentally challenged children.

All fees are offered on a sliding-scale basis, but there is almost always a waiting list for this center.

Starrett Children's Center
73 Waldo Ave., Belfast • 338-1751

The Starrett Children's Center is licensed for 24 but prefers the intimacy of from 16 to 18 children (depending on age). This is a relatively quiet center, with a Montessori-like respect for children's interests and for letting children develop their own fascination and creativity. Art supplies are always within reach, pet animals hang out in cages and tanks, and a large block room allows children to build all sorts of creations. Outside is a small play yard with access to the larger playground of an adjacent elementary school after school hours.

Children ages 2½ through 10 attend (the older kids come for after-school programs). There are two full-time staff members who have been on board for years, one part-time person and several volunteers. The center is open from 7:30 AM to 5 PM Monday through Friday.

Inland to Bangor

Bangor Hilltop School
218 Ohio St., Bangor • 945-3705

At this large center, 87 children ages 2½ to 5 are cared for in various groups: two groups of 3-year-olds, with about 10 to 13 children per group; four groups of 4- and 5-year-olds; and a kindergarten program. The center is open from 6:30 AM to 5:30 PM.

There are 12 full-time staff members plus part-time staff. Staff turnover is low among full-time staffers.

Since 1975, the center has been housed in a three-story building with seven different rooms. The philosophy here is to provide for the child's health, safety and social and emotional growth while also offering a rich and stimulating environment.

The week is organized by themes applied to both free play and more organized activities. There's a library, a physical education room and a playground with four areas, including a cabin, woods and trees marked for climbing.

There is sometimes a waiting list; priority is given to maintaining a gender balance.

Building Blocks Inc.
200 Hogan Rd., Bangor • 947-5117

Housed in the United Technology Center, Building Blocks Inc. has been open since 1995, serving children of state employees and a few kids whose parents don't work for the state. Currently, there are 46 children ages 6 weeks to 6 years. Hours are 6:30 AM to 5:30 PM Monday through Friday. The center also has a certified kindergarten program. There are 11 full-time and five part-time staff members. Rooms are divided into infant, toddler, preschool and kindergarten groups.

As children grow older, they are offered a more structured and academically focused environment. For toddlers, the center focuses on socialization issues, such as using words rather than gestures. Older kids work on sitting in one place and on pre-academics such as numbers and letters. The overall philosophy is that children are individuals who need to be respected and must learn how to make choices. As much as possible, children learn by doing here.

The center is in an open space with small dividers to keep areas intimate. Free time comprises about two-thirds of the child's time, with projects and small-group activities and large-group circle time composing the remaining third.

Outside are two playgrounds: one close to the building for younger children, and a large open field with playground equipment for older children.

There is frequently a waiting list here.

Penquis Child Care Center
120 Cleveland St., Bangor • 941-2841
Job Core Site
1375 Union St., Bangor • 990-1682

These two centers are run by the Penquis Child Care Resources. Both offer a substantial amount of subsidized child care for those who meet minimum requirements. Both centers are open from 7:30 AM to 5:30 PM Monday through Friday, and each takes about 40 children. The philosophy at each center is to offer children firsthand experience in a safe, warm atmosphere. Staff turnover is low at both centers, and many children attend the center for several years as well.

The only difference between the two centers: Job Core Site takes children from 6-weeks-old to 5 years, while Penquis Child Care Center takes children from ages 2½ to 5 years.

Roots & Wings Day Care
274 Western Ave., Hampden • 862-4595

Roots & Wings Day Care accepts children 6 weeks and older, offering after-school care for school-age children. It is licensed for as many as 24 children, but because it's a relatively new program, it often has space. Hours are 6:30 AM to 5:30 PM Monday through Friday.

The day is broken into a morning of structure and free play, with learning activities such as letters, numbers, music and outdoor play. Materials available during free play include blocks, household-like equipment including a stove, a dress-up center, a castle, books and other toys. Afternoons are less structured, with a lot of time spent outdoors.

University of Maine Children's Center
113 College Ave., Orono • 581-4076

The University of Maine offers a large child-care center with 79 full-time slots for kids ages 6 weeks to 6 years. These are divided into three infant and toddler programs and two preschool programs in two separate locations.

There are 20 full-time staff members plus a number of part-time staffers, including students in the university's child-development program. The programs open at 7:30 AM and close at 5:30 PM Monday through Friday. This center is open only to children of university employees and students as well as children of those meeting income guidelines for subsidized care.

Wing Park Children's Center
412 State St., Bangor • 945-9981

Administered by the Bangor YWCA (see subsequent entry), the Wing Park Children's Center offers care for employees of nearby Eastern Maine Medical Center. It's a large center, with 70 children ages 6 weeks to 5 years, and there are frequent openings that can be filled by the general public. This center includes an infant room, a pre-toddler room, a toddler room and two preschool rooms. Child-to-adult ratios meet state guidelines, and frequently there are fewer children per care-giver then the state requires.

YWCA
17 Second St., Bangor • 941-2808

The YWCA offers several programs for children ranging from infant care (in Wing Park Center; see previous entry) to after-school programs. The basic child-care center is called Discovery House. It serves 90 to 100 children and is open from 6:30 AM to 5:30 PM Monday through Friday for kids 2½ years to kindergarten-age. There's a toddler room, two preschool classrooms and kindercare. All but the toddler rooms have two staff members each, meeting or exceeding state requirements. The philosophy is a focus on the child's total development. Self-esteem is enhanced by featuring the child's positive qualities. Activities are either directed by the teacher or by children, with lots of choices.

Lots for Tots One and Two are the Y's nursery school programs. The two programs each meet from 8:30 to 11:30 AM. Three-year-olds go Tuesday and Thursday; 4- and 5-year-olds go Monday, Wednesday and Friday. One program has 25 children each day; the other has 20 children.

Y-Works is the Y's before- and after-school program. Buses pick children up from Bangor, Brewer, Eddington, East Holden, even farther away. As many as 105 children are cared for in this program. Three days a week, the children choose one of five activities that may include swimming, gym, arts and crafts, quiet activities, etc. The other two days are group days, spent with peers of the same age.

Bucksport to Gouldsboro

Blue Hill Village Day Care
Pleasant St., Blue Hill • 374-5476

The Blue Hill Village Day Care has been open for 13 years; for the past eight it's been in an old chapel next to the First Baptist Church in Blue Hill. With a staff of two, the center cares for up to 12 children ages 2 to 5 from 7 AM to 5 PM Monday through Friday.

The focus is on learning through play, with the day including free play, art activities, circle time, theme work, finger play and outdoor activities. Outside, there's a barn-like playhouse with a swing set, sandbox, bikes and a small slide.

Castine Community Child Development Center
Perkins St., Castine • 326-0600

A dozen children from 18 months to school-age are cared for in the two rooms of the Castine Community Child Care Development Center, which is in an old stone church not far from the harbor. The center is open from 7:30 AM to 5 PM Monday through Friday. The working philosophy here is family-oriented, nature-based care. There's no television, few plastic toys and an emphasis on outdoor play in a small playground-area equipped with a play set. There are two full-time and one part-time staffers.

Because Castine is a small town, there are frequently part-time, drop-in slots available. There is also an after-school program.

Live "Y"er
Downeast Family Y, State St., Ellsworth • 667-3086

About 28 children are cared for at this YMCA-based child-care center from 7:30 AM to 5:30 PM Monday through Friday. Children must be 2½ years old and toilet trained to stay at this center. When in 1st grade, they can join the Y's after-school program, held in a local elementary school. The program includes use of the Y's facilities. Children get a swimming lesson once a week, and more lessons are possible. The gym is also available, as is gymnastics. Otherwise, the philosophy enhances curiosity and learning. There are field trips and school readiness programs as well as general play time. Half-time and full-time slots are generally available.

The Kid's Place
Maine Hwy. 15, Deer Isle • 348-2428, 348-2351

The Kid's Place is a day-care center at a nursing home. Day-care providers give priority to children of the nursing home's workers, but there are also slots for community residents. The children have a separate room in the facility with their own play and sleeping areas, but the day is organized for frequent interaction with the nursing home residents. Children go to the nursing home for songs, games and celebrations; residents come to the day care for story hours. This is truly an inter-generational experience.

Photo: Bangor Daily News

Giant sunflowers grow skyward during the summer months in Maine.

The Kid's Place is licensed for 25 children from 8 weeks old to kindergarten-age. It is open from 7 AM to 5 PM Monday through Friday. Because there are a lot of part-time children, there are often part-time slots open.

Mount Desert Island

Kid's Corner
81 Mt. Desert St., Bar Harbor • 288-9503

On a triangular corner as you enter the town of Bar Harbor, Kid's Corner offers day care for about 38 children, infants to kindergarten-age, from 6:30 AM to 5:30 PM Monday through Friday. There are 12 full- and part-time teachers on staff.

The philosophy here is a child-centered, play-oriented approach, with children being offered activity choices and clear, simple rules. Teachers talk with and observe the children. There is a lot of opportunity for art and other forms of expression, but the day's activity depends upon the season, the weather, the composition of the group and the children. Kid's Corner also has three age-appropriate outdoor playgrounds for infants, toddlers and preschoolers.

There is frequently a waiting list here.

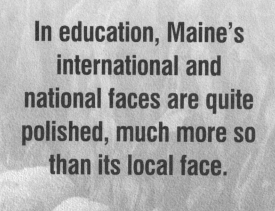

In education, Maine's international and national faces are quite polished, much more so than its local face.

Education

Tell a glassblower in Austria, a photographer in Japan, an ecologist in Brazil, a cellist in Australia or a boat builder in the Netherlands that you are traveling to Maine, but don't be surprised if they've already been here. Places such as Haystack Mountain School of Crafts, Maine Photographic Workshops, Kneisel Hall, WoodenBoat School and College of the Atlantic have such reputations for excellence and innovation that they draw people from around the world.

In education, Maine's international and national faces are quite polished, much more so than its local face. Maine's public schools are striving to make an impact on a population that at times needs a great deal of special services. Parent illiteracy can be a problem in some districts; so can a mistrust of book learning. In a state that, until recently, lived off the land, the woods and the water, how well a child knew the three R's mattered considerably less than the three S's: soil, sea and sky. Notions like that change slowly, but more and more families are realizing the necessity of at least a high school diploma. Maine's 4th-grade reading scores are among the nation's best. The state's upper-grade math scores have been too. The high school dropout rate has been reduced statewide to 2.92 percent (a bit lower in the Mid-Coast area). But still, only about 58 percent of Maine students go on to higher education. In some Mid-Coast districts, that number is as low as 50 percent; in other districts, it's beyond 75 percent.

The Mid-Coast area includes some of the best public schools in the state: Camden-Rockport, Bangor, Orono, Ellsworth, Blue Hill and Mount Desert Island all have stellar high schools as measured by test scores, activities and college admissions. Other districts stand out in other ways. For instance, a little multi-age classroom at the Searsport Elementary School is getting national recognition for its use of Howard Gardner's theory of multiple intelligences (in which all children's achievements are recognized, whether they be in mathematics, rhythm or turning somersaults). In two of the past three years, Rockport's elementary school has received Milken Family Foundation National Educator Awards; the Medomak Valley High School of Waldoboro puts on unusually high-quality musicals; and Deer Isle-Stonington students are national chess champions.

You'll also find some excellent private schools in the Mid-Coast region. The Waldorf education method is popular among those who came to Maine for the back-to-the-land movement of the 1970s. In Camden, Blue Hill and, most recently, on Mount Desert Island, philosophically minded souls have created schools that feature the gentle play- and work-oriented ideas of Rudolf Steiner.

Maine's colleges and universities have excellent reputations. The Mid-Coast region boasts the University of Maine in Orono, the Maine Maritime Academy in Castine, and College of the Atlantic in Bar Harbor. These institutions could hardly be more diverse. UM is large and multi-disciplined, with a huge campus inland. MMA continues the Maine maritime heritage, populating Castine with seamen who are trained to ship out around the world. COA, elegantly situated on Frenchman Bay, offers a degree in only one subject, human ecology, to all its 250 students.

Maine has long been a popular site for children's summer camps. Most are inland, but we'll tell you about a few in the Mid-Coast area.

Then there are the workshops, something of a summer camp for adults — delightful and intensive. Come to Maine in summer to learn how to smith or blow glass, build a boat, shoot a movie, photograph children, make furniture or practice, practice, practice as a musician. Come if you are an amateur wanting to learn a new craft, a novice needing a boost, or a professional looking to experiment in a parallel career field.

Finally, if you are older than 62 and wish to spend a learning vacation on the coast of Maine, write Elderhostel, 75 Federal Street, Boston, MA 02110. Maine locales, such as the Hersey Retreat in Stockton Springs and the Tanglewood 4-H Camp in Lincolnville, host several sessions each summer.

Public Education

Most Maine school districts cross town lines, and some even cross county lines. To administer them, the state has established a few different kinds of associations. Cities and large towns operate school departments. Groups of towns pooling their resources to educate students comprise School Administrative Districts (with the unfortunate acronym SAD). School Unions are looser and less common: Individual towns have their own school boards but share the cost of a superintendent. Rather than have a common high school, these towns frequently offer a set amount of tuition to students to attend school in a district of their choice.

Like many states across the nation, Maine has established educational standards through the federally funded Goals 2000 program. Maine's standards are called Learning Results. Before graduating, students must demonstrate competency in eight academic areas: English language arts; modern and classical languages; social studies; mathematics; science and technology; visual and performing arts; health and physical education; and career preparation.

While the state is developing its own standards, individual districts are as well. With the help of a $1.5 million federal grant, district administrators are meeting with community members, business leaders, teachers and students to determine what students need to learn now to be full participants in the 21st century.

For a time, all Maine schools were required to offer gifted-and-talented programs and a full range of art education. But, since the recession of the late 1980s, such requirements have been waived. A few devoted schools still offer gifted-and-talented programs. Others, recognizing the need for art education, continue to offer complete art and music curricula. Maine schools have one of the most comprehensive online networks in the country, with Internet and e-mail access in most school libraries and many classrooms — some beginning in kindergarten. Internet access comes from a deal worked out with NYNEX (the phone company) in early 1996, after NYNEX was caught overcharging Maine customers. As repayment, NYNEX agreed to establish a statewide telecommunications network, the Maine School Library Network (MSLN).

Every Maine school child is required to take a Maine Educational Assessment (MEA) test in grades 4, 8 and 11 to gauge his/her level of proficiency in reading, writing, math, science and social sciences relative to peers in the same school and statewide. Though these test scores are not intended to be used to rank schools, they nonetheless paint a picture of differences among systems.

Unfortunately, the health of a school system rides on the wealth of a district. Stand-out schools generally are in wealthy and/or well-populated areas. But the correlation isn't totally consistent. If you're moving to the Mid-Coast area and school systems are a concern, talk to other parents, check out MEA scores, or make an appointment with the principal. A good principal can make a major difference in motivating teachers and helping a school progress.

Following is a district-by-district rundown of public schools in our Mid-Coast region, including respective phone numbers.

FYI

Unless otherwise noted, the area code for all phone numbers listed in this guide is 207.

Waldoboro to Stockton Springs

In SAD 40, 832-5358, the high school is in Waldoboro, but the school district also includes Friendship, Union, Warren and Washington — serving about 2,450 students. Each town has its own elementary school; Warren's elementary school is divided into two schools (K through 2nd grade; 3rd through 6th grade). In grade 6, students from most towns are bussed to the middle school in Waldoboro; Union, the exception, retains its own middle school. The one district high school is Medomak Valley High School. It's known for its drama program, for exuberant and well-crafted productions of anything from *On the Town* to *A Midsummer Night's Dream*.

Thomaston, up U.S. Highway 1, is the location of the high school for SAD 50, 354-2555, a long, narrow district stretching 15 miles and spanning both banks of the St. George River as it widens near Muscongus Bay. SAD 50 encompasses Cushing on the western bank, St. George on the eastern and Thomaston where the two peninsulas nearly join. The five schools in the district serve fewer than 1,200 students. St. George's school serves children through grade 8. Cushing students go to the local elementary school but at grade 5 are bussed to the Thomaston Grammar School in Thomaston. All students are served by Georges Valley High School, which is most proud of its students' high reading scores. In 1997, about 50 percent of graduates went on to post-secondary education.

SAD 5, 596-6620, is centered in Rockland. It covers a relatively modest area geographically, encompassing roughly 50 square miles and including South Thomaston, Owls Head and Rockland. Some 1,500 students are served. This small district incudes a surprising number of schools. Students in Owls Head and nearby South Thomaston all begin school in South Thomaston. At grade 3 they switch to Owls Head. Rockland elementary schools also are divided, with students entering a new school at grade 3. At grade 6, all students attend the Rockland District Middle School; at grade 9, Rockland High School. Come September, students in grades 6 through 8 will attend the brand-new Rockland District Middle School. The high school is known for its drama, mathematics and music departments as well as for recent state championships garnered in golf and boys and girls basketball.

Offshore, Vinalhaven and North Haven each have their own (small) school districts. Vinalhaven, SAD 8, 863-4800, teaches its 200 students in one building divided into a K-through-6 school and Vinalhaven High School (grades 7 through 12). Because of the school's

size, students get a lot of faculty attention. Thirty teachers serve on staff.

North Haven, SAD 7, 867-4707, is even smaller. Its 80 students attend one school, North Haven Community School, from kindergarten through grade 12. They are served by a teaching staff of 20, including electives. North Haven students have reaped the rewards of living on an island with a strong summer community. Folks who have summered here for years were so entranced by recent drama productions that they offered the young actors a whirlwind New York theater vacation. Some island families, however, were displeased by the focus on drama and other arts, launching a statewide drama all its own by attempting to dismiss the art-supporting principal, Barney Hallowell. As of press time, he seems to have held on, but the arguments have caused a breach in the community.

The Camden-Rockport school district, SAD 28, 236-3358, has been twice-blessed by Milken Family Foundation grants to the Rockport Elementary School. The grants are awarded annually — two per state — by merit, and it's unusual for the same school to receive them in succession. The district has four school buildings, including two elementary schools, a middle school and the Camden-Rockport High School. The Elm Street School, on U.S. Highway 1 as you enter Camden from the south, is a historic building that serves kindergartners and 2nd-graders only; all children in SAD 28 go to Rockport Elementary for grades 1, 3, 4 and 5. Since the school also has multi-age classrooms, some also go for kindergarten and 2nd grade. The middle and high schools are in Camden.

The 1,500 students in the district are served by approximately 130 teachers. The high school is experimenting with mentors (students spend some time outside the school with community members). The school district as a whole is relatively well-off financially, which might explain why the district has retained an excellent gifted-and-talented program, called Horizons, and a broad selection of after-school activities including athletics, creative writing and other arts such as industrial arts. About 74 percent of students go on to higher education. The district's enrollment has mushroomed, so that Rockport Elementary is a maze of trailers and temporary housing. Pending all necessary approvals, a new high school will be built on Maine Highway 90 in Rockport to open in the year 2000, easing current crowded conditions.

Lincolnville Central School, 763-3366, is an anomaly here. Neither a school union nor a school district, Lincolnville simply runs one K-through-8 school in one building for a current student body of 235. It offers the option of one multi-age classroom for grades 3, 4 and 5 plus a gifted-and-talented program.

Moving offshore again, the Islesboro School, Alumni Drive, 734-2251, serves 106 students in grades K through 12. Islesboro School has about eight or nine students per grade and offers several multi-age classes. Despite its isolation on the island, this school housed in an old mansion offers art, music and honors classes. Students participate in state science fairs and intramural sports. Athletes venture off-island for basketball, soccer, hockey and other games. (If the teams are too late for the ferry, they hitch a ride on a Coast Guard-certified private boat.) At least 90 percent of students go on to college.

SAD 34, 338-1960, is a large district, encompassing five towns and one city and serving 2,000 students in 10 schools (eight elementary schools, a middle school and a high school). The high school, Belfast District High School, is in Belfast; elementary schools are in Northport, Morrill, Searsmont, Swanville, East Belfast and Belfast. All elementary schools are split (grades K through 2 or 3 and grades 2 or 3 through 5), except for the K-through-5 Drinkwater School in Northport.

Belfast Community's Outreach Program in Education (BCOPE), 338-6456, an alternative high school down the block from the larger high school, serves 40 students. BCOPE is geared to those students who don't function well in a conventional high school setting.

Belfast District High School has won state championships in football, field hockey, gymnastics and wrestling. The school also has benefited somewhat from the opening of a large credit-card company processing center

in town: MBNA has offered incentives to employees who volunteer at the school for a certain number of hours each month. Currently, only about half the district's high school graduates go on to higher education.

Farther up U.S. 1, SAD 56, 548-6643, is another widespread district, spanning at least 15 miles along U.S. highways 1 and 1A and serving about 900 students in five schools. Each of the three towns in this district — Searsport, Stockton Springs and Frankfort — has an elementary school. The middle school and Searsport District High School are in Searsport. Elementary schools run from kindergarten through grade 5; middle school includes grades 6 through 8.

This is not a wealthy district, but Searsport Elementary School is gaining some attention for its dedication to Howard Gardner's theories of the seven intelligence areas — logical-mathematical, linguistic, kinesthetic, spatial, musical, social and emotional — that each child draws from as both a learner and a participant. The school has a strong arts program. Artistic and physical activities are incorporated into classroom learning, thus children can draw or act out book reports as well as write them.

In 1997, however, after taxpayers turned down a request from the district to fund a new facility, Searsport District High School lost its accreditation. Students are now literally taking to the streets to raise money for needed improvements in hope of winning back their regional accreditation. Of the 1997 class, nearly 70 percent (33 of 48) sought advanced instruction, either in the military, a two-year college, a vocational-technical institute or a four-year college.

Inland to Bangor

SAD 22, 862-3255, has seven schools spanning two counties - Waldo and Penobscot. It serves 2,350 students. In the Hampden area, Hampden Academy (high school) serves students from Hampden, Winterport and Newburgh, west of Winterport. SAD 22 also has two middle schools — one in Hampden and one in Winterport — and four elementary schools. The Hampden elementary school is divided age-wise into two schools, with 3rd-graders attending an upper primary school; the Newburgh elementary school continues through grade 5.

Hampden Academy sends about half its students through a college-preparatory curriculum with a focus on either behavioral sciences or science and engineering. The remainder of its students go through a technical-preparatory curriculum. There is also an alternative education program at the high school serving about 18 at-risk students.

Specialized classes, such as the bible and myth, psychology, publishing and architectural drawing, are part of the behavioral-science program.

The Bangor School Department, 945-4400, serves the 4,500 students in Bangor. There are 10 schools: seven elementary schools, two middle schools and Bangor High School. The elementary schools are all divided by age, so students attend one school from kindergarten through grade 3 and another for grades 4 and 5. Then, students attend one of the two middle schools for grades 6 through 8. Elementary-school classes have a 20-to-1 student-teacher ratio. The entire school department has a strong gifted-and-talented program beginning in lower elementary grades. In 4th grade, a program of accelerated classes begins. Throughout the system, students pursue special projects, like architectural reviews of the city, the building of electric racing cars, Math Olympiads and Odyssey of the Mind.

Bangor High School has an excellent reputation, with scores on the Maine Educational Assessment tests running 10 to 20 percent above the Maine average.

School Union 87, 866-5521, includes Orono and Veazie, two separate school departments with a total of 1,200 students, all of whom feed into Orono High School. There are three schools in the district: Veazie has an elementary school; Orono has an elementary school and a combined middle and high school. Education is particularly important here: The schools serve many children of University of Maine faculty. Orono High School has a roster of excellent writers and scholars on its faculty, among them novelist Sanford Phippen; it also features an orchestra — un-

usual for such a small high school. Its student-athletes have won state championships in several sports, including field hockey, football and both boys and girls basketball.

Orono High School has instituted an innovative service learning project, developed throughout the first three years of high school, in which students design and complete a community-service endeavor with the help of mentors. About 75 percent of graduates go on to higher education.

The Brewer School Department, 989-3160, serves 2,000 students in six schools. There are four elementary schools. Each school serves a different age group, so all students attend all schools. There's a school for kindergarten and transitional K-grade 1; a school for grades 1 and 2; another for grades 3 and 4; one for grade 5; a middle school; and a high school. Brewer High School has a strong AP program. About 66 percent of students go on to post-secondary education.

School Union 91, 469-2331, is an anomaly in the Maine school districting system. The union serves Orrington and Orland, towns connected by letters (O and R), but by neither geography nor county. Orrington is in Penobscot County; Orland in Hancock County. Between them is Bucksport, not a part of the union, though the union's offices are there. We'll talk about Orrington now. For Orland, see the subsequent "Bucksport to Gouldsboro" section.

Orrington has two schools, a K-through-5 school and the Center Drive School (grades 6 through 8), serving a combined 420 students. The Center Drive School has a strong volunteer program. The school, with multi-age classes, also has received attention for its excellent Maine Studies program, taking students on ambitious field trips and overnight camping trips. The program is also responsible for the dramatic mural on a barn on Maine Highway 15 in Orrington, depicting the rural history of the state. Students repainted the mural in 1997.

Because the union has no high school, students may go to any school they choose. The Town of Orrington pays each child's tuition — up to $5,400 to attend a private school or $4,900 for a public school. The town also offers transportation to the two schools most commonly chosen by its students: Brewer High School and John Bapst Memorial High School, a private high school in Bangor (see subsequent entry in our "Private Schools" section).

Bucksport to Gouldsboro

The Bucksport School Department, 469-7311, serves Bucksport as well as the students of school-less SAD 18, composed of long, narrow Verona Island (in the middle of the Penobscot River) and Prospect (across the Penobscot River in Waldo County). There are more than 1,300 students at four schools: two elementary schools (grades K through 3 and grades 4 through 6); a junior high school for grades 7 and 8; and a high school for grades 9 through 12. Look for the work of art teachers and students in the waterfront mural or inside MacLeod's Restaurant (see our Restaurants chapter), and look for the children's video about ghost houses of the region in the archives of Northeast Historic Films (see our Arts chapter). The school is proud of its emphasis on continuous student improvement. About 70 percent of students plant to pursue post-secondary education.

We're back to School Union 91, 469-2331, this time in Orland, where 271 students attend grades K through 8 at Orland Consolidated School. As in Orrington (see previous section), the town pays tuition for students to attend high school out of the area (commonly known as being "tuitioned out," and, conversely, "tuitioned in"). The union offers students transportation to George Stevens Academy, a public-private school in Blue Hill (see subsequent information), or Bucksport High School in Bucksport.

On the Blue Hill Peninsula, Union 93, 374-9927, is composed of four K-through-8 schools serving 600 students in Castine, Penobscot, Brooksville and Blue Hill. Each has its strong points. Blue Hill has an excellent arts curriculum. Recently, the Blue Hill Consolidated

School got involved in asking 3rd graders to take the oral histories of seniors, create plays from the information and perform them for the public. In Castine, each student works on his or her own educational plan, thereby allowing each student, from special-education to gifted-and-talented, to get what he or she needs. Students are tuitioned out for high school; most attend George Stevens Academy.

School Union 76, 348-7777 serves Deer Isle, Stonington, Brooklin and Sedgwick. Deer Isle and Stonington, both on the island of Deer Isle, comprise a community school district of about 550 students. They share two elementary schools, sending students to Deer Isle village for grades K through 2 and to Stonington for grades 3 through 6. The junior and senior high schools are currently in one building; there are plans to build a new K-through-8 school. As of press time, the decision was to put the school in Deer Isle, next to the current junior-senior high school, but those in Stonington, farther down the island, are miffed enough to make that decision still an uncertainty. Brooklin, with just fewer than 100 students, and Sedgwick, with just more than 100 students — both of which face Deer Isle across Eggemoggin Reach — have their respective K-through-8 schools.

Students in Deer Isle go to the local Deer Isle-Stonington High School whose champion chess team placed among the top-three teams nationally in 1996. In 1997, both an elementary team and the high school team competed at the nationals. Students in Sedgwick and Brooklin have an option for high school. Some tuition in at George Stevens Academy (see subsequent entry) in Blue Hill, others at the Deer Isle-Stonington High School on the island or at the fledgling Liberty School (see subsequent entry), also in Blue Hill.

School Union 96, 422-3522, has five schools in an area encompassed by the broad Schoodic Peninsula. Its 1,200 students attend K-through-8 schools in Gouldsboro, Winter

Photo: Bangor Daily News

Two students sit under a shade tree at the University of Maine in Orono.

Harbor, Steuben and Sullivan, where about 360 attend Sumner Memorial High School. Most students in Union 96 go to Sumner High.

The union is part of a state program known as Jobs for Maine Graduates, in which children are given experience in the job market by interning in local businesses for part of the day during part of the school year. About 50 percent of Union 96's students go on to post-secondary education.

Mount Desert Island

The Mount Desert Island School Department, 288-5049, serves nine schools, including eight K-through-9 schools, four of which are on remote islands.

Let's talk about the remote islands first. The largest island school is Swans Island, with 43 students served by three teachers. Islesford, also known as Little Cranberry, has 19 stu-dents and two teachers. Frenchboro, the most distant of the islands, has four students and one teacher. Then there's Great Cranberry Island whose two students barely outnumber their one teacher.

Back on Mount Desert Island, the system serves the rest of the 1,880 students with elementary schools in Bar Harbor, Mount Desert, Tremont and Southwest Harbor. All students, including those from the island who board in town, end up at Mount Desert Island High School. It has an excellent reputation and consistently sends 70 percent of its students to two- or four-year colleges — and recently as many as 85 percent of its students.

Private Schools

Educational theories of Rudolf Steiner and Maria Montessori dominate the philosophy of Maine's private schools. We'll cover the general philosophies first, then talk about individual schools.

Steiner founded the first Waldorf school in Stuttgart, Germany, in 1919. The focus is on feeling and doing as well as learning — engaging heart, head and hand. Children are encouraged to learn about the natural world, to follow the seasons in their celebrations, and to use natural materials in all their play. Young children are told stories and frequently are not taught to read until age 7.

A Montessori education is based on the premise that if you offer children a creative environment filled with materials to spark curiosity, they'll set out on their own explorations. Learning is self-directed and child-paced. Listen to children, listen to their imaginations, say Montessori educators, and they'll tell you what needs to be done. It's a philosophy ultimately built on respecting and trusting each individual. As with many alternative schools, a hands-on approach is basic to all areas of learning.

That said, we should also note that Mainers, feisty and independent as they are, don't always send their children to school at all: About 1.5 percent of the state's student population (3,154 students) is home-schooled. The reasons are as varied as the families who home-school, but frequently it's an accommodation to various limitations of formal schooling: Some ardent Christians keep their children at home so as to offer a more religious education; others use home-schooling as a bridge through the difficult middle school years, or simply to offer a more holistic, home- and family-based environment. Finally, artistic children might be home-schooled so as to afford them more art time. (We know one young woman who spent much of her high school years apprenticed to a children's theater.)

Waldoboro to Stockton Springs

Ashwood Waldorf School
180 Park St., Rockport • 236-8021

One of the best introductions to the Ashwood School is their May Day celebration, held annually on a weekend close to May 1. Amazingly, no one gets tangled up as flower-decked children and adults dance, binding ribbons around the Maypole. There are food sales and craft sales: The food is healthful and the crafts homemade of true wool and cotton.

The Ashwood Waldorf School moved to its permanent home on 15 acres of land in Rockport in 1995. A grand celebration accompanied that move, a homecoming of sorts after being scattered in three locations since it opened in Lincolnville in 1986.

The school now enrolls more than 90 students who are taught in small, multi-age classes. The student-teacher ratio is no greater than 18-to-1. Additional instructors come in to teach German, French, Spanish, chorus, stringed instruments, gym and handwork.

The core curriculum for students of all ages includes language arts, math, history, geography and science. Additional courses include French, German, music, painting, drawing, modeling, drama, handwork, woodwork and physical education. Reading starts in 1st grade and is approached through writing; it's encouraged in 2nd grade, as students write, illustrate and bind their own books. Grade 3 focuses on practical life skills, including farming and house building. Grade 4 includes a study of animal life. In 5th grade, students focus on geography; in 6th grade, geometry and causal relationships in history; and in 7th grade, physical sciences. This year graduates the first 8th-grade class.

Students come from as far south as Boothbay, as far north as Belfast and as far west as Jefferson. Ashwood is a member of the Association of Waldorf Schools of North America.

Children's House Montessori School
205 West St., Rockport • 236-2911

The Children's House Montessori School takes its name from the first school started by Dr. Maria Montessori in 1907 in a desperately poor neighborhood of Rome, Italy. Montessori's ideas have since spread across the globe, coming to rest at the Children's House in Rockport, among other places. The school offers an open, self-directed learning environment to children ages 18 months to 10 years. Annual enrollment averages 120 students.

Stuart Finkelstein still directs the Children's

House program he started as a preschool 18 years ago. The school's toddler program is offered two mornings a week; the preschool program runs three mornings a week. The primary program runs five mornings a week, with the option of an extended day. The school offers two multi-age classes in 1st through 3rd grade. Fourth-graders have their own class.

The school has open classrooms and an individualized curriculum. Lessons are given one-on-one or in small groups. Students do not receive grades. The arts are integral to the curriculum, as is language. Children are offered swimming and gymnastics in addition to other sports.

In 1995, the school bought a 14-acre parcel of land in Rockport. It has since moved into its own large facility with a spacious playground. There are plans to extend its curriculum into grades 5 and, possibly, 6 in 1998. The school also offers before- and after-school care and a summer camp (see our subsequent "Summer Camps" section).

Community School
79 Washington St., Camden • 236-3000

Not every child thrives within the regimen of a traditional high school, public or private. Some of the best and brightest students, some of the most sensitive and creative, are distracted by drugs, alcohol and basic adolescent trouble. The Community School offers a way out of trouble and back to a diploma to a handful of high school dropouts, enrolling about a dozen at-risk kids at a time who are willing to work hard in an intensive, emotion-sensitive learning environment. Created in 1975, the school is the longest-running alternative program in the state.

While it takes only about six months to achieve a Community School diploma, it takes a lot of hard work. Students live together in a large frame house on a Camden side street. They find and hold down jobs during their six months of study and pay tuition with their earnings. They perform social services and care for their home and fellow students through a series of daily chores including a turn or two each week cooking dinner for fellow students and resident faculty. Students must also swear off drugs and alcohol and confront their problems during weekly community (school) meet-

ings. And yes, they also study, mostly at night, after all their daily responsibilities are complete. The idea is to channel a teenager's vast energy to turn an accumulated sense of failure — potentially a huge burden in a 17-year-old's life — into competency.

Admission to Community School is by application.

Riley School
Warrenton Rd., Glen Cove • 596-6405

Developmental theories of Jean Piaget, focusing on the whole child and his or her capacity to learn spontaneously, are what guide the educational philosophy of the Riley School.

The school was founded in 1972 by Glenna Plaisted, who still serves as director. Currently, 70 students in grades pre-K through 9 attend the school. Classes are small, with an average of eight students per teacher.

There are no grades. Students attend the lower, middle or upper school. Twice a year, teachers offer a full portrait of each student. Working with students, a head teacher prepares each child's schedule according to his or her needs and desires.

The focus is on learning by doing and by questioning. Creativity is important, as are responsibility and discipline. Ultimately, the focus is on childhood wonder and play. The curriculum includes reading, writing, comparative literature, science, math, cultural studies and geography. Other subjects include philosophy, computers, humanities, conversational French, beginning Latin, drama, art, music, photography and reflection.

The school spreads out in six buildings over 45 acres of woods, fields and shore on the coast of Penobscot Bay in Glen Cove, near Rockland. Children come to the school from 24 Maine towns, some as far away as Wiscasset, Damariscotta, Appleton and Belfast.

Toddy Pond School
Oak Hill Rd., Swanville • 338-3848

Toddy Pond School, a small alternative school begun in 1979, is housed in a bright, naturally lighted new building with lots of windows. The school is just over the border from East Belfast. The school takes a developmental approach to education, focusing on individualized, cooperative learning, with attention to a student's emotional, creative and physical as well as academic needs. Parental involvement is essential to the school's function. Parents teach some courses and assist with cleaning the facilities.

Rather than instructing children, teachers at Toddy Pond School encourage children to learn. For math class, students might be given counting or estimating problems to solve cooperatively, or be asked to create forms with the series of Oriental shapes known as tangrams.

The curriculum consists of basic reading, writing, math, science, social studies, painting, pottery, drawing, music, dance and drama. Toddy Pond students are known for their chess-playing expertise, having garnered state honors and competing in national competitions.

Classes are arranged in multi-age groups from kindergarten through grade 7. The school's 21 students are taught by two full-time teachers plus a part-time life sports and art teacher. Students come from a wide range of towns around the Belfast area.

Inland to Bangor

John Bapst Memorial High School
100 Broadway, Bangor • 947-0313

There's sometimes a brain-drain from public schools in the greater Bangor area. Many of the best and brightest students opt out of local high schools, electing John Bapst Memorial High School instead. Perhaps its because John Bapst dubs itself "a place to think."

The 467 students at John Bapst come from a 50-mile radius of Bangor for this rigorous but traditional school. Average class size is about 17. This is a college-preparatory school: 90 percent of the students go on to four-year colleges, with an additional 2 to 5 percent going on to two-year colleges. Students consistently score at the top of the Maine Educational Assessment tests. They are also renowned musicians. At President Clinton's invitation, the band performed at his 1997 inauguration. While in Washington, they were asked to give a second performance.

The school offers honors or advanced-placement classes in English, calculus, chemistry, physics, biology, history and Spanish. It also offers art classes, music, creative writing, journalism, psychology, sociology and college-level accounting.

Stillwater Montessori School
775 Stillwater Ave. and S. Brunswick St., Old Town • 827-2404

We've expanded our northern boundaries a bit to include the Stillwater Montessori School, which offers multi-age classes for kids ages 2½ to 12. About 70 students attend Stillwater; many are associated with the University of Maine in Orono. The student-teacher ratio is about 8-to-1. In 1997, the honor of Maine Teacher of the Year was awarded to a teacher here.

FYI

Unless otherwise noted, the area code for all phone numbers listed in this guide is 207.

As with other Montessori schools, Stillwater is child-centered, based on respect for the nature of each child, for others and for the environment. Children work independently and at their own pace for as long as they want in a noncompetitive environment. The idea is that learning is fun and children want to learn.

Hands-on education is fostered through frequent field trips. Specific curriculum elements include language instruction beginning in preschool, environmental and cultural education and a working knowledge of computers and the Internet.

Currently, the school operates in two locations, with kindergarten and preschool in a separate building from the old religious school that houses the elementary grades. School leaders hope to consolidate or to build a new facility elsewhere.

Bucksport to Gouldsboro

The Bay School
Maine Hwy. 172, Blue Hill • 374-2187

Families move to Blue Hill so their children can attend The Bay School. Sometimes, they even leave upscale Mount Desert Island for the school.

The Bay School offers a Waldorf-inspired

education from pre-kindergarten through grade 8. Unlike the Ashwood School in Rockport (see previous entry), the Bay School is not a strict Waldorf School; rather, it derives some of its curriculum and focus from Maine's natural resources. Still, it remains close to the Steiner philosophy of gentle, creative learning by focusing a child's attention on the surrounding world, including daily and seasonal rhythms, nature and natural materials. One of us brought our sleeping child there one night for a meeting when he was about 4 years old. Hearing the soft voices of adults singing a folk song nearby, he awoke, saw the pale blue ceiling painted with rainbows and clouds and started crying. "I've gone to heaven!" he sobbed.

Some 103 students attend this quiet haven — if not heaven — of a school. They come from the Blue Hill Peninsula, Deer Isle, Ellsworth, Mount Desert Island, Orland, even as far away as Milbridge (Downeast) to attend. The Bay School has multi-age classes (pre-kindergarten and kindergarten, grades 1 and 2, grades 3 and 4, and so on). There are seven full-time and seven part-time teachers. Reading and math are introduced in grade 1 utilizing picture books; students move on to chapter books by grades 2 and 3.

The arts are an essential component here. Music, drama, movement and visual arts are taught; creativity in learning is encouraged. Among each child's necessities for the school year is a recorder (that's the instrument, not the electronic gadget). Handwork, especially traditional crafts, also is taught. Languages are introduced at an early age. On a daily basis, children write and draw their day's work into their own book, which ultimately serves as a reflection of the year's growth at school.

George Stevens Academy
Union St., Blue Hill • 374-2808

Housed in an elegant white building in the center of Blue Hill, George Stevens Academy is a private school that serves as the de facto public high school for the town's population. Students living within the auspices of one of the Blue Hill Peninsula's public school unions receive funds from their town to go to George Stevens. Parents from other towns sometimes pay to send their children to George Stevens

because it's such a strong school. As a young published poet who recently graduated from the school explained, "You're in a rural area, and you can take anthropology. I think that's pretty good."

The school was founded in 1803 as Bluehill Academy, the first secondary school east of the Penobscot River. Today, some 400 students attend grades 9 through 12. They are taught by 37 full-time and five part-time instructors. The combination of strong faculty, an open-education policy and interested parents makes this school one of the best in the state and consistently among the top 10 scorers in the Maine Educational Assessment tests. Each year, from 70 to 85 percent of graduates go on to higher education. The 1996 valedictorian went to Harvard; her best friend went to Yale.

George Stevens Academy has a strong arts program. Its yearly arts festival draws artists, musicians, craftspeople, even karate champions to the school for a week of specialized instruction. It also participates in the National Arts Honor Society. The school has a jazz band and jazz combo as well as a steel band (see the related Close-up in our Arts chapter). In athletics, George Stevens Academy has won regional championships in boys baseball and soccer.

Selected students can participate in a two-week independent-study internship in their junior and senior years — a time to focus on their goals.

Liberty School – A Democratic Learning Community
Maine Hwy. 172, Blue Hill • 374-2886

This fledgling school, serving grades 9 through 12, is based on the idea of true democracy: Students help run the school and their own curriculum needs. Arnold Greenburg, a great initiator (he launched two schools in Pennsylvania before moving to Maine to launch the popular Left Bank Cafe; see our Restaurants and Arts chapters), founded Liberty, which opened for the 1997-98 school year. The school struggled to receive state approval (it ultimately did), precisely because it's so student-directed. (State approval is important because it allows towns that tuition students out to other high schools to pay tuition to Liberty School.) Currently, the school enrolls 40 students, taught by six full-time and four part-time teachers.

Mount Desert Island

Chickadee Tree Children's Center
Northeast Harbor • 276-5247

The Acadia Waldorf Association, composed of a group of concerned parents, has been meeting for a few years to organize a school based on Waldorf ideas on Mount Desert Island. Chickadee Children's Center is its fledgling school. During the 1997-98 school year, the school welcomed children ages 3½ to 6 in a three-day nursery school and a five-day kindergarten. Some 30 children attend, led by two teachers in each of the two classrooms. The school plans to grow with its students, though the first year of 1st grade might wait until the 1999-2000 school year.

The school had not yet determined its 1998-99 location as of press time. Call to find out where classes will be held.

Colleges and Universities

Waldoboro to Stockton Springs

Rockport College
2 Central St., Rockport • 236-8581

The widely known and wildly popular Maine Photographic Workshops recently initiated undergraduate and graduate curricula. It now offers a two-year Associate of Arts degree (students may continue elsewhere to pursue a four-year BFA degree) and a Master of Fine Arts (MFA) degree to students interested in pursuing a dedicated program in photography or film and video.

The fledgling college curriculum, described as a conservatory for photography, cinema, writing and digital media, is based on a previous 15-year relationship with the University of Maine, through which the Maine Photographic Workshops previously offered a degree. Currently, 10 students are working toward the MFA

degree, and 28 are in the undergraduate program, a two-year course of study.

Students take both traditional and nontraditional courses. In the college, the first-year curriculum offers a foundation in art, communication studies and history. Classes include communications (speech and writing), history of image making, social systems and power, writing as thinking, and two- and three-dimensional design plus electives in photography and film and video production.

Interested students at other colleges may also elect to pursue an intense semester-long residency at Rockport in the fall or spring, receiving in-depth training in photography, film and digital media (for graphic designers).

The graduate school offers studies in photography, cinematography, film production, writing, directing, editing and acting, digital media, graphic design, and arts administration. Students might be newcomers to the field embarking on a career in communication arts or working professionals pursuing personal mastery, thus attending the Workshops for only the minimum eight weeks each year (see also the subsequent "Workshops" section).

Inland to Bangor

University of Maine
Office of Admissions, Chadbourne Hall, Orono • 581-3743

Maine's university is on a 660-acre parcel of land beside the Stillwater River in Orono, just north of Bangor.

It is the central university for the seven campuses of the UMaine system (the other major campuses are in Fort Kent, Presque Isle, Augusta, Machias, Farmington and Portland). The University of Maine, or UMaine, awards 43 percent of the system's four-year degrees each year, 64 percent of master's degrees and all of the Ph.D.s, Ed.D.s and C.A.S.s.

Some 9,800 students register at the university each year. About 2,000 are graduate students. In addition to Maine residents, students from 43 states and 70 countries attend.

UMaine offers about 80 degrees in five colleges: Business, Public Policy and Health; Education and Human Development; Engineering; Liberal Arts and Sciences; Natural

Students hoist the sail aboard one of the many vessels used by schools that specialize in maritime studies along Maine's coast.

Sciences, Forestry and Agriculture. An honors program is available for first- and second-year students.

UMaine students are engaged in some active, unexpected projects. Engineering students have assisted in important genetics research at Jackson Laboratory on Mount Desert Island by developing an automated chromosome scanning system. Business majors manage a $250,000 portfolio for the University of Maine Foundation. Performance groups participate in concert tours throughout the world. Anthropology and geology students work on local archeological digs.

The Raymond H. Fogler Library, on campus, is the state's largest, with more than 860,000 volumes, 5,400 periodicals and online hookups to the other UMaine system libraries.

The university offers a comprehensive athletic program. The Harold Alfond Sports Arena has hosted numerous championship games. Especially notable are the champion Maine Black Bears hockey team and the women's basketball team featuring legendary point guard Cindy Blodgett, a record-breaking, homegrown roundball phenom (see the related Close-up on Blodgett in our Spectator Sports chapter).

The university is also the state's land- and

sea-grant institution, meaning it is Maine's public research university. To this end, the university has more than 20 active, organized research centers including the Bureau of Labor Education, Cooperative Extension, Franco-American Centre, Institute for Quaternary Studies, Lobster Institute, Maine Agricultural and Forest Experiment Station, Margaret Chase Smith Center for Public Policy, Pulp and Paper Foundation, Wabanaki Center, Water Research Institute and Women's Resource Center.

A full season of music, theater and dance takes place at the university's elegant Maine Center for the Arts (see our Arts chapter). The surrounding community has flocked to the center for opera, symphonies, circuses, dance performances, even for folk legend Bob Dylan. The auditorium borders the university's excellent Hudson Museum (see Arts), whose collection includes art and artifacts from around the world. The three-story museum remains open during arts performances, offering patrons an additional attraction.

University performers have access to the new School of Performing Arts, a $6 million state-of-the-art facility. Students keep these facilities active with Maine Masque performances of William Butler Yeats' *On Baile's*

Strand, Tom Stoppard's *Arcadia* and the popular musical *Pump Boys and Dinettes*; jazz concerts; faculty and student orchestral concerts; and dance performances.

The university's Museum of Art maintains a strong collection of contemporary works by Roy Lichtenstein, Pablo Picasso, Diego Rivera, Winslow Homer and a host of Maine artists. Shows include avant garde book-art exhibitions (the book is both form and content), exhibits from UMaine faculty, traveling shows and looks into the museum's great collection, especially of works on paper. (See our Arts chapter for more information.)

Bucksport to Gouldsboro

Maine Maritime Academy
**Pleasant St., Castine • 326-4311,
(800) 464-6565 (in-state admissions),
(800) 227-8465 (out-of-state admissions)**

At the head of a historic harbor, the Maine Maritime Academy (MMA) offers 650 students a marine-oriented undergraduate or graduate education.

The school was established in 1941; by the end of World War II, more than 300 MMA graduates served at sea in every aspect of operations. Since then, the school has provided nautical engineers, ocean-science experts and officers to the U.S. Merchant Marine and U.S. military.

The academy's mark on Castine is unmistakable. Even the captain of a 120-foot-long yacht will find his vessel dwarfed by the academy's 500-foot-long training ship, *State of Maine*.

The training ship, one of a fleet of nearly 100 vessels, takes freshmen and juniors seeking U.S. Coast Guard licenses on a two-month cruise each spring to domestic and foreign ports. The tug *Pentagoet* and the barge *Central* are used to instruct students in the nation's

only tug and barge program. MMA also maintains the research vessels *ARGO Maine*, the only oceanographic platform north of Cape Cod, and *Friendship*, equipped with sonar and a remote-control vehicle. The schooner *Bowdoin*, a National Historic Landmark that's famous in Maine waters, has taken students as far as Labrador and Greenland for training in traditional sail techniques and navigation as well as ocean studies.

Elsewhere on the academy's 35-acre campus are advanced facilities that include a power-plant simulator, a 1,200-horsepower engine, a cargo-system simulator for liquefied natural gas tankers, a small-scale steam plant and a state-of-the-art Navigation and Shiphandling simulator that replicates maneuvering a 1,000-foot-long container or tank vessel into anything from a small port to the Port of New York, through seas both stormy and crowded — and many another scenario as well.

In addition to its extensive book and periodical collection, the Nutting Memorial Library is a repository for U.S. government documents as well as charts and maps of the National Oceanic and Atmospheric Administration, U.S. Geological Survey, the Central Intelligence Agency and the Defense Mapping Agency.

The school offers three degrees: an Associate of Science, a Bachelor of Science and a Master of Science. Undergraduate majors include International Business and Logistics, Marine Engineering Operations, Marine Systems Engineering, Marine Transportation, Nautical Science and Ocean Studies; graduate studies include Maritime Management and Port Management. While this is not a military academy, some students — those pursuing a U.S. Coast Guard license — do wear uniforms. A requirement of a U.S. Coast Guard licence is that students wear uniforms and be trained in a regimental format. So don't be surprised to see students

INSIDERS' TIP

Teachers visiting Maine might want to coordinate with some of the state's many summer educational seminars. In summer, both the University of Maine and College of the Atlantic offer programs such as workshops in science or nature studies for gifted and talented children or for regular middle school students.

marching through town in response to barked-out orders.

Mount Desert Island

College of the Atlantic
105 Eden St., Bar Harbor • 288-5015

Whether your senior project is a report of your own investigation into whale mating songs, a book of oral histories and photographs of winter residents on an offshore island, or poems written on paper you made, you will get one degree at College of the Atlantic: Bachelor of Human Ecology.

After the 1947 fire that devastated Mount Desert Island, the community spent a number of years looking for some sort of year-round activity to revitalize the island. It decided upon an educational institution. By then (the late 1960s), experimental colleges were the rage. With the desire to have a curriculum focused on societal and environmental problems, the founding trustees began the college, popularly known as COA.

The school opened in 1972 with four professors who taught literature, law, biology and anthropology to 32 students. Today, the school enrolls its maximum 250 students, who are taught by 26 full-time professors and about the same amount of adjuncts.

Classes include Biology of the Rapidly Changing World; Ornithology in the Lab and Field; Historic Landscape Preservation Studio; Bread, Love and Dreams; and Environmental Education: Nurturing the Child's Ecological Mind.

To graduate, students must not only fulfill the academic credits, but also do community service, complete a term's internship, write an essay about their development as a human ecologist, and undertake a final project that consists of a major piece of independent work. Classes are held in a former summer cottage and in a series of contemporary, award-winning shingle-style buildings, most of which were designed by local architects.

When *The Princeton Review of Colleges* polled students, they found that College of the Atlantic had the happiest students of all schools in the country. They also found the school had the most politically active students — and some of the best food.

Workshops

Maine's Mid-Coast region is comparable only to the largest cities when it comes to the extent and intensity of adult learning available. Whether in music, craft, art, photography, filmmaking or pottery, Maine institutions rank with the best in the world.

Waldoboro to Stockton Springs

Downeast School of Massage
99 Moose Meadows Ln., Waldoboro • 832-5531, 832-0504

Since 1981, the Downeast School of Massage has been training people as massage therapists. Students study a course that includes Swedish massage under three different programs: shiatsu, sports massage and a body-mind program, which includes deep-tissue massage. Graduates land jobs in health spas, sports medicine and as private practitioners. Several graduates work for Olympic teams. Students must be 18 years old with a high school degree to enroll in the program, which can be fulfilled as a 10-month intensive program or a two-year part-time program. About 60 students graduate each year.

Hurricane Island Outward Bound School
75 Mechanic St., Rockland • 594-5548, (800) 341-1744

Outward Bound has become synonymous with confidence, or at least with the concept of using physical challenges to build confidence in one's self and trust in others. It was founded in 1941 in Wales, with the intention of training sailors stationed in the North Atlantic during World War II. Younger sailors had been faring worse than their older counterparts, and educator Kurt Hahn, founder of Outward Bound, thought the problem might be the young sailors' lack of confidence. He developed a training program geared to leading the seamen to recognize their strength and capacities.

The idea spread worldwide. Hurricane Island Outward Bound, taking its name from the school's island base off Vinalhaven, was founded in 1964. Today, it has year-round offices in Rockland.

Adults often enroll in Outward Bound during transitional passages in their lives. To this end, Outward Bound offers special courses geared to adult renewal.

Courses for families with children 14 and older are intended to bring family members together. Other courses are offered for women only or for educators. There are also semester-length courses for college students.

Among the various skills featured in Maine are sailing, sea kayaking, canoeing, backpacking and hiking (all in summer); backpacking, cross-country skiing and dog-sledding (in winter). Additional courses are offered in Florida, Maryland and Ontario, Canada.

For information about youth programs, see the subsequent "Summer Camps" section.

The Maine Photographic Workshops
2 Central St., Rockport • 236-8581

You can't help but notice them if you venture into Camden or Rockport in summer: young women with shaved heads, middle-aged women juggling jangling bracelets, men and women sporting multiple earrings and elderly gentlemen with canes. They have one thing in common: They're all dangling multiple cameras. Is your dog cute? Your child cunning? Are you and your mate done up in matching yellow rain gear? Beware: You're likely to be the subject of a photograph.

In 1973, writer and photojournalist David Lyman decided to gather a group of artists, photographers and students to Rockport Harbor for some summer workshops. Film and video workshops were added after. A quarter-century later, Lyman runs the largest summer photography, film and video center in the world, with as many as 2,500 people attending workshops throughout summer in groups of 100 to 200 per session. Recently, the school has begun offering winter sessions in Oaxaca, Mexico; spring sessions in Tuscany, Italy, and Provence, France; August sessions in Martha's Vineyard; and high school, undergraduate and graduate programs throughout the year. Most sessions last one to two weeks, though some extend to three and four weeks. In Rockport, sessions continue from the end of May through mid-November.

What most distinguishes the workshops is the faculty: The list of members reads like a who's who of photography, film and video. Photographers Mary Ellen Mark, Gary Braasch, Chris Rainer, David Alan Harvey and John Paul Caponigro; cinematographer Stan Waterman; and producer Mimi Edmunds are among the steady staff of the workshop. Call the listed number for a current catalog of offerings.

Professionals flock here to broaden or hone their skills. Amateurs or professionals seeking career changes or career enlightenment also attend. More than a fifth of the students are international. These workshops can turn lives around, launching people on new careers and getting others deeper into the soul of their craft. At very least, people leave here better trained to be more effective at their work.

High school students might be interested in the program for young filmmakers, actors, digital imagers and photographers. At least a dozen such two-week sessions (18 young people per session) take place from June through August.

As for boarding options, the school owns some houses, rents others and puts up the majority of its students at the nearby Windjammer Hotel. Some students rent rooms in private homes.

Students thrive in this atmosphere: With so many photographers, filmmakers, actors and writers gathered, the sessions can't help but be intense.

Penobscot School
28 Gay St., Rockland • 594-1084

This nonprofit center for language learning and international exchange offers courses taught by native speakers in a variety of languages including French, Italian, Spanish, Russian, German, Chinese, Japanese and more. The school also offers a summer immersion program in English as a second language. For this program, foreign nationals come to Rockland and are hosted by local residents for a period of three weeks between July and September. The school also offers intense enrichment, like native-speaking lunches, evening events and immersion weekends. On an immersion weekend, 10 students spend Friday through Sunday taking classes, going on excursions and, above all, speaking only their one chosen language with native speakers. There are also immersion weekends for high school students, children's weekly classes and a children's Window on the World social studies and language program for 4th-graders.

Bucksport to Gouldsboro

Haystack Mountain School of Crafts
off Sunshine Rd., Deer Isle • 348-2306

Even in Maine, there is little to match the sheer beauty of Haystack Mountain School of Crafts, with its weathered shack-like studios perched on a series of pink cliffs cascading down to Jericho Bay. The way we see it, the architecture mirrors the Haystack experience, which is about shaping natural materials into striking objects.

Between early June and the end of August, 85 people at a time come from around the world for expert instruction by artists, likewise from around the world. Four or five separate workshops comprise each of the six summer sessions. Most last two weeks, though one runs for three weeks.

You have to be 18 or older to attend regular summer sessions. Generally you don't have to be an expert in the craft; commitment is all that is necessary. Instruction is organized around set sessions, but studios never close. It's not unusual for people to work through the night on a special project, or to return from the evening session — a group lecture, slide show, poetry reading or dance performance — schmooze a bit with friends, then go back to the studio for a midnight session.

Haystack has had such an impact on some students that they never leave. Deer Isle and nearby Blue Hill are sprinkled with weavers, potters, jewelers and other craftspeople who were introduced to the region via a summer session at Haystack. Many others have found their career paths altered or focused by a session at Haystack; according to these artists, it's due not only to the instruction, but also to the quality of attention they can give their work in this intensive setting between forest and sea — a place where all minds are geared to the aesthetics of the object.

New England residents can take a post-season extended weekend at Haystack for a slightly reduced fee. Haystack also offers special sessions for local and regional high school students and for Maine adults.

Kneisel Hall
Maine Hwy. 15, Blue Hill • 374-2811

Fifty serious students of chamber music — pianists, violinists, violists and cellists — can spend seven weeks in intensive study and rehearsal at Kneisel Hall.

Franz Kneisel, a young, celebrated Austrian violinist, came to the United States in 1885 to join the Boston Symphony Orchestra. He later taught at what became the Julliard School in New York and also established Kneisel Quartet, the first professional string quartet in America. Kneisel summered in Blue Hill and in 1902 began taking his most gifted students with him for a summer of intensive study.

Kneisel Hall began in 1953, after Franz Kneisel died, when his daughter and a group of musicians decided to revive the tradition of year-round musical intensity.

Students spend 4½ hours each day rehearsing by themselves and an equal amount of time rehearsing with two ensembles. Weekly ensembles are coached by instructors, including artistic director/pianist Seymour Lipkin, violinist Roman Totenberg, cellist Barbara Stein Mallow and violists Doris Lederer and Katherine Murdock. Admission is by application and must include an audio tape.

Faculty give two concerts each week — on Friday nights and Sunday afternoons. (See our Arts chapter for more on Kneisel Hall concerts.)

Pierre Monteux School for Conductors and Orchestra Musicians
U.S. Hwy. 1, Hancock • 422-3931

In 1943, Maestro Pierre Monteux fled occupied France and moved with his family to Hancock, where he started his School for Conductors and Orchestra Musicians. During the years Monteux continued his summer school in Hancock, he served as director of the Metropolitan Opera, Boston Symphony, San Francisco Symphony and London Symphony. After Monteux died in 1964, the school went into hiatus for a few years, but it began again under Monteux's first student, Charles Bruck, in 1970.

The Hancock program is an intensive six-week session for about 20 conductors who are also among 63 members of the school's orchestra. Monteux believed that conductors need to be conducted in order to apply their trade, so the program includes the 40 or so orchestral musicians. Musicians come to Hancock from across the United States and Canada as well as from Mexico, France, Taiwan, Italy, Japan and Switzerland.

Current music director Michael Jinbo is an alumnus of the school. So is Andre Previn, Neville Mariner and many other current conductors of major orchestras. For information about Sunday orchestral concerts and Wednesday night chamber music concerts, see our Arts chapter.

WoodenBoat School
Naskeag Rd., Brooklin • 359-4651

To us, it's the ultimate romantic dream: spending a week in one of the most beautiful harbors of Maine while building a wooden dory. Bring along your spouse, your son, your daughter . . . make it a family thing.

Since 1976, *WoodenBoat* magazine has been synonymous with exquisite design and fine craftsmanship in building wooden boats. In 1981, the WoodenBoat School opened to actualize the dreams and images promoted in the magazine.

Want to try boat building? You can take a two-week course in fundamentals and plunge into building difficult boats with the idea that if you learn the basics of the hard ones, you can do anything else. In this course, you start one boat, plank another and finish a third.

Other courses focus on the details of boat building such as joiner work, lapstrake construction and varnishing. Still others send you home with your own kayak, canoe, shellback pram or sailing dinghy for the price of tuition and a building kit.

Some courses teach the basics of boating, whether it be sailing or motor boating, night sailing or navigation, or handling the 28-foot-long *Friendship Sloop*, a 39-foot-long John Alden ketch or the *Lewis R. French*, the oldest schooner operating in Maine.

Classes are small, and accommodations are simple (mostly double rooms with shared baths). You can also camp at the resident campground (especially good if you bring family), stay on your own boat for the price of a mooring fee, or book a room at a local inn. Call for a catalog.

Specialty Classes

Maine Writers and Publishers Alliance
12 Pleasant St., Brunswick • 729-6333

Writers need not suffer from a workshop void. The state's alliance of writers and publishers offers an annual slate of weekly workshops. Though the alliance is based in Brunswick, southwest of our Mid-Coast area, classes are frequently held farther up the coast, closer to our region. The kinds of workshops fluctuate widely. Summer offerings include outdoor writing and field trips for those interested in improving their writing while also learning about the outdoors. Call to find out about current workshops.

Summer Camps

It used to be that every New York and Boston suburb had its army-navy supply shop, each with lists of the uniform needs for scores of Maine summer camps. Then, one day in late June, the local train station would be filled with tearful parents and excited kids bound for camp somewhere in Maine. While parents wrapped their kids in last-minute hugs, porters loaded heavy camp trunks filled with uniforms, each one labeled with the camper's name.

Today the scene may be similar, though the setting is usually a bus station or an airport. Perhaps there are not as many camps in Maine as in the 1940s and '50s, but you still can find plenty.

For a summer sleep-away camp, you'll need to apply as much as a year in advance. Day camps offer more leeway; but even so, some fill up early.

Camping can be important to children. According to psychologist Alice Van Krevelen, "[At camp] a child can find success away from the failures and frustrations of home and school."

For more information on camps, contact the Maine Youth Camping Association, P.O. Box 455, Orono, ME 04473.

Waldoboro to Stockton Springs

Hurricane Island Outward Bound School
Mechanic St., Rockland • 594-5548, (800) 341-1744

Outward Bound courses are tough, warns the Hurricane Island Outward Bound Program. They are designed to test and challenge participants as well as to offer fun and adventure.

Groups of six to 12 youths 14 and older first receive instruction in safety, first aid, wilderness cooking, knotting, boating, rock climbing and other skills, depending on the course. At the end of most courses, students use this instruction to take a final expedition, usually solo — a period of a few hours to three days of solitude at an isolated campsite.

There are Outward Bound programs for middle-schoolers (ages 14 and 15), high school students (ages 15 to 17) and college students (ages 18 to 21), and a myriad of courses for adults and families (see the Outward Bound entry in our previous "Workshops" section). Some youth classes last a week, but the school prefers the intensity of the two-week programs. Special expeditions can last from three to four weeks.

On one excursion, for instance, youths go out in open boats, powered by oar and sail. They learn sailing, navigation, small-boat handling, basic seamanship and leadership skills while watching for dolphins, seals and even whales off the coast of Maine.

Alford Lake Camp
Alford Lake Rd., off Maine Hwy. 17, Hope • 785-5290

A camp for 175 girls ages 8 to 15, Alford Lake prides itself on its small size and long history. There's one counselor for every three campers. In summer 1998, the camp celebrates its 92nd year. A special part of this camp is an International Exchange, welcoming campers from some 15 nations. Sports, wilderness skills and the arts are the three foci, and outdoor living is the overall emphasis. A full season runs seven weeks; two half-sessions also are offered.

Tanglewood 4-H Camp
Tanglewood Rd., Lincolnville • 789-5868, 832-0375 (winter)

Tanglewood 4-H camps, on the Ducktrap River in Lincolnville, have become a year-round source of nature education for children of all ages.

Summer programs include six week-long and one two-week-long residential sessions for kids ages 8 to 14, with a focus on either Maine's natural resources or the creative arts — the children decide. Afternoons are spent doing activities such as cooking, woodworking, hiking, poetry writing or sports. Sessions usually begin the end of June and end sometime in mid-August.

Youths ages 14 to 17 are eligible for two- or three-week leadership programs in which communication, teamwork and leadership are taught in addition to outdoor skills. For campers ages 12 to 14, the camp offers special group challenges and trust activities. Enrollment is limited to 10 per session.

Other discovery programs include living in a forest, living at a wilderness base or tenting on an island. In addition, school groups frequently take advantage of Tanglewood's spring and fall ecology offerings, spending two to five days of intensive time at the camp.

Hidden Valley Camp
New Ireland Rd., off Maine Hwy. 220, Montville • 342-5177, (800) 922-6737

Just about every aspect of Hidden Valley Camp is documented in its annual yearbook; campers write, take photographs for and publish the book. Hidden Valley's arts- and nature-based summer curriculum includes llama treks, canoe trips, poetry writing, theatrical productions, dance performances, rope climbing, horseback riding, an Indian camp (housed in tepees), swimming and much more.

The 250 campers, ages 8 to 13, come from around the nation and the globe. They stay at the camp for either one month or two. Here's a chance to learn unique skills such as caring for animals, making a musical instrument, cutting stained glass or, for those who chose to live in tepees, cooking food over an open fire. There's also an adventure program for 14- and 15-year-olds, taking three- and four-day trips around Maine and using Hidden Valley as a base camp.

Bucksport to Gouldsboro

Flying Moose Lodge
Craig Pond, East Orland
* **(508) 420-0813 (in winter)**

The emphasis at Flying Moose Lodge is on outdoor adventure. The camp has neither a phone nor electricity. Each week, boys are sent off to different adventures in groups of six. It might be a canoe trip one week, mountain climbing or deep-woods hiking another week, and fishing or bicycling a third week. The boys leave on Tuesday, return on Friday and spend weekends swimming in Craig Pond, building a wood and canvas canoe and honing camping skills.

Flying Moose Lodge is for boys ages 10 to 16, though most are ages 11 to 13. Forty-eight boys come to the camp, which includes 15 counselors.

Robin Hood
Herricks Rd., South Brooksville
* **359-8313, (978) 276-5600 (in winter)**

For children who love athletics, Robin Hood Camp fills the bill. With access to fresh and salt water, the camp offers an extensive range of activities: sailing, water skiing, windsurfing, whitewater rafting, crew shell rowing, swimming, kayaking, canoeing, fishing, basketball, baseball, riflery, fencing, archery, soccer, lacrosse, martial arts, rock climbing, ropes, dance, horseback riding, golf, gymnastics, mountain biking, tennis, even week-long scuba

clinics. Quieter activities include photography, arts, crafts, music and drama. Most counselors are top athletes and Ivy League students.

Robin Hood was founded in 1928. Graduates of the camp have become so attached to the area that they return yearly, booking summer weeks at the Oakland House, run by cousins of Robin Hood's Rick and Robin Littlefield.

For more information call the listed numbers or write to 172 Haverhill Street, North Reading, MA 01864.

Mount Desert Island

Acadia Institute of Oceanography
off Maine Hwy. 3, Seal Harbor
* **276-9825, 384-4155 (in winter)**

Children ages 12 to 18 who are fascinated by the ocean will find a formative experience exploring the world of marine science at Acadia Institute of Oceanography.

Waters rich in plankton attract many species of fish; rivers and estuaries serve as ocean nurseries. The coast of Mount Desert Island is an excellent laboratory in which to introduce young scholars to oceanography.

The institute offers five two-week sessions between the end of June and the end of August, serving 42 participants at a time. Basic sessions are for students ages 12 to 15. Advanced sessions are for kids ages 15 to 18 who have completed high school biology or chemistry.

At the institute, which has operated since 1975, participants study the coast's bird and sea life, dissect squid and shark, build a saltwater aquarium and spend time on a boat conducting a water survey. Participants need not have experience in marine studies, but they do need recommendations from their science teachers back home.

The program is housed in the Dunham Schoolhouse, a remodeled school building

FYI

Unless otherwise noted, the area code for all phone numbers listed in this guide is 207.

INSIDERS' TIP

Has your chosen workshop been closed for weeks? Keep trying. Cancellations occur.

Cadets from the Maine Maritime Academy train on a street in Castine.

built by John D. Rockefeller in 1931 on the border of Acadia National Park.

For more information, write Sheryl Gilmore, P.O. Box 98, South Berwick, ME 03908.

Day Camps

Waldoboro to Stockton Springs

Colonial History Camp
Conway Complex and Camden Historical Society, off U.S. Hwy. 1, Camden
• 236-2257, 832-6340

During the first week in August, a dozen children ages 8 to 10 learn to make historic crafts, like checkerboards and Victorian sachets. They also learn about local history, ex-plore adjacent Merryspring Park or downtown Camden, and climb Mount Battie. They might even visit a windjammer and learn about the seafaring history of the region, including the lime trade of Rockport.

Camden Summer Recreation Program
Camden Snow Bowl, Hosmer Pond Rd., Camden • 236-3438

Camden's parks and recreation department offers a six-week-long summer recreation program for residents and visitors. Weekly programs run from Monday through Thursday, and parents can sign up children for a week at a time or for all six weeks. Activities include swimming at Lake Megunticook, visits to local beaches, roller skating, arts and crafts, field games and some canoeing. There's also a week-long baseball camp. Call the recreation department for more information.

Children's House Montessori School
63 Pearl St., Camden • 236-2911

Following the Montessori philosophy of child-guided, individualized education, the Children's House Montessori School (see the previous "Private Schools" section) offers two summer programs for children ages 3 to 5 and 6 to 10. The eight week-long sessions are held from the end of June through mid-August. The program focuses on learning through hands-on experiments and games, with field trips to state parks and beaches.

Tanglewood 4-H Camp
Tanglewood Rd., Lincolnville • 789-5868, 832-0375 (in winter)

The Tanglewood 4-H Camp, on the Ducktrap River in Lincolnville, offers a day camp for children ages 6 to 8. The camp reflects the 4-H concern with the natural world and child involvement. (See the previous "Summer Camps" section for related information.) Activities include art, drama, hiking, games, wading and exploring the natural world. Five sessions are offered, with a dozen children per session, for one or two weeks.

At the end of August, there's also a week-long science camp for girls in grades 4 through 6.

Inland to Bangor

Summer Theatre Camp
Penobscot Theatre Co., 183 Main St., Bangor • 942-3333

The Penobscot Theatre Company gets children involved in its theater through summer workshops in Shakespeare. Two programs are offered, both for two weeks in June and July. There's a program for ages 8 to 13 and one for ages 14 to 18. There is no audition to participate in the program — just desire. Students work toward an in-house children's theater production at the end of the program. The 1998 play is *A Midsummer Night's Dream*. Teachers include cast members of the theater's Shakespeare on the River (see our Annual Events and Arts chapters). It's not unusual for students at the camp to go on to work as interns, either backstage or with walk-on parts during the Shakespeare performances.

Bucksport to Gouldsboro

Apple Blossom Acres
Maine Hwy. 184, Lamoine • 667-9214

Owner Bonnie Moretto runs a week-long children's camp for horseback riding. This is not a babysitting service: Your child has to be ready for hard work, sweat and bugs; but if he or she loves horses, you could offer no better vacation. They'll get two lessons a day and lots of training in caring for horses. (See our Parks and Recreation chapter for related information.)

MERI Community Resource Center
Maine Hwy. 175, Brooklin • 359-8078

The Marine Environmental Research Institute (MERI) is in a Brooklin storefront. The MERI Community Resource Center offers marine-science programs for children and adults that focus on the impact of global pollution and on the preservation of the marine environment. Visit the small library and the small aquarium, and sign up for daytrips into the marine environment. About five different programs are available.

Kids ages 7 to 12 can take a daylong boat trip to an island where they can learn about wildlife, habitats, the food chain and human impact on all three. Programs run 9 AM to 3 PM Tuesday and Thursday. The per-child cost is $18 a day.

For more extensive involvement, children ages 8 to 12 can sign up for a series of four excursions on the RV *MERI* from 10 AM to 4 PM on Wednesdays in July or August. The cost is $18 a session or $64 for all four sessions.

Friday is an on-land day. Children ages 7 to 12 can take discovery walks on the beach, conduct marine-science experiments and learn about the creatures living in the center's sea aquarium discovery tank — part of a program that runs from 9 to 10:30 AM. The cost is $8. Little ones ages 4 to 6 can come Friday from 1 to 1:45 PM for storytelling, videos, games and crafts for a fee of $8 each.

Whole families can tour the oceans on the RV *MERI* with a naturalist aboard Monday and

Friday from 10 AM to noon, or they can go to an island for a naturalist-led walking tour from 1 to 3 PM. The cost for either outing is $20 for each adult or kid 10 and older and $12 for each child younger than 10.

Mount Desert Island

Harbor House
Main St., Southwest Harbor • 244-3713

Harbor House offers a full round of day-camp activities for resident and nonresident children between the end of June and the end of August.

Scamper Camp is for children ages 2½ to 5. Sessions run from 7 AM to 5 PM Monday through Friday for eight weeks, with half- and full-day options available. The emphasis of the camp is on the natural wonders of the area, with walks, hikes, swims and field trips to places such the Acadia Zoo and the Abbe Museum (see our Acadia National Park chapter).

For children ages 6 to 8, Harbor House offers Explorer Camp for eight weeks from 8:30 AM to 3:30 PM Monday through Friday. Activities include frequent visits to Acadia National Park, swimming and arts and crafts. Daily and weekly rates are available.

Children ages 9 to 14 who are interested in boating can learn to sail and get basic water-safety instruction during two- or three-week sessions. Morning and afternoon options are available. Classes use the town dock on Clark Point Road.

Harbor House also sponsors the Summer Festival of the Arts, a three-week arts intensive for more than 200 children entering grades 3 through 11. Areas of focus include dance, drama, theater design, visual arts, music, graphic arts and writing.

Spaces are limited, so it's necessary to reserve ahead. Scheduling happens at a "scheduling fair" held in late June at the Mount Desert Island School cafeteria.

Summer Field Studies
The Natural History Museum, College of the Atlantic, 104 Eden St., Bar Harbor • 288-5015

Following its basic approach of a human ecological, nature-oriented basis for all study, College of the Atlantic offers summer programs for young ones. The Summer Field Studies program has developed a widespread reputation and great popularity. We know families who happily make the daily drive from Bangor to Bar Harbor just so their children can reap the rewards of this field camp. Reserve early.

Sessions feature various aspects of coastal and inland ecology. During two weeks of day-camping, well-trained and good-humored counselors teach children about tidepools, animal hideouts and the differences among the area's ecosystems. Daily activities are hands-on, fun and filled with all sorts of adventures, including discovering tadpoles and searching for animal tracks. Younger children might learn noncompetitive games by the shore; older children might head out together in kayaks for a day of island discovery.

Programs for kindergartners run Monday through Thursday for a week at a time from early July through late August. Programs for children entering 1st through 9th grades run for two weeks during the same time period.

As is true elsewhere, the healthcare trend in Maine is to keep people away from hospitals as much as possible and to organize continued-care clinics and home-healthcare services to assist with aftercare.

Healthcare

The population of Maine's Mid-Coast region is relatively small; the geography is not. This is a long, complex coastal area with many peninsulas. To provide for the health and wellness of people living along such a lengthy expanse, the area has many small health clinics and centers, each of which is connected to one of several small regional hospitals. These facilities generally are able to handle a wide range of healthcare needs. Whatever needs can't be handled by the small hospital (or by such rural saviors as a mobile Magnetic Resonance Imaging (MRI) unit and a mobile nuclear medicine unit that regularly serve rural hospitals) are referred to one of several larger hospitals.

The largest hospital in our area is Eastern Maine Medical Center in Bangor. The largest facility in the state, however, is the Maine Medical Center, 871-0111 or 871-2381 (for emergencies), in Portland. Transfers also go inland to the Mid-Maine Medical Center in Waterville. In this chapter we do not include facilities outside the Mid-Coast area, except for the Miles Memorial Hospital in Damariscotta, 563-1234, just south of the Mid-Coast, used by people from Waldoboro and Friendship. As is true elsewhere, the healthcare trend in Maine is to keep people away from hospitals as much as possible and to organize continued-care clinics and home-healthcare services to assist with aftercare.

Being independent freethinkers, Mainers have also explored a range of alternative therapies. Several good homeopaths practice in the region as well as numerous chiropractors, herbalists, massage therapists, acupuncturists and at least one naturopath. And osteopaths train at the University of New England in the southern Maine town of Biddeford. Women giving birth can chose among doctors, certified nurse-midwives and home birth using the assistance of trained midwives.

This chapter is arranged geographically by the type of facility. In order of appearance, look for hospitals, clinics, psychiatric facilities, specialized-care facilities and alternative healthcare centers. At the end of the chapter, we include some home healthcare services and hospice organizations. Refer to our gray box for emergency numbers and hotlines.

Referrals and Information

General

Info Line
973-6815, (800) 204-2803

This data bank offers information on various community and social services, especially useful for those needing help with chemical dependency, crisis intervention, hospice care, elderly care, and for those seeking family and child services, physicians, AIDS information and dental assistance in the greater Mid-Coast area. It is funded by the United Way of Eastern Maine.

Physician Referrals

If you need advice about choosing a physician in the Mid-Coast area, or need to know about an urgent care center, the following referral lines can help you find what you need. The 800 number is best to call for general information on hospital services and urgent care in the region. Call the other numbers for names of physicians affiliated with local hospitals who are accepting new patients.

Anywhere in Maine: (800) 439-2111
In Rockland: 596-8315
In Belfast: 338-2500
In Bangor: 973-7999
In Ellsworth: 667-8095

Hotlines
24-hour Emergency Numbers

Maine Poison Control Center, (800) 442-6305

Phone Help (crisis intervention), (800) 245-8889

Downeast Sexual-assault Hotline, (800) 228-2470

Blue Hill Memorial Hospital, Blue Hill, 374-2836

Eastern Maine Medical Center, Bangor, 973-8000

Maine Coast Memorial Hospital, Ellsworth, 667-4520

Mount Desert Island Hospital, Bar Harbor, 288-8439

Penobscot Bay Medical Center, Rockport, 596-8000

St. Joseph Healthcare, Bangor, 262-5000

Waldo County General Hospital, Belfast, 338-2500, (800) 649-2536

AIDS Hotlines

AIDS CDC National STD Hotline, (800) 227-8922

Bangor STD Clinic Wellcare Program, 947-0700

Downeast AIDS Network, 667-3506

Eastern Maine AIDS Network, 990-3626

Eastern Maine HIV Information Line, 990-2095, (800) 429-1481

National AIDS Hotline, (800) 342-AIDS

Maine AIDS Hotline, (800) 581-AIDS

Hospitals

Waldoboro to Stockton Springs

Miles Memorial Hospital
Bristol Rd., Damariscotta • 563-1234

Although it's just south of our Mid-Coast area, Miles Memorial Hospital frequently admits people from Waldoboro and the St. George Peninsula to its 40 beds. It offers a 24-hour emergency room, surgery, internal medicine, obstetrics, gynecology, radiology, ophthalmology, family/pediatric practice, a women's center with prenatal care, physical and respiratory therapy, home health, hospice, a nursing home and a retirement facility. For visitors or locals without a doctor, the hospital offers after-hours care (for emergencies that aren't life threatening) between 5 and 9 PM daily.

The hospital accepts insurance, Medicare, Medicaid and credit cards, but as a community hospital, it will administer to anyone who walks through the door, whether or not they can pay.

Penobscot Bay Medical Center
6 Glen Cove Dr., Rockport • 596-8000, 596-8315 (emergencies)

Penobscot Bay Medical Center is a 106-bed modern hospital facility. It offers several special care units, such as a 14-bed Psychiatric and Addiction Recovery Center, a family room where family members of critically ill patients can meet with physicians and counselors or can relax and sleep, five orthopedic surgeons, a cardiac rehab center for aftercare of people with heart "events," chemotherapy, and an inpatient/outpatient physical- and occupational-care department. Its ambulatory-care services focus strongly on community education. Pen-Bay, as it is popularly known, has adopted a model of patient-focused care. Under this structure, patients are placed in proximity according to their physician in a group of rooms known as a care center. This care center is overseen by a registered nurse coordinator. The nurse leads a team of care givers and is responsible for each patient's 24-hour care. Recently, Pen-Bay affiliated itself with local health organization Kno-Wal-Lin (see the "Clinics" and "Home Healthcare" sections). Together, the three are under Northeast Health's umbrella.

Waldo County General Hospital
118 Northport Ave., Belfast
• 338-2500, (800) 649-2536

Waldo County General Hospital is part of Waldo County Healthcare, an extensive

healthcare organization that offers many outpatient services throughout the county. The 45-bed hospital is a full-service center, with a 24-hour emergency department, inpatient and outpatient surgery, intensive- and critical-care units, family practice, pediatrics, internal medicine and such specialties as cardiology, gastroenterology, gynecology/obstetrics, nephrology, neurology, ophthalmology, orthopedics, otolaryngology and urology. Hospice care also comprises a wing of the hospital.

Inland to Bangor

Eastern Maine Medical Center
289 State St., Bangor • 973-7000, 973-8000 (emergencies)

Perched in a tall building on the banks of the Penobscot River, Eastern Maine Medical Center is the region's major hospital, where many acute- and specialized-care patients get transferred. The scope of this 400-bed hospi-

tal is vast. In addition to 24-hour emergency care, general surgery, obstetrics/gynecology, internal medicine and treatment of mental illnesses, there are more than 30 family practitioners associated with the hospital plus several specialists in cardiology, dermatology, endocrinology, gastroenterology, hematology, oncology, infectious disease, dentistry, neurosurgery, ophthalmology, oral surgery, nephrology, neurology, pulmonary medicine, rheumatology, orthopedics, pathology, pediatrics, allergy, immunology and neonatology. The diagnostic services are extensive, as is the variety of therapeutics.

As is common practice in this region (and elsewhere), EMMC has associated itself with regional clinics offering outreach care to the broad geographic area, such as its nine oncology clinics in northern and eastern Maine, including Blue Hill and Belfast. It also has joined five other community hospitals and several medical staffs as part of HealthNet, a regional managed-care organization.

Finally, if beauty alone could heal, this hospital would have a 100 percent success rate. EMMC gets the award, hands down, for the most soaring vistas; many rooms have staggering views over the wide Penobscot River.

St. Joseph Healthcare
360 Broadway, Bangor • 262-1000, 262-5000 (emergencies)

This Catholic, community healthcare organization offers innovative, cost-effective healthcare with 100 beds and 35 local primary-care providers working in association with NorthEast MSO, a managed-care plan. It also offers the only Problem, Wound and Hyperbaric Medicine Center in Maine and the only Lymphedema Clinic in the area. As is the case at many healthcare institutions, the focus is on keeping people out of hospitals. Techniques applied to this end include lithotripsy, a nonsurgical removal of kidney stones, and the use of a preventative bone densitometer to detect osteoporosis and begin preventative measures before deterioration gets too serious. The hospital also has a sleep-studies laboratory and offers a range of diagnostics, including computer tomography (CT) scans.

Outpatient care is provided at the St. Joseph Healthcare Park, 900 Broadway, home of HealthWORKS, offering businesses on-site rehabilitative services and preventative analysis of potential occupational problems, and the St. Joseph Hospital Regional Breast Care Center, with mammography screening and a department of nutritional therapy.

Bucksport to Gouldsboro

Blue Hill Memorial Hospital
Water St., Blue Hill • 374-2836, (800) 488-2836

Like many hospitals in the region, Blue Hill Memorial Hospital has reorganized, consolidating what used to be five health organizations into one large family known as Peninsula Primary Care (PPC), a subsidiary of the hospital. The hospital is a genuine community healthcare provider, with children's toys in every waiting area, hand-knit goods on sale at the hospital store and comfortable birthing rooms. Blue Hill Memorial Hospital now sees itself as the support system for its five associated regional medical centers, admitting patients to fill its 26 beds only when necessary. Specialties include obstetrics/gynecology, general practice, internal medicine, gastroenterology, ophthalmology, oncology, surgery, urology and physical, occupational and speech therapies. Acute-care patients who need additional services are sent to Eastern Maine Medical Center.

Maine Coast Memorial Hospital
50 Union St., Ellsworth • 667-5311, 667-4520 (emergencies)

Maine Coast Memorial Hospital has recently undergone rapid growth. Its medical staff now includes more than 40 healthcare practitioners. It has 64 beds. In addition to providing general medical services and such specialized services as a breast clinic and the Mary Dow Center for Cancer Care, the hospital offers special units devoted to rehabilitation, such as physical and occupational therapies; pulmonary rehabilitation services for sufferers of emphysema, chronic bronchitis and asthma; PremierCare for pediatric rehabilitation; and a lab for sleep studies. The hospital also provides physical therapy to patients from other clinics.

Mount Desert Island

Mount Desert Island Hospital
10 Wayman Ln., Bar Harbor • 288-5081, 288-8439 (emergencies)

The hospital offers a wide range of services including acute and emergency care, surgery, obstetrics, gynecology, pediatrics, geriatrics, community health education, chemical-dependency counseling and ophthalmology. Diagnostics include pulmonary foundation testing, CT scan, color ultrasound, nuclear scan, EKG and X-ray. Therapies include respiratory therapy, chemotherapy, physical therapy and cardiac rehabilitation. The hospital has six associated clinics on the island.

FYI

Unless otherwise noted, the area code for all phone numbers listed in this guide is 207.

Regional Health Centers and Clinics

Waldoboro to Stockton Springs

Waldoboro Family Medicine
27 Mill St., Waldoboro • 832-5291

Working 8 AM to 8 PM Monday through Thursday and 8 AM to 5 PM Friday, Waldoboro Family Medicine's staff of three doctors and one osteopath offers adult and pediatric medical care and health maintenance, including minor surgery such as wart removal. Appointments are necessary. The center will bill insurance companies, Medicaid and Medicare, otherwise cash or credit card payment is expected at the time of the visit. If necessary, a payment plan can be arranged. The center refers patients to Penobscot Bay Medical Center (see the previous "Hospitals" section).

Mid-Coast Family Planning
Elm St., Damariscotta • 563-1224
22 White St., Rockland • 594-6880
132 Church St., Belfast • 338-3736

These three facilities offer gynecological exams, birth-control screening, sexually transmitted disease screening and treatment, pap smears, breast exams, anonymous HIV testing and pregnancy testing and counseling. Males are seen for STD screening and treatment and for HIV testing. While appointments are generally necessary, teenagers can come to a weekly walk-in clinic in Rockland Mondays after 1 PM. The staffs at these clinics include nurse practitioners and counselors, with nurses rotating between clinics, so examinations are scheduled for the days the nurse is present. Services can be covered by Medicaid, private insurance and credit card payments. A sliding-scale fee is an option.

Hours for the Rockland office are 8:30 AM to 7 PM Monday, 8:30 AM to 5 PM Tuesday through Thursday and 8:30 AM to 4:30 PM Friday.

Hours for the Belfast office are 8:30 AM to noon and 1 to 5 PM Monday through Thursday. The Damariscotta office (serving Waldoboro) is open 9 AM to 5 PM Monday through Thursday.

QwikCare
231 S. Main St., Rockland • 596-7838
45 Park St., Camden • 236-8647

One doctor runs one walk-in clinic in Rockland and another in Camden. One of the clinics is open seven days a week for ambulatory care for problems such as colds, flu, aches and pains. This is not an emergency room, however, so if you suspect that your problem is very serious, go to an emergency room.

The Camden office is open 2 to 4 PM Monday through Friday; the Rockland office is open 9 AM to noon Saturday and Sunday and 6 to 7 PM Wednesday. Payment is expected at the time of services. Medicaid is accepted, but neither Medicare nor insurance can be used for payment.

Coastal Medical Care
Professional Building 119 Northport Ave., Belfast • 338-8412

Originally a sports-care clinic, Coastal Medical Care, associated with Waldo County Healthcare, now serves a wide range of related ambulatory-care needs including sports care, athletic training, physicals, occupational health, rehabilitation for sports and work injuries and various diagnostic services such as a sleep lab and hearing diagnostics. The center works closely with area manufacturers to prevent on-the-job injuries and improve employee wellness and healthcare. Appointments are necessary since the one doctor is available only three days a week. There is also one nurse practitioner. The center is open 8 AM to 5 PM Monday through Friday. Payment for sports physicals is expected at the time of the visit. Other services are usually covered by worker's compensation, Medicare, Medicaid or other insurance, which the facility will bill.

Stockton Springs Health Center
Cape Jellison Rd., Stockton Springs • 567-4000

Opened in 1996 by Waldo County Healthcare, this rural health center serves the region through adult and pediatric services, sports medicine, employment physicals, immunizations, stitches and such diagnoses as pap smears, urinalysis and blood-sugar analysis. Walk-ins are accepted, but appointments are not hard to come by at this small center staffed by one doctor and one nurse practitioner. The center bills insurance companies for clients, accepts credit cards and submits bills to Medicaid and Medicare. Sliding-scale fees and payment plans also can be arranged. Hours are 1 to 7 PM Monday, 1 to 5 PM Tuesday and Wednesday, 9 AM to 4 PM Thursday, 8 to 5 PM Friday and 9 AM to 1 PM Saturday.

Inland to Bangor

Bangor STD/HIV Clinic
City of Bangor Health and Welfare Dept. 103 Texas Ave., Bangor • 947-0700, 941-0256 ext. 410

The City of Bangor, through its STD clinic, offers confidential, comprehensive checkups for and treatment of sexually transmitted diseases. It will also assist with treatment of sexual partners. All tests are anonymous and confidential, including HIV antibody testing. All treatment is offered with complete confidentiality as well.

This is not an all-encompassing primary healthcare facility but a well-care and health-maintenance center for people living with STD or HIV. It offers routine health monitoring, basic preventative and maintenance treatment, referrals, laboratory for monitoring of health status, T-cell counts, interpretation of results, monitoring of medications, routine examinations, treatment of acute HIV problems and community education.

Walk-ins for clinical services are welcome 5 to 7 PM Monday and Wednesday and 10 to 11:30 AM Friday. Appointments are necessary for HIV Ab testing and counseling. Office hours for counseling and consultation are by appointment between 8:30 AM and 4 PM Monday through Friday. No client is turned away for lack of funds. Medicaid is accepted.

Brewer Walk-In Center
399 S. Main St., Brewer • 989-1192

If you need someone to look at a rash or your child's ear infection, or if you've been flattened by the flu, you can visit the Brewer Walk-In Center, associated with St. Joseph Hospital. No appointments are necessary, though they can be made. While the director is an MD, the staff consists of a physician's assistant and nurse practitioner, with other doctors coming during specific time slots. Full payment or insurance plan information, including Medicaid or Medicare, is expected at the time of your visit, but no one is turned away. Credit cards also are accepted. Hours are 8 AM to 6 PM weekdays, 9 AM to 3 PM Saturday.

Eastern Maine Medical Center Walk-In Care
289 State St., Bangor • 973-7000

Eastern Maine Medical Center offers a walk-in center open daily from 10 AM to 9 PM. The center is in the same room as the emergency room, and ER staff will assist you if the Walk-In Center is not open. When the center is open, however, this branch allows people to receive acute, non-emergency care at times when there is no doctor available. As with the ER, no appointment is necessary; but unlike the ER, the center is not an expensive solution to healthcare. Cash is not required at your visit; EMMC will bill. It also accepts credit cards and submits to insurance companies, Medicaid and Medicare. Payment plans can be worked out with the billing office.

Mabel Wadsworth Women's Health Center
Intown Plaza, Harlow St., Bangor • 947-5337, (800) 948-5337

The Mabel Wadsworth Women's Health Center considers itself a feminist organization geared to empowering women in their sexual and reproductive lives. Mabel Wadsworth is a real person who has been struggling for Maine women's control over their reproductive health since the 1940s. The clinic offers annual exams, pap smears, breast exams, pregnancy testing and options, abortion services, prenatal care, adoption and parenting, lesbian healthcare, contraception, STD diagnosis and treatment, and community education. Payment

is expected with services; the center will help with insurance reimbursement. It is a Medicaid and Medicare provider. Hours are 8:30 to 4:30 PM Monday through Friday; appointments are necessary.

Orono Medical Center
303 Main St., Orono • 866-5561, (800) 439-5561

The two doctors and three physician's assistants at Orono Medical Center, formerly known as MedNow, serve as a general family medical practice and also provide walk-in urgent care. The center offers diagnostic services such as X-rays and basic lab work as well. It is open 8 AM to 8 PM daily. Payment is expected at the time of the visit, through insurance company billing, credit card or cash.

Penquis Health Services
262 Harlow St., Bangor • 973-3650

A family-planning clinic with five nurse practitioners that also serve the satellite clinics to the north and west, Penquis cares for women's health needs at any age, including pap smears and breast exams. Penquis will bill insurance companies and accepts Medicaid and Medicare. It offers a sliding-scale fee for women's health services. Hours are 8 AM to noon and 1 to 4 PM Monday to Friday and variable times in the evening (please call). Visits are by appointment.

Bucksport to Gouldsboro

Bucksport Family Medicine
285 Main St., Bucksport • 469-6880

One family physician and one physician's assistant attend to a full range of family practice needs, including pediatric care, OB/GYN and counseling services. The clinic is one of five organizations connected with Peninsula Primary Care Association, a nonprofit affiliate of Blue Hill Memorial Hospital. Walk-ins are

---

INSIDERS' TIP

Interested in alternative therapies? Maine's Mid-Coast area is unusually rich in alternative practitioners, including acupuncturists, chiropractors, homeopaths, massage therapists and naturopathic healers.

accepted. Payment is by cash or credit card. The center also will bill insurance providers, Medicare and Medicaid. Payment plans and sliding-scale fees are available. Hours are 8 AM to 7 PM Monday and Tuesday, 8 AM to 5 PM Wednesday through Friday.

Bucksport Regional Health Center
Broadway Ext., Bucksport • 469-7371

The friendly staff at this regional healthcare center provides primary care from pediatrics to geriatrics. Lab and X-ray services are available at the large facility near the local high school. There are five physicians, two nurse practitioners and two mental health counselors on staff. When necessary, health center staff make house calls. The center accepts all forms of payment, including insurance, Medicare, Medicaid and cash.

Castine Community Health Services
Court St., Castine • 326-4348

Castine Community Health Services is a small outpatient clinic staffed by a family physician, a family nurse practitioner and a part-time counselor. Services include pediatric care, assistance with simple lacerations and fractures, diagnostics (including X-rays), OB/GYN and a laboratory. The clinic is one of five organizations connected with Peninsula Primary Care Association, an affiliate of Blue Hill Memorial Hospital. Walk-ins are accepted. Payment is by cash or credit card. The center will also bill insurance, Medicare and Medicaid. Payment plans and sliding-scale fees are available. Hours are 8 AM to 4 PM Monday through Friday.

Blue Hill Family Medicine
Sussman Medical Building, Water St., Blue Hill • 374-2311

Like other members of Peninsula Primary Care Association, Blue Hill Family Medicine offers complete coverage for all family members. The practice is on the campus of Blue Hill Memorial Hospital. There are four full-time family physicians and one part-time family nurse practitioner. If necessary, patients are referred to the Blue Hill Memorial Hospital. Payment by cash or credit card is accepted, and the center will also bill insur-

ance, Medicare and Medicaid. Payment plans and sliding-scale fees are available. Hours are 8 AM to 4:30 PM Monday through Friday.

Blue Hill Women's Health Care
Sussman Medical Building, Water St., Blue Hill • 374-5161

Loosely affiliated with Blue Hill Family Medicine, Women's Health Care offers a full range of women's healthcare through the services of one OB/GYN and one certified nurse-midwife. Payment is by cash or credit card. The center bills insurance, Medicare and Medicaid, and payment plans and sliding-scale fees are available. Hours are 8 AM to 4:30 PM Monday through Friday.

Tenney Hill Family Practice
Sussman Medical Building, Water St., Blue Hill • 374-5000

Two physicians and one physician's assistant staff this family practice serving infants through the elderly. The practice covers all general family-practice services, including OB/GYN, pediatrics and most geriatric care. Walk-ins are accommodated when possible. The practice is part of the Peninsula Primary Care Association. Payment is by cash or credit card. The center will also bill insurance, Medicare and Medicaid. Payment plans and sliding-scale fees are available. Hours are 8 AM to 4:30 PM Monday through Friday.

Island Medical Center
Airport Rd., Stonington • 367-2311

Four doctors staff this medical center, which is a member of Peninsula Primary Care Association. As with other members of PPCA, extensive primary care is offered, including basic pediatric and adult care, assistance with lacerations and fractures, OB/GYN and laboratory services. Those who need hospital care are admitted to Blue Hill Memorial Hospital. Walk-ins are accepted. Payment is by check or credit card. The center submits to insurers and Medicare. Payment plans are possible. There is also a sliding-scale fee for those who need it. Appointments are scheduled from 8:30 AM to 4:30 PM Monday through Friday.

A new crop for Maine is the cranberry. A number of farmers
are turning farmland into cranberry bogs.

Downeast Health Services and Downeast Family Planning
Christian Ridge Rd., Ellsworth
• 667-5304, (800) 492-5550

This small clinic, consisting of a counselor and nurse practitioner, offers a wide range of family-planning services as well as testing for HIV and other sexually transmitted diseases. It also offers maternal-child health visits. The clinic is associated with regional social service agencies. Appointments are necessary for annual checkups. A sliding-scale fee is available. Hours are 8 AM to 4:30 PM Monday and Wednesday and 8 AM to 8 PM Tuesday. The clinic bills a limited number of insurance providers as well as Medicaid. Medicare patients must submit their own claims.

Healthcare Express
Maine Coast Memorial Hospital, 50 Union St., Ellsworth • 667-0156

Healthcare Express handles immediate healthcare needs in association with the hospital's 24-hour walk-in emergency room. Healthcare Express, which operates like a clinic, is open daily from noon to 8 PM and accepts all major credit cards, most major insurance carriers and Medicare.

MedNow Clinic
194 High St., Ellsworth • 667-4655

The MedNow Clinic is open 8 AM to 6 PM Monday through Friday and 9 AM to 4 PM weekends, offering emergency care and treatment, minor surgery, children's care, some continued care including pediatrics, women's health needs and limited on-site testing. The clinic sees mostly walk-ins, though it sometimes schedules appointments. Payment is through insurance providers (the clinic will bill), Medicare or cash. The clinic will also bill its patients; payment plans are available.

Eleanor Widener Dixon Memorial Clinic
Maine Hwy. 186, Gouldsboro • 963-4066

The Eleanor Widener Dixon Memorial Clinic is proud of its reach throughout the Downeast region. In 1995, the clinic served 16,735 patients. This basic health clinic offers family practice, obstetrics and emergency care. The clinic is affiliated with Maine Coast Memorial Hospital (see previous "Hospitals" section) in Ellsworth.

The clinic is open 8 AM to 4:30 PM Monday through Friday. Walk-ins are accepted. The clinic will bill most insurance companies and also accepts credit cards, Medicare and Medicaid.

Mount Desert Island

Mount Desert Island offers six year-round clinics, with a seventh open only in summer. Six clinics are affiliated with Mount Desert Island Hospital in Bar Harbor; the seventh, Southwest Harbor Medical Center, is affiliated with Maine Coast Memorial Hospital in Ellsworth.

FYI

Unless otherwise noted, the area code for all phone numbers listed in this guide is 207.

All the island clinics accept Medicaid, Medicare, most insurance plans and credit cards, but expect to pay when you visit. Sliding-scale fees are available; ask for an application.

Cooper-Gilmore Health Center
17 Hancock St., Bar Harbor • 288-5024

For years this health center across the parking lot from Mount Desert Island Hospital has worked cooperatively with the hospital. In late 1997, the two organizations became officially connected. This full-service health center staffs five doctors covering a wide range of needs, including general family-practice services and an on-site lab. As previously mentioned, the hospital is just across the way. Hours are 8 AM to 5 PM Monday through Friday, with possibly longer hours in summer.

Family Health Center
9 Hancock St., Bar Harbor • 288-5606

In a remodeled home and affiliated with the adjacent Mount Desert Island Hospital (see previous "Hospitals" section), the Family Health Center is a hospital-based clinic focused on community health. All staff members are employed by the hospital.

The center accepts some walk-ins but mostly works with appointments. Three doctors and one physician's assistant provide for all primary-care needs. Lab services are handled through the hospital. Hours are 8 AM to 5 PM Monday through Friday, with longer hours in summer.

High Street Health Center
3 High St., Bar Harbor • 288-5119

The High Street Health Center is a rural facility in the center of Bar Harbor. A staff of two physicians and a nurse practitioner assist with all primary-care needs. The focus is on treating the needs of the whole family. It is affiliated with Mount Desert Island Hospital (see the previous "Hospitals" section). Appointments are necessary, but emergency walk-ins can be handled. The center is open 8 AM to 5 PM Monday through Friday year round. Major insurance providers plus Medicare and Medicaid are accepted.

Women's Health Center
8 Wayman Ln., Bar Harbor • 288-8100

The Women's Health Center offers general health maintenance and deals with women's health issues at its location near the Mount Desert Island Hospital, with which it is affiliated (see previous "Hospitals" section). The center prides itself on its attention to the woman's whole being. Routine examinations, obstetrics, educational programs and referrals to both traditional and nontraditional care providers are offered. Appointments are necessary. The Women's Center is open 8 AM to 5 PM Monday through Friday, until 8 PM Tuesdays.

Northeast Harbor Clinic
Kimball Rd., Northeast Harbor • 276-3331

The Northeast Harbor Clinic is an outreach facility geared to visitors and summer residents. A physician staffs this office 20 hours a week from late June through Labor Day, offering limited assistance in treating colds, flu, bruises, cuts and other basic, acute-care needs. It is affiliated with the Mount Desert Island Hospital (see previous "Hospitals" section). Call for hours. Walk-ins are accepted.

Community Health Center
9 Village Green Way, Southwest Harbor • 244-5630

Physicians from Mount Desert Island Hospital (see previous "Hospitals" section) staff the Community Health Center on a rotating basis. Together with a nurse practitioner, they maintain a full-service care center and a clinic with a full lab, X-ray services, physical therapy and chemical-dependency counseling. The center is open 8 AM to 7 PM Monday and Wednesday and 8 AM to 5 PM Tuesday, Thursday and Friday.

Southwest Harbor Medical Center
45 Herrick Rd., Southwest Harbor
• **244-5513, 244-5514**

The staff of Southwest Harbor Medical Center includes three physicians, one nurse practitioner and a laboratory and radiology technician to assist with general healthcare for adults and children as well as geriatric care, emergency care, diagnostics and minor surgery. This health center is affiliated with Maine Coast Memorial Hospital in Ellsworth (see previous "Hospitals" section), and continued care is available through that hospital. The clinic is open 8 AM to 5 PM Monday through Friday, until 8 PM Wednesday and 9 AM until 1 PM Saturday. Walk-ins are accepted, but appointments are preferred.

Psychiatric Hospitals

Inland to Bangor

The Acadia Hospital
268 Stillwater Ave., Bangor • **973-6100, (800) 640-1211**

In association with Eastern Maine Medical Center, The Acadia Hospital is an acute-care hospital with 100 beds that focuses on treating people suffering from mental illness and chemical dependency. Inpatient psychiatric units assist people suffering from depression, schizophrenia, dual diagnosis, childhood disorders and other conditions, including chemical dependency. Acadia focuses on getting people back into the community as quickly as possible. There is a unit for children ages 3 to 11, an adolescent unit for children ages 12 to 17 and two adult units. Individual, family and group therapies are available, as is medication and education about mental illness. Adolescents can be served at a transitional home called Aspenledge. There are also intensive day programs for adolescents and adults. Days are spent at the hospital for group work, education and coping training; nights are spent at home.

Ambulatory Services offers outpatient diagnosis, treatment and education, while Behavioral Neurology Services offers outpatient evaluation and treatment for neurological disorders, especially those associated with head injuries. For those in crisis, a consultation service provides emergency evaluation and assessment either at The Acadia Hospital or the emergency department of Eastern Maine Medical Center. The referral leads to the least restrictive level of care at the hospital or through another provider. Support groups, outpatient chemical-dependency services and educational offerings are also available at The Acadia Hospital.

Bucksport to Gouldsboro

KidsPeace National Centers for Kids in Crisis – New England School
Graham Lake, Maine Hwy. 180, Ellsworth
• **667-0909, (800) 992-9KID**

For children with severe emotional or behavioral problems, KidsPeace National Centers for Kids in Crisis offers a broad range of assistance, beginning with a comprehensive, multi-disciplinary diagnostics program. Children referred to the program are admitted for a 45-day individualized diagnostic process. While at the center, 11 at a time may attend school in the program's classroom and receive short-term counseling and therapy while still maintaining contact with their families (unless otherwise indicated by law). The Diagnostic Acute Care Program deals with male and female children ages 8 to 18 who are socially and emotionally distressed and developmentally delayed, including those with dysfunctional behavior patterns, mild neurological impairment or needing 24-hour supervision. The 45-bed center also offers a residential treatment program and private education for children and teens through 12th grade.

Mental-health Clinics

Although this section includes clinics dedicated to mental-health issues, many regional clinics also have counselors on staff. Check the Yellow Pages for a list of private doctors and counselors.

Waldoboro to Stockton Springs

Mid-Coast Mental Health Center
12 Union St., Rockland • 594-2541, (800) 540-2072
28 Cedar St., Belfast • 338-2295

A staff of more than 70 professionals, including licensed social workers, psychiatrists, psychologists, substance-abuse counselors and mental-health workers, offer counseling and psychiatric services to individuals, families and schools as well as to the elderly in their homes. Mid-Coast Mental Health Center also offers 24-hour crisis and emergency services, substance-abuse programs and case management for children and adults.

Services can be paid by most private health insurance, Medicaid or Medicare, or based on a sliding-scale fee.

Inland to Bangor

Community Health and Counseling Services
42 Cedar St., Bangor • 947-0366 (for adults)
900 Hammond St., Bangor • 947-0366 (for children)

Community Health and Counseling is a large-scale, nonprofit clinic serving families and children with welfare, mental health and abuse-treatment needs. The Bangor office has a staff of about 470 mental-health professionals and 100 health-services professionals. The organization offers comprehensive mental-health programs such as supportive counseling, advocacy and vocational training for adults. For children, it offers day treatment, assessment centers, crisis

intervention and stabilization, therapy and supportive counseling. It also offers youth-crisis intervention and substance-abuse assistance. Since 1948, CHC has been involved in placing children in adoptive and foster care. It also maintains Ellsworth offices (see subsequent entry). Payment by Medicaid, Medicare, insurance, state contracts or out-of-pocket is accepted.

Bucksport to Gouldsboro

Peninsula Counseling
Sussman Building, Water St., Blue Hill • 374-5780

Outreach counselors working with the Blue Hill hospital and its associated clinics are headquartered in the Sussman Building, behind the hospital.

Community Health and Counseling Services
1 High St., Ellsworth • 667-5357 (for adults)
204 Water St., Ellsworth • 667-2061 (for children)

The nonprofit, community health organization offers individual, group and family therapy, youth-crisis stabilization and adult community-support services. (See the previous Bangor entry for details.)

Mount Desert Island

At this time, there are individual, private practitioners on the island, but no mental health centers or groups. See the Yellow Pages for names of local practitioners.

Alternative Healthcare

The Mid-Coast area has a wide range of alternative health providers. Rather than list

---

INSIDERS' TIP

Medical care played an indirect role in developing the Mount Desert Island community. At the start of the century, when Abby Aldrich Rockefeller was pregnant with Nelson, her doctor decided to spend the summer in Bar Harbor. The Rockefellers followed him there that summer (and many summers afterward), altering the very nature of the island by their presence.

individual practitioners, we offer a discussion of the kinds of therapies available. For practitioners, we suggest you check the Yellow Pages, or the local health food store or co-op.

Acupuncture

Acupuncturists work not only with needles, but also with pressure points and Chinese and other herbs in a 5,000-year-old process that helps the body heal itself by re-establishing harmony or balance in a person's vital energy. Providers in Maine have organized themselves under the Maine Association of Acupuncture and Oriental Medicine, P.O. Box 10912, Portland, ME 04104.

Chiropractic Medicine

Chiropractors manipulate the skeletal system as a first line of healing. Considering their prevalence nationwide, practitioners of chiropractic medicine are hardly considered alternative therapists these days.

Homeopathy

Homeopathy is based on helping the body heal itself through the principle that "like cures like." The medications, known as remedies, use doses so minuscule there is no chemical trace of them in the pills — and yet they can cure everything from ear infections to depression without side effects. Homeopathy is still a basic European form of treatment: The Queen of England has her own homeopath. Homeopathic doctors handle as wide a range of illnesses as allopathic (read American Medical Association-licensed) doctors. There are both M.D. homeopaths and lay practitioners in the region.

Massage Therapists

Massage therapists (a.k.a. bodyworkers) frequently employ a range of healing techniques, from hands-on body manipulation (therapeutic massage) based on relieving pain, stress and limited motion to a variety of hands-on healing.

Shiatsu, meaning "finger pressure," is an Oriental form of bodywork focusing on the 14 meridians and the pressure points, which are pressed to stimulate Ki, or energy.

Hypnotherapy uses hypnosis in conjunction with counseling for healing physical and psychological stress.

Reiki utilizes universal life energy to restore the body to natural wellness.

Naturopathic Medicine

Based on the principle that nature heals, naturopathic healers work with patients to find the root cause of an illness, then employ a wide range of alternative medicines to assist the healing: nutrition, herbs, homeopathic medicine, hydrotherapy, physical therapy, craniosacral therapy and counseling. Wellcare and physical exams as well as assistance with chronic and acute conditions are available.

Home Healthcare Services

One benefit of the trend to limit hospital stays has been an increase of home healthcare services. Maine's Mid-Coast region includes several organizations dedicated to bringing care to people's homes. Generally, such organizations offer a registered nurse to perform such care as changing dressings, managing IV therapy and catheterization. Physical and occupational therapists work on exercises and skill development for the homebound.

Medicaid and Medicare usually certify people for home-health services, or patients can be covered by private insurance.

Waldoboro to Stockton Springs

Kno-Wal-Lin Home Health Care
605 U.S. Hwy. 1, Newcastle • 563-5719
170 Pleasant St., Rockland • 594-9561,
(800) 540-9561
33 Front St., Belfast • 338-2002,
(800) 540-9561
This service includes a full range of home

healthcare on a 24-hour basis in three Mid-Coast counties: Knox, Waldo and Lincoln. Kno-Wal-Lin offers companion homemakers, personal-care assistants, private-duty nurses, an enterostomal therapist and a lactation consultant. Through Northeast Health, Kno-Wal-Lin is now associated with Penobscot Bay Medical Center in Rockport (see the previous "Hospitals" section), providing continued care for clients.

Waldo County Home Health Care
119 Northport Ave., Belfast • 338-2268, (888) 254-5133

Waldo County Home Health Care offers a full range of home healthcare 24 hours a day for those who need it in Knox and Waldo counties. Services include home mental-health care as well as more typical home nursing care (see this section's preamble). Waldo County Home Health Care is associated with Waldo County Hospital for continued care.

Inland to Bangor

A Loving Touch Inc.
149 Cedar St., Bangor • 990-1995

A Loving Touch provides home healthcare for those in need of assistance after surgery or because of a temporary disability. Care includes daily living assistance; therapy for depression; assistance to mothers of newborns, recent widows or widowers; prescription pickups; and even care for pets. Clients are billed for payment; services are not insurance-reimbursable.

Bangor Area Visiting Nurses Inc.
80 Exchange St., Bangor • 947-0589, (800) 745-0589

This corporation offers assistance to those who need home healthcare within a 25-mile radius of Bangor. A lot of the work of the 24 nurses is education, but they also see women with pregnancy complications, visit post-operative clients and monitor at-home safety. Clients are referred from Bangor-area hospitals, doctors, families and other sources. Payment is by insurance, Medicare, Medicaid or out-of-pocket.

Community Health and Counseling Services
42 Cedar St., Bangor • 947-0366

Community Health and Counseling offers home-health services for the home-bound. In addition to basic nursing and rehabilitative services (see this section's preamble), this office offers AIDS care, psychiatric services, geriatric mental-health services, early maternity and orthopedic discharge services, spinal cord- and head-injury care, high-risk pregnancy monitoring, chemotherapy and hospice services.

Home Health & Hospice of St. Joseph
900 Broadway, Bangor • 262-1810, (800) 646-5000

The staff at St. Joseph believe that people recover from illness and maintain better health in the comfort and security of their own home. To this end Home Health of St. Joseph helps people live independently at home with registered nurse services; home-health aid; nutritional counseling; diabetes education; occupational, physical, IV and respiratory therapies; chemotherapy; and respite care. Coverage areas range beyond the Bangor area to Bucksport, Belfast and farther Downeast.

Bucksport to Gouldsboro

Hancock County Home Care
Blue Hill Memorial Hospital, Water St., Blue Hill • 374-5510

A division of Blue Hill Memorial Hospital (see the previous "Hospitals" section), Hancock County Home Care offers long-term–care planning and assistance with other agencies while also providing in-home care. While there are no psychiatric nurses, medical social workers can come to the homes. All methods of payment are accepted, including Medicaid, Medicare, insurance and out-of-pocket.

Community Health and Counseling Services
415 Water St., Ellsworth • 667-3626

Community Health and Counseling Services offers home healthcare in the greater Ellsworth area. See the previous Bangor entry for specifics.

Mount Desert Island

Hancock County Home Care
93 Cottage St., Bar Harbor • 288-5584

Hancock County Home Care in Bar Harbor offers the same range of assistance as its Blue Hill office (see previous entry): in-home care for patients, planning for long-term care and assistance with referrals to other agencies.

Hospices

Waldoboro to Stockton Springs

Kno-Wal-Lin Home Hospice
170 Pleasant St., Rockland • 594-9561, (800) 540-9561

Working in Knox, Waldo and Lincoln counties and linked with their home-health services, Kno-Wal-Lin offers basic hospice care by trained volunteers, including bereavement counseling and caring for the care giver. Spiritual counseling from a pastoral counselor also is available.

Belfast Hospice
Waldo County General Hospital, 119 Northport Ave., Belfast • 338-2500, (800) 649-2536

Waldo County Home Healthcare offers a wide range of collaborative care by coordinating in-home hospice care with a physician, home nursing staff, trained volunteers and bereavement counselors. For a patient's final stages of life, the hospital offers inpatient hospice care, if necessary, that also accommodates family members with an overnight guest room and comfortable family room. The organization also has overnight respite care for families, either at home or in the hospital, for up to five days.

Inland to Bangor

Home Health & Hospice of St. Joseph
900 Broadway, Bangor • 262-1810, (800) 646-5000

St. Joseph provides in-home services for people with terminal illnesses, 24-hours a day, if need be. Known as Terminal Long Care (or "TLC"), the hospital offers at-home chemotherapy and symptom management for those with kidney, lung or neuromuscular disease. Home Health & Hospice of St. Joseph prides itself on its sense of respect for the needs of the patient and the family and its continued commitment to quality of life. Hospice volunteers are assisted by a multi-disciplinary team of spiritual, social and medical advisors.

For good local news,
small-town weeklies
can't be beat.

Media

The media in Portland and Bangor cast wide, sometimes overlapping nets across the state. Portland radio, TV and newspapers serve the southern part of the Mid-Coast area, while Bangor's media cover the northern and eastern sections. Fortunately, the state's excellent public broadcasting network — television and radio — reaches almost everywhere.

Some of us, residents and visitors alike, can't live without the Sunday *New York Times* or *Boston Globe*. Try grocery stores, drugstores or convenience stores.

For good local news, small-town weeklies can't be beat. They have a proud tradition here, covering their areas with a thoroughness the dailies can only approximate.

Yes, but how do locals get their news? The old-fashioned way — through the grapevine. Many towns still have volunteer fire departments, and the low chatter of police scanners can be heard in some kitchens. News travels fast at grocery stores, the post office and the dump, and telephones ring all over town after particularly heated public meetings. Visitors may not have the same network available to them, but it's worth noting that the art of conversation is alive and well.

Newspapers

Dailies

Bangor Daily News
491 Main St., Bangor • 990-8000

The *Bangor Daily News*, which for more than 100 years called itself Maine's largest daily newspaper, has a circulation area that boggles the mind: basically the entire eastern half of the state. A network of 10 bureaus (some are one-person outposts) makes it possible — and a great source for statewide news. Its big weekend paper has seven sections, runs around 60 pages and is published on Saturday. That's the edition to check for job listings. The paper also has strong sports coverage and boasts syndicated columns by Molly Ivins, Maureen Dowd, Cal Thomas, Mary McGrory, and yes, Dear Abby.

A local historian says Thomas J. Stewart started the paper in 1889 when he couldn't get the daily *Whig and Courier* to support his run for Congress. "Fashioned after James Gordon Bennett's famous *New York Herald*, the *News* was an immediate sensation," writes Alan Robert Miller in *The History of Current Maine Newspapers*. Today, the paper is owned by the Bangor Publishing Company.

Circulation figures are 70,000 weekdays (60¢ a copy) and 90,000 for the weekend edition ($1.50 a copy).

Portland Press Herald
390 Congress St., Portland • 791-6650

The *Portland Press Herald* has a big-city newspaper feel and runs considerable national and international news. The paper's layout is clean and easy to navigate, the weather map is in glorious color, and syndicated features include George Will, Ellen Goodman and Judith Martin's "Miss Manners."

The late Guy Gannett consolidated the *Portland Daily Press* and the *Portland Herald* in 1921, and acquired the *Maine Sunday Telegram* in 1925. His company, now Guy Gannett Communications, which is currently for sale ,owns four newspapers and seven television stations, including WGME Channel 13 in Portland.

This paper's circulation is 74,000 weekdays (60¢ a copy), 130,000 Sunday ($1.75 a copy).

Weeklies

Maine Times
9 Union St., Hallowell • 623-8955

"Fighting for a better Maine since 1968"

is how this statewide alternative weekly describes itself. Critics call it an advocate for leftist causes, but that's a badge of honor in some quarters. Where else would you learn who broke the story on health-and-safety violations at the DeCoster egg plant? The enormous federal fines imposed were plastered all over the big dailies, but only in the *Maine Times* did we read that a weekly journalist discovered conditions at the plant and fought to expose them.

Courier-Gazette
1 Park Dr., Rockland • 594-4401

While the *Courier-Gazette* is now the flagship of a chain of newspapers owned by Courier Publications in Rockland, it was founded more than a century ago. The *Gazette* began in 1846; the *Courier*, in 1874; the two joined forces in 1882. An energetic staff covers news and features all over the area. Reporters regularly write columns on the editorial page as well — don't miss David Grima's.

Free Press
6 Leland St., Rockland • 596-0055

One or two features lead this free weekly, supplemented by every community press release it can fit in its pages. The *Free Press* also runs TV listings, a crossword puzzle and popular syndicated columns by *The Miami Herald's* Dave Barry and by Tom and Ray Magliozzi, "Click and Clack" of National Public Radio's *Car Talk*.

Camden Herald
69 Elm St., Camden • 236-8511

The *Camden Herald*, founded in 1869, is now owned by the Courier Publications chain. The change, which includes new staff and design, was greeted with mixed reviews by the community. The paper covers Camden, Hope, Appleton and Lincolnville. It's always had strong sports coverage, and it's a great place to look for upcoming yard sales.

Republican Journal
71 High St., Belfast • 338-3333

Established in 1829, the *Republican Journal* is Maine's oldest weekly. Now owned by

Courier Publications in Rockland, it shares resources and stories with its sister papers. An editorial staff of seven covers all of Waldo County.

Waldo Independent
107A Church St., Belfast • 338-5100

In 1985, *Republican Journal* editor Jay Davis resigned over a disagreement with the publisher. Most of the staff resigned shortly after, when a new editor was hired. Together they launched the *Waldo Independent*. Employee-owned, it manages to produce very strong local news coverage with an editorial staff of three.

The Enterprise
P.O. Box 829, Bucksport, ME 04416 • 469-6722

The Enterprise, a solid weekly newspaper, covers Bucksport, Orland, Verona and neighboring towns. During the winter '98 ice storm, the front page covered the storm's effect on the timber industry — an ambitious undertaking for overworked weekly reporters. Sports, area history, reminiscences and recipes round out the mix.

Maine Coastal News
P.O. Box 847, Brewer, ME 04412 • 990-4436

Maine Coastal News is a 24- to 28-page tabloid that comes out biweekly from April to September and monthly from October to March. Publisher/editor Jon Johansen covers the coast from Kittery to Eastport, writing about anything maritime-related: history, builders, boatyards, marinas.

Castine Patriot
P.O. Box 205, Castine, ME 04421 • 326-4383

Island Ad-Vantages
P.O. Box 36, Stonington, ME 04681 • 367-2200

Weekly Packet
P.O. Box 646, Blue Hill, ME 04614 • 374-2341

Nat Barrows bought the *Island Ad-Vantages* in 1968, the *Weekly Packet* in 1981, and the

---

FYI

Unless otherwise noted, the area code for all phone numbers listed in this guide is 207.

Castine Patriot in 1990. Summer swells their circulations and page counts, but they average a combined circulation of 5,800 to 6,000. They share a core pullout section on events and activities, but the rest of each paper is unique. Like any good weekly, these publications reflect the communities they cover. Stonington revolves around fishing and tourism, Castine has a large retirement community and the Maine Maritime Academy, and Blue Hill has a large hospital. The news sections of each paper cover town government, the school board, births, deaths and other news of note.

Ellsworth American
63 Main St., Ellsworth • 667-2576

Founded in 1855, the *Ellsworth American* is an oversize broadsheet that can run to as many as four sections. It's best known — and loved — for editor John Russell Wiggins, who bought the paper in 1966. Former editor of *The Washington Post* and ambassador to the United Nations, he's been called the grand old man of Maine journalism, and his newspaper has the prizes to prove it. No weekly worth its salt is universally loved, but this paper is an example of what's possible in a relatively affluent community. Look for first-rate reporting, quality photography, even poetry.

Bar Harbor Times
76 Cottage St., Bar Harbor • 288-3311

Now owned by Courier Publications, the *Bar Harbor Times* has returned to broadsheet format. It has a bold layout and a tradition of strong reporting. Writer Nan Lincoln has worked at the paper in various capacities for years, and she's a community treasure. Her obituaries are sensitive, thorough and an extraordinary window on the community. Check out the paper's annual *Bluebook*, a guide to towns and services in Hancock County.

Magazines

HOPE
P.O. Box 160, Brooklin, ME 04616
• 359-4651

Jon Wilson of *WoodenBoat* is at it again, launching this national bimonthly magazine in 1996 "to inspire a sense of hope among read-

ers." The stories focus on people, businesses and organizations all over the country that make a difference. One memorable issue described a sculptor who makes plaster masks of famous people and displays them so blind people can feel the faces and "see" what they look like.

Down East
P.O. Box 679, Camden, ME 04843
• 594-9544

Maine's statewide glossy, this four-color monthly focuses on all aspects of living in Maine — for people who live here and people who want to live here. It includes a calendar of events, some history and an interesting range of light features. The classifieds are a gold mine for real estate and summer rentals.

Island Journal
410 Main St., Rockland • 594-9209

This is the annual publication of the Island Institute, a nonprofit organization dedicated to sustaining islands and their communities. While the stories reflect the institute's mission, they would stand alone in any magazine as quality writing. Poems and extraordinary photographs round out the package. Most copies go to Island Institute contributors, but the *Journal* is available in many Maine coastal and island bookstores.

Maine Antique Digest
911 Main St., Waldoboro • 832-7534

This 31,000-circulation monthly covers the antiques and art market for a national readership of dealers and collectors. A thick, folded broadsheet on newsprint, each issue might run more than 400 pages. Editor Sam Pennington prides himself on taking an independent journalistic approach to market prices and market news, sending out reporters in cases where others might simply run press releases. (See the "Antiques" section of our Shopping chapter for information about the vast antiques market in Maine's Mid-Coast region.)

Maine Boats & Harbors
21 Elm St., Camden • 236-8622

The name says it all. Founder and publisher John Hanson started at *WoodenBoat*, then launched this title independently in 1987. While the focus is on living, working and cruising the Gulf of Maine, subjects include houses, food, history and almost anything nautical. The "Boatyard Dog" column, a picture and description of dogs (and cats) in marine-management positions, is worth the price of the magazine.

People, Places and Plants
35 Cambell Shore Rd., Gray • 428-4001, (800) 251-1784

This magazine, launched in 1996, is a great find for anyone interested in gardening and living in Maine. It comes out five times a year and takes a more European view of gardening, including all aspects of plant care in Maine's sometimes quirky climate.

Salt
19 Pine St., Portland • 761-0660

Salt, a nonprofit, runs an educational program on documentary work for photographers and writers, publishing the best work in a quarterly of the same name. Topics range from Elvis impersonators to the tension between aquaculturists and lobstermen to the evolution of traditional crafts. Because the intent is to document, the photos are stunning and sometimes gritty, and the writing very precise.

WoodenBoat
P.O. Box 78, Brooklin, ME 04616 • 359-4651

They said it would never succeed, but after 23 years, Jon Wilson and his crew are thriving. This is *the* magazine for wooden boat owners, builders and designers nationwide. Niche magazines are always full of good information; this one is full of good writing. We've seen novelist Tom McGuane's byline on its pages.

Television

Network television in Maine's Mid-Coast region is as easy as chocolate, vanilla or strawberry. There are two NBC affiliates, two ABC affiliates and two CBS affiliates. One of each flavor originates in Portland (or nearby Auburn), and one of each originates in Bangor. A small Fox affiliate broadcasts out of Port-

land as well. That said, the big question is whether your TV can pick up these stations. Antennas can greatly help reception, especially in hilly sections. A satellite dish or cable hookup accomplishes the same end, while adding a world of choices.

As you can see, what's available on the television set you happen to be watching can vary wildly. Our best advice is to ask your host and check whatever listings are available. The TV sections of the Portland and Bangor weekend papers are a good place to start.

Network Affiliates

WLBZ Channel 2 (NBC)
329 Mount Hope Ave., Bangor • 942-4821

Channel 2 went on the air in 1954, the second TV station in Bangor. Together with sister affiliate WCSH Channel 6 in Portland, WLBZ Channel 2 claims to broadcast more news than any other Bangor station. Their shared StormCenter programming is very popular (see the subsequent WCSH entry for more on that). WLBZ also sponsors a "People Make the Difference" campaign, which is also the subject of some of its local programming.

WABI Channel 5 (CBS)
35 Hildreth St., Bangor • 947-8321

WABI was the first TV station in the state of Maine, and it's big on sports. Look for high school basketball tournaments, local stock car racing, and selected University of Maine games — women's basketball and men's basketball, football and hockey. Its news anchor, Don Colson, is a veteran, and his experience shows in an appealing informality. The station is in its seventh year of Weather School, a free classroom curriculum on weather, geography and general science for area students; and it has weather tracking stations in several area schools.

WCSH Channel 6 (NBC)
1 Congress Sq., Portland • 828-6666

Channel 6 is the larger of two sister NBC affiliates, and a good deal of their shared programming is produced at its studios. StormCenter, in particular, is very popular. The station calls it Maine's first full-service winter storm news and information source, and it includes school closings, cancellations and driving conditions. The station also produces more than 27 hours of newscasts every week. Watch for segments by lawyer/reporter Susan Kimball — she's a real asset to the news operation.

WVII Channel 7 (ABC)
371 Target Industrial Cir., Bangor
• 945-6457

Channel 7 is the place to find *Wheel of Fortune* and *Jeopardy*, two of the hottest game shows on the air. The station also added Rosie O'Donnell to its lineup, and it's done very well. While WVII news, weather and sports personalities change fairly frequently, Bangor is one of the smaller markets and is often a proving ground for young talent. Selected Bangor Symphony concerts are rebroadcast on the station a few weeks after the performances. Watch the listings for broadcast times.

WMTW Channel 8 (ABC)
99 Danville Corner Rd., Auburn
• 782-1800

Channel 8 is strong on news, with a 5 PM newscast, the first segment in a block that runs to 6:30 PM. Sports coverage is another claim to fame. The station is positioning itself to be the pro sports station, with live broadcasts of the Portland Sea Dogs baseball games and a monthly local sports show. *This Week in New England*, a show on community issues, is produced at its studios as well. Martha Stewart fans can find her TV show here seven days a week.

MPTV Channels 10 and 12 (PBS)
65 Texas Ave., Bangor • 941-1010

Maine's Public Broadcasting Network (MPBN) has studios in Bangor and Lewiston, and while the station lists five different sets of call letters from five different towns, the programming is the same statewide. And the pro-gramming is excellent. Public affairs shows such as *Capitol Connection*, *Quest* and *RFD Maine* explore statewide issues in depth and detail — and with flair. *Masterpiece Theater* and *Mystery* are welcome parts of the mix. Strong children's programming runs throughout much of the day.

WGME Channel 13 (CBS)
1335 Washington Ave., Portland
• 797-9330

Anchor Kim Block is a veteran, and the weather segments are based on advanced weather-tracking technology. (The maps are great!) Local reporter Amy Sinclair won an Emmy for a feature she did on singer/songwriter Dave Mallet. For talk-show junkies, this is one place to find Oprah Winfrey and Maury Povich.

WPXT Channel 51 (Fox)
2320 Congress St., Portland • 774-0051

A relative newcomer to the market, WPXT was started 11 years ago and broadcasts straight Fox programming. It runs a half-hour news show Monday though Friday at 10 PM, and two local shows over the weekend: *Maine Outdoorsman* and *Mark Stimson Real Estate Digest*. Syndicated shows include *NYPD Blue*, *X-Files* and *Walker, Texas Ranger*.

Cable

Cable is only available in towns that have awarded a cable franchise, and even then cable lines tend to run only to more populated areas. This has caused an enormous amount of contention in some towns, and it explains the satellite dishes that sprout from lawns and houses on the back roads.

While cable providers vary from town to town, the following are the major players. Most offer various levels of service, from a basic cable package to a lineup of premium channels including HBO, Cinemax and The Disney Channel.

INSIDERS' TIP

Want to know what's really going on in town? Read the letters to the editor in the local weekly.

Linconville Communications
P.O. Box 200, Lincolnville, ME 04850
• 763-9900

The basic service includes 33 channels. Premium services such as HBO, Showtime, Cinemax, Disney and the New England Sports Network are available for an additional charge and in certain discount combinations. The company serves Lincolnville and Hope.

FrontierVision
400 Old County Rd., Rockland
• 596-6622, (800) 336-9988
149 Target Industrial Cir., Bangor
• 942-4661, (800) 432-1648

FrontierVision bought out Cablevision last year, so it's the big player in the Mid-Coast region. Because franchise agreements differ from town to town, the channel lineup can't be easily summarized. The marketing director says some towns might be contracted for 20 to 40 channels, some for more than that. The basic lineup usually includes Arts & Entertainment, the Turner superstation, Nickelodeon, CNN Headline News and ESPN. Premium channels usually include HBO, Showtime and Disney.

Communities served include Bangor, Bar Harbor, Belfast, Blue Hill, Bradley, Brewer, Bucksport, Camden, Castine, Cushing, Deer Isle, East Sullivan, Eddington, Ellsworth, Franklin, Friendship, Hampden, Hancock, Holden, Indian Island, Lamoine, Mount Desert, Newport, Northeast Harbor, North Sullivan, Old Town, Orono, Orrington, Otter Creek, Owls Head, Port Clyde, Rockland, Rockport, Seal Harbor, South Thomaston, Searsmont, Sorrento, Spruce Head, St. George, Searsport, Southwest Harbor, Stockton Springs, Stonington, Sullivan, Sunset, Surry, Tenants Harbor, Thomaston, Tremont, Trenton, Union, Veazie, Vinalhaven, Warren, Winterport and Verona Island.

Unity Cable Television Inc.
15 Main St., Unity • 948-2288

Basic service includes 31 channels and five premium services: HBO, Showtime, Cinemax, Disney and the New England Sports Network. The fee schedule offers a set price for basic cable and a fee for each additional premium channel. Burnham, Thorndike and Unity are the communities served.

Radio

An incredible number of radio stations broadcast in the Mid-Coast area, so we can merely point listeners in the right direction with the following list. The FCC opened some new channels in the late 1980s, apparently to ensure that the little towns along the coast were getting served. The move seemed to offer an embarrassment of riches for the listener — at least that's what it looked like at the time. What's happened is that it splintered the market, cutting the revenue pie into increasingly smaller slices, and some stations are barely making it. Some simulcast, fewer do local news, and many go to satellite programming for part of the day. The Mid-Coast region encompasses a wide area, and its hills can make radio reception a trial. We've added the town of origin after each listing so you can find the nearest stations.

Adult Contemporary
WCME 96.7 FM, Boothbay Harbor
WDEA 1370 AM, Ellsworth
WEZQ 92.9 FM, Bangor
WKSQ 94.5 FM, Ellsworth
WMGX 93.1 FM, Portland
WQSS 102.5 FM, Camden
WRKD 1450 AM, Rockland
WWBX 97.1 FM, Bangor

Christian
WBCI 105.9 FM, Bath

INSIDERS' TIP

Stores that carry the Sunday *New York Times* often reserve copies for residents and summer visitors. Get on their list if you plan to be in town for any length of time. If you're a weekend visitor but just can't bear to be without the *Times*, call ahead and ask if you might reserve a copy on a one-time basis.

WHCF 88.5 FM, Bangor
WLOB 1310 AM, Portland
WMDR 1340 AM, Augusta

Classical

WAVX 106.9 FM, Thomaston
WBYA 101.7 FM, Searsport
WMEA 90.1 FM (Public Radio), Portland
WMEH 90.9 FM (Public Radio), Bangor

College Radio

WHSN 89.3 FM, Bangor
WMEB 91.9 FM, Orono

Community

WERU 89.9 FM (Alternative music and local info), East Orland

Country

WBFB 104.7 FM, Belfast
WEBB 98.5 FM/WTVL 1490 AM, Augusta
WKCG 101.3 FM, Gardiner
WLKE 99.1 FM, Bar Harbor
WMCM 103.3 FM, Rockland

WPOR 101.9 FM/1490 AM, Portland
WQCB 106.5 FM, Brewer

News/Talk

WGAN 560 AM, Portland
WJTO 730 AM, Bath
WVOM 103.9 FM, Bangor
WZAN 970 AM, Portland
WZON 620 AM (Sports), Bangor

Nostalgia/Oldies

WABI 910 AM, Bangor
WYNZ 100.9 FM, Westbrook

Rock

WBLM 102.9 FM, Portland
WCYY 94.3 FM, Portland
WKIT 100.3 FM, Bangor
WMDI 107.7 FM, Bar Harbor

Top-40

WBZN 107.3 FM, Brewer
WJBQ 97.9 FM, Portland
WMME 1400 AM/92.3 FM, Augusta

Unlike many urban areas, churches here still have a strong presence in the community, both in a religious sense and as centers for social activity.

Worship

Places of worship are bigger than their walls — they are our community at its best — but there are so many choices in Maine's Mid-Coast region, it would be impossible to list them all. For the times and services of a particular denomination, check the local newspaper or the Yellow Pages. What we want to do in this chapter is address the spiritual life of the community and indicate some of the tangible ways it is expressed.

When we first moved to the Mid-Coast region, a native Mainer told us that small-town life was based on giving . . . giving time to the community, giving money to good causes, giving help to the less fortunate, even giving way at intersections. He said Yankees weren't all smiley and happy, but when you needed a hand, they were there.

Not surprisingly, the churches and synagogues in the area are practical and active. They sponsor food pantries, rummage sales, holiday food baskets and bean suppers. Second-hand clothing sales are popular, especially with older members on fixed incomes. The fact is, unlike in many urban areas, churches here still have a strong presence in the community, both in a religious sense and as centers for social activity.

Think for a minute about the geographic area we've described as the Mid-Coast. While most visitors zoom through, seeing only what is on either side of U.S. Highway 1, the region actually spans hundreds of miles, including islands and peninsulas. The population is sparse in places, and consequently not every denomination is represented in every community. People frequently drive miles to join together to worship. While there is an impressive array of choices, visitors need to dig a little and, like the rest of us, might need to go out of their way to find the church or synagogue or assembly of their choice.

Since so many religious groups meet in other quarters, you might have to watch the listings in the newspapers (under churches or even community events) to find them. It might be easy to locate a Congregational church (this is New England, after all!) or a Roman Catholic church, but it might be a challenge to find a Quaker meeting or your nearest Zen practitioners.

Amazing Grace

What are the religious and spiritual choices? The range is as broad as the people who've settled here. The Native American population is still on these shores, endeavoring to preserve its spiritual heritage. The earliest European immigrants were predominantly Protestant, the next wave brought their Catholic faith, and now, according to the Maine Council of Churches, Roman Catholics are far and away the majority denomination.

In the 17th century, the meetinghouse style of architecture was popular for churches, and *Maine Forms of American Architecture*, edited by Deborah Thompson, indicates Maine was slow to abandon it. Thompson writes, "Calvinist doctrine rejected the concept of holy places, [so] there was no bar to using the meetinghouses for all decent business requiring public assembly, as well as for worship."

In the 1800s communities started building specialized edifices for worship services, and you see them set like architectural jewels in the center of town after town. In Searsport, the Second Congregational Church was built in 1812; in Holden, the Congregational Church was built in 1828; and in Bucksport, the Methodist Church was built in 1839. One of the best examples, though, is the Union Meetinghouse in Winterport. Now a community hall, it was begun in 1832, dedicated in 1834 and cost a total of $2,875 to construct. The bell was cast by the Revere Copper Company, which was founded by Paul Revere. It's one of only 112 Revere bells still in existence. The four-faced clock was installed in the steeple in 1861.

The First Church in Belfast (United Church of Christ), 104 Church Street, 338-2282, built in 1818 by Samuel French, is said to best represent the architectural style of the Federal period. The church itself was founded in 1796 by Rev. Ebenezer Price and seven other members. *Historic Churches and Homes of Maine*, by the Maine Writers Research Club, is full of charming detail on the subject: "The 'raising' came on June 13, 1818. Capable men from neighboring towns were invited to lend a hand; and with a barrel of punch, furnished by the parish committee, and a brief address by Judge Crosby, the day must have been a memorable one." The church bell, hung in the belfry in 1820, was made by Paul Revere. In 1836, a town clock was placed in the steeple. Today, the 250-member church has undertaken a 200th anniversary fund-drive to rebuild the steeple and address a number of other repair projects. It offers Sunday services, with a nursery and several member clubs.

First Congregational Church in Ellsworth, Church and State streets, 667-8321, is one of the finest Greek Revival churches in New England. Built in 1846, it's worth a visit — the portico, tower and spire are lovely. Denys Peter Myers, writing in *Maine Forms of American Architecture*, says it looks exactly like most people's mental image of a typical New England church. Today, the congregation numbers between 100 and 150, and the church offers a Sunday service, Sunday school, a youth group, various women's groups and a morning nursery during the school year. The church also opens its doors to nonprofit groups wishing to meet there, including AA, Al-Anon and Next Step. Indeed, many 12-step programs hold meetings in church assembly rooms.

The Chestnut Street Baptist church in Camden is a community treasure. (It's across from the U.S. Post Office, next to the town green.) The steeple was an Eagle Scout project for a boy who lived across the harbor and thought the church needed one. The clock was recently refurbished by a volunteer group that planned the project and raised the funds.

FYI

Unless otherwise noted, the area code for all phone numbers listed in this guide is 207.

From Hand to Hand, the Blessings Flow . . .

Once these handsome churches were built, their uses changed as the population changed. There is a wonderful contemporary example of this in Bangor. The Reform Jewish synagogue, Congregation Beth El, 183 French Street, 945-4578, formed in 1984. For its first 12 years the fledgling group rented quarters from the Unitarian Church, then on Union Street.

"On Friday nights and Saturday mornings, we were permitted to transform their sanctuary into a synagogue in which we could pray and feel comfortable," wrote Sidney R. Block, past president of Congregation Beth El, in a letter to the *Bangor Daily News*. He was writing to thank the Unitarians for sharing their quarters. Block noted that their graciousness extended to putting notice of the Jewish service on their sign.

The Unitarian Church has since merged with the First Universalist Church, 120 Park Street, Bangor, 947-7009, and Congregation Beth El bought a building vacated by the Messiah Baptist Church. We've read that Catholic, Congregationalist, Christian Scientist and Baptist churches have met on or near the site during Bangor's 160-year history.

The Torah at Congregation Beth El also has an interesting history. It was written in Moravia in central Europe during the 1730s, taken by the Nazis during the Holocaust and stored in Prague with other Jewish artifacts. The Holocaust Torahs, as they have come to be called, were acquired by the Westminster Synagogue of London in the 1960s and distributed to Jewish congregations around the world.

As we've said, it's not unusual for churches to share space, and in at least one case, they share ministers. Rev. James Wood and a part-time assistant are the pastors of five Waldo County Congregational (UCC) churches. Each congregation had its own building, but none could support a full-time pastor. The "parish" covers about 30 miles, encompassing the Frankfort Congregational Church, U.S. High-

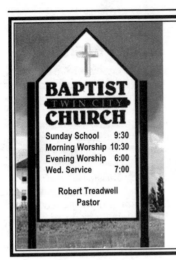

Twin City Baptist Church

Robert Treadwell
Pastor

559 North Main Street
Brewer, ME 04412

Church: 207-989-6852
Home: 207-947-3557

BAPTIST
TWIN CITY
CHURCH
Sunday School   9:30
Morning Worship 10:30
Evening Worship   6:00
Wed. Service   7:00

Robert Treadwell
Pastor

---

way 1A; the Monroe Community Church, Maine Highway 139; the Jackson Congregational Church, Maine Highway 7; the First Congregational Church of Brooks, Maine Highway 7; and the Freedom Congregational Church, Academy Hill Road. Wood works fulltime, and there is a central parish office, P.O. Box 188, Brooks, ME 04921, 722-3614.

Lest you think all the churches here are long-established, consider Twin City Baptist in Brewer. In 1984, it had 52 charter members, and they met in a converted warehouse. In 1987 the members built its present structure on Main Street, and now the church has close to 200 members. Why the need to organize? The other Baptist churches in the area are members of conventions, either the American Baptist Association or the Conservative Baptist Association. Twin City Baptist is independent and governed by its members.

A Place of Diversity

A number of religious groups are growing so fast that they have a congregation but no structure. The Muslim community in the Bangor-Orono area plans to build the state's first mosque. The community's numbers are growing, but the nearest mosques are in Quincy and Cambridge, Massachusetts. "Orono is a place where diversity has been celebrated," said one community member in support of the proposal at a planning board meeting to discuss constructing the mosque. The group now meets at the Robert R. Drummond Chapel at Memorial Union, University of Maine, Orono, 581-1406.

The Drummond Chapel, a 17-by-26-foot room on the third floor of the union, has become a place of worship for many congregations without buildings, including a Zen meditation group, the Maine Christian Association, followers of Baha'i and a yoga group.

Maine Council of Churches, 15 Pleasant Avenue, Portland, 772-1918, publishes the "Directory of Maine Churches, Assemblies and Synagogues 1990." It lists 1,600 churches representing more than 50 denominations and a number of independent churches. An updated version is expected in the next year or two. It's a good place to start, especially if you want to do some research before visiting the area.

Of the mainline congregations, it might be worth noting that in Rockland, the First Universalist Church, 345 Broadway, 594-8750, is reaching out to welcome gays, lesbians and bisexuals into their church community. The church has held educational workshops, made a declaration of inclusivity, added relevant books to its religious library and held social events designed to welcome the newcomers. In 1995, the Unitarian Universalist Association

Built to the Memory of All Young People . . .

We've talked of congregations with and without buildings. Now we'd like to tell you about a building that has no congregation. At least no specific congregation. Vesper Hill Children's Chapel, Beauchamp Point, Rockport, is one of our favorite places, and because it can be difficult to find, it is a consummate Insiders' place.

Built on a stone foundation, the post-and-beam, open-air chapel offers glimpses of Penobscot Bay. The gardens are beautifully maintained, and it is a favorite place for weddings.

The area was donated by the late Helena Bok, and a ceramic plaque hung under the eaves reads: "This chapel is built to the memory of all young people who have passed through this world and gained God by so doing. It stands for freedom of thought, prayer, and action. It stands for holiness within the heart and wholesomeness within the body and for God in the heart each waking hour. May the Lord bless all young people who come here for spiritual and mental refreshment."

Here's how to get to the chapel: From U.S. Highway 1 in Camden, turn onto Chestnut Street (between Camden National Bank and the Town Green). Drive 1.8 miles, turn left on Calderwood Lane, drive .6 miles and turn right. The words "Vesper Hill" are carved into a large low stone on the far side of the turn. The entrance is the first drive on your left.

Caveat: Visiting the chapel early one morning last summer, we were reminded again that it is used as such, and so should be approached quietly. We tramped up the stairs only to discover a young couple huddled up front on one of the wooden benches, wrapped in their own private sorrow. Please be respectful of the chapel and those who might be using it.

The area is maintained by the Vesper Hill Foundation, HCR 60, Box 3090, Camden, ME 04843, and may be reserved for weddings, baptisms and memorials from April 15 to October 31.

Photo: Bangor Daily News

Vesper Hill Children's Chapel, in Rockport, is a haven for
quiet reflection and spiritual refreshment.

in Boston recognized it as a "Welcoming Congregation."

If music might affect your choice of church, Bangor's St. John's Episcopal Church, 225 French Street, 947-0156, has a notable choir. It has recorded a CD and several cassette tapes. In 1996 the choir toured churches in Great Britain and Scotland — its third trip in 10 years. The choir performs at Sunday services as well as at evensongs once a month during the school year. The church building itself is handsome. Richard Upjohn designed a Gothic Revival structure for the congregation in the 1830s. *Maine Forms of American Architecture* notes a perspective drawing clearly suggested masonry construction, but the design was executed in wood. The building burned in the Great Bangor Fire of 1911 and was replaced by a design in the late 19th-century Gothic Revival style. The architect of the more recent structure was Upjohn's grandson, Hobart B. Upjohn.

Reaching Out

We should mention that there is activity in a range of spiritual disciplines. There are t'ai chi classes and shiatsu practitioners. There is an active Spiritualist community in Etna, near Bangor. The Etna Spiritualist Association, chartered by the American Federation of Spiritualist Churches, offers summer programs at Camp Etna, U.S. Highway 2. Contact Rev. Irene Harding, 269-3323, for more information. The 27-acre camp is 120 years old and open to the public during August, when there are daily church services and a variety of seminars. There is an inn and a few small apartments available for visitors. Another Spiritualist community, chartered by the National Spiritualist Association of Churches, operates in Temple Heights, in Northport.

In Bangor, the Silo 7 Bookstore, 7 Bomarc Road, 942-5590, stocks titles on religion and philosophy. Owner Stephen LeBel said he expected Native American and Buddhist texts to be the most popular when he opened the store, but he was surprised to find that "European earth religions" such as Wicca, Druidism and Celtic studies sold best. He said there is rising interest in the field of Reiki, theraputic touch and alternative or complementary healing. His daughter, Lisa LeBel, sees people in the mainstream reaching out, particularly for books on near-death experiences and spiritual development. The New Age Emporium, once of Camden, has moved to Rockland and changed its name to New Horizon, 596-6764, It offers books, a reading area, and other materials for the body, mind and spirit.

If your impression is one of a tolerant community rich in religious and spiritual resources, then you've gotten the point of this chapter. Nowhere is this more evident than in the resurgence of the Baccalaureate in area high schools. Optional and interfaith in its newest incarnation, it's been embraced by students, parents and school boards alike.

In Camden, a bagpiper led a procession of robed clergy, school administrators and graduating seniors down the center of town to the Congregational church. Police cars with flashing lights kept traffic at bay. The sun cast long shadows, proud parents snapped photos, shopkeepers and passers-by waved and cheered. It was a lovely moment — the community at its best.

Index of Advertisers

Index

Going Somewhere?

Insiders' Guide presents 48 current and upcoming titles to popular destinations all over the country (including the titles below) — and we're planning on adding many more. To order a title, go to your local bookstore or call (800) 582-2665 and we'll direct you to one.

Adirondacks	Minneapolis/St. Paul, MN
Atlanta, GA	Mississippi
Bermuda	Myrtle Beach, SC
Boca Raton and the Palm Beaches, FL	Nashville, TN
Boulder, CO, and Rocky Mountain National Park	New Hampshire
Bradenton/Sarasota, FL	North Carolina's Central Coast and New Bern
Branson, MO, and the Ozark Mountains	North Carolina's Mountains
California's Wine Country	Outer Banks of North Carolina
Cape Cod, Nantucket and Martha's Vineyard, MA	The Pocono Mountains
Charleston, SC	Relocation
Cincinnati, OH	Richmond, VA
Civil War Sites in the Eastern Theater	Salt Lake City
Colorado's Mountains	Santa Fe
Denver, CO	Savannah
Florida Keys and Key West	Southwestern Utah
Florida's Great Northwest	Tampa/St. Petersburg, FL
Golf in the Carolinas	Tucson
Indianapolis, IN	Virginia's Blue Ridge
The Lake Superior Region	Virginia's Chesapeake Bay
Las Vegas	Washington, D.C.
Lexington, KY	Wichita, KS
Louisville, KY	Williamsburg, VA
Madison, WI	Wilmington, NC
Maine's Mid-Coast	Yellowstone

THE INSIDERS' GUIDE ®

Insiders' Guide • P.O. Box 2057 • Manteo, NC 27954
Phone (919) 473-6100 • Fax (919) 473-5869 • *www.insiders.com*